Two Worlds

He iwi kee
He iwi kee,
Titiro atu
Titiro mai!

One strange people
and another
looking
at each other!

FROM A HAKA BY MERIMERI PENFOLD

Two

WORLDS

First Meetings Between
Maori and Europeans
1642–1772

Anne Salmond

UNIVERSITY OF HAWAII PRESS
Honolulu

Published in North America by
UNIVERSITY OF HAWAII PRESS
2840 Kolowalu Street
Honolulu, Hawaii 96822

First published in New Zealand by
PENGUIN BOOKS (NZ) LTD
182–190 Wairau Road
Auckland 10, New Zealand

Design and production by Richard King
Typeset in Compugraphic Perpetua
by Typocrafters Ltd, Auckland
Printed in Singapore

LIBRARY OF CONGRESS CATALOGING-IN-PUBLICATION DATA

Salmond, Anne.
Two worlds: first meetings between Maori and Europeans,
1642–1772 / Anne Salmond.
p.   cm.
Includes bibliographical references and index.
ISBN 0-8248-1467-3

1. Maori (New Zealand people) — First contact with Europeans.
2. Maori (New Zealand people) — History — Sources.
3. Maori (New Zealand people) — Social life and customs.
4. New Zealand — Discovery and exploration.
5. New Zealand — History — To 1840.
I. Title.

DU423.F48S25   1992   91-45422
993.01 — dc20

To my teachers in two traditions:
Eruera and Amiria Stirling, and Merimeri Penfold
Bruce Biggs, Ralph Bulmer and Ward Goodenough

Contents

Acknowledgements

It has often been remarked by European scholars that there is no precise word for 'gratitude' in Maori. This is probably because words are an inadequate return for kindness, or help in time of need. It is in a spirit of heartfelt obligation, therefore, that I acknowledge the many people who have been both kind and helpful during the writing of this book.

First, Sir Robert Hall, Sheila Robinson and Wayne Orchiston of the Gisborne Art Gallery and Museum, Darcy Ria, Peggy Kaua, Ingrid and Monty Searancke, Bino and Francis Reedy, Witi Ihimaera, Dorothy Clark, Paaki Harrison, Graeme Hingangaroa Smith, elders of Hauiti Marae in Uawa, John Laurie and Patrick Parsons offered invaluable advice and assistance on research matters in Tuuranga-nui (Poverty Bay), Heretaunga (Hawke's Bay) and the East Coast.

Ngawhira Fleet, Patricia McDonald and Peter Johnston of Ngaati Hei guided my thoughts on Whitianga. It is my hope that they will see the return of their tuurangawaewae at Wharetaewa and Wharekaho, in recompense for the many harms that Ngaati Hei have suffered.

In Tai Tokerau (Northland), Merimeri Penfold, Pineaha Murray, Waerete Norman, Margaret Mutu, Tuhoe Manuera, MacCully Matiu, Patu Hohepa, Sir Hugh and Lady Freda Kawharu, Jane McRae, Te Aniwa Hona, Jack Lee and Cleve Barlow all checked my attempts at understanding the intricacies of tribal histories.

In Raukawa-moana (the Cook Strait area) I am indebted to Atholl Anderson, John Tait, Motueka elders and Nola Arthur for their comments and advice.

Archaeological colleagues have been both patient and generous with their knowledge of particular landscapes and prehistoric sequences. Kevin Jones, Janet Davidson, Roger Green, Douglas Sutton, Geoffrey Irwin, Caroline Phillips, David Simmons, Louise Furey, Ian Barber, Mark Allen and Mary Jeal all offered expert assistance.

On matters of historic research I am greatly indebted to Barry Reay, Leonard and Barbara Andaya, Grahame Anderson, George Hill and Judith Binney. Raewyn Dalziel, Dame Joan Metge, June Starke, Bruce Biggs, Janet Davidson, John Morton and Jeremy Spencer (in a detailed commentary of more than a hundred pages) read and checked the entire manuscript — needless to say, any errors that survived their meticulous scrutiny are mine alone.

Isabel Ollivier has been my mainstay on the French manuscripts throughout the project, and Cheryl Hingley and Jeremy Spencer added invaluable contributions to the translation and interpretation of those texts. I am indebted to

James Traue, Sharon Dell and Anne Upton of the Alexander Turnbull Library for unstinting help, and to the Alexander Turnbull Library Endowment Trust, Indosuez New Zealand Limited, the French Government, the University of Auckland, the Nuffield Foundation and the Scientific Research Distribution Committee of the Lottery Board for their generosity in funding various aspects of our research.

During 1980–81 King's College, Cambridge, and the Department of Anthropology at the University of Cambridge gave me warm hospitality, and for that I am grateful to the late Sir Edmund Leach, and Jack Goody and Stephen Hugh-Jones among others. My thanks also to Sir Raymond and Lady Rosemary Firth for many kindnesses. From 1987 to 1989 the Royal Society of New Zealand and the New Zealand Government, with their award of the seventh Captain James Cook Fellowship, made it possible for this work to be written in peace and quietness. My particular thanks to Lionel Hetherington, Patricia Bergquist and Ross Moore of the Royal Society for their encouragement and support.

Rangimarie Rawiri typed innumerable versions of the manuscript with good-humoured accuracy, and my publisher Geoff Walker, editor Linda Cassells and designer Richard King have been encouraging and wise in their advice.

Finally, as always, I thank my family and friends, without whose company and comfort writing (and life) would be a barren affair.

E aaku hoa, ka nui ngaa mihi me te aroha ki a koutou katoa.

Anne Salmond
March 1991

Preface

At the Hokianga discussions of the Treaty of Waitangi on 12 February 1840, Mohi Tawhai spoke to the assembled gathering of Europeans and Maori and said:

> Let the tongue of everyone be free to speak; but what of it. What will be the end? Our sayings will sink to the bottom like a stone, but your sayings will float light, like the wood of the whau tree, and always remain to be seen. Am I telling lies?

The image was that of the net — a seine net that might be a thousand metres long, with whau-wood floats along its top edge and sinker stones woven into a seam along its base. Like the net of memory, the seine was not cast at random; and when it was hauled it was pulled in by the combined labour of many people.

In some ways Mohi Tawhai's metaphorical statement was prophetic. Maori commentaries and points of view have often been forgotten when popular tradition and historians have cast their narrative nets. The tapu-laden talk of tribal elders has been concealed or is inaccessible, while stories based on European documents have 'floated light, like the wood of the whau tree, and always remain to be seen'.

This may have been inevitable, for parts of tribal knowledge have been closely guarded, and documents can have the advantage of a vivid proximity to the events that are being described. On the other hand, not everything in tribal history is hidden, and many early documents in Maori as well as those in English still survive. If history is to be faithful it cannot afford to be ignorant, and events that involved protagonists from different societies cannot be fairly interpreted from just one point of view.

The unpredictable, dramatic, action-packed first meetings between Maori and Europeans in New Zealand provide a case in point. From one contemporary perspective they were simply puzzling, extraordinary interludes in the life of various tribal communities. The ships — floating islands, mythological 'birds' or canoes full of tupua or 'goblins' — came into this bay or that, shot local people or presented them with strange gifts, were welcomed or pelted with rocks, and after a short time went away again and were largely forgotten. Local comment might well have echoed a proverb quoted by Ngai-te-Rangi chiefs when they farewelled Governor Grey in 1853:

> Haere ana koe ko ngaa pipi o te aaria; ka noho maatou ko ngaa pipi o te whakatakere.
> You go, the shallow-rooting shellfish, while we, the shellfish of deep waters stay behind.

From another contemporary vantage-point, however, that of their seventeenth- and eighteenth-century European chroniclers, the same encounters were simply episodes in the story of Europe's 'discovery' of the world — more voyages to add to the great collections of 'Voyages' that had already been made. The genre of discovery tales was an ancient one in Europe, with a well-worn narrative line — explorers ventured into unknown seas, found new lands and named their coastal features, described exotic plants, animals and inhabitants, and survived attacks by tattooed savages (or worse still, cannibals) with spears. These stories were very popular with ordinary people at the time, for they defined Europeans as 'civilised' in contrast with the 'savages' and 'barbarians' to be found elsewhere, and told exciting tales of giants and 'opposite-footers', 'Indians' with outlandish customs, lost continents where people cooked in vessels of gold and silver, and humans with tails or the heads of dogs.

After two hundred years or more of shared history in New Zealand, one might have thought that scholars would have considered each of these interpretative traditions, if only to set them to question each other, but by and large this has not happened. Modern histories of these first meetings, although they are meticulous and well documented, clearly trace their lineage from the ancient European discovery tales. Europeans are depicted as being in charge of the drama, the explorers are the heroes, while Maori people either sit as passive spectators or act anonymously behind cloaks and tattooed masks. Just as clearly, though, this is not the way it was. Both Maori and European protagonists were active in these meetings and fully human, despite their mythologies of each other, and followed their own practical and political agendas, quite unlike those of their modern-day descendants in many ways.

For the sake of accuracy as well as fairness, the story of the first meetings between Maori and Europeans in New Zealand — and that of European 'discovery' in general — has to be rethought. In this experimental account I have tried to respect the perspectives of both sides, while taking the narratives of neither side for granted. This has required an ethnographic approach to the past, reflecting upon manuscripts in ways drawn from tribal knowledge as well as European history, and grounding the 'sayings' of both Maori and Europeans about these meetings in the physical detail of their daily lives. If in consequence some common misconceptions and bigotries that appear in popular talk can be recognised as mythological, and sink without trace into the sea, I will be content. This may be too optimistic an expectation, however, for I do not think that Mohi Tawhai was telling lies.

The Research

The idea of this book began in 1970–72, as I travelled to marae (ceremonial centres) in different parts of the North Island of New Zealand with Eruera and Amiria Stirling, elders of Te Whaanau-a-Apanui and Ngaati Porou. Eruera Stirling had been my teacher in Maori matters since 1964, and he had suggested that I should take huihuinga (ceremonial gatherings) as the topic of my doctoral thesis. He told me that if I truly wanted to learn about Te Ao Maori (the Maori world) the marae was the place to do it.

He was quite right. As we travelled from one marae to another, we became immersed in the rhythms of tribal time, the taste of food, the sound and lilt of voices, the way people moved. There were graphic lessons to be had in tribal and regional difference, as we visited various areas with their distinctive landscapes, carving styles, histories and ceremonial practices. I began to see what mana was, and ihi, and the force of tapu. Great orators spoke, and voices of the kai-karanga (ceremonial callers) rang out across the marae. In reading the explorers' accounts of their first meetings with Maori people I have been constantly reminded of things I saw and heard on various marae, and it would have been impossible to grasp what they were describing in many cases but for those experiences.

Until 1970 most of what I knew about Te Ao Tawhito (the ancient Maori world) was based on the classic works of the great nineteenth- and early twentieth-century scholars — Elsdon Best, Te Rangihiroa (Sir Peter Buck) and Sir Raymond Firth. They portrayed a society that had an orderly structure, broadly the same from one end of the country to the other, and relatively static and unchanging; and described it with sympathy and eloquence from a wide range of sources. Above all, they made the Maori past acceptable and accessible to most New Zealanders.

What I saw on marae around the country, however, was a robust and resilient way of life that showed continuity with the past but also the effects of innovation and change, and which differed remarkably from one tribal area to another. It was difficult to believe that such diverse tribal traditions, 200 years after the arrival of Cook and Surville, could have developed out of a static, standardised pre-contact way of life. I began to wonder how far the classic portrait of traditional Maori society was real, and how far it was the product of particular scholarly images of tribal life.

Obviously it was not possible to visit the various tribal areas as they had been in 1642 or 1769, to see for myself. It seemed, however, that the next best thing might be to look closely at the reports of the first Europeans who came to New Zealand, for after all they had visited particular places and described their experiences and what they saw. I began to read the explorers' journals, and to my fascination they gave a sense of immediacy and familiarity that had been missing from the scholarly accounts. There were the recognisable ancestors of the people of Tuuranga-nui (Gisborne), of Anaura, of the Bay of Islands, of Whitianga — vigorous, various and playing out ritual forms and political strategies still used on the marae. There were also the sorts of details that had been so instructive during my travels with Eruera and Amiria Stirling, and some of these were surprising — women with patterns like kowhaiwhai (rafter paintings) tattooed round their necks, nets a thousand metres long, double and outrigger canoes, people painted with red ochre from head to foot and vast gardens without a weed in sight.

The perspective of these records felt comfortable because it seemed close to tribal accounts of the past, based on particular landscapes and particular successions of ancestors. It became apparent that it might be possible to add to the physical detail of the explorers' descriptions the political and genealogical detail of tribal histories, and to draw on archaeology and local knowledge to investigate what these particular places had been like at the time of first European arrival. Finally, there were the sketches and drawings — glorious images of coastlines, people, canoes and settlements, capturing information that could not have been conveyed in words.

It was clear that to do the research properly it would be necessary as a first step to find all the surviving documents from each voyage — journals, logs, charts and sketches and, if possible, descriptions of any objects that the voyagers had collected. If I had known what a job that would prove to be, I might never have started. The documents were scattered in archives around the world, and in the case of some of those in languages other than English, there were no reliable translations to be had. In 1978 the project began, and a documents index was set up, with a card for each manuscript or published version, and researchers were located to begin work on the French accounts. This phase of the research would have been impossible without the help of the Alexander Turnbull Library, which supplied copies of the first documents that we worked on, and I was very fortunate to find Isabel Ollivier and Cheryl Hingley, graduates in French from the University of Auckland, who carried out the first translations. Eventually we established a format of facsimile transcriptions in typescript with parallel translations for each document, and Isabel Ollivier was awarded a scholarship by the French Government to work in French archives to complete this part of the research. Her meticulous translations of the documents from a number of early French voyages have been published by the Alexander Turnbull Library, and form the basis for the last two chapters in this work. Jeremy Spencer, a scholar with a great interest in the early explorers, worked on the charts of the Bay of Islands and Tokerau (Doubtless Bay) and correlated them with the modern landscape. My own research during this phase concentrated on the documents in English, and in 1980–81 I spent a year at King's College in Cambridge, visiting

English archives and collecting copies of all the documents of early English voyages to New Zealand.

At the same time as these early documents were being collected, I was working with Eruera Stirling on his autobiography, based on his own writings and a long series of taped conversations we had had together in 1978–79. Eruera was an eminent authority on tribal history and a well-known orator, and in many ways he handled those sessions as though I was a tauira (student) of his, observing many of the tapu restrictions involved in such teaching and instructing me in his philosophies about the nature and uses of knowledge. I became very interested in the differences and relationships between Maori and European systems of knowledge,[1] and began to read European philosophers — Heidegger, Foucault, Ricoeur, Gadamer, Habermas, Hesse, Derrida, Eco and others who I thought might help me to understand some of the essential questions involved, while at the same time studying early Maori texts and cosmological accounts to try to grasp some of the pivotal concepts — tapu, mana, waananga (godly knowledge), tipuna (ancestors) and the like — in Maori interpretations of the world.

It was probably because of this that when the explorers' accounts were examined in close detail, something unexpected began to happen. Snippets of information in their journals made me think that the European explorers were very different from anything I had expected. I began to wonder about their daily lives, and why they reacted as they did in their dealings with Maori people. I came to see that, like most New Zealanders, I had been assuming that my ancestors were rather like myself, and that this assumption might be quite mistaken. When I realised, for instance, that when the explorers described Maori men at an average height of five feet eight inches to five feet nine inches, as 'tall', it was because the average height of European men in the mid-eighteenth century was about five feet two inches (or according to Voltaire, five feet[2]), and that when they called Maori people 'healthy' it was because contemporary European populations were riddled with infectious diseases, then it became plain that the explorers themselves were an ethnographic problem. It was at that point that the study of Te Ao Tawhito (the ancient Maori world) became a study of 'Two Worlds', and the idea of a mirror-image ethnography — in which each side saw the other through a haze of their own reflections — began to develop.

The final stage of the research was sponsored by the Royal Society of New Zealand, when as the seventh Captain James Cook Fellow I tried to draw all these different themes and threads together. The assembled documents were collated day by day and hour by hour (often a complicated task, since some journals were kept in civil time — midnight to midnight, and others in ship's time — noon to noon), and local histories, early Maori accounts, archaeological studies and environmental reconstructions of the places that the explorers visited were collected and examined. The work of previous scholars on these voyages — J. C. Beaglehole, John Dunmore and Andrew Sharp in particular — proved to be invaluable, for they have studied the ships' tracks, identified places, fish and birds, and provided essential information on the voyagers themselves.

Whenever possible I have had my reconstructions checked by those with the relevant expertise, and in some cases it has been possible to give talks in the places described, so that local elders, historians and residents could assess the accuracy of my accounts. As at every other stage, the research has been a collaborative effort, and I am profoundly indebted to all those people — some hundreds by now — who have so freely offered their help and expertise. Errors in the text will inevitably remain, despite my best efforts, however, and I hope that the process of checking and correction will continue as the work is more widely read.

In discussing 'Two Worlds' — Te Ao Maori and Te Ao Pakeha (the Maori and European worlds) — I have drawn inspiration from the knowledgeable traditions of both, therefore:

> Mauria ko oku painga, waiho ko oku wheruu.
> Take what is good in this, and leave the rest behind.

Judge things by reason's way, not by popular say.

MONTAIGNE, *OF CANNIBALS*, 1578

Kia maarama taku titiro.
Let my sight be clear.

A CHANT BY ERUERA STIRLING, 1980

Two Worlds

THUS APPEARS . . .

Around noon on a bright summer's day, 13 December 1642, two Dutch ships riding a South Pacific swell sighted a new coastline. The land seemed high and mountainous, with its summits buried in clouds and the shoreline in huge, hollow waves. The *Heemskerck* turned south-east towards the land, fired a gun and hoisted a white flag to signal a meeting of officers. A cockboat was lowered from the *Zeehaen*, and the sailors rowed her master, the supercargo and the first mate across to the other vessel. On board the *Heemskerck* the officers of the two ships convened a council meeting and passed a formal resolution 'to touch at the said land as quickly as at all possible',[1] recorded this in the ship's register, and ordered that the new coast be marked on the shipboard charts and coastal views be drafted.

'Thus appears the Sand Dunes'. A view sketched in Abel Tasman's Journal, based on a sketch by the draughtsman Isaack Gilsemans, showing Farewell Spit sheltering Taitapu (Golden Bay).

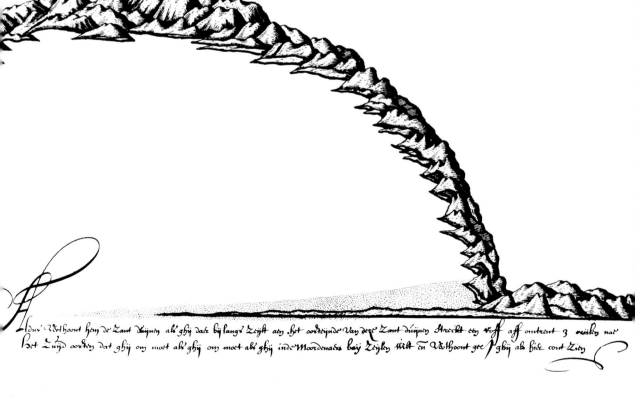

On shore it seems likely that nobody had noticed. No signal fires were lit, and no canoes came out to investigate. The population on that part of the coast[2] must have been sparse and mobile, and in any case the Dutch ships were a long way out at sea. During the next three days the *Heemskerck* and the *Zeehaen* edged north along a rocky coastline at about nine miles distance, naming one low, cliff-edged reef 'Clyppyge Hoeck' ('Rocky Point', now Cape Foulwind), another to the north 'Steijle Hoeck' ('Steep Point'), and looking in vain for signs of people or fires. On 16 December they approached what seemed to be the end point of the land, turned east-north-east in light winds, sailed on through the night and at daybreak found themselves close to the coast, while smoke plumed up in various places from fires on the shore.

The fires were no doubt signals of consternation, lit at the sight of this unprecedented arrival. The *Heemskerck* was a 120-ton war yacht with a crew of sixty sailors, while the *Zeehaen* was a more ponderous but sea-kindly 'fluyt'[3] with a crew of fifty. To the coastal people these vessels must have seemed fantastic and more on the scale of islets than of boats, with their high-looming sides, flagged masts, tangled rigging and square, bellied sails. The figures on the decks must also have seemed extraordinary, with their weird hats and clothing just visible from the shore.

Later that day the Dutch ships approached a sandspit and anchored at dusk beside it, with a view across to a large open bay (Taitapu — Golden Bay, sheltered by Tahuroa — Farewell Spit). On the morning of 18 December they sailed slowly into the bay looking for a good anchorage, with the pinnace and the cockboat searching out ahead. That night at sunset the ships dropped anchor, and about an hour later two canoes from a group of four approached them as lights flared up on shore. After a long, silent inspection,

> the men in the two prows[4] began to call out to us in a rough, hollow voice, but we could not understand a word of what they said. We, however, called out to them in answer, upon which they repeated their cries several times, but came no nearer than a stone-shot; they also blew several times on an instrument of which the sound was like that of a Moorish trumpet.[5]

The rough calling was probably an incantation or a haka, a chant for war, and the instrument played from the canoes was almost certainly a shell trumpet, sounding to challenge the strangers and signalling that the people in the bay were on the alert.[6] A sailor on the *Heemskerck* was ordered on deck to play some tunes in answer, and the second mate of the *Zeehaen*, who had come out to the Indies as a trumpeter, did the same. After these brief and ambiguous exchanges the men in the canoes paddled back to the land in darkness. On board the two ships double watches were set, muskets, pikes and cutlasses made ready, and the guns on the upper deck cleaned and placed in case of trouble.

It was not a promising beginning. Neither group knew anything of the other, and the meeting, when it came, seemed likely to prove bloody. The Dutch were not much surprised by anything they had seen so far, for new coasts were not uncommon on voyages of this sort and their routine patrols in the Dutch East

'Staete Landt', based on a draft by Visscher, showing the western coast of the upper South Island and the North Island of New Zealand. Note that Raukawa-moana (Cook Strait) is shown here as a bay, although the Huydecoper copy of Visscher's chart showed a tentative open channel in the same location.

Indies had brought them into frequent contact with islanders in 'prows'. For the country that lay in front of them, it was not so much this short meeting that would matter but its description in Abel Tasman's journal, the coastal sketches and the charts of 'Staete Landt', as they called it. It was the survival and publication of these documents that would eventually bring two worlds, of Western Europe and this southern Pacific archipelago, tangling together.

Chapter One

TE AO TUATAHI: WORLD 1

The archipelago that the Dutch had found, and which they later called 'Zeelandia Nova' (New Zealand),[1] was one of the most remote places on earth. Surrounded by a vast expanse of green sea,[2] the islands were so inaccessible that they were the last landmass of any size in the world to have been colonised by human beings. In claiming to have discovered the land, however, the Dutch over-reached themselves, for 'Zeelandia Nova' had been settled since about AD 800,[3] when the Netherlands were still a patchwork of marshes interspersed with mediaeval towns, England was an Anglo-Saxon kingdom and Charlemagne ruled much of Europe.

The ancestors of the islanders had arrived in one of the last great voyages of a canoe-borne expansion that began in Island South-East Asia about four thousand to six thousand years ago.[4] Groups of Austronesian-speaking[5] colonists moved eastwards across the Pacific in outrigger canoes, carrying with them pigs, dogs, rats and chickens, South-East Asian cultivated tree and root crops, and technologies for woodworking, house-building, making pottery and harvesting the sea. In New Guinea, New Ireland and Buka, they found long-established populations,[6] and so the new arrivals settled in villages on outlying islands and in coastal bays. There they entered into long-distance exchange networks and perfected a sea-going tradition that combined navigational systems with double or outrigger sailing canoes.

These East Oceanic Austronesians were almost better adapted to the sea than to land, and their detailed knowledge of the ocean and its moods, and their fast and seaworthy voyaging canoes gave them the confidence to explore further to the east. They went on to discover Tonga, Fiji, Samoa, Futuna and Uvea in Western Polynesia, where they became the founding population of Polynesia, making successful voyages to Eastern Polynesia by about 200 BC or earlier.[7]

The 1,650-mile gap between Rarotonga and New Zealand proved to be a formidable obstacle, even for these experienced navigators, and it was not until about AD 800 that they reached this southernmost Polynesian archipelago for the first time. Their long-range voyaging into Polynesia was an achievement based on sophisticated craft and navigational expertise, and it preceded the Viking oceanic explorations out of Europe by about 2,000 years. The rapid seaborne expansion of the Austronesians is one of the great colonising movements of human history, and it is only the arrival of their Eastern Polynesian descendants that can rightly be called the 'discovery' of the land that they (or their descendants) named Aotearoa.[8]

Very little is known about early Maori deep-sea navigational techniques, and perhaps our best chance of understanding their sea-faring methods comes from Polynesian voyaging, and the studies of navigational systems in Micronesia, where related traditional techniques have continued to be used into modern times.

In Puluwat, one of the Caroline Islands in Micronesia, ancestral sailing directions are still being taught in traditional navigational 'schools'. In addition to their practical training in sailing the 'wa', or single outrigger canoes of Puluwat, the initiates must memorise complex metaphorical maps of the seascape and its guiding stars, covering a wide oceanic radius. The night sky is mapped around the compass by named stars, and the ocean by reference to sea features which include islands, reefs, sand-banks, swells, areas of persistent rough water or flotsam, and sea creatures living in particular places. Sets of sailing directions locate the navigator under guiding stars or by seamarks, which change according to season, destination, stage of the journey, current, swell and wind conditions.

The imagery of Puluwat navigation is in some respects incompatible with the way Europeans orient themselves at sea. Under the 'etak' system of reference, for instance, a voyage from one island to another is visualised as being divided into stages with reference to an island that lies to one side of the course. As the voyage progresses, it is the islands, not the canoe, that move. At each stage of the journey the destination island is visualised as coming closer towards the vessel, while the 'etak' or reference island moves back from beneath one star point to the next.[9] The navigators are well aware, of course, that islands do not really move, but this system acts as a mnemonic device that helps them locate themselves accurately at sea. Back-bearings from landmarks and bearings from the sun are also taken.

The confidence with which an experienced navigator might travel in such conditions is well described by David Lewis, in his account of the first stage of a 550-mile journey from Puluwat to the island of Saipan also in Micronesia, under the sole guidance of Hipour, a graduate of the Puluwat Warieng navigational 'school', in 1969:

> The first stage was from Puluwat to Pikelot, to the west-north-west . . . The land receding astern was carefully observed to assess the direction and strength of the current as alternative star courses were available to suit different conditions . . . In the event it proved to be north-going and strong. The initial course in these conditions is laid down as towards the setting Pleiades (Doloni Mariger) or about west-north-west. Under the influence of the current, this course leads over the edge of a submerged reef east of Pikelot. After identifying the reef, the navigator turns west towards the island. When the Pleiades had set, we steered for the rest of the night by keeping the Great Bear (Doloni Wole) and Polaris (Fii He Magid) about 20° before the starboard beam, a task rendered no easier by columns of cloud streaming overhead.
>
> The rising sun and a rather complex beam swell replaced the stars for orientation at dawn . . . About 10.00 we duly passed over the edge of the deep reef,

which was detectable by the light blue colour of the sea over it, and altered course towards the west. An hour later Pikelot topped the horizon ahead.

This 100-mile passage to a 500-yard-long target is commonly held to be so navigationally straightforward on account of the safety 'screen' provided by the deep reef (and the zone of homing birds that surround all islands) that parties frequently set out towards Pikelot from Puluwat on the spur of the moment and when drunk on palm toddy. They always arrive.[10]

The details of early Polynesian navigational techniques may have differed from those now practised in Puluwat, but the broad methods and the quality of their relationship with the sea seem to have been very similar. Familiar stretches of ocean had their own known features, and the sea was not empty but marked by 'sea-paths' between known seamarks, located under a series of named horizon stars, which rose or set over a given destination. Particular swells and their deflection patterns off particular islands were identified, and these, together with land clouds and reflections from the land, the flight paths of land-roosting birds at dawn and dusk, and patterns of underwater luminescence streaking out from islands, helped to expand identifiable targets at sea by a radius of perhaps twelve to thirty miles. Voyages of exploration were often sailed upwind, allowing a safe and rapid downwind journey home.[11] In unfamiliar waters a skilled navigator could recognise and name new swells by studying the sea hour after hour, and the 'star-path' (or succession of guiding stars), the wind and current patterns and numerous other items of navigational information were memorised for the return voyage. During such expeditions the navigator slept as little as possible, ceaselessly scanning the sea and the night sky and keeping watch for land clouds and homing birds. It was said that you could always recognise a star navigator by his bloodshot eyes.[12]

The favoured Polynesian craft for long-range voyaging were middle-sized out-rigger or double canoes about fifteen to twenty-five metres long. Double canoes had the advantage of stability in rough weather and extra space for people and supplies in the hulls and on the sailing platform. These craft were flexible and fast, sailing at about four to seven knots and often faster in a good wind, and capable of covering between ninety and 150 miles a day[13] on a course where tacking was not necessary. The voyaging canoes could carry forty or fifty people and sometimes many more. Fewer probably travelled on voyages of exploration, when food and water for a long journey as well as domestic animals, cultivated plants and personal goods had to be carried. It must have been a canoe of this sort, perhaps a craft ancestral to the double-hulled Tahitian 'tiipaerua' with its thatched hut amidships and high carved stern-posts, a Rarotongan variant, or the two-masted double-hulled 'pahii' with its crab-claw sails curving in the wind, that carried the East Polynesian forebears of Maori people on their voyage of discovery to New Zealand.

This first voyage must have been a deliberate expedition, perhaps from Tahiti, the Australs or the Southern Cooks, because computer simulations of Pacific voyaging have shown an almost nil probability of drift voyages from East Polynesia arriving in New Zealand.[14] The difficulties that confronted the first

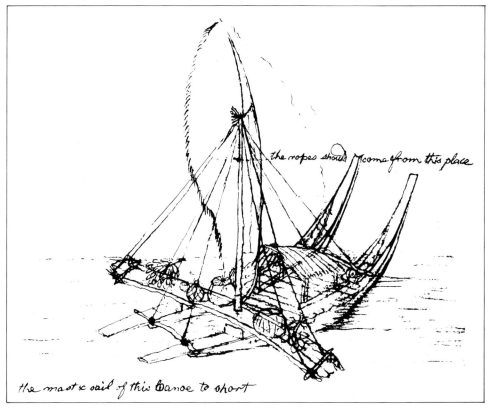

the ropes should come from this place

the mast & sail of this Canoe to short

Above: *A sketch by Sydney Parkinson of a tiipaerua double canoe from Raiatea, during the Endeavour's visit to the Society Islands in 1769.*

Below: *A pen-and-wash drawing of a pahii double canoe, with raised ends fore and aft. Sketched by Parkinson in Raiatea.*

explorers included the need for downwind sailing past the tropics into colder waters, the variable winds that are common in the lower reaches of the voyage and the strong westerlies that sometimes blow. Their inability to predict these conditions must have made such expeditions very difficult and dangerous.[15]

The first successful voyagers may have later returned home to East Polynesia to pass on sailing directions for future journeys or to recruit colonists, although it would have been difficult to sail far enough east through the tradewind belt;[16] and in that case a series of subsequent voyages to New Zealand is likely.[17] All that we can say for certain, however, is that the East Polynesian ancestors did arrive, and not by accident; and that on this or later voyages there were women as well as men on board, and also dogs, rats, and cultivated plants including kuumara (sweet potato), taro, yam, gourd, aute (paper mulberry) and the tii pore variety of cabbage tree.[18] The journey may have been arduous or uneventful, lasting maybe a month — as was the case for the *Hawaiki-nui*, a voyaging canoe which sailed from Rarotonga to New Zealand in 1985; or perhaps just sixteen days, averaging over 100 miles a day, as was the case with the *Hokule'a*, a Hawaiian double canoe which had sailed from Rarotonga in favourable winds just days before. No doubt there were other voyagers to the south who were lost at sea, or who returned home after a futile search of the southern ocean to tell of vast empty wastes of water, rolling in the westerly winds.

When it finally came, the landfall must have been exhilarating. Perhaps it was birds wheeling in the sky in large numbers that warned the voyagers that land was near, an interruption of the western swell, drifting logs and seaweed or, as in the case of the *Hokule'a*, a refracted image of the reddening disc of the sun, setting over a long grey landmass.[19] Whatever the homing signs were, as they sailed closer to land the shoreline would have stretched out along the horizon as far as the eye could see. After centuries of occupation of low atolls and small high islands, the East Polynesian ancestors must have known at once that this was something very different. Once part of the southern edge of the enormous ancient continent of Gondwanaland, these were continental islands with a landmass of over 250,000 square kilometres, more than all the rest of Polynesia put together. Accounts of this first moment of recognition may not have survived, however, for even the stories of Kupe, often held to be the discoverer of New Zealand, sometimes mention previous inhabitants, as in this manuscript account by Wirihana Aoterangi of the Ngati Taahinga tribe of Raglan:

> Kupe then embarked upon his canoe. Aotearoa was the name of the canoe, Turi was his companion. On arrival at this Island they found that the people who dwelt here were fairies. They were, in fact, of goblin-like appearance; such were those people, the descendants of those that were with Maui when he fished up this Island. Those people were the Mamoe, the Turehu, the Tahurangi, the Pokepokewai, the Hamoamoa, the Patupaiarehe, and the Turepe. This Island was the one he discovered first. He thereafter rowed over to the other Island; when he reached there he named the place where he reached the shore Taonui a Kupe.
>
> On his returning from an exploration of the Island, he passed by Rangitoto Island, he left his daughter there; there was a tuna (eel) there, also a rock. He

crossed over to Whanganui-a-tara, that is to say Poneke. When he looked backwards he felt regret for his daughter. He cut his skin and wept, and blood gushed forth and so reddened the herbage on the cliffs, also the fish there, as also the paua of that locality. On his coming hither northwards he came to Aotea and examined Karioi, when he discovered the inhabitants who dug up fern roots with wooden spades. The men of old say those people were the Ngati-matakore. They were not the Ngati-matakore of our race, they were of ancient times and belonged to this Island.

At this Kupe wished to return to Hawaiki; he asked his slave to remain and take care of his Island. He called it after his canoe — that is to say, he named it Aotearoa. He spoke a word to the slave Powhetengu, 'O Po, do you remain and take care of our home.' He did not consent from fear of that people. When Kupe returned and was out beyond Aotea he took off his belt and cast it on the sea, so that the sea might become rough, in case that Po should try and return to Hawaiki. After that Po built his canoe, which when finished he gave it the name of Rewatu. He stated that it was to go fishing, but it was not so, it was for the purpose of returning to Hawaiki. When he put out to sea it swamped and he perished. The canoe turned into stone and also the man; here indeed it still is at the harbour entrance at Aotea. Kupe sailed away to Hawaiki, where he announced that he had discovered a large and splendid Island and that the inhabitants there were like goblins.[20]

The histories of those tribes which tell of Kupe[21] sometimes state that Kupe passed on sailing directions for the new land, and that other voyagers later followed on his sea-path to Aotearoa. In one Whanganui tradition the directions were given to the ancestor Turi (described above as Kupe's travelling companion), who was fleeing from Hawaiki to escape the consequences of a murderous local vendetta. Kupe would not go with Turi but told him to direct the prow of his canoe 'to the rising of the star and the sun'.[22] The canoe Aotea was loaded with a type of kuumara called the kaukau, karaka berries, dogs, rats and puukeko birds among other things, and Turi and his people travelled south-east until they came to an island called Rangitahua (sometimes identified as Raoul Island in the Kermadecs), where they refitted their canoe, built a sacred altar, made offerings and called upon their god:

Nau mai e te atua	Come, god
E kore au e whiti ki raawahi?	Will I not reach the other side?
Nau mai ka whiti au.	Come, I will cross safely!

After further ceremonies and adventures at sea, which included a heated dispute over the correct bearings for the voyage and a childbirth on board, they came to the new land. As the Aotea sailed in to shore the raataa trees were in flower, and in their jubilation the crew threw their prized red feather headdresses into the sea, thinking that here were decorations that were finer still.

Other tribal groups tell of other canoes in their histories, and of different arrivals. Sometimes the founding ancestor is said to have come on a bird or a whale from Hawaiki, while other lines of descent are traced from ancestors who had always lived in Aotearoa from the time of the gods. In Northland some tribes claim Kui, a person who lived beneath the ground, as their ancestor, while others are descended from the union of Tumutumu-whenua, a man who came up from the ground, and his fairy wife.

Of the many voyaging sagas, most tell of planned expeditions from Hawaiki to escape quarrels and dissension in that land, and some also describe return voyages to seek the kuumara, or to revisit kinsfolk. The voyaging traditions exist in exuberant and sometimes contradictory variety, and the versions told by different authorities differ in details such as navigational directions or the lists of plants and animals brought to New Zealand by the voyagers. In the past some scholars have regarded the canoe sagas as largely historical and have used their details to retrace old migrations, while others have preferred to interpret them as myth;[23] but these distinctions mark a line between what Europeans can and cannot believe in these accounts, and do not much illuminate Maori tribal thought. What one can say is that recent research tends to support rather than deny traditional claims for planned voyages of exploration, without at all suggesting that the voyaging sagas were ever meant to answer European questions. Rather, they celebrate the arrival of the ancestors at a new place, and tell how they shaped and named a marvellous new landscape.

At the time of the first Polynesian arrival, the islands of Aotearoa had existed in isolation for about eighty million years. The vegetation was diverse and luxuriant, often coming right down to the water's edge, so that on stretches of the east coast, for instance, red-flowering pohutukawa trees grew along the shoreline with their roots almost in the sea.

The great evergreen forests were dominated by beeches in the south and podocarp and broad-leaved trees in the north, and the floors of the northern rainforests were covered with ferns and mosses and layers of rotting wood, sheltering below a complex canopy of shrubs and seedlings, smaller and larger trees, and sprawling tangles of climbers and lianes.

Numerous species of flightless moa grazed on vegetation in forest clearings and at their fringes — bizarre birds like big-legged ostriches that ranged from about three metres tall to smaller species about the size of a large turkey. Small flightless kiwi, tailless and bewhiskered, scuffled and whistled in the undergrowth at night, and other flightless birds, mostly now extinct, included several types of rails, a parrot, a duck and a goose.

Other ancient relics included the tuatara, sole survivor of a reptilian order, Rhynchocephalia, that had flourished in Gondwanaland; several primitive species of frog; and species of geckos and skinks that are thought to have migrated from New Caledonia and Australia on rafts of driftwood.[24] There were no mammals at all except for two native species of bat, and because there were no large ground-living predators the landscape teemed with birds, living in rocks in the mountains, nesting in the bush, roosting around lakes and swamps and on the banks of rivers, and wheeling and squawking over tussock grasslands or along the coastline.

The sea was also full of life, with galaxias and eels moving up and down the rivers in spawning migrations; kahawai, kooheru, snapper, barracouta and kingfish schooling offshore and a host of home-ranging fish living in the rocky reefs.

Spiky kina (sea-eggs), crayfish and shellfish such as paaua (abalone), oysters and mussels clung to coastal rocks, and along the tideline there were tuatua and toheroa molluscs in sandy beaches and vast productive flats of pipi (cockles) and snails in estuaries and harbours. Large colonies of seals and sea-lions lived on the rocky edges of the land, and whales and dolphins swam offshore.

It was a prolific, archaic environment, until then completely undisturbed by human beings.

After the first canoe grounded and the East Polynesian ancestors established themselves on shore, it seems that the islands were quite rapidly explored, because the earliest settlement sites in Aotearoa investigated by archaeologists include stone tools made from rocks from many different parts of the country. In Palliser Bay by the twelfth century, for instance, the local people were using obsidian from Northland, the Coromandel Peninsula, Mayor Island and the central North Island; chert from south-east Wairarapa; and metasomatised argillite from Nelson and D'Urville Island. They also had nephrite in small amounts, probably from Arahura on the West Coast; schist, which was probably from Nelson; schistose-greywacke from the Kaimanawa Ranges in the central North Island; serpentine and talc from Nelson; and silcrete, which may have come from Oturehua in Central Otago.[25] If these sourcings are accurate, they cover most of the 1,500-kilometre north–south sweep of the two main islands.

The initial survey and naming of the new environment was followed by a period of population expansion when scattered settlements were established in optimal sites along the coasts (especially the east coast) of the North and South Islands, linked by efficient canoe-borne exchange networks and working a wide range of resources from seasonal camps as well as base villages. The local animals would have been easy to catch at first, and their populations had not yet been compromised by human predation; and the wide range of micro-climates may also have helped the East Polynesian ancestors to make the transition from life in small tropical islands to life in this temperate archipelago.

Current evidence suggests that the first settlers brought a range of cultivated plants with them, but if they tried to establish coconuts, breadfruit, sugar cane, banana and pandanus, they failed. Even the Polynesian plants that did survive, particularly yams, taro and aute, were at the limits of their climatic tolerance. Probably the first experiments in local horticulture were carried out in the warmer temperatures of the north, where kuumara (sweet potato), taro, aute (paper mulberry), yams and the introduced species of tii (cabbage tree — *Cordyline terminalis* or *C. fruticosa*) grew reasonably well. It may have been in a sheltered northern east-coast bay that the Polynesian ancestors of the Maori lit their first forest-clearing fires, made their gardens on north-facing slopes or terraces, propagated their cherished crops from tubers or plants brought from the homeland and grew them in mounds or basins, mulched with gravel and protected where possible from the wind.

Overleaf: *Map of New Zealand place-names.*
(Detailed maps are provided in the following chapters for those areas indicated *.)

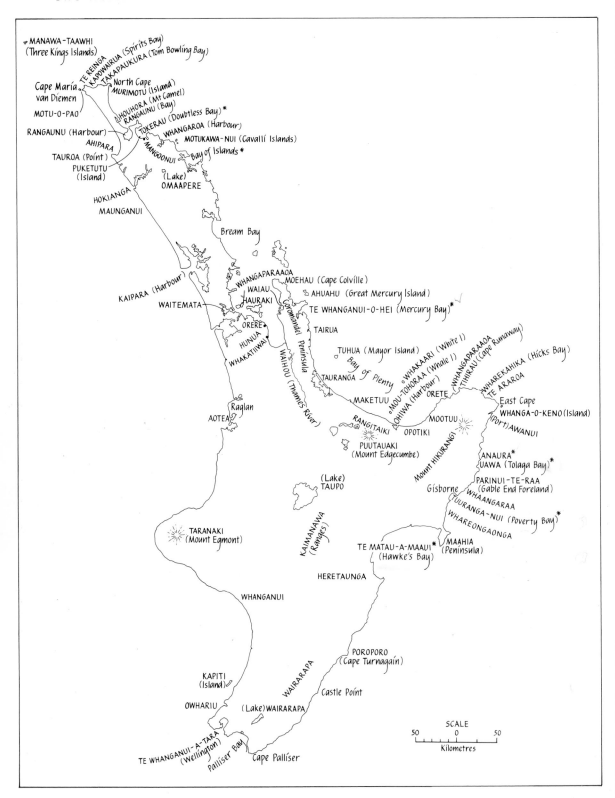

MANAWA-TAAWHI
(Three Kings Islands)

TE REINGA
KAPOWAIRUA (Spirits Bay)
TAKAPAUKURA (Tom Bowling Bay)

Cape Maria
van Diemen

North Cape
MURIMOTU (Island)

MOTU-O-PAO

HOUHORA (Mt Camel)
RANGAUNU (Bay)

TOKERAU (Doubtless Bay) *

RANGAUNU (Harbour)

WHANGAROA (Harbour)

AHIPARA

MOTUKAWA-NUI (Cavalli Islands)

TAUROA (Point)

MANGOONUI

Bay of Islands *

PUKETUTU
(Island)

(Lake)
OMAAPERE

HOKIANGA

MAUNGANUI

Bream Bay

KAIPARA (Harbour)

WHANGAPARAAOA

MOEHAU (Cape Colville)

WAIAU

AHUAHU (Great Mercury Island)

HAURAKI

WAITEMATA

TE WHANGANUI-O-HEI (Mercury Bay) *

ORERE

TAIRUA

HUNUA

WHAKATIIWAI

TUHUA (Mayor Island)

WHAKAARI (White I)

WHANGAPARAAOA

WHAREKAHIKA (Hicks Bay)

MOU-TOHORAA (Whale I)

TIHIRAU (Cape Runaway)

TE ARAROA

Coromandel Peninsula

Bay of Plenty

TAURANGA

OHIWA (Harbour)

ORETE

East Cape

WAIHOU (Thames River)

MAKETUU

WHANGA-O-KENO (Island)

Raglan

(Port) AWANUI

AOTEA

RANGITAIKI

MOOTUU

OPOTIKI

Mount HIKURANGI

ANAURA *

PUUTAUAKI
(Mount Edgecumbe)

UAWA (Tolaga Bay) *

PARINUI-TE-RAA
(Gable End Foreland)

(Lake)
TAUPO

Gisborne

WHAANGARAA

TUURANGA-NUI (Poverty Bay) *

TARANAKI
(Mount Egmont)

KAIMANAWA
(Ranges)

WHAREONGAONGA

TE MATAU-A-MAAUI
(Hawke's Bay) *

MAAHIA
(Peninsula)

HERETAUNGA

WHANGANUI

POROPORO
(Cape Turnagain)

KAPITI
(Island)

WAIRARAPA

Castle Point

OWHARIU

(Lake) WAIRARAPA

TE WHANGANUI-A-TARA
(Wellington)

Palliser Bay

Cape Palliser

SCALE

50   0   50

Kilometres

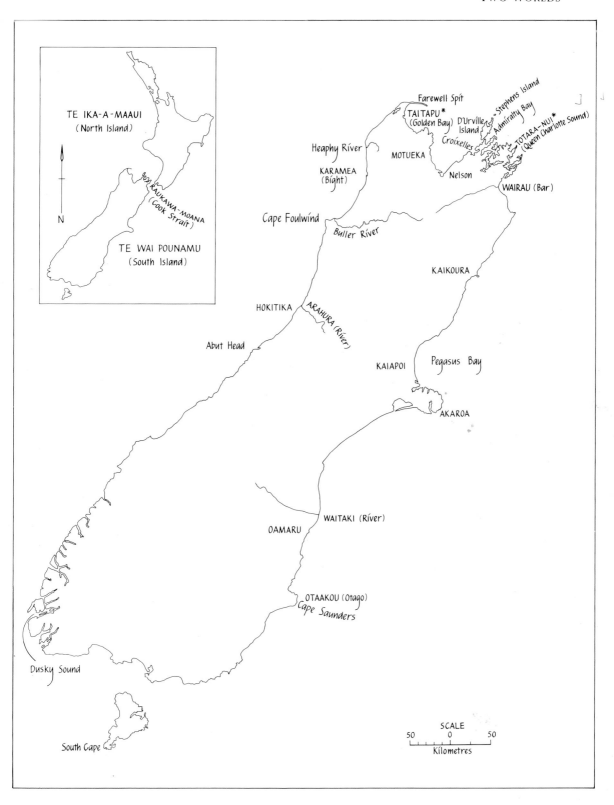

TE IKA-A-MAAUI
(North Island)

N

RAUKAWA-MOANA
(Cook Strait)

TE WAI POUNAMU
(South Island)

Farewell Spit

TAITAPU *
(Golden Bay)

Stephens Island

D'Urville
Island

Admiralty Bay

Croixelles

TOTARA-NUI *
(Queen Charlotte Sound)

Heaphy River

MOTUEKA

Nelson

WAIRAU (Bar)

KARAMEA
(Bight)

Cape Foulwind

Buller River

KAIKOURA

HOKITIKA

ARAHURA (River)

Abut Head

KAIAPOI

Pegasus Bay

AKAROA

WAITAKI (River)

OAMARU

OTAAKOU (Otago)
Cape Saunders

Dusky Sound

South Cape

SCALE

50   0   50

Kilometres

33

Archaeology depends on accident almost as much as it does on science, and so far no site that appears to be one of these very earliest settlements has been discovered. The one tangible link with East Polynesia that has survived is a single trolling-lure shank made from pearl shell, identical to early Marquesan examples and presumably brought from Polynesia, which was found in an excavation at Tairua in Coromandel in 1967.[26] For an overall impression of the founding ancestors, therefore, one must turn to archaeological studies of their tenth- to thirteenth-century settlements, and of these Mount Camel in the Far North, Palliser Bay on the Wairarapa coast, Wairau Bar on the north-east coast of the South Island, and Waitaki Mouth north of Oamaru offer an interesting range of examples.

The Mount Camel site, for instance, is located on a low coastal platform at the mouth of the Houhora Harbour in Northland, which was occupied on a number of occasions between about AD 1100 and 1250. The inhabitants of this summer camp hunted seals, dolphins and moa in some quantity. They also made large catches of snapper, with smaller numbers of trevalli, kahawai and other species being taken. Dogs and rats were eaten, and the remains of various smaller birds including extinct swan and extinct crow have also been found in the middens. It seems that several small family groups, totalling perhaps less than fifty people, came to Mount Camel over a series of summers during the twelfth century to catch seals, dolphins and fish. They also hunted moa elsewhere and brought the trimmed carcasses back to the beach camp to butcher and cook. For their tools they used obsidian from Mayor Island, and basalt and sileceous sinter from Coromandel as well as local stones, and their equipment included one-piece bait hooks, trolling lures, tattooing chisels, and ornaments of perforated seal teeth and small bone and ivory reels.[27] It seems likely that the Mount Camel people were also gardeners, because the Far North was a favourable location for growing Polynesian cultigens, and horticulture was well established in the area later on.

Palliser Bay in the eastern Wairarapa, on the other hand, was a marginal environment for root-cropping in the twelfth century. Early settlement in this area has been particularly well studied, and it includes extensive stone-walled gardens.[28] The East Polynesian settlers at Palliser Bay in the twelfth, thirteenth and fourteenth centuries established a number of small villages at the mouths of streams and rivers, linked by an exchange network (most probably by sea) with other communities throughout the North and South Islands. Soon after settling the area they began to burn the vegetation off the coastal platform and the lower slopes around the bay, and divided up the land into rectangular plots, often laid out at right angles to the beach and marked by low stone walls or stone alignments. In this early period their root crops (which seem to have been mainly kuumara) were stored either inside the houses or in small round or oval pits in sand within the settlements. It was only later that large storage pits were constructed in the area.

In addition to working their gardens the people collected berries and caught birds in the bush behind the bay, especially tui, parakeets and pigeons; they

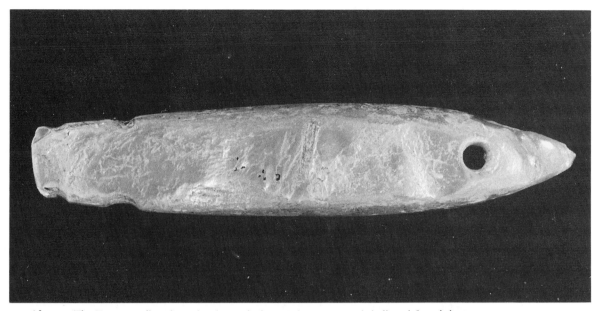

Above: *The Tairua trolling-lure shank, made from Polynesian pearl-shell and found during a Coromandel excavation in 1967.*

Below: *An artist's reconstruction of the Moikau village in Palliser Bay, approximately twelfth century. The house has a cooking area nearby and a group of underground kuumara storepits.*

trapped rats in some numbers, especially in the autumn and early winter; they caught eels and ducks in the rivers and fished using lines and baited hooks around the coastal rocks, trolled for pelagic fish from canoes out at sea and collected crayfish and numerous species of shellfish along the rocky inter-tidal platform. Seals, porpoises and dogs were eaten, and also the occasional moa, but these seem to have been caught elsewhere and it is possible that by the twelfth century moa were already locally extinct.

The early settlers of Palliser Bay were vigorous and healthy, but as they aged, their energetic lifestyle took its toll. Back damage and osteo-arthritis were common, and tooth damage and loss caused serious health problems in early middle age. The women generally bore between two and four children, and most people (as is common in non-industrial societies) died before they were fifty years old. Some of the settlers, including women, were buried with grave goods, and several of them had died violently. In this early period the people followed an ancient Polynesian pattern and buried their dead within the settlements, near the sleeping houses, cooking sheds, small storage pits, drying racks, ovens and fire pits.

Palliser Bay must have been a comfortable home for these hunter-gatherer-gardeners for several centuries, but eventually their slash-and-burn horticulture and the intensive exploitation of marine resources, especially the larger shellfish, began to affect the local environment. Once the coastal forests were burnt off, erosion began to damage the gardens, and the rivers carried an increasing load of sediment onto the beaches, eventually killing off local colonies of filter-feeding shellfish. The people had to travel further inland to catch birds and by about AD 1600 it seems that the local population, who may have also been threatened from the outside, finally gave up and moved out of the area.

Much less is known about the way of life of the people who lived at Wairau Bar, on the north-east coast of the South Island, from the twelfth to the fourteenth centuries, because this site was excavated in the 1940s when archaeological methods in New Zealand were relatively rudimentary.[29] All the same, this settlement on the bar at the mouth of the Wairau River in Marlborough still stands as one of the richest representations of the portable material culture of the early East Polynesian ancestors in Aotearoa. The excavations focused on a series of burials, including one group of seven high-ranking individuals, each of whom had been buried with a perforated moa's egg, and most of whom were also accompanied by magnificent adzes, or necklaces of 'whale tooth' units in whale ivory or moabone, reel-shaped beads with whale-tooth pendants, or porpoise teeth. In three cases the head had been removed after burial with the accompanying necklace, presumably for ritual reasons. Some of the other burials investigated also had grave goods, including reel necklaces in fossil shell, serpentine and human bone, fish-hooks and nephrite adzes. Both men and women were buried with grave goods at Wairau (although those of the men tended to be more elaborate), suggesting a system in which both men and women could have high status.

The people at Wairau Bar evidently hunted moa in some quantity, because moa bones (particularly of the squat and massive *Euryapteryx* species) were scattered all over the site. Water fowl including paradise and grey ducks and the extinct swan were caught on the nearby lagoons with their extensive (but apparently later) systems of man-made canals.[30] It is evident from the trolling shanks and bait hooks found at Wairau that the local people also line-fished and trolled from canoes out at sea. Bone awls and needles were common, and the finer needles were no doubt used to sew skins either edge to edge or onto garments made of flax. Tattooing chisels were also found, and harpoon points, which were probably used to kill dolphins and perhaps also skates and sharks. Fowling does not appear to have been common at Wairau, for only one bird-spear point was found; nor is there any evidence of horticulture.

The Wairau Bar settlers may have been adze-traders as well as accomplished moa-hunters, and at this time in their history they seem to have been wealthy. Nevertheless, current evidence suggests that they died quite young, with an average lifespan of twenty-eight years, and none of those buried had lived beyond their early forties.[31] This was not because of ill health, for the people were vigorous and strong and their teeth in fact suffered much less damage (perhaps from a less fibrous diet) than those of their contemporaries in Palliser Bay. Rather, the life expectancy in early Aotearoa as reconstructed by physical anthropologists (on the basis of rather limited evidence and methods) seems to have been quite short compared to modern times, although it is very much on a par with other predominantly hunting and gathering societies, and often longer than the lifespan in twelfth- and thirteenth-century Europe where the people were plagued by a variety of epidemic diseases.

Finally, the tenth-century site at Waitaki Mouth on the south-east coast of the South Island appears to have been a moa butchery on a vast scale. Hundreds of ovens distributed over an area of more than seventy hectares were used to cook the meat of moa, most of which were probably hunted inland, trimmed into carcasses, piled on reed rafts and floated down the Waitaki River to the coast for processing. The moa legbones were often smashed, possibly to extract the marrow to use in processing the meat; alternatively the meat may have been smoked and hung up to dry in the warm, desiccating coastal winds.[32]

It has been suggested that at places like Wairau and Waitaki, moa were herded up and driven into the water or into traps, and then killed, but this no longer seems likely. The living relatives of the moa are all competent swimmers, and there is no good archaeological evidence for large-scale trapping. Most moa evidently moved in small flocks, and the larger species, including *Euryapteryx geranoides*, must have been formidable birds to hunt, since on the basis of comparisons with related species it seems likely that they could run faster than a man and disembowel an over-confident hunter with one slash of their claws.[33] Most often they must have been ambushed and killed with spears thrown at close range, snared, or bailed up by hunting dogs especially bred for their powerful jaw and neck muscles. It has been estimated that at least 100,000 moa were killed during the early period in southern New Zealand alone,[34] and in the non-horticultural south this concentrated supply of meat must have been of inestimable value.

It is not easy to generalise about early Polynesian life in Aotearoa, if only because the habitats in which different communities lived were so diverse. Perhaps it is best to think of the country at that early period of human settlement as an archipelago of islands, divided from each other by hills and mountains as well as by sea, with their inhabitants living mostly at peace with one another and maintaining an extensive network of exchange and communication along rivers, land paths and by sea. The climate seems to have been relatively calm and mild, and local variations in conditions allowed the ancestors to adapt Polynesian gardening methods and to experiment with new ways of storing their crops. The bell-shaped pits and bin pits that were commonly used in tropical Polynesia for storing fermented breadfruit paste came to be used here for storing root crops over the winter,[35] and raised rim pits and roofed rectangular pits were developed to cope with the large-scale winter storage of kuumara and possibly yams. By about the twelfth century a wide variety of storage pits were being built in and around settlements in those areas where gardening was possible.

In all coastal regions the settlers also fished from the shore and out at sea, collected a wide variety of shellfish, foraged in the bush for berries and hunted birds both in the forests and along the beaches. In some places seals were a major source of food, while in others moa were hunted in large numbers and their meat preserved, very likely for exchange to other groups as well as for subsistence. Useful rock resources throughout the country were quickly identified, and stone-working quarries at Mayor Island (obsidian), Tahanga in Coromandel (basalt), and D'Urville Island and Nelson (argillite) produced rocks or adzes and adze blanks that were exchanged over long distances, while a distinctive early blade-making industry remained largely restricted to the southern South Island.[36] Nephrite (or greenstone) does not seem to have been extensively worked during this early period. Inland exploration for rock sources and for moa was apparently commonplace, and the rock shelters in which hunters and travellers stayed during these expeditions, particularly in the South Island, were often decorated with charcoal and red ochre drawings of people, birds, dogs and other creatures. In the main villages, rectangular wood-framed houses with partly enclosed porches were built early on, for example, in the twelfth century at Moikau in Palliser Bay,[37] but lighter shelters and circular and oval huts, as well as cooking sheds, drying racks and storage platforms were also constructed. Fighting seems to have been uncommon and episodic, and the early settlements do not appear to have been fortified.

Life in early Aotearoa was never static, and from this initial phase of human settlement a counterpoint of exchanges between people and land and sea began that has continued ever since. Once the first forest-clearing fires were lit, people began to compete with the land-living creatures, especially birds, for the use of the environment. The intensive hunting of moa and seals, and the gathering of the larger shellfish began to tip the balance against their survival in some parts of the archipelago. The rat (kiore) and dog also hunted for food, and the depredations of the rat in particular may have driven the lizard-like tuatara out of its mainland habitats.

By the fourteenth century the larger species of moa and elephant and leopard seals were scarce in the South Island[38] and almost non-existent in the North. The native swan, the flightless goose, Finsch's duck, the New Zealand eagle and the native species of goshawk, coot and crow had all become extinct.[39] By the fifteenth century fewer birds of fewer species were being caught in most North Island communities,[40] while all species of moa were virtually extinct in the North Island and had become rare in the South.[41]

The reason for these declines in various animal populations is not certain; climatic changes may have played their part, but hunting, the introduction of dogs and rats, and forest clearance for stands of fernroot and cabbage trees, gardens and villages were almost certainly more significant factors. The settlers in their turn were then forced to adapt to changing conditions. From about AD 1350 onwards, fishing and shell-fishing became more important than hunting in most coastal settlements, and fibrous foods (which must have included both fern-root and cabbage tree, or tii, roots) were more commonly eaten. Settlement expanded into the interior of the North Island and intensified, especially along the coastline. In all horticultural regions by about AD 1500, population pressures and a growing competition for resources and prestige were being reflected in the construction of elaborate fortified villages (paa) and foodstores, the secret burial of the dead, and the display of wealth in greenstone ornaments and probably also in carving. Warfare apparently intensified, evidence of cannibalism begins to appear, and life in many parts of the country became increasingly militarised, with consequences that are recorded in the tribal histories — surprise attacks, inter-group vendettas, social upheaval and forced migrations.

Many practical details of everyday life in early Aotearoa can be retrieved by archaeological excavation, but the question of how that world or series of kin-based worlds were understood is another matter altogether. Pre-European ideas about the world were often influenced after contact with European beliefs and thinking; but if one relies mainly on early recorded statements in Maori and compares those with cosmological accounts from other East Polynesian societies, there is a fair chance of identifying those descriptions of reality that are authentically pre-European. On such a basis it seems clear that in early Aotearoa people lived in a world where gods, people, land and sky, plants, birds, reptiles, fish and other animals shared in a unity of being which was expressed in a language of common descent. There were various accounts of how that world began, but in one cosmological chant recorded from Te Kohuwai of Rongoroa,[42] the universe began with a stirring of primal energy that produced thought and then consciousness, in a series of genealogical stages that eventually also produced lands, gods and people:

Na te kune te pupuke	From the conception the increase,
Na te pupuke te hihiri	From the increase the thought,
Na te hihiri te mahara	From the thought the remembrance,
Na te mahara te hinengaro	From the remembrance the consciousness
Na te hinengaro te manako.	From the consciousness the desire.

Ka hua te wananga	Knowledge became fruitful
Ka noho i a rikoriko	It dwelt with the feeble glimmering;
Ka puta ki waho ko te po	It brought forth night
Ko te po nui, te po roa,	The great night, the long night,
Te po tuturi, te po i pepeke	The lowest night, the loftiest night,
Te po uriuri, te po tangotango,	The thick night, to be felt,
Te po wawa, te po te kitea,	The night to be touched,
Te po te waia	The night not to be seen,
Te po i oti atu ki te mate.	The night of death.
Na te kore i ai	From the nothing the begetting,
Te kore te wiwia	From the nothing the increase,
Te kore te rawea	From the nothing the abundance,
Ko hotupu	The power of increasing,
Ko hauora	The living breath;
Ka noho i te atea	It dwelt with the empty space,
Ka puta ki waho,	and produced the atmosphere which
te rangi e tu nei.	is above us.
Ko te rangi e teretere ana	The atmosphere which floats above
i runga i te whenua,	the earth;
Ka noho te rangi nui e tu	The great firmament above us, dwelt
nei, ka noho i a ata tuhi	with the early dawn,
Ka puta ki waho te marama	And the moon sprung forth;
Ka noho te rangi e tu nei,	The atmosphere above us, dwelt with
ka noho i a te werowero	the heat,
Ka puta ki waho ko te ra	And hence proceeded the sun;
Kokiritia ana ki runga,	They were thrown up above, as the
hei pukanohi mo te rangi	chief eyes of Heaven:
Ka tau te rangi	Then the heavens became light,
Te ata tuhi, te ata rapa	The early dawn, the early day,
Ka mahina, ka mahina te ata	The mid-day. The blaze of day
i hikurangi.	from the sky.
Ka noho i Hawaiki	The sky above dwelt with Hawaiki,
Ka puta ki waho	and produced land,
Ko Taporapora, Ko Tauwarenikau	Taporapora, Tauwarenikau, Kuku-paru,
Ko Kuku-paru, Ko Wawau-atea,	Wawau-atea, Wiwhi-te-Rangiora.
Ko Wiwhi-te-Rangiora.	
Ko Ru, no Ru, ko Ouhoko	. . . And now Ru (a god) was born,
	and from Ru, Ouhoko;
Na Ouhoko, ko Ruatapu,	From Ouhoko, Ruatapu
Ko Ruatawito, no Ruatawito	and Ruatawito; from Ruatawito,
Ko Ruakaipo, no Ruakaipo	Ruakaipo; from Ruakaipo,
Ko Ngae, Ngae nui, Ngae roa	Ngae (a man), Ngae nui, Ngae roa
Ngae pea, Ngae tuturi	Ngae pea, Ngae tuturi
Ngae pepeke, ko Tatiti,	Ngae pepeke, and then Tatiti,
Ko Ruatapu, ko Toi,	Ruatapu, Toi
Ko Rauru . . .	and Rauru . . .

Opposite: *Uenuku-tuwhatu. Carved resting-place of a god.*

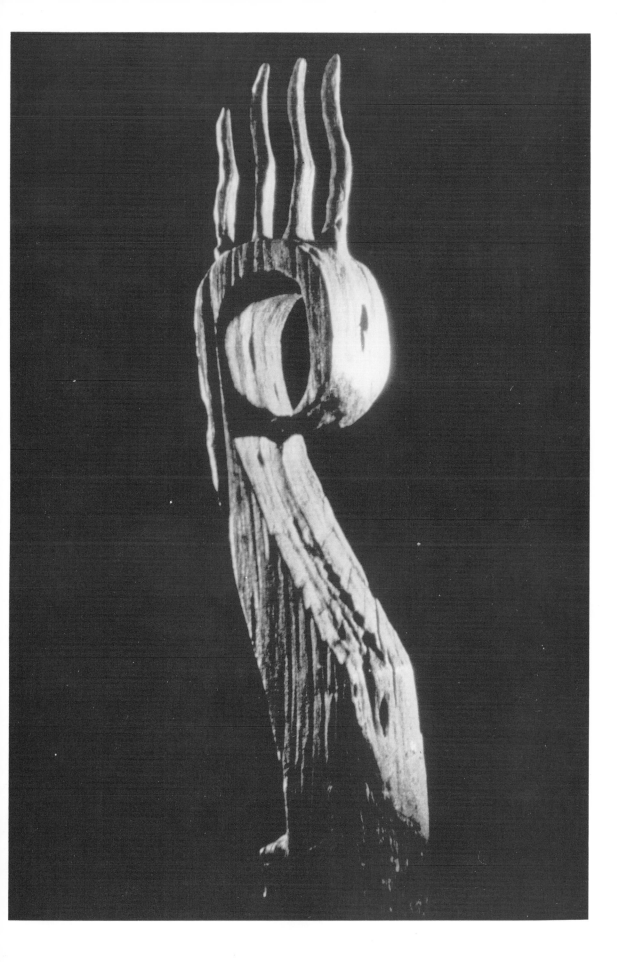

Other chants used metaphors of plant growth to describe the beginnings of the world,[43] or began with the god singing or talking the cosmos into life.[44]

Whakapapa (genealogy) was the central principle that ordered the universe and this, too, was often expressed in metaphors of plant growth, so that a descent-line might be described as a gourd plant, with the main line as its stem and sub-sidiary lines branching off like twining tendrils which might either flourish, or wither away and die. All things in the world were held to share common qualities of life:

> All things unfold their nature (tipu; also 'grow'), live (ora) and have form (aahua), whether trees, rocks, birds, reptiles, fish, animals or human beings.[45]

This kinship was elaborated in magnificent accounts of the mating and separation of the Earth Mother and the Sky Father, when the world and its familiar creatures were formed. Nepia Pohuhu, a priest from an East Coast school of learning, recorded one such description in 1865:

> Ranginui (great sky), which stands above, felt a desire for Papatuanuku (the earth), whose belly was turned up; he desired her as a wife. So Rangi came down to Papa. In that period the amount of light was nil; absolute and complete darkness pre-vailed; there was no sun, no moon, no stars, no clouds, no light, no mist — no ripples stirred the surface of the ocean; no breath of air, a complete and absolute stillness.
>
> So Ranginui took Papa-tua-nuku as his wife; and then he set plants to cover her nakedness, for her armpits, her head and the body; and after that the smaller trees to clothe them both, for the body of the earth was naked. Then he placed the upstanding trees of the forest, and now Papa felt a great warmth, which was all-embracing. After this he placed insects of all kinds and the ancestors of the tuatara amongst the smaller bushes, in the clumps of smaller trees, and in the great forests. Next he put the crabs and the shellfish of various kinds on the earth and in the sea. Finally Rangi and Papa created their children the gods — first their eyes, then the 'house' to hold them (the head); and then the chest and body and the bones of the legs.
>
> Because Ranginui over-laid and completely covered Papa-tua-nuku, their chil-dren could not grow and mature, nor could anything bear fruit; they were in an unstable position, floating in darkness: some were crawling like lizards, some were upright with the arms held up, some were lying with the knees partly drawn up, some lying on their sides, some were lying stretched out at full length, some on their backs, some were stooping, some with their heads bent down, some embracing, some kicking out with legs and arms, some kneeling, some standing, some inhaling deep breaths, some with exhausted breath . . . they were all within the embrace of Ranginui and Papa.[46]

Eventually a faint glimmering of light penetrated this darkness, and the children of Rangi and Papa began to plan their escape. First Uepoto, and then the god Taane reached the outside world, but it was so bitterly cold there that they returned to their mother's side. Now Taane persuaded his brothers to help him force their parents apart, to allow light to enter the world. Taane used four props to separate Rangi and Papa but they still held fast to each other, so he used the sacred adzes Te Awhiorangi and Te Whironui to sever his parents' arms; and in the angry quarrels that followed, the brothers went their separate ways. Once the earth and sky had been forced apart the cosmos became established as a world with twelve (or eleven, or ten in various tribal versions) layered heavens above the earth, and a number of layered regions beneath it. According to a description given to Richard Taylor in the 1850s, the lowest heaven was separated from the earth by a solid transparent substance like ice or crystal, and above this pavement was the reservoir of the rain, and above that the spirits and and winds.[47]

Now the gods created the first woman and took control of earth and sky, and Taane mated with her to begin the human race. Taawhiri-matea went to the seventh layer of the sky to command the winds; Tama-te-uira became the guardian of all different forms of lightning, Parawhenua-mea married Kura and they made the sea; Tuu-te-ahunga married Hine-Pike and they produced all kinds of insects, and Takoto-wai married Tua-matua and they became the origin of the various rocks and stones. By the mating and reproduction of these and other gods the world was progressively differentiated, and within each family the children quarrelled and went to their own places to live. Mangoo (shark), for instance, debated with Tuatara about whether they should live on land or sea. Tuatara suggested that they should live on the land, Mangoo preferred the sea, and they argued bitterly until finally Mangoo said, 'Enough! You stay or show as an object of disgust for people!' and Tuatara replied, 'Very well! That will be my mana, I will live. As for you, you will be hauled up with a hook in your mouth and thrown into the bottom of a canoe; your head will be broken with a fernroot beater and you will be hung out to dry in the sun like a menstrual cloth!'[48]

In the aeons that followed, demi-gods such as Maaui and Mataora brought gifts of godly knowledge to the world, and in particular Maaui stole fire, slowed the passage of the sun in the sky, fished up the North Island of Aotearoa with his grandmother's jawbone and unsuccessfully tried to conquer death. He lived in Hawaiki, that remote ancestral homeland, and subsequent stories in the various tribal histories tell of events in Hawaiki that led to the migrations of the ancestors to Aotearoa.

These and other stories emphasised the kinship between people and their ancestor-gods, and people learned to call on those gods who looked after particular aspects of their daily lives. To do this they used rituals and karakia (chants), learned from senior relatives or in the schools of learning, which summoned the gods to join their junior kinsfolk and to lend their mana (godly efficacy) to human pursuits. Sometimes these gods were remote ancestors who controlled whole areas of life, such as Taane for forests and the birds, or Tangaroa for the sea; but quite often they were family ancestors who looked after their direct descendants, communicating with them through priests, mediums, dreams or omens, or coming to rest in particular animals, or in their skulls which had been kept and cherished by their successors.

People prized this contact with the gods and safeguarded it by observing the laws of tapu, which set apart those people, times and places where the gods were present and in communication with the human world. All living things had a mauri, or life principle, and the mauri of particular places could be represented in material form, often in a sacred stone. Gardens, fishing grounds and forests were protected during their growing seasons by raahui, ritual prohibitions which placed an area under the mana of a particular leader and his or her gods. The gods were always more or less present in some of their descendants, particularly those of chiefly rank, for when a chiefly child was born the priests called up the ancestor gods and the spirits of local forests and mountains, and focused them in a koromiko branch, which was then placed on the child's head, transferring the ancestral mana to the child.[49] Both men and women had gods who governed their characteristic activities, so that work such as weaving and war were surrounded by tapu restrictions, while shared activities such as gardening were controlled by rituals in which senior men and women played parallel parts.

Mana was the practical force of the gods at work in everyday affairs, and the need to defend mana against attacks by insult, excessive generosity, war or witchcraft, (through utu, the principle of equal return), made life turbulent at times. The tribal histories tell of disputes that were solved by gifts of land or diplomatic marriages, or that led to further insults, killings, and embittered wars in which entire kin-groups were virtually wiped out. It was in this context that the bodies of enemies might be ritually eaten, their bones turned into fish-hooks or forks for food, their heads preserved and taunted and their wives and children enslaved. Equally, on the other hand, the assertion of mana inspired hospitality and feasting, aristocratic rituals and alliances, the construction of great fortifications (paa), carved houses and canoes in some parts of the country, the weaving of fine textiles, and the celebration of ancestral deeds in tribal histories, oratory and song.

Ancestor-gods gave people courage and confidence in their daily lives — although ritual errors or attacks by hostile gods could cause intense fear and even death; but this did not lead to a neglect of practical knowledge. The life of particular communities in pre-European Aotearoa was based on a close and devoted study of the physical environment, and a detailed knowledge of plants, animals, rocks, the sea, fish, the weather and the stars. These matters, however, unlike more abstract notions about the world, were relatively accessible to European observation, and they can be safely set aside until the visits of specific European expeditions to particular Maori communities are described.

Chapter Two

WORLD 2: TE AO TUARUA

Half a spin of the earth away, seventeenth-century Europeans lived in a landscape that had been inhabited by humans for about 350,000 years[1] — not so long in the scope of human history, perhaps, but long enough for much of its surface to have been extensively reshaped. The great European plain was edged by an ancient rocky plateau to the north, a belt of hills to the south, and it was punctuated by the high branching ridges of the Alps, which divided and isolated one area from another. Most Europeans lived in scattered homesteads and hamlets surrounded by cultivations and pastures, or in small, walled towns whose people still owned and worked in the fields outside. Villages were built along the network of country roads, sometimes clustering around village greens. The towns had narrow streets, with a central open marketplace overlooked by the church of its oldest parish and often a market house, where the town leaders conducted most of their business. Street life was bustling and boisterous, with goods being sold and made, and in the village greens and town marketplaces the people held their festivities, with singing, dancing, drinking, pageants, processions and other entertainments.

The houses in these settlements were built of wood and clay (or less commonly of stone or brick), with thatched or tiled roofs. Inside the houses there might be stools, a chest, a bench, a bedstead, even a tapestry bedcover, but the poor slept 'on straw . . . with no bed or furniture . . . and only separated from the pigs by a screen'.[2] Many families were virtually homeless, living in makeshift shelters in towns or in the countryside. The rich were sometimes very rich, building magnificent mansions in the cities and on their rural estates which housed large retinues of servants and armed retainers. As a French observer wrote in 1622:

> Oh, golden age! Now we see our countryside enriched with superb buildings, the sight of which wipes out antiquity; and not only are there houses of the bourgeoisie but also superb chateaux of judges, nobles and financiers which in less than a year have destroyed a thousand peasant homes in order to build one noble one.[3]

There were perhaps five to six thousand cities and towns in Europe at this period, ranging from a few giant cities with more than 100,000 inhabitants to several thousand small towns with populations of less than 1,000 people each.[4] The towns were defended with ditch, bank and wooden palisades or stone walls with gun platforms and embrasures, and they clustered most thickly in those areas of dense population — the Low Countries, the Rhineland, central Germany and northern Italy. The large cities were often political capitals, or trading centres with good harbours and navigable rivers for their fleets of wooden sailing ships and barges. About eighty to ninety per cent of the population lived in the countryside, however, with its patchwork of pastures and hedged, walled or open fields set out amongst the retreating masses of broad-leaved woodland. 'Our old Fathers can tell us how Woods are decayed, and People in the room of Trees multiplied,'[5] said one seventeenth-century writer of this human expansion into the forests.

Europe in the mid-seventeenth century was in a ferment — restless, energetic, and pushing at the known edges of the world. New ways of living were beginning to emerge. In the Netherlands, for instance, a free-thinking society of traders sent their ships around the world, while in England a domestic revolution overturned the divine right of kings, and the foundations of British imperialism were laid. None of these changes guaranteed a comfortable life for ordinary folk, however. Most people made a precarious living in seventeenth-century Europe, and famines were commonplace. The climate was becoming colder, and crop failures affected most of the continent in 1649, 1660–61 and during the 1690s, with many local famines in between. Many peasants lived on a diet of rye bread, milk, and soups and porridges of oats and barley, with a few wild fruits and garden vegetables. In famine years, however, they were forced to eat grass, hay, the roots of wild plants, bark, bran, acorns and even partially rotted chestnuts.[6] The parish register of La Croix-du-Perche in France recorded the consequences of one such famine in its entries for 1662:

> Buried 4 March 1662, the child of the late Bignon, died of actual starvation.
>
> Buried 2 January 1662, in our church, the child of the late Jean Vedys, died of starvation in a cowshed.
>
> Buried in our cemetery 20 January 1662, a man named David and his wife, died of starvation at Les Charnois, together with a man named La Gravière, died of starvation.
>
> Buried in our cemetery in March 1662, Anne Rochelte, who died of starvation with her two children.
>
> Buried in our cemetery 28 April 1662, the son of the late Jacques Drovin, died of starvation, like his father.[7]

Contagious disease was a frequent affliction, with devastating epidemics of smallpox, influenza, typhoid and bubonic plague in the rat-infested cities, while typhus, which was carried by rat fleas and human lice, marched in the wake of local armies. Warfare caused widespread social disruption and the destruction of

Opposite above: *An aristocratic picnic in France, painted by Nicholas de Bruyn, illustrating the lavish costumes, architecture, pleasure gardens and entertainments enjoyed by the French nobility.*

Opposite below: *This watercolour by Adrian van Ostade shows the poverty of a seventeenth-century Dutch family. Housing and furniture were rudimentary, and food was often scarce.*

crops and villages. Child mortality was high, with forty to fifty per cent of all children in seventeenth-century rural Spain dying before the age of seven, for example, and twenty-five per cent of children in northern France dying before they were one year old.[8] Industrial disease also caused major health problems, as an early Italian professor of practical medicine described:

> miners: . . . they come up into the untainted open air looking as ghastly as the retinue of the god of the underworld because of their stay in those foul dark places. Whatever metal they mine, they invite dreadful diseases which too often mock at every remedy . . . But it is from mercury mines that there issues the most cruel bane of all that deal death and destruction to miners. . . In the mines of Meissen where black pompholyx is found, the hands and legs of the miners are eaten away to the bone . . .
>
> gilders: . . . we all know what terrible maladies are contracted from mercury by goldsmiths, especially by those employed in gilding silver and copper objects. This work cannot be done without the use of amalgam, and when they later drive off the mercury by fire they cannot avoid receiving the poisonous fumes into their mouth, even though they turn away their faces. Hence craftsmen of this sort very soon become subject to vertigo, asthma, and paralysis. Very few of them reach old age, and even when they do not die young their health is so terribly undermined that they pray for death . . .
>
> glass-workers: . . . During the process of making glass vessels the men stand continually half-naked in freezing winter weather near very hot furnaces . . . they are liable to diseases of the chest . . . Pleurisy, asthma, and a chronic cough are the natural result. But a far worse fate awaits those who make colored glass for bracelets and other ornaments for women. In order to color the crystal, they use calcinated borax, antimony, and a certain amount of gold; these they pound together to an impalpable powder and mix it with glass to make the paste needed for this process, and however much they cover and avert their faces while they do this they cannot help breathing in the noxious fumes. Hence it often happens that some of them fall senseless, and sometimes they are suffocated; or in the course of time they suffer from ulcers in the mouth, oesophagus, and trachea. In the end they join the ranks of consumptives, since their lungs become ulcerated, as has been clearly shown by the dissection of their corpses . . .[9]

The average lifespan was short — in seventeenth-century Paris, the average life expectancy was twenty-three years (although some people lived into their eighties and nineties), while in the ruling families of Western Europe during this period, the average male lifespan was twenty-eight years and the average female lifespan was thirty-four years.[10] On current evidence it appears that seventeenth-century Europeans lived about as long as pre-European Maori, but that overall they were more prone to disease and quite often less well fed.

Nevertheless, population densities were high in much of Europe — perhaps forty to fifty people per square kilometre[11] in many areas, and the overall population of continental Europe during this century was approximately a hundred million.[12] This great conglomeration of people gave impetus to travel, trade, internal as well as external migration, and the growth of industry and capitalist exchange. In the seventeenth century overseas trade items became used as everyday goods for the first time — sugar from the West Indies, spices, Asiatic textiles and, by the end of the century, coffee and tea; and European colonists were moving in a steady stream to other parts of the world — America, India and the East and West Indies.

The economy of Europe was still solidly based on localised production and exchange, however, and the social order was locally various and small-scale. Peasants and agricultural labourers pastured their animals, and worked small parcels of land with various types of wooden ploughs, sometimes harrows, and sickles and scythes, to produce grain, live cattle, milk, butter and cheese, fruit, beer, wine, or cider, and wool, skins and hides for use at home, to pay their rents and tithes, or for sale at the local market. In many cases they could not afford to consume the best of their own produce, as Richard Baxter explained in the *Poor Husbandman's Advocate* (1691):

> If their sow pig or their hens breed chickens, they cannot afford to eat them, but must sell them to make their rent. They cannot afford to eat the eggs their hens lay, nor the apples nor the pears that grow on their trees (save some that are not vendible) but must make money of all. All the best of their butter and cheese they must sell, and feed themselves and children . . . with skimmed cheese and skimmed milk and whey curds.[13]

Sowing and harvesting were carried out collectively, and peasants relied on common lands and woods for pasture, firewood, building materials and wild foods. Most households also had gardens where they grew fruit, vegetables, herbs and sometimes flax for spinning. Everyone in the family worked, either in the fields or in the case of children, gathering wood, carrying water, spinning, or guarding sheep, goats and cows. Peasant families were also often bound to labour for the local lord in return for his care in times of need, but in Eastern Europe in particular, the nobles tightened their control over the peasants until by the end of the century, most had been declared serfs. The economic lot of most European peasants was accurately described by a French commentator in 1622:

> If, when he sowed his ground, the peasant really realised for whom he was doing it, he would not sow. For he is the one to profit least from his labour. The first handful of grain he casts on the soil is for God, so he throws it freely. The second goes to the birds; the third for ground-rents; the fourth for tithes; the fifth for . . . taxes and impositions. And all that goes even before he has anything for himself.[14]

Not surprisingly, many free peasants became indebted and left the land, going to the towns to look for work or drifting miserably around the countryside as vagabonds and beggars. In 1634 it was estimated that there were 65,000 beggars in Paris, and by 1641 that 'the fourth part of the inhabitants of most of the parishes of England are miserable poor people and (harvest-time excepted) without any subsistence'.[15] Most of the poor were women and children, and while the churches encouraged Christian charity, local authorities concerned about prostitution, robbery and violence passed laws ordering vagrants to be whipped out of town or put into workhouses and houses of correction. Those who were caught in criminal acts faced even harsher punishments — hanging,

*A sixteenth-century German print illustrates the various punishments meted out to criminals —
birching, beheading, hanging, drowning, burning, quartering, eye-gouging and other forms of
maiming.*

burning, the amputation of a hand or an ear, beheading, disembowelling, drowning in a barrel of water or branding as well as imprisonment and transportation.
Vagrants and criminals could also be enslaved, along with war captives and those
taken as slaves in Muslim countries, Africa or European territories overseas.

Rural workers included blacksmiths, carpenters, millers, and spinners and
weavers doing piece-work in their homes. In the towns small urban workshops
run by a master with his few apprentices and journeymen were common. Prosperous craftsfolk, petty traders, minor officials, bureaucrats, doctors, lawyers
and money-lenders made up the ranks of the urban bourgeoisie, and they formed
a mobile group between the rich and those in society who toiled or starved.
Successful bourgeois invested in public loans, bought public offices and sometimes became landowners, while those who failed suffered an ignominious
descent into poverty. Seventeenth-century European society was divided
between the poor and the relatively few who led comfortable and sometimes
luxurious lives. Aristocrats and the gentry held an almost complete monopoly
over political power and social position and controlled much of society's wealth,
frequently spending it in gorgeous display — large masonry mansions and
palaces, elaborate food, clothing and furniture, and magnificent entertainments.
They also travelled widely, and despite the political fragmentation of Europe,
male nobles in particular made excursions to the courts of other countries, to
war, to overseas universities or simply to gain a wider experience of the world.
As Sir Thomas Bodley put it in 1647:

I waxed desirous to travel beyond the seas for attaining to the knowledge of some special modern tongues and for the increase of my experience in the managing of affairs, being then wholly addicted to employ myself and all my cares into the public of the state.[16]

Some aristocrats gained large incomes from public office, but most of their wealth, which they invested in the few large-scale commercial enterprises of the time (mining, the Baltic and North Sea fisheries, shipping, textiles and trading companies), was ultimately derived from the land. Noble estates varied in size from several thousand hectares or more to units of twenty hectares or less.[17] Except in Eastern Europe, most were leased out in small parcels to peasant tenants or farmed in larger units by the more prosperous peasants.

In most European countries, however, the greatest overlords were the monarchs, who headed the machinery of state and disbursed patronage to nobles and bureaucrats alike. States could be transferred from one European monarch to another by marriage, barter, sale, bequest or treaty, and family and religious quarrels among the ruling dynasties led to frequent battles fought by cavalry and foot-soldiers armed with muskets and pikes on land, or by cannon-laden fighting ships at sea. The scale of warfare escalated during this century until some states mustered armies of 200,000 to 300,000 soldiers, and great stretches of country-side were left devastated in their wake. An ecclesiastical report described the area around Paris in 1652 after one large-scale campaign:

Villages and hamlets deserted and bereft of clergy, streets infected by stinking carrion and dead bodies lying exposed, houses without doors or windows, everything reduced to cesspools and stables, and above all the sick and dying, with no bread, meat, medicine, fire, beds, linen or covering, and no priest, doctor, surgeon or anyone to comfort them.[18]

Ex-soldiers often turned to theft and were hanged by the military authorities. From 'The Horrors of War', 1633, a series of engravings by Jacques Callot.

51

It is little wonder that popular rebellions and uprisings were common around mid-century, as war, taxes, epidemics, drought and famine combined to make life intolerable for the poor. Tax collectors and the property of rich officials and profiteers were attacked by angry mobs. In 1636 at Saintonge, a tax collector was cut up alive and his flesh nailed to the doors of the people's houses. In 1647 in Naples, the tax collector Moschetola was chased over rooftops and all his belongings burnt.[19] Uprisings in Russia, Poland, Normandy, the Spanish provinces, Switzerland, the Fronde rebellion in France and the Levellers in England flared up in protest against exploitation and the sufferings of ordinary people, but by 1650 the riots had been quelled and absolutist power had become even more entrenched.

As in the Maori case, however, the practical details of everyday life do not fully explain the ways in which the world was understood. People in seventeenth-century Europe conceived of reality in ways that were influenced by Christianity, ancient philosophy and by popular beliefs in the supernatural. The universe was thought to be made up of basic primary matter, which had four properties: hot, cold, moist and dry. Hot and moist together made up air; cold and moist made water; hot and dry made fire, and cold and dry made earth. Since earth was the heaviest it lay at the centre of the universe, surrounded by the moon, the planets and the stars, which encircled it in perfect spheres.[20] The earth was seen not as an inanimate object but as alive — living, breathing and even thinking, and the universe was inhabited by a hierarchy of beings which stretched downwards in a 'Great Chain of Being' from God through cherubim and seraphim, archangels and angels, kings, princes of the Church, magistrates and merchants, to the great mass of peasants and labourers; and beyond the human order to animals and plants and finally stones and earth, which had no soul at all. God was worshipped in churches and cathedrals built with high, vaulting arches and spires, carvings and stained glass; and common notions of how the world began were based on the opening verses of Genesis, quoted here in the stately language of a 1611 English Bible:

> In the beginning God created the Heaven, and the Earth.
> And the earth was without forme, and voyd, and darknesse was upon the face of the deepe: and the Spirit of God mooved upon the face of the waters.
> And God said, Let there be light: and there was light.
> And God saw the light, that it was good: and God divided the light from the darknesse.
> And God called the light, Day, and the darknesse he called Night: and the evening and the morning were the first day.
> And God said, Let there be a firmament in the midst of the waters: and let it divide the waters from the waters.
> And God made the firmament; and divided the waters, which were under the firmament, from the waters, which were above the firmament: and it was so.
> And God called the firmament Heaven: and the evening and the morning were the second day.
> And God said, Let the waters under the heaven be gathered together unto one place, and let the dry land appeare: and it was so.

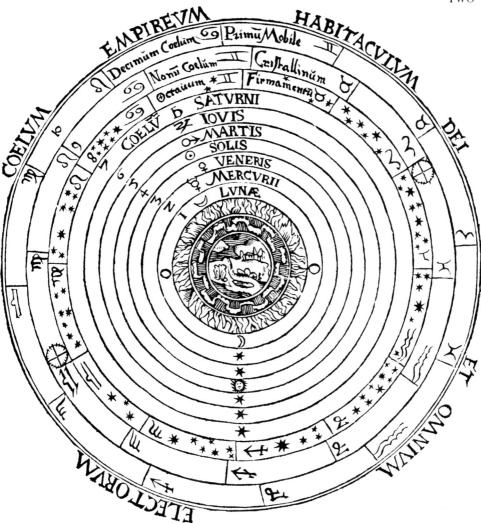

A universe of concentric spheres surrounded the Earth. Illustrated here by Peter Apian in Cosmographicus Liber, *Antwerp 1533.*

And God called the drie land, Earth, and the gathering together of the waters called hee, Seas: and God saw that it was good.

And God said, Let the Earth bring foorth grasse, the herbe yeelding seed and the fruit tree, yeelding fruit after his kinde, whole seed is in itselfe, upon the earth: and it was so.

And the earth brought foorth grasse, and herbe yeelding seed after his kinde, and the tree yeelding fruit, whole seed was in itselfe, after his kinde: and God saw that it was good. And the evening and the morning were the third day.

And God said, Let there bee lights in the firmament of the heaven, to divide the day from the night: and let them be for signes and seasons, and for dayes and yerres.

And let them be for lights in the firmament of the heaven, to give light upon the earth: and it was so.

And God made two great lights: the greater light to rule the day, and the lesser

Mathew Hopkins was the most notorious of all the English witch-hunters during the Civil War. This anonymous sketch shows him confronting a witch and her bevy of demon familiars — dogs, rabbits and other animals.

Sourcerers are too common; cunning men, wizards and white-witches, as they call them, are in every village, which if they be sought unto will help almost all infirmities of body and mind . . . 'Tis a common practice of some men to go first to a witch and then to a physician; if one cannot help the other shall.[24]

Folk medicine considered particular parts of the body to be under the rule of the different signs of the zodiac, and the collection and preparation of herbs, and the best times to take particular medicines depended on the positions of the stars. Plants resembling parts of the body were used to treat the corresponding part; for instance, a potion made from maidenhair fern was used to make the hair grow, and walnuts were thought to be good for the brain and mental disease.[25] Ghosts, hobgoblins and fairies were believed to exist, along with God and the Devil or Antichrist. Witches were agents of the Devil, with powers to curse people to death, blight crops and cause quarrels, barrenness and accidents, and they were assisted by familiar spirits which might take the form of a toad, a mouse, a dog, a cat or some other small animal. The familiars carried out the orders of the witch and were rewarded by being able to suck drops of blood from her body. It is clear from contemporary records that most suspected witches were old women, and poor, and in the witch-hunts of the seventeenth century they were tortured or suffered trial by immersion, as an English diarist records:

July 13, 1699. The Widow Comon was put into the river to see if she would sink, because she was suspected to be a witch — and she did not sink but swim. And she was tryed again July 19th, and then she swam again, and did not sink.

July 24, 1699. The Widow Comon was tryed a third time by putting her into the river, and she swam and did not sink.

December 27, 1699. The Widow Comon, that was counted a witch, was buried.[26]

By mid-century, however, the power of supernatural beliefs began to be eroded by new forms of scientific understanding, at least among the educated classes, and witch mania began to ebb.

Schooling amongst the common people depended on local schools run by the church, and the Protestant churches in particular promoted literacy so that people could read the Bible in their own vernacular languages. In England at about 1650, it has been estimated that there was a school for every 4,400 of the population and one about every twenty kilometres. In rural Surrey at the same time, of 1,265 people who signed a loyal petition, about two-thirds made marks, while a third were able to write their names.[27] The distribution of literacy varied widely by class and country, however, and while the Catholic Church promoted education, it was mistrustful of anything but the most elementary literacy for ordinary people.

Those who believed that knowledge was a privilege for the few promoted the use of Latin, and printed works ranged from pamphlets, flysheets and popular booklets written in vernacular languages to scholarly and theological books, which were usually written in Latin. Censorship was often attempted but did not always succeed, and in times of political turmoil leaflets were produced in quantity and distributed widely to those who could read. As a Paris printer commented in the midst of the Fronde uprisings in 1649, 'One half of Paris prints or sells pamphlets, the other half writes for them.'[28]

In the seventeenth century most European universities were dominated by a conservative male élite, training lawyers for public office and functionaries for the churches, and the great intellectual advances of this age occurred mainly in the scientific academies or amongst scholars and writers supported by the courts. Dramatists such as Shakespeare and Molière reached the common folk as well as the nobles who patronised their companies, but scientific thinkers such as Descartes, Galileo, Kepler, Boyle and Newton communicated through scientific publications and directed most of their efforts at defining a mathematically measured universe towards an educated élite. Their work was eventually to transform popular European understandings of the world from a spirit-ridden place populated by ghosts, demons and sorcerers to one planet among many in a cosmos ruled by scientific laws. Changes in common thought were uneven and slow to come about, however, and in the seventeenth century many of the great scientists themselves still believed in witches.[29]

The invention of the telescope in the late sixteenth century and subsequent observations by astronomers pushed back the limits of the known universe, and exploration and new discoveries expanded knowledge of the earth's geography. Travel literature and collections of 'Voyages' became freely available in Europe from the late sixteenth century onwards, and descriptions of mermaids and monsters, and specimens of plants, animals, sea creatures, rocks and people brought back from distant places prompted popular and scientific curiosity about the outer reaches of the world. Many educated Europeans were still intensely parochial, however, and regarded their own familiar territories as the centre of civilisation, as a comment by John Evelyn in 1645 reveals:

> From the reports of divers curious and expert persons I've been assured there was little more to be seen in the rest of the civil world after Italy, France and the Low Countries but plain and prodigious barbarism.[30]

By far the greatest volume of trade occurred within Europe itself. The transport of goods was slow and expensive because Europe was divided into a great number of independent jurisdictions, and the roads were poor, with only horses and mules as motive power. The rivers offered reliable passageways but they were divided into numerous toll zones, and on the Rhône in the seventeenth century, for instance, the short stretch between the Savoy frontier and Arles alone had forty tolls.[31] The profits on maritime trade were much greater, despite the long distances often involved and the risks of piracy and loss at sea. During the first half of the seventeenth century the colonial powers of Spain and Portugal began to wane and the Dutch and the English began a programme of vigorous overseas expansion, financed by chartered companies operating large fleets of merchant ships and singlemindedly pursuing commercial and national

Opposite: *Pierre Descelier's 1550 map of the world shows Java as part of a speculative great continent, inhabited by strange animals and people.*

advantage. Local peoples in the colonial territories were not much considered in this process, as Jan Pieterz Coen, the founder of the Dutch empire in the East Indies, made clear:

> May not a man in Europe do what he likes with his cattle? Even so does the master here do with his men for these with all that belongs to them are as much the property of the master as are brute beasts in the Netherlands.[32]

Harsh words from an unkind age. Yet in a Europe where misery, exploitation and starvation were commonplace, such sentiments might have sounded almost matter-of-fact.

II

OPPOSITE-FOOTERS

A Pakepakeha Vessel

It was during the nights of Tangaroa [the 23rd to 26th nights of the moon], on the night called Whatitiri Papaa [Crashing Thunder]. The seas were calm and there was no wind. Before dawn when everything was still, the canoes floated, waiting to catch the hau taaraki [land breeze]. They sailed out and as dawn came, they reached the fishing-grounds. There they floated and let down their anchors, and began to fish for tarakihi.

When the sun was up, a boat was seen paddling towards them, coming from far off. It was a long boat, with many paddlers on either side and rows of people in the middle, with a fugleman standing up and also a man in the stern. It came straight towards them. The crew of the fishing canoe were afraid, thinking that this was a war canoe . . . As the boat floated towards them however, its paddles were lifted on board . . . It turned and floated just like the fishing canoe. Then the local people saw how long it was, and the numbers of people that sat in the middle.

Now the men on either side of that boat took up their fishing-lines, baited them and threw them into the water. Soon they were all hauling in fish, four, five or six on the hooks of each line, on both sides of the boat. The people in the local canoe no longer felt afraid, they were excited to see these people catching so many fish. Their steersman ordered them to raise their anchor and they paddled towards the place where the tarakihi were biting. As they paddled closer, the people on the boat rolled up their lines. The local canoe floated, and its crew looked at those people — they appeared very strange. The man in the stern of the boat stood up to haul in the anchor, all the people in the middle grabbed the anchor rope, and as they hauled it in, they chanted. This is how the words sounded:

> Ka whakatakotoria
> Ki te ika te wa o Tu

> E ko te tae o Tu
> E kore rarii

Once the anchor was on board those people took up their paddles, and as they all moved, they spoke in their language. This is what it sounded like:

> Pakepakeha, pakepakeha
> Hoihoi hii, hoihoi hii
> Hihi hii, hihi hii

Now they could be plainly seen. They were turehu [fairy people], punehunehu [misty-looking], ma [fair], ma korako [pale, like albinos], whero takou [red, like red ochre] — that was the way their faces looked. The prow of the boat turned and they paddled back the way they had come. The fugleman and the steersman stood up again. In no time their boat seemed to rise up on the sea, it looked as if they were paddling in mid-air, and finally they were lost in the clouds.

Then the local people knew that these were turehu [fairy people], patupaiarehe [fairies], aparangi [evil gods], atua kahukahu [still-born spirits], kowhiowhio [whistling spirits]. They were sighted many times, before and after that. Their haka [chants] are still remembered, and the place where they chanted was called 'Haka of the god'.

The sighting of this turehu boat was long before the arrival of Captain Cook's ship. When the old men and women saw Captain Cook's ship, they called out 'It is an island, an island floating from afar. Here it is, coming towards us.' When they saw its sails, they cried out 'Aha, ha! The sails of this travelling island are like clouds in the sky! . . .'

Written by Mohi Turei — a Ngaati Porou leader born about 1830, south of East Cape, scribe for Pita Kaapiti of Taapere-nui Whare Waananga (School of Learning). Transcribed by Reweti Kohere from *Te Pipiwharauroa* 1911, ATL MS189, File 63. Translated by Anne Salmond and Merimeri Penfold 1991.

A tribal account (discovered as this book went to press) of a visit by pale-skinned people to the East Coast, well before Captain Cook's arrival. Taken in conjunction with the 'Dieppe' maps of the mid-sixteenth century that mark 'Cap Fremose', identified by some experts in historic cartography as the East Cape of New Zealand (see Colour Plate 1), and Hervé's controversial arguments about a landfall by a Spanish caravel just south of East Cape in 1526 (Hervé 1983), this manuscript adds further interest to speculations about a possible Portuguese or Spanish 'discovery' of New Zealand. 'Pakepakeha' is a fair-skinned, human-like being, and its use in the haka above is a possible origin for the term 'paakeha' — European.

Chapter Three

TASMAN IN TAITAPU (GOLDEN BAY)

December 1642

Between Europe and the Pacific archipelago of Aotearoa stretched an immensity of space and experience. The two places were as far apart as one could physically get and still be in this world. The common folk in seventeenth-century Europe speculated about 'antipodes' or 'opposite-footers', people who lived on the opposite side of the globe and exhibited bizarre, anti-human qualities — barking like dogs, wearing skins and walking upside down on the world.[1] Seventeenth-century Maori were given to speculations about white-skinned people living in the hills, flying men and guardian monsters (taniwha), although they also remembered distant island homelands and the oceanic voyages of ancestors.

But while Maori sailors in the seventeenth century largely satisfied the urge for exploration by their frequent local journeys and migrations, Europe was still in the grip of a phase of expansion that had begun two centuries before. Internal struggles fuelled contests for the control of overseas territories, in which success depended upon effective navigational techniques and ships, and a refined use of force — ultimately, fighting men armed with hand guns and artillery, carried to sea on vessels mass-produced in European shipyards, and backed by organisations which supplied them with orders, information, food, water and clothing. These formidable navies were turned upon local peoples as well as upon European competitors, and in the process of expansion new discoveries were jealously guarded. Perhaps for this reason it has so far proved impossible to establish whether or not Spanish or Portuguese ships visited the New Zealand archipelago in the century before the Dutch arrived, despite a handful of enigmatic clues, some hints in local traditions and the 'Dieppe' series of sixteenth-century maps, which include a line that could conceivably represent East Cape.[2]

As Europe's known world expanded, maritime supply-lines became increasingly attenuated. To reach the East Indies, for instance, ships had to be provided with nine months' rations for a crew of perhaps 200, and the usual sailing time was between five and a half and eight months. A voyage from the East Indies to the southern Pacific meant sailing into largely uncharted waters, and ships were accordingly fitted out for a minimum of twelve calendar months at sea, with additional supplies of trading goods to exchange with any people they might encounter. The logistic and financial demands of such expeditions were heavy, and could only be met by a mercantile state at the height of its powers. In Europe at this time such a prescription pointed to the United Provinces, more commonly known as the Netherlands.

NETHERLANDS IN THE 1640s

The Netherlands in the 1640s were prosperous, bustling, and relatively free of aristocratic control. The Dutch had fought a bitter war against Spanish rule, and in 1588 established a Calvinist republic based on a union of autonomous towns and provinces. The towns opened their gates to political and religious refugees, and, as their populations grew, they vigorously resisted all attempts at external rule. By 1640 Amsterdam had become one of Europe's greatest cities, with a population of some 140,000, and the Dutch had built up a merchant marine of about 2,000 vessels, manned by 60,000 to 80,000 seamen. 'The prodigious increase of the Netherlands in their domestic and foreign trade, riches and multitude of shipping,' wrote Sir Josiah Child in 1669, 'is the envy of the present and may be the wonder of future generations.'[3]

The Exchange and Deposit Bank opened in Amsterdam in 1609 and the Exchange in 1611, and the city became a stronghold of European capital. A con-

In the mid-seventeenth century Amsterdam was one of the great maritime capitals of the world. Engraving by O. Dapper, 1663.

temporary description shows the awe in which this great financial centre was held:

> In this City of Amsterdam is the famous Bank, which is the greatest Treasure, either real or imaginary, that is known anywhere in the World. The place of it is a great Vault . . . made strong with all the circumstances of Doors and Locks, and other appearing cautions of safety, that can be: And 'tis certain, that whoever is carried to see the Bank, shall never fail to find the appearance of a mighty real Treasure, in Barrs of Gold and Silver, Plate, and infinite Bags of Metals . . . 'Tis certain that in no Town, Strength, Beauty and Convenience, are better provided for, nor with more unlimited Expence, than in this, by the Magnificence of their Publick Buildings . . . The Number and Spaciousness, as well as Order and Revenues of their many Hospitals; The Commodiousness of their Canals, running through the chief Streets of passage; The mighty strength of their Bastions and Ramparts; And the neatness, as well as convenience of their Streets, so far as can be compassed in so great a confluence of Industrious People.[4]

Amsterdam was organised around a series of semi-circular canals, and throughout this period it was the scene of feverish construction, with docks, warehouses, canals and houses being built everywhere. In the more affluent parts of town paved roadways ran on either side of a canal, lined with linden or elm trees and two- or three-storeyed brick houses ornamented with sandstone. Bourgeois houses were equipped with massive wooden tables, chairs, cupboards and beds, and their inhabitants lived very well, eating four good meals a day and owning an array of pewter, glass, and porcelain tableware, and extensive personal property.[5]

Prosperity was relatively widely distributed in Dutch society at this time, but still there were many poor people, who lived crammed into the attics, basements and subdivided rooms of ancient timber houses in the more squalid parts of town, or in the countryside in one-roomed mud or wooden houses furnished with perhaps a table, chairs, painted chests and a spinning wheel. As in other parts of Europe, many of the poor were completely destitute, and those who turned to crime were harshly punished. Murder, arson and forgery led to sentences of hanging, burning alive and flogging, and torture was routinely used to get suspects to confess. Patrols of armed guards paraded the streets at night, and town magistrates presided over sessions where criminals were meted out their sentences — amputation of the right hand, of the nose, of one or both ears; gouging of eyes; burning of the tongue or tormenting on the rack.

Life was not always harsh, however, and there were also times of merriment and feasting, even for the poor. The tenor of everyday life was generally good-humoured, and during festivities the Dutch capacity for enjoying their creature comforts became positively flamboyant. Dutch 'kermises' were local festivals that lasted for several days, with market stalls, fairground attractions, dancing, and orgiastic drinking that often led to wild brawls and disorders. Bourgeois banquets and drinking bouts were more decorous, but still incredible amounts of food and drink were consumed. Bourgeois families also read avidly and commissioned works of art, including the paintings of Rembrandt, Rubens, Hals, Steen and others. Their ruling passion, however, was profit. As the provinces of Holland, Zeeland and Utrecht became a major centre of world trade, the local surpluses that resulted were invested in canal-building, drainage schemes, forest clearance, mines, and shipping. Factories powered by windmills mainly used wooden machinery for the manufacture of gunpowder, paper and textiles. The Dutch of this period were inventive and energetic, and in the pursuit of material goods they formed great chartered companies such as the Dutch East India Company (VOC),[6] which sought to monopolise the Asiatic spice trade and wrest its control from the Portuguese. Their enthusiasm for commerce is well recorded in an ode

In Dutch taverns the customers drank together, played games, sang and flirted with the serving-maids. This scene was painted by Jan Steen.

written by the Dutch poet Vondel in 1639, to celebrate a visit by the Queen Mother of France to East India House in Amsterdam:

'Twas not enough they'd won the field in Netherlands;
They sailed the earth to distant and exotic lands,
As far as shines the sun, resolved the sun would see
Their mighty deeds. Our Holland serves as granary
For all the Indies grow. The North has filled its ships
With Eastern crops. The Winter Prince who warms his lips
With pepper, guards in these domains the boast
Of all that heavenly fires of summer cook and roast . . .
Great Java shares with us her treasures fair,
and China, porcelain. We Amsterdammers journey
Where Ganges casts its waters down into the sea:
Wherever profit leads us, to every sea and shore,
For love of gain the wide world's harbours we explore.[7]

THE DUTCH EAST INDIA COMPANY

From its foundation in 1602 the Dutch East India Company built up a network of trading posts from Bengal to Batavia, and by 1644 it was claimed that the Company controlled 150 ships and more than 15,000 men.[8]

The Company's affairs were run by seventeen directors chosen from the 'regent' class of principal merchants, and it eventually owned its own docks, warehouses, banks, war fleet, and a large army.[9] The Company's charter gave it the power to make treaties and war, and in the East Indies (which included what is now Indonesia, Malaysia and the Philippines) it fought against the Portuguese and English, and waged ruthless campaigns against local princes who tried to circumvent VOC control of the trade in nutmeg, cloves, pepper and other spices. In 1621, for example, almost the entire population of the Banda Islands was put to the sword for smuggling spices to other islands. The survivors were exiled or enslaved and their land allotted to former company servants who agreed to trade only with the VOC.[10]

The Company's East Indies headquarters was at Batavia, a Dutch-style fortified city built on the ruins of the conquered port of Jakarta, where company officials lived in state with their Dutch or Asiatic wives, families and retinues of domestic slaves. Common sailors and soldiers, however, were largely recruited from the poor, both in the Netherlands and from other European countries, and they were paid miserable subsistence wages. The death rates on Dutch East Indiamen were often high, and life expectancy on shore in the East Indies was low, so the Company had great difficulty in recruiting its crews. In 1640 a ship's surgeon described the sufferings of the crew on a voyage to Batavia, during which eighty of the 300 men on board died:

It was as if the plague was in the very Ship, and the men were tormented and half-crazed. Some of them had to be tied to their Bunks . . . Teeth simply fell out of the mouths of many because of Scurvy, and their gums were so swollen, blackened and rotted that we had to cut and wash away the flesh every day.[11]

According to Edward Barlow, an English sailor captured by a Dutch East Indiaman in 1674, such loss of life was in part because the conditions on board were even worse than those that prevailed in other merchant navies at that time:

> The ship being very leaky, and the leak increasing, and their men very sickly through means of their bad provisions, having no bread but eating all rice and their salt beef and pork, very old and stinking, and having no other drink but water, drinking much water, and the rice being of a waterish nature, bred a kind of dropsical disease, which swelled them up with water, and in a short time killed many of the men in their ships.
>
> Our English ships commonly make shorter passages and are better provided with provisions, having for the most part bread, and our salt provisions not so old, few of our men dying on our homeward bound voyages: but many of their men die, both going out and coming home in their ships: and their men are kept three and five years in the Indies before they can come home again, going from one ship to another in the country, which trade from one place to another, their conditions being so made before they go out of Holland, so that a third part of those that go out never come home again.[12]

Life at sea was quite as harsh as that on shore, and shipboard justice as rough. Murder, mutiny and sodomy were punished with death, while other offences might lead to sentences of keel-hauling, ducking from the yard-arm, flogging with anything from ten to 500 lashes, and imprisonment in irons. Conditions varied with the character of the skipper. Some captains cheated the crews of their proper rations and sold the surplus in port, or were particularly brutal in their punishment of minor offences. Company officials sometimes justified such tough handling on the grounds that the sailors 'behave like wild boars. They rob and steal, get drunk and go whoring so shamelessly that it seems to be no disgrace with them . . . [Thus] they must be ruled like untamed beasts, otherwise they are capable of wantonly beating up anybody.'[13]

In the East Indies the Company's ships were sent on short trading voyages, raids on smugglers and routine patrols carrying messages and supplies. Sailors who survived this service could rise rapidly through the ranks to become captains, and sometimes even company officials. Abel Janszoon Tasman, a sailor from a small village in the province of Friesland who signed up with the Dutch East India Company in 1633, was one such survivor. He began his service in the East Indies patrolling off the coast of Ambon, where the Company was trying to enforce a monopoly of the spice trade. After being promoted to skipper he took part in a long and arduous expedition in search of islands east of Japan which were rumoured to be rich in gold and silver. In the course of these and subsequent voyages to Formosa, Japan, and Sumatra, Tasman became an experienced commander, and learned to manage cranky, ill-provisioned ships for long periods at sea.

During an early patrol he lost some men in an ambush by local villagers, and at least once he faced a formal complaint from his men for trading their rations of oil, vinegar and arrack to friendly locals.[14] Despite these mishaps, he developed a reputation as a knowledgeable, competent skipper who could be entrusted with difficult assignments. Certainly Tasman was used to sailing in unknown or inaccurately charted waters, and like all of the Company's captains he consulted closely with his senior officers in calculating the latitude, shooting the sun, checking the variation of the compass, altering course[15] and, in the case of disputes, settling the matter in a full meeting of the ship's council.

At this period Dutch cartographers were regarded as the best in Europe, and the company's charts were constantly updated as new information came to hand. Charts, sea atlases, books of sailing directions and navigating manuals were issued to skippers at the beginning of each voyage. The ship's journal and any new charts drafted at sea had to be handed in with the other documents at the voyage's end. While Polynesian navigators relied essentially on the oral transmission of sailing directions and navigational information, European navigators communicated more commonly by means of documents — texts, tables and charts — that recorded the cumulative results of astronomical observation, mathematical calculation and experience at sea.

It was therefore almost impossible to control access to navigational knowledge, since ships and their documents were constantly being seized and pilots bribed or captured. Furthermore, while Polynesian navigators calculated their position by direct reference to the sun, named stars and sea signs, European seamen relied on instruments that translated their observations into locations on an abstract grid, oriented to true north and divided into degrees of latitude and longitude at measured intervals.

Dutch navigators used the magnetic compass to find true north and the Jacobs-staff and back-staff to measure the altitude of the sun, thus fixing their latitude with the help of declination tables. They were however, rather approx-

These illustrations by Sir Jonas Moore in his A Newe Systeme of the Mathematicks, *1681, show the use of the cross-staff (left) and the back-staff (right) as navigational instruments.*

imate in dealing with magnetic variation, and their use of dead-reckoning to measure the ship's speed meant that estimates of longitude were often wildly wrong. An English source described methods that were still being used a hundred years later:

> The Dutch manner of navigating is peculiar to themselves. They steer by the true compass, or rather endeavour to do so, by means of a small moveable central card, which they set to the meridian: and whenever they discover the variation has altered 2½ degrees since the last adjustment, they again correct the central card. This is steering within a quarter of a point, without aiming at greater exactness. The officer of the watch, likewise, corrects the course for lee-way, by his own judgment . . . They heave no log. Their manner of computing their run, is by means of measured distance of forty feet, along the ship's side: they take notice of any remarkable patch of froth, when it is abreast of the foremost end of the measured distance, and count half-seconds till the mark of froth is abreast of the after-end. With the number of half-seconds thus obtained, they divide the number 48, taking the product for the rate of sailing in geographical miles in one hour, or the number of Dutch miles in four hours . . . From all this it is not difficult to conceive the reason why the Dutch are frequently above ten degrees [or six hundred sea-miles] out in their reckoning.[16]

The result of these navigational crudities can be seen in the peevish comments that recur in ship's logs of the period, when land unexpectedly appeared over the horizon, or failed to appear when it was most urgently required.

Despite such difficulties the Dutch contributed largely to charting the Pacific seas. It was this combination of maritime power and mercantile ambition that inspired the VOC council in Batavia to draft the following orders in 1642, instructing Tasman to sail south-east into the Pacific in order to discover the 'Unknown South-land':

> It is well-known that a hundred and fifty years ago only a third part of the globe (divided into Europe, Asia and Africa) was known, and that the Kings of Castile and Portugal caused the unknown part of the world, commonly called America or the New World, to be discovered by the highly reknowned naval heroes Christopher Colombus and Americus Vesputius, who thereby achieved immortal praise . . . With what invaluable treasures, profitable trade-connections, useful trades, excellent territories, vast powers and dominions the said kings have by this discovery and its consequences enriched their kingdoms and crowns; what numberless multitudes of blind heathen have by the same been introduced to the blessed light of the Christian religion; all this is well-known to the expert, has always been held highly praiseworthy by all persons of good sense, and has consequently served other European Princes as an example . . .
>
> For all which reasons we, the Council of India, have determined no longer to postpone the long contemplated discovery of the unknown South-land, but to take the matter in hand forthwith, using for the purpose the ship Heemskerck together with the flute de Zeehaen, placing the said vessels under the command of your persons.[17]

ABEL TASMAN'S EXPEDITION

The 'Unknown South-land' had featured on European world maps for centuries as a necessary counterpoise to the great landmasses of the north, and a place of marvellous geographic fantasies. Marco Polo's descriptions of a country called Locac, where fine timber, gold and elephants could be found in plenty, had been projected onto Terra Australis under the corrupted name of 'Beach', and so it appeared in the maps of the late sixteenth century as 'Beach the gold province to which come few foreigners because of the inhumanity of its people'.

The Dutch had, in the forty years that the VOC had been established, charted much of the northern, west and southern coastlines of Australia and discovered

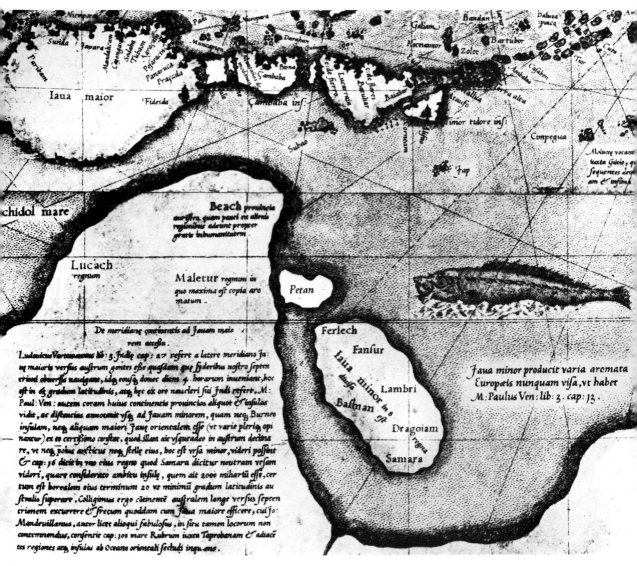

Beach, the golden province, is shown in this detail from Mercator's world chart of 1569, between Java Major and Java Minor, in a sea inhabited by monsters.

that Java and the Solomons were islands, although they were still unsure whether or not New Guinea was joined to Australia. The 'Unknown South-land' allured them as a place where gold and silver mines, and large populations living in fertile, temperate regions might be found. Tasman's instructions dwelt upon these pleasant fantasies and advised him how to conduct himself with any 'civilised men' he might encounter in the South-land:

> You will give to them greater attention than to wild barbarians, endeavouring to come into contact and parley with [the] magistrates and subjects, letting them know that you have landed there for the sake of commerce, showing them specimens of the commodities which you have taken on board for the purpose . . . especially trying to find out what commodities their country yields, likewise inquiring after gold and silver whether the latter are held [by them] in high esteem; making them believe that you are by no means eager for precious metals, so as to leave them ignorant of value of the same; and if they should offer you gold or silver in exchange for your articles, you will pretend to hold the same in slight regard, showing them copper, pewter or lead and giving them an impression as if the minerals last mentioned were by us set greater value on.
>
> You will prudently prevent all manner of insolence and all arbitrary action on the part of our men against the nations discovered, and take due care that no injury be done them in their houses, gardens, vessels, or their property, their wives, etc.; nor shall you carry off any of the inhabitants from their country against their will . . .[18]

The best guess of that period was that 'Beach' might be found in the lower latitudes of the Indian and Pacific Oceans, in a great sweep south-eastward from Mauritius and across past the longitude of the Solomon Islands. The pilot-major Frans Visscher, in his 'Memoir touching the discovery of the South-land' addressed to the VOC's council in Batavia in 1642, speculated that the elusive continent might finally be located if a voyage was carried out from Batavia to Mauritius in August or September, running southward from Mauritius during the summer months to 52° or 54°S latitude, and eastward on that latitude several hundred miles past the longitude of the Solomon Islands until land was discovered.

Tasman's instructions laid down such a course, and also advised him how to conduct negotiations if, as seemed likely, the inhabitants of the South-land should prove to be 'wild savages':

> In landing with small craft extreme caution will everywhere have to be used, seeing that it is well-known that the southern regions are peopled by fierce savages, for which reason you will always have to be well armed and to use every prudent precaution, since experience has taught in all parts of the world that barbarian men are nowise to be trusted, because they commonly think that the foreigners who so unexpectedly appear before them, have come only to seize their land . . . On which account you will treat with amity and kindness such barbarian men as you shall meet and come to parley with, and connive at small affronts, thefts and the like which they should put upon or commit against our men, lest punishments inflicted should give them a grudge against us; and by shows of kindness gain them over to us, that you may the more readily from them obtain information touching themselves, their country and their circumstances, thus learning whether there is anything profitable to be got or effected.[19]

In order that any local people encountered could be enticed by offers of trade goods, the expedition was supplied with a cargo that included a thousand small Chinese mirrors, a hundred knives, assorted ironmongery and pots, spices, twenty packets of Chinese goldwire, tinsel, wax, coral, thirty-nine pounds of elephants' tusks, 5,050 Chinese needles, silver, lead, pewter, brassware, twenty Golconda blankets and an array of textiles.[20] These were loaded into the two ships set aside for the voyage, the *Zeehaen* and the *Heemskerck*, along with water, wood, canvas, cordage, rice for eighteen months and victuals for twelve months, four hogsheads of arrack and 110 able-bodied men.[21]

Tasman's ships each had three masts and were rigged with five or six mainsails, which on average carried them along at four to five knots in good sailing weather. The *Zeehaen* was in poor condition and put to sea with her upper-work half rotten, while the state of the expedition's supplies led the commander at Mauritius to remark 'how hopelessly unsatisfactory was the outfit of the ships for a voyage of such a nature, so that we have been compelled to provide them with firewood, canvass, cordage and various other necessaries'.[22]

Nevertheless, the ships made good time on the first leg of their voyage, from Batavia to Mauritius, and after sailing south-west from Batavia on 14 August 1642, they averaged 120 miles a day.[23] The expedition was run by a ships' council consisting of Abel Tasman as skipper-commander, skipper T'Jercxzoon, pilot-major Frans Visscher (whose memoir had formed the basis of their sailing

Isaack Gilsemans sketched the Zeehaen *and* Heemskerck *at Mauritius in 1642.*

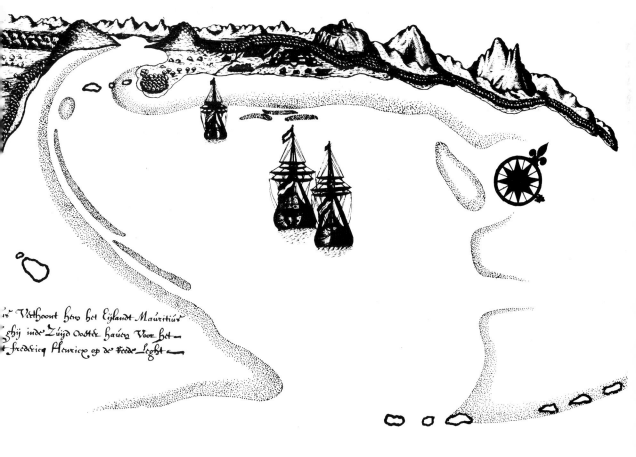

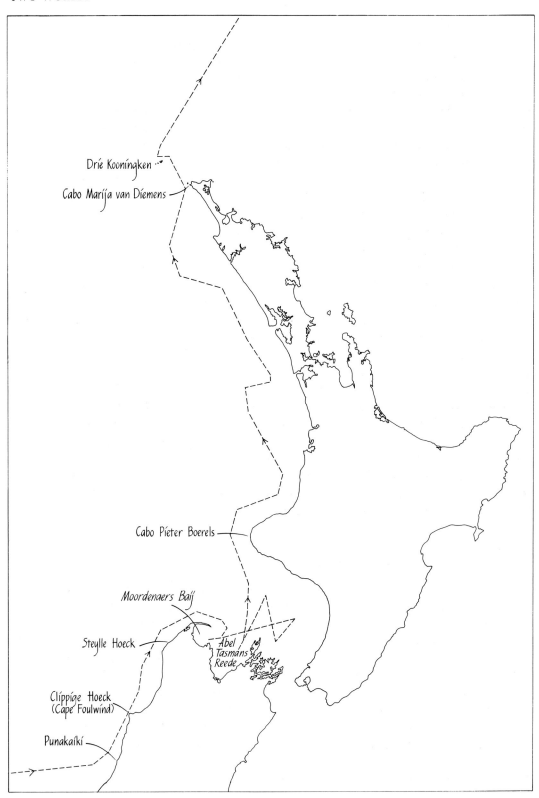

Drie Kooningken

Cabo Marija van Diemens

Cabo Pieter Boerels

Moordenaers Baij

Steylle Hoeck

Abel
Tasmans
Reede

Clippige Hoeck
(Cape Foulwind)

Punakaiki

instructions) and subcargo Abraham Coomans, from the *Heemskerck*; and skipper Gerrit Janszoon, Isaack Gilsemans, merchant and the expedition's draughtsman (who was to produce a series of meticulous coastal views of New Zealand) and the first mate, Henrick Pieterszoon, from the *Zeehaen*.

Upon their arrival at Mauritius the ships were refitted and loaded with pigs, goats, timber, firewood, water and provisions, and on 8 October they sailed south-east from Mauritius, heading for 52–54° South latitude. At 43°S a mass of floating seaweed was sighted, and the officers of the two ships met in council and decided to post a constant lookout at the masthead, offering a reward of three pieces-of-eight and a can of arrack to the first man to sight land.[24] At about 49°S the weather turned stormy and bitterly cold, and it was resolved on Visscher's advice to go back to 44°S and turn east.

On 24 November, at about forty miles distance, they sighted the mountainous coastline of Tasmania, which they recorded in charts and coastal profiles, and named 'Anthonij Van Diemens Landt' in honour of the Governor of Batavia. After some days of coastal sailing Visscher led an expedition on shore during which they heard human voices and the sound of a gong, and saw earthen fireplaces and tree trunks notched for climbing at such great intervals that they thought the local people must be extremely tall.[25] Here, as in later comments about the Three Kings, one can detect a lurking expectation that the Southlanders might be giants.

The next day the ship's carpenter swam ashore in high surf and set up a carved staff with a prince's flag on top to claim the land for the Company. Two days later the ships set off east again in search of the South-land. On 13 December they sighted 'a large land, uplifted high, bearing south-east of us'[26] at a point we would now describe as somewhere off Punakaiki on the west coast of the South Island of New Zealand. From there the ships edged north-east along the coast — Gilsemans producing coastal views as they sailed — until they rounded a sandspit (now known as Farewell Spit), and on 18 December cast anchor in a large, open bay.

TAITAPU (GOLDEN BAY) 1642

Taitapu (tapu coast), as the bay was known in the days of early land-sales to Europeans,[27] is a deep curve cut into the north-western tip of the South Island, and guarded from the western swell by a thirty-five-kilometre sandspit. In 1642 much of the shoreline was fringed with a coastal forest of ngaio, mahoe, and probably northern raataa, kawakawa and niikau palms,[28] with clumps of karaka trees planted here and there. Scattered gardens were located on river terraces and raised coastal flats, or on warm north-facing hillsides, because kuumara, gourd and taro[29] could be grown in the bay in soils mulched with gravel or sand, and spread with burnt-off vegetation.[30] On other hillsides and ridges there were extensive patches of maanuka and bracken fern, and fern also grew on the coastal strip between

Opposite: *The track of* Zeehaen *and* Heemskerck *off the New Zealand coastline, December 1642.*

Waikaho Inlet and Taupata Flat.[31] Two large rivers, the Aorere and the Takaka, ran into the bay, creating sandy estuaries where pipi, cockles, scallops and mud-whelks grew abundantly. Their rivers teemed with eels, smelt, freshwater crayfish and inanga (whitebait), which could be caught in flax nets set into trenches on the riverbanks during the spring migrations.[32] Shaggeries were located up the Aorere and Parapara Rivers, at least in early historic times, and also at Onekaka Inlet.[33] Pakaki, or chewing pitch, washed up on the western beaches around Whanganui Inlet,[34] and the bay was one of the few places in the South Island where the whau, or cork tree, with its light wood invaluable for net floats, could be found.[35]

The sea provided excellent fishing grounds frequented by thirty-kilogram hapuku (groper) off Matau (Separation Point),[36] shark off Puponga[37] and blue cod off Onekaka.[38] Snapper were the most common local fish, but barracouta, kahawai, mullet, herrings and red rock cod were also plentiful.[39] On the rocks around the coastline oysters, mussels, catseye, paaua (abalone), kina (sea-egg) and crayfish were numerous, although these species are not consistently represented in the prehistoric middens that lie scattered throughout Taitapu.[40] Flounder could be speared at night by fishermen carrying flax torches,[41] while whales and dolphins often visited the bay. Seals migrated up the West Coast and swam round the sandspit from January onwards each year to their colonies at Matau or on the offshore islands. In April blackfish came into the bay and sometimes stranded on the shoals around Taupata Point.[42] Flocks of seabirds — gulls, shags, pied stilts, pied oystercatchers and godwits — wheeled about the coastline, and small blue penguins surfed onto the beaches and waddled inland to their burrows, where they howled and wailed like banshees, especially at night.[43]

Swampy areas were common on the coast and along the inland valleys, with kahikatea and matai trees, mamaku tree-ferns and stands of flax and raupo. Behind the coastal bush there were luxuriant rainforests, with concentrations of berry-bearing trees (rimu, matai, hinau, miro, lowland tootara and titoki) which supported large populations of birds — tui, kaakaa (parrots), bellbirds, native pigeon and vivid yellow, blue and green parakeets.[44] Kiwi and weka (wood-hen) scuttled through the undergrowth, while in the mountainous hinterland beech forests sheltered moss-cushioned floors. To the south of the bay there was an ancient belt of marble rock, weathered into a tormented landscape of sinkholes, caves, shafts and fluted outcrops. The local people used argillite from D'Urville Island or the Nelson mineral belt for most of their stone tools, although a local quartzite found near Puponga made excellent sharp-edged knives.[45] There was also a major deposit of iron ore at Parapara which provided red ochre for local use and trading,[46] and greenstone was brought into the district along a West Coast trail that came inland up the Heaphy River or across the Whanganui Inlet.

The current archaeological knowledge of Taitapu is scanty, but a small number of fortified paa sites have been identified on coastal headlands, including Puponga Point, Puramahoi and possibly Taupo Point, and numberous middens and possible habitation sites have also been located.[47] Some of the paa include living terraces and storage pits, so they were probably not simply places of refuge.

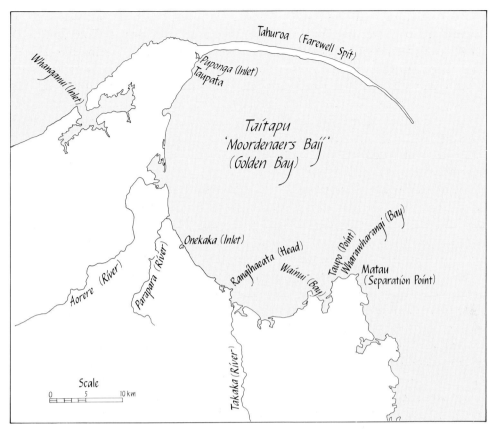

Map of Taitapu (Golden Bay) in 1642.

From the little that is known of local tribal history, the people who occupied Taitapu at the time of Tasman's visit had dominated the district for some generations, and were known collectively as Ngaati Tumatakokiri.[48] They had originally migrated from Taupo to Wanganui in the North Island, and then settled at Arapaoa in Queen Charlotte Sound, from where they had moved westward as far as Taitapu.[49] Political control in this part of the country was evidently difficult to maintain, for the tribal stories tell of a series of migrations from the North where groups landed, fought with the local people and enslaved them or intermarried with their women. Ngaati Tumatakokiri was one such group of migrants from the North Island who, after a long period of local occupation, were attacked in their turn by both Ngaati Apa from Wanganui and Ngai Tahu in about 1813, and according to some accounts lost control over the region. In a document dated 1873 and titled 'The Traditionary History of the Natives of the South Island', their history is described as follows:

> This tribe appear to have held undisturbed possession of the country to the north of the Buller for over a century, after the first settlement of the Ngaitahu in the Middle Island, when their territory was invaded by a division of the Ngatihapa [Ngaati Apa] tribe, from the neighbourhood of Wanganui, in the North Island, who partially conquered them, but after a time, withdrew again to their own district.

The Ngatitumatakokiri, with a view to avenge themselves on this tribe, determined to cross the Strait and attack them at Kapiti, where they then resided, but in attempting to .cross over, large numbers were drowned, and the remainder who landed were so few in number that they fell easy victims to their enemies. No further attempt at conquest appears to have been made by the Ngatihapa until about 60 years ago, when, taking advantage of a war then raging between the Ngai-tahu and Ngatitumatakokiri, they crossed over to Massacre Bay (Taitapu), and again attacked them. The Ngatitumatakokiri having about this time, unfortunately, killed a Ngaitahu Chief named Pakeke, at Maruia, it was determined by both the Ngati-tuahuriri and Poutini Ngaitahu to take revenge. Two fighting parties started unknown to one another, almost simultaneously, one from Kaiapoi and one from Arahura . . . At Karamea they joined forces and proceeded to West Wanganui, led by Tuhuru. There they attacked the Ngatitumatakokiri, and killed large numbers, but, after a time, retired to Arahura.

The Ngatitumatakokiri were shortly afterwards again attacked by the Ngati-hapa, and driven on to the West Coast; and the last of them, consisting of Te Pau and Te Kokihi, two of the principal Chiefs, and a few followers, were killed by Tuhuru and his people, on the Paparoha range, dividing the Valleys of the Grey and Buller. The Ngatihapa had now entire possession of the country formerly occupied by the Ngatitumatakokiri.[50]

Archaeological and historical evidence suggests that the population in the bay has never been large, perhaps no more than 400 to 500 people at any one time. No doubt Ngaati Tumatakokiri at the time of Tasman's visit lived in small villages very similar to those described by later visitors, with houses built low to the ground, curved-roofed cooking shelters, storage pits, and high storage racks, set on coastal promontories in bays or by a river estuary on a sandy beach.[51]

When the Dutch ships sailed into the bay on 18 December 1642, they anchored at sunset somewhere off the Wainui Inlet[52] in fifteen fathoms of water, about four miles from the shore. We can be sure that there had been meetings and debates all of that day, as the people of the coastal villages tried to work out what sort of waka (canoes) these were, and what sort of beings were the white-skinned folk on board. The crews of the two canoes which warily approached the Dutch vessels that evening (perhaps from Taupo Point) must have included some of the most courageous toa (warriors) of Ngaati Tumatako-kiri, who paddled out to inspect the ships more closely and challenge them with incantations and ritual blasts of their shell trumpets. It is possible they had decided that these were spirits of some sort, since in early times when people were afraid of ghosts at night, they commonly blew trumpets and shouted to frighten them away.[53]

As the Dutch replied in darkness with shouts and trumpet calls from the decks of their ships, the warriors must have been mystified by these creatures who entered into their rituals, yet used exotic instruments and spoke an unintelligible tongue. The first published summary of the voyage, which was. based partly on information from the ship's barber-surgeon, Henrik Haelbos, recounts that after these initial exchanges, the Dutch then fired a cannon, provoking an immediate and angry reaction:

The Southlanders began to rage terribly, tooting on a horn, and returned to land. Tasman ordered a watch kept, and equipped the rest with swords, pikes and muskets.[54]

The next morning a canoe with thirteen people on board came out to the ships and the Dutch sailors unsuccessfully tried to persuade them to come closer, showing them white linen and knives and attempting to interpret their shouted messages with the help of a vocabulary supplied by the VOC council at Batavia. As Tasman wryly commented in his journal:

> We did not understand them, their speech not bearing any resemblance to the vocabulary given us by the Hon. Governor-General and Councillors of India, which is hardly to be wondered at, seeing that it contains the language of the Salamonis (Solomon) Islands [in fact Tonga and the Horne Islands].[55]

He also described the visitors in some detail, and it was probably at this time that the merchant-draftsman Gilsemans sketched them in their canoe:

> As far as we could observe, these people were of ordinary height; they had rough voices and strong bones, the colour of their skin being between brown and yellow; they wore tufts of black hair right upon the tops of their heads, tied fast in the manner of the Japanese at the back of their heads, but somewhat longer and thicker, and surmounted by a large, thick white feather. Their boats consisted of two long narrow prows side by side, over which a number of planks or other seats were placed in such a way that those above can look through the water underneath the vessel; their paddles are upwards of a fathom in length, narrow and pointed at the end; with these vessels they could make considerable speed. For clothing, as it seemed to us, some of them wore mats, others cotton stuffs; almost all of them were naked from the shoulders to the waist.[56]

Were these 'civilised men' or 'wild barbarians'? It did not seem likely that this was the fabled 'Beach', with its gold and silver mines, and elephants and kings. Nor would Ngaati Tumatakokiri yet have been able to decide whether the Dutch were human, or perhaps white-skinned patupaiarehe (fairy folk) or some other kind of fabulous being.

The Dutch descriptions of their visitors, in both text and illustration, contain some curious features. There is no indication of facial or body tattoo, nor of any carving on the canoes that came out to their ships, although Tongan tattoo is mentioned in the Haelbos text and shown on one of the sketches, and carved canoes are depicted in the New Ireland drawings from the voyage. In Gilsemans's sketch the double canoes are drawn with their hulls lashed directly together (in contradiction to Tasman's text), and one canoe is shown sailing with a yard-sail or boom-rigged sail. The paddles have large blades with a central ridge. Some of the men are shown with beards, and the man who stands up in the prow of the front canoe wears his cloak with its central seam fastened by corners brought over his shoulders and held together by a knot or a ring. The account derived from Henrik Haelbos added extra details:

> These people were rough, uncivilised, strong, full of verve; the hair on the crown of their heads was smoothed round and tied in a bun at the crown. The crown itself

A. Zijn onze Schepen.

B. Zijn de prauwen, die om ons boort quamen

C. is der Zeeluws practiken dat-na ons boort quam Schepen
   Van Frisson des des landts vermaeckt En dat naer onze
   Schicten wederom Maetty hielt door vij zegen dat zij de
   Prauwn velackt Badory is onze Schepit met onze Scheloup
   Wederom gebalt

D. in de Voetkomingh van hare prauwen in het fokven Vant

E. zijn onze Schepen die onder Zeyle gaen
F. is onze Schaloup die de Prauwen wederom Jacker

Aen t'Voothoort de Moordenaers
Baij als gbij L 15 Vademen
Sate 10 graden het leght

was decorated with a stiff white feather; round the neck hung a square plate [perhaps a pectoral amulet or a tiki[57]]; over the chest was a long white stripe; they wore a square cloak tied in front of the neck.

In the middle of the little boats, bound together in pairs, was the captain who led the rowers. Among those in authority an old man was prominent, who came close to the ship and called out with a rough, loud voice. All used blunt staves.[58]

The 'rough, loud' calling was probably a haka (war chant), provoked by the exchange of ritual challenges the night before. The Dutch completely misunderstood these signals, however.

Shortly after this visit the Zeehaen's officers crossed over to the Heemskerck for a council meeting, and it was decided 'to go as near the shore as we could, since there was a good anchoring-ground here, and these people apparently sought our friendship'.[59] While they were still on board seven more canoes came out from the shore. One, 'high and pointed in front, manned with 17 natives', paddled behind the Zeehaen, while another with thirteen men on board approached the Heemskerck. The crews of these canoes called out to each other and waved their paddles as the Dutch tried to persuade them to come on board with offers of trade goods. The Zeehaen's skipper sent his cockboat back to his vessel to warn the second mates to be on their guard, and not to allow too many visitors on board.

Just as the cockboat left the Zeehaen on its return trip, the crew of the canoe near the Heemskerck paddled furiously towards the cockboat and rammed it at high speed, hitting the quartermaster in the neck with 'a long, blunt pike' and knocking him overboard, killing three of the sailors with short hand-clubs and 'paddles' and mortally wounding one other. The surprise was complete. The victors took one dead body into their canoe, threw another overboard and set the cockboat adrift. The two canoes were then paddled 'with unbelievable skill to the shore,'[60] avoiding musket shots and shots from the Heemskerck's guns. The quartermaster and two of the sailors managed to swim to the Heemskerck, which

Opposite: 'Thus Appears the Murderers Bay'. Isaack Gilsemans's 1642 sketch graphically depicts the ambush in Taitapu, the fleet of canoes that afterwards approached the Dutch vessels, the retrieval of the sloop and the departure of the Dutch ships from the bay. Note the double canoe in the foreground with its hulls lashed directly together; the bearded men with tufts of hair on the crowns of their heads, the absence of carving and tattoo; their leader's garment, and the yard-sail hoisted by one of the fleet of canoes as it returns to land. The coastal profile accurately represents the coastline of Taitapu.

The written captions read:
A: Are our Ships.
B: Are the canoes which came round our ships.
C: Is the Zeehaen's small Boat which came Rowing towards our ship and overpowered By Inhabitants of the land and after that [they] because of the Shooting Abandoned Again when we Saw that They had Abandoned the Boat it was brought Back by our Skipper with our Sloop.
D: Is the View of their canoes and the appearance of the people.
E: Are our Ships which go under Sail.
F: Is our Sloop which brought back the small boat.

sent her pinnace, bristling with armed sailors, to pick them up and recover the cockboat with its cargo of one corpse and a mortally wounded man.

On their return the Dutch ships weighed anchor and set sail. By now there were twenty-two canoes gathered on the shore, and of these, eleven paddled towards the Dutch vessels, including one large canoe with a man standing in her, holding a small white 'flag', probably a sign of peace.[61] When they came within range both the *Heemskerck* and the *Zeehaen* fired, canistershot rattled against the canoe hulls and the man holding the flag was hit and fell. Two of the canoes hoisted yard-sails as they sped back to the shore, where the entire fleet stayed, watching the Dutch. After another council meeting on board the *Heemskerck* a resolution was drawn up:

> to wit: Seeing that the detestable deed of these natives against four men of the *Zeehaen*'s crew, perpetrated this morning, must teach us to consider the inhabitants of this country as enemies; that, therefore, it will be best to sail eastward along the coast, following the trend of the land, in order to ascertain whether there are any fitting places where refreshments and water would be obtainable.[62]

When the council meeting was over, the two ships hoisted anchor and sailed east-north-east into Raukawa-moana (Cook Strait), having named Taitapu 'Moordenaers Baij' (Murderers Bay).

After the challenges, counter-challenges and the cannonshot of the night before, an attack was not surprising, and indeed Tasman had been warned of such a possibility in his instructions. The Dutch sailors were used to bloodshed and fighting, and had often enough been the aggressors against islanders in 'praus'. Nevertheless, they were outraged and their descriptions of this encounter gave Maori a bloodthirsty reputation in Europe when abstracts of Tasman's journal were published there. Van Nierop's 1674 summary of the voyage mused about 'opposite-footers' in telling about this meeting:

> When the sun rises for us, then for them it sets; when it sets for us, then it rises for them. Our noon is their midnight, and our summer is their winter, and so everything goes in opposites, and the ancient scholars have discussed this in amazement and at some length. Perhaps this newly discovered New Zealand is equivalent to our [Netherlands] 'opposite-footers'.[63]

In such a case the Dutch would have expected New Zealanders to have been exactly as they were described, both savage and inhuman. The only surprise was that they were not in some way physically monstrous as well.

For the local people, too, the episode was bizarre. They experienced the crack and flash of firearms for the first time; they had seen high ships with their windows lit at night and captured a white man's body. Perhaps because of its near-fictional quality, and because Ngaati Tumatakokiri ceased to exist as an effective unit before the period of European settlement, Maori records of this meeting are sparse. One likely memory was collected by James Mackay from a few surviving Ngaati Tumatakokiri who were living in the Croixelles in the 1850s. They said that a ship with white men on board had come to 'Whanawhana' near Separation

Point a very long time before, where their ancestors had killed some of them; and probably this referred to the events in 1642.[64]

During the next week the ships tacked around Raukawa-moana, and rode out a storm anchored in the lee of Stephens Island. Tasman suspected from the current that a passage through to the open South Sea must exist but was unable to find it. Christmas Day was celebrated with wine and a festive meal of freshly slaughtered pork. On 26 December they sailed north along the west coast of the North Island, seeing no signs of life until they passed Motu-o-pao (an island off Cape Maria Van Diemen) and on 5 January came to Oo-hau (Great Island) in Manawataawhi (the Three Kings).

Tasman was still anxious to get fresh water for his men, and sent out the pinnace and the cockboat to look for a safe watering-place. They found a small bay with water pouring down a steep hill but were unable to land because of high surf, and returned to the ships reporting that they had seen about thirty or thirty-five very tall men on the hilltops, who called to them in rough, loud voices and walked with enormous strides. A fragmentary surviving journal was evidently written by a sailor who went on one of these ships:

> The said island is all over very quiet and stony; in the higher places verdure is very scarce; few trees; the Island is about two miles in circumference; on the west there are three more small islands and some rocks . . . and coming near the land we saw in one place the water running down from above; we also saw some plantation and also people who cried to us; it was a kind of people almost like the people who

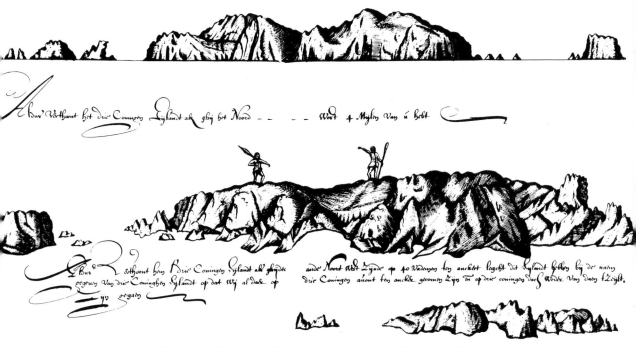

'Thus Appears the Three Kings Island'. Isaack Gilsemans represented the Three Kings from the south-east, and tall armed sentries on the crest of the hills of Oo-hau (Great Island) during Tasman's visit in 1642.

killed our three comrades on the mainland; they came up to us; had wooden sticks about 2 fathoms or one fathom and a half long, and about 2 feet at the end; were very thick, as if the end were very thick, as if they were clubs; they threw stones down upon us from above.[65]

The cultivations were laid out in square beds beside the running water, 'looking green and pleasant',[66] and on the beach two canoes were hauled up, one of which was broken. Haelbos described these as 'boats of straw matting',[67] which might indicate that they were reed vessels of some kind. The next morning the pinnace and the cockboat again tried to approach the bay but they were caught in a strong current and had to go back, watched by a tall man armed with a weapon like a pike, who called out to them in a very loud voice. This was probably a sentry raising the alarm, and with his cry ringing in their ears the Dutch weighed anchor and sailed east into the Pacific.

Not much can be learned about Maori life from this voyage. The contacts were brief and tenuous, and all attempts at communication failed. Each side had its ways of handling meetings between strangers, and the men of Ngaati Tumatakokiri tried both ritual challenges and shouted messages, while the Dutch responded with trumpet calls, cannonshot and words from a Tongan vocabulary. In the end the strangers were sent away, repelled by a maritime ambush in Taitapu and a barrage of rocks in the Three Kings. Some impression of Taitapu's population can be gained from a fleet of twenty-two canoes assembled at short notice, with male crews ranging in size from thirteen to seventeen people, and one can note that naval tactics (including ramming) were used, although their double canoes were evidently small compared with those seen in later visits to other parts of the country; but such details are a fragile basis for reconstruction. After Tasman's visit the European records fall silent about 'Zeelandia Nova' for more than 120 years, while six or so local generations lived through their battles, alliances, marriages and migrations, recorded in the intricate memories of tribal histories.

'TUPUA'
GOBLINS FROM
THE SEA

Chapter Four

COOK'S CIRCUMNAVIGATION
1769–70

In November 1769, when the *Endeavour* sailed into Whitianga harbour during her circumnavigation of New Zealand, Horeta Te Taniwha was a small child on shore. The *Endeavour* spent twelve days in the bay, and during that time her captain, James Cook, visited various settlements, while Joseph Banks and Dr Solander, the naturalists who represented the Royal Society on this expedition, scoured the coast for new species of plants and useful minerals. Much later in his life Te Taniwha described his memories of their visit:

> In the days long past, when I was a very little boy, a vessel came to Whitianga (Mercury Bay). Our tribe was living there at that time. We did not live there as our permanent home, but were there according to our custom of living for some time on each of our blocks of land, to keep our claim to each, and that our fire might be kept alight on each block, so that it might not be taken from us by some other tribe.
>
> We lived at Whitianga, and a vessel came there, and when our old men saw the ship they said it was an atua, a god, and the people on board were tupua, strange beings or 'goblins'. The ship came to anchor, and the boats pulled on shore. As our old men looked at the manner in which they came on shore, the rowers pulling with their backs to the bows of the boat, the old people said, 'Yes, it is so: these people are goblins; their eyes are at the back of their heads; they pull on shore with their backs to the land to which they are going.' When these goblins came on shore we (the children and women) took notice of them, but we ran away from them into the forest, and the warriors alone stayed in the presence of those goblins; but, as the goblins stayed some time, and did not do any evil to our braves, we came back one by one, and gazed at them, and we stroked their garments with our hands, and we were pleased with the whiteness of their skins and the blue of the eyes of some of them.
>
> These goblins began to gather oysters, and we gave some kumara, fish, and fern-root to them. These they accepted, and we (the women and children) began to roast cockles for them; and as we saw that these goblins were eating kumara, fish and cockles, we were startled, and said, 'Perhaps they are not goblins like the Maori goblins.' These goblins went into the forest, and also climbed up the hill to our pa (fort) at Whitianga (Mercury Bay). They collected grasses from the cliffs, and kept knocking at the stones on the beach, and we said, 'Why are these acts done by these goblins?' We and the women gathered stones and grass of all sorts, and gave to

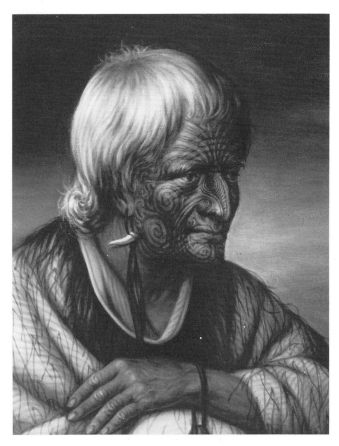

Horeta Te Taniwha, painted by Gottfried Lindauer.

these goblins. Some of the stones they liked, and put them into their bags, the rest they threw away; and when we gave them the grass and branches of trees they stood and talked to us, or they uttered the words of their language. Perhaps they were asking questions, and, as we did not know their language, we laughed, and these goblins also laughed, so we were pleased.

. . . There was one supreme man in that ship. We knew that he was the lord of the whole by his perfect gentlemanly and noble demeanour. He seldom spoke, but some of the goblins spoke much. But this man did not utter many words: all that he did was to handle our mats and hold our mere, spears, and waha-ika, and touch the hair of our heads. He was a very good man, and came to us — the children — and patted our cheeks, and gently touched our heads. His language was a hissing sound, and the words he spoke were not understood by us in the least. We had not been long on board of the ship before this lord of these goblins made a speech, and took some charcoal and made marks on the deck of the ship, and pointed to the shore and looked at our warriors. One of our aged men said to our people, 'He is asking for an outline of this land;' and that old man stood up, took the charcoal, and marked the outline of the Ika-a-maui (the North Island of New Zealand).[1]

Tupua were visible beings or objects of supernatural origin, regarded with a mixture of terror and awe and placated with karakia (ritual chants) or offerings. If they took a human-like shape, it was thought that they could not eat human foods.[2] It is obvious from Te Taniwha's account that the local reactions he described rested firmly on Maori assumptions about the world, and that Europeans and their behaviours were grasped (with some puzzlement) in the light of local experience and expectations.

In a similar fashion the *Endeavour* party also mirrored the society from which they came, not only in their accounts but in their reactions to the local people, their social rankings, their routines, their food, their clothing, their guns, their ship, their intentions and their very presence in a South Pacific bay. Cook's expedition was a side-show of Georgian England, touring the New Zealand coastline, and to grasp its purposes and practices it is to that society that we must briefly turn.

THE ENGLISH BACKGROUND TO COOK'S VOYAGE

Like the Netherlands in 1642, England in the mid-eighteenth century was at the crest of an expansionary wave — confident, materialistic, and worldly. The English had won mighty and lucrative victories in the War of Spanish Succession (1702–13) and the Seven Years' War (1756–63) against much more populous European opponents, and 'John Bull' was in swaggering, patriotic mood.

> As trade enriched the citizens in England, so it contributed to their freedom, and this freedom on the other side extended their commerce, whence arose the grandeur of the state. Trade raised by insensible degrees the naval power, which gives the English a superiority over the seas, and they are now masters of very near two hundred ships of war.[3]

By 1769 England was ruled by George III (a constitutional monarch) and a clique of noble families who dispensed patronage and good fortune to the lower orders. The grandees were not numerous — fewer than 200 peers — but they were fabulously rich and controlled great political power, and perhaps twenty per cent of England's land.[4] Below the peers were the heads of landed families, from baronets to squires; then the clergy, officials and officers, professionals, freeholders and tenant farmers, craftspeople and traders; and finally, the great mass of wage labourers and the poor.

Except at the very highest echelons, status in this finely graded social order depended as much on wealth as upon birth, as Daniel Defoe's classification of English society in 1709 made clear:

1. The Great, who live profusely.
2. The Rich, who live very plentifully.
3. The middle Sort, who live well.
4. The working Trades, who labour hard, but feel no Want.
5. The Country People, Farmers etc; who fare indifferently.
6. The Poor, that fare hard.
7. The Miserable, that really pinch and suffer Want.[5]

Within this system those who succeeded could rise, and indeed England was regarded as a remarkably free and open society by European contemporaries; but in its ruthless protection of property, Georgian England bore hard upon the poor. Theft, poaching, forgery, burning hayricks, destroying turnpikes or sending threatening letters to the powerful were harshly punished, as sessions reports from the Old Bailey show:

> The same day, at noon, the Sessions ended at the Old Bailey, when the 2 following persons received sentence of death, viz. John Turner, for breaking into the apartments of Mrs Turner, who was an intimate of his father's, near Queenhithe, and stealing from thence 1 guinea, £5 1s in silver, and several wearing apparel; and Anne Palmer, alias Hinks, for stealing £8 1s in money, and goods to the value of 38s, the property of Mr Sam. Ruffel . . . Five were burnt in the hand, and 30 were cast for transportation . . . Seven were burnt in the hand and about 20 ordered for transportation . . . Eight were burnt in the hand.[6]

During the eighteenth century capital offences multiplied from fifty to 200 (although there were fewer actual executions).[7] Customary rights were whittled away by law, and debtors were clapped into jail without trial.

Wealth in Georgian England was founded primarily on the land, and about seventy-five per cent of the population were involved in agriculture.[8] The old open fields and clustered villages of Anglo-Saxon times still dominated the landscape, but this was a period of great changes in farming. Wastelands and commons were divided up and cultivated, fallowing was increasingly replaced by manuring and fodder crops, new staples (including maize and potatoes) were introduced and larger farms were created which were then fenced off from the rest of the community. During this agricultural revolution the countryside was reorganised into a grid of fields enclosed by hedges, banks and ditches laid out across its contours. Many smallholders were forced out as they lost their commons rights, and agriculture increasingly became a large-scale business, run by the wealthy few.[9] At the same time tenant farmers in particular often profited from the new regime. Food supplies stabilised as agricultural production increased, and death from starvation became much less commonplace.

In other parts of the country, particularly in the north, cottage industry intensified as families took up carding, spinning and weaving textiles at home to supplement their incomes. In the 1760s John Kay's 'flying shuttle' came into common use, allowing weavers to speed up their work. After 1769, when Richard Arkwright invented a power-driven spinning machine and later set up textile factories where workers operated an array of large machines, the industrial revolution with its system of factory labour was under way.

In this bustling, business-like climate, roads and vehicles were improved to allow a quicker, safer passage for goods and people from place to place. New financial institutions were established, changing patterns of work allowed people to marry earlier, and England's population began to rise rapidly, for the first time transcending the old regime of biological control by periodic mass starvation and hunger-related diseases. Between 1701 and 1801, England's population grew from five million to eight and a half million people,[10] provincial towns expanded and trade and commerce boomed.

Country and provincial people lived according to their means, from labourers

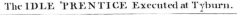

This engraving by William Hogarth shows a public hanging in England in 1747.

in one-roomed wattle and daub cottages to magnates in their mansions, lavishly furnished and set in landscaped grounds complete with grottoes, follies and ha-has. Growing prosperity meant that more of the population lived above the poverty line than in many parts of Europe, and inventories of ordinary people's belongings revealed arrays of pots, pans, kettles, skillets, pewter dishes, tables and chairs, feather beds, blankets and sheets, clocks and candlesticks among their household possessions.[11] According to Dean Tucker in 1758:

> The English of these several Denominations (Peasants and Mechanics, Farmers, Free-holders, Tradesmen and Manufacturers, Wholesale Dealers, Merchants . . .) have better Conveniences in their Houses, and appear to have more in Quantity of clean, neat Furniture, and a greater Variety (such as Carpets, Screens, Window Curtains . . . Bells, polished Brass Locks, Fenders etc. Things hardly known among Persons abroad of such a Rank) than in any other Country in Europe (Holland excepted).[12]

Not only material possessions but also knowledge became more widely disseminated through the academies and charity schools. Many more people read books, magazines, newspapers and pamphlets. Playhouses sprang up everywhere, and writers (including Dr Johnson, Smollett, Fielding, Pope, Defoe), artists

91

(Hogarth, Reynolds) and musicians (Handel, J. C. Bach) made an independent living. In provincial towns, scientific lecturers performed experiments and extolled the findings of Newtonian science; and 'improvement' — technical, scientific and moral — became a matter of popular enthusiasm.

Yet in the Age of Reason witches were still hounded in rural villages, and people treated their ailments with the most extraordinary folk remedies. Entertainment was by and large an uproarious affair — pelting people in the pillory, bear-baiting, cock-fighting, prize-fighting, gambling and public hangings. A whole array of places and clubs focused on drinking — gin shops, taverns, chair clubs, chanting clubs and cock and hen clubs, where youths and prostitutes met to drink and sing songs.[13] Street life was rowdy and riots were commonplace, as Benjamin Franklin noted with some surprise in 1769:

> I have seen, within one year, riots in the country, about corn; riots about work-houses; riots of colliers, riots of weavers, riots of coal-heavers; riots of sawyers; riots of Wilkesites; riots of government chairmen; riots of smugglers, in which custom house officers and excisemen have been murdered, the King's armed vessels and troops fired at.[14]

In the midst of all of this ferment was London, the country's financial power-house, home of the Court and Parliament, and at this time one of the largest and

In this 1759 engraving Hogarth shows the popular sport of cock-fighting.

A curricle, horsemen and pedestrians in fashionable Hanover Square. The scene shown in this coloured engraving by R. Pollard and F. Jukes after E. Dayes, 1787, was typical of the more elegant parts of Georgian London.

fastest-growing cities in the world. Between 1700 and 1820 its population almost doubled (from 674,000 to 1,274,000),[15] provoking bemused comment from contemporaries; for instance, Tobias Smollett in 1771:

> London is literally new to me; new in its streets, and even in its situation; as the Irishman said, 'London is now gone out of town.' What I left open fields, producing hay and corn, I now find covered with streets and squares, and palaces, and churches. I am credibly informed, that in the space of seven years, eleven thousand new houses have been built in one quarter of Westminster, exclusive of what is daily added to other parts of this unwieldy metropolis.[16]

The physical fabric of London faithfully reflected the English social hierarchy, with its elegant new West End squares in stark contrast with the stinks and stews inhabited by the poor. According to von Archenholz in 1780, 'the east end, especially along the shores of the Thames, consists of old houses, the streets there are narrow, dark and ill-paved; inhabited by sailors and other workmen who are employed in the construction of ships'.[17] Conditions inside these houses were described by a number of observers, for instance, Dr Willen in 1801:

> It will scarcely appear credible, though it is precisely true, that persons of the lowest class do not put clean sheets on their beds three times a year; that even where no sheets are used they never wash or scour their blankets or coverlets, nor renew them until they are no longer tenable; that curtains, if unfortunately there

should be any, are never cleansed but suffered to continue in the same state till they fall to pieces; lastly, that from three to eight individuals of different ages often sleep in the same bed; there being in general but one room and one bed for each family . . . The room occupied is either a deep cellar, almost inaccessible to the light, and admitting of no change of air; or a garret with a low roof and small windows, the passage to which is close, kept dark, and filled not only with bad air, but with putrid excremental effluvia from a vault at the bottom of the staircase. Washing of linen, or some other disagreeable business, is carried on, while infants are left dozing and children more advanced kept at play whole days on the tainted bed: some unsavoury victuals are from time to time cooked: in many instances idleness, in others the cumbrous furniture or utensils of trade, with which the apartments are clogged, prevent the salutary operation of the broom and white-washing brush and favour the accumulation of a heterogeneous filth.[18]

About one-eighth of the population of Georgian London numbered among the really poor,[19] who lived in situations such as this or worse, and life at that level was wretched, violent and often brief. Children were frequently abandoned, child mortality was high, and in the workhouses it was nothing short of catastrophic. Of 2,339 children received into London workhouses in the five years after 1750, for instance, only 168 were still alive in 1755.[20]

Many seamen were used to such conditions, because the expansion of population, production and commerce in eighteenth-century England was accompanied by a sharp increase in sea power. Sailors were often recruited from miserable surroundings, either by the Marine Society, which clothed and kitted out impoverished men and boys and enlisted them in the Navy;[21] by the 'crimps' (who got men into debt then procured them a ship, taking all of their wages and prize money until the debt was discharged);[22] or by the press-gangs, which seized seamen by force for naval service in times of war.

From the late 1600s the Dutch had begun to lose their supremacy at sea, and as England and France emerged as the key European contestants for naval and commercial power, English merchant shipping almost trebled (from 3,300 to 9,400 vessels between 1702 and 1776),[23] and the wartime Navy expanded to about 85,000 men.[24] The colonies were also voracious consumers of labour. Of an estimated six million slaves taken from West Africa during this century to work in American and West Indian plantations producing sugar, tobacco, rice and cotton, at least a million and a half were transported in British ships.[25] In India, French and British state-supported trading companies fought commercial and military battles, and in 1756 this rivalry flared into open warfare, both in Europe during the Seven Years' War (which also involved Prussia as Britain's ally, and Austria and Russia, who fought with France) and during the Great War for Empire in North America, India and the West Indies. It was in this context of bitter Anglo-French rivalry for colonial control that James Cook's first voyage of Pacific discovery, and Jean François de Surville's almost simultaneous venture into the South Pacific took place.

THE *ENDEAVOUR* VISIT

The lure that brought James Cook's expedition to New Zealand in 1769 was that same fantastic continent which Abel Tasman had sought: Terra Australis Incognita. Since 1642 Europeans had been preoccupied with their own endemic wars and with colonial struggles elsewhere, but now and then Terra Australis featured in some plan for southern exploration, fostered by thoughts of gold and silver, rich trade opportunities and wondrous natural discoveries. In 1744 John Campbell urged the merchants of Great Britain to explore and colonise the region, and in 1756 Charles de Brosses published a detailed plan for the French settlement and exploration of the Southern Continent which included a rhapsody on its likely marvels:

> How many people differing among themselves and certainly very dissimilar to us, in appearance, manners, custom, ideas, religion. How many animals, insects, fishes, plants, trees, forests, medicinal herbs, rocks, precious stones, fossils and metals. There are doubtless, in all fields, countless of species of which we have not even a notion, since that world has never had any connection with ours and is, so to speak, almost as alien as if it were another planet.[26]

The curving line from Visscher's charts which appeared on a number of world maps[27] under the name of Zeelandia Nova was widely thought to represent part of the continent's coastline, while of the various bowdlerised versions of Tasman's voyage that were published in European travel anthologies,[28] at least one included speculations about 'The Giants of Terres Australes' to titillate the reading public.[29] Even scientists proved credulous on this matter, for in 1767 an account of 'giants' at Patagonia, based on descriptions given by Charles Clerke (who later sailed as master's mate with Cook on the *Endeavour*) was published in the Royal Society's *Philosophical Transactions*.[30] After 1766–69, when both Britain and France sent exploring expeditions into the South Pacific in search of Terra Australis, further fantasies about the inhabitants of the elusive continent emerged. Reports came back from the brief visits of Wallis and Bougainville to Tahiti, and Europeans were enchanted by glimpses of a South Seas paradise, fragrant with flowers, where women welcomed sea-weary travellers with luxuriant caresses.

Like Te Taniwha's people in Whitianga, eighteenth-century Europeans drew upon their own traditions to describe exotic groups, and two main strands can be traced in their accounts of non-literate societies. One was the image of the bestial savage, sometimes gigantic and physically monstrous as well as brutally cruel, which derived from mediaeval bestiaries and theories about demons. The other was the 'savage' as an innocent, happy child of Nature, free of the corruptions of 'civilised' society, the Utopian inheritor of the biblical Garden of Eden.

At about mid-century, Enlightenment thinkers were crafting these ideas into evolutionary schemes that described the transition from savagery to civilisation as deterioration (Rousseau) or progress (Adam Smith, Adam Ferguson, Buffon and De Pauw), depending on whether the idyllic or the bestial image of the

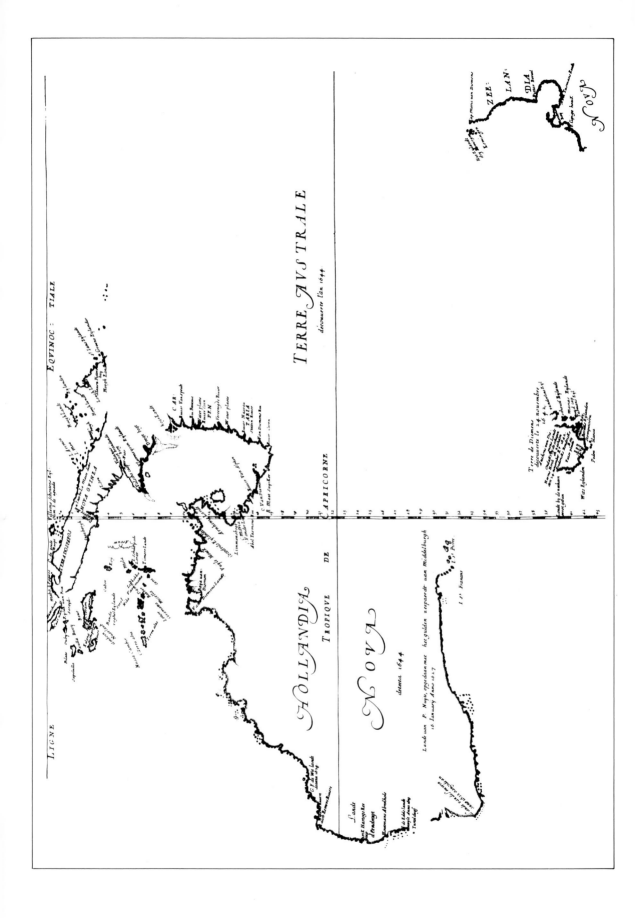

savage was being used. In Britain in particular, rapid changes in technology and material conditions led local philosophers to conclude that 'property is a matter of progress'[31] for 'without private property there would be no industry, and without industry, men would remain savages forever',[32] thus arriving at a judgment in favour of 'civilisation' that was never seriously disturbed thereafter.

In the mid-1760s the search for Terra Australis had intensified. In the aftermath of the Seven Years' War, France hoped to overcome a humiliating defeat by discovering new riches in the hidden continent, while Britain was determined to maintain its maritime and colonial supremacy. In each country there was also tremendous curiosity about new places, and Bougainville's 1768 expedition into the Pacific carried both a botanist and an astronomer on board. Since 1765 the Royal Society had been promoting an expedition into the South Seas to observe the transit of Venus in 1769,[33] and as arrangements for this scientific mission were made they were combined with plans for a probe into the far south of the Pacific to look for Terra Australis. Thus it was that when James Cook was appointed to command the *Endeavour* expedition in 1768, he had instructions from both the Royal Society and the Admiralty to guide him.

THE ROYAL SOCIETY

The Royal Society, chartered in 1662, was involved from the outset in the extension of practical knowledge. Its founders were much influenced by the ideas of Sir Francis Bacon, who argued for a philosophy that would build up practical knowledge on the basis of meticulous observation and experimental testing, for the benefit of humankind. In 1627 he wrote a Utopian account of a marvellous South Sea island, the 'New Atlantis', whose inhabitants spent their time in the study of nature, 'to the effecting of all things possible'. Here there were towers half a mile high for experiments on refrigeration and deep caves, lakes and parks containing a variety of beasts and birds, artificial wells and fountains and a great collection of engines, furnaces and astronomical instruments to assist in making mechanical, astronomical and chemical observations.[34]

When the Royal Society was established in London it had no such magnificent facilities, but it did concern itself with many useful matters, including improvements in agriculture and mining, discoveries in manufacturing and navigation, and the communication of findings from voyages to distant parts of the world. Its journal, *Philosophical Transactions*, became a focus for the international circulation of scientific ideas, and many of the great thinkers of the late seventeenth and early eighteenth century were numbered among its members. The Royal Society also persistently involved itself in practical affairs, and in its connections with provincial societies, its publications and its fostering of scientific debate, it was a main contributor to the enthusiasm for knowledge and material

Opposite: *Tasman's curving line appears as 'Zeelandia Nova' in this chart from M. Thévenot's* Relation de Divers Voyages Curieux, *1663. Note that the incomplete coastlines of Australia, Tasmania and New Zealand suggest the possibility of a vast continent, here labelled 'Terre Australe'.*

improvement that so characterised Georgian England.[35]

Throughout the eighteenth century, science in Europe transcended national boundaries. By 1750, co-operative projects between the various national scientific societies were under way. In 1761, for example, in the midst of the Seven Years' War, the Royal Society participated in an international series of observations of the transit of Venus co-ordinated by the Paris Academy (where one set of French observers was carried to the Indian Ocean in a naval vessel commanded by Marion du Fresne, captain, and Julien Crozet, his lieutenant). In 1763, just after the Peace of Paris, the Royal Society and the Paris Academy jointly conducted trials of Harrison's chronometer, a marine clock that for the first time allowed accurate calculations of longitude to be made at sea.[36] The 1761 observations of the transit of Venus, aimed at calculating the distance of the sun from Earth, had been inconclusive, and so another major project was planned to observe the transit when it recurred in 1769. As victors in the Seven Years' War the British were determined not to be outdone by the French on this occasion, and in the event the Royal Society co-ordinated the international effort, which saw 151 observers making observations of the transit from seventy-seven different stations around the world.[37]

PREPARATIONS

As the Royal Society began to plan its participation in this project, Alexander Dalrymple, a hydrographer who had just returned from service with the English East India Company, urged that any voyage to a South Seas station should be combined with an attempt to find the Southern Continent.[38] In late 1767 the Royal Society recommended that such an expedition should proceed with Dalrymple as its leader. The Royal Navy was to supply transport and Dalrymple helped to select the *Endeavour*, a broad-beamed Whitby collier, as the expedition's vessel. The Navy, however, would not allow a civilian to command one of its ships, and Dalrymple refused to share control of the venture with a naval commander. In 1768 this impasse was resolved when James Cook, a Royal Navy master whose observations of an eclipse of the sun had previously been published in *Philosophical Transactions*, was appointed as captain of the *Endeavour* with the rank of first lieutenant. Charles Green, a former assistant to the Astronomer Royal, was chosen to help Cook with the astronomical observations of the transit of Venus. Joseph Banks, a wealthy young landowner and botanist who had been a Fellow of the Royal Society since 1766, joined the expedition with Dr Solander, a Swedish naturalist, and a retinue of assistants to represent the Royal Society's general scientific interest in the voyage. On 30 July 1768 Cook received two sets of instructions from the Admiralty, the first of which began:

> Secret
>
> Whereas we have, in Obedience to the King's Commands, caused His Majesty's Bark the Endeavour, whereof you are Commander, to be fitted out in a proper manner for receiving such Persons as the Royal Society should think fit to appoint to observe the Passage of the Planet Venus over the Disk of the Sun on the 3rd of

June 1769, and for conveying them to such Place to the Southward of the Equi-noctial Line as should be judged proper for observing that Phaenomenon; and whereas the Council of the Royal Society have acquainted us that they have appointed Mr Charles Green, together with yourself, to be their Observers of the said Phaenomenon, and have desir'd that the Observation may be made at Port Royal Harbour in King Georges Island lately discover'd by Captn Wallis in His Majesty's Ship the Dolphin . . .[39]

Wallis had arrived back in England a little over a month before with tanta-lising reports of a newly found island Eden (Tahiti), which he had named King George's Island, and the Royal Society's planning group had realised that this would make an ideal station for the South Sea observations of the transit. In addition Wallis reported a sighting of mountain tops twenty leagues south of Tahiti which he thought must surely be part of the Southern Continent. It was this claim (which the Admiralty tried to keep secret) that prompted Cook's second set of instructions:

Secret
Additional Instructions for Lt James Cook, Appointed to Command His Majesty's Bark the Endeavour.

Whereas the making Discoverys of Countries hitherto unknown, and the Attaining a Knowledge of distant Parts which though formerly discover'd have yet been but imperfectly explored, will redound greatly to the Honour of this Nation as a Mari-time Power, as well as to the Dignity of the Crown of Great Britain, and may tend greatly to the advancement of the Trade and Navigation thereof; and Whereas there is reason to imagine that a Continent or Land of great extent, may be found to the Southward of the Tract lately made by Captn Wallis in His Majesty's Ship the Dolphin (of which you will herewith receive a Copy) or of the Tract of any former Navigators in Pursuits of the like kind; You are therefore in Pursuance of His Majesty's Pleasure hereby requir'd and directed to put to Sea with the Bark you Command so soon as the observation of the Transit of the Plant Venus shall be finished and observe the following Instructions.

    You are to proceed to the southward in order to make discovery of the Con-tinent above-mentioned until you arrive in the Latitude of 40° unless you sooner fall in with it. But not having discover'd it or any Evident signs of it in that Run, you are to proceed in search of it to the Westward between the Latitude before mentioned and the Latitude of 35° until you discover it, or fall in with the Eastern side of the Land discover'd by Tasman and now called New Zeland.[40]

These supplementary orders instructed Cook to explore the coasts of the Southern Continent and, failing that, of New Zealand; to describe the soil, animals and birds, fish, mineral resources and flora; to cultivate a friendship with the inhabitants and to observe their 'Genius, Temper, Disposition and Number',[41] and with their consent to take possession of convenient situations in the country in the name of the King of Great Britain. All logbooks and journals were to be collected at the voyage's end and sealed for delivery to the Admiralty. None of the crew was allowed to discuss the voyage with anyone until given permission to do so.

Cook's instructions made it clear that whatever anybody else may have

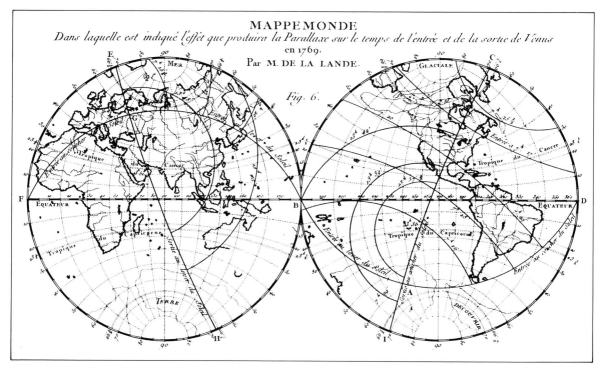

MAPPEMONDE
Dans laquelle est indiqué l'effet que produira la Parallaxe sur le temps de l'entrée et de la sortie de Vénus en 1769.
Par M. DE LA LANDE.

Fig. 6.

In M. de la Lande's Mappemonde *for Transit of Venus in 1769, Tasman's coast of New Zealand appears as the west coast of a speculative peninsula of Terra Australis.*

thought, the Admiralty considered it unlikely that the Southern Continent and 'The Land discover'd by Tasman and now called New Zeland' were one and the same, despite Dalrymple's arguments and a Mappemonde prepared by de la Lande for the 1769 transit observations which showed Tasman's coastline as the probable western edge of a vast southern landmass.[42] Tahiti, the Southern Continent and New Zealand were each to be investigated, and thus by the end of July all the main elements of the voyage had come together. In the following weeks stores, water and liquor were loaded, a contingent of twelve marines was allocated to the expedition, cabins were refitted for the 'Gentlemen', and Banks's party came on board. Cook's journal entry for 26 August laconically records the *Endeavour*'s departure from Plymouth:

> At 2pm got under sail and put to sea having on board 94 persons including Officers, Seamen Gentlemen and their servants, near 18 months provisions, 10 carriage guns 12 swivels with a good store of Ammunition and stores of all kinds.[43]

THE *ENDEAVOUR* PARTY

The 'wooden world' of the *Endeavour* carried a remarkable physical and cultural cargo, and Cook's instructions made certain that Pacific peoples would have an unusually extensive opportunity to examine it. The astronomical aspect of the voyage meant that Cook had to reach Tahiti at least six weeks before the transit.

Peaceful relationships with the local people had to be established so that the portable observatory could be set up and fortified and all its instruments tested. An array of surveying and astronomical instruments including a theodolite, a plane table, a brass scale, dividers, parallel ruler, proportional compasses,[44] several telescopes with stands, a Dolland's micrometer, an astronomical quadrant, several thermometers, a barometer and three clocks[45] were supplied by the Admiralty and the Royal Society, and many of these were used on land in Tahiti and later at Whitianga harbour in New Zealand. Both the instruments themselves and the ritual manner in which they were used (to examine the heavens no less) must have aroused intense interest, and when the quadrant was stolen in Tahiti, curiosity as well as cupidity may have been the reason. Sextants, hour-glasses, logs and compasses as well as the Nautical Almanac were routinely used on board to fix the ship's position. Moreover, Banks had made an extraordinary investment in the voyage, for in addition to employing two artists and an assistant naturalist,

A sketch of the Endeavour *at sea by Sydney Parkinson.*

he had purchased a magnificent array of equipment, as another Royal Society Fellow reported to Carl Linnaeus at the time:

> No people ever went to sea better fitted out for the purpose of Natural History. They have got a fine Library of Natural History; they have all sorts of machines for catching and preserving insects; all kinds of nets, trawls, drags and hooks for coral fishing, they have even a curious contrivance of a telescope, by which, put into the water, you can see the bottom at a great depth, when it is clear . . . in short Solander assured me this expedition would cost Mr Banks £10,000.[46]

During the voyage Banks and Solander collected plants, rocks, animals, insects, birds and fish. Interesting specimens were sketched as soon as possible, pressed (between sheets of Milton's *Paradise Lost*)[47] or planted out if vegetable, eaten or preserved in glass jars supplied by a London surgeon if animal. These activities and their products must have greatly entertained and baffled Polynesian witnesses. The inveterate botanising of Banks and Solander meant that Cook landed more often than the processes of exploration and charting strictly required, and frequently (as Te Taniwha reported) they involved local people in their pursuits.

The libraries on board were extensive and eclectic, including a large collection of 'Voyages' and sailing directions (a translation of van Nierop's account of Tasman's voyages, Campbell, de Brosses, Anson, Dampier, Byron, and manuscript journals from Wallis's voyage among others); de la Lande and Pingré's memoirs on the transit; an advance copy of Dalrymple's 'Voyages in the South Pacific Ocean' with its map showing Torres' passage through Torres Strait; large illustrated volumes to assist in the identification of plants, animals, insects, birds and fish, including several by Linnaeus, and Buffon's *Histoire Naturelle*; and the artist Parkinson's private library of histories, poetry, classical texts, the works of Shakespeare and Cervantes and various writings on aesthetics.[48] Cook had also ordered large quantities of paper[49] for the voyage and journals were regularly being written on board, so it seems reasonable to assume that Polynesian visitors to the *Endeavour* (especially those who stayed on the ship for a time) would have had a fair exposure to the European practices of reading and writing.

The artists were also active on shore, sketching places and people, another activity that presupposes time and reasonably peaceful relations, and this, too, was unusual in European voyages of the period.

Other more prosaic aspects of the *Endeavour* must have likewise seemed peculiar to Polynesian visitors. The food on board was limited in range — bread baked in the form of biscuits, flour, salted and pickled beef and pork, water, 2,900 gallons of beer, spirits and arrack, with lesser amounts of suet, cheese, raisins, peas, oatmeal, wheat, sugar, oil, vinegar and salt.[50] Cook supplemented these rations whenever possible with fresh meat, fruit, vegetables and fish, but after some time at sea the water became extremely foul and the bread crawled with weevils, as Banks described with some feeling after their departure from Tahiti:

> Our *bread* indeed is but indifferent, occasiond by the quantity of Vermin that are

in it, I have seen hundreds nay thousands shaken out of a single bisket. We in the Cabbin have however an easy remedy for this by baking it in an oven, not too hot, which makes them all walk off, but this cannot be allowd to the private people who must find the taste of these animals very disagreable, as they every one taste as strong as mustard or rather spirits of hartshorn. They are of 5 kinds, 3 *Tenebrios*, 1 *Ptinus* and the *Phalangium cancroides* this last is however scarce in the common bread but was vastly plentifull in White Deal bisket as long as we had any left.[51]

Other creatures on board the *Endeavour* included cockroaches and other unpleasant insects, European rats, a cat, Banks's greyhound and a nondescript bitch, a milk-goat that had already sailed around the world with Wallis, and a motley collection of pigs, sheep, ducks and chickens in pens on the forward deck. Of all of these animals only the rats, ducks and the dogs (although local varieties were quite different) would have been in the least familiar to Maori visitors to the vessel.

Thomas Hearne's 1775 watercolour of the Deal Castle *shows a goat, penned animals and the man at the wheel sheltering under an awning on the quarter-deck.*

The ship itself was an exemplar of European technology in its physical construction, equipment and processes of maintenance. The *Endeavour* was a flat-bottomed, serviceable craft just 106 feet long overall, 29 feet 3 inches at the widest point and of 368 tons burthen.[52] She was a 'cat-built' former collier, with a bluff, wide bow, double-sheathed on the hull and extensively altered for the voyage to provide more accommodation on a lower deck and in the cabins. She had three masts, square-rigged and carried ten four-pounder carriage guns,

Admiralty records of the Endeavour's *deck-plans, July 1768, showing the ship's internal lay-out.*

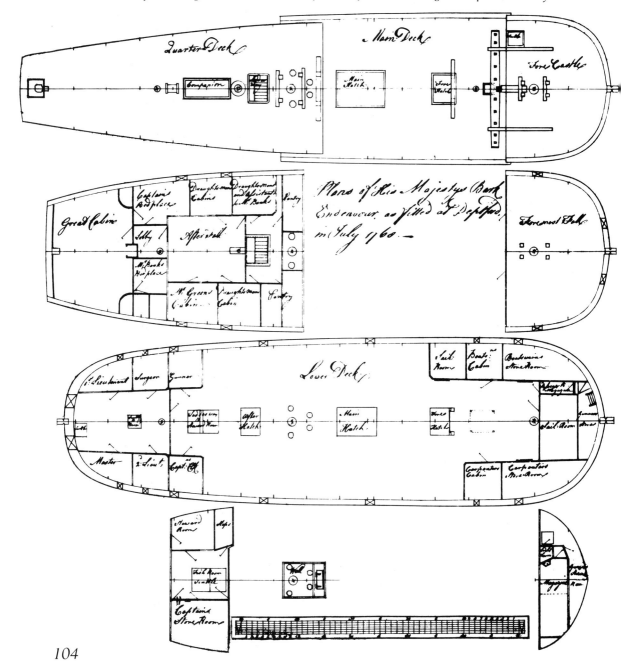

twelve swivels and a miscellany of muskets, pistols and swords. In length the *Endeavour* was within ten or twenty feet of a large war canoe in northern New Zealand, but in height, weight and breadth it was a massive craft by local standards.

The physical fabric of the ship was cared for by the carpenter and his mate, the sailmaker and the crew, while the gunner looked after the all-important guns and ammunition. A forge on board worked by the armourer could be set up for metalworking and repairs, and there were also a number of pumps and other mechanical devices including the capstan and the windlass on deck.[53] Stews and soups were cooked in the galley by the one-handed cook John Thompson, and sanitation was handled by the minute 'heads' for senior officers and 'gentlemen' in the for'ard corners of the great cabin, or otherwise by the miserable seamen's perch exposed to flying rain and spray at the bowsprit. The officers and the 'gentlemen' slept in small cabins (eight feet square or a little larger), and even the great cabin was much smaller than usual, only fourteen feet by twenty-three feet at its widest points, where thirteen men ate their meals, stored their books, dissected specimens on the table, drew them and drafted journals and descriptions.[54] Still, this was luxurious accommodation compared with the quarters down below, where the rest of the ninety-four men on board slept according to the naval rule of fourteen inches to a hammock and one watch always on deck.[55]

If the *Endeavour* was unusual as a Royal Navy craft (for colliers might act as storeships or transports sometimes, but rarely if ever as the main vessel for an expedition), her human cargo was also quite extraordinary. Cook was a skilled and experienced seaman and hydrographer who had served a late apprenticeship in the Whitby coal trade and later as a mate and master in naval vessels off Canada and Newfoundland. His previous commands had been small in scale, however, and the voyages seasonal and relatively short. As it turned out, he was a brilliant appointment, both in his management of the ship and the men on board, but that could not necessarily have been expected. Charles Green, the astronomer, was to work with him closely throughout the voyage, making navigational observations and calculations. He and Cook were to act as joint observers of the transit at Tahiti. Banks's party included Sydney Parkinson, a thoughtful, well-read Quaker who had worked previously as a botanical draughtsman for Banks; John Buchan, an epileptic landscape artist; Dr Solander, a vastly experienced Swedish naturalist who was Linnaeus's favourite pupil, and (like Banks) a Fellow of the Royal Society; and Herman Spöring, a former watchmaker turned assistant naturalist who was also to demonstrate an aptitude for sketching people and coastlines.

Joseph Banks himself had organised his way into the expedition in a thoroughly eighteenth-century fashion, by talking to his friend the Earl of Sandwich, sometime First Lord of the Admiralty, and to members of the Royal Society council, and by offering to invest some of his very considerable wealth in the voyage in the interests of science. If James Cook was the very model of a self-made sailor, rising through the ranks by dint of sheer hard work and mathematical study, Joseph Banks with his £6,000 a year was an exemplar of the cultivated

Above: *An engraved portrait of Sydney Parkinson, the studious Quaker.*

Above left: *A portrait of James Cook painted by Nathaniel Dance after the master mariner's second voyage, of 1772–75.*

Left: *Joseph Banks, painted by Benjamin West in a Maori cloak with a magnificent taaniko border, with a taiaha and painted paddle from New Zealand, and other Pacific 'curiosities'.*

young Georgian gentleman, devoted to botany, zoology and most of the natural sciences (with the curious exceptions of mathematics and astronomy) and carrying out his 'Grand Tour' on an unprecedented scale. His party also included two retainers from the family estates at Revesby, two black servants who died in the snows of Tierra del Fuego before they reached the South Pacific, and two dogs, one of which was an aristocratic greyhound.

In the interests of the safe conduct of the expedition on shore, twelve marines had been detailed to join the *Endeavour*, including one sergeant, a corporal, a drummer and nine private marines,[56] so that military rituals as well as naval ones were enacted in various places in the Pacific (including Tuuranga-nui, or Poverty Bay). The naval complement included forty able seamen, five of whom were from Cook's previous command; eight officers' servants; the boatswain and his mates; the gunner and the armourer; the sailmaker, 'an old man about 70 or 80 years';[57] the carpenter and his mate; the master Richard Molyneux and his mate Richard Pickersgill (both good cartographers), and mate Francis Wilkinson, each of whom had circumnavigated the world with Wallis. There were also Charles Clerke, the high-spirited master's mate who had earlier convinced the Royal Society that there might be giants at Patagonia; Cook's second-in-command Zachariah Hicks, competent and reliable but consumptive; his third lieutenant John Gore, a fine practical seaman who had sailed the Pacific with Byron and Wallis; William Monkhouse, the surgeon, not much of a healer but the writer of a vividly descriptive journal; his assistant William Perry; Orton the clerk, whose ears were cropped in drunken foolery later in the voyage; two quartermasters; and three midshipmen.

As far as we know, all on board except for Banks's two black servants were Caucasian, and all (unlike Bougainville's expedition, where Commerson the botanist had an assistant who had disguised herself as a man) were male. Women sometimes went to sea in the Georgian navy as wives or lovers, but not on this occasion. No wonder the Tahitians were delighted when they (and not the Frenchmen) uncovered the French assistant botanist's disguise, for otherwise they must have thought that women in Europe had not yet been invented. Most of the men on board were aged between eighteen and thirty, as one might expect from demographic patterns at the time; Cook at forty was relatively elderly, and John Ravenhill, the seventy-year-old sailmaker, was a veritable Methuselah. There was also a number of young boys aboard, including some of the officers' servants (or apprentices) and the midshipmen, who worked hard but also entertained themselves and sometimes quarrelled heartily. Nearly all of the crew were British, although they did include one American (James Magra); a Venetian, one Brazilian and another who joined them at Rio.[58] Unlike most of their British compatriots, they were cosmopolitan and widely travelled, familiar with sea ports as well as their own home towns and villages, and a number of them had visited the Pacific before.

At sea or on shore the *Endeavour*'s men formed a tightly ordered, hierarchical society, where the quality of access to food, grog, clothes, accommodation and leisure depended on social class and rank. All on board were subject to the

'Portsmouth Point', a satirical cartoon by T. Rowlandson, showing the sailors' riotous life in port.

rigorous routines of shipboard life, marked out by bells and the boatswain's pipe signalling watches, calling the hands to breakfast or dinner, and piping the hammocks up or down. There was a kind of rough democracy involved, for naval hierarchies were not absolute and men of no particular rank on land could win promotion at sea (as Cook had done) by sheer application and dogged effort. One could scarcely find a more precise illustration of the Georgian theme of 'self-improvement' than Cook's wry preface to his journal of a later voyage:

> I have neither natural or acquired abilities for writing. I have been I may say constantly at sea from my youth and have dragged myself (with the assistance of a few good friends) through all the stations belonging to a seaman, from a prentice boy to a commander. After such a candid confession I shall hope to be excused for all the blunders that will appear in this journal.[59]

Social relations on board were regulated by informal co-operation, backed up in moments of conflict by more formal disciplines that included floggings and confinement. Royal Navy captains were permitted to give their men maximum sentences of twelve lashes for minor instances of insubordination and drunkenness. More serious offences were tried by court martial, and crimes of cowardice, buggery, murder, desertion and treachery could be punished with hanging or sentences of 400 or 500 and up to 1,000 lashes.[60] Casual violence and flogging were in fact common in Georgian England, for disputes often turned into brawls, and children and adults alike were frequently thrashed for domestic misdeeds. Cook's shipboard sentences of twelve or twenty-four lashes for disobedience to an officer, theft or desertion were taken as a matter of course by the *Endeavour* company, although Polynesians who witnessed floggings were aghast to see men tied up to a grating and whipped, and very often they wept or tried to stop the punishment.[61]

Officers were not flogged, however, and in this and other respects the hierarchies of rank were obvious. Officers had their own small cabins, while the men slept in hammocks on the lower deck. They ate separately and dressed differently, with an everyday uniform of frock jacket with breeches and stockings or a dress uniform with white facings and a profusion of gold lace, while the seamen wore blue frock jackets, checked shirts, red waistcoats and canvas trousers or canvas 'petticoats' for boatwork.[62] The marines had their own distinctive dress uniforms of red coats, grey trousers and high steeple hats, while Banks and the other 'gentlemen' wore civilian clothes, which in Banks's case could be quite splendid. In Tahiti, for instance, he had his 'white jacket and waistcoat, with silver frogs' stolen one evening while he slept on shore.[63]

In this sketch by George Cruikshank, a seaman is flogged at the gratings while all hands watch and marines stand guard at the forecastle.

'A Lieutenant' (left), by Dominic Seres, 1777, showing his uniform hat, coat, waistcoat and breeches. His 'Seaman' (right) wears petticoat breeches and a jacket.

The officers and 'gentlemen' ate better than the men most of the time, and Banks had brought rations for his own party on board. The diet, like the accommodation, however, was far more spartan than Banks and others of his party were used to, while many of the seamen found it a marked improvement on their diet and living conditions at home. Most poor families would have considered a hot meal every day and meat four days a week good eating, even though the meat was rarely fresh and the cooking rudimentary; and the lower decks were regularly cleaned and ventilated, and clean clothing was issued as often as conditions at sea allowed.

In addition Cook had been instructed to carry out experiments against scurvy, and supplies of 'portable soup' (dried meat stock that was boiled and mixed with oatmeal, peas, and other vegetables), dried malt, 'saloup', cabbage, mustard seed, lemon and orange 'robs' (essence of juice) and carrot marmalade were loaded on board. Fresh meat and vegetables were collected at every possible opportunity, and Cook ordered one man flogged for refusing to eat fresh meat early in the voyage. There were still cases of scurvy, but none of these proved fatal and the health record of the *Endeavour* was good until they reached Batavia, despite the presence of several men infected with tuberculosis on board and a major outbreak of venereal disease after their stay in Tahiti.[64] This was just as well, because the surgeon William Monkhouse had skimped on his medical supplies, and in any case eighteenth-century medicine was ineffective in its treatment of most serious complaints. Monkhouse, too, like many men on the ship, suffered from 'intemperance' or persistent drunkenness, fuelled by the daily ration of a gallon of beer a man, or a pint of wine or half a pint of arrack, rum or brandy during long passages.

The men purchased rations of tobacco, fished at sea for entertainment as well as food, played music, sang sea songs and danced on the deck. Banks went shooting as a gentleman should, potting gulls at sea and ducks on shore, and in a calm he was rowed around the ship so that he and Solander could use their trawls and other devices for catching specimens from the sea. In leisure as in work, in its taken-for-granted patterns of patronage and loyal support, shipboard life on the *Endeavour* faithfully reflected many aspects of life in Britain, for as a recent study of the Georgian navy has pointed out:

> In the middle years of the century the Navy, considered as a society in miniature, was very much a microcosm of British society in general. It was peculiar in almost all its superficial aspects; it had its own customs and traditions, its dress and language . . . But in its fundamentals, in the ways in which people dealt with one another and thought of one another, it closely resembled British society ashore. In the last analysis, the wooden world was built of the same materials as the wider world.[65]

THE VOYAGE

During the voyage from Plymouth to Madeira the *Endeavour* passed through severe gales and then calms, and while the ship sailed quietly in light breezes Banks's assistants caught various sea creatures with lines and casting nets. Banks and Solander worked industriously to record and classify these creatures and birds caught in the ship's rigging, and Parkinson and Spöring sketched and described their finds. At Madeira, Banks and Solander explored the area around Funchal, collecting eighteen fishes and 246 plants as they went,[66] while 3,000 gallons of wine, some fresh water, meat, fruit and onions were loaded on board the *Endeavour*.[67] This pattern of industrious collecting and description became a daily routine, and during the passage to Brazil, Banks recorded an impressive number of marine animals and birds in his journal. At Rio de Janeiro the Portuguese viceroy kept the *Endeavour* under close surveillance, and no one but the captain and the men required to take on fresh food and water was allowed to land. Banks slipped ashore on one occasion to botanise, but this proved to be too risky, and it was not until the *Endeavour* reached Tierra del Fuego in January 1769 that he and Solander could organise another expedition. They met briefly in the Bay of Good Success with some local Indians and presented them with beads and ribbons, and the next day Banks, Solander, Green the astronomer, Monkhouse the surgeon, the artist Buchan, Banks's four servants and two seamen set off to explore the interior. It proved to be a disastrous excursion, for late in the afternoon as they struggled through marshy scrub Buchan had an epileptic fit. After that it began to snow and some of the party became exhausted and had to stop. The others made their way to a place where they built a fire and spent the night, returning in the morning to find Banks's two black servants frozen to death in the snow. After this sobering experience they returned to the vessel and spent several more days botanising, briefly visiting an Indian settlement before the *Endeavour* again sailed south. Cook took his ship around Cape Horn and down to 60°S, then turned north-west and crossed a great stretch of the supposed southern continent, prompting Banks to comment:

> When I look on the charts of these Seas and see our course, which has been Near a streight one at NW since we left Cape Horne, I cannot help wondering that we have not yet seen land. It is however some pleasure to be able to disprove that which does not exist but in the opinions of Theoretical writers, of which sort most are who have wrote any thing about these seas without having themselves been in them . . . The number of square degrees of their land which we have already chang'd into water . . . teaches me at least that till we know how this globe is fixd in that place which has been since its creation assignd to it in the general system, we need not be anxious to give reasons how any one part of it counterbalances the rest.[68]

On 11 April, after sailing through the island screen of the Tuamotus, the *Endeavour* came to Tahiti and on 13 April anchored in Port Royal Bay. In Tahiti, Cook's third set of instructions drafted by the Earl of Morton, then president of the Royal Society, came into play. The Earl had written a series of 'Hints', which among other things advised Cook, Banks, Solander and others how to handle their meetings with local peoples, how to carry out the observations of the transit, how to recognise any continent that might be discovered and describe its inhabitants, how to examine metals and precious stones, and how to label plants collected during the voyage. His instructions on meetings with local peoples are worth quoting in full:

> *'Hints'* offered to the consideration of Captain Cook, Mr Bankes, Doctor Solander, and the other Gentlemen who go upon the Expedition on Board the *Endeavour*:
>
> To exercise the utmost patience and forbearance with respect to the Natives of the several Lands where the Ship may touch.
>
> To check the petulance of the Sailors, and restrain the wanton use of Fire Arms.
>
> To have it still in view that sheding the blood of those people is a crime of the highest nature:- They are human creatures, the work of the same omnipotent Author, equally under his care with the most polished European; perhaps being less offensive, more entitled to his favor.
>
> They are the natural, and in the strictest sense of the word, the legal possessors of the several Regions they inhabit.
>
> No European Nation has a right to occupy any part of their country, or settle among them without their voluntary consent. Conquest over such people can give no just title; because they could never be the Agressors.
>
> They may naturally and justly attempt to repell intruders, whom they may apprehend are come to disturb them in the quiet possession of their country, whether that apprehension be well or ill founded.
>
> Therefore should they in a hostile manner oppose a landing, and kill some men in

112

the attempt, even this would hardly justify firing among them, 'till every other gentle method had been tried.

There are many ways to convince them of the Superiority of Europeans, without slaying any of those poor people — for Example. —

By shooting some of the Birds or other animals that are near them; — Shewing them that a Bird upon wing may be brought down by a Shot. — Such an appearance would strike them with amazement and awe. — Lastly to drive a bullet thro' one of their hutts, or knock down some conspicuous object with great Shot, if any such are near the Shore.

Amicable signs may be made which they could not possibly mistake. — Such as holding up a jug, turning it bottom upwards, to shew them it was empty, then applying it to the lips in the attitude of drinking. — The most stupid from such a token, must immediately comprehend that drink was wanted.

Opening the mouth wide, putting the fingers towards it, and then making the motion of chewing, would sufficiently demonstrate a want of food.

They should not at first be alarmed with the report of Guns, Drums, or even a trumpet. — But if there are other Instruments of Music on board they should be first entertained near the Shore with a soft Air.

If a Landing can be effected, whether with or without resistance, it might not be amiss to lay some few trinkets, particularly looking Glasses upon the Shore: Then retire in the Boats to a small distance, from whence the behaviour of the natives might be distinctly observed, before a second landing were attempted.

Other and more important considerations of this kind will occurr to the Gentlemen themselves, during the course of the Expedition.[69]

In this opening section of the 'Hints' the Earl asserts that 'natives' are human, the legal possessors of their lands, and yet in his view undoubtedly inferior to Europeans, as the power of European guns would always in the last resort convince them. By placing 'savages' below Europeans in a hierarchical arrangement he echoed the old idea of the Great Chain of Being, which in Georgian England was still a powerful metaphor for organising both nature and society. The Earl understood that humans, like other forms of life, could be systematically described, and in his 'Hints' he included a list of headings under which this might be done:

The natural Dispositions of the people: Their progress in Arts or Science, Especially their Mechanics, Tools, and manner of using them; Their notions of Astronomy &c are principal objects of attention.

Or if they have any method of communicating their thoughts at a distance, As the Mexicans are said to have done by painting, and the Peruvians by the Quipos.

Next, the Character of their Persons
Features
Complection
Dress
Habitations
Food
Weapons

Then may be considered, their

*Their tokens for	Religion
Commerce and if	Morals
they have any currency	Order
that passes among them	Government
in lieu of money, to	Distinctions of Power
bring home several	Police
Specimens from the	*
highest to the lowest	
denomination	

. . . the Natural productions of the Country, in the

Animal
Vegetable and
Mineral Systems.

Their powers in Medicine, whether Salutary or noxious, — The other uses to which they are put by the Natives.

Lastly, to form a Vocabulary of the names given by the Natives to the several things and places which come under the Inspection of the Gentlemen.[70]

'Natural History' in this period covered the study of people as well as plants, animals and minerals, and the Royal Society had previously published instructions for travellers (by Robert Boyle among others) in the *Philosophical Transactions* to guide them in writing useful accounts of the peoples they encountered. Mariners also kept careful 'Sailing Directions', which included comments on 'natives friendly or hostile'. When Cook, Banks, Parkinson, Solander, Monkhouse and others described Polynesians, therefore, in the same systematic fashion that they described coastlines, fish and plants, they were faithfully reflecting the structures and strategies of mid-eighteenth-century European science.

The Earl's advice about how to handle hostile opposition to a landing proved unnecessary in Tahiti, for Tahitians had already been given a practical demonstration of their place in the hierarchy of nature. During Wallis's visit they had attacked his men with stones and were shot at first with muskets and then by the *Dolphin*'s guns, which killed a great number of people. As one of the *Dolphin*'s crew wrote in his journal, 'How terrible must they be shockd, to see their nearest and dearest of friends dead, and toar to peces in such a manner as I am certain they neaver beheald before — to attempt to say what this poor ignorant creatures thought of us, would be taking more upon me than I am able to perform.'[71] When the *Endeavour* anchored in Port Royal Bay therefore, the local people reacted cautiously, trading 'very quietly and civily' and enacting a ritual of peacemaking with the Europeans as soon as they landed.

Even so, Cook was not immediately able to check the 'petulance of the sailors', for on the third day after their arrival a midshipman, provoked by the seizure of a sentry's musket, ordered the marines to fire into a large crowd of Tahitians, killing the offender and wounding some others. The Tahitians' propensity for absconding with the Europeans' property greatly aggravated the *Endeavour* party. Banks remarked that 'great and small cheifs and common men all are firmly of opinion that if they can once get possession of any thing it immediately becomes their own',[72] and this opinion was frequently acted upon at the Europeans' expense. There were a number of such incidents and considerable mutual ill feeling, but Cook ordered his men to set aside their accustomed notions of punishment for 'stealing' and further bloodshed was avoided. Other events during their stay included the death of Buchan, the landscape artist, which compromised Banks's plans to take home a full pictorial record of the people and places visited on the voyage; and the transit of Venus, observed in perfect conditions seven weeks later, although conditions created by the planet's atmosphere made it impossible to accurately measure the precise moments of contact between Venus and the sun.[73]

This is not the place to dwell in detail on the *Endeavour*'s visit to Tahiti, except to say that it profoundly influenced the Europeans in their subsequent observations of Maori life. During their three-month stay on the island they produced numerous descriptions of Tahitian life and collected Tahitian material goods, and many of the *Endeavour* contingent (including Banks, Parkinson and Green) learned to speak some Tahitian. They entered into sexual liaisons with Tahitian women, took part in Tahitian domestic life, ate Tahitian food, slept in Tahitian houses and were guests (and sometimes participants) at Tahitian rituals

A romantic drawing by Giovanni Battista Cipriani of an entertainment inside a house at Raiatea, based on drawings by Parkinson.

and entertainments. On the whole they enjoyed themselves immensely, and in the process began to see Tahitians as individuals with their own interests and stratagems.

It is not surprising, then, that some· of the more stereotypical schemes for classifying human groups with which they were familiar (for instance, Linnaeus's classification of human beings into two species, *Homo sapiens*, which included American Indians, Asiatics and Africans, and *Homo monstrosus*, which included Patagonians and Hottentots),[74] did not survive this intimate exposure to a 'savage' way of life. All the same, their assumptions of European superiority remained virtually untouched. One example of this was Banks's self-justification for adding Tupaia, a priestly ariki (high chief) and navigator from Raiatea, to his entourage, when he drew a commonplace European analogy between animal and human 'curiosities':[75]

> The Captn refuses to take him on his own account, in my opinion sensibly enough, the goverment will never in all human probability take any notice of him; I there-fore have resolvd to take him. Thank heaven I have a sufficiehcy and I do not know why I may not keep him as a curiosity, as well as some of my neighbours do lions and tygers at a larger expence than he will probably ever put me to; the amusement I shall have in his future conversation and the benefit he will be of to this ship, as well as what he may be if another should be sent into these seas, will I think fully repay me.[76]

During their stay Banks's scientific party worked industriously to produce a range of documents on Tahitian life, and Banks himself wrote a lengthy account under a range of headings broadly based upon the Earl of Morton's list. Parkinson and Spöring sketched places and structures, while Parkinson also sketched the people and (like Molyneux) collected an extensive Tahitian vocabulary. Banks used this vocabulary to make comparisons with some other Oceanic languages, suggest-ing on this basis that their speakers 'have originaly come from one and the same place and brought with them the same numbers and Language, which latter especialy have remaind to this time not materialy alterd'.[77] In Tahiti and other islands of the Society group they developed their descriptive skills and exhausted some of their curiosity about Polynesians, for it is notable that their accounts of Maori life are not as detailed and extensive as those written in Tahiti. Most subtly perhaps, they were to take their impressions of this particular Polynesian society and add them to their everyday experience as Europeans, in reacting to and assessing Maori social and physical life.

When the *Endeavour* left Tahiti in mid-July Tupaia travelled with them. He piloted the ship to Huahine, Raiatea, Tahaa and Rurutu where further sketches and descriptions were made. Tupaia also guided their ceremonial encounters with local people and forewarned them of local practices and politics, communi-cating with his fellow voyagers in Tahitian and a smattering of English. After leaving Rurutu they sailed south-west for some weeks, making intermittent false sightings of the southern continent (called by Banks 'Cape Fly-away'), and Banks and Solander resumed their shipboard routine of collecting and describing marine plant and animal species.

On 3 October, as they sailed towards 'Zealandia Nova', Banks wrote in his journal:

> Now do I wish that our freinds in England could by the assistance of some magical spying glass take a peep at our situation: Dr Solander setts at the Cabbin table describing, myself at my Bureau Journalizing, between us hangs a large bunch of sea weed, upon the table lays the wood and barnacles; they would see that not-withstanding our different occupations our lips move very often, and without being conjurors might guess that we were talking about what we should see upon the land which there is now no doubt we shall see very soon.[78]

Three days later, on 6 October 1769, their patience was rewarded when the surgeon's boy Nicholas Young sighted land from the *Endeavour*'s masthead:

> At ½ past one a small boy who was at the mast head Calld out Land. I was luckyly upon deck and well I was entertaind, within a few minutes the cry circulated and up came all hands, this land could not then be seen even from the tops yet few were there who did not plainly see it from the deck till it appeard that they had lookd at least 5 points wrong.[79]

Overleaf: *'New Zeland' is part of Cook's 'Chart of the Great South Sea or Pacifick Ocean shewing the Track and Discoveries made by the Endeavour Bark'.*

NEW ZELAND

Var 11°.25'E
Var 12°.42'E
CAPE NORTH
Sandy Bay
Three Kings
Bay of Iſlands
Cape Brett
Mount Camel
Bream Bay
Barrier Iſle
False Bay
Cape Colvill
Var 11°.9'E
Mercury Bay
Bay of Plenty
Var 13°.50'E
C. Runaway
Var 13°.0'E
Gannet Iſle
EAST CAPE
Tolaga
Poverty Bay
Cape Egmont
Var 14°.56'E
Table Cape
Hawkes Bay
C. Hidnappers
Var 14°.10'E
Turnagain
Cape Farewell
Cape Palisser
Cape Foulwind
Admirally B.
Charlottes S.
Cook's Straits
Var 15°.4'E
Cape Campbell
Caſcades Point
Var 14°.30'E
Var 14°.31'E
Bankss I.
Var 15°.20'E
Doubtfull Har.
CAPE WEST
C. Saunders
Solanders Iſle
Var 16°.16'E
CAPE SOUTH
Var 16°.29'E
Var 16°.34'E
The Traps

Chapter Five

TUURANGA-NUI (POVERTY BAY)

6–11 October 1769

The place where the *Endeavour* first anchored in New Zealand was Tuuranga-nui, a wide bay on the east coast of the North Island. According to early Land Court evidence, the area was occupied at that time by four main tribes — Rongowhakaata, Ngai Tahupoo (later known as Ngai Tamanuhiri), Te Aitanga-a-Maahaki and Te Aitanga-a-Hauiti.[1] Inland, the bay was sheltered by ranges covered with thick forest, while the hills nearer the flats were sparsely clad in scrub, with fern and grasses on the ridges. The central plains were braided by the courses and fertile fans of three major rivers, where taro, kuumara, gourds and probably yams flourished in sunlit gardens.[2] Gardens were also cleared on frost-free hillsides near the rivers, and fernroot diggings were scattered around the bay.[3] Grasslands, wetlands, swamps, scrub and great stands of kahikaatea, pukatea and tawa trees on the flats provided a variety of foods and materials for weaving and building.[4] Large fortified villages, or paa, were built on river bends or strategic hills, protecting houses, cooking sheds and storage pits for root crops — up to 1,300 cubic metres of storage in some places.[5]

Pigeons, kaakaa, puukeko and parakeets were plentiful on the plains, and thousands of ducks lived by the rivers and the Awapuni Lagoon.[6] Creeks leading into the main rivers on either side of the central plain were crossed by eel weirs with names such as Makaroro, Te Rua-o-Mapewa, Arowhati,[7] built and maintained by particular families. Mullet, eels and whitebait swarmed in season in the tidal waterways.[8]

The bay was famous for its crayfish, caught off Titirangi or further north along the coast, and the reefs and tidal flats harboured quantities of shellfish. Paaua were plentiful off Onepoto (now Kaiti), and there were beds of white pipi off Oneroa, where the taamure (snapper) came to feed, crunching the shells in their powerful jaws.[9] Sharks, kahawai, kingfish, flounder and many other species of fish were caught in the bay, and there were a number of favourite fishing grounds, including Te-Wai-o-Hii-Harore at Waikanae, where a spring seeped into the ocean, attracting kahawai, which, according to one early Land Court witness, came there to drink the fresh water.[10] Now and then whales stranded on the beaches, to be claimed by the chiefly leaders of whichever kin-group controlled that part of the shoreline.[11]

The northern end of the bay was dominated by the high hill of Titirangi, facing the offshore island of Tuamotu with the sacred pool Pipitaiari nearby, which had been magically brought there from Hawaiki by the priestly ancestor Ruawharo.[12] At the southern end lay Te Upoko-o-Te-Kuri-a-Paoa, the white-cliffed headland named after the head of the dog of Paoa (or Pawa, as he is sometimes called), an ancestor who commanded the *Horouta* canoe.

Tribal history in the bay is well documented and extremely complex. Each of the major tribal groupings was divided into many sub-groups, or hapuu, linked by a maze of intermarriages and keeping in active contact with other groups both to the north and the south of the bay. People summoned distant relatives in wartime and often lived for a while in the villages of their kinsfolk on either the mother's or father's side. As Rutene Te Eke said in an 1875 Land Court hearing, 'My ancestors were in the habit of going to and fro to other places, we do the same.'[13] Despite the fluidity of the local population, it is likely to have been large, for the first missionary congregations in the bay were estimated at 2,000,[14] and

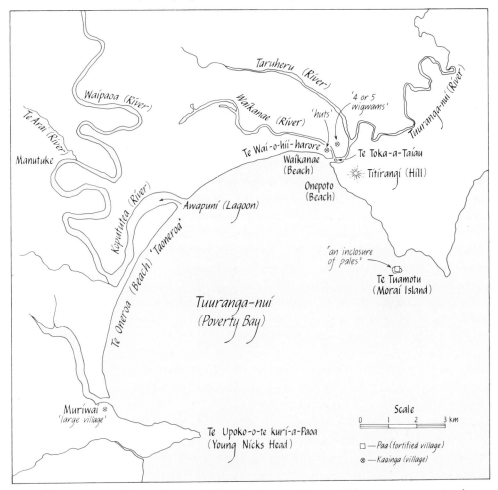

Map of Tuuranga-nui (Poverty Bay) in 1769. (The Awapuni Lagoon follows a reconstruction by Kevin Jones. European names after original map by Cook and Smith.)

120

recent calculations based on local volumes of crop-storage pits suggest that from 300 to 1,000 people could have been fed from gardens on each of the major river fans in the bay.[15]

The people of Tuuranga-nui traced their remote ancestry from the demi-god Maaui, who fished up the North Island and whose canoe is said to have stranded on Mount Hikurangi, near East Cape; from the ancestor Toi; and from three main groups of migrants from Hawaiki. One early migration was that of Paikea, son of Uenuku, who came to Whaangaraa from Hawaiki in the shape of a whale, and whose descendants eventually spread along the east coast from Opotiki to Wairarapa, and to the South Island. Another group came on the *Horouta* canoe, which was wrecked at Ohiwa in the Bay of Plenty before it reached Tuuranga-nui.[16] According to some accounts, the captain Paoa then led a group overland to Tuuranga,[17] while according to others the canoe was refitted and brought a number of the travellers including Paoa to the bay, where it now rests in the depths of the Muriwai Lagoon.[18] The high priestess of this canoe, Hine Haakiri-rangi, waited for her family to join her, and as she waited she named the beach from the Tuuranga-nui River to the cliffs Oneroa (long beach).[19] She then walked inland with a precious bundle of kuumara tubers, looking for a place to plant a garden. When the tubers finally sprouted, she was so pleased that she named the place Manawaruu (delighted).[20] A number of other place-names in the bay record the exploits of Paoa, the captain of *Horouta*.[21]

The sacred canoe *Takitimu*, which brought tapu axes, stones and a number of gods from Hawaiki, arrived at Tuuranga at about the same time as *Horouta*, and according to some accounts its captain Kiwa planted a mauri there as a link between people and the land,[22] while its chief priest Ruawharo established a house of learning called Tokitoki in the bay.[23] The two names alternately given to the district — Tuuranga-nui-a-Kiwa or Tuuranga-nui-a-Rua (Kiwa's or Rua's great standing-place) — recall a contest of mana between Ruawharo and Kiwa, the captain of this canoe.[24] The descent-lines from *Horouta* and *Takitimu* came together in one of the great founding ancestors of Tuuranga-nui, Ruapani, who traced his descent in senior lines from both Paoa of *Horouta* and Kiwa of the *Takitimu* canoe.[25]

A final migration was that of the ancestor Maia, who quarrelled with Uenuku in Hawaiki and escaped by sailing to this country on a raft of gourds (or according to other authorities, on the *Maataatua* canoe),[26] which brought him to Tuuranga-nui. He landed at the eastern bank of the Tuuranga-nui River and, after planting gourd seeds at Maakaraka and other places inland, built a house by the river, which he called Puhikaiiti after the decorative canoe streamer that had held his raft of gourds together. According to Rongowhakaata Halbert, one day Maia called a small girl named Taiau to bring his canoe across the Tuuranga-nui River. When it arrived he drowned her, and she was transformed into the rock Te Toka-a-Taiau, which formerly stood in the river opposite the mouth of the Waikanae Creek.[27] According to Apirana Ngata, on the other hand, Taiau was a great-grandson of Porourangi, the ancestor of the East Coast tribe of Ngaati Porou, and the rock Te Toka-a-Taiau marked the southern boundary of Ngaati

Porou tribal territory.[28] At other times Te Toka-a-Taiau has also been claimed as the northernmost boundary of the Ngaati Kahungunu tribes.[29]

Tribal histories record a number of later migrations from Tuuranga-nui itself — by the ancestors of Ngaati Kahungunu, for instance — provoked by disputes over mana and the control of local resources. Through all of these ancestors the people of Tuuranga-nui were linked with many other places in an intricate web of kinship, where lines could be traced back to common progenitors through male or female forebears for any one of a number of reasons — to claim relationship, seniority, alliance, access to particular resources, residence or the right to travel and trade safely, without fear of attack.

Once the *Endeavour* had arrived at Tuuranga-nui, life in this and other districts of New Zealand was never the same again. Abel Tasman had anchored briefly off Taitapu, where several of his men were killed and some local warriors were wounded and perhaps killed by musket and cannonfire. After that the Dutch sailed up the west coast of the North Island, sighted the Three Kings and were largely lost to local memory. Other visits by European vessels may have followed, but if so we have no conclusive evidence of such arrivals, from either Maori or European records, until the *Endeavour* arrived in 1769.

The *Endeavour*'s visit, on the other hand, involved a six-month circumnavigation of the New Zealand coastline where the vessel anchored in one harbour after another, meeting local people at sea and on shore, visiting their settlements and welcoming Maori visitors on board. Not only did the Europeans have extensive opportunities to observe Maori life in different parts of the country, Maori people of various tribes had their first opportunity to examine Europeans at close quarters — to trade with them, to fight with them, to become infected with European diseases and to work out strategies for dealing with these unprecedented visitors. After the *Endeavour*'s visit, too, European ships began to visit New Zealand, at first sporadically and then in ever-increasing numbers, guided to its coastlines by Cook's meticulous maps.

For the Europeans, the 'discovery' of the east coast of New Zealand on 6 October 1769[30] was a cause for celebration. Nicholas Young, the surgeon's boy, was given the gallon of rum promised as a reward to the first person to see land, and Te Kuri-a-Paoa, the white-cliffed peninsula at the south end of Tuuranga-nui was afterwards named Young Nicks Head in recognition of his sighting. Very little is known about 'Young Nick', source of the first English place-name in New Zealand, except for an indignant scrawl in midshipman John Bootie's journal: 'Evil communications corrupt good manners N. Young is a son of a Bitch.' That evening was spent merrily as the *Endeavour*'s people 'regaled ourselves . . . upon the occasion'.[31] The next day as the ship approached to within about twenty miles of the land, Banks wrote jubilantly in his journal:

> Land . . . appears larger than ever, in many parts 3, 4 and 5 ranges of hills are seen one over the other and a chain of Mountains over all, some of which appear enormously high. Much difference of opinion and many conjectures about Islands, rivers, inlets &c, but all hands seem to agree that this is certainly the Continent we are in search of.[32]

The winds were light and variable, and it was not until four o'clock on the afternoon of 8 October that the *Endeavour* finally anchored in Tuuranga-nui harbour, at a depth of eight fathoms and about a mile off the shore. The land seemed rich and fertile, with a backdrop of 'fine green trees'.[33] From the deck they could see a fenced hilltop (which the Europeans thought must be an enclosure for sheep, deer or oxen but which Tupaia thought was a Tahitian-style marae) on an island,[34] and some neatly built houses on the foreshore, near one of which a crowd of people sat, intently observing the *Endeavour*.[35] A number of large canoes were out on the water and smoke plumed up from the beach, the valleys and far inland, possibly from fires lit to signal the *Endeavour*'s arrival in the bay.

According to William Williams in 1888, the Rongowhakaata people first thought that the *Endeavour* must be a floating island.[36] Joel Polack, a European trader who recorded an account given by the grandchildren of some of those who

View of the North Side of the Entrance into Poverty Bay, & Morai Island, in New-Zealand.
1. Young Nick's Head.
2. Morai Island.

a

b

S. Parkinson del.

R. B. Godfrey Sc.

View of another Side of the Entrance into the said Bay.

Two coastal views of Tuuranga-nui (Poverty Bay), engraved by R. B. Godfrey after lost sketches by Parkinson.

(a) *shows Te Tuamotu ('Morai Island') at the northern end of the bay;*
(b) *shows Te Kuri-a-Paoa ('Young Nick's Head') at the south end of the bay. Note the tall trees in the vicinity of Muriwai.*

lived at Tuuranga-nui when Cook arrived, said that the *Endeavour* was mistaken for a great bird, and the local people had marvelled at the beauty and size of its wings. When it came right into the bay, however, and they saw 'a smaller bird, unfledged (without sails), descending into the water, and a number of parti-coloured beings, but apparently in the human shape, also descending, the bird was regarded as a houseful of divinities. Nothing could exceed the astonishment of the people.'[37] The 'smaller bird' must have been one of the *Endeavour*'s two small boats, which were lowered that afternoon to take Cook, Banks, Solander, Monkhouse, Green, Gore, some seamen and marines ashore to look for a watering-place. The Tuuranga people had a legend of a great bird that had carried one of their ancestors back to Tuuranga after he fetched kuumara tubers from Hawaiki,[38] and perhaps this influenced their interpretation of the *Endeavour*'s arrival.

As the boats landed on the east bank of the Tuuranga-nui River, some people who had been seen on the west bank vanished abruptly from sight. Cook ordered the pinnace to stay at the river mouth while the yawl ferried the rest of the men across the river to search for them. About 300 yards from the water's edge they found a collection of houses that had evidently just been abandoned, and another small hamlet nearby across the Waikanae Creek. The ship's surgeon, William Monkhouse, described these hamlets in some detail:

> These huts were very low, the walling of reeds, and thatched with a kind of rush and course grass. Part of these huts were of the wigwam construction consisting of a roof supported by a poll on one side, and a small or narrow piece of walling on the other; but here was one tolerable house about eight yards by six, the end wall of which where the door, and a window to answer the double purpose of admitting light and giving passage to the smoak, were situated, was placed about two feet within the roof and side walls; the doorway was exceedingly low and narrow so that it was necessary to crawl in. Here we found the remains of an old net made of a strong grass, and an old dress of one of the natives which seemed to be made of much the same kind of materials; the fireplace, that is, some burnt sticks lay nigh the farther end of the house. Contiguous to these huts was the burnt stump of a tree on which was placed a piece of white pumice Stone formed into a very rude resemblance of a human figure . . . Here were also two pretty large fish-pots very well made of withys, of a circular form nearly resembling a common bread-loaf. On the other side the river [probably this refers to the Waikanae Creek] we found four or five wigwams, a quantity of limpet shell, the Shell of a lobster and a ground oven in the Otaheite Style.[39]

These two hamlets, the first Maori settlements to be recorded by Europeans, were almost certainly fishing villages. The hamlet nearest the sea[40] was sited on a block of land known as Te Wai-o-Hii-Harore, which was later described in Native Land Court hearings as a canoe landing-place, a place where fish were netted, and a site much used by the local tribes for their summer fishing camps. According to those accounts, the Waikanae Creek, which formed the northern boundary of this block, had eel weirs right along its course[41] and 'the people lived in villages on either side of the river'.[42] The 'large fish-pots' described by Monkhouse were probably crayfish pots, for there were good crayfishing grounds nearby, while the pumice carving may have represented a sea god, although such figures have usually been described as kuumara gods. The large house was probably a whare toko, described by a later tribal expert as the chief shelter for food gatherers in such villages in the bay.[43]

The Europeans, remembering the Earl of Morton's 'Hints', left some nails and beads by the carved figure in this village as a gesture of respect, and Banks and his companions wandered by the Waikanae, shooting some large ducks and gathering 'a variety of curious plants in flower'.[44]

While they were thus occupied they heard musket shots and hurried back to the west bank of the river. Four young boys had been left in charge of the yawl, and as they played on the beach four men armed with 'very long lances' (or spears, which according to Wilkinson were sixteen to eighteen feet long)[45] came out of the woods on the foothills of Titirangi, on the east side of the Tuuranga-nui River. The boys ran to the yawl and rowed frantically towards the river mouth, trying to escape, while the coxswain in the pinnace fired first a musket and then a musketoon in the air to try to frighten the warriors away. In response they brandished their weapons and continued to advance. When their leader lifted his lance and prepared to hurl it at the boat the coxswain shot him through the heart. His companions carried this man for about 100 yards, but when they realised that he was dead they took his weapons and retreated into the woods. According to early European settlers in the bay, this man was Te Maro of the Ngaati Oneone hapuu of Te Aitanga-a-Hauiti,[46] a tribe that in 1769 occupied lands around Titirangi and as far north as Uawa (Tolaga Bay).

Like the first encounters in Taitapu, this meeting was probably intended as a ritual challenge rather than an ambush. The local people had had a day to muster their forces, and there would have been many more than four warriors on hand. In traditional times one form of ceremonial challenge was to send out a warrior to throw a spear towards an approaching stranger group, although in more recent times this has been muted to a display of weapon handling. The Europeans did not know this, however, and their response was swift and lethal. Te Maro was shot, and as he lay dead on the eastern bank of the Tuuranga-nui, Cook's party crossed the river to inspect his body more closely. Monkhouse wrote a detailed account of Te Maro's physique, dress, hairstyle and facial tattoo:

He was a short, but very stout-bodied man — measured about 5f 3i. Upon his right cheek and nose were spirals of tattaou or punctuation of the skin — he had three arched tattaous over his left eye drawn from the root of his nose towards the temple; each arch about four lines broad — the interval between each about a line broad; . . . his hair, coarse and black, was tied upon the crown of his head — his teeth were even and small but not white — his features were large but proportional — his nose well formed — ears bored — his beard short. He had on him a dress of singular manufacture . . .

Banks described him more succinctly as

a middle sizd man tattowd in the face on one cheek only in spiral lines very regularly formd; he was coverd with a fine cloth of a manufacture totaly new to us, it was tied on exactly as represented in Mr Dalrymple's book p. 63; his hair was also tied in a knot on the top of his head but no feather stuck in it; his complexion brown but not very dark.[47]

'Mr Dalrymple's book' referred to Dalrymple's version of Tasman's voyage, which included an engraving of Taitapu men in canoes, one of whom wore a short garment seamed down the front with its rear corners brought forward, and tied to a frontal central seam. This man's hair was tied in a tuft decorated with a large feather, and clearly Banks wrote his journal entry that evening with his copy of Dalrymple open on the table before him. The Europeans now placed nails and beads on Te Maro's body and returned to the *Endeavour*. That night they heard people talking very loudly on shore, no doubt discussing what had happened that day and what to do about it.

At eight o'clock on the morning of 9 October the longboat, pinnace and yawl rowed through high surf, carrying a large armed party of officers, 'gentlemen', seamen and marines back to the landing-place on the east side of the river. A group of about fifty to 100 local men had gathered on the western bank, apparently unarmed although three or four had long 'pikes' (probably ordinary fighting spears) in their hands. At first only Cook, Banks, and Solander landed and called across the river in Tahitian to the assembled warriors. The warriors immediately rose up, and each produced either a fighting spear or 'a small weapon of well polishd stone about a foot long and thick enough to weigh 4 or 5 pounds'[48] (described by the Europeans as 'patta-pattoos' (patupatu) or 'war bludgeons'[49]). They began a war dance, 'by no means unpleasing to Spectators at a distance — they seemed formed in ranks, each man jump'd with a swinging motion at the same instant of time to the right and left alternately accommodating a war song in very just time to each motion; their lances were at the same time elevated a considerable height above their heads'.[50] According to Gore, as they danced, the warriors 'distended their Mouths, Lolling out their Tongues and Turned up the Whites of their Eyes, the whole Accompanied with a strong Hoarse Song, calculated in my Opinion to Chear Each Other and Intimidate their Enemies, and may be call'd perhaps with propriety A Dancing War Song'.[51]

A musket was fired across the Tuuranga-nui so that the ball struck the water (in keeping with the Earl of Morton's instructions), and the haka ended abruptly. Cook's party retreated a little until the marines had landed and marched with a Union Jack to a small bank about fifty yards from the river. A party of seven, which now included Tupaia, Green the astronomer and William Monkhouse, returned to the river, and this time it was Tupaia who called out in Tahitian to the warriors. They seemed to understand him perfectly, so he told them that the Europeans wanted food and water and offered iron in exchange. The Europeans displayed beads and nails and threw a nail across the river, but it fell short and dropped into the water. The warriors responded with bitter complaints about the killing the day before, and demanded to know where the Europeans had come from. They refused to lay down their weapons, and Tupaia warned the Europeans to be on their guard. According to Monkhouse:

Their pronunciation was very guttural, however Tupaia understood them and made himself understood so well that he at length prevailed on one of them to strip off his covering and swim across — he landed upon a rock surrounded by the tide, and now invited us to come to him. C. Cook finding him resolved to advance no farther, gave his musket to an attendant, and went towards him, but tho' the man saw C. Cook give away his weapon to put himself on a footing with him, he had not courage enough to wait his arrival, retreating into the water, however he at last ventured forward, they saluted by touching noses, and a few trinkets put our friend into high spirits.[52]

According to William Williams, this rock was none other than the legendary Toka-a-Taiau, a portentous, powerful place for the first formal greeting between a Maori and a European.[53] After the two men had saluted each other with a hongi (pressing noses), two other men swam to the rock and Cook gave them gifts; but when their companions began a war dance on the western bank Cook retreated to his own party on the east side of the river. Twenty or thirty other warriors now swam the river, bringing their weapons with them. As they in turn were given beads and iron (which they did not seem to value at all) they performed another exuberant haka and tried to exchange weapons with the Europeans. When the Europeans refused, however, the warriors snatched at their weapons and finally one man seized Green's short sword and waved it jubilantly above his head. Banks, who thought it 'nescessary for our safeties that so daring an act should be instantly punish'd',[54] shot him in the back with smallshot, and Monkhouse, whose musket was loaded with ball, shot and wounded him mortally. This man managed to speak to Tupaia before he died. One of his companions took his greenstone hand weapon while another tried to retrieve the sword, as Monkhouse jabbed at them with his bayonet.

The other warriors had retreated to Te Toka-a-Taiau, and when some of them started to swim back towards Cook's small party, Cook, Green and Tupaia fired, and killed or wounded three more men with smallshot. These men were carried away by their comrades, who 'set up a most lamentable noise and retired slowly along the beach'.[55] According to Monkhouse, 'the Shot man had a human tooth hanging at one ear and a girdle of Matting about four inches broad was passed twice round his loins and tied. He had a paddle [probably a weapon called a pouwhenua] in his hand which, tho' drawing his last breath, he would not part with without the greatest reluctance.'[56] Of the other warriors, he said that one was clad in a 'skin dress' (a dogskin cloak) with a pattern of broad black and white perpendicular stripes, another had his face smeared with bright red paint (or kura, a sign of tapu), most had their hair tied up with a white feather stuck in the tie, while those who stayed on the west bank of Tuuranga-nui wore shaggy rough cloaks which hung from their shoulders to mid-thigh.[57]

There is some confusion about the identity of the man who was shot by Banks and Monkhouse on this day. According to Polack in 1838, the dead man's grandson, Manutai, identified him as Te Ratu, an important local chief.[58] This would perhaps explain why this name was thereafter mentioned to the Europeans in a number of places on a number of occasions. Later tribal accounts, however, while agreeing that a chief named Te Ratu was alive during Cook's visit,[59] do not say that he was shot by the Europeans. Moreover, both Bishop William Williams and Edward Harris, whose forebears had settled in the bay in the 1830s and knew the local people very well, identified this man as Te Raakau[60] of Rongowhakaata, and it is probable that Polack simply misunderstood what he was told. Williams added that Te Raakau and his companions had come from Orakai-aa-puu,[61] a Rongowhakaata stronghold on the bank of the Kopututea River at the junction of the Waipaoa and Te Arai rivers, to try and seize the European vessel.[62] Furthermore, in 1851 Donald McLean recorded in his diary:

> Thursday 15 Feb Started at 5 a.m. . . . for Turanganui where I met an old deformed woman shrunk up from age who had seen Capt. Cook named Hine Kapu she gave an account of a native named Rakau having been killed by Cooks party and another wounded, at the time she describes herself to have been 16 years old. She is quite clear in intellect and retentive in memory describing minutely every small circumstance connected with Capt Cook's visit.[63]

The Europeans were greatly impressed by the bravery of these men. As Pickersgill wrote that night:

> this Reine of courage is unparrelled and is greatly to be Admir'd for its allways been remark'd amongst Savages lett them be ever so much used to fire arms that as soon as they see a man or two fall that they immediatly fall in to disorder and give way yet these People was so far from shewing any kind of fear that when saw the man fall they immediately had ye Presence of mind to attemptd it a second time.[64]

Sickened by the bloodshed, they now left the landing-place, and Cook directed the boats to the south end of the bay to look for another watering-place.

Towards the middle of the bay they saw a long sandy beach, with a lagoon (where the old course of the Kopututea River ran into the sea)[65] behind a sandbar with houses and canoes on it, but they were unable to land there because of the high, pounding surf. Beyond the lagoon Gore described 'a fine Country being well wooded with fine Tall Trees and in all probability well Inhabited from the Number of Smoaks we saw there'.[66] In the south-west corner of the bay, at Muriwai, there was a grove of high trees with canoes drawn up on the beach and a large village nearby. This village was later marked on Cook's East Coast chart,[67] while Parkinson showed the trees clearly in one of his coastal profiles.[68] At about two o'clock as the boats approached Te Kuri-a-Paoa, a breeze blew up from the sea and two canoes came in towards the river, the larger one with a number of paddlers and a smaller one about thirty feet long under sail. Cook was by now convinced that it was futile to try and parley with these people, since their meetings seemed inevitably to end in violence. He decided instead to try to capture some of the canoeists, transport them to the *Endeavour* and there treat them kindly in an attempt to gain their friendship. Very likely he had in mind a section of the Earl of Morton's instructions:

> If during an inevitable skirmish some of the Natives should be slain; those who survive should be made sensible that it was done only from a motive of self-defence . . . But the Natives when brought under should be treated with distinguished humanity, and made sensible that the Crew still considers them as Lords of the

Country. — Such behaviour would soon conciliate them to a familiarity with the Crew, and raise friendly sentiments towards supplying their wants.[69]

He therefore ordered the pinnace to cut off the canoes, and they managed to get quite close before they were noticed. The crew of the larger canoe flew to their paddles and shot rapidly towards the land. Tupaia called out to the crew of the small canoe to come peacefully alongside. Instead they struck their sail and also tried to escape by paddling. Cook ordered a musket fired over their heads, and the seven men and boys on board at once stripped off their cloaks and began to hurl 'great stones' (possibly anchor stones), paddles and other missiles, including a parcel of fish, at the pinnace. Cook's men now shot at them and four of the crew were wounded; two of these fell overboard and were drowned. The survivors tried to hoist their sail again, but two (who were just boys) were taken by the *Endeavour* sailors while the other dived overboard and for ten minutes managed to elude the pinnace, diving and swimming with great agility. Finally he too was captured, and the canoe was allowed to drift ashore with its cargo of two dead or dying men.

The three boats returned to the *Endeavour*, where the captives were clothed and fed with salted pork, bread and biscuit. According to Banks, the names of these young fishermen were 'Taahourange', 'Koikerange' and 'Maragooete',[70] they were aged about eighteen, fifteen and ten years respectively, and the two oldest were 'brothers'. From later tribal accounts it seems probable that they were members of the Rongowhakaata tribe.

At first the young fishermen were terrified that they might be eaten, but when they were reassured that the Europeans 'detested such a thing' they 'put on chearfull and lively countenances and askd and answerd questions with a great deal of curiosity'.[71] They told the Europeans (undoubtedly through Tupaia) 'that the Country was very Extensive that they had no kind of animals except doggs their chief diet being fish and roots; they likewise told us that the People of our side the bay [i.e., the north] eat men'.[72] Parkinson listed the root crops that they mentioned as 'Taro, Eape, Oomara [kuumara] and yams',[73] and the names of three of their gods, or 'Eatuas', as 'Toronomy — Tahougoona — Ohyere'.[74] It was probably these young men who gave Parkinson and Banks the place-names 'Taoneroa', or Te Oneroa (actually the name of the beach from the Tuuranga-nui River to Te Kuri-a-Paoa, which the Europeans applied to the entire district) and 'Tettuamotu' (Te Tuamotu) for the island at its northern end. As one of the better linguists on board, Parkinson said of their speech that 'they spoke the Otaheitean language, though in a different dialect, speaking very guttural, having a kind of *hec*, which some of the people of Yoolee-Etea [Raiatea] have in their speech. Toobaiah understood them very well, notwithstanding they make frequent use of the G and K, which the people of Otaheite do not.'[75] They also promised that the *Endeavour* would be supplied with all its requirements if they were returned to their own place, six miles southward.

At sunset the young men ate large quantities of bread[76] and drank more than a quart of wine and water at a draught, surprising the Europeans both with their

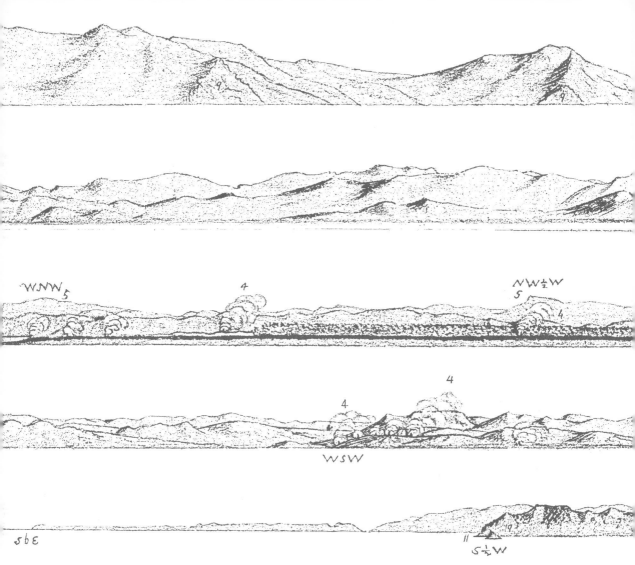

appetite and their good humour. They then performed a dance (evidently a precursor of the action-song) for their hosts, which Monkhouse vividly described:

> The Heiva or Dance is thus performed — They first prepared themselves by passing some Cloth, which they borrowed for the occasion, round their loins, till now totally without any covering: then placing themselves back to back a little asunder the foremost begins, the others following his motions minutely, with lifting up his right leg, at the same instant raising his arms to a horizontal Position, and bending his forearm a little, he trembles his fingers with great quickness — begins a kind of song, and the right leg being raised as above, off they go, beating time singing & trembling the fingers in the most exact uniformity — the body is now and then inclined to one side or the other — sometimes they bend forwards exceedingly low and then suddenly raise themselves, extending their arms, and staring most hideously — at one time, they make a half turn and face one way, and in two or three seconds [return] to their former position, in doing of which they bend forwards make a large sweep downwards with both Arms, extended, and as they turn upon the left foot, elevate their arms in the curve, stare wildly, & pronounce a part of the song with a savage hoarse expiration — this part of the ceremony generally closes the dance.[77]

130

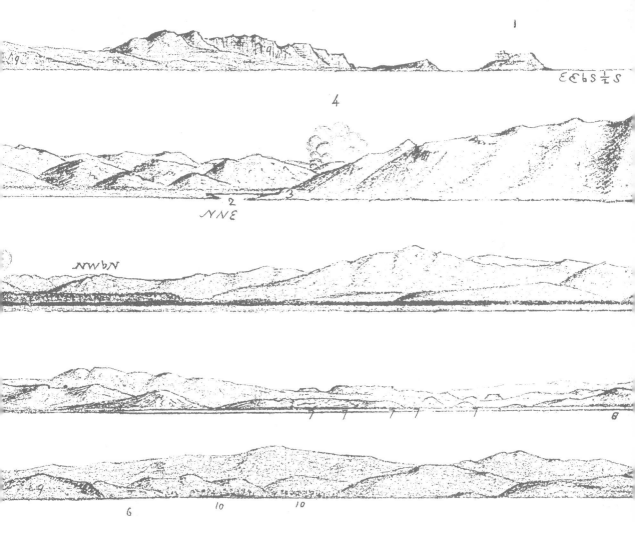

Coastal views of 'Taoneroa' (Te Oneroa, or Poverty Bay) sketched by Herman Diedrich Spöring.
An accompanying key in Banks's handwriting gives the following captions:

1. Tettuamotu the peninsula on which a paling was observd in coming into the harbour.
2. River of salt water about 40 yards wide where we landed.
3. Bank on which the marines and seamen were drawn up.
4. Several large smoaks seen at some distance in the country which were every day repeated about noon and ceasd towards night whence it seems probable that they were for the purpose of dressing victuals. (A meticulous translation of Spöring's bearings for the WSW 'smoaks' carried out by Jeremy Spencer indicates that they pass directly through the site of Ora-kai-aa-puu paa. Pers. comm. 1990.)
5. high mountains very far inland.
6. The place of our boat when the canoe was taken.
7. a lagoon seen from the tops
8. Entrance into it seen likewise from the tops when we were near it in the boats there was a heavy surf in the bay which broke quite across the mouth of it, *the Indians talked much of a river of fresh water somewhere hereabouts
9. White Clifts like the chalk Clifts of Dover & the Island of wight.
10. Groves of large trees.
11. Young Nick's Head.

131

After dark they lay down on some lockers in the great cabin and went peacefully to sleep, despite a loud clamour of voices from the shore.

It must have been these three young fishermen who spoke of a 'king' in their district named 'Te Ratu', or so the Europeans understood them to have said. There was certainly a Rongowhakaata chief named Te Raatuu who was alive during Cook's visit,[78] and he is named in the genealogical records of his tribe and is represented as a carved figure in their main meeting-house, Te-Mana-o-Tuuranga, along with a number of his ancestors.[79] During Native Land Court sittings in the 1870s, Rongowhakaata elders told many stories about this Te Raatuu, his father Te Ika-Whaingata, his grandfather Huukaipuu and his great-grandfather Mokaiohungia,[80] all senior lineal descendants of Rongowhakaata, the founding ancestor of their tribe.

It is perhaps ironic, though, that this man was the first Maori leader to have been described by Europeans as a 'king'. His father Te Ika-Whaingata was portrayed in the Land Court evidence as a vigorous and ambitious leader, but according to some accounts Te Ika was killed when he tried to claim control over the fisheries and foreshore in the centre of the bay,[81] and his son Te Raatuu was less powerful than his father had been. More recent Rongowhakaata accounts say that Te Raatuu maintained his father's mana over the Oneroa fisheries, a feat that is commemorated in a carving in Te-Mana-o-Tuuranga meeting-house at Manu-tuke.[82] Whichever account one upholds, however, it was clearly difficult for any chief in Tuuranga-nui to act the autocrat, for Tuuranga-nui was known to other tribes as Tuuranga-taangata-rite — Tuuranga where all people are equal.[83]

Neither James Cook nor Joseph Banks were contented with the way this day had gone. Banks, the young aristocrat, had discovered that shooting men was less entertaining than potting birds. In his journal entry that night he wrote: 'thus ended the most disagreable day My life has yet seen, black be the mark for it and heaven send that such may never return to embitter future reflection.' His remorse was evidently not sufficient to quell his scientific curiosity, however, for he added in the next line: 'I forgot to mention in its proper place that we pickd up a large pumice stone floating in the bay in returning to the ship today, a sure sign that there either is or has been a Volcano in this neighbourhood.'[84]

Cook, on the other hand, was worried about his repeated breaches of the Earl of Morton's instructions, which said that local people might

> naturally and justly attempt to repell intruders, whom they may apprehend are come to disturb them in the quiet possession of their country, whether that apprehension be well or ill founded. Therefore should they in a hostile manner oppose a landing, and kill some men in the attempt, even this would hardly justify firing among them, 'till every other gentle method had been tried.[85]

By that evening, however, at least nine local men had been killed or wounded by musket or pistol fire, and the shootings out at sea at least could have been avoided. Cook was aware that the Earl of Morton would not be pleased with these events, and tried to explain what had happened in his journal:

> I am aware that most humane men who have not experienced things of this nature

will cencure my conduct in fireing upon the people in this boat nor do I myself think that the reason I had for seizing upon her will att all justify me, and had I thought that they would have made the least resistance I would not have come near them, but as they did I was not to stand still and suffer either my self or those that were with me to be knocked on the head.[86]

During the night of 9 October one of the fisherboys sighed often and miserably until Tupaia got up to comfort him, and then in the dark the three young men sang a song 'like a Psalm tune and contain many notes and semitones; they sung it in parts which gives us no indifferent Idea of their taste as well as skill in musick'.[87] These hours on the *Endeavour* must have been an extraordinary experience for the three young fishermen. They had eaten European foods and drunk considerable quantities of wine and water; they had talked with a Tahitian high priest as well as with the Europeans, and seen the inside of the 'wooden world' of the *Endeavour* as well as its exterior at close range. Given that Maori people had lived in considerable isolation (except from each other) for almost a thousand years, it must have been both astonishing and frightening, like being taken on board a spaceship full of aliens.

On the morning of 10 October a wooding party went ashore early, and at eight o'clock the young fishermen, dressed and ornamented richly with 'bracelets, ancklets, and necklaces [presumably collected in Tahiti] after their own fashion',[88] reluctantly accompanied Cook, Tupaia, Banks, Solander and others to the landing place on the eastern bank of the Tuuranga-nui River. The party crossed to one of the fishing camps on the western bank, where Monkhouse noticed a tree stump that had been carved to resemble some kind of quadruped (probably a dog). Here the fisherboys pleaded to be taken to the south end of the bay instead, saying that they feared that their enemies on this side would kill and eat them. The Europeans were sceptical about this but were preparing to take them back to the boats when suddenly the boys, with tears in their eyes, gave up the argument and went off inland.

The *Endeavour* party now went to a swampy area by the Waikanae Creek to shoot ducks, but before very long some marines who had been posted on the ridge of a nearby sand bank warned them that two separate groups of 'Indians' were creeping up on them. These groups (which included no women or children) increased in size so rapidly that 'in a short time the earth seemed to move with the numbers according to the report of our guards'.[89] The *Endeavour*'s men beat a hasty retreat to the Tuuranga-nui, accompanied by the three fisherboys who had been following them through the bushes. When they reached the west bank they found to their consternation that the pinnace had left its station, but fortunately the yawl had stayed behind and was able to ferry them across the river.

As the *Endeavour* group assembled on the east bank of the Tuuranga-nui the warriors approached in twos and threes, until about 100 to 150 armed men were gathered on the opposite side of the river, headed by two 'chiefs' dressed in white.[90] The oldest of the young fishermen recognised some of this party, and he now took a garment that the Europeans had given him and carefully placed it on the body of Te Raakau, which was still lying on the eastern river bank, with Te

Maro's corpse not far away. No doubt this garment was the red serge cloak that later became famous as Te Makura (according to Harris[91]) or Te Hinu-o-Tuhura (according to Williams[92]), which was worn into battle by Rongowhakaata chiefs. It was said that Te Makura had been laid on Te Raakau's body by Cook himself; and that if the cloak shone in battle it was a omen of victory for Rongowhakaata, but if it seemed dull that was an omen of defeat.[93]

The young men displayed the clothes and ornaments they had been given to their compatriots, and told them about Tupaia, saying that 'he was almost one of themselves'.[94] Tupaia then approached the river's edge to talk to them across the water, and bitter recriminations were exchanged about the killings of the previous day. Eventually an old man carrying a green bough swam the river and embraced the three young fishermen, while the youngest boy, who was said to be the old man's 'nephew', wept over him. After this the old man stood and, passing Te Raakau's body, presented the green bough to Tupaia in a gesture of reconciliation, and in turn was presented with nails, beads and ribbons. As he went back towards the river he broke another branch from a nearby bush:

> Turning his back towards the Body, he approach'd it with the bough in his hand looking behind him, to direct his steps I suppose, alternately over either shoulder — his gait was singular, nor can I compare the manner of his lifting his legs to any thing better than that of a Cock sideling to his antagonist on the Sod.[95]

These ritual movements must have been part of a tapu-raising ceremony, for the old man now stripped off his clothes (as men used to do in battle, and in handling the dead), threw the branch towards the body, then picked up his garments and went back across the river. There he was surrounded by the warriors, who formed into a kind of triangle about him.

During all of these ceremonial exchanges nothing was done about the body of Te Maro, the Ngaati Oneone challenger who had been shot on the Europeans' first landing in the bay. His body still lay on the eastern bank of the river, and the beads that had been placed on it were untouched. Land Court evidence of the 1870s made it plain that in or before the generation of Te Raatuu, Te Aringa, an ancestress of Te Aitanga-a-Maahaki (who had their main lands on the west side of the river), had entered into a dispute with Tuapaoa, an ancestor of Te Aitanga-a-Hauiti (who had most of their lands to the east of the Tuuranga-nui and further north). After an exchange of insults, fighting broke out between the groups which was not settled until several generations later, when a diplomatic marriage reunited the two sides.[96] Tensions around the river at the time of Cook's visit were evidently so acute that Te Maro's people were unable to recover their dead kinsman, and the two warrior parties who now confronted the Europeans (probably of Rongowhakaata and Te Aitanga-a-Maahaki) left his body strictly alone.

The *Endeavour*'s men now went back to their ship, accompanied by the three young fishermen, who preferred to go with them rather than to join their relatives. Perhaps they hoped to join the expedition, either out of curiosity or because their close contact with the Europeans had jeopardised their relationship with their own people. From the *Endeavour*'s deck, Banks and others trained their spyglasses on the shore and watched three men cross the river on 'a kind of raft or Catamaran'[97] (probably one of the fishing rafts that were common on the East Coast a little later[98]). They performed some ceremonies and then carried Te Raakau's body back to the raft. Once they reached the western bank Te Raakau's body was trussed to a pole and carried away by four men. After dinner the young fishermen were landed on the east side of the river, but as soon as they saw people approaching they waded into the water and begged to be taken back to the *Endeavour*. They were left behind, however, and two men crossed the river on a raft and took them to a group of about fifty people gathered near Te Oneroa. At sunset the young men left their companions and walked slowly to the water's edge, where after lowering their bodies they rose suddenly and threw their arms up and out towards the ship three times, perhaps signalling a ritual separation from these uncanny visitors. Then they rejoined their people and walked back with them towards their own part of the bay.

Monkhouse summarised his impressions of Tuuranga-nui in his journal that evening as follows:

> A pretty large flat extends itself along part of the north side of this Bay and across its head the soil of which is mostly a Sand, but about the lagoon we visited the soil is a rich marle : this flat is covered with a coarse grass and low shrubbery, along the south side there appeared to be several fine groves of well grown trees — the back land consists of a group of hills of good height and are pretty well cloathed with wood. The north head forms a peninsula ending in a high bluff on the summit of which is one of the fortified villages of this country, which we now took to be a Marai or Burial ground from the opinion of our friend Tupia; there appeared to be a large village within the South head; and from the fires and smoaks we saw at the head of the bay we believe this country to be well inhabited.[99]

Summary
THE *ENDEAVOUR* ACCOUNTS OF TUURANGA-NUI

The physical topography of Tuuranga-nui's coastline was well recorded by the *Endeavour* journalists and artists in 1769. They described the bay as open and unsheltered, with white cliffs to the south and a high hill to the north, and wooded hills inland. At the foot of the northern cliffs was a small island, whose name Parkinson accurately recorded as 'Tettuamotu' (Te Tuamotu), with a fortification on its summit — possibly the paa called Ruruhangehange, or another called Rarohau, both of which were said in early Land Court evidence to have been strongholds on the island at about that time.[100] A very ancient paa on the high hill of Titirangi was not described by the Europeans, and it may have been in ruins in 1769.[101] To the west of the Tuuranga-nui River, and close to the sea they saw a small fishing village of 'wigwams' and thatched houses, including one twenty-four feet long by six feet wide, with a porch two feet deep, and this settlement was marked on Cook's fair chart of the East Coast. On the other side of the Waikanae Creek there was a smaller settlement of four or five 'wigwams', which were simply roofs supported by a pole on one side and a low wall on the

135

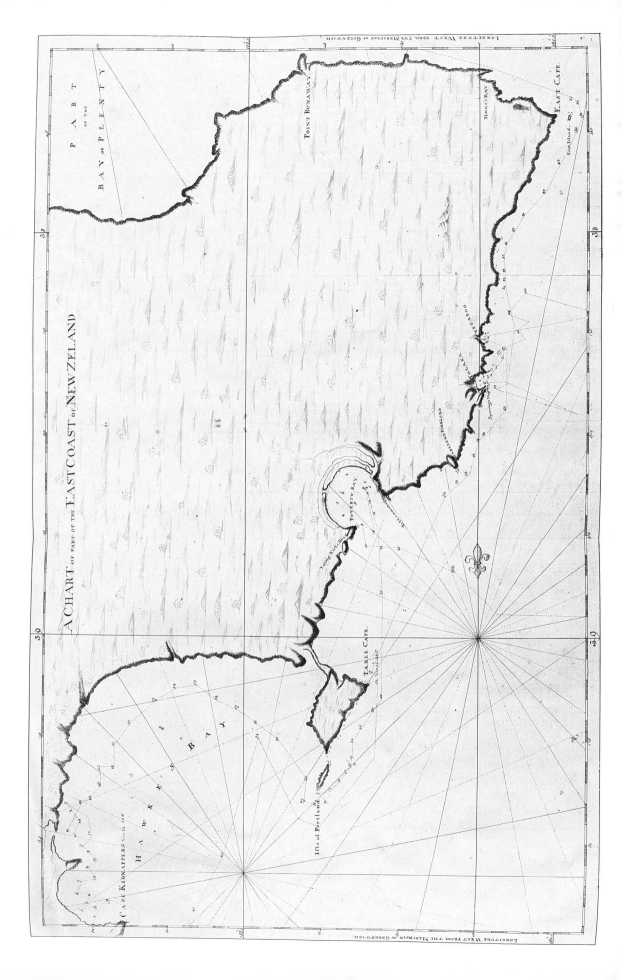

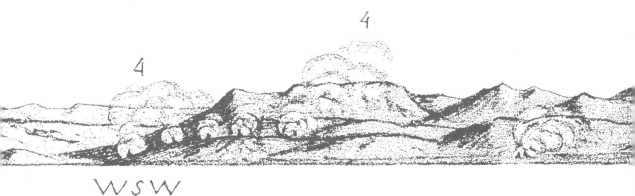

Enlargement of a section of one of Spöring's coastal views of Tuurangi-nui, showing several of the 'large smoaks' in the vicinity of Orakai-aa-puu paa. These and other pencil sketches by Spöring and Parkinson have been printed (and sometimes enlarged) from microfilm of the originals, and the foxed backgrounds delicately cleaned out (following a suggestion by Jeremy Spencer) by scraping the print. The aim is to show as clearly as possible all detail of the original sketch.

other. Within the southern head was a large village, which was clearly marked on Cook's chart of the East Coast; and Gore also described houses and canoes on the sand bar at the mouth of the Kopututea River.

Despite the excellence of their descriptions, however, it is important to remember that the *Endeavour*'s men never ventured more than about a kilometre inland, and that their impressions of the bay were in some respects misleading. Sea foods were important to the economy of the district, but so was agriculture, and the *Endeavour* observers saw no gardens. Because they explored neither the Kopututea River, which was obscured from their view by its sand bar, nor the upper reaches of the Tuuranga-nui, they did not realise that there were fertile gardens and large fortified settlements inland. In his frustration at being unable to secure food and water Cook named Tuuranga-nui 'Poverty Bay', a most inaccurate description.

Nor did the expedition gain a reliable impression of the local population, although they suspected from the many 'large smoaks' they saw that the bay was well inhabited inland. Women, children, the ill and the very old must have been evacuated to the paa of their various descent-groups when the *Endeavour* arrived, and apart from the fishermen the expedition met only groups of warriors. On one occasion these fighting-men were led by an 'old man' (who may not in fact have been very old in modern reckoning, given the average life expectancies of both Maori and European populations at that time), and two of the fisherboys were young, but otherwise the *Endeavour* group saw mainly mature men, and they saw no women at all during their time in Tuuranga-nui. The first group of Ngaati Oneone challengers numbered only four; the second group which con-

Opposite: *Cook's chart of the East Coast at original scale shows a village in Tuuranga-nui near Muriwai, and another (the fishing-camp) on Te Wai-o-Hiiharore at the mouth of the Tuuranga-nui River. It also marks the fortified village at Kahutara (Table Cape) and two others on the east Maahia coastline.*

fronted them from the western bank of the Tuuranga-nui on 9 October (said by Williams to have been Rongowhakaata warriors from Orakai-aa-puu paa) numbered about fifty (with the European estimates ranging from fifty to 100); while on 10 October they were approached by two groups operating independently at first, which jointly numbered about 150.

These numbers suggest a scale of social organisation in which groups of perhaps 500 people could each quickly mobilise a force of about fifty to seventy-five warriors, on occasion joining forces with other groups. This may under-estimate group sizes, however, for Orakai-aa-puu (which was abandoned in 1839, the year before a mission station was established very near the paa)[102] was later described by Williams as a palisaded settlement covering an area of three acres, with many fenced enclosures inside where the houses were built — rather a vast (and possibly exaggerated) construction for a group of 500 people.

It is evident from the *Endeavour* accounts that the Tuuranga-nui people were well practised in resisting outside intrusion; and from the fears of the young fishermen, their tales of enemies at the northern end of the bay who might eat them, and the desertion of Te Maro's body on the Tuuranga-nui's eastern bank that there were major internal disputes and tensions within the bay at this time.

During the expedition's first three days on shore in New Zealand the *Endeavour* journal-keepers and artists described a number of individuals; hair-styles; clothing styles (which included the use of penis strings[103]); personal decoration; facial tattoo (the first man shot had spirals tattooed on his right cheek and arches tattooed on his left temple, while the oldest fisherboy had only his lips tattooed); weapons (including spears of different sizes, patupatu, or hand clubs, and a weapon like a paddle); canoes (including one thirty feet long and another that was larger); fishing nets and pots; a possible fishing god; and houses, shelters and settlements (including one fortified paa). Coastal views of Tuuranga-nui were produced from the deck of the *Endeavour*, and there were also charts, forty species of plants collected by Banks and Solander and at least one weapon, which was taken from Te Raakau.

All the same, these first encounters between Cook's men and Maori people had been short, suspicious and violent, and not a great deal was learned about life on shore. According to Polack, the Tuuranga-nui people described the discharges of the muskets as 'waititiri, or thunder,' and reported feeling ill when these 'atua' (supernatural beings) simply looked at them.[104] On the whole, the local people must have been profoundly relieved when on the morning of 11 October, the *Endeavour* raised its anchor and sailed south out of the bay.

138

Chapter Six

COASTING TE MATAU-A-MAAUI (HAWKE'S BAY)

12–18 October 1769

The south-eastern region that the *Endeavour* was now about to visit was, according to local tribal histories, dominated at that time by a loose-knit grouping of sub-tribes known as Ngaati Kahungunu, a prosperous and powerful people who traced their descent from Kahungunu and his father Tamatea-ariki-nui (or Tamatea-mai-Tawhiti), of the *Takitimu* canoe.[1] One heartland of this region was Heretaunga, described by other tribes as Heretaunga-hauku-nui (Heretaunga of the heavy dew) — in other words a rich place, laden with resources.[2]

Te Matau-a-Maaui (Maaui's fish-hook) was a large bay backed by a rampart of hills, covered with beech forests that were criss-crossed by the trails of kiore (Polynesian rat).[3] From these high ranges, rivers ran down the coastal hills to the flats, giving access to fortified villages and hill and valley gardens in the interior.[4] Inland lakes swarmed with wildfowl and harboured eels, kookopu (galaxias), inanga (whitebait), freshwater pipi and mussels. Muttonbirds nested at Puke-ti-tiri and at Titi-o-kura, about twenty-five kilometres inland, where they were trapped in nets hung on the ridges as they flew home at dusk to their burrows.[5] Wood pigeons, tui, huia, bellbirds, parrots and parakeets lived in patches of bush on the flats. Fern-clad hills ran down to extensive grasslands, swamps and a large lagoon behind Ahuriri Bluff, famous for its succulent paatiki (flounder).[6]

In 1769 this lagoon formed a sheltered harbour for local canoes, accessible from the sea by an inlet to the north of the bluff. There were dense beds of shellfish on both sandy beaches and rocky shores in the bay, and good fishing grounds out at sea. Whales often visited Te Matau, drawn there by the force of their mauri (the material symbol of their life-principle) located at Maahia to the north. Some of these whales acted as sea guardians for local descent-groups, protecting canoes from capsize and other disasters.[7] All of these features contributed to the reputation of the bay as a wealthy, prestigious place.

Like Tuuranga-nui, the ancestral history of the region was complex, with genealogical lines from Maaui (whose hook snagged on the southern promontory of the bay when he fished up the North Island), from Mahutapoanui (of Lake

Waikaremoana), from Toi's son Awa-nui-a-Rangi, his grandson Whaatonga and his great-grandson Tara, and from Paikea. By 1769 it seems that Taraia, a descendant of Tamatea-ariki-nui, had long since established his mana over the bay.[8] The local landscapes were full of reminders of the ancestral canoe *Takitimu*, which according to early accounts from Ahuriri had left Hawaiki because of quarrels over cultivated lands.[9] After an arduous voyage *Takitimu* had arrived at Tauranga, where Tamatea disembarked and married a local woman by whom he had a son, Kahungunu. Meanwhile the canoe carried on around the eastern coast, visiting various bays, and after a stay at Tuuranga-nui it travelled on to Te Matau, where the priest Ruawharo left several of his children, providing them with various species of fish and shellfish as food supplies. Other local traditions say that Ruawharo settled at Oraka on the Maahia Peninsula, planting the mauri for whales along

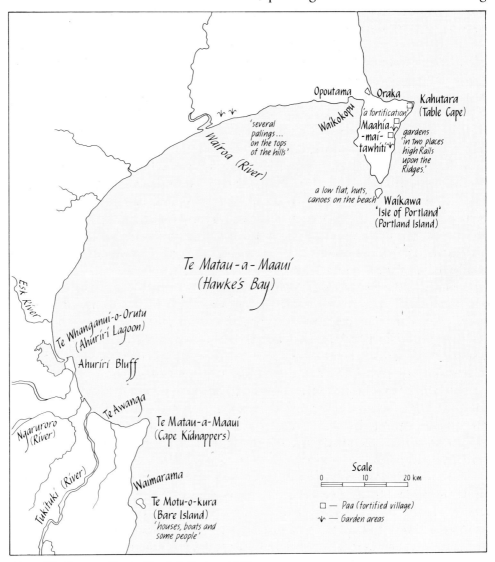

Map of Te Matau-a-Maaui (Hawke's Bay) in 1769.

140

the sea coast and placing sands from Hawaiki at Maahia and Wairoa as burial grounds for his descendants.[10] According to these stories the canoe then landed at Opoutama, where the god of that name was left behind in the form of a rock, while at Wairoa wooden skids were left at Makeakea and in the riverbed at Whakapau.[11] At Te Awanga a man called Karotimutimu was landed with supplies of whales, mussels and a small fish named koroama, while at Waimarama four men went ashore and more skids and two stone anchors were left behind.[12]

In later years Tamatea's son Kahungunu grew to manhood and travelled down the eastern coast, making a series of important marriages as he went, and when he arrived at Maahia he married his fourth wife, Rongomaiwahine, from whom the chiefly lines of Ngaati Kahungunu descend. It was not until three generations later, however, when some of Kahungunu's descendants were expelled from Tuuranga-nui that his great-grandson Taraia established effective control over this district, and Ngaati Kahungunu became the local 'people of the land'. There were still people with strong Kahungunu links in Tuuranga-nui when the *Endeavour* visited there in 1769, but now as the ship sailed south she was heading towards undisputed Ngaati Kahungunu lands.

After leaving Tuuranga-nui on 11 October, the *Endeavour* sailed south along the coast at a distance of three or four miles, heading towards the Maahia Peninsula. In the afternoon the wind died, and as the vessel lay becalmed off Whareongaonga six canoes approached her from the land. Tupaia called out to their crews and tried to get them to come closer, but they stayed at a discreet distance until a canoe from Tuuranga-nui (or nearby) came out to the *Endeavour*, and its crew of four went straight on board. Both Gore and Banks recognised one of these men as the warrior who had saluted Cook on Te Toka-a-Taiau several days earlier, and Banks asked him how the young fishermen from Tuuranga-nui were faring. This man said that they were at home and unhurt, and that they had given a very good report of their treatment on board the *Endeavour*.

The other canoes now gathered alongside, and of fifty men about twenty came on board, where they traded their clothes, ornaments, weapons (including spears twenty to forty feet long and a whalebone and a greenstone patu) and even their paddles, which Parkinson described as 'curiously stained with a red colour, disposed into various strange figures; and the whole together was no contemptible workmanship'.[13] He later sketched these or very similar paddles in ink and watercolours,[14] and a paddle likely to be one of those traded on this occasion still survives in the British Museum.[15] Tupaia gratified these visitors with a sight of his tattooed hips, and when most of them left about two hours later, they took away with them trade goods including beads, trinkets, glass, white Tahitian tapa cloth and, according to local tradition also an axe and a tomahawk.[16]

Banks and Monkhouse described these men at length, saying that they ranged between five feet to six feet one inch in height, were dark brown in colour, with aquiline rather than flat noses and discoloured teeth. According to Banks, they had tattooed lips with spiral facial tattoos cut as deep as one-sixteenth of an inch in some cases, and of these men the oldest and 'those who appear as chiefs'[17] had the most complete and deepest patterns. Monkhouse observed that

A well finished face has no part untouched but the upper part of the forehead: and in this state they look as black as any Negroe whatever. All below the forehead is done in Spirals — over each eye are broad arches. But among these People I saw but two or three compleatly tattaoued — the lips seem to be the first part subjected to this marking, and I observe one or two with the under lip only tattaoued.[18]

A number of sketches of tattoo patterns (moko) by Parkinson and Spöring were probably made on this occasion,[19] and the prevalence of partial moko was subsequently confirmed by other observers in both this and later voyages.

Banks added that some of these men had their faces either fully or partially painted with 'a red colour in oil'; and their hair was oiled and tied up on the top of their heads, decorated with feathers and sometimes a wood or bone comb which 'they seem'd to prize much'.[20] Others had regular scars on their faces and arms, which they said had been self-inflicted in mourning ceremonies.

The Europeans gave excellent descriptions of both garments and canoes. Monkhouse classified the cloaks he had seen so far into three categories, the first sort being woven with warps of bundles of fibre and a widely spaced weft, and worn around the torso with the upper corners turned back and tied. Some of this type of cloak had widely spaced threads of black in the warp and beautifully woven borders (taaniko) about two and a half inches deep, worked in diamond patterns, some half black, half white; others half black, half brown or cinnamon.[21] The second sort of cloak was closely woven of twined threads; and the third sort was the shaggy, rough cloak described earlier in Tuuranga-nui, which might be worn over the shoulders or around the waist, where it was tied on by a woven girdle. Each of the last two types of cloak was sometimes decorated along its lower edges by dogskin; and a number of such garments collected by the *Endeavour* expedition (including girdles of the finest weaving, stained with red ochre from the bodies of their original wearers) still survive in various European museums.[22]

By way of personal ornament, these men — who must have been either Rongowhakaata from Tuuranga-nui or from the most northerly hapuu (sub-tribes) of Ngaati Kahungunu — wore white bundles of down, greenstone pendants or human teeth in their ears; a triangular piece of greenstone or a flattened oval pendant soaked in fragrant oil around the neck, and in some cases a knot made of a seabird's feathered skin split in two over their shoulders.

Their canoes were about forty feet long and four feet wide at the most, with seats for the paddlers and a steersman at the stern. Banks described these vessels as follows:

Their boats were not large but well made, something in the form of our whaleboats but longer; their bottom was the trunk of a tree hollwd and very thin, this was raisd by a board on each side sewd on, with a strip of wood sewd over the seam to make it tight; on the head of every one was carvd the head of a man with an enormous tongue reaching out of his mouth. These grotesque figures were some at least very well executed, some had eyes inlaid of something that shone very much; the whole servd to give us an Idea of their taste as well as ingenuity in execution, much superior to any thing we have yet seen.[23]

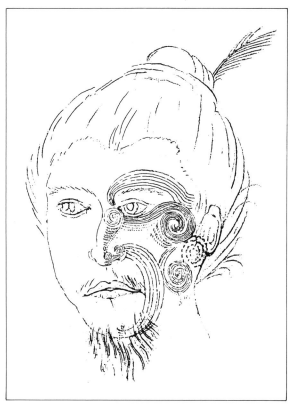

These portraits by Parkinson very likely represented one of the men who visited the Endeavour *off Whareongaonga on 11 October 1769, conceivably the man who saluted Cook on Te Toka-a-Taiau. Note that the partial moko of the pencil sketch was transformed into a fully symmetrical facial tattoo in the reversed pen-and-wash version. Interesting features of the pen-and-wash portrait include the curvilinear facial moko patterns, the top-knot decorated with three white feathers and a carved comb, the greenstone ear-pendant and hei-tiki worn around the neck.*

Parkinson added that the prow carvings were painted red;[24] and Monkhouse that some of the canoes had flat stern pieces four to six feet high.[25] After trading all of their paddles the crew of one of these canoes even offered to trade the canoe itself to the Europeans. Before they left the *Endeavour* the man from Tuuranga-nui invited Cook to return to their bay in peace. Although Banks was enthusiastic, Cook decided to carry on in search of a more sheltered harbour, where the *Endeavour* could safely ride at anchor and fresh food and water could be loaded on board.

As the canoes departed, three young men were left behind by their own group and the others refused to take them ashore, so they spent the night on board. According to Monkhouse,

> one of them was well-featured, of a make somewhat delicate and was the person whose face was daubed with red paint — on the upper part of his forehead were a number of lines or scratchings of some cutting tool, which he said he had inflicted upon himself in a mourning ceremony. Another had an effeminate voice and was

still less masculine in his figure — the third was altogether a bad and miserable figure and stupid.[26]

These young men performed a dance for the *Endeavour*'s people 'striking the thighs almost the whole time of the dance instead of trembling the fingers',[27] ate bread, salted meat and a gruel of wheat and sugar, and like the three young fishermen in Tuuranga-nui, seemed quite cheerful and eventually went to bed on a steering-sail under the forecastle. When they woke in the morning, however, and realised that the *Endeavour* had travelled south during the night, they began to cry, saying that they were being taken among their enemies. Evidently another descent-group boundary had been passed, for as Banks now commented, 'the countrey is certainly divided into many small principalities'.[28]

At about seven o'clock two canoes came out from two to three miles south of Kahutara (which Cook named Table Cape 'on account of its shape and figure'[29]) at the northern end of Maahia Peninsula (whose name Pickersgill recorded as 'Terato'). The *Endeavour*'s passengers waved out and eventually persuaded one of these canoes to come alongside. They told the crew that they had been left on board the *Endeavour* and explained that the Europeans 'neither beat nor *eat* their country men, which was farther illustrated by striking with the hand, and afterwards fixing the teeth in the flesh and giving a horrid picture of tearing it from the bone'.[30] With this reassurance a tall, well-built, middle-aged man, whom they described as an 'Earee or Chief' was persuaded to come on board. This man carried a whalebone patu and wore a new, closely woven cloak edged with dogskin, while his facial tattoo was the most complete and deeply engraved the Europeans had yet seen. According to Monkhouse, he

> very readily came into the Ship, but tho' his countenance betrayed no marks of fear he would not be prevailed on to move from the gangway. He saluted those next him; and contemplated the objects about him with a kind of look of consequence. He answered the questions put to him with a peculiar indifferency.[31]

One can imagine the astonishment with which this ariki (high chief) must have regarded the *Endeavour*, and yet clearly he was determined to maintain his composure even in so extraordinary a circumstance. Unfortunately the name of this high chief was not recorded, for he must have been a man of great mana and undoubtedly would still be remembered in the historical records of his tribe.[32] The crew of his canoe included three or four men, one of whom wore an ankle bracelet of cylindrical white shells (probably *Dentalium nanum*) and others perfumed neck pendants, plus two women and a girl. These were the first Maori women to be seen by Europeans, but their presence was simply noted with Monkhouse's appreciative comment that 'the Womens lips were tattoued — one of them was jolly and had large breasts'.[33] At about this time another canoe appeared but stayed at a distance, and the ariki took away the three men who had slept on board the *Endeavour* the night before, promising to return later with sweet potatoes, taro and yams.

At Kahutara Monkhouse noted a fortification with a ditch and high palisade strengthened with a cross-rail. Further south along the peninsula he described a fortification on a hill with a few straggling huts on the flats and two outrigger canoes nearby, a rare sighting of this type of vessel in New Zealand. Cook's chart of the East Coast marked three settlements along Maahia's east coastline, which probably record these sightings. Banks also described some gardens, evidently planted in sequence since some showed earth freshly turned up in furrows while others had plants at various stages of growth.

Before noon another canoe, carrying four people, came out to the *Endeavour*, and from a distance of about a quarter of a mile several ceremonies were performed. A man in the bow holding a green branch chanted and sang, sometimes seeming to threaten the *Endeavour* and at other times seeming to offer peace. Tupaia talked with this man, who made signs that the *Endeavour* should wait for them to come alongside. Just then a breeze blew up and the ship sailed off. In frustration his crew shouted and brandished their paddles, and 'one of them very civilly turned up his breach and made the usual sign of contempt amongst the Billingsgate ladies'[34] — the first recorded instance of the ritual insult known as whakapohane, or exposure of the anus.

The peninsula that the *Endeavour* was now coasting was Maahia-mai-tawhiti, also named Tuara-hiwi-Ohenga[35] after the back of the captain of the ancestral canoe *Karamu-rau-nui*.[36] Ruawharo, the priest of another canoe, the sacred *Taki-timu*, had brought sand there from Hawaiki and formed a mound where he implanted the life-force of whales. The *Endeavour* was following in *Takitimu*'s wake when it rounded Waikawa ('Isle of Portland' — now Portland Island), where Ruawharo had built a shrine that sheltered the mauri for the eastern coast.[37]

Waikawa was a small island that appeared to be quite barren, but on its inner coast there was a flat with some houses on it and canoes drawn up on the beach. A great number of armed men with long spears had gathered on the cliffs, so that the horizon seemed to bristle with spears. As the *Endeavour* hauled around the southern end of the island she was caught in turbulent shoal waters, and during the resulting confusion four canoes full of armed men raced out from the island to threaten the ship, and attempted to capture the small boat that had been lowered alongside to take soundings. These men threw several spears at the hull, addressed the *Endeavour*'s people in long speeches, and chanted and shook their paddles, challenging them to fight. Monkhouse was on the taffrail and, noticing one warrior brandishing his spear with particular fury, he imitated the insulting gesture that he had seen earlier that day:

> I was induced to retort the compliment we had recieved in the morning merely to try its effect upon this Quixotic hero — enraged at the insult he instantly threw his lance towards me with all his might, and took up another to try a second effort: he bid his Comrades pull up a little higher and held his lance poized ready to throw while I put myself in the same attitude with a long telescope — thus full of wrath we both stood staring at each other when C.C. observing these threats began to be uneasy about the man in the boat astern and therefore ordered a musket loaden with small shot to be fired at the very Canoe I was engaged with. Mr —— who was below and hearing the order threw a loading of small shot so nigh the ear of my Antagonist that it produced the most ludicrous change in his Countenance I ever saw

. . . Immediately after the discharge of the muskets a great gun loaden with musket-ball was fired upon the water which threw them into great consternation. Yet in the midst of all this they felt the sting of our laughing at them, and by a kind of involuntary impulse shook their paddles and gave a shout — but their fears instantly succeeded this flash of Courage — they Stared wildly round them for a moment, and then retiring, collected themselves to hold a conference on matters of the most extraordinary nature that they would perhaps allow they had ever seen.[38]

This was the first time that the *Endeavour*'s cannons had been fired in New Zealand, and it must indeed have seemed an extraordinary occurrence to the local people. Monkhouse's taunting gesture, the whistling smallshot and the smoke, roaring and sea spouts created by the cannonfire can only have been interpreted as a display of supernatural power, and all the more threatening for being directed towards an island that harboured the sacred mauri of the region.

Several of these canoes had outriggers, and one a vertical prow-board about two feet in diameter, carved with a double series of spirals and arches in filigree style.[39] According to Monkhouse, the warriors on board another canoe had red earth paint (kura) daubed over their facial tattoos to frightening effect. Cook decided that since night was coming on and the waters were evidently shoaling, it might be best to drop anchor, and so the *Endeavour* spent the night anchored about three miles north-west of Waikawa. In the evening two canoes visited the vessel, one a war canoe with armed men and the other a small fishing canoe with a crew of four. Tupaia talked with these people but could not persuade them to come on board, although they willingly answered any questions that he asked. It was probably they who told the *Endeavour* party that the peninsula was named 'Teracaco' and Portland Island 'Teahoura' (or 'Teahowray' [Te Ahorei] according to Parkinson).[40] These visitors took gifts with them when they left, and fires were kept blazing all that night on shore, 'possibly to shew us that our freinds there were too much upon their guard to be surprizd'.[41]

On the morning of 13 October a northerly breeze blew up and the *Endeavour* steered toward Waikokopu in search of fresh water and a safe anchorage. On closer inspection this bay seemed unpromising, so they coasted the shoreline at a distance of two or three miles, pursued for a time by a fleet of nine canoes. In this interval Cook, Parkinson, and others noted houses, canoes on the beaches, four palisaded hilltops and a number of square cultivations. Cook described the countryside as 'very pleasant and fertile',[42] with a foreshore of sandy beaches and white cliffs, a hinterland of wooded hills and several high mountains inland. Towards evening a large canoe carrying eighteen or nineteen people armed with long spears came out from a small village (probably around Wairoa), and threatened the *Endeavour* from about a mile's distance, at nightfall returning to the land.

On the morning of 14 October the *Endeavour* approached Ahuriri in light drizzle, and as mist rose up in the valleys they saw a fine river (probably the Esk) with a patch of yellow 'flaggs' (perhaps toetoe) on low ground and several groves of tall, tapering trees (probably kahikatea) on the flats at a distance. On either side of Ahuriri Bluff there was a narrow stone or sand beach with a very large lagoon behind it, set in a landscape of 'fine sloping hills, which stretched out into beautiful green lawns, though not covered with wood, as other parts of the coast are'[43] — Te Whanganui-o-Orotu or the old Ahuriri Lagoon. This place was a sheltered canoe harbour, famous for its paatiki (flounder) and other fisheries, and a site of dense Ngaati Kahungunu settlement at this time.[44]

The *Endeavour*'s longboat and pinnace were lowered to take soundings and to search for fresh water, but as several canoes approached they were called back to the ship. At ten o'clock four canoes came out from the land, two from Ahuriri and two from the mainland, carrying a total of sixty-eight men apparently intent on attacking the *Endeavour*. A 'very aged man' stood at the centre of one of these canoes, carrying a weapon (evidently a taiaha) decorated near its point with red and white materials, and he and another man in the same canoe armed with a similar weapon seemed to be directing the attack. These canoes came up yelling and shouting at a furious rate, and as they approached the ship a Tahitian cloak was thrown overboard as a peace offering, which the crew of one canoe picked up, and then a flannel cloak, which none of them would touch. When they were about 100 yards from the ship a cannon loaded with grapeshot was fired in front of the leading canoe, and when the water shot up in the air they all abruptly fell silent and paddled rapidly away. A fifth canoe now joined this group, and four more came into sight. As these four canoes approached, the *Endeavour*'s people called out to them that 'we were freinds if they would only lay down their arms'.[45] These people put down their weapons and quietly approached the ship. One man took off his cloak and offered it for barter, but his companions let their canoe fall back and refused to come any closer.

By now the *Endeavour* was off the Ngaruroro River, a place famous for its kahawai,[46] where a large canoe came out from the land. When its crew were told about what had just happened, they in turn paddled furiously towards the *Endeavour*, thundering out a war chant, brandishing their paddles in the air and throwing a spear at the stern, which bounced off and sank into the sea. Most of the other canoes joined them. Before long seven canoes carrying about 160 men were gathered under the *Endeavour*'s stern, where they performed a war dance, which Monkhouse vividly described:

> They treated us with a kind of *Heiva* or war dance performed by striking their paddles upon the gunwell, laid across for that Purpose, beating time in exact regularity to the parts of a Song which they chanted in a very martial tone. A Man in the headmost Canoe at the same time, standing erect, Shouldered, poized and brandished his paddle with the true spirit of a Veteran. In some of his gesticulations great savageness was expressed — in bending forward, throwing his Arms behind him, elevating his head, staring wildly upwards, and thrusting his tongue forward, he exhibited a figure very like that expressed in the heads of their Canoes. He did this at the close of the song, pronouncing the last sentence with a strong hoarse expiration [according to Parkinson, 'Epaah'][47] — the rest followed his example in the last manoeuvre. We commended the performance and they obliged us with a repetition of it.[48]

Parkinson also described these people and their canoes, saying that one man

Parkinson's sketch 'New Zeland War Canoe bidding defiance to the ship' was a later composite showing the haka with which local groups often greeted the Endeavour. *Note several women (wearing greenery on their heads), a child and a dog on board this vessel. The weapons displayed included mere (hand clubs), taiaha, kotiate (a lobed form of mere), tewhatewha (with an axe-shaped head), a spear and paddles.*

'who seemed to be a chief' was covered with red paint and wore a red cloak, while others wore striped cloaks and many of the rest, who seemed to be their 'servants', went quite naked.[49] The man who was painted with red ochre must have been intensely tapu, for kura was a sign of godly presence and red feather cloaks were rare and very precious. The leading men also had their hair tied up on their heads, and some wore the perfumed pendant with feathers, or pieces of a pellucid green stone around their necks. Their 'halberts' (taiaha) were decorated with red and white tassels (probably red kaakaa feathers and white doghair), while one man held a greenstone 'hatchet' shaped like a Tahitian hand club. Some of their canoes were between fifty and sixty feet long, carrying on average eighteen to twenty-two people; decorated with carved gunwhales, filigree prow-boards ending in carved heads, each with large paaua eyes and a protruding tongue, tall carved stern-posts fringed with feathers and trailing long streamers made of dark feathers stripped from the quill and woven together with 'thread'.[50] According to Monkhouse, these craft were also equipped with bailers made out of hollowed gourds.[51]

The men in the large canoe now ordered the others to fall back, and when this canoe came to the stern, Tupaia talked with its crew about 'the names of the countreys kings &c',[52] asked them to sing and dance, which they did, and invited them to come alongside, leaving their arms behind. These people piled all of their weapons into one of the other canoes, and the rest of the canoes then approached the *Endeavour*, where their crews were given presents before returning to the land. That evening both Banks and Monkhouse described groves of high trees standing on the coastal flats with a square palisaded enclosure nearby. Monkhouse also noted a small village on the shore with a small fortification on the thinly covered hills behind it, probably at Te Awanga.

The next morning, 15 October, the *Endeavour* was off Te Matau-a-Maaui (Maaui's fish hook), the promontory where Maaui's hook had snagged as he fished up the North Island. Five or six fishing canoes carrying about thirty people came out from Te Matau (whose name was recorded as 'Mattaruwhaow' [Mataruahou is the name of Scinde Island[53]] on Molyneux's map of New Zealand) to threaten the *Endeavour*. As they approached they were shown a Tahitian cloak, which induced them to come alongside. According to Monkhouse:

> We now saw that they were fishermen indeed, a miserable looking, half starved crew — their hair uncomb'd, ungreased, unornamented — their few Ahous old and dirty — their boat old, and without ornament or weapon. But they had got fish and these were pleasing objects — we soon made them understand our wants and they begun to trade with us; but willing to give us a specimen of their abilities and make a good market they sent us up two or three stones in their small baskets instead of fish: Upon detection of the cheat we only desired them to keep their stones for a better purpose — the fish they had were lobsters, sea ears [paaua], a kind of cod, two or three smaller kinds of fish, and part of a Shark; their fishing tackle consisted of hoop nets about three feet diameter — a kind of Trawl, fishing lines and hooks made of wood & bone — the hooked part was bone and bearded — the lines formed of a kind of grass two platt. Some of these People were dressed in the third kind of Ahou [kahu, garment] — one of these Canoes had a roll of straw mat — It might be a sail.[54]

When they were reproached for trading unfairly and all of their fish were gone, these unfortunate fishermen dropped reluctantly astern. Shortly after this a large canoe from the north side of the bay paddled towards the *Endeavour*, followed by seven others. After an exchange with the fishermen this canoe

Spöring's views of Te Matau-a-Maaui (Cape Kidnappers) from the north-east (above) and south-east.

approached the ship directly. It carried twenty-two men, including one old man who stood with a long staff in his hand repeating 'certain sentences in a tone very similar to that in which our Otaheite friends repeat their religious forms or Church Liturgy',[55] no doubt a karakia of some kind. Two of these men each wore a double topknot, greased and ornamented with three feathers. According to Parkinson, the dialect of these people was less guttural than that in Poverty Bay, and more similar to Tahitian.[56]

They were given some Tahitian garments and Cook received a taiaha, and then he tried to barter an old black cloak for a brown furred garment edged with white worn by an old man sitting in the stern of this canoe. The old man preferred a piece of red baize that had been held up, but when this was lowered overboard he coolly packed up both baize and his own cloak in a basket and held up a paddle, asking if that was wanted instead. He then told his crew to let go of the rope that held them to the *Endeavour* and his canoe dropped rapidly astern.

The Europeans were infuriated by this instance of 'cheating'. When trade resumed and the old man's canoe came alongside again, some of the *Endeavour* crew decided to trepan it, hoisting it up by a bowline around the prow to the anchor chains. Instead the local people took the initiative, attempting to seize first the captain's steward and then Tayeto, Tupaia's boy, as he climbed down the ship's ladder to take their fish. This second attempt succeeded and two men held Tayeto fast in the front of their fishing canoe while the rest of their crew paddled rapidly away, defended by the large canoe whose men now adopted a fighting posture. The marines were already lined up on the *Endeavour*'s deck, and when they were ordered to shoot at Tayeto's abductors, they killed one of the men who held him so that the boy was able to leap into the sea. The large canoe paddled forward to try to recapture him, but one of the great guns was fired overhead. As they in turn were fired on by the marines the crew of this canoe held up cloaks and nets in a hopeless effort to protect themselves, and two or three were killed. The canoes now raced back to land, where three dead or wounded men were carried ashore, and one of the *Endeavour*'s boats picked up Tayeto and brought him back on board.

As soon as he had recovered from his fright Tayeto brought a fish to Tupaia to offer to his god in thanksgiving for his escape. Tupaia approved the gesture and instructed him to throw it into the sea. In 1851 William Colenso talked to Waimarama men about this affray, and reported their conversation as follows:

> 25:3:1851.
>
> I received an interesting account from Zechariah Ngarangikamau, concerning Capt. Cook's visit to these parts in 1769; and the plan and abduction of 'Tayeto', the son of Tupaea the Otaheitian, who accompanied Capt. Cook. This was done by Zechariah's maternal grandfather, Te Ori. In this affair (which took place on the 15th of October in that year, and which has given name to the S. Cape of Hawke's Bay) the Natives lost 2 men, Whakaruhe and Whakaika; Te Ori himself being also badly wounded by a ball, which lodging under the knee and never extracted, caused him to limp to the grave . . . Zechariah and other old men, in relating the circumstance, said, that their fathers were warned by Tupaea not to approach the

ship hostilely; he saying, 'Mai, mate koe' (here, thou wilt be killed); but that their priests and chiefs contemptuously overruled all Tupaea said, with, 'Kahore he rakau o te hunga o Hawaiiki; he pu kakaho, he korari!' (The people of Hawaiki have no other arms than reeds, and stalks of flax — ie. Phormium.) It was, however, from this vessel, and at this time, that these Natives received the cabbage, and another plant which they call a 'Haaria'; this latter has become extinct, but, from the Native's description, and from their identifying and confounding it with my sunflowers at the Station, I presume it to have been an artichoke, or its near ally a Chardon.[57]

Tupaia and the Europeans alike had apparently been identified as people from Hawaiki, whose weapons need not be feared. The comment that the cabbage and a plant similar to an artichoke were introduced at this time is interesting, for Colenso was a fluent Maori speaker and a fine amateur botanist who was unlikely to have been confused about these identifications.

The *Endeavour* now left Te Matau-a-Maaui, which they named Cape Kidnappers in memory of this incident, and sailed south past Motu-o-Kura (which they named Bare Island for its barren appearance). Here they saw about a dozen houses, some canoes and people, and other people in a small bay on the mainland directly opposite. During the night the *Endeavour* brought to, and on the morning of 17 October sailed along a coastline of smooth rolling downs, white cliffs, sandy beaches and snow-clad inland mountains, passing several villages, 'smooks' and one garden before they reached Te Poroporo (Cape Turnagain) at 40°34′S. As always obedient to his instructions (for the Admiralty had ordered him to go to 40°S in search of the Southern Continent), Cook now reversed his course and turned north, sailing back towards Hawke's Bay during the night while several huge fires flared up on the hills inland. Banks attributed these fires to forest clearance for gardening,[58] while Forwood thought that they must be 'burning mountains'.[59]

During the next day the *Endeavour* turned to windward off the bay, and on the evening of 18 October a canoe came out from the southern end of Maahia Peninsula with five men on board. Two who seemed to be chiefs were readily persuaded to come on board, leaving their 'servants' to look after the canoe, and one of these men greatly impressed the *Endeavour* observers with his open, free and gentle manner. He had a very light facial tattoo and a fine new cloak bordered with black, white and red taaniko 'more curiously chequered than can possibly be described — the border was also broader than any yet seen'.[60] This man wore a greenstone pendant in his ear, 'formed somewhat like a french bean', which he would not part with, saying it was the 'tooth' of a deceased person worn in memory of a friend.[61] His companion had a deeper facial tattoo and mourning scars on his arms, and he wore a human tooth in his ear and a greenstone tiki with paaua eyes around his neck, which Monkhouse dubbed 'the monkey face'. This tiki was sketched by Spöring in a drawing dated 'Hawkes Bay October 18 1769'.

These men insisted on spending the night on board, so Cook ordered their canoe hoisted up alongside and their servants brought into the ship. The chiefs

Paikea rides his whale at the gable of Whitireia meeting-house, Whaangaraa.

The key ancestors for both Anaura and Uawa were Porourangi's great-great-grandson, Hingangaroa, and Hauiti, Hingangaroa's son by his second wife Iranui (who was the sister of Kahungunu, ancestor of the Hawke's Bay tribes). Iranui and Hingangaroa lived at Uawa, where he established the school of learning known as Te Raawheoro and founded a carving tradition which spread right around the East Coast.[14] Hauiti was his youngest son, who established his mana over the lands around Uawa after a dispute over fishing rights with his elder brothers Taua and Maahaki. Hori Mokai told the tale of this dispute in the Land Court in 1889:

> Hauiti occupied the land on the south side of this stream (S.W. of Uawa river . . .) as far south as Gisborne. The land on the north side belonged to Taua and Maahaki. When Hauiti had his fishing [net] made [which according to Mohi Ruatapu's version of the story was of an immense size[15]] he came across to his brothers' side to fish. When fish had been caught, Hauiti's brothers took the fish. The third time they, Taua and Maahaki took the fish Hauiti was grieved and went to Gisborne, inland to see Marukakoa the chief there. Hauiti went into Marukakoa's house. Hauiti said I have come to you for aid against my brothers. Marukakoa made a great smoke and left Hauiti inside and shut the door. Then he listened to the sufferings of Hauiti. In the morning he found Hauiti was not dead, so he went to kill birds for Hauiti, to strengthen Hauiti to conquer his brothers. Marukakoa said now go back and when [you] get there you will conquer your brothers. Hauiti came back and built a pa called Takitaki-a-Hauiti in Uawa near the

158

present [1889] church. He then again put his net in the water. Taua and Mahaki came again to take the fish, but the net turned over on them and their men were killed. [Ruatapu's version makes it clear that the fish-robbers were seized in the net by stratagem and killed.] Then a fight began. A chief called Karaka of Taua and Mahaki was killed. He [Hauiti] got close to a pa called Weriweritukua where he had some friends. He called to them to come to him at the foot of the hill. When they knew it was Hauiti they came to assist and there was a big fight called Para-weraru and Taua and Mahaki were defeated . . . Taua and Mahaki's descendants scattered, some north, some going south.

Taua and Mahaki were not killed but went on to this block to Whakatiki-a-Hauiti, the fighting then ceased and they all lived at peace . . . Hauiti then gave a feast at Whakatiki-a-Hauiti. Hauiti made a pile of food as high as Puketapu. He collected food from all parts. Taua and Mahaki were ashamed at the generosity of Hauiti so they went north to catch fish of a certain sort, but they could not do so. Then Hauiti sent a man to Te Koka to have them killed, Taua and Mahaki, and they were killed at Te Koka.[16]

Kahukuranui, Hauiti's son, completed this process of conquest when he had Taua's son Apanui killed for insulting him, and went to live at Anaura with his sons Kapihoromaunga and Tautini. There Tautini took over his elder brother's mana in a dispute over fishing rights at Tokomapuhia, and he became the founding ancestor for Anaura Bay.[17]

ANAURA ('TEGADOO')
20–22 October 1769

Anaura is a small bay ten kilometres north of Uawa and sixty kilometres north of Tuuranga-nui, carved out of rugged hill country and edged by mild slopes and flats that lead down to beaches to the north and south of the bay. On the morning of 20 October, as the *Endeavour* approached Uawa, two canoes, soon joined by another eleven, came out to the vessel. When it became evident that the *Endeavour* could not tack into the bay the occupants of the canoes invited the Europeans to enter Anaura instead, where they said there was plenty of fresh water. According to Cook, these people had heard about the shootings at Tuuranga-nui[18] but they did not seem to be in the least afraid of the Europeans, preferring perhaps to exchange gifts with them rather than to treat them as enemies. The *Endeavour* sailed into Anaura and at eleven o'clock anchored in the shelter of Motuoroi, a large island at the southern end of the bay, on which Monkhouse noted two stages about twenty feet high that he thought might be racks for drying fish. Below these stages on the south side of the island was a large fenced village, which apparently had been abandoned for some time. Most likely these stages were fighting-towers, although Monkhouse's guess that they were for drying fish was also plausible.

By the time the *Endeavour* came to anchor, seventeen canoes had gathered alongside. Two old men who seemed to be chiefs were invited to come on board, which they did without any hesitation. One of these men wore a fine cloak, decorated with narrow transverse stripes of white dogskin and a chequered border. His face, chest and arms were tattooed in spirals, and he wore human

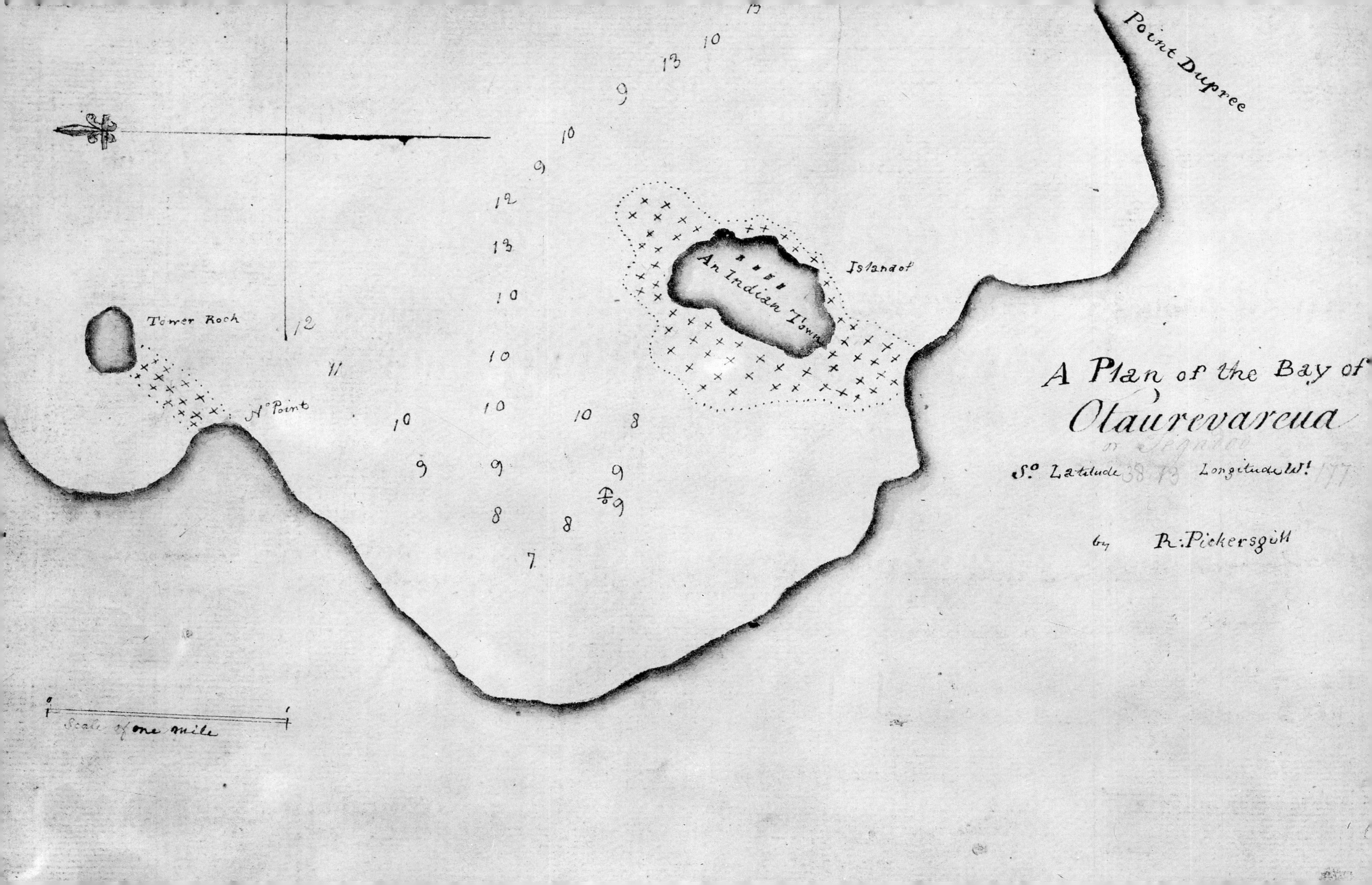

A Plan of the Bay of
Otauwawrua

S.º Latitude 38 70 Longitude W! 177

by R. Pickersgill

Point Dupree

Island?

An Indian Town

Tower Rock

Scale of one mile

teeth suspended from one ear, and a large piece of armbone thrust through a great hole in the lobe of the other. The other man wore a cloak decorated with tufts of red parrot feathers, and he had extensive face and chest tattoos. These two chiefs stayed with the Europeans while they ate dinner, examining everything they saw but refusing to eat anything themselves. During the meal another old man was seen alongside in a canoe brandishing his paddle, apparently inciting the assembled warriors to attack the vessel. There were about 130 men in the canoes gathered around the *Endeavour*, some dressed in shaggy 'thrum' capes, and one man wearing a closely woven cloak dyed in black. One of the chiefs on board leaned out the window of the great cabin and 'threat'ned them in very warm terms',[19] perhaps warning them by reminding them of the killings by whaitiri (musketfire) in Tuuranga-nui.

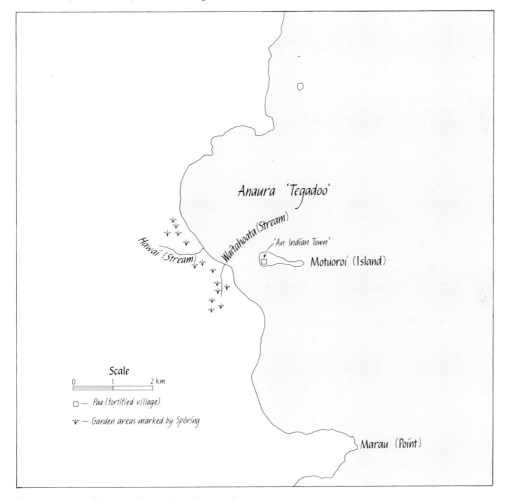

Above: *Map of Anaura ('Tegadoo') in 1769.*

Opposite: *Pickersgill's 'A Plan of the Bay of Otaurevareua or Tegadoo' shows 'An Indian Town' on Motuoroi, the island at the south end of Anaura Bay. This was the deserted village described by* Endeavour *journal-keepers.*

After dinner these chiefs were presented with four yards of linen each and a spike nail; they were delighted with the cloth but did not seem to value the nails at all. In exchange they gave 'several trifles' to the Europeans. Cook, Banks, Solander and a number of armed men went with them in the small boats to look for fresh water. When it began to blow and rain and the surf ran high, Cook called a canoe to take his guests ashore and returned to the ship. By now many people had gathered on the beach, and although they seemed peaceful, the Europeans had earlier observed them walking around trailing spears. Cook did not want to risk a landing with wet powder and flintlocks that might prove useless in an emergency. Later that afternoon, when the wind died down, the landing was made. According to Banks:

> We were received with great freindship by the natives in general who seemd carefull of giving us umbrage by collecting in too great bodies : each family or the inhabitants of 2 or 3 houses which generaly stood together were collected in a body, 15 or 20 men women and children, these sat on the ground never walking towards us but inviting us to them by beckoning with one hand movd towards the breast. We made them small presents, walkd round the bay, and found a place for watering where the people are to land tomorrow and fill some at least of our empty cask.[20]

Since the people seemed friendly, Cook decided to stay on at least one more day at Anaura to collect fresh water and to allow Banks and his party to look for plants and other 'curiosities'.[21]

In the morning Lieutenant Gore went with a large party of men to begin filling the water casks from two small streams on shore, but the sea was so rough that it was very difficult to get the casks back to the ship. Both on shore and out at the vessel the local people began to exchange 'whatever they had' for cloth with the sailors. They preferred Tahitian barkcloth to European fabrics, although by night its value had fallen more than 500 per cent.[22] At the watering-place about sixty of the local people, supervised by two 'chiefs' wearing superior garments of the loose-woven kind, watched the Europeans intently but did not mix with them. It is said that a Ngaati Porou ancestor called Te Rangitautia had prophesied that 'when the roots of the slow-growing hinahina tree had spread over his grave, he would hear the clattering of a foreign tongue and the noise of numbers'[23] Perhaps some of the more thoughtful of these people were reflecting on his prediction as the sailors talked among themselves.

Spöring's coastal views of Anaura show a number of hillside gardens in the centre of the bay, laid out in a chequerboard pattern and evidently either fenced, or edged by the cut margins of the adjoining scrub. These were the first Maori cultivations that the *Endeavour* observers had seen at close quarters, and Monkhouse described them in some detail:

> We had an opportunity to examine their Cultivations more at leasure to day and found them very far to surpass any idea we had formed of them. The ground is compleatly cleared of all weeds — the mold broke with as much care as that of our best

Opposite: *Spöring's panorama of 'Tegadoo' (Anaura Bay), 20 October 1769.*

SE

SEbS

S½S

Watering place

NbE¼E

gardens. The Sweet potatoes are set in distinct little molehills which are ranged some in straight lines, in others in quincunx. In one Plott I observed these hillocks, at their base, surrounded with dried grass. The Arum [taro] is planted in little circular concaves, exactly in the manner our Gard'ners plant Melons as Mr ——— informs me. The Yams are planted in like manner with the sweet potatoes: these Cultivated spots are enclosed with a perfectly close pailing of reeds about twenty inches high . . . We saw a snare or two set upon the ground for some small animal, probably of the Mus Tribe [the kiore or Polynesian rat]. The radical leaves or seed leaves of some of these plants are just above ground. We therefore suppose their seed time to be about the beginning of this month. It is agreed that there are a hundred acres of ground cultivated in this Bay — the soil is light and sandy in some parts — on the sides of the hills it is a black good mold. We saw some of their houses ornamented with gourd plants in flower. These, with the Yams, sweet Potatoes and Arum are, so far as we yet know, the whole of what they Cultivate. Whether the Cloth Plant, which we now became acquainted with, is at all cultivated is not without some doubt.[24]

One of Spöring's sketches 'Tegadoo' shows a vertical burn-off high on the hills, either for fernroot or for swidden gardens. According to Banks, the seed leaves of the taro had just appeared in the gardens, while the yams had not yet sprouted above ground. He added that the cultivations ranged between one and two to between eight and ten acres each, with a total of 150 to 200 acres in the bay.[25] Banks estimated the population of Anaura at not more than 100, although Monkhouse had said there were 130 people out by the *Endeavour* the day before.[26] It is also possible that some of the local people had moved to their fishing stations or had gone inland once planting was over. Even if the local population was 150 to 200 people, however, that was still about half a hectare of cultivation per head, which indicated a very high investment of labour in gardening in the bay.

Watering-place

Enlargement of one of Spöring's views of Anaura, showing the watering-place and hill gardens on the sunny slopes.

A recent archaeological study of horticulture in Anaura correlated the 1769 records with local topography and soil types, and concluded that the historic estimates of garden sizes, area and population were about accurate. Spöring's coastal views were evidently sketched close into the shore, using a spy-glass to detect detail. Many north-facing slopes were thus not visible, the true extent of the coastal flats and mild slopes behind the beach was minimised, and the slope of the gardens shown was exaggerated.[27] His representation of the coastal gardens were therefore somewhat misleading, and most of them seem to have been made in fact on milder slopes between the beach and the hills, with storage pits on the ridges above them. It appears that the mounds in which both kuumara and yams were grown served to concentrate nutrients and to warm the soil, while the mulching observed at the base of some mounds and the circular hollows in which taro were grown helped to keep the ground moist. The low reed fences served as wind-breaks.[28]

The local people traded only fifteen or twenty pounds of sweet potatoes to the Europeans, for by this time of the year they had planted out most of their seed kuumara and other supplies were running low.[29] They were eating mainly fernroot and seafoods, as Monkhouse recorded:

At Poverty Bay we had obvious reasons for thinking that some part of the food of these people was very course — this was now fully cleared up. In contemplating the people as they were moving about me I observed two old men, who appeared as chiefs, going to dinner — glad of the opportunity I immediately introduced myself by means of my beads &c. and was recieved very cordially. They were seated upon the grass — a young man had made a fire a short distance from them — he had a quantity of roots each about nine inches long, a flat large pebble, and a wooden mallet by him — some of these roots were roasting upon the fire he attended and turned them till they were thoroughly heated — he then beat them, one at a time, doubled and beat them again, and when fully softned he threw them to the Chiefs, who were now employed eating a lobster that had been dressed but was now cold. A woman had brought them this lobster, and afterwards brought them another, from a contiguous hut. They eat the lobster and roots just as we would lobster and bread. I partook with them of the repast — but we had nothing to drink — I pulled out my brandy bottle and took some to invite them — they tasted with me, and did not seem much to dislike it which surprized me exceedingly. Several other people of both sexes were sitting by us but no-one eat besides these two chiefs . . . At another place I saw a parcel of old and middle-aged men sitting in a range nigh a fire where a person was roasting and beating these roots and throwing them to each in turn — they chewed them for a considerable time and then spit them out — this was an evening's amusement. These roots are those of a fern which grows every where in great plenty in every port we visited in this Country.[30]

According to Banks, the cooked fernroot had a sweetish, clammy taste and was not unpleasant to eat, except that it was so stringy that most people kept a basket by them during meals so that they could spit out the chewed fibres.[31]

During the day Monkhouse and some others wandered off into the hills to the south side of the bay, where they came across a single house in a pleasant location. A man, a woman, their two sons and two women 'servants' greeted them, and the woman gave them a cloak she had been making. Her husband showed them paddles, two digging sticks (one short and pointed, about three inches wide and thirty inches long and the other the same width and about six feet long), some burnt red ochre, and barbed bird spear points about six inches long made of wood and bone. The house itself was very neatly built, with reed walls (probably of raupo) about four inches thick, a thatched roof covered with bark, which was held down by a net, a door about two-foot square with a carved board over the lintel, a mat on the floor and a small wooden chest with cord hinges (perhaps a burial chest) just inside the door. The man would not let them go in, but crawled into the house himself and brought out the mummified body of a child, which Monkhouse understood him to say was his own child who had died soon after birth. This body he readily exchanged for a 'trifle' — a most puzzling transaction.[32] Perhaps he thought that he was making an offering to a spiritual being of some kind.

Banks and Solander also spent the day wandering around Anaura, collecting plants and shooting birds for specimens. They saw some 'very small and ugly' dogs (the Polynesian kurii), which according to Magra had small pointed ears, and visited several households where Banks approvingly noted latrines for each cluster of houses and a rubbish heap for food scraps and other waste. The people received them affably, and it seems that some of the Europeans tried out Tahitian-style familiarities with the women. Banks ruefully observed:

> [The] red ocre and oil which generaly was fresh and wet upon their cheeks and fore-heads [was] easily transferrable to the noses of any one who should attempt to kiss them; not that they seemd to have any objection to such familiarities as the noses of several of our people evidently shewd, but they were as great coquetts as any European could be and the young ones as skittish as unbroke fillies.[33]

Banks had greatly enjoyed his love affairs in Tahiti, and perhaps he assumed that sex in the Antipodes would be as unabashed. If the local women were reluctant to sleep with the Europeans, however, they were wise, for the women in Tahiti had been infected with venereal diseases during the visits of Wallis and Bougainville to the island, and more than half of the *Endeavour*'s crew had shown symptoms of gonorrhoea and syphillis after only a short time on the island.[34]

That evening a number of local people visited the ship, where they danced for the Europeans, rolling their eyes (puukana), poking out their tongues and adopting postures that may have been sketched by Parkinson on that occasion.[35] Monkhouse must have had their appearance vividly in mind when he wrote his last surviving journal entry that night, for it included detailed descriptions of tattoo patterns, their strong physique and various styles of dress. He observed that in this place tattoo seemed to be carried out first upon the lips, and that the women, the young men and some older men had no more tattoo than this. Men aged between about twenty-five and forty had perhaps one cheek and one eye-brow tattooed, while older men and 'those people who appear as Chiefs' had full facial tattoos, and in addition sometimes body tattoos — a spiral tattoo on the right chest, on the right arm or on the outside of a leg. The facial tattoos were often very deeply cut, while the body tattoos were much more superficial.

The women, who used red ochre more often than the men, wore a waist girdle plaited from a highly perfumed grass with the leaves of some fragrant plant 'by way of figleaves' beneath their cloaks. Unlike the men they did not tie up their hair, grease it or ornament it with feathers and combs, although sometimes they plaited the leaves of a plant similar to coltsfoot (possibly kawakawa) into the hair over their foreheads. The men also wore ear ornaments — human teeth, pieces of human and bird bone, fingernails or carved pieces of wood — more often than the women, and some of them had pierced their ears and stuffed the holes with birds' down to stretch them out. One of these men had a greenstone axe with him, but he would not part with it for anything the Europeans had to offer.

According to Spöring and others, the local name for the bay was 'Tegadoo' (perhaps Te Karu),[36] while Pickersgill's chart of the bay was labelled 'Otaurevareua' (Otaurewarua).[37] The other name recorded in Anaura was 'Peritoto', described in Parkinson's vocabulary as 'Tupia's freind at Tegadu',[38] but this man is otherwise unknown.

Summary
THE *ENDEAVOUR* ACCOUNTS OF ANAURA

Anaura in 1769 was a small community of about 150 people who supplemented their diet of sea and wild plant foods with kuumara, yams, taro and gourds from about sixty hectares of meticulously tended gardens. The combination of Spöring's coastal views of Anaura, which show nine garden areas on the hill-sides, and Monkhouse's and Banks's very detailed descriptions of garden layout, the maturity of particular crops, the size of particular gardens and the overall area in cultivation provides the best early European description of Maori horti-culture, and the only detailed account of gardening that included neither Euro-pean cultigens nor any influence from European tools or agricultural techniques. The level of investment of effort in gardening at Anaura (at just under half a hectare per person) must have been very high indeed, and it is likely that some of these crops were exchanged for specialist products (including greenstone and adze blanks, for the region had no suitable rock types for adzes) from other districts. Perhaps their agricultural wealth also secured a peaceful life for the local people, for the only plausible paa observed in the bay was in ruins. The local people (who may have been joined on this occasion by visitors anxious to see the Europeans) appeared to be prosperous, because a number of old 'chiefs' among them wore fine cloaks and had extensive moko on both face and body, and there were a good number of canoes in the bay.

Archaeological surveys in Anaura show a number of likely paa, one on Motuoroi Island and the rest quite close to the coast, although gardens and storage pits are found on both sides of the bay. The fenced settlement that was observed in ruins in 1769 was probably the paa on Motuoroi, and it seems likely that if any of the other paa were in use as defended sites at this time, they would have been observed by the Europeans as they wandered about the bay. Partly because the atmosphere was so tranquil in Anaura, the *Endeavour* journal-keepers were able to observe Maori domestic life for the first time, and their descriptions of houses, domestic furniture, meals and routine fishing expeditions (when the canoes went off in the morning) give an impression of unhurried peace. The neatly constructed houses in the bay sometimes had a square area enclosed with a fence of reeds in front, and were often built in a cluster of two or three dwellings with a common 'dung-hill' and latrine. These dwelling units were occupied by 'families' (probably extended families, or whaanau) of fifteen to twenty men, women and children. Other houses were built on their own, however, and the house visited by Monkhouse was occupied by a single family composed of a man, a woman, two sons, and two women 'servants' who may have been war captives, either taken in some campaign or obtained by exchange. Domestic furniture in this household was scanty — just a mat, a wooden chest and some everyday tools and supplies of useful items such as red ochre, although the description may not be comprehensive, since Monkhouse was not invited inside. At mealtimes chiefs ate apart from the others, with both men and women cooking for them, and men and women also seemed to eat apart. Meals at this time of the year were based on crayfish and fernroot, although other foods were no doubt also eaten. This suggests that for at least five or six months of the year fernroot (rather than kuumara, yams and taro) was the staple diet.

Men and women may have eaten separately but on other occasions family groups (where children are mentioned for the first time) met the Europeans together. Wilkinson reported that 'the men in general have more than one wife',[39] a reference to the practice of polygyny that was usual in chiefly families. Wives were handed presents that had been given to their husbands and did not appear to be servile to their menfolk, nor were they prepared to sleep with the Europeans, although some of them were willing enough to flirt.

Once again in Anaura there was straightforward evidence of social hierarchy. Two heavily tattooed 'old men', one wearing a dogskin cloak and the other a red parrot feather cloak, played significant roles and observed restrictions on eating on board the *Endeavour*, while three others (also in distinctive garments) incited attacks at sea or supervised the local people on shore. Cannibalism was apparently practised, for according to Wilkinson in his general comment on 'Tagadoo':

> Government of this Country, Each Family as its chief likewise Every Village but thier Connections Appears to have no great Extent as we found that 3 boys that we had in our Custity was afraid of being Eat by there Enimise on the North Side of Poverty Bay; Customs of the Country, as yet we can give but a very Improper Account of our Indian has Convirs'd with them on these Subjects, which is that they all agree that they kill and eat all there Enimies when ever they take any.[40]

Of the gifts that the local people were given, they seemed to value Tahitian barkcloth most highly, at least to begin with, and it is significant that Monkhouse recorded barkcloth plants as growing wild in the bay. There were good descriptions in the journals of canoes, clothing, ornaments (including fingernails worn as earrings and an armbone thrust through a large hole in the earlobe) and tattoo, which included spiral body tattoos on the chest, arm and leg.

Red ochre was commonly used in the bay. Monkhouse was shown a quantity of red ochre that he was told was burnt before use, and he described it as being rubbed dry onto bodies and fine cloaks, or in another form painted onto faces. In 1841 Colenso noted prodigal quantities of 'red oxide of iron' on the cliffs at Whareponga, north of Anaura, which he said was made into a coarse red pigment for decorating canoes, architraves of chiefs' houses, kuumara stores, carved work and mausoleums, 'every article, in fact, which they may please to make sacred; red being invariably their sacred colour'. The red pigment used on faces and bodies, on the other hand, was collected by laying fern fronds in streams of 'chalybeate' water, and as the pigment was deposited on the fronds it was collected, rolled into balls and baked for use. According to Colenso, 'the red pigment they here call Takou, while among the northward tribes it is known by the name of kakooe [kokowai]'.[41]

Perhaps the most surprising thing about these meetings in Anaura was that the local people seemed neither hostile nor afraid, despite their evident familiarity with what had happened in Tuuranga-nui. Skirmishes and inexplicable deaths were a fact of life in most Maori communities, and although the Europeans and their vessel provoked considerable interest, there is little to indicate that they were regarded here with other than cautious curiosity and as a source of valuable and exotic items for exchange.

UAWA (TOLAGA BAY)
23–29 October 1769

The *Endeavour* left Anaura on 22 October because the surf on the beach there made it almost impossible to complete the watering. The vessel spent a day and night tacking in foul winds before being directed by local people to Uawa, a little south of Anaura, where there was a safe anchorage and accessible fresh water. After sending in two armed boats to inspect the watering place Cook brought the vessel into Uawa on 23 October and anchored at the centre of the bay in the early afternoon. Banks and others understood the local people to say that this place was called 'Tolaga' or 'Tollago',[56] another name that is now quite unknown and apparently represented a linguistic misunderstanding of some kind. According to local traditions, when the Europeans asked for the name of the place the people thought they were asking about the wind, for Taaraki was the wind off the land, which made sea conditions dangerous for canoes or ships.[57]

Uawa was a stronghold of Te Aitanga-a-Hauiti descent-group, the location of the whare waananga (house of learning) known as Te Raawheoro, and in 1769 home of the high chief Te Whakataatare-o-te-rangi and his cousin Hine Matioro, descendants of some of the most aristocratic ancestors of the East Coast. At the time of Cook's visit Te Whakataatare-o-te-rangi was a great chief who received the foods produced from lands around the bay. It was later said of him that 'Whakataatare is the top of the karaka tree and Ngaati Kahukuranui and Ngai Taawhao [sub-tribes of Te Aitanga-a-Hauiti] are the branches underneath'.[42] Hine Matioro is said to have been a young girl in 1769,[43] but in later life she was described as 'a great queen . . . with a large territory and numerous subjects'.[44] Te Whaka-taatare-o-te-rangi's headquarters were at Te Pourewa, an island off Opoutama at the south end of the bay.[45]

Uawa, like Anaura, was a small bay set in rugged country, but it was distinguished from Anaura by two meandering rivers, the Uawa and the Mangaheia, which ran down to the sea through inland valleys and coastal flats, creating swamps and rich alluvial soils along their courses. The cultivable areas in the bay were thus far more extensive than in Anaura, although more likely to be affected by frost. According to a recent archaeological analysis, the population was likely

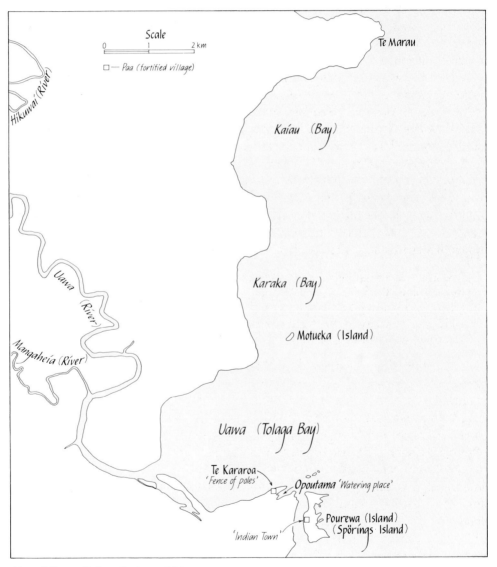

Map of Uawa (Tolaga Bay) in 1769.

170

to have been about five times as large;[46] indeed the earliest missionary estimate of population for Uawa gave a figure of 1,200 people.[47] Settlement in Uawa extended far inland, where there were fortified villages, eel weirs, cultivations, stands of karaka trees, and bush where kiekie, berries of various kinds and birds were taken along the creeks and rivers.[48] Gardens were made on the rolling hills and in alluvial soils along the river valleys, and raupo pollen was collected from the swamps, beaten out of male raupo flowers, mixed with water, kneaded and baked to make a delicacy that Colenso reported in 1838 looked and tasted very like gingerbread.[49] Tutu shrubs grew on the scrub-covered hills, and their berries were collected and the juice squeezed into calabashes, straining out the poisonous seeds in the process. A large succulent kelp (rimurapa), dried and cooked in squares, was often mixed with tuupaakihi or tutu juice and stored in calabashes, where it became very sweet and tasty.[50] The flour of roasted fernroots, pounded and mixed into a paste (aruhe kohere), was also mixed with tutu juice to make it sweet and pleasant.[51]

Along the adjacent coastline there were a number of well-known crayfishing stations, including Te Haha, Taoparapara, Te Ika-a-Tauira, Tatara (a reef off Motueka) and Maitara.[52] Shellfish, crayfish and kehe (granite trout) were taken around Motueka Island;[53] and Toka-mapuhia was the famous fishing ground for kahawai south of Te Marau, where Tautini had usurped the mana of his elder half-brother Kapihoromaunga by knocking down his raahui marker and fishing there without permission.[54] There were also haapuku fishing grounds offshore, where fish were taken using the techniques described by Colenso at Kawakawa in 1841, with flax lines, hooks made out of the tough forked branches of taanekaha or kahikaatoa trees, and baits of crayfish flesh or tarakihi in season, when that fish migrated towards the coast in shoals in summer. According to Colenso:

> [haapuku were] common on the New Zealand coasts; the natives having their marked spots for fishing, near rocks and shoals lying off the land in deep water . . . These preserves are all 'raahui' i.e. private; and scrupulously descend from the chief to his nearest relatives. Any infringement on such a fishing preserve was invariably resented, and often ended in bloodshed.[55]

Altogether the resources in the bay were rich and relatively compact, thus providing a strong economic base for the many sub-groupings of Te Aitanga-a-Hauiti.

As the *Endeavour* anchored in Uawa on 23 October, a number of canoes came alongside and brought them fish and kuumara. Of the things they were offered in exchange, however, they wanted only white cloth and glass bottles, so that the Europeans found it difficult to trade. Some of these people had greenstone axes and earrings which they would not exchange at any price, and they also set a very high value on the kuumara they had.[58] Wilkinson described their canoes as being from fifteen to forty feet long, having a hollowed-out hull built up with a broad plank lashed on, the join being covered by a rail with white feathers held in each turn of the lashing; and carved prows, stern-posts and side-strakes.[59]

Parkinson described the countryside around the bay as 'agreeable beyond description . . . The hills are covered with beautiful flowering shrubs [maanuka], intermingled with a great number of tall and stately palms [probably cabbage trees in flower], which fill the air with a most grateful fragrant perfume.'[60] He thought that with proper cultivation, particularly in the inland valleys, Uawa might be made 'a kind of second paradise' — the first time that any of the *Endeavour*'s people had hinted at the idea of settling the new land.

Monkhouse's meticulous journal ended at Anaura, and the information on Uawa is much less detailed as a result. Banks was preoccupied in Uawa with botanising amongst a marvellous variety of plants, but both Parkinson and Cook evidently spent considerable time ashore, and their accounts are relatively informative and vivid. Samples of twenty new species of tree were brought on board the *Endeavour*, one of which yielded a whitish gum and good firewood (the tarata, or 'maple'), while another (the tii, or 'cabbage tree') produced a cabbage which they later boiled and ate. Wild celery and scurvy grass were gathered to provide the men with greens, and maanuka for brooms, and about ten boatloads of firewood were cut. Parkinson noted ferns, parasitic plants, seaside plants and a 'sort of Hemerocallis' whose leaves yielded 'a very strong and glossy flax, of which their garments and ropes are made'.[61] Magra added that there were cloth plants (aute) growing wild in the bay.[62]

There were many beautiful varieties of birds at Uawa, including parrots, pigeons and quail but no domestic poultry, and the sober Mr Spöring claimed to have seen a strange brown bird like a kite which trailed a most enormous tail fly over his head at Pourewa Island.[63] Probably this was a kite, for these were flown in traditional times both for entertainment and in rituals of divination.[64] The only quadrupeds seen were a very few kiore (Polynesian rats) and dogs like those from Tahiti, Cook noting that the flesh of the latter was eaten and their skins used to decorate clothing.[65]

Out at sea there were many varieties of fish, including flounder, 'soals', 'skipjack or horsemackerel' and abundant shellfish and crayfish, the latter weighing up to eleven pounds and being eaten with fernroot as a kind of staple at this time of the year.[66] The hilltops and ridges around the bay were covered with fern, and the hillsides and valleys were covered with woods made almost impenetrable by supplejack. In some places hill-gardens on light, sandy soils had been made where kuumara and also yams in lesser quantities grew in mounds in neatly cultivated rows, surrounded by low fences that probably served as windbreaks. Cook climbed up into the hills (perhaps up Titirangi) on 24 October to get a view of the countryside, but found that

> I could see but very little the sight being bound'd every where by still higher hills. I found the tops of the hill Barren at least nothing grow'd upon them but fern but the Vallys and Sides of many of the Hills wher luxirous clothd with several sorts of trees, and little Plantations of the Natives lying dispersd upon and down the Country[67] [probably on the rolling hills to the south side of the bay].[68]

According to Banks, there were many deserted houses in the valleys and the people were living in light shelters on the hill ridges, a settlement pattern that puzzled him since it was obviously hard work carrying fishing tackle and crayfish pots up to these higher locations.[69] Parkinson added:

> Adjoining to their houses are plantations of koomarra and Taro. Their grounds are cultivated with great care, and kept clean and neat . . . The natives build their houses on rising ground under a tuft of trees; they are of an oblong square, and the eaves reach to the ground. The door is on one side, and very low; their windows are at one end, or both. The walls are composed of several layers of reeds covered with thatch, and are of considerable thickness. Over the beams, that compose the eaves, they lay a net made of grass, which is also thatched very close and thick. Their fires are made in the center upon the floor, and the door serves them for a chimney. Their houses, therefore, of course must be full of smoke, and we observed that everything brought out of them smelt strong of it . . . We saw but few of their houses, and those few were mostly deserted, their inhabitants having forsaken them through fear of us, who, doubtless, appeared as strange beings to them as they did to us.[70]

Parkinson and Banks also both commented on the amount of carving in the bay. On 28 October Banks, Solander and Spöring, and probably also Cook, visited Te Pourewa Island (whose name Banks recorded as 'Tubolai'), where they saw a large carved canoe sixty-eight and a half feet long, five feet wide and three feet six inches high, built out of three pieces of hollowed log, with a finely carved prow and one-piece gunwhale planks. At the same place they also saw the unfinished framework of a large house about thirty feet long, still full of chips, with all the woodwork squared and smoothed and 'the side posts carvd . . . in a masterly stile of their whimsical taste which seems confind to the making of spirals and distorted human faces. All these had clearly been removed from some other place so probably such work bears a value among them.'[71] Pickersgill's chart of Uawa marked an 'Indian town', which was probably the site of this house, on the landward side of the island.

Chiefs' houses were often decorated with carved sideposts, or poupou, and indeed these were quite commonly shifted from old, decaying houses to a newer structure. It seems probable that Banks took one of the carvings from this house back to the *Endeavour*, for just such a poupou is represented in a pen and wash drawing made after the voyage.[72] No other opportunity presented itself to acquire such a carving while the *Endeavour* was off the coasts of New Zealand, and it is possible that the local chiefs presented it to him as a gift, although carvings embodied ancestors and this house must have been highly tapu. The canoe was drawn on site by Solander in a series of sketches, one showing the entire canoe and others showing the elaborately carved prow, identified by the inclusion of the canoe's overall measurement for length.[73] Parkinson added that the tops of walking-sticks (tokotoko), boards to put on their houses and paddles were also carved

> in a variety of flourishes, turnings and windings, that are unbroken; but their favourite figure seems to be a volute, or spiral, which they vary many ways, single, double and triple, and with as much truth as if done from mathematical draughts;

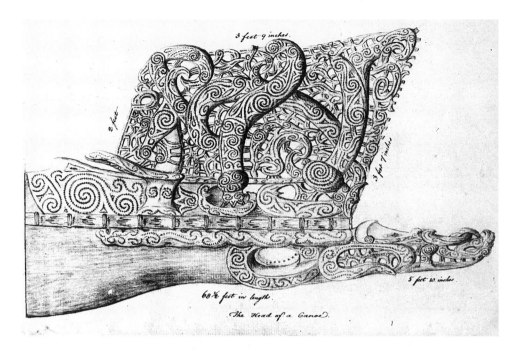

3 feet 9 inches.

2 feet

3 feet 7 inches

5 feet 10 inches

68½ feet in length.

The Head of a Canoe.

Above: *Spöring sketched this canoe prow on Pourewa Island in Uawa (Tolaga Bay) on 28 October 1769. It is a detailed depiction of an elaborate, sinuous piece of carving, associated with Te Raawheoro carving school.*

Left: *'Carved Plank from New Zeland', engraved in England by John Frederich Miller after the voyage in 1771. This poupou (carved wall post depicting an ancestor) was almost certainly collected from the carved, abandoned house visited by Banks, Solander and Spöring at Pourewa Island on 28 October 1769. The original, an irreplaceable exemplar of Te Raawheoro stone-tool carving style, cannot be traced.*

yet the only instruments we have seen are a chizzel, and an axe made of stone. Their fancy, indeed, is very wild and extravagant, and I have seen no imitations of nature in any of their performances, unless the head, and the heart-shaped tongue hanging out of the mouth of it, may be called natural.[74]

According to local histories, even before Hingangaroa had established his carving school at Uawa the ancestor Rua-te-pupuke had brought back carved posts from the sea-god Tangaroa's house and built them into his own house Te Raawheoro at Mangaheia in the bay, so that carving at Uawa traced back to ancient times.[75] It is likely that carvers from Uawa, like master carvers in historic times, moved widely around the country and that their products could be found as prized possessions in many different districts. Pickersgill thought that the people at Uawa were 'more mark'd on their faces armes etc' than those at Anaura, so tattoo (moko) may also have been a local speciality.

From a comment by Parkinson it appears that while men did the carving, women wove the fine cloaks, and he added that they also carried burdens and did 'all the drudgery'. On the other hand he noted that the women at Uawa 'seem to be proud of their sex, and expect you should give them every thing that they desire, because they are women; but they take care to grant no favours in return, being very different from the women in the islands who were so free with our men'.[76] Cook added that the Uawa women were very modest:

> One day at Tolaga I saw a strong proff that the women never appear naked at least before strangers. Some of us happen'd to land upon a small Island where several of them were naked in the water gathering Lobsters and Shell fish. As soon as they saw us some of them hid themselves among the rocks and the rest remain'd in the Sea untill they had made themselves aprons of the Sea weed and even than when they came out to us they shew'd manifest signs of Shame and those who had no method of hiding their nakedness would by no means appear before us.[77]

According to Magra, on the other hand, many of the young women went to the watering-place, where they 'granted their last favour to all that sollicited them, and on very reasonable conditions'.[78] He also told the story of an officer who, while wandering about the bay, was invited to enter an enclosed group of houses where about two dozen people were eating a meal of kuumara and cray-fish. He was asked to join their meal and in return offered beads and cloth as a gesture of appreciation. They later singled out a beautiful young girl and indicated that he 'might retire with her'. After their love-making they returned to join the others, and an elderly man with two women entered the enclosure, saluting everybody present by pressing noses (hongi). When the officer took his leave he repeated this gesture, which they greatly enjoyed. They sent a guide with him who carried him on his back over the many 'drainage ditches' around the cultivations that they passed[79] (possibly along the fertile flats beside either the Uawa or the Mangaheia Rivers, or to the south of the Uawa River).

Although these accounts of the sexual behaviour of local women appear to be contradictory, each may in fact be true. High-born young women and married women were sexually inaccessible, although a very important guest might be offered an aristocratic sleeping-partner as a gesture of hospitality and honour (manaaki). Captive women might be made quite freely available to visitors, and young women were generally at liberty to sleep with whomever they pleased, and at this first meeting there was no way of anticipating the dangers of venereal infection from European men. On balance it seems likely that both here, and possibly at Anaura, at least some of the sailors found women to sleep with, and in that case it can be assumed that venereal diseases and perhaps other infectious diseases were passed on to the local people.

Like most of the *Endeavour* party, Tupaia spent a good deal of time ashore at Uawa. On 25 October Banks reported him deep in conversation with one of the local priests (probably a tohunga from Te Raawheoro whare waananga (house of learning)): 'They seemd to agree very well in their notions of religion only Tupia was much more learned than the other and all his discourse was heard with much attention.'[80] Learned men of other tribes (particularly from the East Coast) are reported in tribal accounts to have regularly visited Te Raawheoro,[81] and such exchanges of ideas cannot have been uncommon, although the widely travelled Raiatean high priest must have been a fascinating guest. Tupaia also questioned the local people about cannibalism, having already heard about this practice in Tuuranga-nui, asking '. . . whether or no they realy eat men which he was very loth to beleive; they answerd in the affirmative saying that they eat the bodys only of those of their enemies who were killd in war'.[82] Although Tahitian myths told of women who ate people,[83] cannibalism was not practised in Tahiti, and Tupaia reacted to the custom with horrified disbelief. In Europe, too, it was held that witches ate people (especially babies), and eating human flesh was generally regarded with fear and loathing, although Cook himself was always matter-of-fact about the practice.[84]

Tupaia was a great favourite with the people of Uawa. Long after this visit he was remembered — children in the bay were named after him, the cave where he had often slept was called Tupaia's Cave and the well that Cook's men had dug around a spring at Opoutama ('Cook's Cove') was called Te Wai Keri a Tepaea (the well dug by Tupaia).[85] Another landmark at Opoutama that is closely associated with Cook's visit was Te Kotore o te Whenua, a natural rock arch facing the sea with a stream running through it. Such grottoes were artificially constructed on noble estates in England and were considered the height of fashion. Quite unaware of its mundane local associations (for its Maori name, aptly enough, means the anus of the land), Banks described this arch as 'the most magnificent surprize I have ever met with',[86] and both Spöring and Parkinson recorded it in a series of romantic sketches.

The bay seemed very peaceful at this time. As at Anaura, the only likely paa described was in ruins. On 27 October Cook and the 'gentlemen' made an expedition around the bay, and Banks climbed a hill above the watering-place to take a closer look at several deserted houses with a curving ditch about 100 yards long nearby (shown in Spöring's sketch of the cove). This ditch was associated with a double row of posts fourteen to sixteen feet high, each post ten feet from the next, the two rows set about six feet apart and occasionally joined at the top

176

Above: *This sketch of Opoutama by Spöring shows the sailors rolling barrels ashore, watched by interested spectators. The brushwood fence curving down the hill in the background is associated with a paa called Te Kararoa.*

Below: *Spöring sketched the arched rock in Uawa known as 'Te Kotore o te Whenua' (The Anus of the Land), which provoked raptures from Banks: 'We saw also an extraordinary natural curiosity. In pursuing a valley bounded on each side by steep hills we on a sudden saw a most noble arch or Cavern through the face of a rock leading directly to the sea, so that through it we had not only a view of the bay and hills on the other side but an opportunity of imagining a ship or any grand object opposite to it. It was certainly the most magnificent surprize I have ever met with so much is pure nature superior to art in these cases.' (Banks* Journal *I: 419.) Given the Maori custom of insult by whakapohane (ritual exposure of the anus), this ranks as a grand cross-cultural joke.*

by a sloping pole — a structure that can only have been part of an abandoned fortification.[87] All the same, the local people were adept at war dances and talked of eating enemies killed in war. Banks had also earlier been treated to a demonstration of weapon-handling by an old man who set up a pole for them and attacked it mercilessly with a hardwood spear about ten to fourteen feet long and a patu, spearing this imaginary enemy through the body and then hitting the upper end of the pole repeatedly and very hard with his hand club.[88]

From this it seems that war was no very distant memory, and it is possible that there were inland strongholds that the *Endeavour*'s men either did not see or did not bother to describe. In his summary description of New Zealand, Banks said of the East Coast area that

> Throughout all this District the People seemed free from apprehension & as in a state of Profound Peace; their Cultivations were far more numerous and larger than we saw them any where else, & they had a far greater quantity of fine Boats, fine Cloaths, fine carved work; in short the People were far more numerous, and lived in much greater affluence than any others we saw.[89]

This account was closely supported in 1814 by Jem, a Tahitian met by the missionary Marsden at North Cape, who told Marsden that the inhabitants of the East Cape area were active, ingenious and peaceful people who possessed larger and better-built houses, more extensive plantations, finer mats and better-finished weapons than all other tribes in New Zealand.[90]

Probably because this was the first place that the *Endeavour* had anchored in peace for any length of time, interesting snippets of information on matters other than dress, tattoo, houses, cultivations and landscape began to be collected at Uawa. Solander acquired a whipping top from some boys at the watering-place, and Wilkinson described the local division of labour; 'the men are empd Hunting or Tilling the ground while the women Doing there Domanstick Business at Home'.[91] Cook's rough notes on Uawa include comments derived from Tupaia's conversations with the many local priests as well as his own observations, which show signs of an awakening ethnographic curiosity:

1. The Religion of the Natives bear some resemblance to the George Islanders
   ———

2. they have god of war, of husbandry &c but there is one suprem god whom the[y] call   he made the world and all that therein is —— by Copolation

3. they have many Priests

4. The Old men are much respected ——

5. they have King who lives inland his name is   we heard of him in Poverty Bay

6. They eat their enimies Slane in Battell — this seems to come from custom and not from a Savage disposission this they cannot be charged with — they appear to have but few Vices — Left an Inscription

7. Their beheavour was Uniform free from treachery

8. The women may be known by thier Voices they paint thier faces red

9. the Womens faces are not tattou'd

10. the[y] seem to live on the ridges of hills in the summer
11. We found several houses not inhabited
12. The frames of some of the house were orimented with Carv'd woork ——
13. Thier Carving good
14. Thier large Canoes
15. Animals none except Dogs and Ratts, the former they eat and oriment thier cloths with the skin ——
16. Plants Birds and Insects, Woods &c
17. Fishes in the sea ——[92]

In these notes, which include the first European record of Maori beliefs, Cook seemed at pains to defend the local people from imputations of 'savagery', saying that they were neither treacherous nor riddled with vice, and that their practice of eating enemies was not a sign of a savage disposition ('this they cannot be charged with'), but rather a matter of custom. His comment about leaving an inscription was confirmed by Magra, who said that it was made on a tree a little to the right of the watering-place.[93] When this was done the *Endeavour* raised its anchors on 29 October and, followed by canoes loaded with fish, sailed north out of the bay.

Summary
THE *ENDEAVOUR* ACCOUNTS OF UAWA

The *Endeavour*'s visit to Uawa was remembered by local people in a number of tribal accounts. In 1874, for instance, Ropata Wahawaha satirised Ngaati Porou memories of the visit in a humorous contribution to the Maori newspaper *Te Waka Maori o Niu Tirani*:

Then Capt. Cook sailed to Uawa and there he saw the chief Whakatatare-o-te-Rangi. He called out to him: 'Tatare! Tatare! Give me some provisions!' and a supply was given to him accordingly. Then said Capt. Cook: 'Tatare is a chief!' — words, which, afterwards, became a proverb. Cook then gave Tatare a bright red scarf, a musket, a keg of powder and a flat lump of lead. Cook invited Tatare to make trial of his skill by firing off the musket. The gun was loaded, and the chief held it close to his cheek and fired it off, but he became so alarmed at the report that he dashed the gun down on the stone and it was broken, and then he threw it into the water.

Afterwards, the natives broke open the keg of powder, and came to the conclusion that it was turnip seed. So they cleared away the bushes, prepared a plot of ground, and planted the supposed turnip seed. Then the people rejoiced and said: 'Our women and children will be satisfied (fed) for the seed of food is in the ground!' Others said: 'Yes, true! No wonder if we rejoice! It is all so very jolly!' And afterwards, when it rained, they said: 'This will bring up our seed!'

Out of the lead they formed an adze, which they sharpened carefully and put a nicely-made handle to it. And the fame of this adze prepared by Tatare spread far and wide among the tribes. At length, many assembled to examine it and witness the trial of its capabilities. On the first blow being struck on the wood, lo and behold! it bent and doubled up. Then all the people, as if with one voice, exclaimed: 'Oh! it has not been subjected to the influence of fire. If it were heated

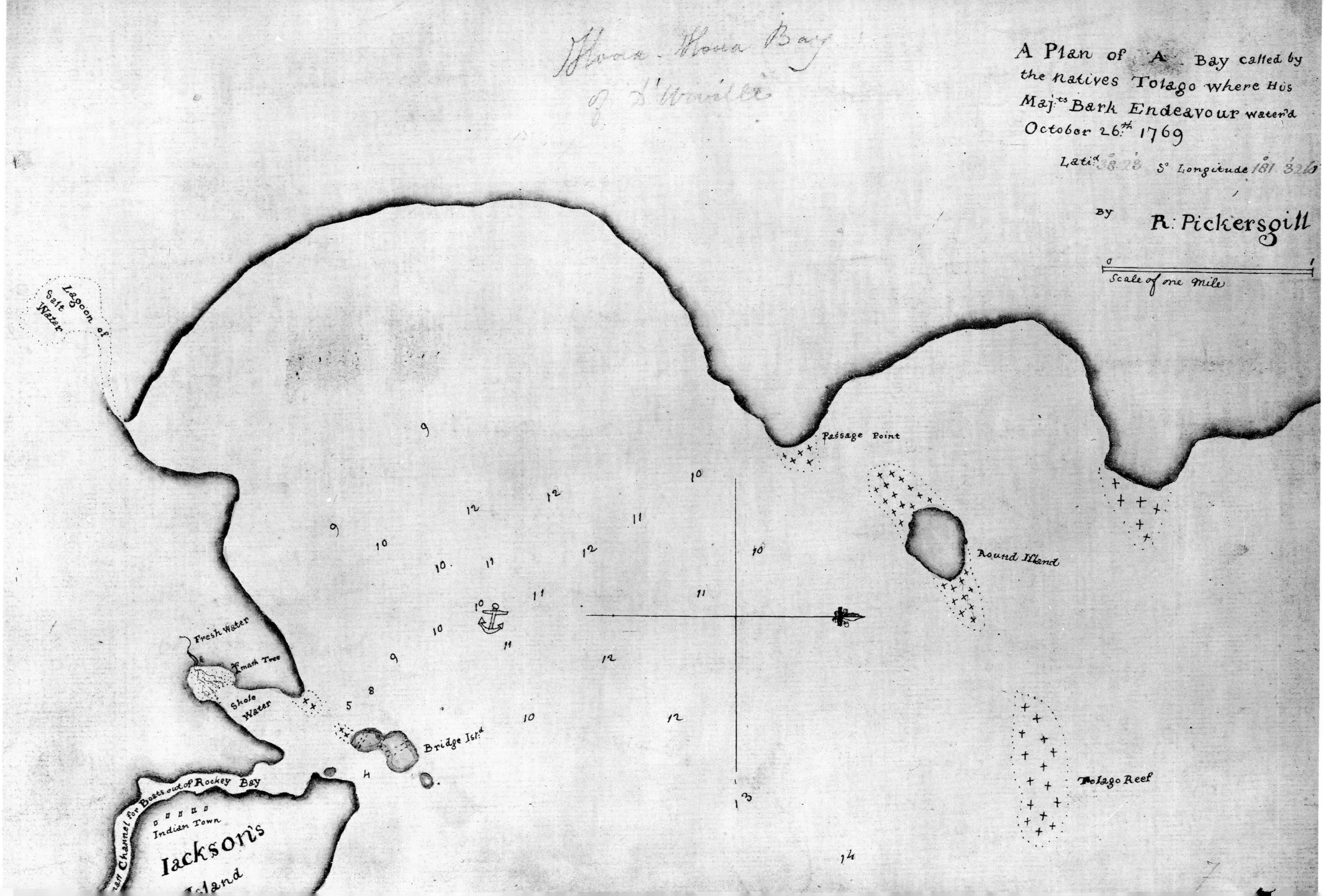

A Plan of A Bay called by
the natives Tolago where His
Maj:s Bark Endeavour water'd
October 26th 1769

By R. Pickersgill

Latit: 38° 8' S° Longitude 181° 32½

Scale of one Mile

Thomas Moun Bay
J. Monille

Tolago Reef

Round Island

Passage Point

Lagoon of
Salt Water

Fresh Water
French Town
Shoal Water

Bridge Isl:t

Jacksons
Island

Indian Town
Bases out of Rockey Bay
Channel for Boats out

10 10 10 10 10
11 11 11 11
12 12 12
9 9 9
8 5
6

in the fire, it would become hard.' Then they said: 'Right! Bring some wood for a fire. Let it be given much wood that the fire may burn long and the adze be well hardened!' [Nephrite and other adzes were heated to harden them.[94]]

So they lighted a fire and cast the adze upon it. But, wonder of wonders, it melted! Then arose a shout: 'Drag it from the fire! we must consider some plan to perfect this adze!' Quite a number rushed to the fire and attempted to pick out the remains of the adze with sticks, but it separated into many parts and was abandoned. And so ignorance came to its natural result![95]

Although none of the journals of this voyage mention a gift of a gun and gunpowder, in 1835 the trader Polack talked with Taatare's grandson Te Kani-a-Takirau, who also said that his 'father' had been given gunpowder by Cook, which the people planted, mistaking it for seed. He added that when it failed to sprout a left-over handful was thrown in frustration into the fire where it exploded, scattering the people, who exclaimed, 'Atua no te Pakeha!' (the Pakeha's god!) Polack was presented with cloaks on this occasion and two spike nails, which were said to have been originally been given by Cook to Tuuranga people and taken from them in battle by Te Kani's father; and he was also shown three light-blue beads from Cook's visit that were worn by Te Kani's wife. Te Kani took him to Tupaia's well and the cave where he had slept, where among other wall drawings in charcoal a sketch of a ship and some boats was pointed out, which everybody present agreed had been drawn by Tupaia himself.[96]

In 1888 Williams reported that Hine Matioro, who was a young girl at the time of Cook's visit, had been introduced to him as a person of high rank, and that he presented her with beads and other ornaments.[97] The puzzling thing is that there are no comments at all about high-ranking individuals at Uawa in the 1769 journals, although this is probably because Monkhouse's records, which were so meticulously detailed, survive only in an early fragment which ended at Anaura. If a community in which some women have always held high-status positions could be described by comments such as Parkinson's 'the women . . . do all the drudgery'[98] during the generation of Hine Matioro, one of the greatest of all East Coast women, then the explorers' descriptions of Maori women must be regarded with caution. Moreover, although Te Whakataatare-o-te-rangi was a man of great mana who is also said to have met Cook, he is not mentioned at all in the *Endeavour* journals, although it is possible that he was the old chief in the red cloak who boarded the vessel at Anaura Bay.

Another early version of Cook's visit to Uawa came from a Tuuranga-nui chief named Te Apaapa-o-te-rangi, who also focused on the gifts that the Europeans were said to have left behind:

But the cat was a new animal which was brought by the Pakeha. When the ship of that Pakeha chief called Cook arrived, it stopped at Uawa and they and their men came ashore to fetch water and firewood for their ship. When the wood and the water were fixed up, that chief wrote his name on the flat surface to stay, and it

Opposite: *Pickersgill's 'Plan of A Bay called by the natives Tolago' locates a row of houses on the inner coast of Pourewa ('Jackson's') Island, and shows a 'mark tree' on the northern side of Opoutama.*

181

is still there. He brought two cats, one male, Puhi [pussy] was the female and Kati [cat] was the male of those two cats which were grey in colour. On coming ashore they were let go — [they] ran into the forest and were lost. The two dogs black with projecting ears and white chests. These dogs were brought for the Maori.

The parareka [potato] was obtained there, that [potato] which is called wae-ruru, the papake, and wiri, that is all those potatoes. He brought corn [maize] too. On its growing tall then the root was uncovered to see if it had fruited — no fruit was seen, then it was said, 'Eh, we have wasted all our work in [trying to get] food [from this]. There's not a single fruit.' The corn was pulled up, and corn was lost.

Cook asked about the food of the Maori, birds were shown, mashed hinau was brought, raupo pollen bread and mashed raupo shoots. That chief approved and he took away those two 'breads' and a bundle of fern root. He brought back seven hats [haatiwhere] and said the name of those cloths was — rari-haate [perhaps fur hats or wigs] ten red blankets — the Maori gave a name to red blankets — paaraikete-tahurangi [fairy blankets]. When this was over he brought two pots and the axe called by the Maori 'Takarita', two iron hoops which were cut into hatchets, many were made from those two hoops. This was the first [gift] of the iron hatchets [given] to our people that is to the east coast. It was these axes which [were used to] hollow out in dressing trees, to adze timber, or to fit house timbers together, [to make] pa palisades, to make earthworks, and food pits. That ends my explanation.[99]

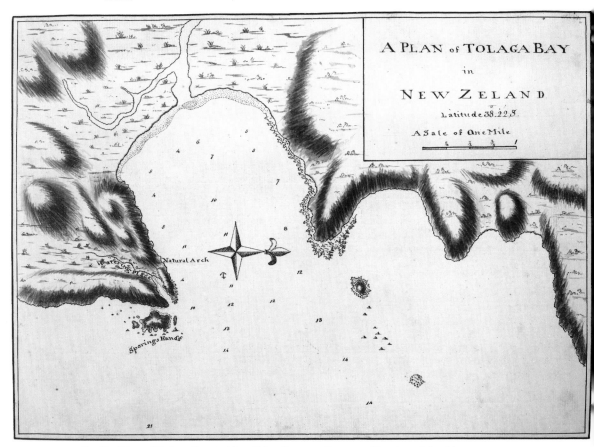

Cook's 'Plan of Tolaga Bay in New Zeland' names Pourewa 'Spörings Islands'.

Spöring's coastal views of 'Tolaga' (Uawa), 23 October 1769. A photographic panorama taken by Jeremy Salmond from the sea at Uawa in 1990 confirmed that Spöring's views are remarkably accurate.

This account gives interesting details on local foodstuffs and suggests that extensive biological (maize, potato varieties, dogs and cats) and technological (hats, red blankets, pots, an axe and two iron hoops) transfers of items took place at Uawa. Some of these details, however, were probably derived from later exchanges with Europeans.

In Uawa the quality of the European descriptions of Maori life started to change. The minute descriptions of physical appearance of people and places that had dominated the early journal entries in New Zealand began to give way to more directed enquiry into aspects of social life, although information on these topics was still very fragmentary. The topography of Uawa was well represented in Spöring's coastal views, but the landscape was only generally described in the written accounts; nor were there population estimates, nor comprehensive day-by-day journal entries (with the inevitable mention of individuals) of visits to particular settlements and gardens, or of what took place on shore. The logs recorded the daily routines of wooding and watering, and regular visits to the ship by local people to trade fish, crayfish and kuumara, but otherwise gave only brief, uninformative comments.

There were good descriptions of the structure on the hills above Opoutama, which seems to have been the remnants of a double palisade and ditch of a paa called Te Kararoa,[100] and of a carved house and a large carved canoe on Pourewa Island (where a settlement was marked on Pickersgill's chart of the bay). Useful generalised accounts of houses, settlement patterns, gardens and personal ornament and clothing were also written. The archaeological record at Uawa suggests that the focus of settlement in the bay was about one kilometre up the Uawa River, at the intersection of the Mangaheia, Waimaunu and Uawa Rivers, and at the entrances to the enclosed valleys of the Mangaheia and Hikuwai Rivers, another two to four kilometres upstream.[101] It seems probable that a number of the *Endeavour* party travelled some way up these rivers, noting deserted houses, fertile lands and gardens drained with ditches along the alluvial flats; but no detailed descriptions of these landscapes have survived. Of the people in the bay, Parkinson noted that they were generally lean and tall with black hair (at Anaura he had seen two brown-haired men), and the men wore beards 'of a middling length'. The women scratched themselves on their faces when mourning for dead kinsfolk, while the men carried such scars upon their bodies, and 'the principal men' wore tattoos whereas the women, servants and particularly handsome men and women wore red ochre on their faces. The interesting thing is that, like the European descriptions, the tribal stories about this visit to Uawa focused on goods they received, indicating that Maori and Europeans in these first meetings shared a fascination with the material possessions of the other side.

Chapter Eight

FROM UAWA TO HAURAKI

30 October–23 November 1769

On the morning of 30 October, as the *Endeavour* sailed about two miles offshore north of Anaura, two fishing canoes tried to catch up with her. The wind was brisk, and the ship soon left them behind. This stretch of countryside was rugged, with small sandy bays, several villages (with one 'large town' marked on Pickersgill's chart near Port Awanui) and areas of garden visible from the sea. A little after noon the *Endeavour* rounded Whanga-o-keno (East Island), the landing-place of the legendary canoe *Mangarara*, which had brought insects and lizards to the archipelago,[1] and sailed along the East Cape into an expansive bay. Parkinson described the coastline west of East Cape as

> considerably higher than the rest. It was divided by fine deep valleys, and had all the appearance of a rich fertile country, being cloathed with large verdant trees, had some parcels of ground cultivated, and several rivulets among them which lost themselves in the sea. We could also discover several villages, which seemed to have been fenced in by art.[2]

The area around Horoera Point was described on Pickersgill's chart as having 'many Indian towns and Cultivated Lands'. Later that afternoon they passed a small bay (Wharekahika) that they named 'Hickes's Bay' (now Hicks Bay) after the first lieutenant, and brought to for the night twenty-four miles west of the cape. Early the next morning the *Endeavour* sailed along a fertile and well-inhabited coastline into the territory of Te Whaanau-a-Apanui, a confederation of kin-groups descended from Taua, Hingangaroa's eldest son, and thus closely related to the people of Anaura and Uawa. As the *Endeavour* approached Tihirau Peninsula, five canoes came out two miles offshore to threaten the ship. One large

NWbN

East Cape Dist 2 leagues

East-Island

NbW.

Spöring's sketch of East Cape from a distance of '2 leagues' shows Whanga-o-keno (East Island) offshore.

swbs.   *sw.*

'View of the Land on the S.W. side of Cape Runaway', sketched by Spöring on 1 November 1769, shows Mount Edgecumbe.

canoe, packed with sixty people all armed with spears and paddled by sixteen men on each side, circled the vessel. A priest recited incantations and some of the crew performed a war dance. According to Parkinson, they yelled out 'Harre yoota patta pattoo' (Haere (k)i uta . . . patupatu) — a garbled fragment of speech that talked of coming to the land, and of weapons, or patupatu. On a signal from a small canoe this craft sped forward to menace the *Endeavour*, stopping only when a volley of grapeshot whistled past them on one side. After a brief consultation the crew paddled forward again. This time Cook ordered a cannon loaded with roundshot to be fired over their heads, which so terrified the people that all the canoes fled back to shore. Tihirau (now known as Tikirau) was named Cape Runaway in memory of this incident.

Just west of Tihirau the *Endeavour* passed Whangaparaaoa, which according to traditional accounts was an ancient landfall of the *Tainui*, *Arawa* and *Maataatua* canoes. Here the countryside was described as well wooded and pleasant with large gardens and small clusters of houses, some fenced with palisades and others quite open, scattered amongst the trees. During that afternoon they approached Orete along a fertile coastline 'full of Plantations laid out in regular inclosers divided by fences, look'd like inclosers in England'[3] — an interesting reference to the chequerboard field systems that were becoming common back home. That evening the *Endeavour* brought to three miles from the shore, twenty-four miles south-east of 'Koakhali', or Whakaari (which they named White Island). Three or four canoes came out but kept at a safe distance from the ship.

The next morning was calm and fine, and forty-five canoes were sighted approaching from different parts of the coast near the mouth of the Mootuu River, suggesting a large local population.

Of the seven canoes that came close to the *Endeavour*, one had a human skull on board which was being used as a bailer. The chief man on the largest canoe made speeches, brandishing his spear, and eventually came alongside, where he pronounced a few words and gently threw a stone against the side of the ship. At this signal his men immediately took up their weapons, but Tupaia warned them that if they attacked they would all be killed, and threw Tahitian cloth down to them (which influenced them far more than his threats had done). They now began to exchange crayfish, large green-lipped mussels (so that nearby Toka-taa Point was named 'Mussel Head') and several conger eels with the officers for small pieces of cloth, which they cut into bits two or three inches square and put

186

into holes pierced in their ears. After a while these people began to take goods from the officers without making any return. When one man defied their threats and laughed at them, a musket was fired over his head, which quickly brought him back to the ship to complete the exchange.

The sailors crowded to the gangway to get mussels and crayfish for themselves, but as their supplies ran low the local people again began to take goods without giving anything in exchange. Finally one man seized a pair of sheets that had been hanging on a rope in the sea to soak, and let his canoe drop astern, laughing at the Europeans. Two musketballs were fired through his boat but this did not deter him, although he deliberately began to plug up the leaks. A charge of smallshot was now fired, which hit him in the back, but even then he continued to repair his canoe, every now and then rubbing the place where the shot had penetrated his flesh. The other canoes quickly retreated with their crews performing war dances while musketballs whizzed around them. When a cannonball was fired between two canoes, narrowly missing them and then skidding several times on the water before sinking, Pickersgill said they made 'the most Precipitated retreat I ever saw'.[4]

The *Endeavour* sailed towards Whakataane, passing several fortified villages that were marked on Cook's chart of this region. By nightfall the ship was just inside Mou-tohoraa ('Mowtohora' or in Pickersgill's journal 'Ohite-horo'[5]), or Whale Island, where a large carved and decorated double canoe made of two canoes lashed together by a narrow deck came out. Its crew of twenty talked with Tupaia, performed songs and dances, made impassioned speeches and then pelted the ship with stones. The *Endeavour* anchored in the shelter of this island opposite a high, rounded mountain inland (Puutauaki), which Cook named Mount Edgcumbe (now Edgecumbe). The next day, 2 November, they continued west, chased by several craft including the carved double canoe that had approached them the night before. This time the canoe was under sail, and it finally caught up with the *Endeavour* inside Rurima Rocks, where it crew sang chants, performed a haka and then again pelted the ship with stones, mocking the Europeans for their cowardice in running away. Spöring sketched this canoe, and one of the *Endeavour*'s journal-keepers described its sail:

> [This was] a sail of an odd construction, . . . made from a kind of matting, and of a triangular figure; the hypothenuse, or broadest part, being placed at the top of the mast, and ending in a point at the bottom. One of its angles was marled to the mast, and another to a spar with which they altered its position according to the wind, by changing it from side to side.[6]

A musket loaded with smallshot was fired at one young man who had proved a good shot with his stones, and he shrank down as if wounded while the sail was lowered and the canoe called off the chase.

By now the *Endeavour* was off the Rangitaiki Plains, where the coast looked low and sandy. Past Matataa the land seemed very fertile, and as they sailed further north they saw large villages built on the clifftops, defended by deep ditches and high palisades, 'so that probably these people are much given to

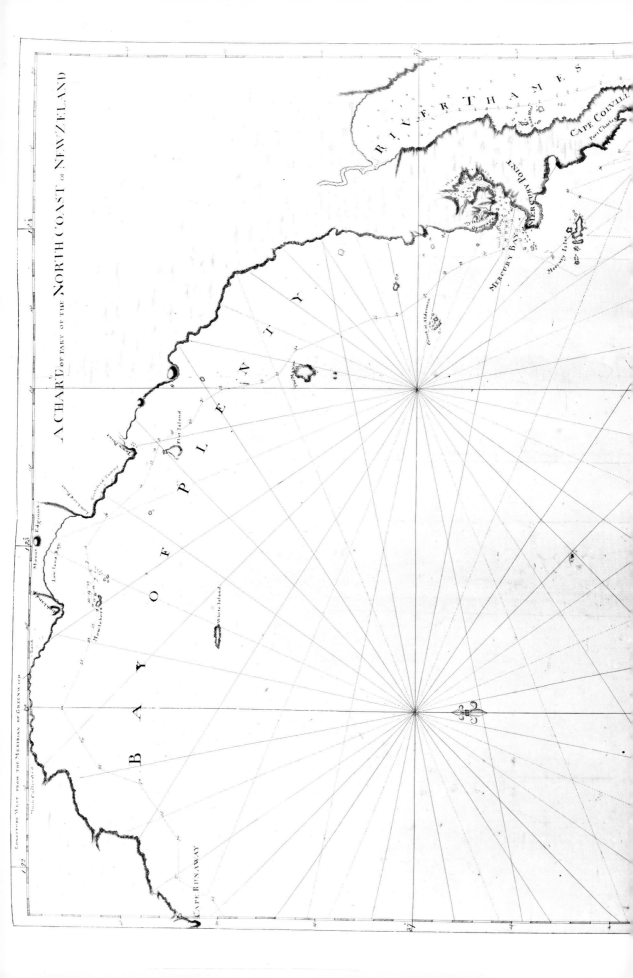

A CHART of PART of the NORTH COAST of NEW ZELAND

Longitude West from the Meridian of Greenwich

RIVER THAMES

CAPE COLVILL

Port Charles

MERCURY POINT

MERCURY BAY

Mercury Isles

Court of Aldermen

BAY OF PLENTY

White Island

Flat Island

Mount Edgcumb

Low land Bay

Newstead

CAPE RUNAWAY

This double canoe under sail, sketched by Spöring on 2 November 1769, chased the Endeavour *off the Bay of Plenty coastline. A chief in the stern of the canoe is depicted brandishing a mere, while another amidships wears a chequered cloak and carries a taiaha. One of the crew is shown using a bailer.*

war'.[7] Near Maketuu the fortified villages seemed larger than ever, always palisaded and built on hill ridges and high places. Hundreds of large canoes were drawn up along the shore, some of which seemed to have awnings, but none of these put out to sea. According to Pickersgill, the largest of these fortified 'towns' was built near the sea, defended by a fence and ditch and containing upward of 500 houses.[8] Banks concluded that this great sweep of coastline from East Cape to Maketuu (which they called the Bay of Plenty) was the richest and most densely populated place they had yet seen, and that it might be the residence of their princes:

> As far as we have yet gone along the coast from Cape Turnagain to this place the people have acknowledged only one cheif, Te ratu: if his dominion is realy so large he may have princes or governors under him capable of Drawing together a vast many people: for himself he is always said to live far inland.[9]

Banks's speculation reflected expectations about Terra Australis, and it was quite inaccurate. Te Raatuu was, as we have seen, a Rongowhakaata chief from

Opposite: *Cook's 'Chart of Part of the North Coast of New Zeland' shows a string of fortified paa east of Whakataane, others between Matataa and Maketuu, several on Okurei ('Town Point'), and Wharetaewa paa in Mercury Bay.*

189

Tuuranga-nui, and the claims to his dominion over so vast a territory can only have been based on linguistic confusions, perhaps between people indicating the west where the sun sets (te raa e too), and their identifications of local leaders. The Bay of Plenty was certainly a region of dense settlement, however, drawing its wealth from fertile coastal lands and prodigal fisheries out at sea, and inhabited by a complex array of tribes descended primarily from Toi, and the crews of the *Maataatua*, *Takitimu*, *Arawa* and *Tainui* canoes. If north of Maketuu few fortified villages were noted, this was because in the region the major paa (according to archaeological surveys) were sited much further inland.

On the night of 2 November the *Endeavour* sheltered inside Tuhua (Mayor Island), a place that supplied obsidian to many parts of the mainland, and the next morning sailed north along a barren, rocky coastline with many islands off-shore, some with fortified towns. Two canoes came out from one of these settlements and chased the *Endeavour*, but could not overtake it. A group of perpendicular rocks whose local name Parkinson recorded as 'Te rooa mahoe' (Te Rua Maahua), was named the 'Court of Aldermen' (now the Aldermen Islands), and the Europeans entertained themselves by naming each rock, whether wide and squat or narrow and tall, after municipal worthies with similar shapes back home in England. On Castle Island (Ngaatuturu) Banks described

> houses built on the steep sides of cliffs inaccessible I had almost said to birds, how their inhabitants could ever have got to them much surpassd my comprehension; at present however we saw none so that these situations are probably no more than places to retire to in case of Danger which are totaly evacuated in peaceable times.[10]

At one o'clock the *Endeavour* was off Te Ooa-a-hei (the exclamation of Hei), now known as Haahei, where the ancestor of Ngaati Hei had claimed the coastline by naming a prominent rock after the curve of his nose (Te Kuraetanga-o-te-Ihu-o-Hei).[11] The houses here were scattered along the coastline, and three small dug-out canoes, uncarved, hollowed out by fire and with twenty-one men

A VIEW of the COURT of ALDERMEN

A VIEW of the ISLANDS and MAIN within the COURT of ALDERMEN

Charles Praval's sketch of Te Rua Maahua, or the 'Court of Aldermen', was probably based on a lost original drawing by Spöring. These craggy islands inspired the Europeans to name each one after a similarly shaped alderman back home.

190

on board, came out to threaten the ship. Those people were dark-complexioned and had stripped off most of their clothes. They performed a vigorous haka (war dance) before approaching the ship, where they threw a spear at a sailor who was letting down a rope to them, and then another, which reached the deck but hit no one. Time and again during the *Endeavour*'s circumnavigation of New Zealand spears were thrown at the ship, usually after a war dance and often after incantations and speeches were given; and these weapons were thrown singly and probably represented ritual challenges rather than all-out attempts at attack. On this occasion two muskets were fired over the challengers' heads, and they all returned to land.

TE WHANGANUI-O-HEI (MERCURY BAY)
3–15 November 1769

Late on the evening of 3 November the *Endeavour* sailed into a bay well sheltered with islands, followed by several dug-out canoes, and anchored just inside the south entrance of the harbour. These canoes (which had neither carvings nor washboards) came to the ship's side, where their crews talked with Tupaia. One of the Europeans shot a bird on the water which they took up and tied to a fishing-line that was trailing behind the vessel. In return for this courtesy they were given some cloth, but they then performed a haka and tried to tow away the anchor buoy, quite undeterred by a volley of two or three muskets that was fired over their heads. These people shouted out that they would return the next morning with allies and attack the *Endeavour*, and sent off a canoe that went away to another part of the bay to get assistance. Sentries were posted on the *Endeavour*'s deck, and during the night canoes came out twice, hoping to surprise the Europeans, but finding men on watch they went back to the land.

During the mid-eighteenth century most of the Bay of Plenty and the Coromandel Peninsula, then known as Te Paeroa-o-Toi (Toi's long mountain ridge),[12] was in a state of readiness for war. The tribes of the western Bay of Plenty, the Coromandel and the Far North were contesting with each other in raids and sieges, recorded in their tribal histories. Fighting was common in the summer, so during November descent-groups in these areas were on the alert, which accounts for their rapid and vigorous response to the arrival of a strange vessel in their waters.

Ngaati Hei, the people of this particular bay, had good reason to be cautious. They and their close relatives Ngaati Huarere were ancient tribes, descended from the earliest inhabitants of the archipelago. Kupe, the explorer, was an early visitor to the bay, crossing the river that was later named after him — Te Whitianga-a-Kupe (Kupe's crossing). Tama-te-kapua, captain of *Te Arawa*, and his uncle Hei, its sailing-master, came later.[13] After *Te Arawa* had landed at Whangaparaaoa (which in some early accounts evidently referred to Whangaparaaoa north of Auckland)[14] it coasted south to Moehau (Cape Colville) at the tip of the Coromandel Peninsula, where their high priest Ngaatoro-i-rangi left a mauri on a small island, and Tama-te-kapua their captain claimed the land by saying that he would be buried at that place.[15] Tama-te-kapua settled first at Maketuu, the final landing-place of the canoe, but after a quarrel over a garden he returned to Moehau, crossing en route the Whitianga Inlet. He did indeed later die at Moehau and was buried on the summit of Moehau Mountain.[16]

Tama-te-kapua's son Huarere went with him to Moehau, while his close kinsman Hei travelled as far as the Whitianga River, where he settled beside the harbour that became known as Te Whanganui-o-Hei (Hei's great bay).[17] The *Tainui* canoe also visited the bay on the way north, where its sail was left leaning against a cliff that afterwards was called Te Raa-o-Tainui (*Tainui*'s sail).[18] The descendants of Huarere and Hei intermarried with local people on the peninsula who claimed descent from Mokoterea of the *Aotearoa* canoe,[19] and together they controlled Te Paeroa-o-Toi for many generations.[20] By the time of the *Endeavour*'s visit, however, they were under attack from several directions — by

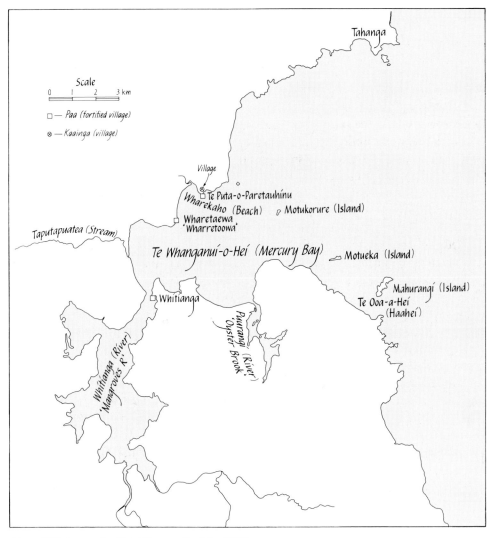

Map of Whanganui-o-Hei (Mercury Bay) in 1769.

192

tribes to the west who traced descent from the *Tainui* canoe, by war parties from Northland and by their own remote relatives from Tauranga and further east.[21]

The district was well worth fighting over. According to the archaeological record, Whitianga (the common name of the area) and other places along the east coast of Coromandel were among the earliest sites of settlement in New Zealand. A pearl-shell lure that must have been brought from one of the islands in Polynesia has been found in an excavation at Tairua, south of Whitianga, and there are archaic settlements and middens all along this coastline. Tahanga at the northern entrance to the bay was the source of a sought-after basalt stone for adzes,[22] very like the volcanic basalts found in high islands in Polynesia. Siliceous sinter, useful for cutting tools, was found on Ahuahu (Great Mercury Island),[23] and there was a place for working obsidian from Tuhua by the Puurangi River.[24] Ahuahu was spoken of in the migration stories of *Te Arawa* and *Tainui*, and of *Horouta* and Paikea from the East Coast. This and other offshore islands around Whitianga had micro-climates where root crops could readily be grown, and the Whitianga people migrated there in spring and autumn for planting and harvesting. The island resources included colonies of grey-faced petrels which could be taken from their burrows when young and cooked and preserved in gourds in their own fat; swarms of small eels in the swamps; large mussels, crayfish, oysters and other shellfish growing on the shoreline; and prodigal fisheries out at sea. The offshore islands and nearby bays were a breeding ground for many species of fish, and these fishing grounds are still famous, although the stocks of most species have been greatly depleted by commercial harvesting. The waters of Te Whanganui-o-Hei were sheltered and calm, celebrated as 'Te tai kau-hoenga tamaahine o Hei, he tai rangimarie te karekare' (Hei's coast for swimming, gentle as a young girl, a peaceful smooth-watered coast)[25] — a fine base for sea-borne warriors and fishermen alike.

In 1769 the rugged, mountainous country of the northern peninsula was covered in a luxuriant rainforest of tawa, rimu, and kauri, with an irregular fringe of shrublands, fernlands and coastal vegetation. A variety of birds lived in the inland bush, including kokako, pigeons, kaakaa, tui, kiwi, huia and parakeet, while native frogs lived in the leafy litter or in the splash zones of the streams. In Whitianga itself a number of streams ran down into the inner harbour, creating expanses of wetlands where raupo, flax and rushes grew in swamps inhabited by eels and ducks. Out in the tidal estuaries there were mangroves and great beds of shellfish, with flocks of seabirds wheeling overhead. There were invigorating hot mineral springs at Taputapuatea, named after one of the most sacred places in Raiatea, and around Puurangi there were excellent freshwater springs.[26] To the south side of the bay the landscape was barren, and ferns and scrub grew on heavily leached soils, while to the north gnarled pohutukawa trees clung to rocky cliff faces with petrels burrowing around their roots, sharing their holes at times with tuatara.[27] The great mountain behind the northern cliffs, Maungatawhiri, was covered with mature rata forest, and on its lower slopes pohutukawa, karaka and puriri grew, with yellow-flowering kowhai on the more exposed stony outcrops.[28] The coastline here was craggy and dramatic, with high headlands and

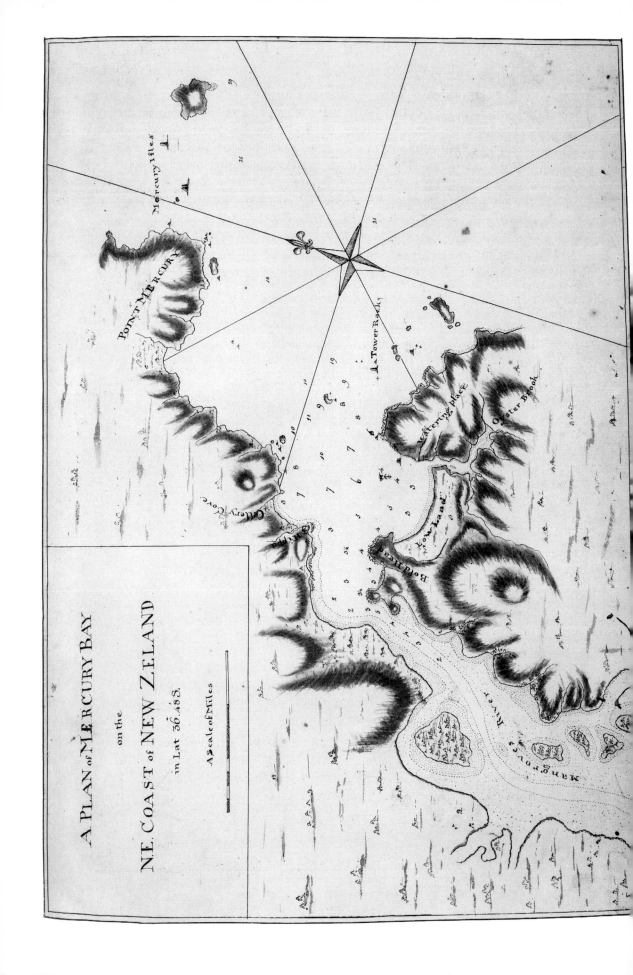

A PLAN of MERCURY BAY

on the

N.E. COAST of NEW ZELAND
in Lat 36.48 S.

A Scale of Miles

Mercury Isles

POINT MERCURY

Cutlery Cove

Watering place

Oyster Brook

A Tower Rock

Low Land

Bold Head

Mangrove River

small islands alternating with stretches of glittering white sand.

Early on the morning of 4 November, as the *Endeavour* lay at anchor in Te Whanganui-o-Hei, ten or twelve canoes carrying about 150 men (Wilkinson thought 170 men; Pickersgill thought 220 men in fifteen or sixteen canoes) armed with spears and stones came out. They paddled about the ship for several hours, sometimes threatening the Europeans, 'staring at us in a wild manner' (presumably widening their eyes in the ritual expression known as puukana, or perhaps attempting to maakutu [bewitch] the Europeans — maakutu means 'to stare at fixedly')[29] and approaching the ship from one side and then the other. According to Banks

> our resolution was that as we had in vain shewd them the power of musquets by firing near them and killing the bird yesterday we would on the first provacation they gave us fire at them with small shot, the last resource we had to show them our superiority without taking away their lives.[30]

Cook was intent on staying some time in this bay because it seemed a suitable place to carry out observations of the transit of Mercury (predicted to take place on 9 November), and thus to accurately fix the longitude of this part of New Zealand for chart-making. He therefore thought it necessary to deter the local people from attacking the *Endeavour* or its crew. They talked with the people in the canoes for a time, and began to exchange trade goods with them for their weapons. One man tried to keep both the goods and his weapon, and as he swaggered in his canoe he and a man next to him were shot with smallshot, and a musketball was fired through the hull of their canoe.

They paddled away, bleeding profusely and ignored by their companions, who after a pause resumed trading their weapons to the Europeans. Finally one man tried to keep two pieces of cloth in exchange for one weapon. As he sat in his canoe about 100 yards from the *Endeavour*, a musket was fired at its hull, holing it twice just above the waterline. The people now began to panic and when they turned their canoes around a cannon loaded with roundshot was fired over their heads, 'ye Noise of which and seeing the Shott rise and fall in the water so Great a distance set them in the [most] Terrible disorder possible to immagine Scarcely knowing which way to take for safety, but recovering their Sences most dextierously puld to the Shore'.[31]

Cook and Molyneux the master shortly afterwards took two boats out to sound the bay and search for a better anchorage, approaching first the north side of the bay, where they were invited on shore by a number of armed men, and then rowing towards the head of the bay, where they saw a fortified village on a high point (probably Wharetaewa paa). Later that afternoon the *Endeavour* was shifted to an anchorage marked on Pickersgill's chart of the bay, one and a half miles south-east of the mouth of the Puurangi River, where an old man named 'Torava'[32] (Toiawa) came on board. According to Banks, this man

> seemd to be the cheif both today and yesterday but in all the transactions of yes-

Opposite: *Cook's 'Plan of Mercury Bay on the N.E. Coast of New Zeland'.*

terday he was observd to behave sensibly and well, laying in a small canoe always near the ship and at all times speaking civily to those on board. With some persuasion he venturd down into the cabbin and had presents, Cloth, Iron &c given him; he told us that the Indians were now very much afraid of us, we promisd freindship if they would supply us with provision at their own price.[33]

Early the next morning two other men came on board the *Endeavour*. They were given two pieces of English cloth and some spike nails each, and exchanged goods for more cloth. They told the Europeans (probably through Tupaia) that they had been very concerned about the arrival of the *Endeavour*, for every now and then some people came from the north to raid them, taking away their wives and children as captives and plundering them of all their possessions. In order to survive these attacks they had been forced to build their houses close together on high rocky places, and they had become very suspicious of strangers. Although the *Endeavour* and its occupants must have seemed extraordinary to these people, they, like many other visitors who came on board the ship, relaxed as soon as they realised that these 'tupua' were not intent on harming them, and became both inquisitive and friendly. After this visit Cook, Banks and a party of sailors took the pinnace to Puurangi River to haul the seine, while Molyneux and another party went in the yawl to sound the bay and dredge for shellfish. As Cook's party arrived at the riverbank a group of local people beckoned to them and unsuccessfully tried to persuade them to cross the river. Later, several sailors who had been left to guard the pinnace saw two men on the other side of the river fighting to settle some quarrel, beginning with spears, which the old men soon took from them, allowing them to continue with their fists. After a while this group went behind a small hill so that the sailors did not see the outcome of the fight. Neither of the fishing parties was very successful. In the afternoon Cook and Molyneux went to another part of the bay (probably to Cooks Beach, since a line of soundings are marked in that direction on Pickersgill's chart) while the local people brought quantities of cockles, mussels and scallops and mullet out to the *Endeavour*, enough to feed everybody on board.

During the next three days Cook ordered the ship heeled and the hull scrubbed, wood cut, water brought on board and wild celery collected as an antiscorbutic to boil and serve at the ship's table. Each day the sailors went fishing, and the local people supplied them with dried fish and fresh mackerel very like those caught in England. Banks and Solander went ashore to collect plants and rocks and often visited the people at Puurangi, who were living out in the open while they collected heaps of fernroot and shellfish to take back to their own settlement elsewhere. Their encampment was surrounded by great heaps of shells, presumably produced as the people scooped out the contents of the shellfish to dry in the sun. Huge middens of this sort were piled up all around the bay, 'many waggon loads together, some appearing to be very old',[34] while on the south side of the bay large ferns grew on the hilltops. The landscape was otherwise quite barren and no cultivations were seen.

On the evening of 8 November Banks and Solander visited their friends at Puurangi to see how they slept at night:

It was as they had told us on the bare ground with no more shelter than a few shrubs over their heads, the women and children were placd innermost or farthest from the sea, the men lay in a kind of half-circle round them and on the trees close by them were rangd their arms in order, so no doubt they are afraid of an attack from some enemy not far off. They do not acknowledge any superior king which all we have before seen have done, so possibly these are a set of outlaws from Teratu's kingdom; their having no cultivation or houses makes it clear at least that it is either so or this is not their real habitation. They say however that they have houses and a fort somewhere at a distance but do not say that even there is any cultivation.[35]

As Banks later commented, these people did not bother to put up any shelter even though on two occasions it rained solidly for twenty-four hours at a stretch.[36] The old man Toiawa appears to have been the leader of this party. Banks's manuscript vocabulary also mentions his sister 'Hinnanato', 'Omoea — my freind at Opoorage [Puurangi]', and 'Tuwhatoo — Tupia's freind at Opoorage'.[37] Horeta Te Taniwha, whose childhood memories of the *Endeavour* visit to Whitianga were quoted at the beginning of Chapter 4, was a little boy among this group. He was a Ngaati Whanaunga from Waiau and other places, for according to the Land Court records, migratory patterns of subsistence were commonplace on the peninsula. According to Te Taniwha, the leader of their party, 'a distant relative of mine', was a chief of Ngaati Pou (or Te Uri-o-Pou) of the Hauraki Gulf, further west,[38] a tribe closely related to Ngaati Hei. It was no doubt because of those kinship connections that this group of people was visiting the bay.

The next day, 9 November, was memorable for several reasons. At daybreak a great number of canoes came out to the *Endeavour*, loaded to the gunwales with mackerel, which they traded with the Europeans. Evidently they had made an enormous catch and were disposing of the surplus, which the Europeans ate fresh, pickling the rest in casks. Later that morning Green the astronomer went ashore on the ocean beach, some 300 metres from the west bank of the Puurangi River to observe the transit of Mercury (at $36°50'18''$ South, $175°45'23''$ East according to Herdendorf's recent calculation), with Cook and Hicks as assistants.

While they were preoccupied with setting up the apparatus and making these observations (a process which must have both puzzled and fascinated local observers) two large and three small canoes packed with armed warriors (one carrying forty-seven men) came out to the *Endeavour*. These men were complete strangers to the Europeans and evidently had come from outside the bay. They may have been Ngaati Hei warriors, returning from their summer settlements on the offshore islands to see what was going on. Their canoes were finely made, not dug-outs, and the people seemed prosperous, wearing fine cloaks and feathers and offering valuable goods for trade. These people seemed to have heard nothing about firearms. One handsome young man called 'Otirreeoonooe' (perhaps Otiriunui) after trading each of his garments, offered a black and white dogskin cloak in exchange for a large piece of cloth. As soon as he had it in the canoe his companions paddled away from the *Endeavour*, singing a war song and shaking their paddles defiantly in the air when they thought they were safely out of range. Lieutenant Gore, whose cloth had been seized and taken, fired his musket at this man and shot him dead. A roundshot was then fired overhead (according to Forwood, to prevent these canoes from landing where Green and Cook were carrying out their observations) and all of these canoes paddled rapidly away.

A boat was sent ashore to tell the people at Puurangi what had happened. At first they retreated from the Europeans, but after a while returned and said that the man had deserved his punishment, 'unaskd by us', said Banks, 'who thought his fate severe knowing as we did that small shot would have had almost or quite as good an effect with little danger to his life, which tho forfeited to the laws of England we could not but wish to spare if it could be done without subjecting ourselves to the derision and consequently to the attacks of these people'.[39] Cook when he returned on board was angry with his second lieutenant:

> I have here inserted the account of this affair as I had it from Mr Gore but I must own that it did not meet with my approbation because I thought the punishment a little too severe for the crime, and we had now been long enough acquainted with these People to know how to chastise trifling faults like this without taking away their lives.[40]

Te Taniwha's account of this affair suggested that the young man was a relative of some kind:

> One of our tribe was killed by the goblins who first came to Whitianga. We — that is, our people — went again and again to that ship to sell fish, or mats, or anything that we Maoris had to sell; and one day one of our canoes, in which were nine persons, paddled off to the ship; but one of the nine was a noted thief, and this man took a dogskin mat to sell to the goblins. [Te Taniwha's earliest version of Cook's visit, given to Lieutenant-Governor Wynyard in 1852, named this man as 'Rimmi, a chief, the grandfather of Paul of Pata-aroha'. According to another account by Te Taniwha, his companions also took pet kaakaa and carved feather boxes out to trade.[41]] There were five of them at the stern of the canoe and four in the bow, and this thief was with those in the stern. When they got alongside of the ship, the goblin who collected shells, flowers, tree-blossoms, and stones was looking over the side [in the Wynyard account, Te Taniwha called this man 'Waro', a man of consequence amongst the white people, who could sell any goods on board the ship, and collected ferns and plants]. He held up the end of a garment which he would give in exchange for the dogskin mat belonging to this noted thief; so the thief waved with his hand to the goblin to let some of it down into the canoe, which the goblin did; and, as the goblin let some of it down into the canoe the thief kept pulling it towards him. When the thief had got a long length of the goblin's garment before him, the goblin cut his garment, and beckoned with his hand to the man to give the dogskin mat up to him; but the thief did not utter a word, and began to fold up the dogskin mat with the goblin's garment into one bundle, and told his companions to paddle to the shore. They paddled away. The goblin went down into the hold of the ship, but soon came up with a walking-stick in his hand, and pointed with it at the canoe that was paddling away. Thunder pealed and lightening flashed, but those in the canoe paddled on. When they landed eight rose to leave the canoe, but the thief sat still with his dogskin mat and the garment of the goblin under his feet. His companions called to him, but he did not answer. One of them went and

shook him, and the thief fell back into the hold of the canoe, and blood was seen on his clothing and a hole in his back. He was carried to the settlement and a meeting of the people called to consult on the matter, at which his companions told the tale of the theft of the goblin's garment; and the people said, 'He was the cause of his own death, and it will not be right to avenge him. All the payment he will obtain for his death will be the goblin's garment which he has stolen, which shall be left to bind around his body where it is laid.' His body was taken and put into one of the ancient cave burial-places. Not any evil came from this death, and we again went to barter with the goblins of that ship, and the goblins came again and again on shore, nor was there one evil word spoken, or any act of transgression on our part for that death.[42]

That evening Banks and Solander shared a meal with their friends at Puurangi, eating shellfish, crayfish, fish and birds that had either been broiled on a skewer over the fire or cooked in earth ovens — 'holes in the ground filld with provision and hot stones and coverd over with leaves and Earth'.[43] As they ate together a woman sat on the ground nearby, comforted by just one other person, weeping, talking out loud and cutting herself on the arms, face and breast with a shell. She must have been mourning for the man who was shot, despite the evident view of the rest of her people that he was responsible for his own destruction.

The next day Cook, Banks and others went in two boatloads to explore the Whitianga River. They rowed about four or five miles up its course, past flat islands covered with mangroves which had lumps of kauri gum stuck to their roots, sand banks with productive beds of cockles and scallops, and beds of rock oysters in some places. There were ducks, curlews (probably godwits), a 'Black Bird about as big as a Crow, with a long sharp bill of a Colour between Red and yellow'[44] (probably oystercatchers) and a colony of shags sitting on a tree by the river. Some of the local people must have accompanied them on this expedition, for Te Taniwha later described the shooting of these shags:

Overleaf: *Pickersgill's 'Plan of Port and River Mercury — call'd by the Natives, Apuragge'*
includes a table of topographical references:

a, a, a   *Small Rivers of Fresh Water*
B, B   *Indian Fortifyde Townes*
C   *Outer Bay*
D   *Inner Bay*
E   *Oyster Banks*
F.   *A Salt Water River*
G   *Place Where the Observation of the Transit of Mercury was observd Latitude 36:49S°*
H   *N° Point of the Bay*
I, I   *Low Isl^ds coverd with Trees like mangroves*
K   *A Rock like a Pillar with a small one on each Side*
L, L   *Sholes Dry at Low Water*
M   *A high Double Peak'd Mountain.*

Wharetaewa, Te Puta-o-Paretauhinu and the small paa on Motukorure Island are each marked B.
The site where the Transit of Mercury was observed on 9 November 1769 is marked precisely in
Cook's Bay, 'G'.

Point Mercury

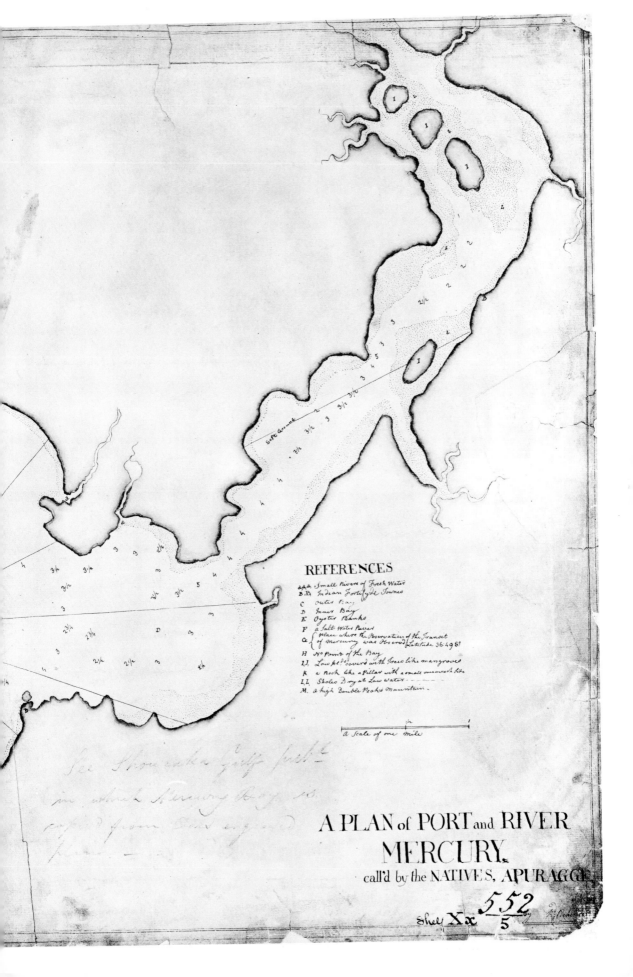

REFERENCES

A.A.A. Small Rivers of Fresh Water
B.B. Indian Fortifyde Townes
C. Outer Bay
D. Inner Bay
E. Oyster Banks
F. a Salt Water River
G. place where the Observation of the Transit
of Mercury was Observed Latitude 36.49 S.
H. No Point of the Bay
I.I. Low Land covered with Trees like mangroves
K. a Rock like a Pillar with a small onewash tide
L.L. Sholes Dry at Low Water
M. a high Double Peaks Mountain.

a Scale of one mile

A PLAN of PORT and RIVER
MERCURY,
call'd by the NATIVES, APURAGGE

$\frac{552}{5}$

Shelf Xx

Now some of the goblins had walking-sticks which they carried about with them and when we arrived at the bare dead trees where the shags roost at night and have their nests, the goblins lifted the walking-sticks up and pointed them at the birds, and in a short time thunder was heard to crash and a flash of lightening was seen, and a shag fell from the trees; and we children were terrified, and fled, and rushed into the forest, and left the goblins all alone. They laughed and waved their hands to us, and in a short time the bravest of us went back to where the goblin were, and handled the bird, and saw that it was dead. But what had killed it?

The Europeans shot twenty of these shags in all and broiled them over a fire for dinner. They had also brought pork and biscuits with them, which Te Taniwha said they shared with their Maori companions. He described the biscuits as a sweet, hard 'pumice-stone' and the pork (which the old people thought was either whale meat or human flesh) as so salty that 'it nipped our throats, and we did not care for such fat food'.[45]

Cook described the country to the east side of the Whitianga River (which he named the 'Mangroves River') as barren, but to the west well wooded, adding that they saw no cultivations anywhere around the upper harbour. On their way back to the ship his party stopped briefly at Whitianga paa, once Hei's own settlement.[46] Here the people of a small nearby village welcomed them, gave them a delicious meal of hot pipi and showed them the paa, which was in ruins at this time. Cook described the place in some detail:

> A little within the entrance of the river on the East side is a high point or peninsula juting out into the River on which are the remains of one of thier Fortified towns, the Situation is such that the best Engineer in Europe could not have choose'd a better for a small number of men to defend themselves against a greater, it is strong by nature and made more so by Art. It is only accessible on the land side, and there have been cut a Ditch and a bank raised on the inside, from the top of the bank to the bottom of the ditch was about 22 feet and depth of the ditch on the land side 14 feet; its breadth was in proportion to its depth and the whole seem'd to have been done with great judgement. There had been a row of Pickets on the top of the bank and another on the outside of the ditch, these last had been set deep in the ground and sloaping with their upper ends hanging over the ditch; the whole had been burnt down, so that it is probable that this place has been taken and distroy'd by an Enimy.[47]

It seems likely that this 'enimy' was a Tauranga chief called Tuuhopetiki, who had lived six generations before 1870, or a generation before Te Raatuu of Tuuranga-nui, and thus about a generation before the *Endeavour*'s visit to Whitianga. According to evidence from his descendants in early Land Court hearings, Tuuhopetiki came from Tauranga to fight the local people and destroyed Whitianga paa, killing its chief Koropiritoetoe. He was so struck by the beauty of Koropiritoetoe's wife, however, that he spared her life and married her, renaming himself Pirimaupakanga (Piri who won the battle) after her former husband, taking over his role as leader and settling down amongst her people in peace.[48] The bases of the palisades of this paa were rotting in the ground, indicating that it had been abandoned for perhaps fifteen to twenty years.

Every now and then during the two weeks that the *Endeavour* was anchored in Whitianga strange canoes came into the bay to visit the ship, and the local people reacted to these arrivals with mingled fear and caution. Early on 12 November two such canoes arrived, and eventually two of their crew were persuaded to come on board, where they exchanged goods with the Europeans. The local people brought out some 'large fish calld yellow tails' (kingfish), and after this the longboats went up the Puurangi River to collect oysters while Cook, Banks and Solander took two boatloads of men to the north side of the bay to visit the strongholds of Ngaati Hei for the first time. First they landed near a picturesque small paa built on top of an arched rock close to the mainland, which was cut off from it at high tide. This paa contained no more than five or six houses, fenced around with a palisade, and accessible only by one very steep and narrow path. The inhabitants of this paa, Te Puta-o-Paretauhinu,[49] invited them in most cordially. Since they were intending to visit a much larger paa nearby, they reluctantly refused, presenting the women of the paa with small gifts. This paa was sketched by Solander and, like the arched rock at Uawa, provoked raptures from Banks, who called it 'the most beautifuly romantick thing I ever saw'.[50]

'Spöring's Grotto' depicts the small paa on the arched rock Te Puta-o-Paretauhinu, seen on 12 November 1769. This paa was reported to hold five or six houses; the male figure waving a cloak in welcome is therefore somewhat out of scale. Note the canoes drawn up on the adjacent coast.

Wharretouwa.   W b N

These enlargements of Spöring's panorama of Mercury Bay show Wharetaewa (above) and Te Puta-o-Paretauhinu — 'Spöring's Grotto' (below).

Spöring' Grotto.
N W b W.

The Europeans now approached the larger paa, whose name they recorded as 'Wharretouwa' (Wharetaewa). About 100 of its inhabitants came down, waving, calling 'Horomai' (Haere mai!) and sitting near the beach to greet the Europeans. This was the first formal welcome the *Endeavour* party had received, and the calls were no doubt karanga (ritual calls of welcome), which would normally have initiated a ceremonial exchange of speeches. Instead the Europeans approached and gave the people gifts (including perhaps the calico, knives, axes and nails later mentioned by Te Taniwha[51]) and asked permission to visit their paa. These people (who must have been Ngaati Hei), 'with a great deal of good nature and friendship',[52] took them up to Wharetaewa and escorted them around, so that both Cook and Banks were later able to write very detailed descriptions of the place.

According to these accounts, Wharetaewa paa was built on a high promontory washed on two sides by the sea, with one side to the land being very steep and providing access by a path, and the other, flatter side being defended by a double ditch, a bank and two palisades. The outer palisade was built between the two ditches and sloped over the inner ditch, while the inner palisade was built on the bank, with space behind it for armed men to move about. The height from the bottom of the ditch to the top of the bank was twenty-four feet. Behind the inner palisade two fighting-stages, or 'Porava' (pourewa),[53] were built at right angles, one defending the double ditch and bank and the other straddling the entrance to the paa. These stages Banks measured at twenty feet six inches high, forty-three feet long and six feet six inches wide, and bundles of darts and stone were piled up on them ready for use. A strong palisade about ten feet high ran right around the paa, inside which the sloping ground was terraced into twenty divisions, each containing from one or two to twelve to fourteen houses. According to Cook, these terraces 'lay in the form of an amphitheatre'.[54] These terraces were individually palisaded round and linked by little lanes with narrow entrances that could easily be blocked up. Immense quantities of fernroot and dried fish were heaped up inside the paa, but there was no water supply except for a spring at the bottom of the hill, so that water had to be laboriously collected in gourds and carried up into the paa. Outside the palisades by the pathway were some houses and outworks, a number of large nets, and about half an acre of land planted in gourds and sweet potatoes, the only garden that the Europeans saw in the bay. At the foot of the promontory there were two steep rocks with houses defended by palisades on their summits.

Two young men showed the Europeans how they fought, one climbing up to the fighting stage and the other acting as an attacker on the outside of the ditch. They performed war dances and displayed their weapons, which included long spears (huata), fighting staffs (including taiaha, pouwhenua and tewhatewha), 'truncheons' (patu) of wood, bone and stone, and throwing spears ten to twelve feet long, barbed at one end. After this demonstration the *Endeavour*'s men returned to their vessel.

From 13 to 14 November the *Endeavour*'s men collected wild celery and boatloads of oysters from the beds at Puurangi, and Banks and Solander completed their botanical collections in the bay. On one of these expeditions Solander saw women catching crayfish by walking at mid-tide among the rocks, feeling with their feet, and then diving down to bring up enormous crayfish one after another.

During 14 November Cook went in the pinnace to a tiny island called 'Poegaig' (Poikeke) with two other small islands, 'Motueike' (Motu Heka — heka being a kind of cod)[55] and 'Motucara' (Motukorure)[56] nearby, where he visited a small palisaded village with fenced terraces inside. The people were hospitable and friendly. Cook observed that, as there was no fresh water on the island and it was only accessible from one side, it was probably a place of last retreat. It may have been on this day that Cook had an inscription cut into a tree near the Puurangi River marking the ship's name and the date of its visit. After displaying the English flag he 'took formal possession of the place in the name of His Majesty'.[57] It is unlikely that this act was legal, however, for Cook does not mention any discussions with the local people on this matter. The Earl of Morton's instructions recognised local inhabitants as the legal possessors of their lands, and the Admiralty instructions required their permission to be obtained before any valid act of possession could take place.[58]

Very early on the morning of 15 November 'the Indians came off in Their Canoes with their wives and Children'.[59] It was probably on this occasion that the young Te Taniwha visited the *Endeavour* with some of his relatives:

> After the ship had been lying at anchor some time, some of our warriors went on board, and saw many things there. When they came on shore, they gave our people an account of what they had seen. This made many of us desirous to go and see the home of the goblins. I went with others; but I was a very little fellow in those days, so some of us boys went in the company of the warriors. Some of my play-mates were afraid, and stayed on shore. When we got on board of the ship we were welcomed by the goblins, whom our warriors answered in our language. We sat on the deck of the ship, where we were looked at by the goblins, who with their hands stroked our mats and the hair of the heads of us children; at the same time they made much gabbling noise in talking, which we thought was questions regarding our mats and the sharks' teeth we wore in our ears, and the hei-tiki we wore suspended on our chests; but as we could not understand them we laughed, and they laughed also. They held some garments up and showed them to us, touching ours at the same time; so we gave our mats for their mats, to which some of our warriors said 'Ka pai', which words were repeated by some of the goblins, at which we laughed, and were joined in the laugh by the goblins.
>
> I and my two boy-companions did not walk about on board of the ship — we were afraid lest we should be bewitched by the goblins; and we sat still and looked at everything we saw at the home of these goblins. When the chief goblin had been away in that part of their ship which he occupied, he came up on deck again and came to where I and my two boy-companions were, and patted our heads with his hand, and he put his hand out towards me and spoke to us at the same time, holding a nail out towards us. My companions were afraid, and sat in silence; but I laughed, and he gave the nail to me. I took it into my hand and said 'Ka pai' ('Very good'), and he repeated my words, and again patted our heads with his hand, and went away. My companions said, 'This is the leader [captain] of the ship, which is proved by his kindness to us; and also he is so very fond of children. A noble man

206

— one of noble birth — cannot be lost in a crowd.' I took my nail, and kept it with great care, and carried it with me wherever I went, and made it fit to the point of my spear, and also used it to make holes in the side-boards of canoes, to bind them on to the canoe. I kept this nail till one day I was in a canoe and she capsized in the sea, and my god (the nail) was lost to me.[60]

According to Te Taniwha, an old chief (probably Toiawa) drew a chart in charcoal on the deck of the *Endeavour* during this visit, indicating the islands off Whitianga, Moehau, Hauraki and North Cape. He tried to explain to the Europeans about Te Reinga, the place where spirits leap off into the underworld, by lying on the deck as though he were dead and then pointing to its location at North Cape on the map. Te Taniwha said that the Europeans were mystified by this performance, but that Cook gave a handful of seed potatoes to this chief. These he took back to his own settlement at Hunua and planted, and they cropped profusely there for many years. According to Banks on the other hand, Toiawa told the Europeans that as soon as the *Endeavour* left the bay he and his people would have to return to their own paa, for the relatives of the man who had been shot by Gore had 'threatened to revenge themselves upon him as being a freind to us'.[61]

If Te Taniwha's account is accurate, there were no such reprisals, but when the *Endeavour*'s crew weighed anchor at seven o'clock on the morning of 15 November and sailed out of Te Whanganui-o-Hei they left a number of very uneasy people behind them. That night Pickersgill summarised his impressions of Whitianga:

The Inhabitants of this Part are very much markd on the faces and are very neat carvers and in every other respect as Described before except their canoes which are very bad — In this bay we likewise got a good deal of black and green jasper [probably black and green obsidian] which the Natives make use of as tools.

WHITIANGA TO HAURAKI
17–23 November 1769

According to Te Taniwha's account, the people of his party had lands at Whaka-tiiwai and Orere on the west coast of Hauraki Gulf, on the other side of the Coromandel Peninsula. As the *Endeavour* left Whitianga they also departed the bay to travel home, and up on the hills between Whangapoua and Waiau (Coromandel Harbour) they caught sight of the *Endeavour* for the last time.[62] As the ship sailed round the peninsula it caused consternation wherever it went. It is said to have been sighted off Whangapoua by a lookout posted on Tokatea (Castle Rock) by a party of Ngaati Maru who were working on a war canoe. They rushed to the crest of the rock to see it, and one man who had been using a prized greenstone adze called Kanohi Pounamu dropped it in a gully as he scrambled up the trail, and the taonga (treasured item) was never found again.[63]

At Moehau (Cape Colville) on the morning of 18 November the Europeans saw a crowd of people gathered on 'a remarkable bare point jutting far out into the sea . . . who seemd to take but little notice of us but talked together with much earnestness'.[64] It is said that the mauri placed on the small island off Moehau (at the tip of the Coromandel Peninsula) by the high priest of *Te Arawa* was one of the most sacred stones of all, so the people must have been concerned to safeguard so intensely tapu a place. After about half an hour two carved canoes put off from the shore, one carrying twenty and the other sixty-two people. These canoes reminded Parkinson of the carved craft that had visited Whitianga on 9 November, with the young man on board who was later shot by Gore. Their crews performed a war dance and threw stones at the ship and then dropped back, but soon returned to challenge the Europeans once more. Tupaia went to the poop and warned them not to attack. They replied that if only he and his companions would come ashore they would all be killed:

> Well; said Tupia [according to Banks], but while we are at sea you have no manner of Business with us, the Sea is our property as much as yours! Such reasoning from an Indian who had not had the smallest hint from any of us surprizd me much and the more as these were sentiments I never had before heard him give a hint about in his own case.[65]

Unimpressed by Tupaia's reasoning, the local people pelted the *Endeavour* again with stones, stopping only when a musketball was fired through the hull of one of their canoes.

On the night of 18 November the *Endeavour* anchored just south of Waiau (which must have been where Te Taniwha's party saw her from the hills), and the next morning cruised down the west coast of the peninsula towards the Waihou River. Two large canoes came out to the ship and several people came on board and told the Europeans that they knew Toiawa and called Tupaia by name. Te Taniwha's reminiscences do not mention Tupaia, but his fame had clearly spread and no doubt the people of Whitianga had reported his presence on the vessel. Shortly after this another canoe came from the west coast of 'Ooahaowragee'[66] (Hauraki), probably from Whakatiiwai or Orere, for it brought a young man who said he was Toiawa's grandson, thus suggesting that Toiawa was indeed an Uri-o-Pou from those places. Some of these people brought a large container of smoked eels as a gift 'which tasted very sweet and luscious', and Cook gave each of them a small gift in return before they left the ship. The *Endeavour* anchored off Te Puru on 19 November, near a coast that appeared to be well wooded and cultivated in places. The men went fishing with hook and lines that evening, catching large numbers of 'bream' (either snapper or tarakihi).

The next morning at daybreak, Cook, Banks, Solander and Tupaia took two boats to the bottom of the bay. Here they found a fine wide river, the Waihou, which Cook named the 'River Thames'. About a mile up this river they came upon a fortified village built on a bank of dry sand which was completely sur-rounded by deep mud. The inhabitants, who invited them in, had heard about the Europeans and mentioned Toiawa's name. A little further up the river they came to another village, with just a few inhabitants, and then about twelve to fourteen miles from the river mouth a great forest of kahikatea, one of which they measured at nineteen feet eight inches round. According to Banks, this was 'the finest timber my Eyes ever beheld', and they chopped down a young tree

(probably a matai) whose wood proved heavy and solid, too much so for masts but excellent for planking.[67]

On their way back to the ship the inhabitants of the fortified swamp paa, seeing them pass by on another channel, came out in their canoes and exchanged goods with the sailors in a very friendly fashion. It seems likely that their settlement was Oruarangi paa, which, with its companion paa Paa-te-rangi, was sited on the east bank of the Waihou at a place where the river divided into two channels around a large island.[68] If this identification is correct, the *Endeavour*'s men had seen one of the most famous of all Hauraki paa, talked of in many tribal stories and the site of a historic conflict between the original people of the district, Ngaati Hako (close relatives of Ngaati Hei, Ngaati Huarere and Te Uri-o-Pou), and Ngaati Maru, who traced their descent from the *Tainui* canoe.[69] Oruarangi and Paa-te-rangi were also the sites where thousands of artefacts — shell war trumpets, fish-hooks, tattooing implements, toggles, pumice bowls, stone tops, stone adzes, fern pounders, bone mere, bone needles, bird spear barbs, greenstone tiki and pendants — were fossicked out of the ground in the 1930s.[70] Many of these articles were eventually deposited in museum collections, where they provided a basis for the archaeological definition of 'Classic' Maori material culture.

This was Cook's longest excursion inland anywhere in New Zealand. During the afternoon the ebbing tide carried the two boats back out to the bay, but night overtook them and at midnight they moored the boats and slept almost until dawn. At 7 a.m. they got back to the ship, and soon after a fresh gale began to blow, making it impossible for canoes to come out to the ships. The next morning Cook took the pinnace to the western coast, 'but found thier neither inhabitants or any thing else worthy of note'.[71] Many canoes gathered around the *Endeavour*, their crews offering cloaks and weapons in exchange for paper and Tahitian barkcloth. When one of these people got on deck and stole a half-minute glass out of the ship's binnacle cupboard, Hicks had him seized and tied to the shrouds for a flogging. His companions began to call for their weapons, but Tupaia reassured them, saying that he would only be whipped, not killed, and they watched without resistance as he was given a dozen lashes with the cat of nine tails. After this an old man 'beat him very soundly and sent him down into the canoes'.[72] All the people left the ship and refused to come near it again.

The Tahitians had been appalled when they saw sailors flogged during the *Endeavour*'s visit, and the people of Hauraki must also have thought this was a barbarous punishment. A man's back was tapu, so to tie and whip him would not only hurt him physically, but also destroy his mana. Other people's taonga (prized possessions) were also tapu, however, and to be caught taking such items without permission was a cause for great shame. Probably this is why the people watched passively as this man was flogged and the old man beat him further before sending him away.

On 23 November the ship weighed anchor, and began to work its way in heavy rains and thunder out of the bay. During the next day Cook drafted his general comments on Hauraki, describing the 'River Thames' as running through flatlands, with hilly land to the east and low country to the west of the bay, all well wooded and apparently fertile. The land around the river mouth was covered with mangroves, but further inland swamps edged the river or 'immense woods of . . . stout lofty timber' grew right up to the banks. He observed posts stuck in the riverbed, probably for anchoring eel and lamprey traps, but few cultivations were visible. The population seemed to be sparse. The local people were strong, active and well built, and all of them painted their bodies with red ochre and oil from head to foot, something the *Endeavour* party had not seen before. Their canoes were numerous, large, well constructed and carved. Pickersgill was very impressed with the region: 'the country on each side appears very delightfull and fertile and seem'd to be very Popoluse'.[73] Certainly the archaeological indications are that in the recent pre-contact past, Hauraki had been a remarkably wealthy place.

Summary

THE *ENDEAVOUR* ACCOUNTS OF BAY OF PLENTY, WHITIANGA AND HAURAKI

The *Endeavour* evidence suggests that from Uawa to Opotiki in 1769, the local communities were generally prosperous and at peace. Cultivations were visible (and therefore accessible) from the sea, and many settlements were undefended. The local people do not seem to have been greatly concerned about raiders from the ocean, although they were quick to challenge the *Endeavour* as the ship sailed into their waters. From Opotiki to Hauraki, on the other hand, many formidable 'towns' and villages were seen, and the gardens must have been inland and possibly hidden away, for they were scarcely mentioned in the European accounts. Both tribal histories and comments reported from the people at Whitianga suggest that at this time of the year in this district, war was an ever-present possibility, and that warriors travelled considerable distances to fight. People also evidently travelled long distances to visit friends and kinsfolk, however, for marriages between partners from widely separated communities are commonly recorded in the tribal accounts.

Around Maketuu and Tauranga the great numbers of canoes and the scale of the fortified 'towns' suggested a dense and wealthy population, and Cook very wisely did not attempt a landing anywhere on this part of the coast (although his main reason for caution was no doubt the safety of the *Endeavour* and the dangers of a lee shore). The people of these places must have been able to gather formidable taua (war parties), for in 1828, when Tauranga was first visited by missionaries, 1,000 canoes were counted on the beach between Otumoetai and Te Papa, and they were told that the local people could muster 2,500 fighting men.[74] Hauraki had been able to muster an even larger force of 4,000 warriors,[75] although at the time of the *Endeavour*'s visit they saw relatively few people, settlements or canoes. It is possible that Hauraki was recovering from one of the episodes of destructive warfare recorded in its tribal histories, or that many of its fighting men were away on some expedition. In Whitianga Parkinson had been told by some men (very likely Uri-o-Pou from the encampment at Puurangi) that they were constantly being raided by people from the north, who 'plundered them of every thing they could find, and carried their wives and children away captives'.[76] Whitianga was the site of the Tahanga quarry, which supplied many regions with basalt for stone tools, and this may have made it particularly attractive to visiting war parties. The tribal histories from Hauraki also tell of Ngaapuhi (used here as a general term for tribes around the Bay of Islands and further north) raiding in Hauraki, and of revenge raids from Hauraki to the north, so it is possible that as Ngaapuhi were expanding from Hokianga into the coastal Bay of Islands at about the time of Cook's visit, they were simultaneously raiding south.

The Coromandel Peninsula, then, was strategically placed within easy sailing distance of a number of wealthy, densely populated districts, including the western Bay of Plenty, Thames and Northland, and it is small wonder that the people there seemed embattled at the time of Cook's visit. The Uri-o-Pou visitors in particular may have been expecting an attack, for dried shellfish and fernroot were classic siege foods, which presumably they were planning to take back to their own settlements. In Whitianga, too, domestic arrangements in groups under external threat were described for the first time. In the camp at Puurangi the warriors slept in a protective half-circle around their women and children; and the paa at Whitianga similarly protected its occupants, with its outer barriers of ditches, bank, palisades and fighting-stages arranged around the inner fenced compounds, where kin-groups lived in one to two, or twelve to fourteen houses (presumably individual families on the one hand, and extended families or subtribes on the other). The demonstration of fighting techniques at Wharetaewa paa was a graphic illustration of how disputes between descent-groups were sometimes resolved. The *Endeavour* accounts of life in this region were also informative about discipline and the resolution of arguments within descent-groups. It is clear that the theft of valuable items was regarded as a serious offence, and European reprisals were accepted with some tolerance. The story of two men fighting first with spears, and then with their fists under the watchful eye of their elders at Whitianga indicates a method for the settlement of disputes within the group, and the likelihood that violence within the community was kept carefully under control.

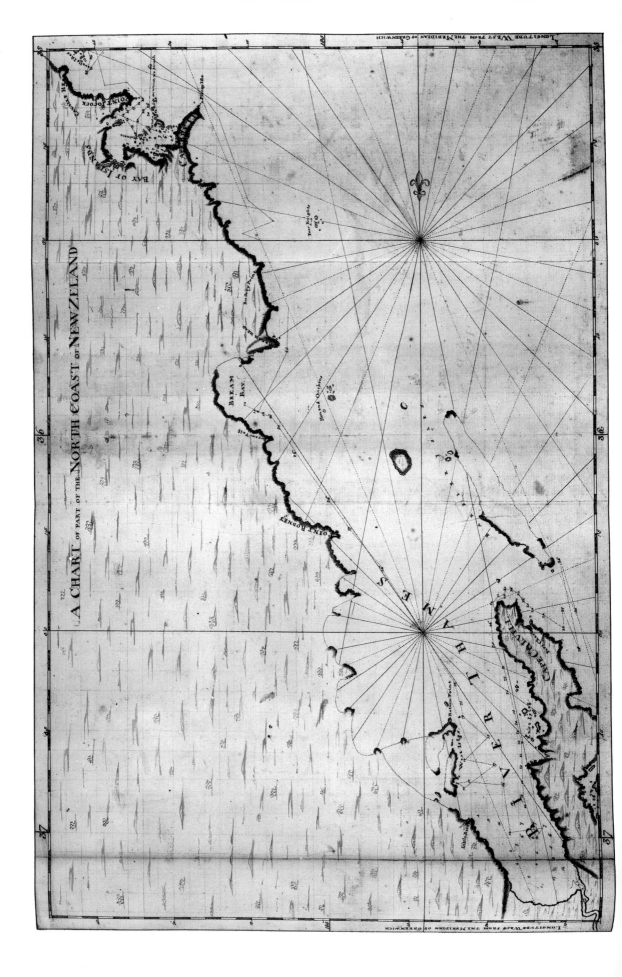

A CHART OF PART OF THE NORTH COAST OF NEW ZELAND

BAY OF ISLANDS

POINT POCOCK

CAPE BRETT

BREAM BAY

POINT RODNEY

RIVER THAMES

CAPE COLVILLE

Chapter Nine

HAURAKI TO THE BAY OF ISLANDS
24 November–5 December 1769

During 24 November the *Endeavour* sailed in a south-westerly gale past the Wai-temata Harbour. After coasting a sandy shoreline the ship anchored in a curving bay, which Cook named Bream Bay after a haul of about 100 'bream' (actually tarakihi[1]) caught by hook and line that evening. Cook noted a freshwater river to the south and described the land between Cape Rodney and Bream Head as 'low and wooded in tufts, and between the Sea and the firm land are white sand banks, we saw no inhabitants'.[2] During the night fires were seen inland, but no canoes came out to the vessel. At daylight on 25 November the *Endeavour* sailed further north, past scattered houses and three or four fortified villages with extensive gardens nearby. That evening seven large canoes came out to the *Endeavour* carry-ing about 200 people, who sang and danced as they paddled around the ship, some-times grinning and sometimes menacing the Europeans. Two men who said they had heard of the *Endeavour* came on board and were given gifts. The last place where the expedition had met with local people was at Hauraki, 200 kilometres to the south, which indicates how efficient and speedy the networks of communi-cation were at this time. Some of these people began to exchange goods with the Europeans, and Parkinson remarked on their tattoo patterns, which were very different from those seen to the south:

> Most of them had the figure of volutes on their lips, and several had their legs, thighs and part of their bellies, marked. One woman, in particular, was very curiously tataowed. The tataow on their faces was not done in spirals, but in different figures from what we had ever seen before.[3]

It seems that in 1769 there was a distinctive style of moko (tattoo) in the North, for over the next few days both Parkinson and Solander sketched a series of remarkable facial and body tattoos. These showed spiral patterns on the but-tocks and in one drawing, on the upper haunch; patterns like those used today in rafter paintings on thighs, neck, cheeks and foreheads; curious jagged marks

Opposite: *Cook's 'Chart of Part of the North Coast of New Zeland' shows the coastline from Mercury Bay to the Bay of Islands. The opening to the Waitemata Harbour was suspected but not detected.*

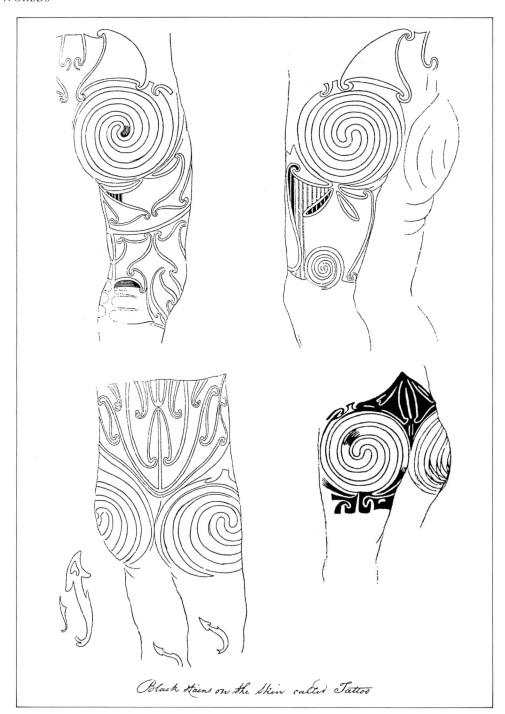

Black Stains on the Skin called Tattoo

Parkinson's 'Black Stains on the Skin called Tattoo' probably represents the tattoos on the crew of seven large canoes that came out to the Endeavour on 25 November, north of Whaangarei. Over the next few days, Banks and Cook remarked on the elaborate thigh and buttock tattoos of the local people — apparently a characteristic Northland style, with motifs reminiscent of koowhaiwhai rafter paintings.

between the eyebrows, and great curving stripes across the back or the chest. Banks also described thighs so closely tattooed that they looked like striped breeches,[4] commenting that:

> In this particular, I mean Amoco, almost every different tribe seem to vary their customs: we have some days seen Canoes where every man has been almost coverd with it, and at the same time others where scarce a man has had a spot except his lipps black'd, which seems to be always Essential . . .[5] The Buttocks which in the Islands was the principal seat of this ornament in general here escapes untouched: in one place only [i.e., the North] we saw the contrary: possibly they might on this account be esteemed as more noble, as having transferred the seat of their ornament from the dishonourable cheeks of their tail to the more honourable ones of their heads.[6]

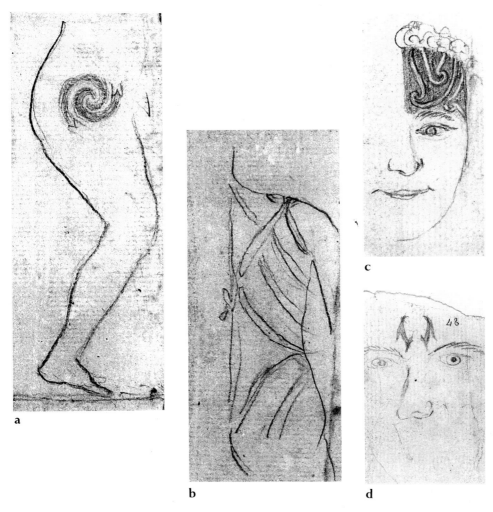

Spöring's sketches of tattoo designs seem also likely to have been made on the stretch of coastline between Whaangarei and the Bay of Islands. Note the spiral haunch tattoo (a), curving striped torso tattoo (b), forehead tattoo (c), and the jagged motifs between the eyebrows (later sketched as calf tattoos in Tokerau by Surville's artist) in (d).

After a series of exchanges the local people returned to their canoes and threw stones at the ship, shaking their spears. When trade resumed they began to keep gifts without giving anything back. One man kept a pair of black breeches without offering anything in return, and was fired on with smallshot. As soon as he saw another musket being aimed in his direction he tried to screen himself with his cloak (a traditional defence against darts and stones), and flung the breeches into the sea.

It is not easy to decipher what was happening in these transactions. Maori gift exchanges did not necessarily involve immediate return gifts, although a return was certainly anticipated at a later date. When trade items were held up by the Europeans, however, and items in the canoes were pointed at, the local people probably understood well enough that an immediate exchange was expected; and no doubt Tupaia was able to make this clear. In fact they usually completed some direct exchanges before someone decided to test the situation by withholding a return gift. At that point the Europeans generally decided that the locals were 'cheating', and reacted violently to discourage such 'dishonesty'. It is unlikely, however, that Maori people shared this perception of what was going on. It may be that they were simply trying to prolong the interaction by holding back return gifts to indicate that the exchange should be completed later on.

After this man was shot, several musketballs were fired, splintering one of the canoes, and the entire fleet rapidly retreated. As soon as they thought they were out of range the people began a haka. The great gun was fired over their heads, which so terrified them that they raced back to the land 'with the most Amaseing Expedition'.[7] Cannonfire must have convinced them that the Europeans could command both thunder and lightning, and hurl mysterious missiles great distances through the air.

The next morning (26 November) the ship was approached by two small canoes whose occupants said they had heard of the events of the night before. They came on board and exchanged goods very quietly. Shortly afterwards two large canoes arrived from a distance, and gathering up some other canoes they approached the *Endeavour* in a fleet carrying about 170 people. These canoes were seventy feet long, well carved and decorated, and their crews appeared prosperous. They carried many patu of stone or whalebone, and weapons made of whale's ribs (hoeroa) or imitations in wood, carved and ornamented with tufts of dog's hair. These people were dark-skinned and had tattoo patterns very like those described by Parkinson the day before. They would not part with their weapons or clothes for anything the Europeans had to offer, until finally one man held up a greenstone axe to exchange for cloth. Once he had the cloth in his possession, however, his canoe paddled away until a musketball was fired overhead, which brought him hastily back to the *Endeavour*'s side to return the cloth. After this his canoe returned to land. That afternoon the ship was off Raakau-mangamanga (which was now named Cape Brett after Rear-Admiral Sir Piercy Brett, the man who had signed Cook's secret Admiralty instructions). Cook jovially named 'Motugogago' (Motukokako) Piercy Island, both after the admiral and because it had a hole pierced through it. From this vantage point off the

Parkinson's portraits of two Maori women may also have been made in the Far North, since the neck tattoos are reminiscent of Northland moko patterns. The woman at left, however, appears to be wearing a feather hat of a kind described during the Endeavour *voyage only in Queen Charlotte Sound.*

southern end of the Bay of Islands they could see villages both on islands and the mainland, and a number of large canoes carrying several hundred people came out to the ship. Cook described their crews in his journal that evening:

> The people in these Canoes made a very good appearence being all stout well made men, having all of them their hair which was black Comb'd up and tied upon the Crown of their heads, and there stuck with white feathers, in each of the Canoes were two or three Cheifs and the habits of these were rather superior to any we had yet seen, the Cloth they were made on was of the best sort and cover'd on the out side with Dogs skins put on in such a manner as to look agreeable enought to the Eye. Few of these people were tattow'd or mark'd in the face like those we have seen farther to the south, but several had their Backsides tattou'd in much the same manner as the Inhabitants of the Islands within the Tropics.[8]

Parkinson added that although these people were reluctant to part with anything else, they had large quantities of fish, which they freely exchanged with the Europeans.[9] These amicable exchanges finally broke down when one man took goods without making a return, and an irate midshipman slung a fishing-line at him, hooking him on the buttock and heaving hard until the shank broke off, leaving the barb embedded in his backside.

The next day the ship sailed in light breezes past a cluster of islands (the largest being Motukawa-nui), where several canoes came out to offer 'cavalle'

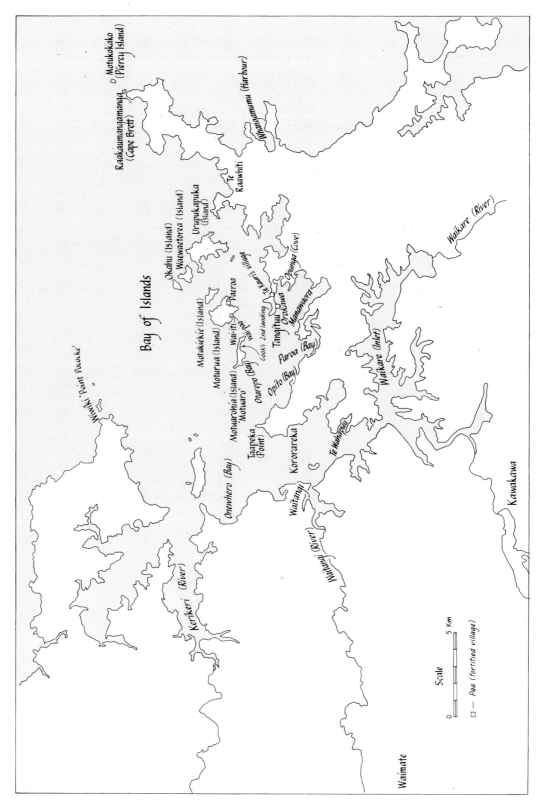

Motukokako (Piercy Island)

Raakaumangamanga (Cape Brett)

Whananamumu (Harbour)

Te Raawhiti

Waikare (River)

Okahu (Island)

Waewaetorea (Island)

Urupukapuka (Island)

Bay of Islands

Opunga (Cove)

Paeroa

Orokawa

Manawaora

Motukiekie (Island)

Kororipo [Te Puna] [Kororipo's village]

Cook's 2nd landing

Tangituu

Wai-iti

Moturua (Island)

Wairoa

Paroa (Bay)

Otarepo (Bay)

Opito (Bay)

Motuarohia (Island) 'Motuaro'

Waikare (Inlet)

Wiwiki 'Point Pococke'

Taapeka (Point)

Onewhero (Bay)

Kororareka

Te Wahapu

Kawakawa

Waitangi

Kerikeri (River)

Waitangi (River)

Scale

5 Km

0

□ — Paa (fortified village)

Waimate

fish (horse mackerel) for trade, inspiring Cook to name this group the 'Cavalles' (now the Cavalli Islands). These people soon began to chant and threw fish at the Europeans, pelting the ship with sticks and stones and behaving 'most abominably saucy'.[10] They would not stop this barrage, even when two musketballs were fired through one of the canoes. Cook climbed on to the poop of the *Endeavour*, where he was showered with rocks, so he aimed a musket loaded with smallshot at a warrior who was about to let fly, and fired. The man clapped his hands to his face and fell flat in his canoe. When another canoe raced forward with a load of stones, ready to pelt the ship, they too were fired on with small shot and quickly returned to land. The coast here was rocky, with rolling country behind the shoreline cultivated in places. Later in the morning several canoes came out but their crews simply looked at the *Endeavour*, and then went back to land. During that afternoon and the next day the wind turned foul. The ship was driven south and was forced to retrace its track. On the morning of 29 November the *Endeavour* bore up for 'a most spatious and well shelterd harbour, or rather collection of harbours almost innumerable formd by Islands',[11] finally coming to anchor in the Bay of Islands southwards and in the lee of Motuarohia (Arohia Island).

THE BAY OF ISLANDS
29 November–5 December 1769

The district the *Endeavour* was now about to visit was a bay with deeply indented inlets and a scatter of craggy islands, sheltered between two headlands, Wiwiki ('Point Pococke') and Raakaumangamanga (Cape Brett).[12] Its hinterland was dominated by a plateau where extinct volcanoes, some topped with fortifications, rose out of a sea of fern and stone-walled fertile gardens. A number of rivers linked the coastline with the interior, allowing canoes to travel some way inland towards Omaapere, a shallow lake whose waters teemed with freshwater fish and wild fowl. Alluvial soils had formed along the courses of these rivers, but much of the rest of the land in the bay was of a poor-quality clay, not very suitable for agriculture. From Omaapere to Hokianga on the west coast, and in a great sweep around Kawakawa and Waikare, grew dense forests of broadleaf trees overshadowed by rimu, totara, kahikatea and miro, with kauri on the ridges. Much of the rest of the countryside had been cleared of forest by fire and felling, and those areas were covered in fern and scrub, with patches of bush in the gullies.

The *Endeavour* had anchored off the south-east end of the bay, which apart from the volcanic plateau was the other main area of good soils in the district. The rolling hills of this region, both on the mainland and the offshore islands, had been largely cleared, providing good sites for slope gardens. Spectacular views in all directions, productive fernlands, forests supplying building materials, berries and birds, long twisting coastlines with headlands for fortifications and sheltered bays for canoe landings and villages made this an irresistible site for settlement.

Opposite: *Map of the Bay of Islands in 1769 and 1772.*

Out to sea the waters were also rich in resources. Dense beds of cockles, rock oysters, scallops and horse mussels grew around the coastline. In sheltered bays flounder, paakati (spotties), rays and dogfish lived on the muddy sea floors, while snapper, trevally and parore swarmed in feeding migrations up the sea channels. Out in mid-water jack mackerel, kahawai and warehenga (kingfish) preyed on schools of yellow-eye mullet, piper and anchovies, and along the semi-exposed rocky edges of the outer islands lived numerous blue maomao, poorae, large snapper, red moki and huge haapuku (groper). Dolphins and humpbacked whales sported near the mouth of the bay, and every now and then the waters were seized with a silvery convulsion of fish, as swarms of krill and small fish were chased to the surface by schools of kahawai, trevally or mackerel, preyed on in their turn by kingfish, mako shark and even marlin, while snapper flicked in to seize the scraps, and seabirds screamed and darted down from the sky.[13]

According to tribal traditions, the bay was one of the very early sites of Polynesian settlement in Aotearoa. The people of the area traced their origins from Kupe, the voyager who first circumnavigated the North Island. Kupe had landed at Hokianga on the west coast opposite the bay, leaving behind two taniwha (fabulous monsters) as its headlands. Other founding ancestors included Tuputupuwhenua (in some accounts Kupe's son), a taniwha who burrowed beneath the land from Hokianga across to Kerikeri in the Bay of Islands;[14] Nuku-tawhiti and Ruaanui, who came from Hawaiki to search for Tuputupuwhenua on the *Maamari*.[15] The tribes of this region also traced lines of descent from Toi through Te Awa-nui-a-Rangi and Puhi-moana-ariki of *Maataatua* canoe, which linked them to the Bay of Plenty, and from Tamatea of the *Takitimu* canoe, which linked them to Tauranga and the East Coast.[16]

At about the time of the *Endeavour*'s arrival, the political situation in the region was extremely volatile. Ngaati Awa, the descendants of Te Awa-nui-a-Rangi, had almost been pushed out of the area around the bay although remnants of that population still remained; and Ngaapuhi, the descendants of Puhi-moana-ariki and his grandson Raahiri, were expanding into the bay from their strongholds in Hokianga and inland. Ngaati Pou lived at Ohaeawai, on the south-east islands, and also to the north at Whangaroa, and Ngaati Miru and Te Wahine-iti (possibly sub-divisions of Ngaati Pou[17]) controlled the Waimate-Kerikeri district. According to some accounts, Ngaati Pou were an offshoot of the Uri-o-Pou people at Hauraki who, after being defeated in an ancient battle,[18] had fled to the north, where their ancestress Marohawea married a man from Hokianga called Tuuiti. The Raawhiti district was occupied by Ngati Wai, a tribal grouping that included Ngare Raumati,[19] and all of these groups were vying with each other for access to the rich resources of the bay and for political control.[20]

As the *Endeavour* sailed south past the mouth of the bay on 28 November several very large 'heppa' (paa) were visible inland, 'one the largest we have seen' (probably Rangihoua).[21] The ship entered the bay on 29 November and at eleven o'clock anchored hurriedly in shoal waters, over a sand bank that extended south-westward from Motuarohia and is clearly marked in Pickersgill's chart of the bay. The master and the mate were sent in the pinnace and the yawl to take soundings, and Molyneux fired warning shots at a canoe whose crew tried to board his boat. At two o'clock as the *Endeavour* was shifted several hundred metres eastwards between Motuarohia and the Orakawa Peninsula on the mainland to the south, canoes put off from every point, until soon there were thirty-seven large and small canoes carrying 300 to 400 people crowding around the ship. Not long before this arrival, it is said that a Ngaapuhi seer named Te Matapoo had prophesied that 'in the future a fair-skinned people will arrive, whose axes will have no lashings, and whose canoes will be coated and painted with gum' ('taihoa ka tae mai teetahi iwi, he iwi kiritea; ko ngaa toki, he toki kaha kore; ko ngaa waka, he waka puni, he mea pau ki te ware').[22] Perhaps some of these inquisitive spectators were checking the accuracy of his predictions.

Cook remarked that many of these people had previously come out to the ship while it was at sea. He invited several chiefs on board, where he presented their leader with broadcloth and his companions with nails and other small items. These people were generally cautious in their behaviour towards the Europeans and seemed very afraid of their guns, although one man while pressing noses with Parkinson managed to pick his watch from his pocket. Their chiefs presented gifts of large mackerel to the *Endeavour*'s people, which as Parkinson appreciatively commented 'ate very deliciously'.[23] It is said that this meeting was one later described by Patuone, a famous Ngaapuhi chief, to a European friend in an account that was subsequently published by John White:

> One day, before Patuone and Nene were old enough to bear weapons, Tapua (their father) and his people were out netting fish at the sea coast at Matauri. They had caught many fish, when the ship appeared beyond Motukokako. Then Tapua and his people left their nets and went in their canoes — Te Tumuaki, the canoe of Tapua and his crew of eighty, Harotu, the canoe of Tuwhare and his crew of forty, Te Homai, the canoe of Tahapirau and his crew of forty, and Te Tikitiki, the canoe of Ne' and his crew of sixty — to look at that ship.
>
> They went to see the vessel because such a ship had never before visited that place. When the canoes were near the ship, the people on board beckoned to them to come closer. So Tapua's men conferred together, and when they had come to a decision, the canoe commanded by Tapua went alongside the ship. Then they threw the fish from the canoe up on to the ship, as an offering to those strange sea-goblins (tupua maitai). The goblins were pleased with the fish, and shouted with joy as they gathered them up.
>
> After this Tapua went on board the ship, and the leader of the goblins presented him with a red garment and with the salt flesh of an animal. It was cooked flesh, with both fat and lean meat on the one piece. Tapua took it and gave it to his son and daughter, Patuone and Tari. Food of this kind had not previously been known to the Maori; they found it to be sweet, and very good.[24]

Tapua, the father of Patuone and Waka Nene, was a 'renowned warrior chieftain of capacious mind'[25] who was also the priest for his people in the Bay of Islands, and his deeds are recorded in many tribal stories. His two sons later became famous leaders of the Ngaati Hao sub-group of Ngaapuhi, their mother's people at Hokianga on the west coast.

According to the *Endeavour* journals, when most of the Europeans went

NWbW   *Here we landed.*

below to eat their dinner after the meeting with these people, a chief signalled to the assembled canoes and they surged ahead of the ship to seize the anchor buoy, ignoring a burst of smallshot that was fired overhead. A gun loaded with ball was fired at them and 'one of their most active leaders' was wounded in the arm. They then seized the buoy, which they had hauled into a canoe and threw it back into the water. To add to the chaos a cannon was fired. The cannonball skipped along the surface of the water and rolled inland, chased by the crews of two or three canoes who rushed ashore to find it. Tupaia called out to these people and after a while they all came back to the ship.

Cook now decided to land on Motuarohia (variously named 'Motuaro', 'Motu-haro' or 'Cumattiwarroweia' in the journals). At three o'clock he, Banks, Solander and an armed party of marines boarded the pinnace and the yawl and were rowed to Otarepo Bay on the western end of the island.[26] No canoes accompanied them, which Banks thought was a good sign. As soon as they landed on the beach, however, all of the canoes paddled at high speed to the island, and people landed on either side of the cove, running concealed behind its rocky outcrops and suddenly approaching in great numbers — at least 500 to 600 people — 'in a confused Stragleing manner'[27] to surround the Europeans. Cook and Banks marched to meet them, and although the warriors had their weapons raised they did not attack. A line was drawn on the sand to indicate that the warriors must not pass it, but other men had already appeared behind the Europeans and mingled with them.

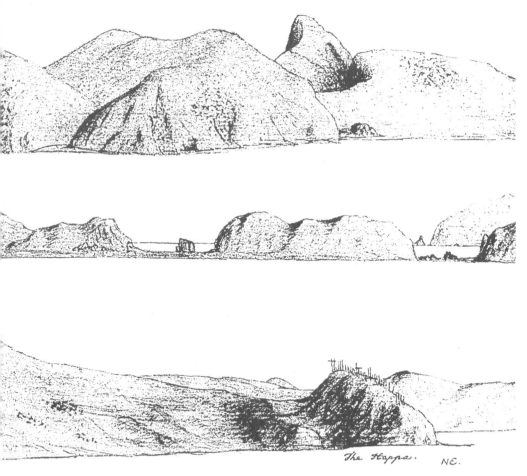

The Heppa. NE.

Spöring's three-part coastal view of 'Motuaro' (Motuarohia) in the Bay of Islands was sketched on 29 November 1769, on the day of the Endeavour *party's dramatic landing on the island. Otarepo Bay is marked 'Here we landed', and the headland paa on the south-eastern end of the island is called 'The Heppa'.*

The massed warriors now began to chant a war song, and three men stepped up to each of the boats and tried to haul them ashore. Cook fired a musket loaded with smallshot at their leader, and Banks and two others fired at warriors who began to attack the *Endeavour* party. The warriors fell back in confusion, but were soon rallied by a man who ran forward waving his patu and calling out to his companions. Solander shot him with smallshot and he fled. The whole group of warriors moved up onto high ground, where the Europeans shot at them with muskets loaded with ball. Several other attacks were repelled before the local people were put to flight by a roaring carronade broadside from the *Endeavour*. The officers on board, seeing their companions in danger, had warped the ship side-on so that its cannons faced the island, and fired three four-pounders, which narrowly missed their aim, the cannonballs flying over the warriors' heads.

According to Cook, only one or two people were wounded with smallshot in this affray, 'for I avoided killing any one of them as much as possible and for that reason withheld our people [presumably the marines] from fireing'.[28] Magra gave a graphic shipboard version of the danger that Cook and his party had been in:

Captain Cook, with several gentlemen, attended by a party of marines, landed on one of the islands, and incautiously suffered themselves to be surrounded by a great body of Indians, a party of them at the same time marching down to the boat to cut off their retreat. These motions being immediately seen on board the ship, a spring was put on her cables, and a broadside brought to bear on the island, and several great shot fired a little over them: our people on the island were, at this time, separated in small parties, none consisting of more than three or four, and so closely prest that they found it impossible to use their arms; and the number of their enemies was so unequal, that they every minute expected death.

In the consternation and disorder occasioned by their dangerous situation, several muskets were confusedly discharged, but fortunately they did no mischief. The natives were, however, greatly terrified by the passing of our cannon balls a little above their heads, and immediately dispersed, at a time when they might with the greatest facility have destroyed every one of our people on shore.[29]

Once the local people had retreated, the Europeans put down their muskets and gathered wild celery. Cook went over to a cave where he had seen people hiding and persuaded some of them to come out. One was the old chief (perhaps Tapua) who had boarded the ship that morning, with his wife and brother — an interesting indication that women could be present on such war-like occasions. The old chief told them that another brother of his had been struck by smallshot in the attack and asked if he would die. The Europeans gave him gifts and tried to reassure him, showing him both smallshot and a musketball and telling him that his brother had only been hit by the first, but that if his people attacked again they would be shot with musketball 'which would infallibly kill them'.[30] Parkinson also reported that 'O te Goowgoow' (possibly Te Kuukuu), a chief's son whom he later sketched, had been wounded in the thigh during the affray.

After this exchange the Europeans went back to their boats and rowed around to another bay on the island, where the inhabitants 'were as meek as lambs'.[31] Cook, Banks and probably Solander climbed a high hill (possibly Paa Hill in the centre of the island) to view the landscape, which Banks later graphically described in his journal:

The bay we were in was indeed a most surprizing place: it was full of an innumerable quantity of Islands forming as many harbours, which must be as smooth as mill pools as they Landlock one another numberless times. Every where round us we could see large Indian towns, houses and cultivations: we had certainly seen no place near so populous as this one was very near us.[32]

More wild celery was collected, rather to Banks's disgust, since he had found no new plants in this place. Accompanied by some local people, they then returned to the boats and were rowed back to the *Endeavour*, where the crews of nine or ten canoes had come on board during the afternoon and traded peacefully.

Early in the morning of 30 November the anchor was raised in the hope of putting out to sea, but the wind died, so Cook sent the master and the mate with two boats to sound 'up the harbour' instead. Three sailors had gone ashore on Motuarohia the night before to steal sweet potatoes from a garden, and Cook ordered them punished with a dozen lashes each, confining one man because he

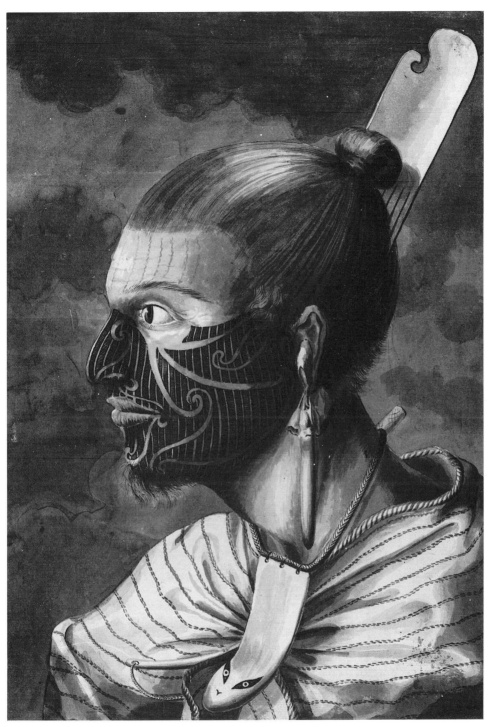

A pen and wash portrait of 'Otegoowgoow' (Te Kuukuu) by Parkinson. This chief's son was shot in the thigh during the affray on Motuarohia on 29 November 1769. Note his magnificent northern-style facial tattoo, the large comb in his top-knot, the greenstone ear-pendant, and the rei puta neck ornament in the shape of a whale's tooth with stylised eyes near the tip.

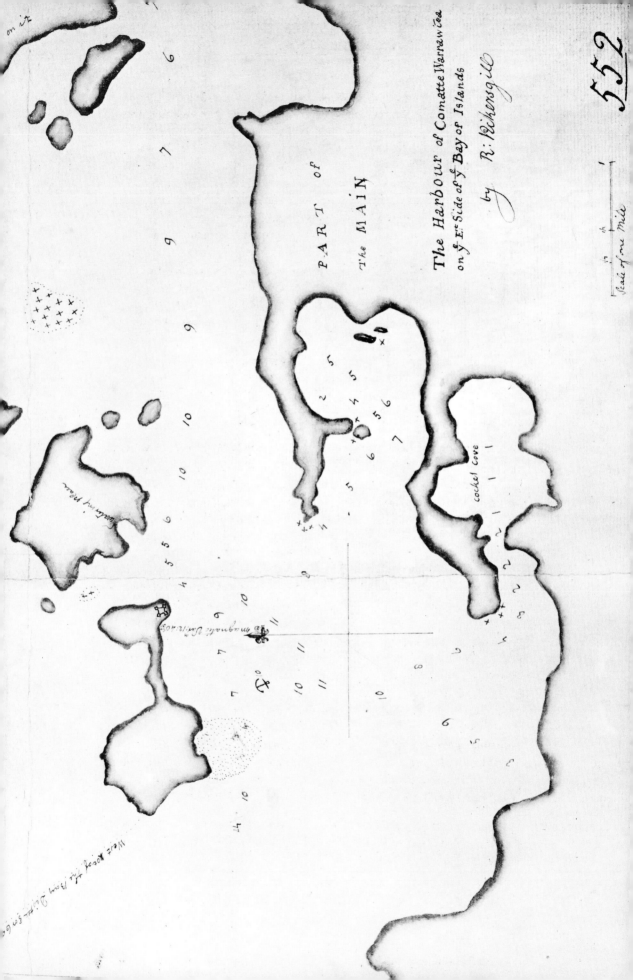

insisted there was nothing wrong with what he had done. A number of canoes came out to the ship but their crews were reluctant to trade for anything the Europeans had to offer. The Tahitian cloth that had been so greatly valued further south was not much sought after in the North. According to Banks, 'they have for some days told us they have of it ashore and shewd us small peices in their Ears which they said was of their own manufacture, this at once accounts for their having been once so fond of it and now setting so little value upon it'.[33] It seems that aute was a specialist product of the North, cultivated and made into cloth in these parts and traded south, where it was greatly esteemed as a rare reminder of the ancestral homelands. Aute grew wild in Anaura and Uawa, but apparently it was not cultivated in either of those places. Their visitors also told them that the man whom Cook shot in the face on 27 November had died, for three smallshot had struck his eye and penetrated to the brain. These people were evidently very cautious in their behaviour towards the Europeans, because as Banks remarked:

> They Always after one nights consideration have acknowledgd our superiority but hardly before: I have often seen a man whose next neighbour was wounded or killd by our shot not give himself the trouble to enquire how or by what means he was hurt, so that at the time of their attacks they I beleive work themselves up into a kind of artificial courage which does not allow them time to think much.[34]

At eleven o'clock a gun was fired as a signal to recall the boats, and at midday they returned to the ship. According to Magra, during that day

> we landed on an island at the west side of the bay where we found good water and cellery in great plenty; and also a town where we drew our nets, but with very bad success, though the Indians at the same time caught large quantities. Their success was occasioned by watching the approach of the fish who came in large shoals; together with a difference in the form of their seines, which were two or three fathom in depth, and of proportionable length.[35]

This expedition is probably the same as one referred to by Cook, Banks, Forwood and others, towards the south-west of the bay that afternoon. Fresh water and celery was found 'on the mainland' (probably at Opito Bay near Russell because a row of soundings on Pickersgill's chart headed in that direction and this bay was clearly marked on Cook's working chart of the region[36]). Cook described the place as a small sandy cove with two small streams, several gardens planted with kuumara and yams, and plenty of trees. The people were extremely friendly and polite, but the Europeans had to cut their visit short because it began to pour with rain.

The next morning the weather was miserable and windy, so when Cook sent a boat ashore to Motuarohia to cut grass for the *Endeavour*'s sheep, Banks and Solander stayed on board. By now Banks was beginning to draw some general conclusions about Maori life on the basis of his experience in the places they had

Opposite: *Pickersgill's chart of 'The Harbour of Comatte Warrawiea' describes Urupukapuka as 'an Isl^d with a great Deal of Cultivated Lands & Townes on it', and marks the fortified paa on Motuarohia and the 'watering place' at Waipao Bay on Moturua.*

already visited. On this day he mused about the subject of cannibalism:

> It is now a long time since I have mentioned their custom of Eating human flesh, as I was loth a long time to beleive that any human beings could have among them so brutal a custom. I am now however convincd and shall here give a short account of what we have heard from the Indians concerning it. At Taoneroa the first place we landed in on the Continent the boys who we had on board mentiond it of their own accords, asking whether the meat they eat was not human flesh, as they had no Idea of any animal but a man so large till they saw our sheep: they however seemd ashamd of the custom, saying that the tribe to which they belonged did not use it but that another very near did. Since that we have never faild wherever we went ashore and often when we conversd with canoes to ask the question; we have without one exception been answerd in the affirmative, and several times as at Tolaga and today the people have put themselves into a heat by defending the Custom, which Tubia who had never before heard of such a thing takes every Occasion to speak ill of, exhorting them often to leave it off. They however as universaly agree that they eat none but the bodies of their enemies who are killd in war, all others are buried.[37]

Banks's statement is an interesting reflection of the interplay of cultural attitudes during the *Endeavour*'s meetings with Maori people. It is clear that he was horrified even by reports of eating human flesh. His reluctance to believe that such a custom could exist can be traced to a natural scientist's scepticism about mediaeval beliefs in baby-eating witches and cannibalistic 'opposite-footers'. Cook on the other hand, as we have seen, was matter-of-fact about the practice, considering it to be the consequence of 'custom' rather than of savagery or vice. Tupaia, like Banks and perhaps influenced by him, thought that cannibalism was appalling and told the local people to give it up. The young fisherboys in Tuuranga-nui had excused the custom by saying that while their tribe did not practise it, other tribes did; and the people at Uawa and in the Bay of Islands angrily defended the practice (which expiated offences against mana by eating the bodies of enemies, just as in Europe crimes were expiated by torturing the bodies of offenders) against both European and Tahitian criticism.

The next day it was still raining and Banks and Solander went ashore on Motuarohia and got drenched. On 3 December the weather cleared. A number of canoes visited the *Endeavour* that morning, and, according to Parkinson, one very large canoe, which had evidently come from outside the bay, 'had eighty people in her, most of whom paddled; the chiefs wore garments of dogs skins, and were very much tatowed, the men upon their hips and the women on their breasts, necks and bellies'.[38] This description suggests that women as well as men paddled this craft. Banks and Solander went ashore on the 'Continent' (for Banks still cherished the idea of Terra Australis), possibly at Paroa Bay, since a row of soundings heading towards 'Cockel Cove' (in Paroa) was recorded on Pickersgill's chart.[39] Here they found few plants and fewer people, but those brave souls who had stayed behind to meet them took them to their village, which was an undefended settlement at the end of an inlet. One old man showed them a set of tattooing instruments that, according to Banks, was exactly like those they had seen at Tahiti. They also met the man who had been shot with

Above: *Spöring's accurate sketch of the fortified paa at the south-eastern end of Motuarohia in the Bay of Islands shows palisades, high structures, low buildings with gabled and curving roofs on the slopes, and rounded hummocks, which were probably the net shelters mentioned in the journals. Note also the small coastal settlement with what seem to be stepped tracks leading to it.*

Below: *John James Barralet's later rendering of the same paa on Motuarohia was based on Spöring's sketch, but adds a canoe in the foreground.*

musketball during the attempt to seize the anchor buoy on 29 November. His wounds, through the fleshy part of his arm and on the chest, were healing well, although they had no dressings on them and were open to the air. Banks showed him a musketball and told him that he was lucky to be alive.

That afternoon Banks and Solander went with Cook to Moturua, an island north-east of the *Endeavour*'s anchorage. Cook described it as about three miles in circumference, with about forty to fifty acres of root crops (according to Banks, 'sweet potatoes, yamms & c') planted around a village. The island was well inhabited and it has been suggested that the village mentioned here was Paeroa paa, a fortified headland that was to figure largely in the accounts of Marion du Fresne's expedition three years later.[40] This seems unlikely, however, for Banks commented that the people here 'livd in the same peaceable stile' as those they had visited earlier in the day, which suggests that like the village they had visited that morning, their settlement was undefended. Cook also described several streams of excellent water in Waipao Bay, a location on the island marked as a 'watering-place' in Pickersgill's chart.

December the fourth was the *Endeavour*'s last day at anchor in the bay. Early in the morning the boats were sent to Moturua to collect water and cut grass. At about breakfast time 'Our Old Man' (probably Tapua once again) came on board with his brother, who had been wounded with smallshot in the skirmish on 29 November. His thigh had been struck by at least 100 shot, but the wounds were healing well and seemed to give him little pain, despite the fact that no dressings had been applied.

After breakfast Cook, Banks and Solander went with the pinnace and the yawl to the mainland. As they rounded a point (probably Orokawa Peninsula in Manawa-ora Bay, from the soundings on Pickersgill's chart) the inhabitants of a large fortified paa (probably Tangituu) waved out for them to land. They went ashore and the people quickly traded almost a boatload of fish to the Europeans, then showed them their village, which was a 'neat compact place and its situation well choose'. There were two or three other settlements nearby, which they decided not to visit, and the people took them to their gardens, which were very extensive and planted with yams, taro and kuumara. This must have been near the coast, for 'after having a little laught at our seine, which was a common kings seine' the people also showed them one of their own nets, whose depth Banks estimated at five fathoms (nine metres) and its length at not less than 400 to 500 fathoms (730 to 1,140 metres). Reports of such vast seine nets are not uncommon in the accounts of early European visitors, at least in the Bay of Islands and the Bay of Plenty, and a great deal of labour must have been required both to make and to work them. Not surprisingly in light of the superb local fisheries, Banks commented that 'fishing seems to be the cheif business of this part of the countrey; about all their towns are abundance of netts laid upon small heaps like haycocks and thatchd over and almost every house you go into has netts in it making'.[41] After this the people took them to see six cloth plants or 'aouta' (aute), which Banks identified as the same species that grew in Tahiti and which the locals cherished as a great rarity.

Later that afternoon they made another expedition to 'a very distant part of the bay', probably in the vicinity of Urupukapuka (again on the evidence of a line of soundings in Pickersgill's chart), where they landed near a little fort built on a small rock, surrounded by sea at high tide and accessible only by a ladder. An old man met them while all his companions ran away, but he was reluctant to take them to the paa:

> He said there was his wife but if we would promise to practice no indecencies towards her he would accompany us; this we most readily did and he was as good as his word. The ascent was so difficult that tho there were stepps and a pole we found it dangerous enough. When we came up there were in it 3 women who on our first coming cried, but presents soon put them in a better humour. There were in all only 3 houses, but the situation as I have before describd was so steep that the inhabitants of them might easily defend themselves against almost any force that could be brought against them.[42]

The old man's uneasiness suggests that there had already been 'indecencies' perpetrated on local women during the *Endeavour*'s stay. No doubt the sailors had also found local women who were willing to sleep with them, in which case venereal infections were probably passed on. The women in this instance may have been crying with fear, or more likely they were weeping in memory of the dead, an element in any Maori ceremonial of encounter. If these were ritual tears, the women would have been extremely surprised to be given gifts to cheer them up.

At four o'clock the next morning the *Endeavour*'s anchors were raised and the ship set sail, followed for a time by 'Several Large Canoes full of Indians who all Seemd very Sorry at our Departure from them'.[43] The wind dropped, and that evening the *Endeavour* was becalmed for a time and almost driven on to the rocks of Okahu Island by an eddying tide. The pinnace was lowered in a panic and got stuck on one of the guns, but eventually it reached the water and took the *Endeavour* in tow, guiding it out of the bay. The ship was so close to the land at one moment that Tupaia was able to talk with the people on the shore. At eleven o'clock that night the ship grounded briefly on a sunken rock (Te Nunuhe), bringing Cook in an instant on deck in his drawers. The *Endeavour* immediately came off, however, and early the next morning they reached the safety of the open sea.

Summary
THE *ENDEAVOUR* ACCOUNTS OF THE BAY OF ISLANDS

The topography of the south-east end of the bay was well described in the *Endeavour* journals, charts, sketches and coastal profiles. Not surprisingly, since Motuarohia was so often visited and the ship was anchored off its coast, this island featured in a number of the sketches and coastal views. There were three consecutive views of the island by Spöring, which showed the island largely cleared of forest except in the gullies and in patches around the coast. The headland paa on the south-eastern end of the island appeared in one of these coastal views and was also very accurately sketched by Spöring. This drawing was

copied later in the voyage by Parkinson in less accurate pencil and pen-and-wash sketches. Spöring's pencil sketch showed palisades and high structures — perhaps a fighting stage and racks for drying fish — and buildings that appeared to have both gabled and curving roofs. At the base of the paa in Parkinson's pencil sketch, hummocks were shown that were probably the net shelters described in the journals, with steps leading down to them. When Parkinson redrew this sketch in pen and wash, he added warriors armed with spears on the fighting stage and outside the palisades, canoes out on the water and up on the beach, and two shelters placed on a ledge on the cliffs. Parkinson also produced idealised compositions in pen and wash based on the eastern lagoon on the island, and 'Paa Hill' on its northern cliffs,[44] showing barrel-vaulted houses on raised ground above the water, one on Paa Hill with its entrance to the side and a window on the end wall, and the other (by the lagoon) with a window above the door. These were presumably sketched during one of the frequent expeditions by the ship's boats to the island.

Pickersgill's chart of 'The Harbour of Comattewarrawiea [possibly Ko Matewarawaia] on ye east Side of ye Bay of Islands' marked the headland paa on Motuarohia, and also lines of soundings indicating routes of exploration taken by the ship's boats; a watering-place on Moturua; and Urupukapuka, which was described as 'an island with a great Deal of Cultivated Lands and Townes on it'. Cook's 'Chart of Part of the North Coast of New Zeland' marked settlements to the north of Poraenui Point on the Purerua Peninsula, on the northern end of Urupukapuka Island, on Motukiekie, on Moturua and two on the Raawhiti Peninsula.

It seems probable that the people the Europeans met at settlements on the islands and near Te Raawhiti were either Ngare Raumati or Ngaati Wai, since they controlled the district at that time. The *Endeavour* was being visited all the time by people who must have come from every part of the bay, and no doubt also from inland Hokianga, Whangaroa and other parts of the North.

Cook said of the resources and the population at Te Raawhiti at this time:

> As this was not the season for roots, we got only fish, some few we caught our selves with hook and line and in the Saine but by far the greatest part we purchass'd of the Natives and these of Various sorts, such as Shirks, Stingrays, Breams, Mullet, Mackarel and several other sorts; their way of catching of them are the same as ours, (viz) with hooks and lines and with saines; of these last they have some prodigous large made all of a Strong kind of grass . . . The Inhabitants of this Bay are far more numerous than at any other place we have yet been in and seem to live in friendship one with another altho it doth not att all appear that they are united under one head. They inhabited both the Islands and the main and have a number of Heppa's or strongholds.[45]

Opposite: *These 'Views in New Zealand', by Parkinson, have been identified by Jeremy Spencer (1983: pp. 271–72) as (above) an idealised rendering of the eastern lagoon on Motuarohia, and (below) as a stylised depiction of Paa Hill, viewed north-eastwards, on the northern cliffs of Motuarohia. Note the barrel-vaulted roof on the houses.*

From these and other comments it seems that the population of the Bay of Islands was both large and wealthy, and this was demonstrated by the number and size of their settlements, their fleets of large carved canoes (one canoe carrying eighty-two people), and their numerous fine cloaks of dogskin, prestige weapons, elaborate tattoos and huge nets. The charts include comments on the density of population, towns and cultivations, and the journals record encounters with large fleets of canoes (thirty-seven on one occasion). About 500 to 600 fighting men combined in one strategically planned ambush on Motuarohia, four times the size of any previous group to have jointly confronted the *Endeavour* party. The *Endeavour* explorers did not go inland, probably thinking it too dangerous, so they did not see some of the largest paa and expanses of gardens in the region. The combination of fertile volcanic soils, large rivers with alluvial soils nearby, rich fisheries both in the bay and inland along the rivers and in Lake Omaapere, productive fernlands and areas of forest made this one of the most desirable and densely occupied areas (apart from the Bay of Plenty) in the country.

As in Tuuranga-nui, another wealthy place, descent-group politics in the Bay of Islands were volatile and complex, and Cook's comments on this topic were perceptive. A number of major confederations were competing for control, and occupied choice territories for as long as they were able. In both of these places, rich resources meant increased competition amongst kin-groups and their leaders, and this in its turn made it difficult for any one group to achieve lasting dominance over the region. The people of the bay were wealthy and powerful, much given to raiding other districts in their formidable fleets of carved canoes, as well as each other, but even here the Europeans looked in vain for the 'kings, princes and governors' of the Unknown Southern Land. It is, however, likely that these groups joined forces in the face of the European arrival, for Cook reported that they seemed to 'live in friendship one with another' and a party of 500 to 600 warriors probably represented an alliance of some kind. Tribal accounts, though, suggest that this was a temporary state of affairs.

At the Bay of Islands the Europeans noted a distinctive tattoo style and were shown tattooing instruments; they visited a number of settlements and gardens, which they barely bothered to describe; they were impressed by the efficiency of Maori fishing and the vast scale of their nets; and came close to being killed en masse on Motuarohia. They described the courage of local warriors, who rallied even in the face of musketfire, and remarked on the rapid healing of wounds caused by both smallshot and musketball. Nevertheless, this visit to the bay by the *Endeavour* expedition, with their high priest Tahitian interpreter, shipload of scientists and hand-picked crew of sailors, many of whom by now could speak a little Maori, was ethnographically a wasted opportunity. Unlike Monkhouse's journal, or earlier entries by Banks and Parkinson, there were few detailed descriptions of particular people, villages or gardens. One is led to conclude that by this time, after nine weeks off the coast of New Zealand, the novelty of Maori life was beginning to wear off.

Chapter Ten

From Bay of Islands to Admiralty Bay

6 December 1769–31 March 1770

After leaving the Bay of Islands on 5 December, the *Endeavour* sailed north in difficult offshore winds past the Cavalli Islands, where several canoes came out to trade, soon leaving them behind as the ship picked up a southerly breeze. On 9 December they sighted Tokerau, 'a deep Bay'[1] that Cook named Doubtless. Later that morning, as the ship lay becalmed off the Karikari Peninsula, five canoes came out but kept at a safe distance. After these canoes returned to land six more canoes visited the ship, whose crews told the Europeans that they had heard of their guns and traded them quantities of various fish and garments. Tupaia asked these people about their country:

> They told him that at the distance of three days rowing in their canoes, at a place called Moorewhennua [Muriwhenua], the land would take a short turn to the south-ward and from thence extend no more to the West. This place we concluded must be Cape Maria Van Diemen, and finding these people so intelligent desird him to enquire if they knew of any Countries besides this or ever went to any. They said no but that their ancestors had told them to the NW by N or NNW was a large countrey to which some people had saild in a very large canoe, which passage took them up to a month: from this expedition a part only returnd who told their coun-treymen that they had seen a countrey where the people eat hogs, for which animal they usd the same name (Booah) as is usd in the Islands. And have you no hoggs among you? said Tupia. — No. — And did your ancestors bring none back with them? — No. — You must be a parcel of Liars then, said he, and your story a great lye for your ancestors would never have been such fools as to come back without them. Thus much as a specimen of Indian reasoning. After much conversation our freinds left us but promisd to return at night and bring with them fish, which they did and sold it very reasonably.[2]

This story of a canoe voyage to a large country north-north-west of Muri-whenua, where the people had 'booah', or pigs, is intriguing, because the only

Overleaf: *'A Chart of the N⁰ Pᵗ of New Zealand taken in His Majˢ bark Endeavour', by Richard Pickersgill, extending from the 'Cavally Islands' to Cape Maria van Diemen ('Discover'ᵈ Anno 1642 by Captⁿ Abel Janson Tasman'), shows Rangaunu Harbour as 'An Entrance into the Land' and describes Mount Camel ('Campbell') as 'a Sandy Hill seen on Both Sides'.*

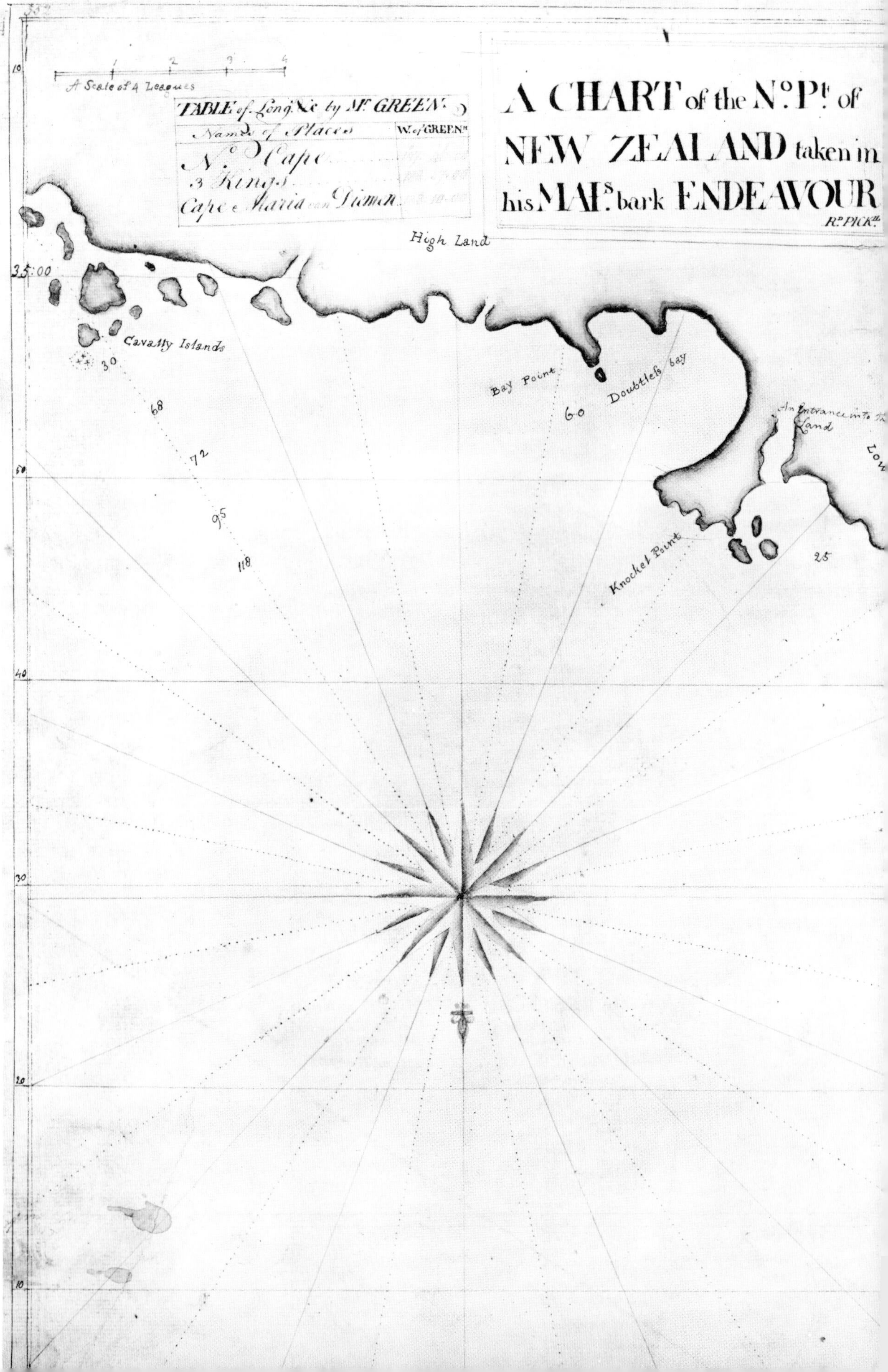

A Scale of 4 Leagues

TABLE of Long. &c by Mr. GREEN.

Names of Places	W. of GREEN.
No. Cape	
3 Kings	
Cape e Maria van Dieman	

A CHART of the No. Pt. of NEW ZEALAND taken in his Majs. bark ENDEAVOUR

Ro. PICK.

High Land

Cavalty Islands

30

68

72

95

118

Bay Point

60

Doubtless bay

An Entrance into the Land

Low

Knockel Point

25

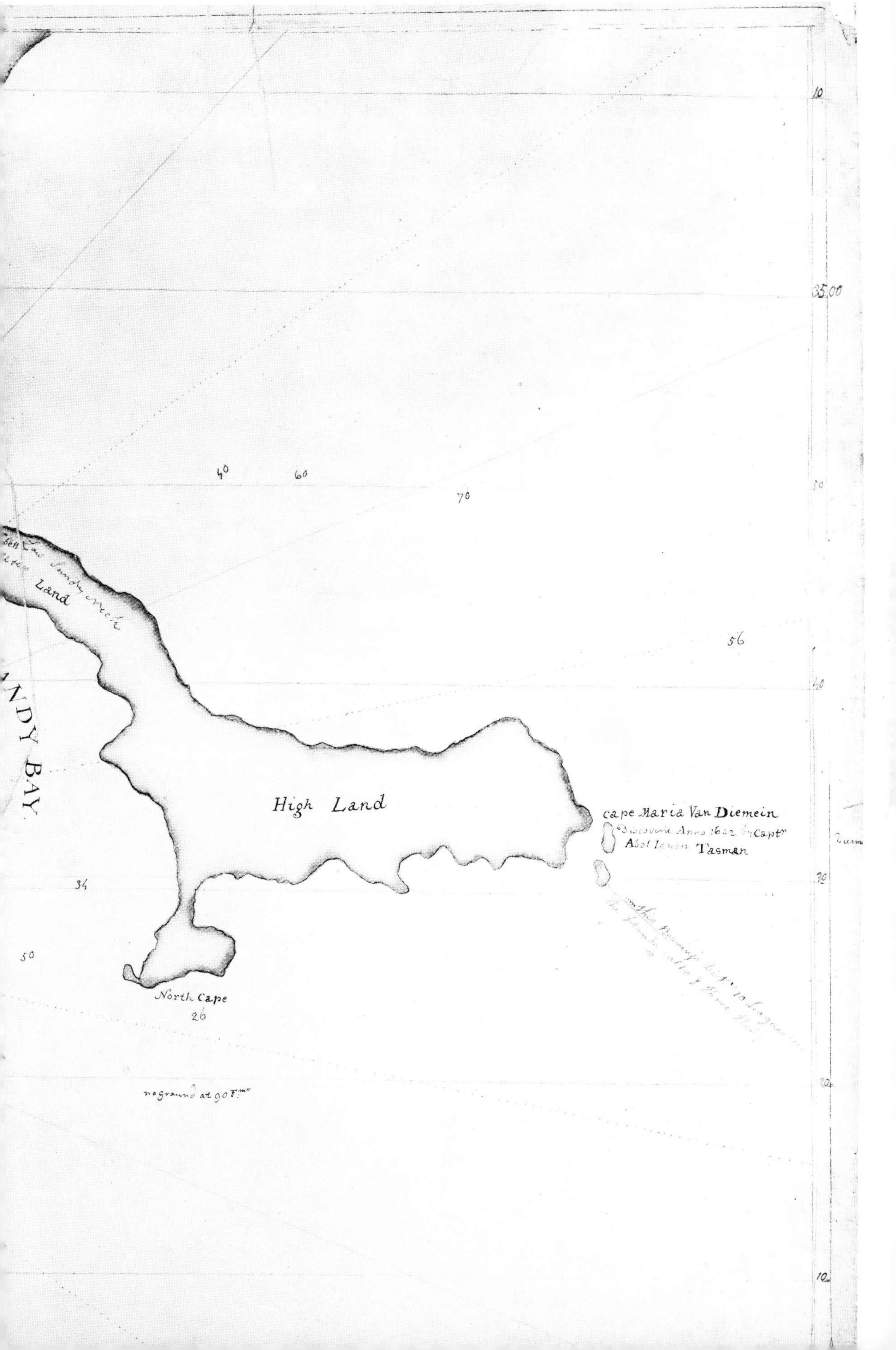

10

35,00

20

40

60

70

56

30

NDY BAY

Sandy Neck

Land

High Land

cape Maria Van Diemein
Discover'd Anno 1642 by Capt:
Abel Janson Tasman

34

50

North Cape
26

no ground at 90 F.ms

10

large island in that direction is New Caledonia. Pigs were evidently not introduced there until Cook's visit in 1774, however,[3] although there were pigs (boa) in Vanuatu at this time. Tupaia was openly sceptical of this story, and in his dismissal of the local people exhibited a Polynesian chauvinism that was to become increasingly evident during the rest of the voyage.

The next morning the *Endeavour* sailed past the entrance of Rangaunu Bay, northwards to Houhora Harbour. At the entrance to Houhora was a high hill that they named Mount Camel. As the ship was abreast of Mount Camel a large fire was seen on the Karikari Peninsula, and Cook described the landscape as follows:

> No Country upon Earth can looke more barren than the land about this Bay doth, it is in general low except the mountain just mentioned and the Soil to all appearence nothing but white sand thrown up in low irregular hills lying in narrow ridges parallel with the Shore . . . The first ridge behind the sea beach is partly cover'd with shrubs Plants &c but the second ridge hath hardly any green thing upon it which induced me to think that it lies open to the western Sea. As barren as this land appears it is not without inhabitants, we saw a Village on the side of Mount Camel [according to Wilkinson, 'several Hipas'] and a nother on the Eastern side [Karikari] besides five Canoes that were pulling off to the ship but did not come up with us.[4]

During the next few days the *Endeavour* tacked on and off the coast in unfavourable winds, leading Banks to comment that 'we turnd all day without loosing anything, much to the credit of our old Collier, who we never fail to praise if she turns as well as this'.[5] On 14 December they sighted land, which Cook thought must be the northern end of the country, for the ship was rolling in huge westerly swells. On 16 December, as the *Endeavour* was driven out to sea by the westerlies, the *St Jean Baptiste*, a French ship that was also on a voyage of discovery, was blown in the opposite direction around North Cape. By an extraordinary coincidence, the first two European ships to visit New Zealand since the mid-seventeenth century sailed past each other in a gale, unaware of each other's presence.

Two days later the *Endeavour* approached Murimotu (the island off North Cape), where some people were sighted and a paa that Banks thought was surrounded by a mud wall. On 24 December Manawataawhi (the Three Kings Islands) came into view. The wind had died down so Banks went out in a rowboat to shoot gannets, which they ate the next day as a Yuletide 'goose pie'.

> 25 Christmas Day. Our Goose pye was eat with great approbation and in the Evening all hands were as Drunk as our forefathers usd to be upon the like occasion.[6]

The *Endeavour* finally turned south on 1 January 1770. During the next two weeks the ship cruised the west coast of the North Island, keeping a respectful distance from the land. Near Taranaki mountain (whose name Molyneux recorded as 'Ohacabeetee', Parkinson as 'Whakapeete' — maybe a confusion with Kaapiti Island — and which Cook named Mount Egmont) they sighted a few houses and a fire, but otherwise no signs of life were seen. On 14 January the ship sailed past Tasman's 'Murderers Bay', sighting a fire on a small island in Admiralty Bay, and on 15 January the *Endeavour* entered Totara-nui (Queen Charlotte Sound) for its last and longest stay in any New Zealand harbour.

TOTARA-NUI (QUEEN CHARLOTTE SOUND)
15 January–6 February 1770

Totara-nui was a maze of deep bays, inlets and islands carved out of the north-eastern end of the South Island. Its waterways wandered far inland amongst steep hills and headlands, which in 1770 were covered with a rain forest of podocarps and hardwoods, although the wind-blown hills around the outer sound were quite barren. Kereruu (wood pigeons), kaakaa (parrots), parakeets, weka, tui and bellbirds lived in the bush, where kiekie and mamaku (tree-fern with its edible root) and tawa, titoki and miro trees, supplejack and fuchsia (with their edible berries) grew in abundance. The landscape was rugged and magnificent, with high hillsides covered in fern above the treeline, alternating with sheltered valleys and gullies where root crops had once been grown.[7] Groves of karaka and ngaio grew along the coast with thickets of maanuka on the promontories, and flocks of seabirds including oystercatchers, herons, shags, petrels, dottrels and little blue penguins wheeled or waddled about the rocky shoreline.[8]

Totara-nui's wealth, however, came from the water, with its coastal beds of cockles, mussels, oysters, scallops, and in some places paaua and crayfish, and inexhaustible supplies of fish, including flounder, mackerel, kahawai, haapuku, barracouta and shark.[9] The creeks that ran down the hills had inanga (whitebait), eels and freshwater crayfish, and fishing of various kinds was the main industry in this water-bound place.

Totara-nui had a complex and ancient history, for it had long been a staging point in migrations from the North to the South Island. The safest and quickest passage across Raukawa-moana (Cook Strait) was the sea-path from Owhariu at the southern end of the North Island to Arapaoa (now Arapawa Island) at the entrance to the Sounds, using Ngaa Whatu (the eyes — the Brothers Islands) as a guide. According to tribal accounts, Ngaa Whatu, placed there by Kupe, were so tapu that only a tohunga or a very high-born person could look at them, and the eyes of the paddlers had to be covered with karaka leaves as they made the crossing, guided by a tapu steersman.[10]

South Island traditions speak of a number of ancestral canoes, including *Taki-timu*, *Te Waka-o-Aoraki*, *Te Waka-huruhuru-manu*, *Arai-te-uru*, and *Uruao* (which was brought by the ancestor Raakaihautuu, who dug many of the South Island lakes with his digging stick). Raakaihautuu's people were the Waitaha, an industrious, peaceful folk who were said to have brought kauru (cabbage trees), aruhe (fernroot) and mamaku with them, as well as many species of birds.[11] They were expert in sacred matters, and most of the South Island rock drawings, executed in a black paint made of the soot of monoao wood, rautawhiri berry juice and weka oil, were attributed to them by later tribes.[12] Another ancient people were the Rapuwai, big clumsy men said to be up to eight feet tall, who were sometimes thought to have come with Rakaihautuu on the *Uruao* canoe.[13] This canoe is reported to have visited the Sounds, then called Te Tauihu o te Waka (the prow of the canoe) after one ancient description of the South Island — Te Waka-o-Aoraki (the canoe of Aoraki).[14]

Kupe also came to the Sounds, chasing a giant octopus all the way from Hawaiki, and this visit was remembered in many local place-names — Arapaoa, after the downward path of his whalebone weapon as he hit the creature's head; Whekenui (big octopus), the bay in Tory Channel where it was killed; Ngaa Whatu-kai-ponu, where the octopus's eyeballs were placed as a witness to Kupe's deed; Kura-te-Au (Tory Channel), where the current ran red with the octopus's blood; Te Mimi-o-kupe (Kupe's urinating), a spring on Wedge Point in Totara-nui; and many other names.[15]

Map of Totara-nui (Queen Charlotte Sound) in 1770.

Successive waves of migrants from the North Island — Ngaati Mamoe, Ngaati Tuumatakokiri, Ngai Tara-pounamu, the Ngaati Kurii of Ngai Tahu, Ngaati Kuia and Ngaati Apa moved through the Sounds, each leaving groups of descendants behind them. By 1769, according to some accounts, Totara-nui was dominated by the latest arrivals, a party of Rangitaane[16] led by Te Rerewa, who had exchanged his lands around Lake Wairarapa for a fleet of seven canoes in which to make the migration across Raukawa-moana. Like all of the previous northern migrants apart from Ngaati Kurii, Rangitaane traced their ancestry from the *Kura-haupo* canoe[17] and Te Rerewa also had close kinship links with Ngai Tara-pou-namu. These kinship ties and a network of intermarriages among the previous occupants of the area may explain why at the time of the *Endeavour's* arrival, each of the tribes mentioned above evidently still had settlements in the various inlets and bays of the Sounds, and according to an early Ngaati Kuia source, Ngaati Apa occupied the outer reaches of Totara-nui.[18]

As the *Endeavour* sailed into Totara-nui on the morning of 15 January 1770, a current swept her towards some rocks at the north-west entrance. The boats were lowered and towed the ship clear, watched by a male sea lion that had surfaced nearby. According to Banks:

> the land on both sides appeard most miserably barren till we got pretty deep in when it began to mend by gradual degrees. Here we saw some canoes who instead of coming towards us went to an Indian town or fort built upon an Island nearly in the middle of the passage, which appeard crowded with people as if they had flockd to it from all parts; as the ship aproachd it they wavd to us as if to invite us to come to them but the moment we had passd by they set up a loud shout and every man brandishd his weapons which none of them were without. The countrey about us was now very fertile to appearance and well wooded so we came to an anchor about long cannon shot from the fort, from whence 4 Canoes were immedi-ately dispatched to reconoitre I suppose and in case they were able to take us, as they were all well armd. The men in these boats were dressd much as they are rep-resented in Tasmans figure, that is 2 corners of the cloth they wore were passd over their shoulders and fastned to the rest of it just below their breast, but few or none had feathers in their hair. They rowd round and round the ship defying and threat-ning us as usual and at last hove some stones aboard which we all expected to be a prelude of some behaviour which would oblige us to fire upon them; but just at this time a very old man in one of the boats express'd a desire of coming on board, which we immediately encouraged, and threw a rope into his canoe by which she was immediately hawld up along side and the old man (contrary to the opinion of all the other Indians who went so far as to hold him fast for some time) came on board, where he was received in as freindly a manner as we possibly could and had many presents given to him, with which he returnd to the canoes who immediately joined in a war dance — whether to show their friendship or enmity it is impossible to say, we have so often seen them do it on both those occasions.[19]

The local people had congregated at a paa on the southern end of Motuara Island, with sentinels posted at 'the point of the bay'[20] (possibly Cape Jackson), for Magra reported that an armed watchman at that location was twice relieved as the *Endeavour* sailed into the Sound. He added that as the ship passed Motuara, 'an old Indian, in a singular kind of habit, came down to the waterside, attended by several of his countrymen, and there performed some mysterious rites, with a matt and feathers, &c'[21] — no doubt a tohunga who was carrying out rituals in an attempt to avert harm from these extraordinary visitors. The four canoes that had been sent from the paa had about sixty-five warriors on board, and the courageous old man who boarded the vessel (later identified by Banks as 'Topaa', or 'Topea' in the Banks vocabulary[22]) must have been an important elder, for Magra said that he was 'apparently of some distinction among them'. As he came on board Tupaia greeted him with a hongi. His companions in the canoes laughed uproariously and then eagerly boarded the vessel themselves.[23]

Later that afternoon the local people returned to Motuara while the *Endeavour*'s men collected wood and water at Meretoto (which Cook named Ship Cove), shot numerous shags, gathered mussels and other shellfish and made a huge haul of 300 pounds of fish in the ship's seine. Parkinson commented that some of these fish weighed up to twenty-one pounds each, and he later listed the fish that they caught in the Sounds as cuttlefish (probably octopus); large bream (probably snapper) some of which weighed twelve pounds and tasted like fine salmon; small gray 'breams' (probably tarakihi); small and large barracouta (makaa); flying gurnards (kumukumu); horse mackerel; dogfish (pioke); soles and dabs (flatfish of various kinds); mullet; drums (sciaenidae); scorpaenas, or rockfish (scorpionfish); colefish (blue cod — raawaru); and 'the beautiful fish called chimera' (elephant-fish).[24]

Despite this splendid variety of sealife, Banks and Solander were disappointed with Meretoto, for they found only two new species of plants there. Cook, on the other hand, was delighted with the place, for it had a fine stream of excellent water, and 'as to Wood the land here is one intire forest'.[25]

At daybreak on the morning of 16 January, three canoes brought about 100 people (including women) from the paa to the *Endeavour*. Banks commented that the presence of women was 'a sign tho not a sure one of peacable inclinations',[26] which suggests that women had been among some of the groups that had previously confronted the *Endeavour*. The ship had been careened for scrubbing, and when the longboat put off with a load of casks these people tried to follow it in their canoes. A musket loaded with smallshot was fired at them, whereupon they immediately returned to the vessel. They now offered 'stinking fish' (probably dried shark) in exchange for European goods, and traded peacefully until two men were barred from coming on board by the master. They threatened him with their spears and were physically forced back into their canoes. Shortly after this another man tried to snatch some goods from the deputy purser, and then threatened him with his patu. As soon as Cook saw this he fired a musket loaded with duckshot, wounding the man in the knee and on the foot. According to Magra:

> His wounds producing a plentiful hemorrhage, [the warrior] bathed them in salt water, and the pain being acute, he angrily threw the fish which he had sold, and for which he had been paid, into the sea. The Indians who were in the other canoes, did not appear surprized either at the report of the gun or the wounds it had made, though they all paddled round and examined them; nor did the

wounded Indian retire, but wrapping himself up in mats he continued about the ship several hours.[27]

After this the people paddled about the ship for a time, eventually approaching the stern, where they talked with Tupaia 'about their antiquity and legends of their ancestors'.[28] They apparently told him that they had never either seen or heard of a ship such as the *Endeavour* visiting their coastline before. This is not surprising, since these were probably quite recent migrants to the area who were unlikely to have heard of Tasman's encounters with Ngaati Tumatakokiri over a century before. Some of this group, both men and women, wore headdresses made of bundles of black feathers that had been rounded and tied to the top of their heads, a dress item the Europeans had not seen before and which Parkinson depicted in a number of sketches.[29] These head-dresses have sometimes since been described as 'mourning hats', although similar feather head-dresses were also worn in historic times as a mark of high rank.

That afternoon Cook, Banks, Tupaia and others went into the pinnace to a cove about a mile to the north, where they saw a woman's body (which at first they mistook for a seal) floating in the water. They rowed past it to the shore, and as they landed all but one member of a small family group that had been cooking on the beach ran off into the woods. After a while these people returned, except for an old man and a child, who stayed in sight amongst the outermost trees. The Europeans examined an earth oven on the beach, which later proved to contain a dog's carcass, and a large number of food baskets nearby. In one of these they saw two bones that had been almost picked clean, which on closer inspection seemed to be bones from a human forearm. Cook traded for one of these bones, and in consternation asked the family members if they were not dog bones. In answer one of them took hold of the flesh of his own forearm and pretended to chew it. As Banks later commented:

> Tho we had from the first of our arrival upon the coast constantly heard the Indians acknowledge the custom of eating their enemies we had never before had a proof of it, but this amounted almost to demonstration: the bones were clearly human, upon them were evident marks of their having been dressd on the fire, the meat was not intirely pickd off from them and on the grisly ends which were gnawd were evident marks of teeth, and these were accidentaly found in a provision basket. On asking the people what bones are these? they answerd, The bones of a man. — And have you eat the flesh? — Yes. — Have you none of it left? — No. — Why did you not eat the woman who we saw today in the water? — She was our relation. — Who then is it that you do eat? — Those who are killd in war. — And who was the man whose bones these are? — 5 days ago a boat of our enemies came into this bay and of them we killd 7,[30] of whoom the owner of these bones was one. — The horrour that apeard in the countenances of the seamen on hearing this discourse which was immediately translated for the good of the company [perhaps by Tupaia or by Parkinson, who later wrote a vocabulary of words from Queen Charlotte] is better conceivd than describd. For ourselves and myself in particular we were before too well convincd of the existence of such a custom to be surprizd, tho we were pleasd at having so strong a proof of a custom which human nature holds in too great abhorrence to give easy credit to.[31]

Banks as a natural scientist was gratified to have proof of the practice of cannibalism, but the seamen were horror-struck to find that the old seafaring tales of 'anthropophagi' (people-eaters) at the edges of the known world were true. Superstition was rife amongst sailors, and fears of witches (who were thought to eat human flesh) were still commonplace. Even the better-educated officers became obsessed with cannibalism during their stay in the Sounds, and often wrote about the custom in their journals. Wilkinson commented, 'These Poor Wretches are at war even with their Next Dore Nabours,' and Pickersgill wrote:

> we saw one of the Bodys and two arms with flesh upon them which we saw them eat this is the first Proof Possitive we have had of the Inhabitants being CANIBALS and I belive these are the only People who kill their fellow creatuers Puerly for the meat which we are well Assured they do by their laying in wait one for another as a sportsman would for his game and they carry this detestable crime so far as to glory in carrieing in their ears the Thumbs of those unhappy sufferrs who fell in their way.[32]

Magra, on the other hand, seemed delighted to be able to contradict those armchair philosophers in Europe who denied that the custom had ever existed. He also made it clear that local people were far from apologetic about the practice:

> Perhaps they thought, like a celebrated philosopher, that it was as well to feed on the bodies of their enemies, (for by their own accounts they eat no other) as to leave them to be devoured by crows. It is however certain that they had no belief of any turpitude in this practice, because they were not ashamed of it; but, on the contrary, when we took up an arm for examination, they imagined us to be desirous of the same kind of food, and with great good nature promised that they would the next day spare a human head ready roasted, if we would come or send to fetch it. Some gentlemen, who never left their own homes, have ventured, on the strength of speculative reasoning, to question the veracity of those travellers who have published accounts of cannibals in Africa and America; treating as falsehoods every relation, which, from their ignorance of human nature, appears to them improbable: but let them not indulge the same freedom on this occasion; the fact will be too well attested to be rendered doubtful by their visionary impertinent objections.[33]

Banks added that the floating corpse of the woman they had seen had been sunk in the sea with a stone by her relatives, a custom of the Sounds, but it had somehow got loose and floated back to the surface, where it was claimed by her 'brother' the next day. Not surprisingly, perhaps, the cove where these observations were made was named 'Canibals Cove', and the sailors called the Sound 'Cannible Harbour'.

Early the next morning Banks was woken by a marvellous carillon of birdsong from the land:

> This morn I was awakd by the singing of the birds ashore from whence we are distant not a quarter of a mile, the numbers of them were certainly very great who seemd to strain their throats with emulation perhaps; their voices were certainly the most melodious wild musick I have ever heard, almost imitating small bells but with the most tuneable silver sound imaginable to which maybe the distance was

no small addition. On enquiring of our people I was told that they have observd them ever since we have been here, and that they begin to sing at about 1 or 2 in the morn and continue until sunrise, after which they are silent all day like our nightingales.[34]

After this avian concert a small canoe came out from Motuara to visit the ship, carrying among others Topaa and a woman whose husband had been recently killed and eaten at a place to the east (presumably somewhere on Arapaoa Island). Her arms, thighs and legs were scarified in mourning. The conversation turned to the topic of cannibalism, and one of the men on this canoe traded Banks a human forearm bone, biting and chewing on it 'in such a manner as plainly shew'd that the flesh to them was a dainty bit'.[35] Tupaia again interrogated these people about the custom:

> But where are the sculls, sayd Tupia, do you eat them? Bring them and we shall then be convinced that these are men whose bones we have seen. — We do not eat the heads, answerd the old man who had first come on board the ship, but we do the brains and tomorrow I will bring one and shew you. — Much of this kind of conversation passd after which the old man went home.[36]

This group also told the Europeans that they were expecting an imminent attack 'over the hills' (probably from Port Gore) by the relatives of the canoeload of people that they had killed. This suggests that they had congregated in the paa on Motuara and posted sentries for that reason, and not because of the *Endeavour*'s arrival.

Most of the sailors were kept very busy during their stay at Totara-nui, scrubbing the ship on both sides and treating the timbers with a 'mixture of Tallow and Venetian red' (an interesting parallel with the Maori practice of painting their war canoes with mixtures of oil and red ochre), caulking with oakum and tarring any gaps, repairing the casks, ironwork and rigging, collecting wood, water and green vegetables, drying out the powder and baking the ship's biscuits to kill the innumerable weevils that infested them.

Only Cook and Banks's entourage had much opportunity to explore the Sounds. On 18 January Cook, Banks and Solander went for an expedition in the pinnace along the western coastline, where they described the landscape as densely wooded, although the eastern coast seemed quite bare. On turning the point into Waatapu (Resolution Bay)[37] they came across a man fishing in a small canoe and rowed beside him for a while. He showed them his hoop-net, which was seven or eight feet in diameter, extended by two hoops and baited with paaua in the bottom. This net was lowered to the sea bottom and when a sufficient number of fish were attracted by the bait, he pulled it up very gradually, so that the fish were scarcely aware of what was happening. Banks commented that they had seen many such nets in almost every place that they had visited. During this excursion the Europeans shot many shags in Waatapu (which they called 'Shag Cove') and roasted them for dinner. Banks added 'between shaggs and fish this is the place of the greatest plenty of any we have seen'.[38] That afternoon some of the *Endeavour*'s people (presumably on a wooding expedition in Ship Cove) found three human hip bones by an oven at the outskirts of the bush, where Parkinson luridly claimed that the local people 'used to partake of their horrid midnight repasts'[39] — an improbable, witch-haunted claim, since Maori people did not eat at midnight.

During 18 and 19 January the people in the paa on Motuara seemed very quiet and did not visit the *Endeavour*. On the 19th a group came by canoe from a paa elsewhere in the bay (probably the paa at East Bay) and traded a large number of mackerel for pieces of cloth, paper and nails, which by now they had begun to value.

On 20 January Topaa came to the ship as he had promised with four preserved heads, which according to Parkinson 'had their brains taken out, and some of them their eyes, but the scalp and hair was left upon them. They looked as if they had been dried by the fire, or by the heat of the sun.'[40] Banks thought that these heads were kept as 'trophies' and indeed the heads of both kinsmen and enemies were preserved, in the former case for affectionate reasons and in the latter as an insult to their mana. One head, which seemed to have belonged to a fourteen- or fifteen-year-old male, had been damaged by repeated patu blows to the forehead, and this was reluctantly traded to Banks for a pair of white linen drawers. The others Topaa would not part with for any price. That morning Cook and Banks continued to survey the west side of the Sound, but saw neither people nor cultivations in the course of this excursion. Banks commented that 'the bay every where we have yet been is very hilly, we have hardly seen a flat large enough for a potatoe garden. Our freinds here do not seem to feel the want of such places as we have not yet seen the least apearance of cultivation, I suppose they live intirely upon fish, dogs and Enemies.'[41]

During 21 January the *Endeavour* party fished both with the seine and hook and lines, making enormous catches, and Jonathon Monkhouse went ashore (possibly at Anakakata Bay, where a number of houses were marked on Pickersgill's chart of the Sound). He later told Banks he had found a number of deserted houses there, and some things tied to the branches of trees, including a quantity of human hair which he took away with him. Monkhouse guessed that this might be 'a place consecrated to religious purposes'. It seems likely that this was indeed a tapu site, for human hair was used as a tapu marker for burials and boundaries, and in maakutu (sorcery); in which case Monkhouse's action was a serious desecration. It may have been detected immediately, because later on that day Parkinson reported that when a group of the *Endeavour*'s men, including Monkhouse, rowed towards the paa on Motuara two or three canoes came out, and the Europeans thought they were about to be attacked. Monkhouse shot at these people, at first with smallshot and then with ball, evidently killing one man, and the canoes hastily retreated 'as well they might', said Banks, 'who probably came out with freindly intentions (so at least their behaviour both before and since seems to shew) and little expected so rough usage from people who had always acted in a freindly manner to them, and whom they were not at all conscious of having offended'.[42] Either Monkhouse's interference with the tapu site had been noticed and the people in the canoes were seeking utu (retribution), or it was (as Banks thought) an innocent visitation and Monkhouse's reaction was

Parkinson's pen-and-wash sketch 'New Zealanders Fishing' is apparently a composite. In the foreground are two fishing canoes with small crews, using the hoop-nets and some wearing the black feather hats and cloak styles described in Queen Charlotte Sound. The large carved canoes in the background probably are northern canoes, introduced into the picture as an artistic conceit.

the result of a guilty conscience. In either case the local people now had serious cause for disaffection with the *Endeavour* party.

On 22 January Cook, Banks, Solander and others went in the pinnace to explore the south-east side of the Sound and landed on Arapaoa, just south of Tikaiope (Blumine Island),[43] possibly in Kaitapeha Bay. Banks and Solander went botanising while Cook climbed Kaitapeha Hill,[44] where he saw a magnificent panorama of hills and islands, and a strait clearly passing from the eastern to the western sea. According to Banks he 'returnd in high spirits, having seen the Eastern sea and satisfied himself of the existence of a streight communicating with it, the Idea of which had occurd to us all from Tasmans as well as our own observations'.[45] This sighting must have been a blow for those on board the *Endeavour* (including Banks) who still believed that they had discovered the Unknown Southern Continent. On their way back to the ship they explored the coastline behind Tikaiope and Motupara (Pickersgill Island), where they saw a sizeable abandoned village and another that was inhabited (no doubt 'Hippah Rocks' paa in East Bay). It was probably on this occasion that Magra saw several deserted villages, one of which has been located as an archaeological site on Amerikiwhati Island[46] and two others whose locations are still unknown. He described the Amerikiwhati paa as follows:

247

> On a small island, lying S.E. from the place where we anchored, was one of those deserted towns, most agreeably situated, and consisting of about eighteen houses, placed in a circular form; it was surrounded and defended by a wall curiously constructed, by driving two rows of long stakes or spars into the ground, at convenient distances, and afterwards filling the intermediate space with what we called broom-stuff, being a small kind of brush, made into bundles like faggots, and placed on end, in double rows, supported by others lying parallel with the ground: in this manner the wall is raised six or seven feet in height, and, not withstanding the simplicity of its structure, it is not easily broken or destroyed, especially when guarded by men, who fight not only to preserve freedom and property, but their own bodies from being cruelly butchered and eaten.[47]

This brushwood palisade would have been even more effective than a timber structure in warding off spear-thrusts from attacking warriors, and was probably built in this fashion because of the difficulty of driving posts into the island's rocky ground.[48]

Near this paa Magra also spotted two other abandoned villages. One was a 'more regular fortification' on a high hill near a pleasant bay. The hill was precipitous and had a level space on top with several large water reservoirs dug into it. This flat area was enclosed by a palisade of logs each two feet in diameter, driven deep into the ground and about twenty feet high, with fighting stages nearby and surrounded by a ditch ten feet wide. Inside the defences there was space for 200 to 300 houses, although none now remained. At the foot of this hill was a second ruined town, which Magra thought had been the ordinary residence of those who had built the fort. In commenting on these structures he remarked that many of the fortified 'castles' they had seen in New Zealand, less well protected by topography than this site, were defended by several ditches, a 'drawbridge', and a palisade that sloped inward towards the defenders. He and others had discussed this kind of arrangement with a chief on one occasion and suggested that the inward-sloping palisades (such as they had seen at the two large paa in Whitianga) might assist an attacking party in their advance. The chief replied that on the contrary, an outward-sloping palisade would provide a secure shelter for a party of attackers who wished to tunnel under the defences, and that such an arrangement would be far more dangerous. He also told them that fortified villages of this sort were never taken except by surprise or in a seige, where the defenders could be successfully cut off from their food and water supplies.[49]

Magra added that during their time on the Sound they had seen a number of deserted villages. Some of these seemed to have been abandoned for about four or five years, for they were overgrown with shrubs and high grass.

The next day was wet and squally, but Cook carried on with his survey, visiting one of the islands (probably Long Island), where he saw a deserted village with a number of houses that Pickersgill subsequently marked on his chart of the Sound.

On 24 January Cook sent a gang of men to an island to cut grass for the ship's sheep, and that afternoon Banks, Cook and others visited the 'Hippa Island' paa at the southern end of Motuara Island for the first time:

> Our freinds the Indians . . . receivd us with much confidence and civility and shewd us every part of their habitations which were neat enough. The town was situated upon a small Island or rock divided from the main by a breach in a rock so small that a man might almost jump over it; the sides were everywhere so steep as to render fortifications even in their way almost totaly useless, accordingly there was nothing but a slight Palisade and one small fighting stage at one end where the rock was most accessible.[50]

The people of the paa brought several human bones to trade with the Europeans, the flesh of which they said they had eaten, for these had become a sought-after souvenir amongst the *Endeavour* sailors. Banks also described a memorial to a dead man within this paa, constructed in the form of a wooden cross ornamented with feathers. The local people assured them that this man's body was not buried there, but refused to tell them where it was. Perhaps they feared that in their ghoulish enthusiasm for collecting bones the Europeans would plunder his grave. After this Cook's party went to the northern end of Motuara to collect water, then crossed to the mainland, where they saw scattered houses (maybe those marked on Pickersgill's chart around Waikawa Bay), the inhabitants of which were out fishing.

On the morning of 25 January Banks and Solander, having now exhausted the local supply of unknown plants, went collecting mosses with considerable success. During the afternoon they accompanied Cook in the pinnace on an excursion towards the mouth of the Sound, and in one of the small coves of Anakakata Bay they shot some shags. According to Banks, the local people were now leaving the paa on Motuara, which seemed to be their refuge in times of danger, and a large group of them came to meet the Europeans.

> These people came a good way to meet us at a place where we were shooting shags and invited us to the place where the rest of them were, 20 or 30 in number, men, women, children, Dogs &c. We went and were receivd with all possible demonstrations of freindship, if the numberless huggs and kisses we got from both sexes old and young in return for our ribbands and beads may be accounted such: they also sold and gave us a good many fish with which we went home well pleasd with our new acquaintance.[51]

It seems that Cook and his party had been treated to the exchange of hongi (pressing noses), which occurred when Maori groups met each other in peace — indeed a significant sign of acceptance.

During the next day Cook, Banks and Solander climbed a high hill on the eastern side of the Sound (probably near East Bay) where they again saw 'Cooks Straights' stretching from east to west, with open sea on either side. They built a cairn of rocks on the summit containing some musketballs, beads, smallshot and other imperishable items, then climbed down to find Tupaia and the boat's crew chatting with a group of local people. As Cook commented, 'Tupia always accompanies us in every excursion we make and proves of infinate service.'[52] They ate a meal of shags and fish, and their visitors showed them where to find fresh water. On their way back to the ship they visited the paa in East Bay, which Cook had sighted on 22 January, after his first hilltop view of the strait. This

'Hippah Rocks' paa was sited on a small, steep island and had just one fighting stage. Cook said 'it containd a good number of people' and Banks estimated that it held about eighty to 100 houses, although archaeological surveys of the island suggest that this paa held no more than forty houses or other structures, and that Banks's estimate was an exaggeration.[53] The people of this paa eagerly traded small dried fish that they had hanging up, for nails, ribbons and paper.

Over the next few days the *Endeavour* party was preoccupied with routine business, completing repairs to the ship. Banks and Solander went botanising without success, for the bush on the western side of the Sound was so tangled with climbing plants that they found it impossible to travel far from the shore in any direction.

On the morning of 29 January Topaa returned to the *Endeavour* with three other men, and Cook was told that on 19 January one of his officers (in this account the master, Molyneux) had shot two men, killing one of them. Soon after, Green the astronomer and Tupaia met some other local people ashore (presumably from another kin-group) who contradicted this account; so that when Tupaia returned to the ship he declared 'that what we heard in the morn was absolutely false, that so far from dead nobody was even hurt by the shot. Our Freind Topaa is he says given too much to Lying.'[54] Later that morning Cook with some of his men climbed a high hill near Cape Jackson and saw an island (Stephens Island) away to the north-west, with other islands in between that seemed to shelter safe anchorages. On the top of this hill he made another stone cairn, which contained a silver coin, beads and musketballs, surmounted by an old flag — all of which were no doubt taken soon after by inquisitive local curio-hunters. On the way back to the ship they met some people on shore and traded a small quantity of fish.

Over the next few days it rained continually and Banks and Solander did little exploring. The routine work of the ship carried on, however, and on 30 January Cook sent a party of men to gather wild celery from one of the islands (probably Long Island). While they were cutting plants near some abandoned houses, a group of about twenty men, women and children landed, and five or six women sat down and began to scarify themselves with flints, shells and chips of green-stone on their legs, arms and faces. While they were doing this the men began to repair the huts, and they explained to the sailors that these women were mourning for their husbands, 'which they told us the Tartars had Come in the Night and kill'd or Matta'd them to eat'.[55]

That afternoon an inscribed post bearing the ship's name, the month and year of its visit to the Sound was set up in Ship Cove, with a Union Jack flying from it. The next morning Cook, William Monkhouse and Tupaia visited 'Motu-ouru' (Motuara) to ask permission to set up a similar post on the highest part of the island. Topaa met them there and Cook questioned him about the two men who had been said to have been killed and wounded on 19 January. He also told Topaa through Tupaia that they had come 'to set up a mark upon the Island in order to shew any ship that might put into this place that we had been here before'.[56] Topaa agreed not only that this should be done, but promised that the post would never be taken down. Cook then distributed silver threepenny pieces dated 1763 and spike nails marked with 'the King's broad Arrow' to several old men who were present, climbed with his men to the highest point of the island and set up the post, hoisting the Union Jack upon it and naming the inlet 'Queen Charlottes Sound'. Having concluded these formalities he 'took possession of it and the adjacent land in the name and for the use of his Majesty, we then drank Her Majestys hlith in a Bottle of wine and gave the empty bottle to the old man (who had attended us up the hill) with which he was highly pleased'.[57] For the local people, the ritual setting up of poles was a familiar method of communicating with ancestor gods. Most likely Cook's actions were interpreted as a tapu act of some kind (perhaps establishing a raahui, which put a place under the mana of a leader and his gods), sealed by the presentation of a bottle to the local chief.

While the post was being raised Cook questioned Topaa through Tupaia about local geography, especially about the strait and whether the land to the south of it was a continent or an island. Topaa assured him that the strait stretched from the western to the eastern sea. According to Pickersgill, he said that 'they knew but of 3 lands one of which lay to the N° which they would be 3 months in going round another which we was upon they could go round in 4 days and a Third lyeing SWtd of which they had but a very Imperfect knolledge and called it Towie poe namou [Te Wai Pounamu, greenstone water — the South Island]'.[58] Cook added that the land to the north was called 'Aeheino mouwe' (possibly Ahi noo Maaui [Maaui's fire] or A, e hiia noo Maaui [fished by Maaui] — the North Island[59]), and it seems that the land that could be circumnavigated in just four days was Arapaoa Island. After this Topaa returned to the ship with Cook and shared food with him, just as one would after any major ceremony.

On 3 February Cook was preparing to leave the Sound. Early that morning he sent the longboat to gather celery. Solander and Tupaia accompanied him to East Bay paa, where they traded for dried fish and bought so much that finally the old men told Cook to leave the island. These people confirmed everything that Topaa had said about the strait and the country's geography, and seemed extremely relieved when Cook's party went back to their ship. Later that afternoon another group of Cook's men went to the north of the ship to trade for more fish, with no better success. At the same time some of the 'gentlemen' on board made last-minute efforts to attend to their creature comforts, as Banks reported with glee:

> One of our gentlemen came home to day abusing the natives most heartily whoom he said he had found to be given to the detestable Vice of Sodomy. He, he said, had been with a family of Indians and paid a price for leave to make his addresses to any one young woman they should pitch upon for him; one was chose as he thought who willingly retird with him but on examination provd to be a boy; that on his returning and complaining of this another was sent who turnd out to be a boy likewise; that on his second complaint he could get no redress but was laught at by the Indians. Far be it for me to attempt saying that Vice is not practisd here, this however I must say that in my humble opinion this story proves no more than that our gentleman was fairly trickd out of his cloth, which none of the young

ladies chose to accept of on his terms, and the master of the family did not chuse to part with.[60]

If this was not good evidence of homosexuality, it certainly pointed to a local sense of humour.

During that same afternoon the yawl went out fishing, and one of the crew 'Brought the Bones of a Young Infant which had lately been killed from one of the Indians he had them all Hanging round his Nack with the flesh on some of them'.[61]

The next day the sailing was delayed because some wet hay for the ship's animals had to be dried, and Banks was told several garbled stories by the crews of two boats that had gone out the day before. One crew claimed to have met a double canoe whose occupants said that they had lost a young girl several days before and feared that she had been eaten; and the other crew said they had met a double canoe whose people told them they had captured and eaten such a child the day before, and traded them her bones. As Banks drily commented:

> I am inclnd to beleive that our two boats who went out at very different times in the morn both in the same direction, one only farther than the other, saw one and the same canoe and only differently interpreted the conversation of the people, as they know only a few words of the language, and eating people is now always the uppermost Idea in their heads.[62]

Most of the Europeans still had only the sketchiest grasp of Maori, and their understanding of local statements could not be relied on. Throughout the circumnavigation the only reasonably successful communications with local people were carried out by Tupaia, who had been able to make himself understood in Maori from the time of their first landing (for Maori and Tahitian were closely related languages); possibly also by Tupaia's 'boy' Tayeto, although he is almost never mentioned in the journals; and by Banks and Parkinson, who from the evidence of their journals and the vocabularies they collected were the best European linguists on board. From the time the *Endeavour* had left the Bay of Islands either Tupaia had become adept at passing on to Banks the content of conversations with Maori (probably in a mixture of Tahitian, Maori and English) or Banks had begun to understand these for himself, for what seem to be verbatim translations of exchanges in Maori between Tupaia and local individuals were scattered throughout Banks's journal from that time onwards. The last such lengthy exchange was reported on 5 February, as the *Endeavour* was being manoeuvred to a better position for sailing out of the bay. Topaa came on board to say goodbye and talked with Tupaia about local traditions, a conversation Banks recorded as follows:

> He knew of no other great land than that we had been upon, Aehia no Mauwe [probably Ahi noo Maaui — the North Island], of which Terawhitte [Te Raawhiti — the south-eastern extremity of the North Island] was the southern part; that he believd his ancestors were not born there but came originaly from Heawye [Hawai'i — Hawaiki] (the place from whence Tupia and the Islanders also derive their origin) which lay to the Northward where were many lands; that neither himself his father or his grandfather ever heard of ships as large as this being here before, but that [they] have a tradition of 2 large vessels, much larger than theirs,

which some time or other came here and were totaly destroyd by the inhabitants and all the people belonging to them killd. This Tupia says is a very old tradition, much older than his great grandfather, and relates to two large canoes which came from Olimaroa, one of the Islands he has mentioned to us. Whether he is right, or whether this is a tradition of Tasmans ships whose size in comparison to their own they could not from relation conceive a sufficient Idea of, and whoom their War-like ancestors had told them they had destroyd, is difficult to say. Tupia all along warnd us not to beleive too much any thing these people told us; For says he they are given to lying.[63]

Topaa's story of the two large vessels that were destroyed by local people may well have been a version of Tasman's visit. Cook's account of this conver-sation spoke of a visit by one small vessel from Olimaroa, a distant land to the north (which had also been mentioned to them by people in the Bay of Islands), when only four people had been killed — perhaps quite an accurate account of the killing of the men from Tasman's cockboat. During Topaa's visit Hicks also reported that one of his companions had tried to take a pistol and a half-hour glass.

Later this day Banks and Solander went ashore at Ship Cove to complete their collections and there met a family of seventeen people, headed by 'a pretty child about 10 years old who was the owner of the land about where we wooded — the only instance of property we have met with amongst these people'.[64] His mother sat beside her son on mats in the open air, slashing herself in mourning for her husband with the rest of the family around them. These people were very friendly to Banks and Solander, inviting them to spend the night with them, but they had to refuse because the *Endeavour* was about to sail. This may have been the first time that any of the Europeans had been invited to sleep on shore, since no such invitations were mentioned in earlier journal entries. As Banks ruefully observed, 'Most unlucky I shall always esteem it that we did not sooner get acquainted with these people, from whoom we might have learnt more in a day of their manners and dispositions than from all that we have yet seen.'[65]

On 6 February the *Endeavour* finally sailed out of the Sound, rounding 'Cape Koamaroo' (Ko Aamaru) and narrowly escaping being swept onto the tapu rocks of one of Ngaa Whatu by the ebbing tide.

Summary
THE *ENDEAVOUR* ACCOUNTS OF TOTARA-NUI

Parkinson described the landscape around Ship Cove in some detail in his account of Totara-nui:

> The country, about the cove where we lay, is entirely covered with wood, and so full of a sort of supplejack, that it is difficult to pass through it: there is also a little sand-fly which is very troublesome; and the bite of it is venomous, raising a bump on the skin which itches very much. The tops of some of the hills, which at first appeared to be bare, we found covered with the fern plant, which grows up to about a man's height. The hills decline gently to the water's edge, and leave no flat land excepting one place.

The woods abound with divers kinds of birds, such as parrots, wood pigeons, water-hens; three sorts of birds having wattles [probably saddleback, huia and kokako]; hawks; with a variety of birds that sing all night. We also found a great quantity of a species of Philadelphus, which makes a good substitute for tea. At one particular place we met with a substance that appeared like a kid's skin, but it had so weak a texture, that we concluded it was not leather; and were afterward informed by the natives, that it was gathered from some plant called Tee goomme [tii-kumu (*Celmisia* sp.)]: one of them had a garment made of it, which looked like their rug cloaks.[66]

Cook, who described the Sound as a 'Collection of some of the finest harbours in the world', reported that there was a variety of excellent timber growing on its high hills and deep valleys, fit for all uses except ships' masts, for which it was too hard and heavy. Fish were available in extraordinary quantities and could be caught with little effort. In this productive environment, he thought that 'the number of Inhabitants hardly exceeds 3 or 400 people, they leive desperse'd along the Shores in search of their daly bread which is fish and firn roots for they cultivate no part of their lands'.[67]

Archaeological studies show ancient evidence of past cultivation in the Sound, including innumerable pits, but in 1770 there was no sign of gardens. Totara-nui was in an uproar at the time of the *Endeavour*'s visit, most likely because of the killings first reported to the Europeans and the expectation of a return attack from over the western hills; and presumably there was little point in planting root crops which could easily be raided. A number of local people had been recently killed, for the *Endeavour*'s men met several family groups in deep mourning. According to Parkinson, 'we heard a great cry, or howling at the Hippa every night, and, most likely, at that time they were cutting and slashing themselves, according to their custom, which is done with a piece of green stone, shell or shark's tooth, which they drive into their flesh, and draw it along, beginning at their feet and continuing it to their heads'.[68] It is also possible that there was raiding amongst groups in the Sound itself, because Cook's men met some small family groups in mourning and others who reported that they had recently killed enemies and eaten them.

All the same, there must have been a degree of political unity in Totara-nui, for at the time of the *Endeavour*'s arrival the paa at Motuara was packed with people, who only gradually dispersed to their small hamlets (shown as eight clusters of scattered dwellings on Pickersgill's chart) along the western coast nearby; and the paa at East Bay remained occupied throughout the *Endeavour*'s three-week stay in the Sound. According to Parkinson, the paa at Motuara held about thirty-two houses, containing up to 200 inhabitants,[69] and archaeological surveys of the paa in East Bay suggest that it was of a similar scale. These may have been the citadels of two opposing confederations of kin-groups in Totara-nui, with Topaa as a key figure in the Motuara group. Banks later described the occupants of these two 'towns' as 'two different societies' who had nothing to do with each other for a time while the *Endeavour* was in the Sound.[70] Whatever the causes of the current turmoil, however, the numbers of deserted fortifications seen in the area suggest that inter-group raiding had been going on for some considerable time.

The pattern of dispersal from Motuara to the nearby coves is interesting, for it suggests how settlement patterns may have ebbed and flowed in times of war. On 15 January, when the *Endeavour* arrived in Totara-nui, all but the small family group in Cannibal Cove were gathered in the paa at Motuara, with sentries posted on the adjoining coastline. On 18 January Cook and others met a man fishing on his own in Waatapu (Resolution Bay), and on 24 January they visited Motuara paa, finding it still well occupied. Later that day they saw scattered houses around Waikawa Bay whose inhabitants were out fishing, and on 25 January Cook and his companions met a group of twenty or thirty people in Ana-kakata Bay. On 30 January about twenty people, including some women in mourning, reoccupied a group of abandoned houses on 'Hamote' (Long Island), and on 5 February, as the *Endeavour* was about to leave the Sound, Banks and Solander met another family group of seventeen, also in mourning, in the vicinity of Meretoto (Ship Cove). Evidently the small extended family (whaanau) was the preferred working group for hunting and gathering, owning houses, mats, fishing gear and canoes, and most likely these operated out of particular coves. There was also evidence of the inheritance of leadership in Banks's report of a ten-year-old boy who was the 'head' of his extended family and 'owner' of the lands around Ship Cove. Usually though, the senior men such as Topaa and the other 'old men' on Motuara were the leaders of kin-groups, in the Sound as elsewhere.

The coves occupied by these groups were ideally placed for hunting and gathering activities, with access to freshwater streams, areas of flat land for dwellings, sloping sandy beaches for canoes and flax, bush foods, and fernroot high on the adjacent hills, as well as abundant fish and shellfish offshore.[71] Consequently the people did not have to range far to collect their food, perhaps within a radius of one and a half kilometres from their hamlets, and were in no danger of starvation. All the same, Cook commented that 'This people are poor when compared to many we have seen and their Canoes are mean and without orament, the little traffick we had with them was wholy for fish for we saw little else they had to dispose of.'[72] Parkinson added that very few of the local people were tattooed, and this suggests that for some time there had been little surplus wealth in the community. It is difficult to know whether this was because they did not practise agriculture, or (more likely) because the area, like Whitianga, was so situated as to be susceptible to frequent attacks by raiding parties.

The appearance of the Totara-nui people was not much discussed in the journals, but Parkinson made a number of sketch portraits of individuals both on land and in their canoes, and one fine pen and wash drawing of people fishing from small canoes with hoop-nets. This sketch has other canoes in the back-

Overleaf: *Pickersgill's 'Plan of Queen Charlo's Sound', S° Sea' shows the paa at the southern end of Motuara, the deserted village (evidently with a ditch or palisade defence) on Long Island and another on Motupara (Pickersgill Island) The* Endeavour's *anchorage off Meretoto (Ship Cove) and scattered houses along the coastline between Meretoto and Anakakata Bay are also marked.*

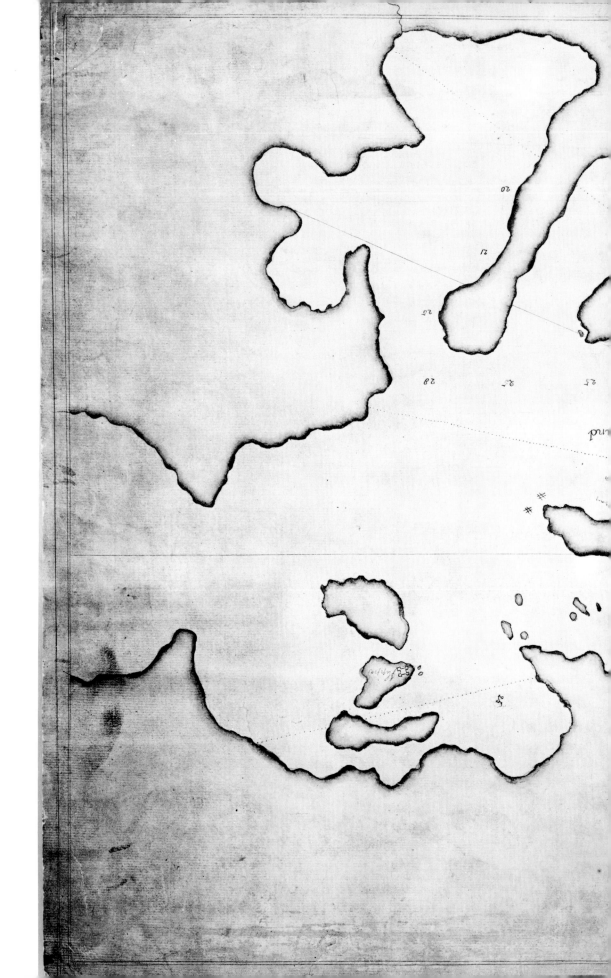

A PLAN of QUEEN CHARLO's SOUND on the No. side of ISLAND; So. SEA.

LATITUDE 41.05.32. LONG: 184.36 Wt.

KNUCKENSGILL

552/6

Shelf X:c

The Natives of this Country are Cannibals

Very High Land overgrown with Woods

A Scale of two Miles

High Land

Good fishing ground

Cannibal Harbour

Muddy ground

MacPherson's Cove

Weeds

Weeds

Queen Cha.

Long Island

Magnetic Var: 13:00 Et.

Best head of the Sound and Wt. head of Cook's Straits

ground which are probably there because of artistic licence, since they seem more like canoes seen in the North than any described in the Sound. The dress styles in the pencil sketches show both rain capes and finer garments worn over the shoulder or fastened in front in the fashion first depicted during Tasman's voyage; rounded feather 'hats' worn by both men and women; ear ornaments (of greenstone, feathers and teeth) and, neck ornaments of the rei puta type; top-knots, combs, feathers placed in the topknot, or in four sketches (which may not have been made in Totara-nui) high-plumed head ornaments, one in the shape of a feathered crest. Many of the men sketched in these drawings had vertical scars on their foreheads, but otherwise no tattoo; and light beards.[73]

One extensive section of the Banks manuscript vocabularies appears to have been collected by Parkinson in Totara-nui, and he also commented in his journal that 'when these people are pleased on any occasion, they express it by crying Ai, and make a cluck with their tongues not unlike a hens when she calls her chickens'.[74]

These two studies of Maori by Parkinson may have been made in Queen Charlotte Sound, or more likely off Cape Palliser. Note the feathered head-crest and the tall feathered head decoration.

258

Cook commented that the Totara-nui people seemed to have some knowledge of iron, for they willingly took it in exchange for their own goods. This information could only have come from the people at Te Poroporo (Cape Turn-again) — about 220 kilometres to the north, which shows how effective the networks of communication were in 1770. They also liked paper at first, but when they discovered that it was spoiled by water they would not take it or Tahitian barkcloth, much preferring to be given English broadcloth or red kersey cloth instead.

This was the *Endeavour*'s longest stay in any New Zealand harbour. The ethnographic information to be derived from the journals and sketches in Totara-nui was relatively rich, although as in the Bay of Islands familiarity had begun to dampen the explorers' curiosity about local ways of life. From the *Endeavour* accounts it seems that life in the Sound was perilous, not so much because of environmental conditions but because of frequent raiding. Its position as one logical landing place for northern war parties intent on plundering southern greenstone meant that Totara-nui's history was turbulent, just as Whitianga's position beside the prized basalt quarries at Tahanga meant that they were also frequently raided.

The political insecurities of life in Totara-nui and the consequent relative poverty of its people led Pickersgill to conclude that they were 'the Poorest and most mizerable sett we saw on New Zealand'.

COOK STRAIT TO ADMIRALTY BAY
7 February–31 March 1770

During 7 February the *Endeavour* sailed south-east down Cook Strait, sighting the highest peak of the inland Kaikoura Range (Tapuaenuku) and a small fire on a barren and sandy coastal plain. In Cloudy Bay they saw a long row of tall trees on the flats, and the next evening Cook tacked north-east on a changing wind. Some of his officers had begun to argue that perhaps 'Aehei no Mauwe' (the North Island) was not an island after all but joined a larger landmass somewhere to the north of the strait. Cook by now was convinced that this was no continent, but to dispel any remaining debate he sailed the *Endeavour* northwards back towards Te Poroporo (Cape Turnagain). Near Cape Palliser three canoes came out to sea and followed the ship, eventually catching up with her. With very little invitation their crews boarded the vessel, where Parkinson sketched them and described them in his journal:

They were much like the natives of Mataroowkaow [Matarukau?], a village in Tolaga Bay; being very neatly drest, having their hair knotted on the crown of their heads in two bunches, one of which was tamoou, or plaited, and the wreath bound round them the same. In one of the canoes there was an old man who came on board, attended by one of the natives; he was tataowed all over the face, with a streak of red paint over his nose, and across his cheek. His brow, as well as the brows of many others who were with him, was much furrowed; and the hair of his head and beard quite silvered with age. He had on a flaxen garment, ornamented with a

Sketches of Natives
of New Zeland

beautiful wrought border; and under it a petticoat, made of a sort of cloth they call Aooree Waow: on his ears hung a bunch of teeth, and an ear-ring of Poonamoo [pounamu], or green stone. For an Indian, his speech was soft, and his voice so low we could hardly hear it. By his dress, carriage, and the respect paid to him we supposed him to be a person of distinction amongst them.

We observed a great difference betwixt the inhabitants on this side of the land, north of Cook's Straits, and those of the south. The former are tall, well-limbed, clever fellows; have a deal of tataow, and plenty of good cloaths; but the latter are a set of poor wretches, who, though strong, are stinted in their growth, and seem to want the spirit or sprightliness of the northern Indians. Few of them are tataowed, or have their hair oiled and tied up, and their canoes are but mean.[75]

Two of these canoes were large and handsome, ornamented like canoes seen earlier in the north or on the east coast of the North Island. It seems probable that at least one set of Parkinson's portrait sketches (which showed men with double topknots, wearing teeth and greenstone ear ornaments and with their brows 'much furrowed' with vertical scarring) were made on this occasion. These were later used together with sketches from Totara-nui in producing two of Parkinson's composite pen-and-wash studies of carved canoes.[76] As soon as these people came on board the *Endeavour* they asked for 'Whow' (Whao — the term for chisel) or nails, yet when some were given to them they asked Tupaia what they were, making it plain that they had not seen such objects before. As Cook reasoned:

> These people asking so readily for nails proves that their connections must extend as far North as Cape Kidnappers which is 45 leagues, for that was the southernmost place on this side of the coast we had any traffick with the natives, and it is most probable that the Inhabitants of Queen Charlottes Sound got the little knowlidge they seem'd to have of Iron by the connections they may have with the Terrawhetteans bordering upon them, for we have no reason to think that the inhabitants of any part of this land had the least knowlidge of Iron before we came among them.[77]

These people, 'who seemed to have been cut and mangled in several parts of their bodies', on being given gifts promptly made gifts in return, which Banks said had not happened before in New Zealand. Inspired by their courtesy to supose that these might be envoys from 'Te Ratu's kingdom', he asked them if Te Ratu was their king, but they replied that no, he was not.

This visit by the wealthy representatives of communities near Palliser Bay suggests that the southern Wairarapa (which climatically was not unlike Totara-nui, and lacked some of its natural advantages) was capable of producing surplus wealth for its inhabitants, and that canoe-borne networks of communication along the east coast of the North Island were as efficient as those across Cook Strait.

Opposite: *It is my guess that these head-and-shoulder portraits were made off the Wairarapa coast — Parkinson described one man encountered in a canoe off that region as having his 'brow . . . much furrowed', probably with the vertical scars (haehae) shown in some of these portraits. Note the combs, feathers, ear ornaments and remarkable top-knot ornaments.*

The next day Te Poroporo was sighted and, having convinced all on board that 'Aehei no Mauwe' was an island, Cook turned the *Endeavour* south to coast the eastern side of Te Wai Pounamu (the South Island). As the *Endeavour* sailed south along the Wairarapa coastline, Banks described the local landscape:

> It made in low hills which seemd pretty well clothd with trees but at the bottom of them was lowish land making in tables, the topps of which were covered with white sand . . . ; between these were a few vallies in which were wood and in one of these we saw a few houses. In the Evening the country rather mended upon us I suppose, as many fires were seen by which I suppose it to be better inhabited.[78]

On 11 February two canoes came out from Castle Point and their crew traded a few fish and some trolling lures, 'made upon a peice of wood, which I beleive serves instead of bait in towing as the Mother of Pearl does on the Islanders towing hooks'.[79] On 14 February, four double canoes carrying fifty-seven men came a long way out to sea from the Kaikoura Peninsula to meet the *Endeavour*. According to Banks, 'we were farther from the shore than ever canoes had come before' — about fifteen to nineteen miles. The weather was calm and Banks was alongside the ship in a rowing boat, shooting seabirds. As soon as his crew spotted the canoes they rowed rapidly to the *Endeavour* and scrambled back on board, apparently without being seen, for their visitors were staring fixedly at the ship. They seemed very timid and, according to Parkinson, 'had some leaves about their heads, but few cloaths on their bodies, and seemed to be poor wretches'.[80] Nor could Tupaia persuade them to come alongside the vessel to trade. After a while they went away, and at sunset their canoes could be seen about halfway back to land. This is an interesting indication of the off-shore range of double canoes (which were much used around Raukawa-moana in early historic times, for their stability in rough seas) out to about fifteen to twenty miles, and the willingness of their crews to stay on the ocean at night is noteworthy. These cautious, astonished visitors were to be the last Maori people whom the *Endeavour* party encountered.

On 16 February a fire was seen on shore in Pegasus Bay, and on 17 February near 'an excellent harbour' (Akaroa), two people were spotted sitting on top of a hill. As the *Endeavour* sailed further south-west no signs of life were seen until a large fire was sighted south of Otaakou on 4 March. Banks took this as 'indisputable proof that there are inhabitants, tho probably very thinly scatterd over the face of this very large countrey'.[81] All this time a debate over the status of the South Island was waged on board between the 'Continents' and the 'no-Continents' — 'one [party] who wishd that the land in sight might, the other that it might not be a continent,' reported Banks. '. . . myself have always been most firm for the former, tho sorry I am to say . . . that there are no more heartily of it than myself and one poor midshipman, the rest begin to sigh for roast beef'.[82]

The further the land extended to the south the more ebullient the 'Continental' party became, until on 10 March the *Endeavour* sailed around South Cape

Opposite: *Cook's 'Chart of Part of New Zeland or the Island of Tovy Poenammu' shows the* Endeavour's *track around the South Island.*

in fresh winds, 'to the total demolition of our aerial fabrick calld continent,' Banks ruefully conceded in his journal. The ship proceeded along a rugged, barren coastline past Dusky Sound, and northwards along the west coast of the South Island without seeing any signs of human life. On 30 March the *Endeavour* anchored in Admiralty Bay to replenish their supplies of wood, fresh water and fish. There they found two or three houses that seemed to have been deserted for a year or more, one at 'the side of a mountain, at a little distance from the bay, and the wreck of an old canoe lying in a cove contiguous to it'.[83] After several days of miserable windy weather Banks and Solander finally ventured ashore and collected three new plants high in the hills, and on Saturday 31 March the *Endeavour* sailed out of the bay, past Cape Farewell and towards the eastern coast of Australia.

Chapter Eleven

THE *ENDEAVOUR* ETHNOGRAPHIC ACCOUNTS OF NEW ZEALAND

When the *Endeavour* sailed from England, the Earl of Morton, then the president of the Royal Society, had given a set of 'Hints' to the expedition's leaders. These included a list of broad headings for their accounts of any people they might meet with on their voyage of discovery. Cook had written a brief 'Description of Georges Island' at the end of their three-month stay in Tahiti, and after visiting others of the Society Islands, Banks provided a lengthy, generalised description of the 'Manners and Customs of the S.Sea Islanders'. These accounts related only very broadly to the Earl of Morton's 'Hints', but Cook and Banks each followed much the same set of topics.

Banks and Cook followed this same list of topics (although each in a somewhat different order) in their 'Accounts' of New Zealand, although those were significantly shorter and less detailed than their descriptions of Tahiti had been. During the visit to Tahiti everything had been exotic and unfamiliar, and the three months spent at Matavai Bay in close contact with local families had given Banks in particular many insights into local life, and a good working knowledge of Tahitian. In New Zealand, on the other hand, only fifty-six days of the *Endeavour*'s six-month circumnavigation were spent at anchor in various harbours, and many of their encounters with local people were hostile, or tentative and uneasy. Tupaia proved to be an invaluable mediator and translator, but this meant that the Europeans had less incentive to learn Maori. Both Banks's and Cook's descriptions of Maori life were noticeably sparse in those areas where conversation and close contact were necessary for good description, especially topics such as religion, healing, the role of priests, and social relationships in general.

Their accounts of the visible, material aspects of life, on the other hand, were meticulous, detailed (especially those written by Banks) and supplemented by the marvellous sketches and drawings by Parkinson and Spöring. What follows is a summary of the generalised descriptions of New Zealand written by Cook ('A short and general description of the Country, its Inhabitants their manners, Customs &c') and Banks ('Account of New Zealand') at the end of their visit. The summary follows Banks's list of topics and includes, where relevant, some gen-

unsafe, much to Banks's chagrin. Cook in his 'Description' noted quantities of iron sand around Mercury Bay; some stones in Admiralty Bay that may have contained minerals, although Solander thought not; and a white stone near South Cape that he thought was probably marble, although 'Mr Banks I afterwards found was of opinion that they were Mineral to the highest degree, who is certainly a much better judge of these things than I am and therefore I might be mistaken in my opinion . . .'[8] He added that at no time had they seen any signs of metals among the local people.

Quadrupeds and animal products

In his 'Account' Banks observed that New Zealand had 'no Quadrupeds realy original natives of it. Dogs and rats indeed there are; the former as in other countries the companions of men [who, according to Cook, 'breed and bring them up for no other purpose than to eat'[9]], and the latter probably brought hither by the men, especialy as they are so scarce that I myself have not had an opportunity for seeing even one.'[10] This last comment was unsurprising, since the kiore (Polynesian rat) lived mainly in the bush and Banks had rarely ventured inland. They saw a few seals and one sea lion, but the only signs of their use by the local people were some sea lions' teeth ornaments, 'which they make into a kind of Bodkins and value much', one of which was sketched by the artist Miller, employed by Banks to sketch his collection of 'artificial curiosities' after the voyage. The other animal products seen were dogs' skins and hair, and birds' skins and feathers used as decoration on clothing; ornaments made of birds' bones and beaks and dogs' teeth; patupatu (hand clubs) made of whalebone and the whaletooth neck ornament (rei puta) reported by Cook and sketched by Spöring, which was evidently very highly valued.

Birds

According to Banks's rather limited observations, there were not many species of birds in New Zealand, and of these only the gannets seemed to be the same as the species in Europe. There were ducks, shags and gulls rather like the European varieties, all of which made good eating, and hawks, owls, quails, and 'several small birds that sing much more melodiously than any I have heard'.[11] The seabirds also included albatrosses, shearwaters, petrels and a few penguins.

Insects

Banks also recorded relatively few species of insects — 'a few Butterflys and Beetles, flesh flies very like those in Europe, Musquetos [mosquitoes], and sandflies maybe exactly the same as those of North America, make up the whole list.'[12]

Fish

'For this scarcity of animals on land,' wrote Banks in his 'Account', 'the Sea however makes abundant recompense. Every creek and corner produces abundance of fish not only wholesome but at least as well tasted as our fish in Europe: the ship seldom anchord in or indeed passd over (in light winds) any place whose bottom was such as fish resort to in general but as many were caught with hook and line as the people could eat.'[13]

Banks described mackerel of several kinds, one of which (the southern mackerel) looked exactly like those in England, and another kind very like the English horse mackerel. These swam in enormous shoals and were caught by the local people in large seine nets. In addition there were 'hakes', 'breams' (snapper and tarakihi), 'cole fish' (blue cod), elephant fish, sting rays or skates, dogfish, flatfish, eels and congers. The lobsters were 'allow'd by every body to be the best they had ever eat,'[14] and were caught by local people who dived close to the shore, feeling for them first with their feet. The Europeans also greatly enjoyed the 'excellent oysters', and the cockles, clams and other varieties of shellfish. Parkinson's vocabulary gave 'hewhai' (he whai) as the term for a skate and 'eraperape' (reperepe) as the term for a 'chimera', or elephant fish.

Plants

Banks's descriptions of New Zealand plants were supplemented by his and Dr Solander's botanical collections, and the sketches of plants by Parkinson that were to form the basis of the 'Florilegium' for the voyage. Banks commented that although the countryside was luxuriantly covered with vegetation, there was no great variety of plants, but that most local species were entirely unknown to botanical science. Sow thistle (puuhaa), nightshade (poroporo), and perhaps one or two varieties of grasses were familiar; three or four varieties of ferns were the same as those seen in the West Indies; but otherwise only about five or six of about 400 species had previously been botanically described.

There were few edible vegetables. The Europeans collected wild celery, a herb called 'fat hen' in England and a kind of cress that grew abundantly on the coast as remedies for scurvy, and on one occasion they made a delicious meal of the cabbage of a 'Cabbage tree' (in this case, probably a niikau palm).[15]

As far as Banks knew, however, the only vegetables eaten by the local people were fernroot (aruhe), a kind of 'Pandanus' (probably kiekie) and their cultivated crops — yams (uwhi), sweet potatoes (kuumara) and taro, all three plants being well known in the East and West Indies. He commented that 'they cultivate often peices of many acres, and I beleive any ship that was to be to the Northward in the Autumn about the time of digging them up might purchase any quantity'.[16] The local people also grew gourds (hue), which they used to make 'bottles' and 'jugs', and a small quantity of the Chinese paper mulberry tree (aute), which the South Sea islanders used to make their garments and was very highly valued. Banks thought that this plant had been brought from a hotter country, since it was very scarce in New Zealand and the plants did not thrive. The people beat it (presumably its bark) into small pieces of cloth, which they wore in the holes in their ears as an ornament.

The local people had no fruits but 'a few insipid berries' (a Maori epicure would have been scandalised to hear karaka, tawa, hinau and the other edible berries so described), yet there was an impressive array of excellent timber trees. The plant that most impressed Joseph Banks, however, was the flax plant, or harakeke, which he described in two varieties distinguished by the colour of their flowers, one (*Phormium cookii*) having a yellow and the other (*P. tenax*) a deep-red bloom. This was a hardy plant, growing on hills, in valleys, in dry soil and most vigorously near swamps. From this plant the local people, with little preparation, made their clothing, both fine and coarse, and their string, lines and nets. Banks thought that 'so usefull a plant would doubtless be a great acquisition to England', a comment that foreshadowed his later role as a collector of plants for Kew Gardens and the patron of several schemes to make use of New Zealand flax — among other things, for ships' cordage and to clothe the convicts at New South Wales.

Population

In his 'Account' Banks reported that when they first came ashore at Poverty Bay they had imagined the country's population to be larger than it afterwards appeared. Poverty Bay and the Bay of Plenty were 'much the best peopled parts of the countrey that we have seen' (although from the evidence of the journal entries, the Bay of Islands should also have been mentioned here), and the smoke from fires in these places suggested that they were well inhabited inland. Elsewhere:

> we have however found the sea coast only inhabited and that but sparingly, insomuch that the number of inhabitants seem to bear no kind of proportion to the size of the countrey which they possess, and this probably is owing to their frequent wars. Besides this the whole Coast from Cape Maria Van Diemen to Mount Egmont and seven eighths of the Southern Island seems totaly without people.[17]

People

In both 'Accounts' the people were described as very strong, fit, active and healthy. According to Banks:

> The men are of the size of the larger Europaeans, Stout, Clean Limnd and active, fleshy but never fat as the lazy inhabitants of the South Sea Isles are, vigorous, nimble and at the same time Clever in all their excersizes. I have seen 15 paddles of a side in one of their Canoes move with immensely quick strokes and at the same time as much Justness as if the movers were animated by one Soul: not the fraction of a second could be observd between the dipping and raising any two of them, the Canoe all the While moving with incredible swiftness: and to see them dance their War dance was an amusement which never faild to please every spectator, so much strength, firmness and agility in their motions and at the same time such excellent time kept that I have often heard above 100 paddles &c struck against the sides of their boats, as directed by their singing, without a mistake being ever made.[18]

Cook added that the men were 'a very dark brown Colour with black hair, thin black beards and white teeth'.[19]

The women, on the other hand, seemed to Banks to be:

> rather smaller than Europaean women, but have a peculiar softness of Voice which never fails to distinguish them from the men tho both are dressd exactly alike. They are like those of the fair sex that I have seen in other countries, more lively, airy and laughter-loving than the men and have more volatile spirits, formd by nature

to soften the Cares of more serious man who takes upon him the laborious toilsome part as War, tilling the Ground &c[20]

This was a far cry from the miserable, toil-worn drudges depicted by some other early European writers. Banks thought that the 'dispositions of Both Sexes seems mild, gentle and very affectionate to eachother but implacable towards their enemies, who after having killd they eat, probably out of a principle of revenge, and I beleive never give quarter or take prisoners' (although in fact prisoners were often taken as servants). He said that whenever the local people met with the Europeans and considered themselves to be in the stronger position they attacked, first using the war dance to fire themselves up to 'a kind of artificial courage', which seemed to be in the nature of a test:

> They always attackd us, tho seldom seeming to mean more than to provoke us to shew them what we were able to do in this case. By many trials we found that good usage and fair words would not avail the least with them, nor would they be convincd by the noise of our firearms alone that they were superior to theirs; but as soon as they had felt the smart of even a load of small shot and had had time allowd them to recollect themselves from the Effects of their artificial courage, which commonly took up a day, they were sensible of our generosity in not taking the advantage of Our superiority and became at once our good freinds and upon all occasions placd the most unbounded confidence in us.[21]

The people were not addicted to stealing, as the Islanders had been, but if after a challenge they could induce the Europeans to place some goods in their hands by offering their own in exchange, they would often 'refuse to return it with all the coolness in the world, seeming to look upon it as the plunder of an enemy' — an interesting explanation of the 'thefts' that provoked so many shootings in these early meetings with Europeans.

Banks considered the local people to be more modest in their behaviour and decent in their conversation than the Tahitians, although if a man wished to sleep with a local woman it was not impossible, providing the proper protocol was followed:

> If the consent of their relations was askd and the Question accompanied with a proper present it was seldom refusd, but then the strictest decency must be kept up towards the young lady or she might baulk the lover after all. Upon one of our gentlemen making his adresses to a family of the better sort the following answer was made him by the mistress of the family: 'Any of these young ladies will think themselves honourd by your adresses but you must first make me a proper present and must come and sleep with us ashore, for daylight should by no means be a witness of such proceedings.[22]

The role of the senior woman in these negotiations is interesting, and also her insistence that the man should spend the night ashore. In such a case he would have been very vulnerable to attack, although this never happened as far as one can tell. It seems clear from various journal entries that there was considerable love-making with local women, which must have resulted both in pregnancies and the transmission of venereal diseases.

'The Head of a Chief of New Zealand, the face curiously tattaowed, or mark'd, according to their Manner'. An engraving by T. Chambers after Parkinson.

The people seemed to wash less often than the Tahitians, probably because the climate was colder. Banks found the smell of the bird or fish oil with which they anointed their hair repellent when it was rancid, and reminiscent of the Newfoundland and Labrador fishing stations: 'the better sort indeed have it fresh and then it is intirely void of smell, but the inferior often use that that is rancid and consequently smell something like Greenland dock when they are trying Whale Blubber.'[23]

Tattoo

Of tattoo (or moko) Banks wrote in his generalised 'Account' that black dye was introduced under the skin by a 'sharp instrument furnish'd with many teeth'. The women had their lips blacked, although sometimes they had patches of body tattoo, while 'the men on the contrary seem to add to their quantity every Year of their lives so that some of the Elder were almost coverd with it'.[24] Cook commented that the tattoo on the face, and less commonly on the buttocks and thighs, was carried out in stages, probably because the operation was almost intolerably painful. Many of the old and some of the middle-aged men had facial tattoos that were deeply cut, perhaps to 'make them look frightfull in war', although the younger men (whom Banks described as those under twenty-five or twenty-six — an interesting definition of 'youth' in the 1769–70 Maori population) might have only their lips blacked. Those a little older often had a patch of tattoo over one eye or on a cheek. While the Europeans found a full facial tattoo very ugly, Banks said:

> it is impossible to avoid admiring the immence Elegance and Justness of the figures in which it is form'd, which in the face is always different spirals, upon the body generally different figures resembling something the foliages of old Chasing upon gold or silver; all these finishd with a masterly taste and execution, for of a hundred which at first sight you would judge to be exactly the same, on a close examination no two will prove alike.[25]

Banks thought that in places where the population was larger the people wore more moko, possibly because in a larger population there would be more individuals to act as an example to others in bearing the pain with fortitude. Both Parkinson and Spöring sketched many examples of both facial and body tattoo.

The people also often decorated themselves with red ochre, both on the face and the body, either by rubbing it dry onto the skin or more commonly by mixing it with oil and painting it on. As Banks commented,

> this latter is generaly practisd by the women and was most universaly condemned by us, for if any of us had unthinkingly ravishd a kiss from one of these fair Savages our transgression were wrote in most legible Characters on our noses [a 'kiss' being a hongi], which our companions could not fail to see.[26]

Clothing

Both Cook and Banks likened the common clothing of the local people to 'the square thrum'd matts that are made [in Europe] of rope yarns &c to lay at the

doors or passages into houses to clean one's shoes upon'.[27] The 'rain capes' were made out of flax leaves each split into three or four vertical strips which were then dried and woven into a mat, with strips eight or nine inches long left on the outer side to keep the wearer dry in wet weather, 'as every strip of leaf becomes in that case a kind of Guttar which serves to conduct the rain down'.[28] One such mat might be worn over the shoulders reaching down to the knees, while another was worn around the waist reaching nearly to the ground; and 'when they have it on [they] resemble not a little a thatchd house'. Several of the *Endeavour* artists' sketches of people show this style of dress.

The finer cloaks were pieces of cloth about four feet long and five feet broad, 'made of the same plant after it is bleached and prepar'd in such a manner that it is white and allmost as soft as flax but much stronger'.[29] One of these cloak types was made like European coarse canvas (Cook mistakenly thought this was done with a needle), only the fabric was 'ten times stronger' (close weave kaitaka); while the other type (open weave kaitaka) had glossy vertical threads which 'shone almost as much as silk', sometimes in coloured stripes, knotted together by widely spaced horizontal threads. Both types of fine cloak often had decorative borders of taaniko, worked, according to Banks, with different colours 'in fine stiches something like Carpeting or girls Samplers in Various patterns with an ingenuity truly surprizing to any one who will reflect that they are without needles'.[30] Other fine cloaks were decorated with spaced strips of dogskin or feathers, and on one occasion (actually on two occasions according to the journals) they saw a man wearing a cloak entirely covered with red parrot feathers (kahu kura). All cloaks were fastened by a string on one corner with a 'bodkin'

274

This pencil sketch by Parkinson seems to be a composite. Note the women and children on board, weapons including a spear, tewhatewha, hoeroa and taiaha, the conch-shell trumpet, garments, and the way in which the sail was being manoeuvred by a man wearing a belt and penis string.

(au rei) at the end of it, which was used to join the two sides of the cloak together. One such 'needle' was sketched by Parkinson with a caption that said that they were sometimes made of 'sea-ear' (paaua). Many cloaks, especially those of the finer sort, were collected during the voyage and are now held in European museums. Striped cloaks, chequered dogskin cloaks, and the open-weave cloak decorated with a border of dogskin were also shown in various of Parkinson's sketches.

The men wore short beards and tied their hair into a small knot on the top of their heads, sticking a comb into this knot and two or three white feathers. Around their waists they wore a belt with a string fastened to it that was tied to the prepuce of the penis. Magra said that local people he had talked to told him that this was to preserve the sensibility of the glans. The men often wore no other clothing than this (as one can see from some of the sketches) but according to Banks, they 'shewd visible reluctance and signs of shame when we desird them to untie it from a curiosity to see the manner in which it was tied'.[31]

The women wore their hair short and seldom tied up — or if it was tied it was at the back of their heads, and never ornamented with feathers. They were very modest about their private parts and never willingly exposed them, but wore a 'girdle of many platted strings made of the leaves of a very fragrant Grass [probably kaaretu]; into this were tuckd the leaves of some sweet scented plant fresh

Spöring's fine sketch of a rei puta neck ornament.

gatherd which like the fig leaf of our first mother served as the ultimate guard of their modesty'.[32] Otherwise they dressed very much like the men, except that they seldom wore fine cloaks.

Both men and women had holes bored in their ears, which were stretched out to at least a finger's width and kept extended by plugs of cloth, feathers, birds' bones, a stick of wood or nails given to them by the Europeans. The women often wore large bundles of snowy-white albatross down at their ears, which 'tho very odd made by no means an unelegant appearance'.[33] The people also suspended greenstone chisels or bodkins, the nails and teeth of deceased relatives (Cook commented, 'I think we were told that they did belong to thier deceas'd freinds'), dogs' teeth or other ornaments from their ears. On just one occasion Banks saw a person with a feather stuck right through a hole in the bridge of the nose. Sometimes women wore bracelets or anklets made of shells or birds' bones, while the men often wore greenstone tiki around their necks — 'the figure of a distorted man'; or the rei puta — 'the tooth of a whale cut slauntwise, so as something to resemble a tongue, and furnished with two eyes', which they valued above all other things. Cook added that at Queen Charlotte Sound many men and women wore round caps made of black feathers, and it was probably these that were described in Parkinson's vocabulary as 'potai' (pootae) 'the feather ornament on their head'. Parkinson also listed 'heebeekee' (he piki) as 'a bunch of scarlet feathers which they stick in their hair'.[34]

Many of these ornamental items were collected during the voyage or were sketched by the artists on board. A number of sketches of men were also made, showing these forms of ornament, although interestingly enough few individual portraits of women were drawn.

Houses

Joseph Banks, who had grown up in the rural grandeur of Revesby Abbey, was not impressed by Maori housing:

> Their houses are certainly the most inartificialy made of any thing among them, scarce equal to a European dog kennel and resembling one in the door at least, which is barely high and wide enough to admit a man crawling upon all fours. They are seldom more than 16 or 18 feet long, 8 or 10 broad and five or 6 high from the ridge pole to the Ground and built with a sloping roof like our Europaean houses. The materials of both walls and roof is dry grass or hay and very tightly it is put together, so that nescessarily they must be very warm. Some are lind with bark of trees on the inside, and many have over the door or fixd somewhere in the house a peice of Plank coverd with their carving, which they seem to value much as we do a picture, placing it always as conspicuously as possible. All these houses have the door at one end and near it [either over it or beside it according to Cook] is generaly a square hole which serves for a window or probably in winter time more for a chimney, for then they light a fire in the middle of the house. At the same end where this door and window are placed the side walls and roof project, generaly 18 inches or 2 feet beyond the end wall, making a kind of Porch in which are benches where the people of the house often sit. Within is a square place fencd of with either boards or stones for the rest, in the middle of which they can make a fire; round this the sides of the house are thick lyd with straw on which they sleep. As for furniture they are not much troubled with it: one chest commonly contains all their riches, consisting of Tools, Cloaths, arms, and a few feathers to stick in their hair; their gourds and Baskets made of Bark which serve them to keep fresh water, provision baskets, and the hammers with which they beat their fern roots, are generaly left without the door.
>
> Mean and low as these houses are they most perfectly resist all inclemencies of the weather and answer consequently the purposes of mere shelter as well as larger would do. The people I beleive spend little of the day in them (except may be in winter): the porch seems to be the place for work, and those who have not room there must set upon a stone or the ground in its neighbourhood.[35]

Cook thought that people often left their houses altogether in the summer, living dispersed in small temporary huts around the countryside. Banks added that 'some few of the better sort' of houses had courtyards enclosed by walls ten to twelve feet high made of timber and hay, enclosing three or four houses. Evidently the size of houses varied with family size, and on this topic Banks commented that 'their families are large'. He reported in his 'Account' that he had seen the unfinished framework of one very large house in Tolaga Bay, thirty feet long, with the sides ornamented with broad, carved planks, 'but for what purpose this was built or why deserted we could not find out'.[36] Very often, however, when the people were gathering fernroots or off fishing they would live in the open air, simply relying on their rain capes for shelter in wet weather.

Food

The people were reported in the accounts as eating food in moderate quantities, including dogs, birds (especially seabirds and albatrosses), fish, sweet potatoes (kuumara), yam (uwhi), 'Coccos', or taro, sow thistle (puuhaa) palm cabbage (niikau), but above all the roots of a species of fern (aruhe) that grew abundantly on the hills and closely resembled English bracken fern.

The question of human flesh as food provoked Banks into a vehement discourse on the 'admirable chain of nature', one of the ruling ideas of eighteenth-century Europe. He argued that although people in New Zealand undoubtedly ate human flesh, it was unthinkable that they did so for nourishment or pleasure but rather from a passionate desire for revenge:

> Nature through all the superior part of creation shews how much she recoils at the thought of any species preying upon itself : Dogs and cats shew visible signs of disgust at the very signs of a dead carcass of their species, even Wolves or Bears were never sayd to eat one another except in cases of absolute nescessity, when the stings of hunger have overcome the precepts of nature, in which case the same has been done by the inhabitants of the most civilizd nations [for instance, in the great European famines]. Among fish and insects indeed there are many instances which prove that those who live by prey regard little whither what they take is of their own or any other species; but any one who considers the admirable chain of nature in which Man, alone endowd with reason, justly claims the highest rank and next to him are placd the half reasoning Elephant, the sagacious dog, the architect Beaver, &c in Whoom instinct so nearly resembles reason as to have been mistaken for it by men of no mean capacitys, from these descending through the less informd Quadrupeds and birds to the fish and insects, which seem besides the instinct of Fear which is given them for self-preservation to be movd only by the stings of hunger to eat and those of lust to propagate their own species . . . , shading itself away into the vegetable kingdom — whoever considers this I say will easily see that no Conclusion in favour of such a practise can be drawn from the actions of a race of beings [presumably here he means fish and insects] placd so infinitely below us in the order of Nature.[37]

Banks's reaction to cannibalism seemed to turn on the belief that it debased human nature and overturned the Great Chain of Being, placing human beings below dogs, cats and even bears and wolves, and alongside such unreasoning forms of life as fish and insects which devoured their own kind without scruple. He recalled the evidence of cannibalism he had seen in Queen Charlotte Sound, which had finally convinced him that the custom was indeed practised in New Zealand, and discussed his attempts to buy a preserved head from Topaa: 'These it seems these people keep after having eat the brains as trophies of their victories . . . ; they had their ornament in their ears as when alive and some seemd to have false eyes.'

Cooking

It was claimed in the 'Accounts' that in New Zealand small fish and birds were generally roasted over an open fire on a long skewer fixed between two stones, the supporting stone being shifted to lower or raise the skewer over the fire. Large fish and dogs were cooked in earth ovens, 'a few stones heated hot and laid in a hole, their meat laid upon them and coverd with Hay seems to be the most difficult part of it'.[38] Fernroot was heated over the fire until the outer skin was charred, and then beaten with a wooden hammer on a stone until the outer layer came off. The inner glutinous pulp was sucked for a long time and the inner fibres spat out. In the South Island fernroot and fish formed the basis of the diet all year, and in the North throughout the summer at least from planting time onwards. Both fish and fernroot were dried in the summer and stocked up in huge piles for winter, when fish in particular were either more scarce or more difficult to catch. The people drank only water, and they appeared to have no intoxicating liquids of any kind.

Health

It seemed to both Cook and Banks that a simple and moderate diet was responsible for the fact that these people were healthy in the highest degree. People had often crowded to meet the Europeans, and Banks said that he could not recall ever seeing anyone with an infected skin, although at first they had mistaken white patches of dried salt on the skins of those who visited them at sea for some kind of disorder. Banks commented that 'such health drawn from so sound principles must make physicians almost useless: indeed I am inclind to think their knowledge of Physick is but small'. Smallshot wounds had nothing applied to them, and yet these healed quickly and without any infection. Both he and Cook thought that there were many old people in the population, although the actual age of these individuals is difficult to guess. The physical anthropologist Philip Houghton has suggested they were probably in their forties,[39] but most other evidence from tradition and early-contact history indicates that people may well have lived into their eighties and nineties in this period:

> Hardly a canoe came off to us that did not bring one or more [old people] and every town had several whoom if we may judge by gray hairs and worn-out teeth were of a very advanced age. Of these few or none were decrepid, indeed the greatest number of them seemd in vivacity and chearfullness to equal the young, indeed to be inferior to them in nothing but the want of equal strengh and agility.[40]

Worn-out teeth were not a reliable indicator of actual age, however, given the highly fibrous diet of fernroot, shellfish and fish.

Canoes

Cook, the practical sailor, in his 'Description' admired the local canoes, commenting that their construction showed great ingenuity and workmanship. They were long (on one occasion, according to Cook, the local people lined their canoe up against the *Endeavour*, evidently to compare their lengths, and it extended from the ship's anchor at the bows to the stern, that is about 100 feet), narrow, and shaped very much like a New England whaleboat. The war canoes (waka taua) carried from forty to 100 men, and were ornamented with fine carved work. The hull was wedge-shaped, and the large canoe seen at Uawa (which was almost seventy feet long) had a hull constructed of three sections hollowed out to about an inch and a half or two inches thick, well fastened together 'with strong plating'. Each side on this canoe was built up with a single long carved plank about ten to twelve inches deep, well fitted and lashed on, with a

A pen-and-wash sketch of a waka taua (war canoe) by Parkinson, probably based on a canoe seen off the Wairarapa coast, showing carved decorations, four women on board, and an array of fine cloaks.

number of thwarts laid across and lashed to the gunwhales to strengthen the canoe. The prow carving projected five to six feet forward and was four and a half feet high, while the stern carving was fourteen feet high, two feet wide and one and a half inches thick. Most canoes were at least twenty feet long, most were carved and a few of the small ones (especially towards the south) had outriggers or were constructed of two hulls joined together. The carved stern-posts and prows of war canoes were decorated with 'loose fringes of Black feathers that had a most gracefull effect', and the carved gunwhale boards were ornamented with white bunches of feathers on a black ground, placed at intervals.

The paddles were light and often carved, with an oval blade, about six feet long altogether, and the paddlers were very expert, working in perfect unison. The canoes were seldom sailed, however:

> we very seldom saw them make use of Sails and indeed never unless when they were to go right before the wind. They were made of mat and instead of a mast were hoisted upon two sticks which were fastned one to each side, so that they requird two ropes which answerd the purpose of sheets and were fastned to the tops of these sticks; in this clumsey manner they saild with a good deal of swiftness and were steered by two men who sat in the stern with each a paddle in his hand.[41]

The canoes were often sketched, and also paddles, bailers, individual prow and stern carvings; and one of Parkinson's sketches shows how the sail was manoeuvred. Some paddles and at least one bailer were collected on the voyage and taken back to London, where they still survive in the British Museum.

Carving

Banks commented that

> for the beauty of their carving in general I fain would say something more about
> it but find myself much inferior to the task. I shall therefore content myself with
> saying that their taste varied in two materialy different Stiles, I will call them. One
> was intirely formed of a number of Spirals differently connected, the other was in
> a much more wild taste and I may truly say was like nothing but itself.[42]

The 'Spiral' style was well represented on some of Spöring's sketches of
canoe prows, and the other style was perhaps that recorded on the Uawa prow,
the poupou (wall carving) from Uawa, or the feather boxes collected during the
voyage. Parkinson's 'Account' also included a sketch of a carved mask, with the
following intriguing comment:

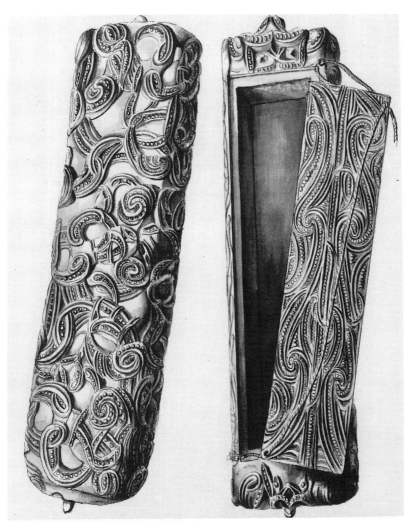

'Carvd trunk or box New Zeland'. A papa hou, or feather box, sketched in pen and wash by John
Frederick Miller after the voyage.

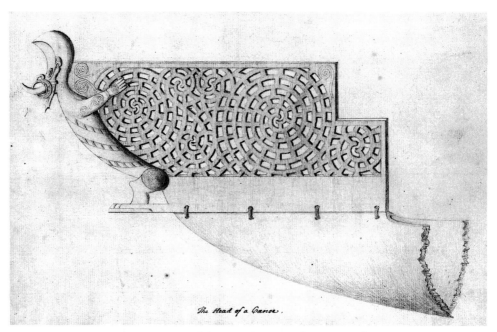

The Head of a Canoe.

Sketches by Spöring of the carved prow and sternpost of a canoe.

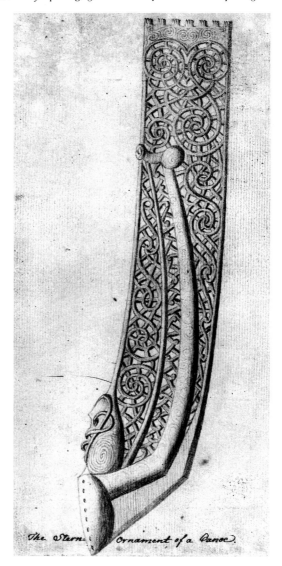

The Stern Ornament of a Canoe.

a favourite Ornament, which resembles a human face, made of wood, coloured red, and is much like some of the Roman masks. The eyes are made of the fine coloured ear-shells [paaua], laid into the wood. This was six inches long but they have different sizes. Some of the smaller ones have handles carved very ingeniously; these they frequently hold up when they approached the ship and perhaps it may be the carved figure of some idol which they worship.

Two of these objects have survived from Cook's voyages, and have subsequently been variously described as canoe prow ornaments, latrine decorations or bird snares.[43]

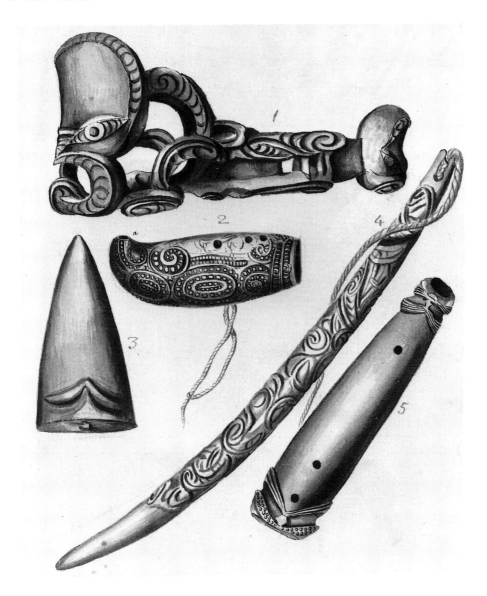

This pen-and-wash sketch by Miller shows a facial mask (as described by Parkinson), two flutes, a carved cloak bodkin and a carved neck ornament of the rei puta type.

Tools

According to Cook's 'Description', the people used adzes or axes (Banks said 'hatchets') of a hard black stone (presumably greywacke, argillite or gabbro), or of 'green Talk' (greenstone), which was both hard and tough. Greenstone adzes were very highly valued, and the people refused to part with them. Cook said that 'I offer'd one day for one, one of the best axes I had in the Ship besides a number of other things but nothing would induce the owner to part with it: from this I inferr'd that good ones were scarce among them.'[44] There were also chisels made of both greenstone and human bones, and for work requiring a very sharp edge, pieces of 'jasper' were broken off a large lump and used until they were blunted. Banks thought that 'jasper' was probably used to bore a hole through a piece of glass that they had given to someone at Uawa, who then converted it into an ornament. He confessed complete ignorance, however, of the method used to cut and shape their stone patu. There is only one sketch of a greenstone

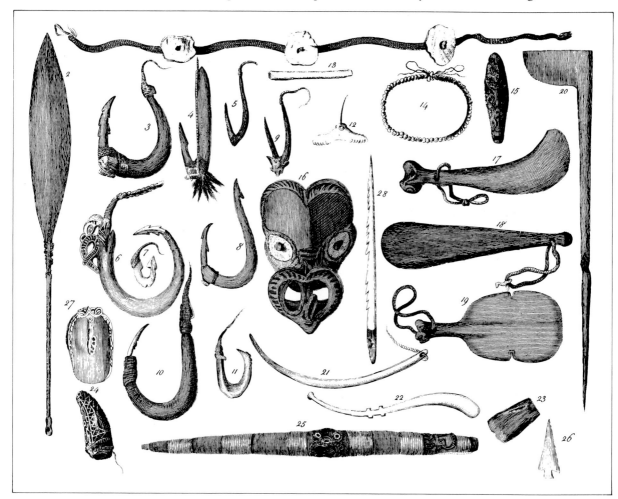

'*Various kinds of Instruments Utensil &c, of the Inhabitants of New Zealand . . .*' engraved by T. Chambers after S. H. Grimm.

stone chisel (captioned 'A Wedge or Chisel, made of the green stone, or Poo-nammoo [Pounamu], as they call it, and sometimes of the Basaltes. These wedges they sometimes tie to a wooden handle, and then use them as hatchets and hoes. They are of various sizes, from one to eight inches in length'). None of the stone implements known to have been collected on Cook's voyages are attributable with any certainty to the 1769–70 expedition.

Weaving and netting

Banks admitted to have seen a cloak being woven only once in New Zealand 'that was done in a kind of frame of the breadth of the Cloth, across which it was spread, and the cross threads worked in by hand'[45] — evidently a reference to weaving sticks. He said he had no idea how the decorative borders (taaniko) were made. Fishing nets were made very like European ones, using unprepared split flax, and they could be extremely long: 'A seine seems to be the joint work of a whole town and I suppose the joint property: of these I think I have seen as large as ever I saw in Europe.'[46]

Fish were also caught with lines and hooks made of wood or bone, with wood, bone or shell points lashed on (some fish-hooks were collected and later sketched and described). Most often, though, they were caught with fish pots and baskets, including the hoop-nets described in Totara-nui, which had hoops seven to eight feet in diameter and were baited with little baskets full of fish guts or paaua tied to different parts of the net, and weighted down with a stone sinker.

Gardening

According to Banks's 'Account':

> In tillage they excell, as people who are themselves to eat the fruit of their industry and have little else to do but to cultivate nescessarily must. When we first came to Tegadu [Anaura — in late October] their crops were just coverd and had not yet began to sprout: the mould was as smooth as in a garden, and every root had its small hillock ranged in a regular Quincunx by lines which with the pegs still remain in the feild.[47]

This added detail about the Anaura gardens indicates the precision and tidiness with which they were laid out. Banks observed that the soil was generally sandy and easily tilled with 'a long and narrow stake flatted a little and sharpned, across this is fixd a peice of stick for the convenience of pressing it down with the foot'[48] (the koo, or digging stick). In his view, gardening, weaving and the other 'arts of peace' were most often practised in the north-eastern parts of the country.

Warfare

War, on the other hand, wrote Banks, 'seems to be equaly known to all tho most practisd in the South West parts. The mind of man, ever ingenious in inventing instruments of destruction, has not been idle here.'

He described the local weapons as spears made of hardwood, sharpened at both ends, fourteen to fifteen feet long and sometimes pointed with human bone, held in the middle; 'battle axes' (or tewhatewha) made of very hard wood and about six feet long, with a pointed handle and a broad axe-like blade used for chopping at the head of an adversary; 'patoopatoo' (patupatu) or 'hand bludgeons' of stone, whalebone or hardwood made in different shapes, sharp-edged, and fastened to the wrist by a strap or stuck in the belt, 'most admirably calculated for the cracking of sculls'; 'darts' (pere), barbed (sometimes with a stingray's sting) and sharp-ended about eight feet long, thrown down on adversaries from a height in defending a paa (these proved useless, however, in attempts to attack the *Endeavour* because of its height above the water); stones that were thrown very accurately and for great distances, much farther than the Europeans could manage; 'halbards' (taiaha), carved and ornamented with dogs' hair, feathers and inlaid shell 'like Mother of Pearl', and carried as a mark of distinction; and 'spontoons' (or hoeroa), 'the rib of a Whale as White as snow carvd very much and ornamented with dogs hair and feathers', which were also carried as a mark of rank. A number of these weapons were collected, and sketched after the voyage.

According to Cook's 'Description':

> Whenever we were Viseted by any number of them that had never Heard or seen any thing of us before they generaly came off in the largest Canoes they had, some of which will carry 60, 80 or 100 people, they always brought their best close along with them which they put on as soon as they came near the ship. In each Canoe were generaly an old man, in some two or three, these use'd always to direct the others, were better Clothed and generaly carried a halbard or battle ax in their hands or some such like thing that distinguished them from the others. As soon as they came within about a stone's throw from the ship ['having no Idea that any missive weapon could reach them farther,' added Banks] they would there lay and call out 'Haromai hareuta a patoo age' [haere mai haere [ki] uta . . . [k]a patua a koe], that is come here, come ashore with us and we will kill you with our patoo patoo's, and at the same time would shake them at us, at times they would dance the war dance, and other times they would trade with and talk to us and answer such questions as were put to them with all the Calmness emaginable and then again begin the war-dance, shaking their paddles patoo patoo's &c and make strange contorsions at the same time, and as soon as they had worked themselves up to a proper pitch they would begin to attack us with stones and darts and oblige us whether we would or no to fire upon them. Musquetary they never regarded unless they felt the effect but great guns they did because these could throw stones farther than they could comprehend.[49]

War songs and music

Banks described the war song (haka or peruperu) as follows:

> The War Song and dance consists of Various contortions of the limbs during which the tongue is frequently thrust out incredibly far and the orbits of the eyes enlargd

Opposite: *Sketches by Miller made after the voyage. Above are various types of patu (hand-clubs): mere, wahaika and kotiate. The long clubs below are: a 'battle axe' (tewhatewha), a 'dart' (kopere), a halbert (taiaha), another 'dart', and a 'spontoon of a Whales Rib' (hoeroa).*

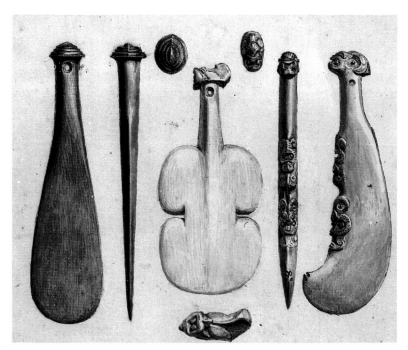

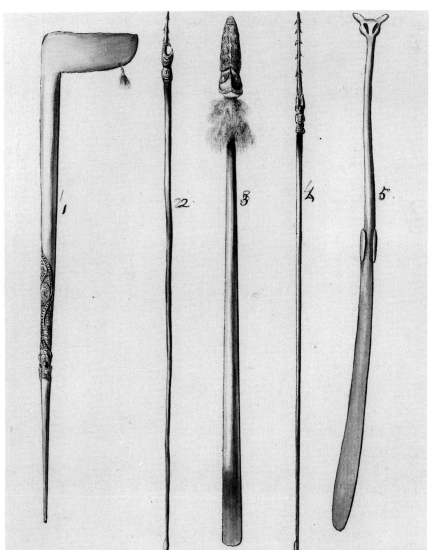

287

so much that a circle of white is distinctly seen round the Iris: in short nothing is omittd which can render a human shape frightful and deformd, which I suppose they think terrible. During this time they brandish their spears, hack the air with their patoopatoos and shake their darts as if they meant every moment to begin the attack, singing all the time in a wild but not disagreable manner and ending every strain with a loud and deep fetchd sigh in which they all join in concert. The whole is accompanied by strokes struck against the sides of the Boats &c with their feet, Paddles and arms, the whole in such excellent time that tho the crews of several Canoes join in concert you rarely or never hear a single stroke wrongly placd.[50]

This song was used both in war and peace, but always before an attack. In addition the women 'sing prettily enough in parts' in a slow melancholy style, songs that Banks commented 'certainly have more taste in them than could be expected from untaught savages'. The local instruments included two or three sorts of trumpets (including 'the shell calld Tritons Trumpet with which they make a noise not much differing from that made by boys with a Cows horn' (puu taatara); and a 'trumpet, 19½ inches in length, made of a hard brown wood which they split, and carefully hollow out each side so as to fit neatly again, leaving an edge on each side; and joining them together, they are bound tight with withes made of cane . . . They produce a harsh shrill sound' (puutoorino)); and a small pipe of wood, 'crooked and shapd almost like a large tobacco pipe head, but it has hardly more musick in it than a whistle with a Pea in it' (nguru). One of these was sketched by Parkinson and described as a carved whistle with a mouth-hole and several finger-holes, about three inches long and worn around the neck and making 'a shrill sound'. Although a number of flutes and at least one war trumpet were collected and sketched after the voyage, Banks says that he never heard the people play or sing with any of these instruments. According to Cook, 'their signs of frendship is the waving the hand or a peice of cloth &c'.

Forts and leaders

According to Banks's 'Account', the people in Mercury Bay, the Bay of Islands and Queen Charlotte Sound, being constantly in danger of attack, lived together in fortified towns sited on steep-sided islands or peninsulas and defended at weak points by broad ditches, strong palisades, and fighting stages (puuhara, pourewa) eighteen to twenty feet high, where the defenders could stand and throw down darts, spears, and stones. Quantities of fernroot and dried fish were stored in these 'heppas' (he paa), but water was not usually available except outside the defences. Most of the people seemed to be living in paa, while others were out in small parties collecting fernroot and fish. In Hawke's Bay, Poverty Bay, Tolaga, and 'Tegadu', however, he claimed that there were no paa (although in fact paa were sighted in Hawke's Bay and one in Poverty Bay, according to the journals), and the people lived in scattered houses. In these districts there were long 'stages' built on the hills as retreats, but most of these were in ruins:

> Throughout all this district the people seemd free from apprehension and as in a stage of Profound peace. Their cultivations were far more numerous and larger than we saw them any where else and they had a far greater quantity of Fine boats,

Fine cloaths, Fine carvd work; in short the people were far more numerous, and livd in much greater affluence, than any others we saw. This seemed to be owing to their being joind together under one cheif or king, so at least they always told us, Whose name was Te ratu and who lives far up in the countrey.[51]

On the basis of his misunderstandings about Te Ratu, Banks managed to construct an illusory kingdom, claiming that from Cape Kidnappers to the Bay of Plenty the people were under Te Ratu's command:

his Dominions are certainly for an Indian Monarch most extensive, he was acknowledged for a lengh of coast of upwards of —— Leagues and yet we do not know the eastern limits of his dominions; we are sure however that they contain the greatest share of the rich part of the Northernmost Island and that far the greatest number of people upon it are his subjects.[52]

Both Banks and Cook thought that the other leaders they met in those areas were lesser chiefs, who received respect and obedience from their tribes and probably administered justice to them. The only instance they saw of this was, however, at Thames, where a man who had tried to steal something from the Europeans was kicked and hit by his 'chief'. The chiefs were usually old men, and the Europeans never found out how they gained their office, although outside Te Ratu's supposed territories 'we plainly learnt that the cheifs whoom they obeyd, of which every tribe had some, receivd their dignity by inheritance'.

The people in 'the Southern parts' seemed to hold many things in common, especially their few fine cloaks and their nets, which they kept in a small hut in the middle of their town. Each house had sections of net being made in them which Banks thought would eventually be joined together to make the long seine nets that they saw. Generally speaking, however, according to Cook:

Whatever place we put in at or whatever people we spoke with upon the Coast they generaly told us that those that were at a little distance from them were their enemies; from which appear'd to me that they were very much divided into parties which make war one with another, and all their actions and beheavour towards us tended to prove that they are a brave open warlike people and voide of treachery.[53]

Division of labour

According to Banks in his 'Account':

The Women are less regarded here than at the South Sea Islands, at least so Tupia thought who complaind of it as an insult upon the sex. They eat with the men however. How the sexes divide labour I do not know but I am inclind to beleive that the Men till the ground, fish in boats and take birds, the Women dig up fern roots, collect shell Fish and lobsters near the beach and dress the victuals and weave cloth, while the men weave netts — thus at least these employments have been distributed when I had an opportunity of Observing them which was very seldom, for our approach generaly made a holiday where ever we went; men women and children flocking to us either to satisfy their curiosity or trade with us for whatever they might have.[54]

289

Religion

The Europeans saw few signs of religious observance, and no public places of worship like those in Tahiti. Banks saw only one private shrine, a small square edged with stones near a kuumara cultivation, which had a spade in the middle with a basket of fernroots hanging from it, 'an offering (I suppose) to the Gods for the success of the Crop so at least one of the natives explain it'.[55] The people acknowledged the existence of superior beings, and had similar ideas about the creation of the world and of people to Tupaia, although he 'seemd to be much better versd in such legends than any of them, for whenever he began to preach as we calld it he was sure of a numerous audience who attended with most profound silence to his doctrines'.

Burial and mourning

Both Cook and Banks reported in their 'Accounts' that in New Zealand, unlike Tahiti, burial was kept secret. They saw no burial places anywhere in the country. In the north the people told them that people were buried in the ground, while in Queen Charlotte Sound they said that a weight was tied to the body and the dead person was sunk in the sea. Mourners slashed (haehae) their bodies, especially on the arms, faces and chests. According to Banks:

> I have seen several with such wounds of which the blood was not yet staunchd and one only, a woman, while she was cutting herself and lamenting. She wept much, repeating many sentences in a plaintive tone of voice, at every one of which she with a shell cut a gash in some part of her body; she however contrivd her cutts in such a manner that few of them drew blood and those that did penetrated a small depth only. She was old and had outlivd probably those violent impressions that greif as well as other passions of the mind make upon young people, her greif also was probably of long standing.[56]

Language

Cook, Banks, Magra and Parkinson were all very struck by the similarities between Tahitian and Maori. According to Magra:

> It deserves to be remarked, that the people of New Zealand spoke the language of Otahitee with but very little difference, not so much as is found between many counties in England; a circumstance of the most extraordinary kind, and must necessarily lead us conclude, that one of these places was originally peopled from the other, though they are near two thousand miles distance; and nothing but the ocean intervenes, which we should hardly believe they could navigate so far in canoes, the only vessels that they appear to have ever possessed.[57]

Banks produced a comparative list of a number of common words in Northern Maori, Southern Maori (where the vocabulary items were collected by Parkinson, who he said 'made use of more letters in spelling the words than were absolutely necessary') and Tahitian to illustrate these parallels, adding two explanatory comments: 'first, that the words were so much disguisd by their manner of pronouncing them that I found it very dificult to understand them till I had wrote them down; secondly that Tupia at the very first understood and conversd

290

with them with great facility.'[58] Tupaia was evidently well travelled within Polynesia and quite likely was familiar with several Polynesian languages, in which
case he would have handled the sound shifts between Tahitian and Maori with
relative ease.

Banks's word lists were as follows:

	Northern	[Modern transcription]	Southern	Otahite
a cheif	Eareete	[he ariki]	Eareete	Earee
a Man	Taat	[tangata]	Taata	Taata
a Woman	wahine	[wahine]	wahine	wahine
the head	Eupo	[he upoko]	Heaowpoho	Eupo
the Hair	Macauwe	[makawe]	Heoooo	Roourou
the Ear	Terringa	[taringa]	Hetaheyei	Terrea
the Forehead	Erai	[he rae]	Heai	Erai
the Eyes	Mata	[mata]	Hemata	Mata
the Cheeks	Paparinga	[paapaaringa]	Hepapaeh	Paparea
the nose	Ahewh	[ihu]	Heeih	ahew
the Mouth	Hangoutou	[he ngutu]	Hegowai	Outou
the Chin	Ecouwai	[he kauae]	Hekaoewai	————
the Arm	Haringaringa	[he ringaringa]	————	Rema
the finger	Maticara	[matikara]	Hemaigawh	Maneow
the belly	Ateraboo	[————]	————	Oboo
the navel	Apeto	[pito]	Hecapeeto	Peto
Come here	Haromai	[haere mai]	Horomai	Harromai
Fish	Heica	[he ika]	Heica	Eyca
a lobster	Kooura	[koura]	Kooura	Tooura
Coccos	Taro	[taro]	Taro	Taro
Sweet potatoes	Cumala	[kuumara]	Cumala	Cumala
Yamms	Tuphwhe	[te uwhi]	Tuphwhe	Tuphwhe
Birds	Mannu	[manu]	Mannu	Mannu
No	Kaoure	[kaore]	Kaoure	Oure
1.	Tahai	[tahi]	————	Tahai
2.	Rua	[rua]	————	Rua
3.	Torou	[toru]	————	Torou
4.	Ha	[whaa]	————	Hea
5.	Rema	[rima]	————	Rema
6.	Ono	[ono]	————	Ono
7.	Etu	[whitu]	————	Hetu
8.	Warou	[waru]	————	Warou
9.	Iva	[iwa]	————	Heva
10.	Angahourou	[ngahuru]	————	Ahourou
the teeth	heenihu	[he niho]	heneaho	Nihio
the Wind	Mehow	[te hau]	————	Mattai
a theif	Amootoo	[————]	————	Teto
to examine	Mataketake	[maatakitaki]	————	Mataitai
to Sing	Eheara	[————]	————	Heiva
Bad	Keno	[kino]	Keno	Eno
Trees	Eratou	[he raakau]	Eratou	Eraou
Grandfather	Toubouna	[tuupuna]	Toubouna	Toubouna

The Banks manuscript vocabularies now held in the School of Oriental and African Studies Library, London, included fifty-five other vocabulary items, in two lists, one of which was headed 'the South part as taken by Mr Parkinson in Queen Charlotte's Sound' and the other, 'the NE and NW Parts taken by myself in Taone roa, Tegadu, Tolaga and Opoorage'. Parkinson's published journal also included a vocabulary, with some items in addition to those in the Banks list attributed to him:

Papa,	Father.	[paapaa]
Hetamaeh,	A boy, or Son.	[he tama]
He aowpoho,	The head.	[he upoko]
He ai,	The brow.	[he rae]
He matta,	The eyes.	[he mata]
He toogge matta,	The eye-brows.	[he tuke-mata]
He gammo,	The eye-lids.	[he kamo]
He eih,	The nose.	[he ihu]
He peeapeea,	The nostrils.	[——]
He papaeh,	The cheeks.	[——]
He gaoowai,	The mouth.	[he kauae (jaw)]
He neeho,	The teeth.	[he niho]
He gooteh,	The lips.	[he ngutu]
Haiaeeo,	The tongue.	[he arero]
Egoorree,	A dog.	[he kurii]
Teyka,	Fish.	[he ika]
Hewhai,	A skate.	[he whai]
Eraperape,	The fish called Chimaera.	[he reperepe]
Hepaooa,	Ear-shells.	[he paaua]
Hekohooa,	Small ear-shells.	[——]
Heraiyanno,	The small biting fly.	[——]
Heaow,	A leaf.	[he rau]
Heanoohe,	Fern root.	[he aruhe]
Tracaow,	Wood.	[he raakau]
Po whattoo,	A stone.	[pohatu]
Whakabeete,	The large peaked hill.	[Hakapiti (Mt Egmont)]
Hewai,	Water.	[he wai]
Heawhai,	A house.	[he whare]
Pateea,	A hedge or fence.	[——]
Ewhao,	A nail.	[he whao]
Tochee,	A hatchet, or adze.	[toki]
Eei,	Victuals.	[kai]
eaowte,	Indian cloth.	[he aute]
Hecacahoo,	A garment.	[he kaakahu]
Opoonamoo,	A green ear-ring.	[pounamu]
Potai,	The feather ornament on their head.	[pootae]
Heebeekee,	A bunch of scarlet feathers which they stick in their hair.	[he piki]
Emaho,	Tataow.	[he moko]

Kaowaowaow,	A small flute.	[koauau]
Hewaca,	A canoe.	[he waka]
Hewhaiwhai,	A bile.	[wheewhee]
Hoggee,	To paddle.	[hoki (return)]
Patoopatoo,	To throw stones, to threaten.	[patupatu (to hit)]
Oweerree,	To roll up.	[wiri (to twist)]
Orero,	To speak, or a speech.	[koorero]
Apoorotoo,	Good.	[——]
Ekeeno,	Bad.	[e kino]
Matto,	Steep.	[——]
Mai whattoo,	Stronger, or very strong.	[——]
Keeanooe,	Too small.	[kia nui — make it large]
Keeamaow,	Larger.	[——]
A, a,	Yes.	[ae]
Kaowra,	No.	[kaore]
Na, na,	What say you?	[na, na]
Eeha, teneega?	Whats that? or what call you that?	[he aha teenaa?]
Eta eta,	Look you; here, here.	[——]
Ma dooge dooge,	Let me see it, or let me look.	[maatakitaki]
Katahe,	One.	[ka tahi]
Karooa,	Two.	[ka rua]
Katarroo,	Three.	[ka toru]
Kawha,	Four.	[ka whaa]
Kareema,	Five.	[ka rima]
Kaonoo,	Six.	[ka ono]
Kawheetoo,	Seven.	[ka whitu]
Kawarroo,	Eight.	[ka waru]
Kaeeva,	Nine.	[ka iwa]
Kacahaowroo,	Ten	[ka kahuru]

Most of the recorded vocabulary items were words for body parts, food or common objects, although a few verbs and phrases were also listed and Banks had learned the possessive particle 'taa/too', the indefinite article 'he' and the specifiers 'ko' and 'oeia' (koia). On the basis of this evidence the Europeans' linguistic skills were very limited, and they must have been largely reliant on Tupaia's ability to make himself understood both by the local people, and by his *Endeavour* companions, especially Cook, Banks and Parkinson.

Magra's general comments in particular made a comparison between Tahitian and Maori customs, appearance and material culture to show both similarities (as evidence of common origins) and differences between the two populations. Like the Tahitians, according to Magra, the New Zealanders cooked their food in earth ovens, tattooed their bodies, tied their hair at the top of their heads, and had similar axes and fish-hooks; but they seemed far more courageous than the Tahitians in war, were browner in complexion, and lacked bows and arrows, which the Tahitians used 'with great dexterity'.

From this last point Magra concluded that the Tahitians must have migrated from New Zealand, and later invented the bow and arrow, 'as it cannot be supposed that the New Zealanders would have lost so beneficial an acquisition, if they had ever been acquainted with it'.[59] Banks, on the other hand, concluded that:

> from the similarity of customs, the still greater of Traditions and the almost identical sameness of Language between these people and those of the Islands in the South Sea there remains little doubt that they came originaly from the same source: but where that Source is future experience may teach us, at Present I can say no more than that I firmly beleive that it is to the Westward and by no means to the East.[60]

In echoing this opinion Cook also made it plain that he did not believe that any Southern Continent existed as a possible common homeland, except perhaps in the high latitudes.

CONCLUSIONS

Taken as a whole — the day-by-day journals and logs; the charts; the botanical, zoological and ethnological collections; the artists' sketches; the vocabularies; and Banks's, Cook's, Magra's and Parkinson's generalised 'Accounts' — the *Endeavour* descriptions of the physical aspects of life in New Zealand were superb. Those observers with some training in natural science (particularly William Monkhouse and Joseph Banks) wrote detailed and meticulous accounts that check well against the surviving evidence of the places and objects which they described. Spöring's coastal views were extremely accurate, as were Cook's charts. The collections of 'artificial curiosities' and the sketches of them made during the voyage by Herman Spöring and afterwards by John Frederick Miller provided an invaluable sample of Maori material culture in 1769–70, even though the places where most of these objects were collected cannot now be reliably identified. Parkinson's and Spöring's pencil sketches of people and places gave a vivid evocation of local landscapes and their inhabitants, although Parkinson's finished pen-and-wash compositions and the engravings based on them were probably the least accurate records produced during the voyage. Joseph Banks's 'Account of New Zealand' and Cook's general description gave a great deal of detail that had not been included in any of the daily journals. Above all, the day-by-day journal entries (although in the case of a number of the surviving journals these were copied straight from the ship's log) together with the logs and charts gave precisely located accounts of events, people and environments in various parts of the country. It is often possible to work out where a writer went on a given day, who went with him and the limits of their communications with the local people; and when a range of such accounts is set alongside other kinds of information (including Maori accounts of those meetings and tribal histories), the reconstruction of many aspects of life in those places in 1769–70 can begin.

None of this is to say, however, that the *Endeavour* accounts were without their limitations. The contacts with Maori groups were brief (the longest was twenty-three days in Queen Charlotte Sound), seasonally restricted (October to March), and none of the *Endeavour*'s people ever travelled far inland (the farthest was a boat trip twelve to fourteen miles up the 'River Thames'). For long stretches of coastline there was no social information at all, either because the *Endeavour* was sailing too far offshore or at night, the local canoes could not catch her up, or simply because the explorers could see nothing of settlement or cultivations from their vantage point on board the ship. The observers were all male, and they noticed very little about women or children, except when they had sexual dealings with the local women.

Communications throughout were limited by the uneasy and often hostile reactions of local groups, and by a combination of Tupaia's limited grasp of English, the Europeans' limited grasp of Tahitian and Maori and difficulties experienced in hearing Maori accurately (because the hearers were using Tahitian or various English dialect sound systems). Details given by different observers were sometimes (although not often) contradictory, and the quality of their descriptions varied according to training, the vagaries of individual interests, and shifting levels of curiosity about local life.

Most fundamentally, the *Endeavour* records were shaped by the standards and expectations of the eighteenth-century societies from which they came. The production of such records in the first place (for the *Endeavour* expedition was, if nothing else, a marvellous artefact of eighteenth-century European seafaring and natural science); their categories of description (from 'halbards' and 'spontoons', to 'governors' and 'kings'); and their judgements of such ineffable qualities among Maori as courage, virtue, beauty, honour and reason, all mirrored Europe at least as much as the realities of Maori life. The observers' unconscious reflections of their own lives shaped their reflections upon others, and in this interplay of images one can see the complexity, as well as the fascination, of these early European accounts.

Despite these limitations, the *Endeavour* records remain invaluable for three main reasons. First, one can be confident that the technology and social practices described had not yet been significantly changed by European technology and practices. After Cook's voyage, one can never be sure of this again. This is not to argue that the people in the various places visited were unaffected by the *Endeavour*'s presence (for as Banks had reported 'our approach generaly made a holiday where ever we went; men, women and children flocking to us either to satisfy their curiosity or to trade with us for whatever they might have'), but rather that the local people responded in ways which were still peculiarly their own.

Second, because this was a voyage of exploration and discovery, and because James Cook was so thorough, the *Endeavour* sailed around both islands and anchored in a number of different harbours. Both at anchor and under sail the observers on board commented on regional differences in canoe architecture, clothing styles, tattoo, dialect, cultivation, settlement patterns and wealth. Cook's voyage to New Zealand is unparalleled among the early meetings between Maori and Europeans for the geographic spread of its observation and its precise evidence of regional variations in tribal ways of life.

Third, the cumulative detail of *Endeavour* observations, their accuracy and the range of media in which they were expressed are unsurpassed in the records of any other early expedition to New Zealand. This was the only scientific expedition to reach New Zealand in this period and one of the great scientific expeditions of its time, and the quality of its records pays an impressive tribute to the qualities of eighteenth-century European science.

At the same time, the *Endeavour* voyage was also a prelude to the European exploitation of New Zealand and the excellence of its records (and Banks's expert advice and advocacy) contributed to the speed and relative ease with which the early stages of that exploitation and then settlement took place.

THE ANTIPODES
OF FRANCE

Chapter Twelve

SURVILLE IN TOKERAU (DOUBTLESS BAY)

December 1769

New Zealand is the place where we should probably put the antipodes of France and where the Dutch were maltreated. They say there are tall men there; whether they are really so or whether fear made them seem so to the Dutch, they are in any case mysterious about giving a full description of them.

Pierre Duval: *La Monde, ou La Géographie Universelle 1670.*[1]

The *St Jean Baptiste*, the ship that had crossed the *Endeavour*'s track off North Cape on 16 December 1769, was a French Indian vessel on a trading expedition bound for 'Davis Land', an island rumoured to be off the coast of Terra Australis. Jean-François-Marie de Surville, the captain, had decided to call in at New Zealand for food and water, because his crew had been stricken with scurvy and they had a desperate need for fresh supplies.

Surville's expedition knew nothing of the *Endeavour*, and like Cook and a later explorer from French India, Marion du Fresne, the *St Jean Baptiste*'s officers were dependent on Tasman's account and charts of the New Zealand coastline. At this period French map-makers were known as the best in Europe, and a number of contemporary charts included Tasman's version of the western coastline of part of the South and all of the North Island. Some French theorists (including de la Lande, map-maker for the French 1769 transit of Venus expeditions) thought this might be part of the Southern Continent, and marvellous fantasies were circulating about what might be found in the Southern Hemisphere's southern seas. To understand the expectations that Surville and, later, Marion du Fresne brought to New Zealand, and their behaviour towards local people, it is necessary to consider briefly the society from which they came.

THE FRENCH BACKGROUND

In the mid-eighteenth century France was by far the most densely inhabited country in Western Europe, with a population of twenty million people.[2] At the height of the Seven Years' War (1756–63), France maintained a standing army of half a million men.[3] It was also the acknowledged centre of European intellectual and cultural life, with one of Europe's most glittering royal courts. The French state had a formidable bureaucratic administration, and along with Britain it was one of Europe's leading industrial powers, producing luxury items, wool, linen cloth and iron, and a range of cheap, low-quality goods.[4] French trade expanded dramatically during this century, due mainly to an increase in colonial commerce, and its navy also grew. By 1750, however, backed by a vigorous and innovative industrial infrastructure, the British Navy gained a numerical advantage over the French of almost two ships of the line to one.[5] This was to prove a decisive factor in British victories over France in various battles both in Europe, and during the 'Great War for Empire'.

Unlike England, France was still ruled by an absolute monarch, and in many ways the 'Ancien Régime' was a conservative, traditionalist society. Few fundamental innovations in agriculture or manufacturing were made during this era, which Pierre Goubert has characterised as:

> the age of patois and witches, shepherds, and millers, seigneurs and tithe-gatherers, salt-tax collectors and tipstaffs, barter and small transactions, moving at the speed of mule and wayfarer, of the seasons and the signs of the zodiac, with a distant King and God who are the ultimate judges and the last resort and consolation.[6]

The common people held the King in awe, and the cry of the army before going into battle was 'Vive le roi!' The Bourbon kings organised a spectacular cultural life centred on Versailles, with opera, dance and drama, hunting, gambling and public rituals, where nobles were encouraged to compete for royal patronage and favours. The monarchs assembled an array of talented administrators and built up a large standing army, but all of this was extremely expensive and had to be financed by direct and indirect taxes. Since the nobles as well as the Church and a host of wealthy commoners were exempt from most direct taxes, the weight of supporting the state fell heavily on the peasants. The attitude of the seigneurs (estateholders) towards the people who paid most of the taxes and worked their lands was often harsh, as a contemporary document from Angevin recorded:

> The seigneurs regard the tenant farmers who work their property as veritable servants, the labourer who feeds them as a slave; if a day-labourer in their employ succumbs under the load, they are less grieved than by the death of one of the horses in their stable. The contempt of the nobility for the commonalty is beyond belief.[7]

The hierarchies of the Ancien Régime were a complex, finely graded combination of birth and wealth, so that while letters of ennoblement or offices that carried noble status could be purchased from the King, nobility was otherwise defined by descent through males, with the ancient virtues of honour and military courage being held to pass down the family line. At mid-century there were perhaps 150,000 nobles in France.[8] Nobility and wealth usually went together, so that even a middling noble might own a house in the country and a 'hostel' in town, two or three seigneuries (estates) where a few thousand peasants lived and paid dues, some mills and wine presses, a park, woodlands and some game preserves.[9] By virtue of their birth, nobles had the privilege of wearing the sword,

Versailles, painted by Pierre-Denis Martin in 1722. The French royal family's great palace had seventeen acres of buildings and 1,400 fountains.

occupying offices in the Army and Navy and the higher positions in the Church, and serving the King at Court. By virtue of their birth commoners had the privilege of engaging in manual labour (which was forbidden to nobles) and paying taxes without relief.

As in England wealth was founded on the land, and eighty-five per cent of the population lived in the countryside, with its great diversity of landscapes and local customs. From the flat cornfields of the north to the vineyards of the grape-growing regions, the woods and pastures of the mountain lands and the hamlets of the west with their concentric rings of gardens and hemp patches, each region had its own nobles, its Parlements, its churches and walled towns, and considerable autonomy from centralised control. Those who created rural wealth by their labour saw little of it, however, and in almost every province the existence of ordinary people was precarious and life was often brief.

In the parish of Auneuil, for instance, over fifty-one per cent of those born died before reaching the age of twenty, although at mid-century as in England, a falling mortality rate coincided with a surge in economic growth.[10] Famines became less severe during this century, but typhoid and tuberculosis were still endemic in many areas, and there were periodic epidemics of typhus, influenza, diphtheria and smallpox. Houses were often poorly ventilated and overcrowded, water supplies were contaminated, and people bathed infrequently and rarely changed their clothes. About half of the average harvest was skimmed off in tithes to the Church, royal land taxes, indirect taxes (including the infamous salt tax), seigneurial dues, rent or sharecropping payments on leased lands and interest on debts; and on top of that about a quarter of the gross harvest had to be set aside for next year's seed.[11] Although some peasant families were independent, most were very poor, and vulnerable to ruination by bad harvests, sickness, accidents, or the forced military service of their men. Vauban described the peasants of Nivernais as an example of rural poverty:

> The general run of people seldom drink wine, eat meat not three times a year, and use little salt . . . So it is no cause for surprise if people who are so ill-nourished have so little energy. Add to this what they suffer from exposure: winter and summer, three fourths of them are dressed in nothing but half-rotting, tattered linen, and are shod throughout the year with sabots, and no other covering for the foot. If one of them does have shoes he only wears them on saints' days and Sundays: the extreme poverty to which they are reduced, owning as they do not one inch of land, rebounds against the more prosperous towns and country bourgeois, and against the nobility and the clergy.[12]

A pattern of late marriage and low illegitimacy rates suggest that peasant families were surprisingly chaste and repressed in their sexual lives. Evidently the Catholic Church had been successful in preaching against premarital sex and adultery, and that married love was intended by God for procreation, not for pleasure.

If disaster struck and an unmarried woman became pregnant or a family lost its lands, they often had to leave their communities and were forced into beggary, vagrancy, prostitution or crime. In 1724 the royal government ordered a round-up of vagrants by the mounted constabulary, and had them incarcerated in poor-houses. In the 1760s, when perhaps one-tenth of the population had become indigent, beggars were swept off the streets and into 'depôts de mendicité' — filthy, disease-ridden places. In such circumstances the poor often resorted to desperate measures, abandoning their children and stealing for survival. In towns up to ninety-five per cent of crimes were directed against property, committed by relatively young, recent arrivals, and were brutally punished by flogging, branding, or condemnation to the galleys. Judicial torture was not abolished in France until 1780,[13] and serious crimes were punished by racking, burning, breaking on the wheel, impalement on spikes or drawing and quartering.

The poor often drifted into the towns, centres for local wealth, influence and culture. The towns had their own administrations, and a complex array of privileges and exemptions which set them apart from the surrounding

Opposite: *'L'Homme de Village'. Nicolas Guérard's engraving of the mid-eighteenth-century French peasant labouring to pay his taxes.*

NÉ POUR LA PEINE

Reveille Matutina de Campagne

Collecteur

LA BEILLE ou Mouche à Miel

Chacun a part à ses travaux

LA VACHE

Par son moyen l'on boit et mange

LE COCHON il est méprisé et necessaire

LA POULE sa journée est d'un petit prix

Attributs du Paysan et des Animaux

l'Homme de Village

Tous les jours au milieu d'un Champ   Travailler tant que l'année dure
Par la Chaleur par la froidure   Pour amasser par son labeur
L'on voit le Pauvre Paysan   De quoi payer le Collecteur.

PORTRAIS DES · SOUFRANCE · DE · R · F · DAMIEN · ATTANTATEUR · DE · LAS
PERSONNES · SACRE' DU ROV · LOUIS · XV · LE · 5 · JEANVIER · ··· 1757

An anonymous artist's portrayal of the brutal punishments meted out to Robert-François Damien after his unsuccessful attempt to assassinate Louis XV in 1757.

countryside. Only fifteen per cent of the French population lived in towns and cities, however, although Paris with its population of 500,000 to 600,000 was the second-ranking city in Europe. Eight French cities had populations of between 50,000 and 100,000 people,[14] but most towns were relatively small, serving as ports, ecclesiastical and judicial centres, or as marketplaces for the surrounding countryside. Many towns were still surrounded by walls, and each had its cathedral or church, its market and perhaps a citadel, surrounded by a teeming jumble of alleyways and streets. There were also meadows, vineyards and large enclosed gardens inside the walls, and often communal herds looked after by the town shepherds and swineherds. Urban foundlings were sent into the country to wet-nurses, and rural people came to town as servants, apprentices and vagrants, so that there was a constant exchange of population and services between the urban centres and their rural hinterlands.

Nobles stood at the apex of urban society, occupying most offices of any importance and owning much of the surrounding land. Below them were wealthy rentiers, financiers, merchants, officials and professionals, and then a middling group of less wealthy people, who included workshop masters and shopkeepers.

Finally, most urban workers were organised into guilds, with skilled workers as their élites, and unskilled, unorganised labourers (including domestic servants) making up the bottom of the urban hierarchy. In towns as in the countryside servants were expected to be subservient, and any pretensions on their part were vigorously protested, as in this outburst by a Montpellier bourgeois in 1768:

> For nothing is more impertinent than to see a cook or a valet don an outfit trimmed with braid or lace, strap on a sword, and insinuate himself amongst the finest company in promenades; or to see a chambermaid as artfully dressed as her mistress; or to find domestic servants on any kind decked out like gentle people. All that is revolting. The estate of servants is one of servitude, of obedience to the orders of their masters. They are not deemed to be free, to form part of the social body with the citizens. Therefore they should be forbidden to mix with the citizenry; and if any such mixing must take place, one should be able to pick them out by a badge indicating their estate and making it impossible to confuse them with everyone else.[15]

Both in towns and in the countryside levels of illiteracy were high — about sixty-five per cent illiteracy overall,[16] with higher rates in many rural districts. The Catholic Church provided those local schools that did exist, and churches were the main social centres for most communities. Patron saints were honoured in local festivities, and other communal celebrations included spring and harvest festivals with eating, drinking, dancing, brawling, merriment and games. During the long winter nights rural women gathered around the fire in each others' cottages to sew and gossip, and the men got together in the taverns to drink, gossip, and play games of skill and chance. Narrative songs, satires and dramas, urban fairs with exotic animals and freak shows, puppets and acrobats, boxing matches, bear-baiting and cock-fights were the stuff of popular culture. Those fortunate few who were literate read out to others miraculous or religious stories, advice on portents and herbal treatments from the chap-books, or the 'bibliothèque bleue'. The piety of ordinary people was thus a combination of fervent church-going (which began to shift towards secularism in the latter half of the century) and magical beliefs in astrology and spells, so that earthworms or wasps might be excommunicated and church bells rung on St John's Eve when witches were about. Ideas about 'savages' were partly shaped from this popular mythology; from ideas about witches; from memories of the 'fureurs' of the previous century (explosions of popular rage in which mobs had committed murders, ritual mutilations and cannibalism); from folktales where people ate their own kin or were eaten by ogres;[17] and the stories in the chap-books of strange tribes who always slept in the shadow of their own feet.[18]

Some of those who were literate attended the colleges, and later the universities, academies and salons where high culture and learning were expressed. Scientists, philosophers, dramatists, theologians and poets were part of an international élite, literate in Latin as well as French, who exchanged ideas and discoveries with their counterparts in other European countries. 'Salons' run by society women brought together artists, aristocrats and philosophers for witty, original conversation, while the state-supported Academy of Science encouraged

research in chemistry, astronomy, mathematics and natural science, disseminating the results to other national academies (including the Royal Society in London) and its provincial counterparts. The role played by the Paris Academy in the 1761 and 1769 observations of the transit of Venus has already been mentioned, and Charles de Brosses, a member of the Dijon Academy (who was also the president of the Burgundian parlement and a shareholder in the French India Company) produced the first great collection of Pacific 'Voyages' in 1756, advocating the exploration of the unknown Southern Continent and expeditions into the Pacific from Pondicherry or Île de France (Mauritius).

Discovery and exploration were important themes in the intellectual life of this period, for the French Enlightenment thinkers used accounts of other societies to question their own, and to investigate the nature of society itself. Their precursor, Michel de Montaigne, had written of Brazilian Indians:

> I think there is nothing barbarous and savage in that nation, from what I have been told, except that each man calls barbarism whatever is not his own practice; for indeed it seems we have no other test of truth or reason than the example and pattern of the opinions and customs of the country we live in.[19]

In his account of Brazilian cannibalism he argued that his compatriots should judge other societies 'by reason's way, not by popular say', for as he said in his essay 'Of Cannibals':

> I am heartily sorry, that, judging their faults rightly, we should be so blind to our own. I think there is more barbarity in eating a man alive than in eating him dead; and in tearing by torture and the rack a body still full of feeling, in roasting a man bit by bit, in having him bitten and mangled by dogs and swine (as we have not only read but seen within fresh memory, not among ancient enemies, but among neighbours and fellow citizens, and what is worse, on the pretext of piety and religion), than in roasting and eating him after he is dead.[20]

He also used comments by some Brazilian Indians who had visited France to satirise the inequalities of his own society:

> Three of these men, ignorant of the price they will pay some day, in loss of repose and happiness, for gaining knowledge of the corruptions of this side of the ocean; ignorant also of the fact that of this intercourse will come their ruin (which I suppose is already well advanced: poor wretches, to let themselves be tricked by the desire for new things, and to have left the serenity of their own sky to come and see ours!) — three of these men were at Rouen, at the time the late King Charles IX was there. The King talked to them for a long time; they were shown our ways, our splendour, the aspect of a fine city. After that someone asked their opinion, and wanted to know what they had found the most amazing. They mentioned three things, of which I have forgotten the third, and I am very sorry for it; but I still remember two of them. They said that in the first place they thought it very strange that so many grown men, bearded, strong and armed, who were around the King

Opposite: *Urban and rural sociability. In the towns, workers came together in taverns, while in the countryside peasant families huddled around the fire in the evening, gossiping and telling stories.*

(it is likely that they were talking about the Swiss of his guard) should submit to obey a child, and that one of them was not chosen to command instead. Second (they have a way in their language of speaking of men as halves of one another) they had noticed that there were among us men full and gorged with all sorts of good things, and that their other halves were beggars at their doors, emaciated with hunger and poverty; and they thought it strange that these needy halves should endure such an injustice, and did not take the others by the throat, or set fire to their houses.[21]

Among the eighteenth-century 'philosophes', Denis Diderot and Jean-Jacques Rousseau echoed Montaigne's arguments most closely. Despite a fascination with the machinery and technological processes documented in detail in his *Encyclopaedie*, Diderot held that 'savages' were more free than 'civilised' men, who suffered from a unjust social order and brutalising forms of work. Jean-Jacques Rousseau argued that technological progress and the invention of private property had been the source of inequality and the ruination of humanity:

As long as men were content with their rustic huts, as long as they confined them-selves to sewing their garments of skin with thorns or fish-bones, and adorning themselves with feathers or shells, to painting their bodies with various colours, to improving or decorating their bows and arrows; and to using sharp stones to make a few fishing canoes or crude musical instruments; in a word, so long as they applied themselves only to work that one person could accomplish alone . . . they lived as free, healthy, good and happy men . . . but from the instant one man needed the help of another, and it was found to be useful for one man to have pro-visions enough for two, equality disappeared, property was introduced, work became necessary, and vast forests were transformed into pleasant fields which had to be watered with the sweat of men, and where starving and misery were soon seen to germinate and flourish with the crops. Metallurgy and agriculture were the two arts whose invention produced this great revolution. For the poor it is gold and silver, but for the philosopher it is iron and wheat that first civilized men and ruined the human race.[22]

Other philosophers, however, inclined more towards the doctrine of the 'ignoble savage'. Buffon, for instance, was in no doubt that technological devel-opment was a form of progress. His sketches of most 'savages' in *L'Histoire Naturelle* were negative caricatures, and he gave credence to descriptions of giants and Pacific peoples with tails. Voltaire used the idea of exploration in an account of conversations between a gigantic extra-terrestrial traveller from Sirius and a shipload of French philosophers to satirise philosophical pretensions, and praised aspects of English society in order to promote religious, intellectual and political liberty in France. In his story 'Lord Chesterfield's Ears', a learned doctor who had travelled round the world with Banks and Solander gave a mock-serious account of Tahitian ceremonial love-making and 'the inhabitants of the immense country called New Zealand' were described as 'the most barbarous of all barbarians'.[23]

In France the inspiration for exploration and voyages of discovery thus owed much to both philosophy and utility, to patriotism and profit. France fought battles with England in trade as well as war, and a hint of English discoveries was enough to impel a French response. Surville's and Marion du Fresne's voyages combined dreams of profit and imperial glory with echoes of the philosophes' fantasies about 'savages', so that while the *St Jean Baptiste* accounts can be characterised as reminiscent of Buffon, Marion du Fresne's experiences in the Bay of Islands were shaped by an idealised version of Montaigne's and Rousseau's 'Noble Savage'. True to Rousseau's depiction of his own society, however, the driving force behind these expeditions was the acquisition of property, both for the voyagers and the King, and it was no accident that they left from French trading centres and were connected with that tattered instrument of French imperial policy, the French India Company.

This satirical engraving by an anonymous artist (c. 1750) shows Rousseau and Voltaire locked in a violent argument.

THE FRENCH INDIA COMPANY

The 'Compagnie des Indes' had been founded with full state support and patronage in 1664, but it attracted little private investment and was a shaky organisation from the beginning. French merchants were wary about investing in so distant a venture, and the royal government was often distracted by wars and its own financial woes. In 1708, plagued by financial insecurities, the Compagnie stopped sending ships to the East and licensed private merchants to conduct the trade instead. In 1719 it narrowly escaped ruin when John Law reorganised France's financial system, amalgamating the Compagnie with a new national bank, which collapsed in spectacular style. Rather than wind up the Compagnie, however, the government decided to reconstitute it and placed its affairs under the control of a council appointed by the King. Under this new regime the Compagnie's Indian trade in silk, fine cotton, indigo (for blue dye), saltpetre (for gunpowder), spices and opium flourished for a time. By 1740 it had forts at Pondicherry and Chandernagore, smaller posts in Bengal and Malabar, and owned the islands of Île de France (Mauritius) and Bourbon (Réunion) and a magnificent base and arsenal at Lorient in Brittany.

The Compagnie waged commercial war in India against its British rival, the East India Company, but in 1742 the contest became diplomatic and military as well. The Mughal Empire was breaking up, and when Dupleix was appointed Governor at Pondicherry he began a series of intrigues with Indian rulers aimed at consolidating the Compagnie's financial position and undermining its British rival. At first the Compagnie made great gains, but expensive sieges and skirmishes with the British soon followed. In 1756, when the Seven Years' War broke out in Europe, pitched battles were fought in India between the two companies, which ended with the defeat of the Compagnie des Indes. Pondicherry, Chandernagore and other posts were destroyed, their walls, fortifications, offices and Governor's palaces blown up by British engineers, and French trade and commerce in India collapsed.

When the Treaty of Paris was signed in 1763 the French were handed back the trading stations they had held in India in 1749, but with the proviso that no fortifications were to be rebuilt in Bengal and no troops were to be stationed there. Britain, adopting Dupleix's tactics of intrigue and military intervention, soon won great influence and financial power in India, while France lost all hope of political dominion. Law de Lauriston was appointed the new Governor in 1764 to try and rebuild the Compagnie's stations, but in 1769 the Compagnie's finances collapsed and all of its remaining possessions — thirty ships, warehouses and buildings in Lorient and in India, naval and military stores and 2,450 Compagnie slaves[24] — were returned to the King. Voltaire penned the Compagnie's epitaph:

> At last there was left to the French in this part of the world only regret for having spent immense sums of money for over forty years for maintaining a Company which never made the least profit, which never paid to its shareholders and creditors from the profits of its commerce, which in its Indian administration lived

only on secret brigandage . . . , a memorable and perhaps useless example of the little knowledge which the French have had so far about the grand and ruinous commerce of India.[25]

BACKGROUND TO SURVILLE'S VOYAGE

The voyage of the *St Jean Baptiste* was a commercial venture that arose out of the rubble of the collapse of the Compagnie des Indes. Jean-François-Marie de Surville was a Breton from a wealthy bourgeois family, who had first sailed in a Compagnie ship when he was ten years old. After a succession of postings he fought against the British in the War of the Spanish Succession and the Seven Years' War, finally winning a wartime commission in the French Navy. He was well regarded by his superiors as 'a great sailor, very good soldier, fit for great things, active, witty, firm and determined, a man attentive to details, who has commanded the King's ships with distinction'.[26] In 1765 he commanded the *Duc de Praslin*, which took the new Governor, Lauriston, to Pondicherry. After this voyage Surville, Lauriston and Jean-Baptiste Chevalier, Governor of Chandernagore, became joint partners in a syndicate to trade in the Indian Ocean. Surville returned to France in 1766 and gained the Compagnie's permission to trade in the area covered by its monopoly, at the same time acquiring two new partners for the venture, Lorient traders called Bourgeois and Callois. He then organised the building of the *St Jean Baptiste*, a 650-ton vessel fitted out with thirty-six guns in the shipyard of Nantes, and sailed her from his home town of Port Louis to India in June 1767.

The ship made several trading voyages along the Indian coast, and a trip to the Philippines was being planned when rumours reached Pondicherry that the English had just discovered a rich South Sea island. In December 1768 Chevalier, one of the partners in the syndicate, wrote to the Minister of Marine to announce that their vessel the *St Jean Baptiste* was being sent on a voyage to investigate this new discovery:

> I must now outline the reasons which decided me to leave on the vessel the *St Jean Baptiste* the European crew she had brought from Europe and even thought it necessary for the good of the service to strengthen it as much as I could. This vessel, as you are aware, my lord, has been built for two purposes, one being to trade in time of peace and the other to carry out raids against the enemy in times of war . . .
>
> But a second motive which is no less important is a plan for a bold voyage she is about to undertake, and which it is my duty to advise you about, on account both of its importance and of its novelty. The suggestion has been inspired by the English following a strange discovery they have just made and which forshadows a success as strange as it is remarkable.
>
> One of their ships, recently arrived at the Cape of Good Hope from the South Sea, was driven by the winds towards an island which did not figure on the charts. Although they have taken every precaution to prevent its latitude from being known, nevertheless certain people from the ship have been so enthusiastic about this discovery that they were unable to stop themselves from gossiping, and this is in broad terms what we have learnt: This island, according to reports, must be situ-

ated in approximately 102° west of the Paris meridian. We suspect it may be the one seen by the Englishman David in 1686 which is marked on the chart. However, the English say that it is not shown on any of theirs. Whatever it is, the adventure is worth attempting and its success could become too important for our nation for me not to be in honour bound to sacrifice everything to make it succeed. In the instructions which I am giving M. de Surville, of which I have the honour to enclose a copy, you will see in detail the plan of this affair and the manner in which we are proposing to carry it out.[27]

These instructions, which have never been found, evidently directed Surville to sail from Pondicherry to Malacca, the China Seas and the Philippines, then to traverse the Pacific in both the northern and southern latitudes, returning by way of Manila (where if all else failed the cargo could be sold at a profit), China and Batavia. For most of the voyage, however, the officers (including Labé, a share-holder in the venture) knew little about what was planned. 'Davis (or David's) Land' was a small sandy island which in 1687 had been reported to have a long, high coastline to its north-west, possibly Terra Australis Incognita. The rumours of its rediscovery that reached the French from the Cape of Good Hope appear to have been a garbled version of the *Dolphin*'s 'discovery' of Tahiti, for that ship had visited the Cape in February 1768.[28] Abbé Rochon, in a later account of Surville's voyage, recounted the story as it was heard in India at the time:

I was in Pondicherry in August 1769 when the rumour spread that an English vessel had found in the South Sea a very rich island where, among other peculi-arities, a colony of Jews had been settled. The account of this discovery . . . became so well known that it was believed in India that the purpose of de Surville's voyage . . . was to search for this marvellous island.[29]

Monneron, the clerk on board the *St Jean Baptiste*, commented later that:

the love of the marvellous common enough among travellers, could well have exag-gerated the advantages of the island in the outfitters' ears; but even discounting much of the tale, it was natural enough to think that the island should be richer than other countries because it lies about 700 leagues to the west of the coast of Peru, in latitude 27° to 28° south, which is the latitude of Copiago [Copiapo], source of immense riches in gold for the Spanish.[30]

This idea — commonplace in the period — that gold and silver, once found at one location on a certain latitude, could be found at other places on the same latitude, was the source of the dreams of great wealth which persuaded even the sober Labé, second-in-command on the vessel, to invest his capital in this voyage.

PREPARATIONS FOR THE VOYAGE

The *St Jean Baptiste* was fully careened and a three-year supply of food was loaded on board, including dried meat, dried biscuits, flour, rice and livestock (nearly all of which had been slaughtered by the time they reached New Zealand). The food was to be a later cause for bitter discontent. Labé complained that the supplies were quite inadequate:

Lastly for a voyage of discovery as hard as this one will be we have not even taken on private mess stores, except for hens and sheep, but I am not counting on them. They are quickly used up and almost all die etc. We should have had various salted meats, pickled beef, stuffed tongues, savaloys, and butter, cheese, hams; but we have none of all that, not even mustard or fajaux [?]. It is pitiful, no desserts at all, we are served any old how, those who have wine drink it . . . I am very much afraid that we will later have to suffer for it.

After some time at sea it seems that the supplies and conditions on board the *St Jean Baptiste* were even worse than was usual on eighteenth-century French vessels, although these (as described by La Gravière) were bad enough:

A cutaway view of a French two-decker warship, showing its internal and deck structures.

THE VOYAGE OF THE *ST JEAN BAPTISTE*

At the beginning of the voyage Surville and his officers spent some time in Chandernagore, which by early 1769 had been extensively rebuilt under Chevalier's leadership. Chevalier had transformed the residence at Goretty into a gorgeous palace, much frequented by both the local French and English élites, and a large defensive rampart and canal were being built around the town. Relations with the English at this time were cordial, and this may have been how Chevalier heard about Wallis's stay at Cape Town. The expedition set out from Bengal in March 1769 for Yanam, a small French settlement further south on the east coast of India, where they took on board bullocks, kids and some bales of textiles, then south to Masulipatam, another small trading-post where further food and textiles were loaded. The ship then sailed further south to Pondicherry, the main remaining French settlement in India.

By this time Pondicherry had also been extensively rebuilt as a town divided by a canal into European and Indian sectors, with the governor's palace beside a tree-lined parade ground at the centre of the European part of town. At this time Surville must have visited Law de Lauriston, Governor at Pondicherry, his other main partner in the venture. Firewood, water, a hundred bales of trade goods, supplies and twenty-three marines were brought on board. Finally, on 2 June 1769, the *St Jean Baptiste* sailed out of Pondicherry on an island-hopping itinerary that took the ship east past the Niccobar Islands to Malacca, and then on to Pulo Tioman in the South China Sea, and to Trengganu and Pulo Condore.

On 21 August the *St Jean Baptiste* anchored off the Batan (or 'Bashi') Islands in the Philippines, where they obtained water, goats, pigs and vegetables, and the crew got blind drunk on local liquor. Three of Surville's crew jumped ship here, so he kidnapped three Batan Islanders to replace them. (These were the crew of the small Batan skiff that the French later used in Doubtless Bay to get themselves dry-footed to the shore.) After this the ship sailed into seas that were barely charted, spending a week in the sweltering heat of the doldrums, where the food rotted and the men succumbed to scurvy. The journals tell a tale of lagging spirits and unrelieved misery, until finally on 7 October a coastline was sighted and on 13 October the *St Jean Baptiste* anchored in 'Port Praslin', a sheltered channel to the north-west of Santa Isabel in the Solomon Islands. Labé went ashore with a party to look for fresh water and food, and was ambushed by the local people. The sergeant of marine was wounded and died several days later, while Labé was wounded twice below the groin — an experience that left him in considerable pain and vitriolic about 'savages' (whom Surville now compared several times to monkeys).

By now Surville was quite unsure of the *St Jean Baptiste*'s true position, since he was forced to rely on a combination of the log and sand-glasses to fix his longitude. The ship had already sailed by his reckoning through several islands marked on the shipboard charts, which located the Solomon Islands well to the east of Tasman's New Zealand coastline. After getting water but very little fresh food in the Solomons the *St Jean Baptiste* sailed east-south-east along a chain of islands, not daring to land for fear of further attacks. The ship left San Cristobal on 7 December, and having consulted their précis of Tasman's journal, Surville and Labé decided to strike south and then east to the coastline of New Zealand. By now many of the crew had died and most of the rest were stricken with scurvy. There were still pigs on board, but otherwise the officers were reduced to eating thick soup for their meals. The ship was leaking badly and the crew were dispirited and wretched. On 9 December Labé recorded that 'according to my reckoning, I find myself 29 leagues inside New Zealand'.[39] The *St Jean Baptiste* had sailed 134 leagues past the New Zealand coastline by his reckoning, when on Tuesday, 12 December 1769, land was finally sighted: 'at 11.15 this morning, saw the land of New Zealand, very high . . . very distant'.[40]

The ship turned north and sailed past Hokianga Harbour along a sandy, inhospitable lee shore. Gales blew up, and more men died. The ship was leaking badly in high seas; and Prévost's précis of Tasman, which described the ramming of the Dutch cockboat in Murderers Bay,[41] had aroused some anxiety on board. Pottier L'Horme reported: 'Our position was fairly critical, embayed on an unknown coast, the people of which are savages of bad repute.'[42] On 15 December the ship was driven in a raging gale past Motu-o-pao (an island off Cape Maria Van Diemen) and Oo-hau (the largest of the Three Kings Islands) towards Murimotu Island (off North Cape). Labé described the high lands around Motu-o-pao and Murimotu as burnt in the gullies, and reported '2 types of straw huts or tombs' on Murimotu. By an extraordinary coincidence, as the *St Jean Baptiste* doubled Murimotu on 16 December, the *Endeavour* was also off North Cape, but the westerlies that were driving Surville's ship eastwards had forced the *Endeavour* far out to sea. The first two European vessels to visit New Zealand since Abel Tasman in 1642 sailed past each other in a gale, completely unaware of each other's presence. Then the *St Jean Baptiste* turned southward into smooth seas, tacking along the eastern coast towards Tokerau, named Doubtless Bay by Cook just a week before.

SURVILLE'S VISIT TO TOKERAU
17–31 December 1769

Tokerau was one of the most northerly havens in New Zealand, guarded by two rocky peninsulas that sheltered a long sandy beach along its western coast, a deep alluvial river valley (Oruru) inland from the bay, and a shallow harbour, the Mangoonui, to the south-east.[43]

According to a recent archaeological study, the Oruru Valley was the most densely inhabited area in the bay, with vertical strip gardens etched across the contours of its cleared hillsides, and wetland gardens on the riverlands below, marked out by extensive systems of drainage ditches and canals.[44] The French did not see Oruru, however, for they spent all of their time off the east coast of the Karikari Peninsula (in ancient times known as Rangiaohia).[45] According to a detailed archaeological study of Karikari,[46] most settlements were clustered near

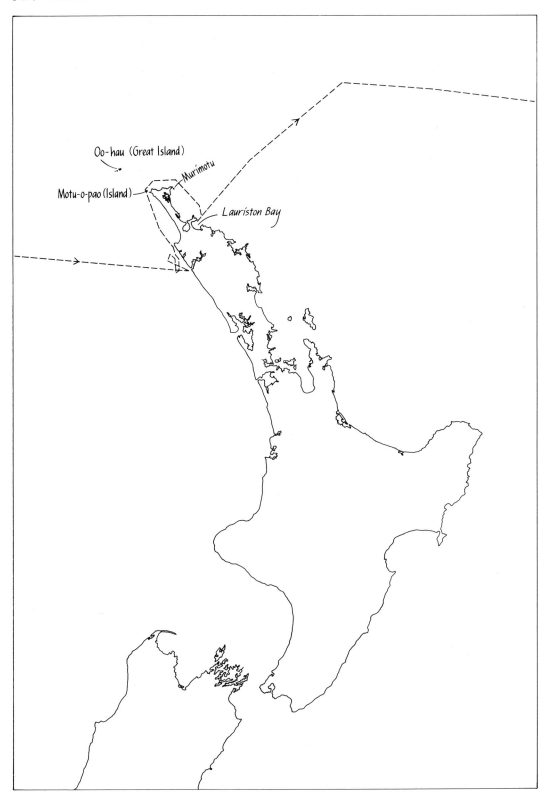

Oo-hau (Great Island)

Motu-o-pao (Island)

Murimotu

Lauriston Bay

the northern end of the peninsula, where patches of agricultural land, bush and permanent water sources were scattered along a coastline of cliffs and rocky outcrops.

On the north-western side of the peninsula there were rich fisheries and tuatua beds in Rangaunu Bay, with its clear sandy bottom and rocky islands and reefs. A variety of shellfish including puupuu (winkle), mussel, oyster, kina, black snail, scallop and crayfish was found along the rugged northern coastline. To the south-east the sandy curve of Tokerau Beach sheltered beds of toheroa and tuatua, and large shoals of fish of many species came there to spawn in the summer months. To the south-west were the silty waters of the Rangaunu Harbour, much

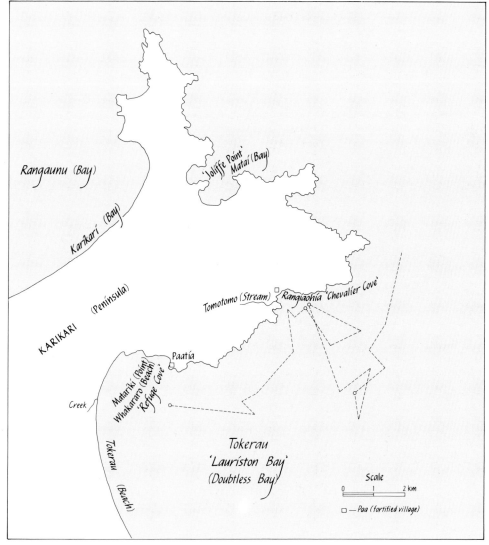

Above: *Map of Tokerau (Doubtless Bay) in 1769, showing the anchorages of the* St Jean Baptiste.

Opposite: *The track of the* St Jean Baptiste *off the New Zealand coastline, 1769.*

319

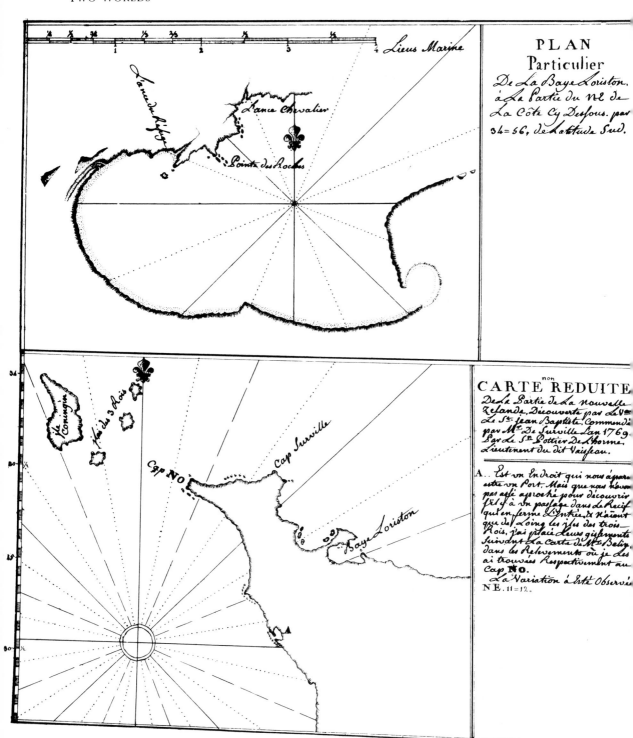

Pottier L'Horme's chart of 'La Baye Loriston' (Tokerau) and the northern part of the North Island, 1769.

frequented by migratory waders. Rangaunu Harbour was a famous shark, flounder and mullet fishery, where dense beds of pipi and mudsnails were also found. The neck of the peninsula was a low-lying expanse of sandy ridges and swamps, covered with a stunted vegetation of scrub and sedges. There were no good garden soils or rock sources in this area and the archaeological evidence suggests that the Karikari people mainly lived on the rocky parts of the coast, where they occupied base villages, gardened, collected stone for tools and oven-stones and shellfish; and travelled in summer to their fishing villages and camps.

There are early historical accounts of great summer fishing expeditions on the Rangaunu Harbour, when canoes were hauled overland from Tokerau and even from Ahipara. According to one account, more than 7,000 dogfish (kape-taa) were caught at Rangaunu on just two days in January 1855 by the crews of fifty canoes, amidst scenes of intense excitement. The dogfish were sun-dried on tall scaffolds and stacked like firewood in the store-houses, and their oil was mixed with red ochre to make a paint for war canoes, burial monuments, carvings in principal houses, and the scraped bones of the dead, or mixed with fragrant plants as a cosmetic for the face and hair.[47] At the time of Surville's visit in 1769, it is probable that most of the local people had already shifted to their fishing villages and were eagerly anticipating the annual shark fishing at Rangaunu.

Rangiaohia, the small cove where the French first landed, was a place with ancient associations. It was said to be the place where humans first learned the art of netting, when a man called Kahukura tricked a fishing party of patu-paiarehe (white-skinned 'fairy people') into abandoning their net, so that he could see how it was made.[48] According to local traditions, it was also the first landfall of the *Maamaru* canoe, which brought the ancestors of the local people (now known as Ngaati Kahu) to the peninsula. *Maamaru* had previously sailed under the name of *Tinana* from Hawaiki to Ahipara, where its commander Tuumoana lived for many years before going back to Hawaiki, leaving his daughter Kahutia-nui behind him. Back in Hawaiki the canoe was re-adzed, refitted and given the new name of *Maamaru*, and it voyaged to Tokerau under the command of Tuumoana's nephew Te Parata. After exploring the bay, Te Parata built his paa at Rangiaohia and married Kahutia-nui, and together they became the founding ancestors of Ngaati Kahu.[49]

As the *St Jean Baptiste* sailed towards Tokerau on the morning of 17 December 1769, a canoe came out to the ship. The French were not sure what to expect. As Monneron wrote in his journal that afternoon:

> Abel Tasman gives an account of a hostile reception accorded him in this region, and after his account we too were apprehensive of some bad treatment from the inhabitants. But we were somewhat surprised to see approaching us a boat manned by 5 or 6 men, who were eager to offer us fish which they had just caught.[50]

These people traded a few fish and shellfish for some white cotton cloth and a knife, and as they left they showed the Europeans where they lived. Shortly afterwards four more canoes came out to about nine miles off the land, showing fish to the Europeans and finally paddling up under the gallery to exchange large

321

quantities of fish for pieces of blue and white cloth, which they put on around their shoulders. According to Labé, their canoes were well carved and twenty-eight to thirty feet long, with wash-boards. Each canoe was crewed by eight to ten men, five feet three inches to five feet seven inches tall, whose long hair was daubed red on their forelocks, and who were wearing dogskin cloaks. They were unarmed except for a few spears. The chief of these people indicated that he wanted to visit the *St Jean Baptiste* and the Europeans beckoned him to come on board. Pottier described this meeting:

> Amongst all the savages in the boat, the one who seemed to be the chief came on board, all alone. When he got to the quarter-deck, he seemed speechless and trembling. He was made much of. Our captain embraced him and led him into his cabin, gave him something to eat, and some liquor to drink. He made him a present of a jacket of coarse red cloth, with green facings and bavaroises and some red trousers. The man let himself be dressed in the jacket, in exchange for which he gave us a dog-skin tunic, which covered him from shoulder to mid-calf. We took him into the wardroom, where one of our officers put a shirt on him, over the jacket. [According to Monneron, at this point his people became uneasy about his absence and 'began to show their disquiet; quite a clamour went up. He showed himself to his people and we understood from his gestures that he was telling them that he was safe.']51 The man went back to his canoe, seemingly well pleased, but when he got there the fancy took him to remove his new clothes. It was quite a joke to see all his companions doing their best to get the shirt off, without success; they pulled it mostly from the bottom, but once they noticed that by pulling it that way they were tearing it, they saw that this was impossible, and would have spent ages without achieving their aim if the chief had not explained to them that to put it on him we had made him lift his arms. After that they took it off easily.52

As Monneron commented, 'it is easy to imagine the joy felt by our unhappy crew at finding themselves among peoples who had already treated us with humanity'.53 At 10.30 a.m. the canoes went back to land and the ship began to follow them into the bay, tacking several times before sailing close to the eastern coast of Karikari Peninsula, which Labé described as 'very high, bare, with scrub in some places, sand in others.'54 Two paa were noted as they approached the land. Spencer has located these on Joliffe Point at the centre of Matai Bay, and on Puketutu Island. Finally, at 9.15 that evening, the *St Jean Baptiste* anchored in Tokerau, about five miles from the shore. Surville named the bay 'Lauriston Bay' after Law, the Governor of Pondicherry, and described the landscape in his journal:

> This bay seems a lovely place. The nearest heights close to the sea look a little arid, except in the hills where there are trees. Near the shoreline, particularly in the curve of the bay there is nothing to be seen but sand dunes [Tokerau Beach]. But the second row of mountains on the mainland side look heavily wooded, with fine trees [i.e., the hills beyond Mangoonui Harbour to the south-east].55

From their anchorage to the south-east of Rangiaohia the French could see a small fort on a high, pointed hill beside a 'pretty cove' (Rangiaohia), with a small sandy beach below it where the people beached their canoes.

At daylight on 18 December eight to ten canoes came out to the *St Jean Baptiste*, bringing a large quantity of fish, and a crew of four to ten (mainly men, but including several women) to each canoe. Some of the larger canoes were fifty feet long and carried up to twenty-four men armed with spears, clubs of 'black stone' and 'ivory' (whalebone), or a sort of 'sabre' tipped with bone. Labé described these people in some detail:

They paint [tattoo] their faces and buttocks like the Kaffirs of the Guinea Coast and put red in their hair, which they arrange like the coiffures of Indian women; their dress consists in some loincloths which they put about their waists. Some have dog skins sewn together, others wear nothing on their bodies but a Thrum mat with broad straws six inches long; by way of ornament they hang round their necks a greenish stone like glass which represents a devil figure — I cannot describe it clearly [greenstone tiki]. Others have in their ears pendants of this same stone, 3 or 4 inches long, ¾ inches thick, thin and pear-shaped but flat. Others have in their ears pieces of dogskin. Some have the skin of a bird to cover their nudity, without passing underneath, others do not hide it at all. They are without modesty and are great thieves, but they do not seem to be dangerous. They do not have fierce faces as do the people at Port Praslin . . .

   I had forgotten to say that these people put tufts of white feathers on their heads, sometimes black ones; some put them across the forehead. They all have pierced ears. The designs they put on their faces and their buttocks are the colour of gunpowder. These designs are embossed and well worked. They also put this colour on their lips, red pigment mixed with oil on their hair and some of them on their bodies. The women do the same.[56]

From the evidence of this account the local people were relatively wealthy, with dogskin cloaks, greenstone tiki and pendants, and plentiful facial and body tattoos. The observation that 'birdskins' (perhaps feathered aprons)[57] were worn (as was later stated, by the women) 'to cover their nudity' is interesting, as a variation on the perfumed grass girdles described by Monkhouse at Anaura. The reference to thieving suggests that as in other districts, goods were sometimes taken without any immediate return being given. In fact vast quantities of fish ('enough to feed 400 men') were piled into baskets during this meeting in exchange for pieces of blue and white cloth and empty bottles, with some bargaining being conducted in sign language (for like Tasman, Surville's men had no useful vocabularies on board). The French were also given several stone patu and one of whalebone. When these exchanges were over several of the local people, including the chief who had previously visited the ship, came on board and were entertained in the captain's cabin.

At two o'clock that afternoon Surville had the longboat lowered with ten soldiers on board and eight oarsmen each armed with a sabre. Pottier later described the scene as they rowed towards the land:

All [the] people were scattered here and there on the hills and the shore, and no doubt were doing honour to the new arrival by waving things constantly to one side, as though to create a breeze, while they bent over — some had long-haired skin cloaks, and others had bunches of grass. This ceremony must have been tiring for them, considering its length, because it started right from when they first saw the boat, and went on until the captain set foot on land.[58]

Surville was not certain 'whether these signals were favourable or unfavour-able',[59] but in fact he was being given a ceremonial welcome (poowhiri) by local people who were arranged around the contours of the natural ampitheatre at the back of Rangiaohia Bay.

As Surville landed from the small Batan Island skiff onto a rocky ledge jutting out from the beach, the chief (now described as a man between forty-five and fifty years old and dressed like the others) came forward and greeted him with a hongi. He seemed terrified of the Europeans' muskets, either because they had already been demonstrated to him on the ship or because he had heard about the *Endeavour* shootings at the Cavalli Islands and in the Bay of Islands just two or three weeks before. Surville asked by signs for water, and the chief led him and his men to a freshwater stream (only 100 metres away). He indicated that they should sit down above the beach and did not invite them up to the paa. Surville could see the paa quite well, however, and described it later from the ship as made

> of grassy earth with a ditch cutting across a little raised mound leading up to that level. Outside the same ditch is a row of palisades, an excellent means of stopping raids which it would appear they carry out on one another constantly. But as for us, neither their feeble arms nor their poor fortifications are capable of stopping us for a minute . . . Besides the collection of huts or grass cabins which were inside the fort there were a few huts spread about here and there in threes and fours [particularly, as he later observed 'on the side where we disembarked (i.e., the south side), where they stretch almost to mid-way point on the hill']. It looked to me as though there were some plantations of sweet potatoes, which were only just starting to grow.[60]

As Surville and his men sat down by the stream, the local men, women and children crowded down from the hills to see them. Some of the men were armed with long or short spears, clubs made of whalebone about four feet long (prob-ably hoeroa) or patu of stone or whalebone. Surville had learned caution from his experiences in the Solomons and he alerted his men to be wary of a surprise attack. The chief sent these people away, however, and they soon came back with dried fish and bundles of wild celery and cress, having no doubt been told that these strange visitors would appreciate such gifts.

Labé had stayed on the ship, and when the shore party returned he asked them what they had seen. The sailors described numerous long-haired domestic dogs, water fowl and wild teal ducks on shore, and in the cove some cultivations, large fishing seines, and a freshwater creek tumbling down from the hills with trees growing almost to its edge. Such resources may have meant wealth to the local people, but the French were obsessed with dreams of the fabled 'Davis Land'. In Labé's rueful comment on these descriptions one can hear their fantasies collapsing:

> We were also expecting to find in this country riches in the form of gold and silver, but our hopes were vain. When the crew is better we will pursue our discoveries

in the east. Perhaps we will be luckier in finding islands rich in metal that we can trade for our merchandise and so recover the time lost to date and the misery suffered through lack of supplies and through illness. For God is merciful. He does not abandon his children.[61]

By now only seven or eight of the *St Jean Baptiste*'s crew were in good health, and that night the last of the black slaves from Malagasy died of scurvy. The conditions on board were wretched, and their need for water, fresh food and wood was desperate. Surville was also eager to get his sick men on shore, for according to medical theory at the time, scurvy was due in part to the foul atmosphere below decks; and land breezes, or even just stepping on the land itself, were held to be a powerful curative.[62] The next morning (19 December), therefore, Surville had the longboat loaded with ten empty water barrels, and set off with eight armed oarsmen and six woodcutters with axes; accompanied by fourteen of the scurvy sufferers who could still walk, in another boat.

As the boats rowed towards Rangiaohia the local people repeated the ceremony of the day before, waving cloaks, a few 'palms' and 'sticks', and the chief again came down to the beach to greet them, 'but less affectionately, I thought',[63] Surville reported later. There is a confusion of dates here in the accounts, but from most of the journals it seems that on this day armed men had gathered on the hills 'in different squadrons'. Some 'who appeared to be chiefs or kings from different villages' were making an uproar, probably urging in haka or speeches that an immediate attack on the French should be made. The chief told Surville to stay on the beach and asked him for his musket ('of which he was familiar only with the sound', according to Monneron). When that was refused he asked for Surville's sword. Surville handed this over and, taking the sword out of its scabbard, the chief displayed it to the men of the different 'squadrons', apparently telling them that the French had come in peace.

According to Labé, the women now approached the sailors, making suggestive signs to them and indicating that they should go with them into the bush. The sailors feared that this might be the prelude to an ambush, however, and stayed on the beach. Eventually the chief, having pacified the assembled warriors, came back to Surville and pressed noses with him, and they walked together to the creek. Surville's men dug a hole by the stream so that the barrels could more readily be filled. At first this seemed to make the local people uneasy, but the chief again asked for Surville's sword and was given it, and took it up to the fort.

After this, most of the people seemed to relax, and they even helped the sailors to roll the full barrels back to the boats. While the axemen were cutting wood, however, some warriors edged down from the hills to surround them, but finding them on the alert they soon withdrew. Surville had food brought from the boats and shared a meal on the beach with the chief and 'some of the principal natives', who particularly enjoyed the pork that was served. The local people probably also cooked some of their own food at this time, for Surville afterwards described their method of cooking in an earth oven: 'At the bottom of the hole they have put stones, and having made a good fire on these so they

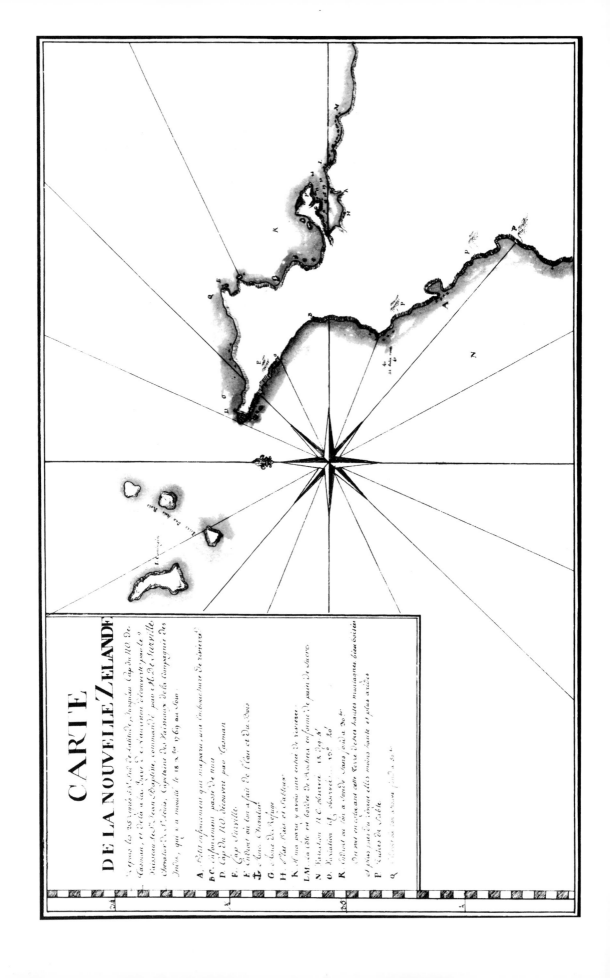

CARTE
DE LA NOUVELLE ZELANDE

Depuis les 35 vents Sud Sud de Latitude jusqu'au Cap du NO De
Tasman, et Dela a du Nord E et Situation découverte par le
Vaisseau le St Jean Baptiste, commandé par M. De Surville,
Chevalier de l'ordre, Capitaine Des Vaisseaux De la Compagnie Des
Indes, qui y a mouillé le 18 a Xbre 1769 au Soir.

A. Petit enfoncement qui na paru aucune embouchure de rivière?

B C. enfoncement passé De nuit

D. Cap Du NO découvert par Tasman

E. Cap Surville.

F. Endroit où l'on a fait De l'eau et Du Bois

G. Anse Chevalier

H. Anse De Refuge

K. Plat Pais et Sablieux

L M. sa tête est Gelée De Ancrées enforme De pain De Sucre

N. Variation H C observée 18° 29 h'

O. Variation h observée 13° 40'

R. Endroit où l'on a Sondé Sans où la 30 b'

S. plus près la rivière elles moins facile et plus aridée

P. Pointe De Sable

Q. Rocher au Sud à Fleur d'eau De 30 b'

are burning hot, they put their fish on top, cover it with leaves, then with earth and make another fire on top of that.'[64]

The people also offered Surville domesticated dogs in exchange for European goods, indicating that these were good to eat. When the meal was over the scurvy sufferers were brought on shore for about an hour to 'take the land air', where their appearance must have startled and perhaps frightened the local people. Tallifer, a surgeon on a later French Pacific voyage, described the symptoms of the disease as follows:

> Swellings covered by black scabs appeared on various parts of their bodies, the skin revealed small wine-coloured stains at the root of the hairs; their joints stiffened, their flexor muscles seemed to shorten and held their limbs half-bent. But nothing was more hideous than the appearance of their face: to the leaden complexion of the victims of scurvy was added the prominence of the gums jutting out of the mouth, which itself showed ulcerated spots. The sick gave out a fetid smell, which, when you breathed it, seemed to attack the very root of life. I have often felt all my strength ebb away when I approached them.[65]

Scurvy sufferers had swollen legs, and shivered and trembled constantly. The local people had never seen Europeans (or for that matter blacks or Indians) before and knew nothing of scurvy or similar diseases, and these sick men must have made a shocking and uncanny sight.

After the barrels of water, firewood and a quantity of cress had been loaded into the longboat, Surville climbed on board, accompanied by the chief. As soon as the people on shore saw this, however, they 'began to weep and cry out like devils'.[66] The local men immediately launched a canoe, and after hesitating a while the chief listened to his people and returned to land, giving his dogskin cloak to Surville (thus placing Surville under his protection) and saying that he

Opposite: 'Chart of New Zealand' is accompanied by a key:
From 35°54' Lat South to Tasman's NW Cape and from there to Lauriston Bay discovered by the ship the St Jean Baptise, commanded by Mr De Surville Knight of St Louis, Captain in the Indies Company, which anchored there on the 18 December 1769, in the evening.

A   Little bay which seemed to me to be a river mouth
BC   Bay passed at night
D   NW cape discovered by Tasman
E   Cape Surville
F   Place where we got water and wood
Y   Chevalier Cove
G   Refuge Cove
H   Flat, sandy land
K   This seemed to me to be the entrance to a river
LM   The coast is fringed with rocks in the form of a sugar loaf
N   Observed variation 12°4' NE
O   Observed variation 13°20' NE
R   Place where we took soundings without finding bottom at 30f. Sailing along this coast you see very high mountains, thickly wooded and close to the shore, lower and more barren ones.
P   Sand dunes
Q   Place where we found bottom at 50 fathoms.

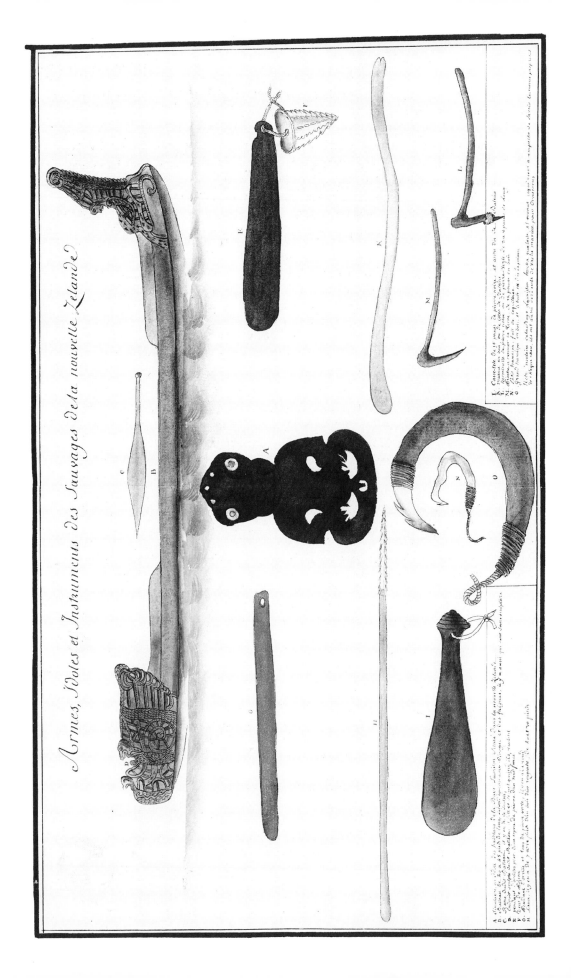

Armes, Pôles et Instrumens des Sauvages de la nouvelle Zelande

would visit the ship the next day. Labé commented, 'We do not know what to make of this performance.'[67]

While Surville's party had been on shore that morning five or six unarmed canoes, each with a crew of twelve to twenty men, came out to the *St Jean Baptiste*. They traded a few large fish, 'each about 20 inches long and shaped like a bonito' (probably trevally), forty to fifty horse mackerel, clams, mussels, some oil that seemed to be made from seeds (probably titoki oil), two bone clubs, a greenstone ear pendant three inches long, a greenstone 'devil' (no doubt a tiki) and two 'mother-of-pearl' fish hooks for heavy Bengal cloth and bottles. Labé added:

> I forgot to say that the islanders of Lauriston Bay have neither iron nor other metals; they use axes of greenstone and shells for knives etc, just as at Port Praslin. They also have a weapon which is a lance 10–12 feet long, made of very heavy wood; at one end there is an axe of greenstone, 6 inches wide and at the other end is a club [a very curious description]. They know what slaves are because they offered to sell some to the captain and even to the soldiers in exchange for pieces of cotton cloth.[68]

The two fish-hooks were probably one-piece hooks of turban shell, and the greenstone ear pendant, the tiki, the hafted adze and the lance are likely to be the artefacts that were later sketched by Pottier L'Horme in his drawing of the 'Arms, Idols and Instruments of the Savages of New Zealand'.

At 5 a.m. on 20 December Surville and Pottier each took a boat to shore, with a contingent of thirteen soldiers, eight rowers, six axemen and the sick who could still walk. This time there were more than 200 warriors drawn up on the hillside, and when the chief came forward to meet the Frenchmen, he signalled

Opposite: *'Weapons, Idols and Instruments of the Savages of New Zealand', sketched by Pottier L'Horme. This sketch shows a paddle, a canoe, two greenstone ornaments, a hei-tiki, a spear, a hoeroa, a mere, two fish-hooks and two agricultural tools. The accompanying key reads:*

A   *Simulacrum or idol of the inhabitants of Lauriston Bay in New Zealand*

B   *Boat 40 to 45 feet long, the base like a canoe, with washboards. There are also some without carving*

C   *Oar of the said boat. There are some sculpted ones*

D   *Carved part of the same boat which can be taken off and put on at will*

E   *Flat ear pendant made of a sort of green stone. There are round ones.*

F   *Fish tooth*

G   *Long ear pendant made of green stone. There are round ones.*

H   *Lance. There are some 7 to 18 feet long made of a hard reddish wood, 20 and 30 feet long.*

I   *Club 15 inches long, made of black stone and another of whalebone*

K   *Bludgeon made of wood or whale-ribs*

L   *Adze made of black or green stone, 3 to 8 inches long*

M   *Pick for working the ground, 12 inches long, made of wood*

N   *Small fishhook made of shell*

O   *Large wooden hook, with a fishbone tip*

Our Islander from Lauriston Bay fell ill and died, which prevented our knowing the proper names for each thing. They also have the teeth of sea-cows as ornaments.

them to go back to the ship. Surville refused, and after a lengthy conference with his people the chief again approached Surville,

> who embraced him, then made him the present of an axe, an empty barrel, and a bucket which he had asked for the day before, and put a beautiful new white ostrich feather around his head (because these people are very fond of feathers, particularly white ones). The savage allowed this ornament to be attached, with a slight air of indifference, and embraced Mr de Surville according to their custom. He then put one of the chief's fingers side by side with his own, and tried to make him understand that he wanted to be on good terms with him. I do not know whether or not he grasped this properly, but despite all these attentions, the savage gave him a cold reception.[69]

Given the intense tapu of a chief's head, Surville's act in placing a white feather ornament on it might well have met with 'a slight air of indifference'. It is impossible to imagine what the chief thought about the symbolic joining of his finger with Surville's. He was also given blue and white calico, some fine red cloth and a garnet necklace. According to Labé, these gifts were given

> to tame and coax them and to avoid any argument with these islanders; however it is not that we are afraid because 10 armed men is more than is needed to drive them from their dwellings, but then where would we find what we need after putting these people to flight? That is the reason we cajole them, that and humanity and nothing else.[70]

Despite these presentations the chief remained cool. The French were allowed to land, however, and fetch water and wood from the cove. At the watering-place, according to Surville,

> an old man who was sitting [there] went on haranguing me continuously in a loud voice, and without making a single gesture that would help me understand what he meant. He annoyed me intensely because he never stopped, and was always looking me in the eye and speaking to me. I let him talk on. I had the refreshments brought and we ate, including the chief and a few others whom he indicated as belonging to him. I also gave some to the old orator, and as the chief made signs that he belonged to him I attached a piece of red ribbon to his spear. From then on he ceased his harangues and seemed happy.[71]

It seems probable (from the fact that he was seated and stared fixedly at Surville while 'haranguing [him] continuously') that this old man was a tohunga (priest) who was attempting to maakutu ('stare fixedly', bewitch) Surville. In that case Surville's gesture in tying a red ribbon around his spear was an extraordinary response. Red was the tapu colour, and the act of tying a cord around something was to claim it, and place it under one's own mana. To meet maakutu (witchcraft) with a direct imposition of one's own tapu was to confront the gods head-on, and to claim that the old man was 'happy' about this was undoubtedly an error of cosmological proportions.

The women now approached the sailors, 'making all the gestures that are not made especially not in public, going as far as drawing aside the bird skin that covers their nakedness and showing everything they have'.[72] This behaviour was interpreted by the French as 'lasciviousness', but under the circumstances of extreme hostility it was more likely to have been the whakapohane (ritual exposure of the genitals), an expression of intense derision and contempt.

When the wood had been cut and the barrels filled, Surville returned to his ship to find that three canoes had visited it during his absence but had traded only five fish before returning to the south-east side of the bay. As he commented in his journal, 'all that smacks of the coldness that was shown us on land'.[73] Later that afternoon the St Jean Baptiste shifted its anchorage closer to the land, and that night another sailor, this time a man from Lyons, died of scurvy. According to Labé, the men who died in the bay were 'thrown overboard', an act that would have polluted the tapu of local fisheries and shellfish beds. The custom of sea burials in Queen Charlotte Sound seems to have been atypical, for in most areas (including the North) the presence of dead bodies in the sea led to a raahui (ritual prohibition) being placed on the fisheries in the area. It is uncertain whether the local people knew that these sea burials were taking place, although the ship would have been clearly visible from the land. During the next day the weather was wet and windy. No canoes came out to the St Jean Baptiste and the French did not venture ashore.

By the morning of 22 December the weather had cleared, and several canoes paddled out to the ship, bringing a little cress, which they presented to Surville. The chief and 'a sort of a chief from another village' came with them. The French indicated to them by signs that they wished to go ashore to fetch food and water, and to anchor still closer to land. The chiefs boarded the St Jean Baptiste and were taken to the captain's cabin, where the second chief was given a red jacket identical to the one that had been previously presented to his companion, and 'a bedspread made of green wool that he wanted'.[74] They seemed eager for the French to go ashore, but the rest of that day was spent manoeuvring the ship to a new anchorage closer to Rangiaohia, which Surville named 'Chevalier Cove' after the managing director of the Compagnie des Indes at Chandernagore.

Very early the next morning the chief came out again to the ship, followed by six other canoes loaded with greens. He was curious to know what a cannon was for, so Surville showed him one and tried to explain how it worked. He and his people watched attentively from the quarter-deck as the cannon was prepared for firing. When it was fired the chief carefully marked the spot where the cannonball hit the water, exclaiming loudly as the water spout rose high in the air. His people were very frightened by the explosion and all the canoes alongside fled when they heard it, but the chief seemed 'greatly astonished, remaining in ecstasies over it'.[75] Surville then showed him the ship's pigs and presented him with a male and a female piglet, 'trying to make him understand that by their copulation if he kept them, he would get many more'.[76] This fact (or Surville's sign language explanation of it) gave the chief great pleasure, and he received the piglets with marked satisfaction. By now it seems likely that the chief and his people had decided that the St Jean Baptiste party were atua (supernatural beings) of some kind — immune to witchcraft, commanding thunder and lightning, possessed of strange animals, and many of them horrible to behold.

At 6.30 a.m. the longboat and the yawl took Surville, the chief, fourteen oarsmen, a group of the sick armed with swords, and twelve armed soldiers back to the bay, while Labé loaded the gundeck with cannonballs and prepared to fire on the local people if they tried to resist a landing. Instead of going to Rangiaohia, however, the chief urged Surville to visit a cove immediately to the south of it, where he said there was a larger stream of fresh water (identified by Spencer as the Tomotomo Stream). They landed but the banks of the creek were strewn with rocks and the cove was out of sight of the *St Jean Baptiste*. Surville re-embarked in the boat and rowed to Rangiaohia, where the local people had just made a large catch of mackerel and other fish in a very long seine net. As Surville commented, 'I think that was what he did not want me to see; as they distribute it amongst everyone and live on it, I harm them.'[77]

Despite his realisation that he might be jeopardising their livelihood, Surville persuaded the local people to trade most of these fish, and sent them back to the ship to distribute to his crew. This time there were no warriors gathered on the hills, and the sailors were allowed to walk a little way inland without opposition. The work of cutting wood and filling the barrels with water went on peacefully until the afternoon, although when the chief again asked Surville for his sword so that he could display it to his people, Surville refused to give it to him. As he explained later in his journal 'this ceremony annoys me, and I refused his request. He was a little hurt, but there was nothing else to be done.'[78] By now Surville was being criticised by some of his officers for humouring the chief, whom Labé in particular regarded as 'tiresome — everything he sees he wants, sometimes we give it to him and we have difficulty refusing him — folly on the captain's part'.[79] Labé was also urging in his journal (and no doubt to Surville) that the local people should be driven out of their cove by force so that the sick could recuperate safely on shore, saving the exhaustion of frequent long trips to and from the ship. Perhaps Surville was influenced by this to harden his attitude towards local demands. The barrels of water and wood were brought back to the ship without incident, and some of the sailors told Labé that the local people had asked them what they did to any prisoners that they took: 'We gave them to understand that we bury them. They told us that in their country when they take prisoners they cut off their heads and show them to the people; next they open their stomachs then they eat them.' The sailors were horrified by this but Labé's reaction was undemonstrative —'from that I conclude that they are cannibals'.[80]

At 4.30 a.m. on 24 December several canoes came out to the ship as usual, bringing the chief, who asked that the Europeans should no longer take their muskets ashore, since they terrified his people. The canoes also brought out two women whom Labé described as very ugly, 'but that does not stop them making the customary extremely immodest gestures'.[81] The journal writers on board the *St Jean Baptiste*, unlike those on the *Endeavour*, were generally very uncomplimentary about the physical appearance and conduct of Maori women. Perhaps this was because the *Endeavour*'s men, unlike those on the *St Jean Baptiste*, had spent three glorious months in Tahiti before arriving in New Zealand and had begun to come to terms with Polynesian mores and physical beauty.

At five thirty that morning the usual flotilla of longboat, yawl and the little Batan Island boat went ashore, carrying twelve soldiers armed with muskets, and eighteen sailors and eighteen sick men, each armed with swords, who landed without any trouble. According to Labé, 'it seems that our firearms have intimidated these people. We have showed them to them and even fired several shots and made them understand that when it fired it killed men and moreover that it was thunder. They believed it and consider us more than men and no longer go near our weapons.'[82]

It seems certain that the local people had heard reports from the Bay of Islands about the shootings there, and when one of the officers inadvertently raised his musket towards a chief on this occasion, the man ran away in fear. Most of the people at Rangiaohia now avoided the Europeans, except for some women and the chief who had so often visited the ship. He clearly considered himself their ally and protector, and when Surville's knife was stolen during this visit, the chief found the thief and soon had the knife returned.

Later that morning, while Surville's party was ashore, a canoe came to the stern of the *St Jean Baptiste* to trade. Labé acquired 'stone axes and dogskins that they cover themselves with, clubs which I think are of whalebone and other similar trash'.[83] Soon after this the people of the canoe cut Monneron's fishing line and paddled rapidly away. Labé was sorely tempted to shoot at them, but did not fire for fear of alarming his comrades on land. In the early afternoon the boats returned with firewood and cress, and later that day several canoes crossed the bay, with people carrying shell trumpets on board.

The next morning was a cheerless Christmas Day. One of the Batan Islanders had died of scurvy during the night, and Labé's impatience with his captain's refusal to allow the sick to recuperate in tents ashore had mounted to a fever pitch:

> This morning dispatched three boats [to carry] . . . the sick who are fit to walk, the others who are on board are in a serious condition. Mr de Surville does not take them ashore. I consider them dead men, being unable to get better on board the vessel. I do not know why the Captain keeps them on board. However I suggested to him that it was advisable to put them ashore, putting up one or two tents there; he replied that it would be to sacrifice them outright. I offered to stay on shore with a guard of 15 to 20 men to protect them from any harassment and from surprise attack, but nothing I could say to him was to any avail. What is going to happen? Our sick will not be able to recover and we will have the unpleasantness of seeing them die on board and then we will be in a serious position as regards running the ship. And then, the Captain will have to reproach himself all his life for the deaths of so many poor wretches, that we could have saved if we acted differently. As for me, I am not involved. I have pointed out everything that could subsequently befall us.[84]

The boats went ashore and came back with water, firewood, sand, and a sack of vegetables, and that afternoon Surville and Labé set off together on a fishing expedition. At first they went to a cove (Tomotomo) just south of Rangiaohia, but

Vue d'une Montagne ou les Insulaires de la nouvelle Zelande sont
retranchés avec leurs maisons

Maison de sauvages de 12 a 20 pieds de long sur 8 a 12 de large
et 6 a 7 pieds d'élevation elles sont construite en natte s'enlevant

Echafaudages qui sont au pieds de leurs montagnes pour observer leurs
prisonniers tiquets pour mettre leur fils ou sec

it was too rocky there to cast the seine. They continued south along the coastline to Whakararo, 'a fine sandy cove . . . without rocky edges, but you can throw the seine three times without fear of striking rocks'.[85] While Labé organised the hauling of the seine on the beach, Surville climbed the bluff (above Paatia paa) and saw a deep bay (Paatia-matariki) on the other side, with sandy coves and a village nearby. From the top of this hill he saw 'lakes of some sort' (presumably Lakes Ohia and Rotokawau at the neck of the peninsula) and a wide bay, and realised for the first time that Karikari was a peninsula. Six or seven people (who on the basis of later tribal accounts were probably of Te Paa-tuu-poo tribe) came to Whakararo with gifts of greens and met Surville as he came back to the beach.He gave them cloth, and they told him that there were many fish at Paatia-matariki, and invited him to go there. Labé later reported that he had seen in this cove an orchard 'bearing a yellowish-red fruit, the size of a large olive, which has a long stone like an olive; this fruit is edible. They are bitter'[86] — a clear reference to a plantation of karaka trees.

At four o'clock on the morning of 26 December a large expedition of officers went with two longboats, the yawl and the Batan Island boat to Paatia-matariki. There they found to their delight a wide sandy bay, a few friendly people, easy access to fresh water and firewood and good fishing. After a successful cast of the net they set up a cauldron on the beach and cooked a fish soup flavoured with herbs, a performance that must have fascinated the local people. They also shot a number of birds on the wing, including 'a sort of blackbird' (tui), curlew, parrots, quail, turtle doves, wood pigeon (or kuukupa) and seabirds. According to Surville, there was no four-footed game, however, and no reptiles except a few lizards. Like the people at Rangiaohia, the people at Paatia-Matariki were very frightened of guns. Labé reported that the shooting of the birds 'surprised them considerably and they must take us for demi-gods and not for men'.[87]

One of the chiefs in this bay, who had met Surville at Whakararo the day before, had a paa (Paatia) 'at the top of a little rocky hill which forms the point of his cove, and the houses come right down to within the cove'[88] — later sketched by Pottier in his 'View of a mountain where the islanders of New Zealand are entrenched with their houses'. He invited the French to visit the place and, according to Labé, there explained to Surville (presumably by sign language) his methods of defence:

> When they come to attack me, I withdraw with my people to my mountain, which is rather difficult to climb, and I defend myself with long lances and heavy stones, which I drop on them, and when I have killed some of them I run at once to get them and cut them into pieces and then eat them . . .[89]

In gratitude for his hospitality Surville presented this chief with two little pigs, male and female, and a cock and two hens.

Opposite: *'View of a Mountain where the Islanders of New Zealand are Entrenched with their Houses'. This sketch by Pottier L'Horme shows Paatia paa, a scaffold for drying fish and a net hung up to dry, and a house ('12 to 20 feet long by 8 to 12 wide and 6 to 7 high').*

Early on 27 December the boats set out again for Paatia-matariki (which Surville had named 'Refuge Cove'), only to find the place almost deserted. The people had abandoned their houses, according to the French from fear of an attack from the mainland. The few people who remained gave them a warm welcome, and they cast the seine net several times, catching a mediocre haul of flatfish and red gurnard. Labé (who had remained on board) observed that for several days now the fishing canoes had stopped coming out to trade with the *St Jean Baptiste*, although he had seen them 'continually seining and catching a lot of fish. I do not know who to blame. It seems it comes from the chiefs of these islanders.'[90] During the day the wind blew up from the east-north-east, and the sea became very rough. One longboat and the yawl managed to struggle back to the *St Jean Baptiste* that evening (Surville encouraging his oarsmen by the offer of a bottle of wine each if they beat the yawl back to the ship), but the second longboat got into serious difficulties, as Pottier later recorded:

> In my boat I had all the sick men, which along with the oarsmen, the surgeon and me, made 33 men. Besides this there were 3 barrels of water, firewood, cooking pots and axes, plus a little boat towed behind mine [the Batan Island boat], which was useful for getting us dry-footed to shore. Leaving the cove, where we had spent the whole day, I put up sail to catch the wind in the bay, from which I would have reached the vessel on the other tack, but the mast was too weak, and it broke. So I had to attempt a return to the ship under oars. But the boat was too loaded up, and the one we were towing stopped us gaining ground. And so, seeing that the wind got stronger and stronger as night was falling, and that there were rocks at the surface of the water . . . and that the oarsmen were tired, I had the grapnel thrown out to give them time for a bit of a rest. I was also hoping that the wind would die down, but on the contrary, it got stronger and stronger, which led me to the resolution about 9.00 to lift the grapnel and go back to seek shelter in the cove we had left . . . The night was so dark we could not see the reefs on to which we nearly ran twice, since we got close enough to touch them with the oars. On the other hand, the little boat we were towing was thrown forward twice by the swell, and got in the way of the oars, and on several other occasions came crashing violently against the coping of our boat. Another problem was that our boat was taking on so much water that our poor sick men were just about afloat. The crowded conditions made it hard to bail it out . . . Finally, just as we were about to reach the cove where we were going to seek shelter, we touched the boat's bow on a rock at the S.E point before we could see it. Fortunately we got off it without taking a lot of water, but the boat remained some time with the bow very high up out of the water, with the coping at water-level. From that moment on I got everyone to keep dead silent in order not to be heard by the savages who live on top of this point [Paatia paa], for fear lest they should think we were taking advantage of the darkness of the night to go and take them by surprise. Once we were far enough into the bay to be in shelter, I had the grapnel lowered, and covered everyone, particularly the invalids, with the boat sail. Then I had the water bailed out, and set a good guard, for fear of savages appearing.
>
> As soon as day had fully broken I had the boat brought inshore and disembarked all my men. I had a big fire lit on shore to warm them up. Some time later a few savages turned up, and came up close to us. The chief of this cove was amongst them. I gave him to understand by signs that our return was occasioned

by the bad weather, which was preventing our getting back to the ship. He quite understood. As we had some fish in our boat, which we had caught in the seine the day before. I divided half of it amongst us all, and kept the other half for the next day, in case it was impossible for us to go back on board ship, because it was all we had to eat. But I was very agreeably surprised when a sort of chief amongst the savages came up to me with some dried fish, which he got another savage to bring me. When I received him, I indicated that I had nothing to give him in exchange. He made signs to say that he asked for nothing, and in addition offered his hut to house us all. This offer appeared to proceed from a heart truly humane, and touched by the accident which prevented our returning to the ship. But I judged it unwise to trust him.[91]

At 8 a.m. on 28 December Pottier sent eight armed men overland to Rangiaohia, with orders to find some way back to the ship to fetch provisions. About three-quarters of an hour later he was woken from an exhausted sleep by shouts from his men, who reported that they had seen the *St Jean Baptiste* wallowing in high seas off the south end of Rangiaohia, where the storm had driven it almost onto the rocks. Thinking that the ship was about to be wrecked, Pottier scrambled up the hill behind Paatia Point and saw the *St Jean Baptiste* rolling heavily close to the land, but finally to his intense relief the ship hoisted its foresail and sailed towards the shelter of 'Refuge Cove', where it anchored in more sheltered waters. He later learned that the *St Jean Baptiste* had dragged on its anchors until it was only a musketshot from the reefs below Rangiaohia paa, when they were forced to cut one anchor cable and let another go. Labé later described what had happened:

> the sea [was] breaking over us and driving us on to the coast. To make matters worse, the vessel stayed for quite a long time without answering to her rudder and we stared death in the face, seeing rocks along the length of the ship fit to make your hair stand on end. However we were lucky enough to stretch from them, the vessel having run forward a little. God has delivered us from danger and has worked a miracle in our favour.[92]

It was the loss of these two anchors (and a smaller one lost off Paatia Point) that later forced Surville to abandon his plans to explore New Zealand in favour of sailing to the east. According to Surville's account of the storm, although the danger to the ship had been extreme he had not been overly concerned about the safety of his men on shore:

> I thought them very safe with the natives, to whom we have only done good since we have been here and this occurrence goes to show that it is always better to begin relations with kindness and patience, than with force and violence, both of which seem to me, besides, a little unfair always towards people who are in their own country, and have never dreamt of coming to trouble you in yours.[93]

Early on 29 December the replacement tiller snapped in heavy seas. After this there was a lull in the storm during which Pottier L'Horme managed to bring his boat with all its men back to the ship. Some of the sick men were in a very bad way, and four more of them died during the next few days, including one

Frenchman, a Moorish lascar and two natives of Pondicherry, all of whose bodies were thrown overboard into the bay.

At 5 a.m. on 30 December Surville, Pottier and Labé went back to 'Refuge Cove', where Surville hoped to make 'a cast of the net, and also [to] see whether I could not capture a native, in order to extract from him afterwards whatever knowledge it would be possible to obtain about this country'.[94]

The local chief greeted them warmly and gave them cooked and dried fish. In return Surville presented him with blue cloth and some wheat, corn and green peas, which he showed him how to plant. After the French had eaten dinner in the shelter of a grove of trees the local people brought them more dried and cooked fish. The chief invited them to a group of houses on a rise below the paa, where several women danced for them:

> There were about 8 or 10 of them grouped around us, amongst whom were three girls or women who danced in front of us for a very long time, trying by all sorts of the most lascivious movements to attract us. Two young men also joined in their dance. Finally, bored with seeing always the same thing (because they went on and on, apparently thinking that we were only difficult to arouse, and that they would succeed in the end), after having traded for some dried fish with this little group we went down. The three females followed us and in a final transport one seized me around the waist, and squeezing me hard in her arms made the most lascivious movements against me. I shook her off and we went about our tasks.[95]

The French crew were so ill and debilitated during their visit to Tokerau that it is unlikely that they had been sexually very active. The women's dancing on this occasion was probably a performance in honour of their guests, although given the lack of response there may also have been an element of teasing and taunting in what they were doing. The *Endeavour* crew after their stay in Tahiti had regarded Maori women as comparatively chaste and modest, and barely commented on the sexual explicitness of some local dancing. The *St Jean Baptiste*'s men had had no such experience, however, and both Labé and Surville reacted with affronted distaste on this occasion. Later that afternoon the wind blew up again and Surville and Labé took the boats back to the ship.

During the great storm on 28 December the *St Jean Baptiste*'s yawl had swamped, and on the night of the 30th it must have washed ashore. Early the next morning one of the officers who was surveying the coastline with a telescope saw the yawl stranded on Tokerau Beach, with several local people (whom Surville now for the first time called 'noirs', or blacks) looking at it. Surville ordered the longboat lowered and hastily set off towards the beach, but when they arrived the yawl was no longer visible. He and his men ran up and down the sand dunes searching for it, until finally they found a trail where the yawl had been dragged over the dunes as far as a deep, narrow creek, and either sunk amongst the reeds or taken along the creek to some nearby lakes. During their search the sailors had shot some birds and finally in weary frustration they heated up the cauldron on the beach and made a meal of birds and wild celery, 'fit for the gods'.

Over the preceding few days Surville had experienced near-shipwreck, criticism from his officers and the deaths of some of his men. The loss of the yawl was the last straw, and he was now intent on revenge. After this meal he led his men to the northern end of the beach where there was 'a fairly big village', with people running up and down the nearby hills, and drawn up in armed parties on the heights. One small group had stayed close to the houses, however, and their leader signed to Surville to approach. Surville beckoned to him in turn, and the man came forward unarmed, carrying a green branch — 'a symbol of friendship among all these people'. Surville angrily reproached him for the 'theft' of the yawl and ordered several of the sailors to 'arrest' him and tie him up with ropes. He was led away to the longboat, and, 'wishing to extend the revenge further', Surville then seized two fine canoes that were beached nearby, loaded with nets. He ordered some sailors to take one of these canoes to the longboat, while all the nets were piled into the second canoe and it was set alight. After this Surville and his men moved on and fired five or six groups of fishermen's huts and fern-root store-houses (about thirty buildings in all) along the nearby creek.

While they were doing this one of the soldiers noticed a group of warriors heading towards the longboat. Surville and two soldiers raced back to the longboat, the soldiers with bayonets fixed, and arrived just in time to drive off five or six warriors armed with spears who were trying to rescue their prisoner. As the warriors ran off, Surville's men set fire to one last village nearby and then returned to the *St Jean Baptiste* in the longboat with the prisoner and the captured canoe. A group of about sixty armed men stood and watched impotently as the fire took hold and spread across the scrublands behind Tokerau Beach.

As Pottier L'Horme reported back on board the *St Jean Baptiste*:

> the prisoner turned out to be the same man who had had dried fish brought to me when I was without food at Refuge Cove in the bad weather. I was touched with the greatest compassion when this poor wretched man came on board. Recognizing me, and not knowing what his fate would be, he flung himself at my knees, embraced them fervently, then got up and embraced my body just as fervently, with tears in his eyes. He said some incomprehensible things to me, but indicated by signs that he was the one who had had fish brought to me at a time when neither I, nor those who had incurred the misfortune of not being able to regain the vessel, had a single thing to eat. This man appeared to be asking for mercy, or begging me to ask it for him. I did my best to console him, and explained to him that we had no wish whatever to harm him. It was useless; he kept on crying, especially when he saw irons put on his ankles to keep him prisoner.[96]

Labé, on the other hand, simply described this man's physical appearance and lamented that Surville had taken only one prisoner:

> The Islander whom Mr de Surville captured and then took on board is a man of about 35 years and seems very vigorous and alert, 5 feet 2 inches tall, squarely built, painted and embossed like the Kaffirs from the Guinea Coast, long hair tied in a knot, his body the same colour as the peoples of the Coromandel Coast. His clothes consist of a type of dogskin cloak which covers his body. His nudity is not covered with linen. This poor man seems very gentle and quite quiet . . . I had him put in irons and manacles for fear that he would escape by swimming away. In my

opinion Mr Surville has made a bad mistake in not carrying off a dozen islanders. They would have served us well on board for the menial tasks, since we have already lost 60 men from the crew and have more than 40 still sick.[97]

From Surville's point of view, the 'theft' of the yawl had provided ample justification for burning houses, canoes, nets, and capturing a local chief. From a Maori point of view, however, it was no theft at all, because canoes, whales, sea-mammals and anything else that washed ashore came under the mana of the chief of that place.[98] The capture of this man (whose name was recorded by the French as 'Naguinoui' or 'Naquinovi',[99] and as 'Ranginui' in local tradition) must have seemed an arbitrary gesture of hostility, as difficult to understand as many other of the French actions had been. A Te Paa-tuu-poo tradition collected by John White, probably in the 1850s, recorded local memories of this episode:

> In the days of ancient times a vessel came to Mangonui [here probably used as a term for the entire bay], this we heard from our old people who related this information about these goblins [tupua] to us. The vessel dropped anchor at Mangonui, and a gale came on and the sick people of these salts [maitai] from the other side of the sea were on shore, and the people of Patuu tribe attended to and fed these sick people, and they were kind to these white skins [Pakeha] till the gale subsided, when the chief of the Patuu tribe paddled on board [sic] of the ship to see the goblins, and to see the ship, and the chief who was called Ranginui was tied by orders of the chief of those salts, and the ship sailed away with Te Ranginui on board, and the vessel was lost to sight out far on the sea and sailed away no one knew where. There was not any cause given for which Ranginui was made prisoner by these salts, nor was there any reason for his being taken out to sea, but for such acts as this the Maori retaliated on the salts who might come to these islands that the Maori might have revenge for the evil brought on them by the salts, or those from over the sea.[100]

Surville, however, had no qualms about what he had done. On 31 December after raising anchor and sailing out of the bay, he wrote in his journal:

> Seeing that . . . the wind was continuing to blow too strongly for a ship that was down to its last cable and anchor, and having in addition just what I would desire, a savage and a native canoe, and our men being also partly rehabilitated and in a state to undergo a small voyage, I ordered the anchor raised. At 9.00 in the evening we were under sail.[101]

The voyage from Tokerau proved to be anything but short. Surville headed his ship towards Peru, a Pacific crossing that wore both the ship and its crew to tatters and which took more than three months. Ranginui was freed from his irons and treated kindly by Surville, who exempted him from work and let him sleep in the council chamber with the captive from the Solomon Islands. At first he 'sighed and cried often', but Labé soon reported that 'he no longer seems sad, laughs with everybody, drinks and eats well and sleeps well; he eats a great deal. From time to time he is afraid that he will be disembowelled then eaten; that is

Opposite: *'Indian of New Zealand called Naguinoui cannibal'. This sketch of Ranginui displays his spiral buttock tattoo and curious horned tattoos on his calfs.*

Indio de la nueva — Zelandia llamado Naguinoui
antropophago

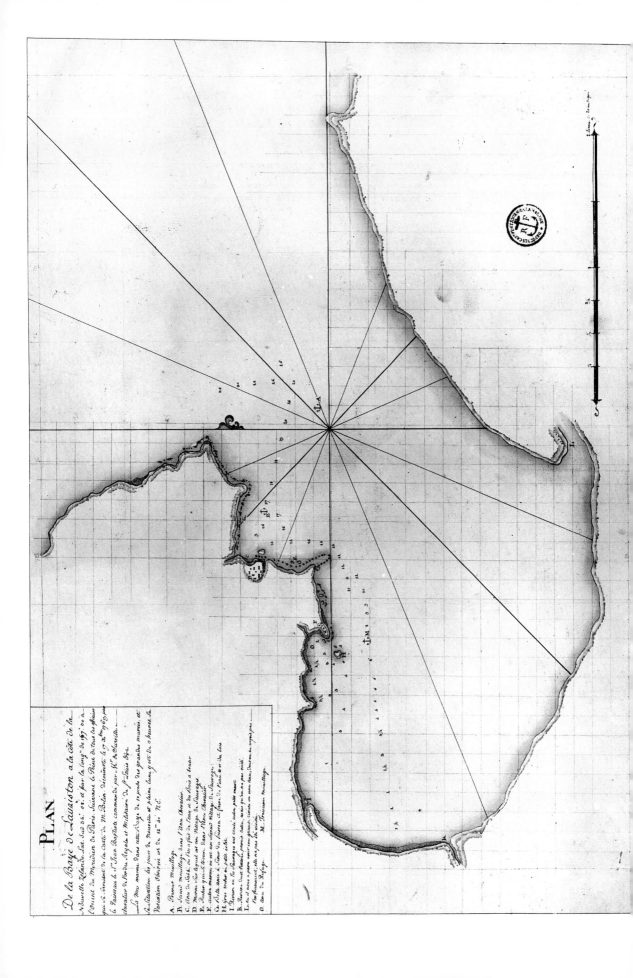

PLAN
De la Baye de Lauriston à la côte de la
Nouvelle Zélande Lat: Sud 34°. 25. et par la long: de 197°. 20. à
l'Orient du Meridien de Paris. Suivant le Point de tous les plans
qui a été trouvé à la Côte du M. Bolin Decouverte le 17. 18. et 19. par
le Vaisseau le S. Jean Baptiste commandé par Mr. de Surville.
Mouillé de Nord: Ayats et Militaire du 1er. Juin 1840.

La Mer monte dans cette Baye de 10 pieds Out grandes marées et
la situation les jour de Nouvelle et pleine Lune. y est de o heures la
Variation observée ac de 18 de NE.

A. Premier Mouillage.
B. Second Mouillage dans l'eau Chevalier.
C. Ance de Sable, où l'on a fait de l'eau et du Bois à terre.
D. Marais: Pùr Baptisé où l'on Mouillage de Sauvage
E. Rocher qui découvrent, Basses Pleine Chenalier.
F. autre marais où est un Grand Village de Sauvages.
G. Ile Ronde ou à Nouv: Vis l'eau et l'isau: 1 s Point de l'Ile loin
H. Gros Rocher de petite Isle.
I. Ruisseau ou le Sauvages ont conté cette petite marée.
K. Ruisseau C'est Portail: paroist Salai, où y a pas pris.
L. où l'eau a paru venir une grand Isante en eau dans Ouvert de rupts par
les faumant, elle ne pas la visite.
O. Ance de Refuge.   M. Troisième mouillage.

what the islanders do to people they take prisoner in their country.'[102] Pottier
L'Horme sketched him in his journal, along with various artefacts including the
captured canoe, but he did not survive the voyage. On 24 March 1770, in sight
of the Juan Fernandez Islands, Ranginui died of scurvy, and less than two weeks
later, Surville drowned in high surf on the bar of Chilca in Peru as he made a
desperate effort to seek help from the Spanish for his crew.

THE *ST JEAN BAPTISTE* ETHNOGRAPHIC ACCOUNTS OF TOKERAU

At the end of their brief visit to Tokerau, Surville, Pottier L'Horme and Monneron
wrote generalised descriptions of the place, in Surville's case contrasting and com-
paring it with 'Port Praslin' in the Solomon Islands. In the 'Description' that follows
I have combined their generalised comments, under the headings used by Pottier
L'Horme in a relatively detailed account that seems to have been prepared for
publication.

The Land

According to Monneron,

> No one, before us, had set foot in this country. It was discovered on 13 September
> 1642 by Abel Tasman, who encountered the same weather on the west coast as we
> did. He followed the coast from latitude 42° 10′ south to 34° 35′ south only. Thus
> everything we have seen in the eastern region has been discovered by the *St Jean
> Baptiste*.[103]

This was not true, of course, as we have seen, even given European ideas
about 'discovery', for the *Endeavour* had preceded them on the eastern coastline.

Height, features, and colour of these people

Pottier L'Horme described the people of 'Lauriston Bay' as:

> fairly tall in general, without being giants [thus contradicting one of the suggestions
> in Tasman's account]; even quite small people are found, as witnessed by the one

Opposite: *'Plan of Lauriston Bay' has an elaborate explanatory key:*
A   *First anchorage*
B   *Second anchorage in Chevalier Cove*
C   *Sandy Cove where we got water and firewood*
D   *Hillock where the savages' village is*
E   *Rock in Chevalier Cove*
F   *Another hillock where there is another of the savages' villages*
G   *Fine cove for seining for fish and getting water and wood*
H   *Big rock or little islet*
I   *River where the savages sank our little boat*
K   *River whose entrance appears to be good but which we did not visit*
L   *Where there appeared to be a big river or a cove whose curve was not visible; it was not visited*
M   *Third anchorage*
O   *Refuge Cove*

chest level with a little piece of string. This mat, which has more or less the effect of an ecclesiastical stole, provided no covering at all for the private parts, which they take no pains to hide. Instead of a mat, the chiefs wear large cloaks made of several dogskins sewn together [huru kurii], and the size of these corresponds to their rank and dignity. They turn the hair outwards when they are on ceremony and turn it inwards in their free time to guard against the cold. [Surville added that the dogskin cloaks could be held in at the waist by a wide plaited belt.]

All the chiefs or principal people amongst them, and even the old men, besides their cloak or their mat, wear around their loins a kind of cloth, which I shall mention later, which covers their organs of generation. But it is worn more to guard against the cold than because of any feeling of modesty, the slightest notion of which is so foreign to them, that they piss wherever they happen to be, paying as little attention to this act as any animal I have ever seen, and never once turning aside for anyone . . . All the women wear either the same loincloth or a bit of matting. They are thus more modest than the men concerning this part of the body, but they also outstrip the men in licentiousness.[110]

One can note this same preoccupation with nakedness and immodesty in Buffon, whose description of various 'savage peoples' cited 'lasciviousness' and sexual liberty as classic markers of a 'rude' and 'unpolished' way of life.

Their normal food

The people ate dog's meat; human meat 'when they can catch one of their enemies'; a lot of fish; a few sweet potatoes; gourds; 'a type of root which has a great deal of similarity with the iris' (probably taro); and fernroot, which was their most common food. According to Surville, the fernroot was put in the fire for a moment, beaten on a stone with a wooden hammer, kneaded and then eaten. 'I tasted it,' he added. 'It is terrible and full of little hard bits, much tougher than the hay our animals eat.'[111] Fish were caught and dried in summer, or wrapped in leaves and cooked in an earth oven. This was made by digging a hole, half filling it with stones, lighting a large fire on top then taking off the stones, putting in the parcel of food, putting the stones back on top and covering these with earth. Pottier remarked that, judging by the appetite of Ranginui, their captive, the people were 'prodigiously greedy' (a comment that conflicted with some of the *Endeavour* observations).

According to Pottier's account, Ranginui ate continually on board ship but seemed to miss his fernroot, and 'we noticed that he had very short teeth . . . As we were examining them he indicated that they had been cut down like that, and that it was the custom in his country. He also had great difficulty pronouncing French words, especially those containing "s".'[112] These patterns of wear on Ranginui's teeth were more likely to have been the characteristic 'fernroot planes' described by physical anthropologists, which have been attributed to a very fibrous diet.

Their ornaments

Pottier L'Horme gave a detailed and interesting description of the local use of tattoo, or moko:

Among their ornaments I number the way they paint the face, the buttocks and other parts of the body. The painting [tattoo] of the face is a mark of distinction, so that they do not all have painted faces, and those that do have the face painted do not all have it done in the same way. Some have ¾ of the face done, which creates a most bizarre and singular effect, because they would need to finish only half the forehead to have the face totally painted. Of these I have seen only one, the chief of all the neighbouring villages. It may well be that this chief had a superior whose whole face was painted. Others are only painted from the two points of the eyebrows and the bridge of the nose, down to the bottom of the face. These people, at the point of each eyebrow on each side of the nose, have two kinds of painted horns which stick up about ¾ of an inch on to the forehead. They are inferior by only one grade to the one who has ¾ of his face painted. Others have only one half of the face painted, in which case the painting goes down the neck to shoulder level. Finally there are others who have only the two horns between the eyebrows. The two horns do not always have the same form. These men would seem to be the lowest rank of the leaders. The same does not apply to the painting they do on the buttocks. All the men and women have them painted, without distinction. They consist of bands, about one inch wide in the form of a spiral. They gave me to understand that this painting was an act of religion. The leaders add a painted decoration to these spirals, which is more or less extensive according to their dignity. There are also those who have on each calf a portion of the same painting which forms the figure inscribed here in the margin. The man we have in our power had the same design on the right leg A and another on the left B.

The women do not have the face painted, except for the lower lip. Even that is not the general rule, because the one who looked the prettiest to me had only two little rectangular patches on the same lip, and 4 other round ones, two on each side of the mouth, above and below. But besides the painting of the buttocks which they have in common with the men, the women have a piece of painting below the breasts, on the stomach. I have not noticed at all that this is a mark of distinction with them, I believe it is more a decoration according to whim; I have seen only 3 or 4 of them and the women who seemed to be attached to the big chief had none.[113]

This description accords well with the *Endeavour* accounts of moko, although Pottier thought that partial tattoo might be a function purely of status, rather than of status plus age. The 'horns' between the eyebrows, the calf tattoos, the description of body tattoos on women's bellies, the squares tattooed on the lower lip and dots at the corners of the mouth of one woman, and the observation that all men and women without distinction had spirals tattooed on their buttocks are interesting items of information. Pottier's colour sketch of Ranginui showed a blue spiral tattoo on his buttock with a curvilinear pattern in a band below it, blue curvilinear facial tattoos reminiscent of those sketched by Parkinson in the Bay of Islands, and two curious blue tattoos on his calf, which were also described in Pottier's journal (as well as a greenstone ear ornament and a red hairband fastening his top-knot).

According to Pottier, the tattoo patterns were 'engraved into the skin' with a wood instrument, one end of which was bent into a right angle and sharpened. This implement was tapped with another piece of wood, and then 'very fine charcoal dust' was put into the wounds to make the tattoo indelible. He saw no children with tattoos.

347

Contrary to the *Endeavour* journal writers, Pottier stated that few of the men had beards, and that they tried to pluck out the hairs as they grew:

> Just the same it grows despite their efforts, and they do not have the skill for cutting it, which greatly annoys them. One day one of the savages came into my cabin while I was in the process of shaving. He seemed so enchanted by the ease with which the razor cut my beard that he asked me to cut his, which I did, as much for my own satisfaction as for his. He did not lack for admirers amongst his companions, who wanted me to do the same for them, but I was not prepared to go to those efforts.[114]

The people had long straight hair, which they tied on top of their heads, and both men and women wore bird feathers, especially white ones, as head ornaments. They also put an oil-based red paint (kura) in their hair, on their foreheads, and in some cases all over their bodies. According to L'Horme, however, 'I thought I noticed that this custom was restricted to the minor leaders.'[115] Surville added that he had also seen some people with yellow paint in their hair.

Both men and women had pierced ears, in which they wore a variety of ornaments, including flat or cylindrical greenstone pendants, 'sometimes pale, sometimes milky and sometimes quite bright, while remaining the same sort of stone';[116] bones; 'fish teeth in the form of snakes' tongues, both sides of which are very finely serrated'; human teeth; and even bits of biscuit given to them by the sailors. Around the neck many people wore 'a kind of idol' made of greenstone (the tiki), and a few wore a sea-cow's tooth or that of a similar animal, well polished, with two eyes drawn in black at the end (rei puta). Monneron said of the tiki that 'this figure seems to be squatting on its heels; the eyes are made of mother-of-pearl, laid into the stone; it is astonishing that they are able to give it such a fine polish, shape it and pierce it without the use of metals'.[117]

Their housing

According to Monneron, 'their houses are like those of all savages, which is to say small and undecorated'.[118] Pottier, however, gave a good description of Maori dwellings:

> Their huts, or dwelling-places, generally have a rectangular shape; the walls would be 3 feet high, and the roof 7 or 8 feet high, 8 to 10 feet long, by 4 or 5 feet wide. They are not all the same size. The entrance is very small; the biggest I have seen was only 2½ feet high by 1½ feet wide. They light a fire at the door of their hut. This doorway, which is the sole opening, is always on the opposite side to the bad weather. These huts are constructed from squared pieces of wood crossing one another at right angles and strongly joined together at all points of intersection, and abutting on posts planted solidly at each corner. They cover this framework with several layers of rushes, which shelters them admirably from the ill-effects of weather. Most of the huts have no doors in the entrances. Those which do, have the jambs decorated with an idol, which I took for the face of their household god. The plank serving as a door is closed in such a way as to be very difficult to open for those who do not know the secret of it. I noticed that the chief had several places to live, and he went there to stay either because he wished to, or because

he was called there on tribal business. When he goes from one home to another like this, he takes all his riches with him. I think private people who also have several huts do the same, in which case the huts stay empty, and for the most part open.

Such is the general construction of their huts. I have nevertheless seen a few built in a circular shape, and covered in reeds. But these ones did not look to me like huts intended for permanent habitation. I shall say later what I thought of these scattered dwellings, which seemed intended as temporary hiding-places. Their villages are composed of only 5 or 6 huts at most, but their towns contain more.[119]

In this account Pottier described small houses, with only a doorway for ventilation, clustered in hamlets of five to six dwellings that were used at different times of the year (no doubt as the archaeological records suggests, for activities such as gardening and fishing). There were also a few circular shelters, which Pottier thought were temporary hiding-places. In consequence there were always a number of empty houses to be seen — an interesting fact to be considered in assessing population estimates based on counting house sites.

Their method of fortifying themselves against their enemies

According to Pottier, the people built their 'citadels' on the steepest place that they could find, arranging their houses in tiers and erecting 'great pillars of wood' outside the paa where fish were dried. At times of threat all of the houses in the countryside were abandoned, and the people moved into these strongholds, living two or three families to a house. Of about fifty houses scattered around the bay that were seen by the French, only one was occupied during their stay, evidently because it was a hiding-place. He added,

> it can be seen from this that these people are inexperienced in the art of warfare; they know no other fortification than places which present difficulty of access due to nature. Aside from this there is no wall to prevent the enemy surprising them. A ditch of average width which I would rather call a dip in the ground behind which they have stuck a few stakes, furnish all the entrenchment for an area which it would be simplicity itself to attack.[120]

Despite these disparaging comments, Monneron admitted that 'few of us dared to climb [up to the paa] because it was too dangerous for us to want to satisfy a mere whim of curiosity. One false step would invariably cost us our lives.'[121]

Their weapons

The local people had 'lances' or spears (huata) up to twenty-one feet long, pointed at one end, sometimes with a sting-ray's tail. These spears were occasionally decorated with a tuft of dog's hair, or some feathers. Once an enemy had been wounded with the spear they jumped on top of him, and clubbed him with a 'spatula' (patu), made of polished slate-coloured stone or whalebone with a carved pommel, about twelve to fourteen inches long and usually worn stuck into a wide plaited belt. The people also had a weapon made of a whalebone rib

349

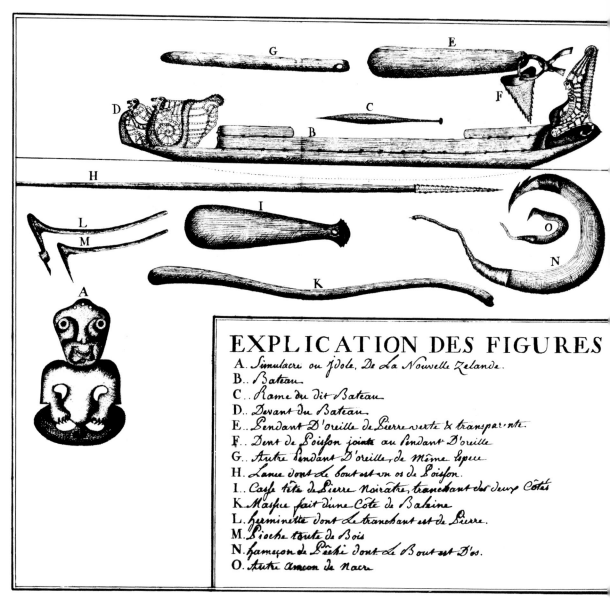

'New Zealand objects', described in a key:

A Image or idol from New Zealand
B Boat
C Paddle of the aforesaid boat
D Prow of the boat
E Ear pendant of green transparent stone
F Fish tooth attached to the ear pendant
G Another ear pendant of the same sort
H Spear tipped with a fish bone
I Truncheon of blackish stone with a cutting edge on both sides
K Club made from a whale rib
L Adze whose cutting edge is of stone
M Mattock completely of wood
N Fish-hook with a tip of bone
O Another fish-hook, made of mother-of-pearl

350

(hoeroa), carved at one end and with a sharp flat blade at the other, or a similar weapon carved in wood. According to Pottier, 'they indicated that they strike the head in the region of the temples with this instrument',[122] an informative, if rather puzzling, comment (given the shape of the weapon), since ethnologists have been uncertain about how these 'hoeroa' were used. A spear and a hoeroa were also included in Pottier's sketch of 'Arms, Idols and Instruments . . .'

Proof of cannibalism

Pottier L'Horme commented that during their visit to Paatia paa the local chief showed them how his people killed and ate their enemies:

> Once we were on the flat area he took a lance, and brandishing it in various directions, he showed us how they defend themselves when attacked. He gave us to understand that if a few enemies were left on the battlefield, they cut them in pieces and distributed them amongst themselves for eating; and these signs were unequivocal. The man we have in our power who I think is one of the leaders in the area, gave even clearer explanations. He made signs to say that they seized their enemies by the tuft of hair they have on top of the head, and struck them with their spatula on the temple. Once having killed them, they cut off the 4 limbs, slit the stomach open in the shape of a cross, ripped out the intestines, cut the trunk to pieces, likewise the limbs, and distributed it to those present for eating. I cannot say whether they eat these frightful viands raw, or whether they cook them.
>
> These people fight cruel wars amongst themselves. The big chief of Chevalier Cove indicated to us that he was in a state of hostility with another chief, and that we were under an obligation to help him make war on his enemy.[123]

Yet, noted Pottier, 'all the time we stayed, we learned of not one act of hostility from his enemies, and the tranquillity that seemed to reign everywhere suggested that peace was general'.[124] He therefore suspected that the chief's request had concealed a stratagem to kill his visitors, so that he 'could then feast to his heart's content on the flesh of these white men, the first he would ever have seen'.[125]

Intelligence and character of these people

Although Pottier's journal entries showed signs of fellow-feeling for local people, particularly for Ranginui, the successive sections of his general account of the place became increasingly harsh and derogatory. These were clear echoes of Buffon, who had written of the American Indians that 'though each nation might have manners and customs peculiar to itself; though some might be more fierce, cruel, courageous, or dastardly than others; they yet were all equally stupid, ignorant, unacquainted with the arts, and destitute of industry'.[126]

Pottier L'Horme was evidently another believer in the myth of the 'ignoble savage', for he described the people of Tokerau as follows:

> [They have] very limited intelligence. Their arms and fortifications are still in their infancy and doubtless their tactics are on the same level of perfection. They do not even have an inkling of the advantages they would derive from using slings — when

they do throw a few stones, it is by hand. They are even further from any knowl-edge of the bow and arrow. They do some pieces of woodwork that seem fairly good from a distance, and look like pieces of ancient fretworked furniture, but seen up close they proved to be very roughly made. It is true that they do not have convenient tools, since they have no knowledge of iron. It can be seen from what I have reported that the talents of these barbarians are no better employed as regards things of the first necessity, such as agriculture and weaving. As for fishing, if they are familiar with the implements for it, they could be said to have been forced into this knowledge by the prodigious abundance of fishes along their coasts.

They have shy natures, but they are lazy to the last degree, treacherous, thieving, defiant, and on the lookout to surprise you without thinking twice, which goes to show their limited intelligence, because from what I could see they paid not the slightest attention to the consequences.[127]

To support his claim that the people were treacherous and careless of the con-sequences, Pottier offered an illustration. On one occasion the ship's chaplain had been invited to accompany the local chief and his wife (probably at Rangi-aohia) to some huts. The chief's entourage increased as they walked, until they were accompanied by a number of armed men. The chaplain, fearing that he was about to be ambushed, decided to return to the beach and was permitted to do so — hardly a compelling example of treachery.

The first paragraph in Pottier's description of local people gave the 'pro-gressivist' argument, which stated European superiority on the grounds of tech-nological advantage. The second paragraph can be contrasted with Cook: 'All their actions and beheavour towards us tended to prove that they are a brave open warlike people and voide of treachery.'[128] European ideas of the 'ignoble' (or the 'noble') 'savage' evidently had more to do with particular European traditions of 'the other', and the character of particular individual Europeans, than with actual Maori patterns of behaviour.

Their instruments of carpentry

Pottier L'Horme described two types of carpentry tool:

an adze, whose butt and handle are made of a single piece of wood. At the end of the butt they attach a stone of the same type as their spatulas [or patu]. It is about 3″ long by ½″ wide, and the cutting edge is cut more or less like a mortise chisel. Apart from the adze . . . they have another tool of which I have seen only the blade. It is a stone about 10″ to 12″ long, by 3″ to 4″ wide, cut like an axe blade as one end. I do not know whether they attach it to a handle when they use it, or whether it is used like a chisel. It is with these two tools that they work their wood, especially when they are hollowing out huge trees to make canoes.[129]

Their fishing implements

The local people caught abundant fish at this time of the year and at first they supplied fish to the French, but stopped when the *St Jean Baptiste* was no longer welcome in the bay. According to Pottier, their fishing nets were extremely large, 'so that it takes all the inhabitants of a village working together to pull one. I assume that it is common property. One certainty is that they share the outcome of the fishing amongst everyone.'[130] The nets were made like European seines, of 'a very fine rush, which knots superbly', with a narrow band filled with stones to act as sinkers. Their fish-hooks were made of shaped roots, fitted with a very sharp bone ('I do not know of what animal,' wrote Surville).

Their canoes were very long and shaped of a single piece of wood, with the sides made higher by planks lashed on by 'cords made of rushes'. Each end was covered in with a fitted piece of wood. Cross-pieces were slotted neatly into grooves in these end boards, and the canoes of the 'greatest chiefs' had prow and stern pieces decorated 'by a kind of fretted sculpture' with feathers and tufts of dog's hair attached. Those of their 'subordinates' had carvings only at the prow, and some canoes had no carvings at all. According to Surville, canoe carvings were painted with oil-based red paint.

A canoe, a net hung up to dry and two fish-hooks were sketched by Pottier after their visit to the bay.

Agricultural implements

Karikari was not a great agricultural area, for the main areas of good soil in the bay were along the Oruru Valley. It is therefore not surprising that the gardens seen by the French on the peninsula were small. According to Pottier, the local people had just two kinds of agricultural implement, one shaped like a trowel and the other like a pick two or three feet long, shown in one of Pottier's sketches.

Their songs, and musical instruments

According to Monneron,

> we saw musical instruments among them. One is a shell to which they fit a cylindrical pipe 3 or 4 inches long; they draw from it sounds like that of the bagpipes; it is no doubt the same instrument that Abel Tasman speaks of [a puu taatara]. The other is about an inch and a half long [shaped like an olive, but fatter and longer according to Pottier]; it is hollow and has only one hole from which they draw 5 or 6 different sounds as sweet as that of the flageolet [nguru]. These people no doubt have a strong taste for music. We heard them singing in chorus several times and they keep in perfect tune. They seem to be very fond of dancing as well.[131]

Their religion

Pottier L'Horme described the tiki as an 'idol', adding that 'the signs they made to tell us that these were their gods consisted in joining their hands together and raising their eyes to the sky'.[132] There were also similar figures, only larger, on the door-posts of some houses, and on the canoes. Not surprisingly, considering that none of the French spoke any Maori, Pottier said, 'I have been unable to ascertain with what kind of cult they honour this god, nor whether they recognize several gods rather than admitting only one.'[133]

Burials and mourning

Pottier reported that when a person died, the local people told them that they buried the corpse in the ground, then they cut their faces, chests and thighs (haehae) with seashells in mourning. He added 'I do not know whether they perform the same for those amongst them who, once killed or taken in warfare, are eaten by their enemies.'[134]

Their style of greeting

Monneron described their manner of greeting [hongi] as follows:

> The one receiving the greeting sits on the ground and the one making it comes and presses his nose against the one who is seated. They stay in this posture without saying anything for about half a minute. Mr de Surville did the same with those savages who made no objection to sitting down to receive his salutation.[135]

Division of labour, and 'their great dirtiness'

According to Pottier, 'the women go in the canoes, and handle the paddles just as well as the men. They carry their children on their backs, covered by their matting. To all appearances they go fishing too, moreover I have not noticed that they take more of a part in the housework than the men.'[136] This comment is interesting, for it indicates a much less gender-based division of labour than has sometimes been suggested for early Maori communities.

Pottier added that the people were very dirty, and that they ate body (but not head) lice and suffered a kind of scabies — here again contradicting Banks, who said that he had 'never seen an eruption on the skin or any sign of one by scars or otherwise'.[137] The comment about dirtiness is interesting, for conditions on board the *St Jean Baptiste* must have been far from clean. French ships at this time had no scuppers to carry away filth and dirty water;[138] rats, lice and cockroaches abounded, and ventilation was poor. Given that the ship was short of water and that so many of the crew were ill (and vomiting was one of the symptoms of scurvy), conditions on board must have been filthy. It is difficult to believe, given the comments of other explorers about the cleanliness of Maori settlements, that conditions on shore were as unpleasant as those on board the *St Jean Baptiste*.

Nature of the terrain

Surville described 'Lauriston Bay' as a place well fitted to the requirements of a European vessel:

> At Lauriston Bay, in all the coves I have explored, water can be collected with the greatest of ease; it is right next to the shore, runs freely, and comes from the hills. The barrels only need to be rolled less than four paces, on very level sand. The air is healthy here. The country is open and the soil seems very good. There are 3 or 4 different types of cress and a kind of wild celery whose effect was singularly prompt on our sick men. Firewood is not lacking here, and although the country

is all bare, almost like the Cape of Good Hope, all the valleys and gullies are wooded, and right up to the seashore there are large trees.[139]

Monneron described the land to the right-hand side of the entrance to the bay (Karikari) as mountainous, and covered with high scrub, with grass on the summits, but around 'Refuge Cove' (Paatia-Matariki) there were streams lined with many trees. At the back of the bay (behind Tokerau Beach) there was 'a fair-sized pond about half a league from the shore' (Lake Ohia) with a well-wooded range of hills beyond. The east side of the bay seemed fertile, but they were not able to explore it. According to Pottier, the soil in the valleys was sandy, covered by a 'thin crust of earth formed by the decomposition of the leaves and grasses', and the mountains were rocky, with reddish clay soil, which was chalky where it was exposed.

Plants

The French noted two main types of tree: one that Surville said was cultivated, with an edible fruit shaped like an olive, yellow when ripe, which grew very high and bushy and had leaves like those of the Spanish laurel (a description of the karaka); and the other, which 'produces huge bunches of flowers, of a quite delicate red. Interspersed among the greenery, they make a very attractive sight. I have seen no fruit on this tree, which grows very high'[140] — the pohutukawa tree. Pottier also described a shrub that looked rather like juniper but smelled quite different — 'if you rub the leaves between your fingers it smells like roses' (perhaps maanuka); and another that was very bushy and beautifully green, with leaves like young barley, but not as long. The plants used by the French included two types of cress and a wild celery, which had an amazingly rapid effect in alleviating scurvy, but caused attacks in which the sufferers became red-faced and breathless.

The cultivated plants included sweet potatoes, which were just starting to grow; another 'similar' root (possibly yam); taro; and 'sweet gourds', grown in small quantities. The staple vegetable at this time of the year, however, was fernroot.

Reptiles and quadrupeds

The only reptile noted in 'Lauriston Bay' was a small black lizard, about four inches long. The only quadrupeds were rats (kiore), and dogs (kurii), which were 'of medium size with long, fairly fine hair. These people feed them, as we do with sheep, and eat them in the same way.'[141]

Birds

There were numerous birds. Pottier thought that this was 'probably because the savages are not energetic enough to kill them'.[142] He mentioned quail; a bird with 'the size and colouring of a blackbird, except that under its beak it has two little red wattles like a hen's' (perhaps the huia); a similar bird with a little tuft of white feathers under the beak (the tui); a bird 'tinier than our wren'; and many other species, all of them very tame. There were also enormous numbers of wild duck, curlews, sea larks, snipe, a bird with 'black plumage, red feet and a red beak shaped like a woodcock's' (the oystercatcher), which they found excellent eating, and a similar bird with a pale yellow beak.

Fish

The fish in 'Lauriston Bay' were listed as flounder, mackerel, 'cavalles' or horse-mackerel, cod, bull-head, gurnard, red gurnard, angler fish, dogfish, bass, gobys, and 'a kind of ray called sea-devil'. On the seashore, added Pottier, they saw pieces of yellow resin, transparent, crumbly, light and inflammable — a description of kauri gum.

Precious gifts

Surville concluded of the people of 'Lauriston Bay' that 'they live miserably in an excellent country, through lack of knowledge'.[143] Pottier remarked that

> we gave [them] some very precious gifts, if they do but know it. One of them was wheat, and we made signs to indicate how it must be sown, then gathered, crushed to make flour, mixed into a dough, and cooked to make bread, which they found very good. We gave them peas, and some rice plants, but I doubt if this terrain is right for rice-growing. Finally we gave them two little pigs, male and female, and a hen and a rooster. These were the only ones we had left, and moreover they are the very tiny kind, white, with feathery legs, which we were raising on board out of curiosity. This was all we could manage in our state of privation. If they know how to take care of all these things, there is enough there to multiply the species, but their laziness is so great that there is reason to fear we have cast our seed on barren ground.[144]

CONCLUSION

The *St Jean Baptiste* had visited Tokerau, been given a formal welcome, and received guarded hospitality (as well as direct displays of hostility) from two different communities within the bay. They had been unable to communicate with the local people except through sign language, so their accounts of local life were superficial and remote, although accurate as to physical detail. Their interpretations of local activities were strongly influenced by the European idea of the ignoble savage, and this influenced not only their descriptions, but also their behaviour. Surville had interpreted the taking of the yawl as treachery and theft, and in retribution destroyed canoes and houses, and captured a man who had offered them food and shelter at a time when they were vulnerable to attack. Unlike the *Endeavour*'s crew, they did not shoot anyone, but some of their descriptions of the local people were extremely unpleasant — the result of their own physical wretchedness, perhaps, as well as their prejudices. The experience of the *St Jean Baptiste* expedition in Tokerau was shaped as much by their own interpretations and behaviour as by those of the local people, and in their accounts of local life they mirrored their own mythologies, which at times they mistook for truth.

356

'Mariao'
The Death of
the Noble Savage

Chapter Thirteen

MARION DU FRESNE IN THE
BAY OF ISLANDS
April–July 1772

The story of Marc-Joseph Marion du Fresne's voyage to New Zealand began with that persistent mirage, Terra Australis Incognita, and a project to return Ahutoru, a Tahitian taken to Paris by Bougainville, back to his home island. As Le Dez, the first lieutenant of the *Marquis de Castries*, explained in the preface to his 'Summary' of the voyage:

> The intention of the Court in proposing the voyage to Cythera and in laying down the course to be followed, was to return the Indian Boutavery [a Tahitian version of 'Bougainville'] to his island, Tahiti, to visit that archipelago, to befriend the various chiefs there and to learn about the products of the island, of which Mr Bougainville's report had given us a very favourable idea, and to make a few discoveries in the southern part of our globe, so little known and, up until then, neglected.
>
> Gonneville's Lands, Circumcision Cape, sighted by Mr Bouvet in 1739, the large number of icebergs he met in those parts (almost sure signs of a large land mass); more recently the land Mr de Kerguelen has just discovered and the islands we ourselves came upon, all these things indicate a third continent, the existence of which seems sufficiently demonstrated by the very form of the globe, which obliges us to attribute to the other hemisphere approximately the same configuration, the same quantity and quality of matter as to ours. There still remains therefore an immense expanse of sea to be explored and it can now be done more successfully than ever before, now that the art of navigation, based on a deeper knowledge of cosmography and guided by astronomy, is subject to far fewer errors; one might also add that ships have never been more apt to make these voyages, both for their solidity and for the ease with which they can be made to perform the various manoeuvres required, and one can truthfully say that we are in the century of modern discovery.[1]

'Gonneville Land' was a place discovered by a French expedition in 1504 when, believing themselves to be in the neighbourhood of the Cape of Good Hope, they were driven to a country where the local people treated them well. In the eighteenth century this was widely believed to be part of the Unknown Southern Continent. In 1739 Bouvet, attempting to follow Gonneville's supposed route (which in the absence of any estimates of latitude, longitude or bearings was largely guesswork), found a cape in latitude 54°, west of the Cape of Good Hope — actually the island now known as Bouvet Island. The fact that Bouvet's island was cited by Le Dez showed how large 'Gonneville Land' was supposed to be, for Marion du Fresne's expedition was looking for it in the southern Indian Ocean, while Bouvet's island was located in the southern reaches of the Atlantic.

Like Surville, Marion du Fresne was a longtime officer of the French India Company whose career had been disrupted when the company collapsed. He had served in privateers during the War of the Austrian Succession, carrying Prince Charles Edward from Scotland to France in his ship the *Prince de Conty* after the Battle of Culloden, and finally winning a posting as a 'blue officer' in the Royal Navy. When the war ended, Marion served in various ships of the Compagnie des Indes, returning to the Navy during the Seven Years' War. In 1761 he again returned to the Compagnie, taking Pingré the astronomer on board his ship the *Comte d'Argenson* to the Indian Ocean to observe the 1761 transit of Venus. In 1766 he settled at Île de France (Mauritius), where he had bought land and was appointed the harbour master at Port Louis. For a time this was a profitable appointment, because between 1768 and 1770 Île de France was strengthened as a naval base from which surprise attacks could be launched on the British settlements in India. Choiseul sent many troops and ships there, hoping by this and other diversionary strategies to weaken the British fleet in the Channel, leaving England vulnerable to an invasion in which France's defeat in the Seven Years' War could be revenged.

In 1770, however, a storm wiped out part of the French fleet in Port Louis, and shortly afterwards Choiseul was dismissed and most of the remaining troops on vessels were recalled to France. Marion du Fresne had a reputation as 'a skilled sailor, energetic, a great trader, rash with neither principles nor restraint, but brave',[2] and it is not surprising that such a man found the prospect of peacetime inaction unattractive. When Ahutoru arrived in Île de France in October 1770, therefore, Marion du Fresne drew up a plan that he presented to Pierre Poivre, the island's civil administrator, proposing a voyage to return Ahutoru to Tahiti and to search for 'Gonneville Land'. Marion du Fresne was prepared to pay for the crew and the incidental expenses of the voyage if the King would provide him with two ships. Poivre sent forward the proposal to the Minister for the Navy, and after some discussions with Abbé Rochon (who had arrived on the island with Kerguelen and who later edited Crozet's account of the expedition) and with Commerson (Bougainville's botanist, who had stayed in Île de France), Poivre approved this plan. Instructions from the court were passed on by Poivre, which, according to Marion in a letter to the minister, suggested that his expedition should

> endeavour to reconnoitre — if as indeed I presume they do exist — the Austral lands, by quartering the Seas to the Eastward between the 43rd and 50th parallels of latitude. Should I come upon no Land, I shall therefore lay my Course for New Zealand . . . If in those Diverse Lands which I intend to Explore I meet with any Good Fortune, I shall at once Dispatch, Monseigneur, one of my Vessels to bear

you News thereof; and I shall Neglect nothing which may bear upon the Manners of the Natives or the Products of their Territories. Of these I shall keep the most precise Record, as best I may.[3]

It is probable that most of what Marion du Fresne knew about Tahiti he had learned from Commerson, who among Bougainville's party had been the most rapturous about 'New Cythera'. In Commerson's manuscript account of the voyage he wrote about Tahiti as follows:

I can assure you that it is the one spot on the earth's surface which is inhabited by men without vices, prejudices, wants or dissensions. Born under the loveliest skies, they are supported by the fruits of a soil so fertile that cultivation is scarcely required, and they are governed rather by a sort of family father rather than by a monarch. They recognize no other God save Love. Every day is consecrated to him, and the whole island is his temple . . .

One must be careful not to entertain such a suspicion as that one is dealing only with a horde of gross and stupid savages. Everything in their homes manifests the greatest intelligence: as regards their canoes, they are constructed on entirely unknown lines; their navigation is directed by observation of the stars; their houses are large, elegant in shape, both comfortable and symmetrical; they have the art, not of weaving their cloth thread by thread, but of suddenly producing the fabric, entirely finished, simply by the blows of a mallet . . . Their fruit trees are so planted at judicious intervals that they have not the tiresome monotony of our orchards, although retaining all that is agreeable and pleasant in the latter; the dangers of the coastline are marked by beacons, and are lighted at night for the sake of those at sea; they know all their plants, distinguishing them by names, and these names even explain their affinities and relationships; although the various tools employed in their arts are made of raw materials, yet so far as regards the shape selected and certainty in operation they can be compared even with our own. For these things they surely deserve our respect, although our intercourse with them endured but for a short period.

. . . Did they not refuse, horrified, the knives and daggers which we offered them, seeming to divine instinctively the abuses that we had committed with such implements? On the contrary, how eagerly they came to examine and to take the dimensions of boats, sails, tents, barrels, and indeed of everything which they supposed could be imitated with advantage to themselves!

Then the simplicity of their moral code: the fairness of their treatment of women, who are in no way oppressed, as is the case with most savages; their brotherly love to each other; their horror at the shedding of man's blood; their deep veneration for the dead, who are supposed to be only sleeping; their hospitality to strangers. As regards all these virtues, one must allow the journals the privilege of description, but only in such terms as our gratitude and our admiration should require of them.[4]

This description was infused with an intoxicated euphoria that far surpassed Rousseau's accounts of 'savage life'. According to Crozet, both l'Abbé Rochon (a member of the Academy of Science and a skilled astronomer) and Commerson were originally intended to accompany the expedition to Tahiti,[5] and so Commerson and Marion du Fresne must often have discussed the voyage together. Bougainville's own account of his voyage to Tahiti was not published in France until 1771, and so it seems certain that Commerson was the key influence on Marion's ideas about Polynesian peoples.

It is not clear precisely how the costs of setting up the expedition were distributed. Bougainville had donated one-third of his personal fortune towards chartering a ship in Port Louis to return Ahutoru to his homeland, and the Duchess of Choiseul, Ahutoru's protector in France, had donated money to purchase implements, animals and seeds to be taken back to Tahiti. It seems that Marion mortgaged his property in Île de France and Magon, another wealthy resident there, agreed to stand surety for him to the sum of 150,000 livres (or about £6,000 in contemporary currency).[6] According to the muster rolls of the two ships, the *Mascarin*, a flute with twenty-two guns, was owned by the King, while the *Marquis de Castries*, described as a 'private ship' with sixteen guns, was owned by Marion du Fresne. The ships were armed at the King's expense, and crews of 140 officers and men for the *Mascarin* and 100 officers and men for the *Marquis de Castries* were recruited at Île de France. Marion described his crews as 'tolerably good',[7] but no detailed descriptions of their ages, origins, or even the names of most of the sailors were given in the muster rolls. There was a black cook (Anthonie) and a number of black slaves on board who were mentioned in the journals. No doubt the crew was ethnically at least as diverse as that of the *St Jean Baptiste*, whose men had mainly been recruited in France.

The officers of the *Mascarin* included Marion du Fresne, 'Fireship Captain'; his former comrade and now second-in-command Julien Crozet, (described by D'Après de Mannevillette as 'a very good sailor, a Scholar and a man worthy of trust on the most vital occasions'),[8] who wrote a detailed journal of the voyage; Jean Roux, an ambitious ensign whose retrospective account of the voyage was also evidently based on a fairly comprehensive journal; and Chevillard de Montaison, ensign and clerk, who wrote a brief retrospective summary of the voyage. Du Clesmeur, the commander of the *Marquis de Castries*, was only twenty-two years old and the privileged nephew of the Governor of Île de France. He kept a journal that was later rewritten as both a history of the voyage and a navigational record of the daily manoeuvres of his ship; while Le Dez, 'first lieutenant second-in-command' of the *Marquis de Castries*, has been identified by Ollivier as the author of an excellent retrospective account that found its way into Bougainville's private library.

The shipboard library on the *Mascarin* included de Brosses' *Histoire des Navigations aux Terres Australes*, for as Crozet said, 'I had it always near me';[9] Prévost's inaccurate summary of Tasman's voyage; and 'Van te Culin's charts' (probably Van Keulen)[10]; while on the *Marquis de Castries* they had de Brosses' book (quoted by Le Dez) and probably also Prévost's *Histoire Générale des Voyages*, since Le Dez mentions 'Bellin's chart', which was included in Prévost's work; 'Anson's book' (*A Voyage Round the World in the Years 1740–44*); and 'some Spanish charts'.

By October 1771 the two ships were ready to sail from Île de France. Marion du Fresne was anxious to leave before Kerguélen, who had arrived in August and also had instructions to search for the Southern Continent; and a smallpox epidemic that broke out on the island gave added urgency to their departure. A cargo of trade goods was loaded on board, and on 18 October the two ships sailed for the Île de Bourbon (Réunion), and then set off for the Cape of Good Hope to collect their main supplies. Almost as soon as they left Bourbon, Ahutoru came down with smallpox. Marion then changed course for Port Dauphin, at the south-east end of Madagascar, where he could be nursed on land. On 6 November, however, only two days after they arrived at Port Dauphin, Ahutoru died. According to Le Dez:

> The event affected us all the more as we feared it would put an end to the voyage, but Mr Marion was determined to go on with it, and the difficulties that he very well saw in store for him could not deter him. There is no doubt that without that man we would have had difficulty insinuating ourselves into the favour of the islanders and we would have needed a lot of time and skill to bring them to the point where we could get from them all the information we wanted.[11]

Marion du Fresne had invested most of his private capital in the voyage, and hoped to make a fortune in trading with the inhabitants of 'Gonneville Land'. The voyage therefore continued towards the Cape of Good Hope, although shortly after they left Fort Dauphin, Chevillard de Montaison and de Vaudricourt, who were on board the *Mascarin,* also came down with the disease. When the ships arrived at the Cape of Good Hope, Marion hid his sick officers in the hold of the *Mascarin,* and permission was given to begin loading twenty months' supplies for the voyage. The ship's biscuit had to be made and the meat salted so that the food was as fresh as possible, and while this was being done rumours spread on shore that there was smallpox on board the *Mascarin.* As soon as the Governor heard of this he ordered the *Mascarin* to anchor off Robin Island, downwind from the town, while the *Marquis de Castries* continued to take on supplies for both vessels. Finally, on 24 December the *Marquis de Castries* joined the *Mascarin* off Robin Island, where Marion told his officers of his strategy for the voyage:

> His plan was first to go in search of the Southern Continent and to this end to shape his course from the moment of departure between the south and the east, according to the direction and varying force of the wind, until he reached the 48th or 50th parallel, then to sail in this latitude between 60° and 70° longitude east of Paris and next to head east as directly as possible . . . until we reached 115° or 120° longitude. If we found we had sailed through this region without coming across any land then we were to shape our course between the north and the east so as to reach 43° and 44° latitude as soon as possible, to go in search of Diemensland, which is situated to the south of New Holland. Only in the case of dire need were we to put in there; from there we were to go without fail to Three Kings Island, which is marked on the charts at the northern tip of New Zealand in 33° or 34° latitude south and 163° or 164° east of the Paris meridian.[12]

In many respects this was a similar course to that first sailed by Tasman, although the starting-point was further west. Soon after they sailed from the Cape on 28 December 1771, they discovered the islands now known as Marion and Prince Edward, but in trying to establish whether these were islands or promontories of 'Gonneville Land' the two ships collided, damaging both and wrecking the *Marquis de Castries*'s foremast and bowsprit. After makeshift repairs they sailed further east, discovering the Crozet Islands and taking possession of them for the King of France. Hopes were high that they had at last discovered the Southern Continent, but visibility was so poor and the ships so battered that it was impossible to make certain of this.

On 3 March the two ships anchored in Diemensland (Tasmania) at Blackman's Bay, where a group of about forty Aboriginals, some armed with spears and stones, had gathered around a fire on the beach. Marion had three boats lowered and sent one to each end of the bay, while the boat carrying him and du Clesmeur rowed in to meet these people. As they saw the boats approaching, the Aboriginals gestured and called out. Wishing to befriend them, Marion sent ashore two sailors, stripped naked like the local people and carrying gifts.

The Tasmanians put down their spears and sang and danced as they approached the naked sailors, inspecting them with obvious astonishment. They handed a flaming brand to one of the sailors and were given a mirror and some necklaces in return. Shortly after this Marion, du Clesmeur and several others landed and presented them with more gifts, including bread, which they tasted and threw away; a bottle of water from which they drank a little and then emptied out the rest, keeping the bottle; a live duck; and a hen, which they soon tore to pieces.

When one of the other boats approached the beach, however, they became alarmed, and gestured to the Europeans to go away. The people in this boat took up their muskets with bayonets fixed, and when the Tasmanians saw this they hurled a shower of stones and a few spears at the Europeans on the beach. Both Marion and du Clesmeur were hit and a musket volley was fired overhead, forcing them to retreat and allowing Marion and his men to get back into the boats.

The boats attempted to make a second landing further along the bay, and the Aboriginals again made hostile gestures, driving the duck before them and throwing spears at it to demonstrate their accuracy, and then throwing spears at the boats. Finally, Marion's men fired a musket volley at them, killing one man and wounding several others. The two ships stayed for several days in the bay, hunting for fresh water and food without success. They visited a nearby island, and Le Dez described the people they met there as 'more like beasts than men'.[13] He speculated that the local people wandered about in bands, eating seafood, sleeping in rudimentary bark shelters and going naked.

On 10 March the two ships sailed out of the bay and headed east towards New Zealand. On the authority of Tasman's journal Marion expected to find a good anchorage there, where he could repair his ships and get fresh food and water. The crossing was uneventful, and at sunrise on 25 March, in calm seas and fair weather, the men on board the *Marquis de Castries* saw land 'in the shape of a sugar-loaf' looming indistinctly to the east. The next morning, as the two ships approached the west coast of New Zealand, they sighted a high mountain with patches of snow on its peak. They named it 'Pic Mascarin' (Mascarin Peak) after Marion's vessel, not knowing that Taranaki Mountain had already been named Egmont by James Cook. The French consulted their copies of Tasman's journal and charts, and decided that this must be the southern cape of Tasman's

Murderers Bay. At dawn on 27 March the ships came within five miles of the land, where they saw people and scattered bushes along a beautiful, low-lying sandy coastline. Du Clesmeur drily observed in his log that 'according to the longitude corrected at Diemensland I am seven or eight leagues inland' (which was better at least than the *St Jean Baptiste*'s 134 leagues past the coastline). That night violent nor'westerlies blew up, forcing the ships to stand off from the coast as fires flared up on shore.

The ships sailed north, coasting the land as closely as they dared, and on 31 March they sighted the inlet of a large cove whose entrance was marked by a line of breakers — the Kaipara Harbour. North of this inlet Roux described an indented coastline backed by high ranges of mountains, 'of handsome appearance and looks very pleasant'. The next day a steep cape (Maunganui Bluff) came into sight, and soon afterwards the headland of Hokianga Harbour, with some men visible in a cove to the south. Further north the ship passed more inlets and then a big sandy point and a beautiful bay with many fires on shore (Ahipara). According to Le Dez, the entire western coastline must have been inhabited, because they had seen fires every day.

On 3 April they sighted 'Cap St Marie' (with Motu-o-pao offshore), where du Clesmeur remarked, 'It gave me great pleasure to see almost within reach the stopover I had wanted for so long'. His pleasure was shortlived, however, for a violent storm forced the battered ships out to sea, and it was not until 12 April that they were able to explore Manawataawhi (Three Kings Islands), where Tasman's journal had led them to believe there was plenty of fresh water and supplies. The French had already learned to be sceptical of Tasman's descriptions of the New Zealand coastline, but now their impatience with its inaccuracies was almost palpable:

> We sighted Three Kings Islands. At first we could not believe it was them, because they were nothing but big rocks. Tasman . . . maintains that on [the largest] island there is a river which falls into the Sea. It will be clear from the following that this navigator gives very false ideas.[14]

The ships sailed round Oo-hau (Great Island), sighting sheer cliffs, smoke and vegetation on its summit, and some men 'who in the distance looked very tall'[15] (echoes of Tasman's 'giants'). They saw one patch of brush, some small trees and several houses, and made several vain attempts to land. They could not find the river that Tasman had described, however, only a ravine in the north-west where water might run in wet weather. Roux commented that since the island was so arid, people probably came there from the mainland to fish. From their accounts and from the charts it seems that they did not closely approach Tasman Bay, where the only permanent freshwater stream in the group could be found, and this misled them about the habitability of Oo-hau, which, as archaeological evidence shows, had often been occupied in the past.[16]

Setting Tasman's account aside, they now headed for the east coast of the mainland to look for water, food and a safe anchorage. The ships sailed southeast past Motu-o-pao and Te Rerenga Wairua (Cape Reinga), the legendary

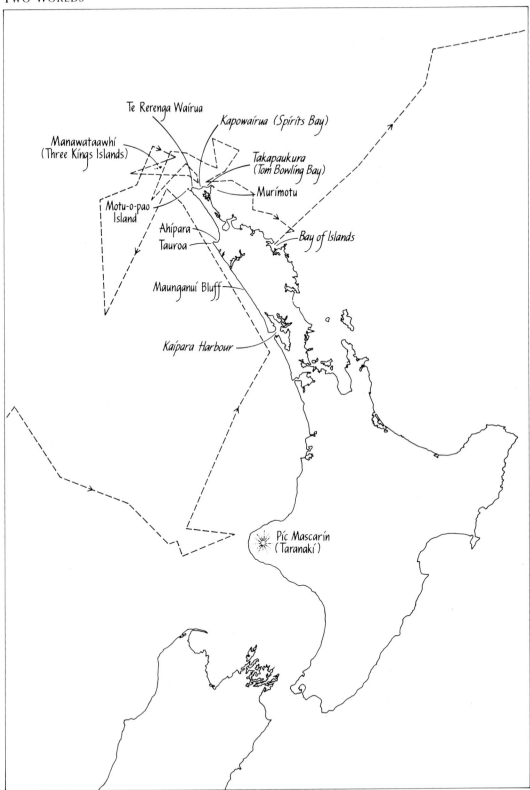

leaping-place of spirits into the underworld. Early on the morning of 15 April Marion sent his second lieutenant Lehoux in the *Mascarin*'s boat to explore 'two beautiful sandy coves' (Kapowairua, or Spirits Bay, and Takapaukura, or Tom Bowling Bay).

Lehoux returned later that day to report that the western bay (Kapowairua) offered a reasonable anchorage and a freshwater river (probably the Waitanoni), and that it was evidently well inhabited since he had seen well-beaten tracks and the ruins of a large village. He had entered some of the houses and described

> windows decorated with lattice work, several carved planks, a fairly large seine made of screw pine [flax] which had, instead of sinkers, little round pebbles in a casing of netting with very much smaller mesh than that of the seine, a marble slab for grinding paint — the one he found was red — a roundish stick and a lot of other trinkets which gave us a high regard for the industry of these people. He left on shore a beautiful canoe made in the manner of the catamarans of India.[17]

Lehoux's account suggests that in 1772 at Muriwhenua, the homeland of Ngaati Kurii, there was an active carving tradition that produced both carved houses and canoes. Fishing was also evidently a major industry, and his description of seine nets with a finely woven band along their base for sinker stones is significant. The 'roundish stick' was probably a fernroot pounder, which Lehoux collected along with other small items to take back to the ship. His boat also visited Takapaukura but found no water there, only a beautifully carved canoe, so early the next morning the *Mascarin* and *Marquis de Castries* sailed into Kapowairua (Spirits Bay). The *Mascarin*'s boat was sent ashore, but later reported that the water in the river was brackish near its mouth. As the winds blew up that afternoon they had great difficulty in returning to the ship with their collection of 'curiosities' or locally made goods. By nightfall the winds were gusting strongly and when the currents also turned against the ships they began to drag their anchors. A huge wave hit the *Marquis de Castries*, snapping two of its anchor cables, and they were forced to cut loose a third cable (which they buoyed first), while the *Mascarin* let loose two. At dawn the next morning the men on board the *Mascarin* found themselves embayed and being driven headlong by high waves and violent squalls towards a rocky coast. Just as they had given up all hope of escaping shipwreck, the wind suddenly shifted and the ship cleared the land by less than a musketshot.

On 23 April the weather finally cleared. Marion called a council meeting of his officers, and after an exchange of letters between the two captains they decided to return to Kapowairua to recover the lost anchors. The *Marquis de Castries* had scurvy cases on board and water was being rationed, so their need for a safe anchorage was becoming desperate. As the ships sailed back past Takapaukura in calm weather, a 'very pretty little village surrounded by ditches and palisades' on a hill came into sight, and Marion sent Roux in one of the boats to look at it more closely.

Opposite: *The track of the* Mascarin *and* Marquis de Castries *off the New Zealand coastline.*

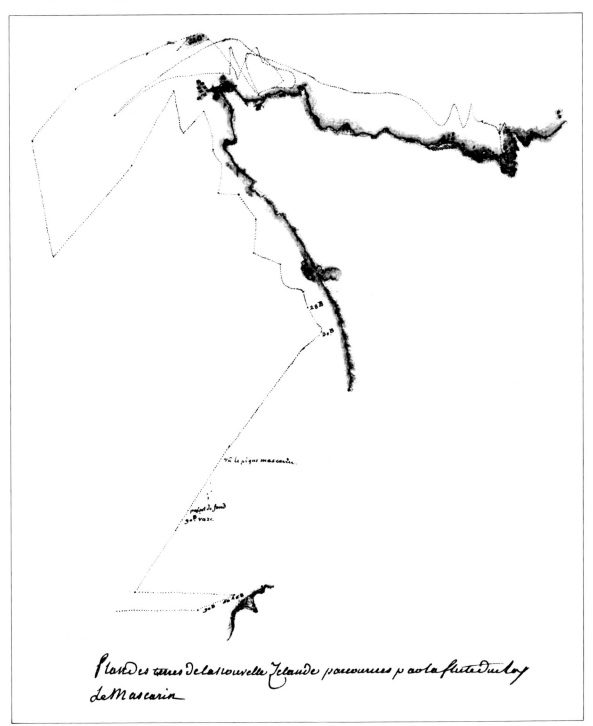

'Plan of the lands of New Zealand . . .' describes the track of the Mascarin *off Cape Reinga and Spirits Bay. This track differs in several respects from that illustrated on page 366, which is based on a reconstruction carried out for the Centennial Historical Atlas project, in which noon sights appear to have been used.*

A small canoe with three or four men on board fled into a cove as the boat approached, and its crew took refuge in their paa. When Roux beckoned to the people from his boat and made gestures of friendship to them, an old man came forward, turning his spear upside down and throwing a large fish into the boat. Roux presented him with several handkerchiefs and a knife, which he tried out at once on his paddle, and in return the old man invited Roux to visit his home. Roux declined, leaving the old man despondent that no one would come ashore. According to Roux, the local people treated this man with great respect, and 'he inspected me closely and seemed very surprised by all that he saw. He asked me an endless number of questions of which I understood nothing. He called over a canoe which was coming back from fishing and he gestured to me to choose the fish that I liked most.'[18] As in so many earlier meetings, an older male leader had taken the initiative, showing both courage and self-possession. The French described the inhabitants of this place as olive-skinned, tall, strongly built and dressed in large skin cloaks (presumably of dogskin).

After this brief encounter the boat returned to the ships, and they carried on to 'Ance aux Ancres' (Anchor Cove, or Kapowairua), where they soon recovered the *Mascarin*'s anchors, which were still safely buoyed. The *Marquis de Castries*'s anchor cables had sunk, however, and could not be recovered. While the work of trying to locate the lost anchors was going on, Roux, Le Dez, du Clesmeur and others visited the shore. Roux inspected the river (probably the Waitanoni) and found its water to be brackish near its mouth, but as he walked inland along its course he noticed irrigation canals 'every ten paces', watering a fertile, grassy plain that had evidently once been cultivated. Plants, including gourds, a kind of daisy, reeds and flax, grew on the plain, the flax being used for 'very fine nets', ropes, and for lashing house-timbers together. He and his companions shot several quail ('partridges' according to Le Dez), and then explored the abandoned village on the left bank of the river that had previously been visited by Lehoux. Several houses in this village had been burnt, others wrecked, and the settlement seemed to have been recently abandoned, since some storehouses containing nets, some quite new, were still standing. The nets that Lehoux had seen proved to be 480 to 600 feet long and five to six feet wide, with round floats of a very light wood along their top edge and sinker stones in a woven pouch along the bottom, and they were covered with flax leaves to keep them dry. Roux inspected the houses very closely, and later wrote a superbly detailed account of their architecture:

> Among other things their houses prompted our admiration, so skilfully were they made. They were rectangular in shape and varied in size according to need. The sides were stakes set a short distance from one another and strengthened by switches which were interlaced across them. They were coated on the outside with a layer of moss thick enough to prevent water and wind from getting in and this layer was held up by a well-constructed little lattice. The interior was woven with a matting of sword-grass [flax] on which there were at intervals, by way of ornament as well as to support the roof, little poles or more accurately, planks, two to three inches thick and rather well carved. In the middle of the house there was also

a big carved pole which supported the weight of the roof (together with two others at the two ends). What surprised us still further was that the whole construction was mortised and very strongly bound together with their sword-grass ropes. On the central pole was a hideous figure, a sort of sea-devil. As we have found this figure in all their houses and in this very same place, which seems consecrated to it, there is every reason to presume that it is their divinity that is represented under this form.

Each house has a sliding door, so low that we virtually had to lie down to enter. Above it there were two small windows and a very fine lattice. Running right round the outside was a little ditch for water to flow in. These houses are roofed with reeds; in some of them there was a rather poorly-made cot and inside it some very dry straw that they sleep on.

In front of each door three stones were to be seen, forming a sort of hearth where they would make a fire: there was another stone a little way off, which they used to grind their red pigment. I had the post taken from one of these houses; it was very well carved and made of the wood of the Sassafras, giving off a very pleasant smell. It seemed to me extraordinary that anyone could do such work without tools such as ours: however, nowhere did we find traces of any metals. We saw trees cut with three faces as we would do. Everything went to prove that the world over necessity makes men invent the means of making life easier . . .

I do not know if there are any quadrupeds in this country, but we found in this village the form of a trough, made like ours, from which I suspected that they apparently had some sort of livestock. We also found a piece of skin rather like a bearskin.[19]

This is the best early contact account of Maori domestic architecture. Evidently the basic framework of the house was made of shaped mortised and tenoned timbers, lashed together. The walls were constructed of a strong wicker-work lattice interlaced around vertical posts, with a thick layer of moss held up by another lattice on the outside to keep the water out. Flax matting (or according to Le Dez reed lining) on the inside provided added insulation. The flax matting on the walls had Polynesian precedents, while the 'reed lining' may have been panels of raupo stalks. The roof was held up by carved wall posts (poupou) two to three inches thick, and three central carved posts, the middle one carved with 'a sort of sea-devil'. According to Le Dez, this carving had a man's head on a lizard's body painted dark red, perhaps a representation of a taniwha, or of the sea-god Tangaroa in this coastal settlement. The description suggests that a number of these houses (not just the chief's house) had carvings inside, although no exterior carvings were mentioned. Roux, like Banks before him, collected a carving (in this case a central pillar) and took it back to his ship.

Inside the houses there were roughly made sleeping-places with a bedding of 'very dry straw', and in front of the low, sliding door a stone hearth and a rock for grinding red ochre. Two small windows were constructed above the door, screened by a fine lattice, and the roof was covered with 'reeds' (toetoe or raupo). The floor of the house was kept dry by an exterior drain. According to Le Dez, these houses were low-built, and about ten or twelve feet square. Roux also noticed a trough in the settlement (probably for dying fibre or steeping food in juices) and some animal's skin (dogskin, which he thought was like bearskin), both of which suggested to him that there might be large animals on shore. He was very impressed with the way that wood had been worked without any metal tools, and commented, 'we imagined, from what we had just seen, that if we did find a port, it would be easy for us to get assistance from these people'.

Very likely this settlement was only temporarily empty. Its occupants may have fled at the sight of the European vessels, and in the shadow of Te Rerenga Wairua these may have seemed like spiritual apparitions of a most peculiar kind. The people of Ngaati Kurii had no doubt heard about the visits of Surville and Cook to the south, and seen the *Endeavour* as she rounded North Cape, but the rumours of musketfire, killings and kidnappings were unlikely to have inspired much confidence in these new arrivals. The charred houses in the village may have previously been burned in a skirmish, or perhaps because of a violation of tapu inside them, but the fact that nets, carvings and other goods were left behind suggests that their owners were not very far away. The European visitation, with its pilfering and prying, must have seemed like a supernatural muru (plundering raid) to appease these multi-coloured ghosts.

On the morning of 28 April 1772 the French ships, having retrieved only two of their five lost anchors, set sail for the east. As the ships rounded Murimotu (the islet off North Cape, which they called 'Cape Eolus') they sighted several islets, tree-covered hills, and to the south a number of deep coves. On 1 May they weathered Raakaumangamanga (Cape Brett, which they named 'Cap Quarré' — Square Cape) at the south end of the Bay of Islands, where they saw more islands and fires blazing up inland. On 3 May the vessels sent out armed boats to look for a suitable anchorage, and two or three canoes came out from Raakaumanga-manga. One canoe with eight or nine men on board approached the *Mascarin*, but stopped at some distance and refused to come any closer. Marion ordered small gifts to be lowered on a lead-line, hoisted the ship's flag and beckoned these people to come alongside. They took the gifts and gave fish and shellfish in exchange, but still stayed at a safe distance.

Finally, after circling the ship for about an hour, the canoe came alongside the *Mascarin* and one old man, who 'had a venerable air about him', came on board. As soon as he was on the ship's ladder his canoe pushed off again. Marion greeted this man warmly and took him to the captain's cabin where he gave him food and wine. The old man was trembling all over and speechless, very likely fearing that like Ranginui from Doubtless Bay he would be seized and carried off. Marion ate bread and then gave him some to eat, and offered him wine which he drank with evident disgust, washing it down with a lot of water. After this Marion, to this old man's astonishment, took off his cloak and dressed him in European garments. For a time he seemed nonplussed, as well he might, since chiefs were intensely tapu and unaccustomed to such casual handling. He soon recovered his self-possession, however, as the French officers showed him axes, chisels and adzes, which he evidently knew how to use, and presented him with several of these as gifts. The old man then asked them a number of questions and went back on deck to signal his companions to come on board. Enticed by the sight of the things that he had been given, they came up the ladder, and each of the officers 'adopted' one of these men and dressed them in breeches and a shirt. According to de Montaison:

> in spite of the satisfaction it gave them and the ease with which they lent themselves to their metamorphosis, their general embarrassment and their awkwardness amused us greatly. After spending about two hours with us, they reembarked quite gaily, taking with them in their canoe a pig and a hen which we had given them.[20]

As soon as these men had reached their canoes they took off the European clothes and dressed again in their cloaks, hiding the gifts they had been given. Other canoes had gathered off the coast, and when they heard how these men had been treated they paddled rapidly toward the *Mascarin* and the *Marquis de Castries*. Their crews 'came alongside at once and came on board as boldly and with as satisfied and confident an air as if they knew us already'.[21] More than 100 men boarded the *Marquis de Castries* and 250 visited the *Mascarin*, where armed soldiers had been posted unobtrusively on the poop. The visitors were unarmed and brought gifts of fish and 'very good potatoes' (kuumara), and in exchange they were given small gifts, and ships' biscuits, which they ate heartily.

On board the *Mascarin* they spotted some red paint, and when they were given some of this they were ecstatic. Some of these men had their hair painted red with kokowai (red ochre), which was a much darker red than the European scarlet. These people were tall and well built, with tattoos on their faces, thighs and other parts of their bodies. The Europeans examined their tattoos, and they in turn pulled back the Europeans' clothes to see if their skin was also white beneath their garments. They exclaimed with amazement to find these creatures white all over, and pressed their lips against the Europeans' hands and faces. After a while they began to dance, making 'terrible grimaces and leapt about showing something of the savage',[22] in very regular time.

On board the *Marquis de Castries* du Clesmeur tried out Bougainville's Tahitian vocabulary on some of these people, and to his surprise managed to make himself understood. Some of his visitors (presumably using body measurements of some kind) took the dimensions of his vessel. They ate bread with pleasure, but like their compatriots on the *Mascarin* they disliked wine and brandy. They explored the ship with confidence, taking the nearest sailor as a guide, and indicated to the French sailors that their women were pretty, 'hoping to attract us by this ploy which is indeed an effective way to unite nations the most disparate in their ways, their manners and their customs'.[23] In an effort to entertain them, one of the French officers played the violin for them, then the drums, which they disliked, and afterwards the flute, which made no great impression on them. After this these people sat on the ship's deck and sang 'chants, with little variation, which rose with effort from their chests', accompanied with actions. They took gifts but immediately returned them until the Europeans showed them by signs that they should keep them; and gestured at the muskets, calling them 'tapou' (tapu or te puu — gun), which the French rightly took to indicate that they had met Europeans before.

Among the canoes that approached the *Mascarin* there was one with carved open work on its prow and stern-post, decorated with feathers. An old man dressed in a dogskin cloak 'had a prouder and more distinguished look about him than the others', and he had stayed on board this canoe with four young women while his companions went aboard. Roux, who decided from the deference paid to this man that he was an important chief, tried to persuade him to come on board. The old man hesitated, indicating that he would like to exchange his dogskin garment, which 'looked quite like our fur greatcoats', for Roux's scarlet jacket. Roux made signs that if he came on board the exchange would be made, so the old man climbed the ship's ladder to the *Mascarin*'s deck, followed by the women. After the exchange had taken place, to his great pleasure, he set about exploring the ship, where 'everything he saw seemed very strange to him; he could not understand what the cannon were for'.[24] Some time later, seeing that the French were ignoring the women he had brought on board he sent them back to his canoe.

According to Roux:

these islanders are generally tall, well-built, and with pleasant faces and regular features, seeming to be very agile and strong and vigorous looking. We measured some of them, who seemed to be the tallest among them, and they were over 6 feet and well-proportioned. Their usual height, as far as I could see, is five foot five to five foot six inches. They are all well built, with beautiful eyes, aquiline noses, well-shaped but large mouths, pronounced chins, in a word they have very handsome faces.[25]

At dinner-time Marion du Fresne invited this chief and one other to join their meal. They ate bread and meat with evident pleasure, but rejected salt meat (as the people at Whitianga had done during the *Endeavour*'s visit) and wine. After they had tasted some white wine, mistaking it for water, they pushed it away and drank large quantities of water instead. That evening the two chiefs stayed on board with two companions, despite the protests of their people, and offered to guide the French to the back of their bay. According to Crozet, one of these chiefs (probably the more senior) was called 'Tacouri',[26] whom several tribal accounts of Marion's visit to the bay identify as Te Kauri, a chief of Te Hiku-tuu sub-tribe of Ngaapuhi.[27] Every time the ship tacked out to sea Te Kauri became exceedingly uneasy and asked the French to go back to the shore, no doubt fearing that like Ranginui of Doubtless Bay he might be carried off. Roux listened carefully to his speech and noted that the language he spoke was very like Tahitian, 'which renewed our regret over the loss of the poor native of that island who died of smallpox on board our vessel'.[28]

At 1 a.m. the next morning the *Mascarin*'s boat, which had rowed south-west of Cape Brett to a 'very deep bay' (probably Whangamumu Harbour), returned and reported that they had found a village with 1,000 houses (500 to 600 houses according Le Dez) where many canoes surrounded them, forcing them to fire several musketshots to frighten them off. The people had lain down in their canoes when the muskets were fired, and then sat up and paddled away. One of these canoes was beautifully carved and held eighty to 100 people. There were many rivers and good timber for masts in this bay, but unfortunately it was not sheltered from the wind.

At the same time the *Marquis de Castries*'s boat, commanded by Second Lieutenant Rasseline, had gone north-west of Raakaumangamanga into a large bay dotted with islands (the Bay of Islands) where all the land was cultivated and densely populated. This bay was sheltered from the easterly and northerly winds, and promised to be a good haven.

Early on the morning of 4 May, therefore, the two ships sent their boats into the Bay of Islands, guided by a local pilot, to make 'the necessary arrangements for anchoring as soon as possible at a land where we imagined we would find everything we needed for the repair of our vessels and the replenishing of water supplies'.[29] The pilot showed them various inlets and places where water might be found, and on shore one man asked an officer to shoot a bird with his musket, thus indicating some familiarity with such weapons. In the evening, guided by its boat, the *Marquis de Castries* anchored north of Motuarohia Island; and in the morning shifted to join the *Mascarin* at their anchorage between Okahu and Motukiekie Islands. Two fortified villages (presumably those marked on their charts at the western end of Motukiekie and the eastern end of Waewaetoorea Island) with their palisades and ditches were clearly visible at this location from the ship's deck.

Early on the morning of 5 May the vessels were surrounded by more than 100 canoes, which brought out fish, shellfish and potatoes, their crews eagerly trading these for glass beads and nails. Bougainville's Tahitian vocabulary again proved invaluable, for Crozet tried it this time and 'saw with the greatest surprise that the savages understood me perfectly'.[30]

In his retrospective account of the voyage Crozet vividly described the welcome they were given by the Bay of Islands people:

> Many canoes came along filled with savages, who brought us their children and their daughters, all coming unarmed and with the greatest confidence. On arriving at the vessel, they commenced singing out *Taro*, the name they gave to ships' biscuit. We gave small pieces to everyone and that with the greatest economy, for they were such great eaters and so numerous that if we had given them according to their appetite, they would soon have consumed our provisions; they brought large quantities of fish, for which we gave them glass trinkets and pieces of iron in exchange. In these early days they were content with old nails two or three inches long, but later on they became more particular and in exchange for their fish demanded nails four or five inches in length. Their object in asking for these nails were to make small wood chisels of them. As soon as they had obtained a piece of iron, they took it to one of the sailors and by signs engaged him to sharpen it at the millstone; they always took care to reserve some fish wherewith to pay the sailor for his trouble. The ship was full of these savages, who appeared very gentle and even affectionate. Little by little they came to know the officers and called

Opposite: *These images of New Zealanders in L'Abbé Rochon's edition of Crozet's journal are somewhat fancifully adapted. Te Kauri (a sketch based on the Surville voyage depiction of Ranginui) is represented at top left. The identity of the artist whose sketches formed the originals of these engravings is unknown.*

TACOURI.

FEMME DE LA NOUVELLE ZÉLANDE.

FILLE DE LA NOUVELLE ZÉLANDE.

HABILLEMENS DES INSULAIRES.
de la Nouvelle Zélande

them by their names. We only allowed the chiefs, the women and the girls to enter the chart room. The chiefs were distinguished by the feathers of egrets or of other aquatic birds stuck in their hair on the top of their head. The married women were distinguished by a sort of straw plait which confined their hair on the top of the head; the girls had no such distinctive mark, their hair hanging naturally over their neck without anything to bind it.

It was the savages themselves who pointed out these distinctions and who gave us to understand by signs that we must not touch the married women, but that we might with perfect freedom make advances to the girls. It was in fact not possible to find any more approachable.

As soon as we discovered these distinctions we passed the word round the two ships so that everyone might be circumspect with regard to the married women, and thereby preserve the good understanding with savages who appeared so amiable, and not to cause them to be ill-affected towards us. The facility with which the girls were approached was the cause that we never had the slightest trouble with the savages on account of their women during the whole time we lived amongst these people.[31]

There are a number of noteworthy things about Crozet's account. The welcome that the French ships were given may have had something to do with local memories of the *Endeavour*'s muskets and cannon fire, which made trade more tempting than attack; but since the time of the *Endeavour* visit the people in the Bay of Islands had also apparently discovered the value of iron, which in 1769 they had treated with complete disinterest. The small chisels that the French sailors made for them were probably used mostly for carving wood, although they would also have been excellent for making holes and grooves for lashings, and other finely detailed wood and bone work. They had also begun to use local terms for ships' biscuit (taro) and muskets (te puu), and to learn the sailors' names.

The French evidently later had affairs with many of the young women, whom they described as 'very amorous' (perhaps out of desire for nails as well as Frenchmen), but the local people warned them against approaching any married women. Crozet and Roux were very unflattering about the local women, describing them as 'very ugly, small and poorly built',[32] and as 'short, very thick in the waist, with voluminous mammae, coarse thighs and legs', an aesthetic judgement that echoed some of the *St Jean de Baptiste* accounts, but not those from the *Endeavour*. It has been suggested in Chapter 12 that this may have been because the English, having already spent three months in Tahiti before arriving in New Zealand, had begun to come to terms with Polynesian forms of beauty.

Crozet went on to comment that it appeared to him that there were 'three kinds of men' amongst the people who came out to the *Mascarin*. The first group, whom he termed 'the true aborigines', were yellowish-white and tall with straight black hair; the second group were shorter, darker people with curly hair; and the third group, whom he called 'true Negroes', had woolly hair, broad chests, and beards.[33] In fact the truly significant distinctions amongst the people they were meeting were genealogical, not physiological, and this is something that the French were never to understand. The political situation in the Bay of Islands was at least as volatile as it had been during the *Endeavour* visit, and no doubt it had become even more complex as a result of the English interventions in local life — shooting people, robbing gardens, 'indecencies' against women, fishing in certain bays and their patterns of trade with particular groups. Some of the individuals who had been wounded by the English were from important chiefly families (for instance, the young chief Te Kuukuu), and this had no doubt intensified the inter-tribal feuding in the region and may have accelerated the process of Ngaapuhi infiltration in the bay.

Three early tribal accounts of Marion's visit to the Bay of Islands survive among manuscripts written and translated by John White in the 1850s and 1860s, two from anonymous Ngaapuhi sources and one from Haakiro, son of the famous Ngaapuhi chief Taareha. One of the anonymous accounts of Marion's visit is particularly detailed and convincing, and it claimed that at that time Ngaati Pou still controlled Te Waimate and the south-east islands: 'Ngaati Pou were the people who lived outside the Bay of Islands, that is to say on Motu-arohia, Te Wai-iti and other islands there. The people of this sub-tribe . . . belonged to Te Waimate, but in the fishing season they lived on these islands in order to obtain seafood.'[34]

The account collected by John White in 1857 from the son of Taareha, however, claimed that Ngaati Wai controlled Te Raawhiti at the time,[35] while much later accounts given to Leslie Kelly described Ngare Raumati (a subgroup of Ngaati Wai) as occupying the entire south-eastern district.[36] This confusion can most likely be attributed to the fact that Ngaati Pou, Ngaati Wai and Ngare Raumati were all essentially remnant hapuu of Ngaati Awa, which were probably not very clearly distinguished at this time.[37] Furthermore, not long after 1772 Ngaapuhi appear to have evicted both Ngaati Pou and Ngare Raumati from the bay. All surviving Maori accounts of Marion's visit were thus from Ngaapuhi sources, the victors being relatively unconcerned about the precise tribal affiliations of those whom they had displaced. To the French, in rather similar fashion, these were all 'savages', a generalisation that was eventually to prove fatal to many of their number.

On the afternoon of 5 May, Marion, Crozet and du Clesmeur visited 'the big island at the foot of a mountain' (Waewaetoorea from a dotted line on one of Marion's charts and a caption on du Clesmeur's chart), guarded by a detachment of soldiers. The local people greeted them warmly. As they walked along the coastline they could see twenty villages, the smallest accommodating 200 people and most having at least 400 inhabitants. That evening they named the bay (which Cook had already named the Bay of Islands) 'Port Marion' after the leader of their expedition. The next morning Marion, accompanied by a party of sailors and an armed guard, went back to Waewaetoorea to cut wood for repairs to the *Mascarin*, and here they found two enemy groups camped ready for battle. The sergeant in charge of the armed guard went a short distance away to shoot birds, and was approched by a party of twenty or thirty armed warriors who laid down their weapons and entreated him to assist them in the impending fight. A chief who had previously visited the *Mascarin* took him by the hand and led him to the head of his party.

The chief now ordered his men to advance, which they did in a very orderly fashion, armed to the teeth with long spears, darts, 'truncheons' (probably taiaha), war clubs (patu), which they said were used for splitting skulls, and a 'sort of assegai with very sharp teeth, such that when a man is wounded by this weapon it is impossible to draw it out because of its teeth or hooks, which are set in the opposite direction' — evidently a particularly lethal form of spear. Their enemies, astonished by the sight of a white man and terrified by the two musketshots he now fired, turned and fled.

The victors shouted for joy and sang as they escorted the sergeant back to the longboat, calling him 'Tetimon', a name they always called him thereafter. It is certain that the defeated party would have stored up the memory of this humiliating retreat, blaming the French and marking them for later retribution. Gratified by the joy of the victors and entirely innocent of any notion of utu (the principle of equal return, or revenge), Roux remarked on this occasion that these were 'a fine people, courageous, industrious and highly intelligent, because they understand very well what we want to make them to understand'.[38]

During the next two days the winds began to gust from the north-east, and the officers sent the boats out to look for a more secure anchorage. Marion and du Clesmeur explored the islands, searching for a convenient place to get fresh water and to establish a store for the ships' supplies and a shore hospital for their sick. Moturua Island seemed the most suitable location, so on 11 May the two vessels sailed into the lee of Moturua, where they finally anchored, the *Mascarin* off Tokotokohau Point and the *Marquis de Castries* a little to the west off Motu-kauri, just a mile away from the *Endeavour*'s anchorage in 1769. Most of the work of charting the bay must already have been completed during the previous five or six days, for on 11 May du Clesmeur was able to comment:

> One can rely confidently on the plan I have given on this port. I have already given warning that it was drawn from estimated bearings and distances, and even supposing that a few errors have slipped into it, they certainly would not be very considerable [although contemporary cartographers consider his charts to the bay much less accurate than Cook's].[39]

As the vessels arrived at their new anchorage many canoes came out to visit them. Their crews exchanged fish, weapons and axes for nails, old knives, iron or bread, presented women to the French (perhaps in gratitude for the victory of 6 May) and seeming to be angry if they were rejected. These people were endlessly curious, asking the French sailors innumerable questions that they did not in the least understand, and were clearly very puzzled by many of the things that they saw. A number of chiefs slept on board that night, to their evident delight.

On 12 May, Marion ordered tents to be pitched by the west bank of a small creek at Wai-iti Beach (on the south-west side of Moturua) as a hospital for the sick. On 13 May a forge was erected on the east bank of this creek, and a guard-house and store-tents by the river in adjacent Waipao Bay, which Cook had also used as a watering-place. Most of the sick were suffering from scurvy, but they soon began to recover with a diet of fresh fish supplied by the people of the local paa and 'wild myrtle' (maanuka or kaanuka), and plenty of exercise and fresh air. A group of huts in the bay were immediately abandoned by their occupants (who later also dug up their gardens and took away building timbers), an action that puzzled the French, who thought that since they had no intention of harming the local people there was no good reason for them to leave. Presumably the inhabitants of the bay, taking a different view of events, had decided that their territory had been occupied — another possible cause for subsequent hostility towards the French. As Roux later reflected:

> I am convinced that they believed very firmly that we would stay there forever because every day we unloaded many items from the vessels. We even took advantage of the grass huts they had abandoned, storing our rigging in them.[40]

On a headland to the south-east side of the island there was a large fortified village with a population of about 300, known as Paeroa paa, which was later mapped and described in detail by the French. Cook and Banks had described extensive gardens on Moturua, but these were not mentioned in the journals of this voyage. South of the vessels, on the Orokawa mainland and sited along a ridge of hills west of Te Hue Bay, was Te Kauri's village. This was fortified only on one side (probably above the Tauri-kura isthmus, across which canoes were hauled), and was the largest settlement that the French knew of at that stage. Roux had already described 'Tacoury' as proud and distinguished in appearance, and now added that he was a subtle, handsome and enterprising man about forty years old, who was regarded as one of the great chiefs of the area. With his ally 'Piquiore' (perhaps Pikiorei), whose fortified village at Tangituu on the Orokawa isthmus had been visited by Cook, he made war on many of the other local chiefs, who frequently asked the French to join them in attacking him. No doubt Te Kauri heard of this, and he may have soon decided that the French represented an intolerable political threat. Certainly he visited the French ships and

Overleaf: *Du Clesmeur's 'Plan of Port Marion' has an extensive key:*

A   *Native villages fortified with palisades*
B   *Villages with few huts*
C   *Fortified villages burnt by the French*
D   *Large village belonging to the chief Tacoury, also burnt*
E   *French masting camp*
F   *Foremast and bowsprit, abandoned*
G   *Wood where the masts were made, one of 65ft, the other 45ft*
H   *East channel*
I   *West channel*
K   *Cove where the killings occurred*
L   *Entrance route*
M   *First mooring*
N   *Second mooring*
O   *Mooring of the Mascarin*
P   *Mooring of the Castries*
Q   *Bank which uncovers and where the sea always breaks*
R   *Outward route*

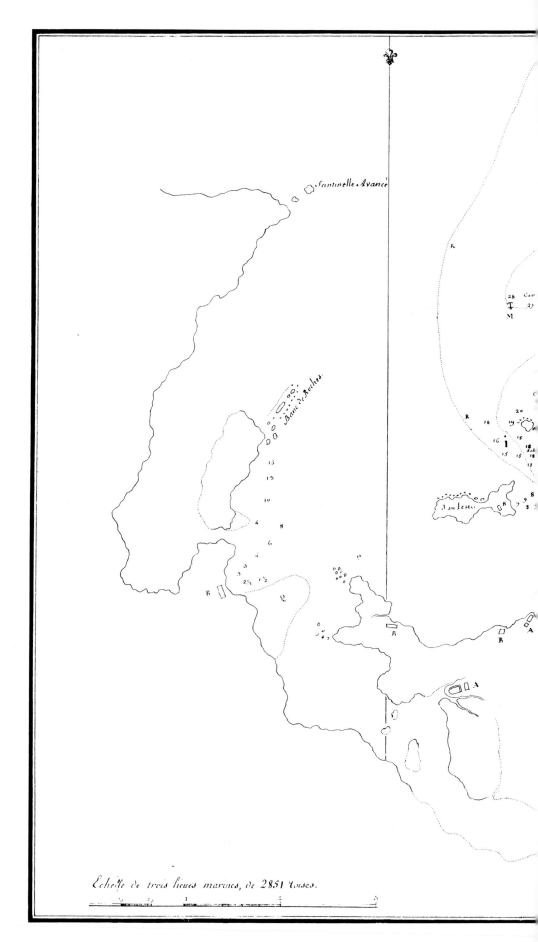

Santinelle Avancé

Banc de Roches

Echelle de trois lieues marines, de 2851 toises.

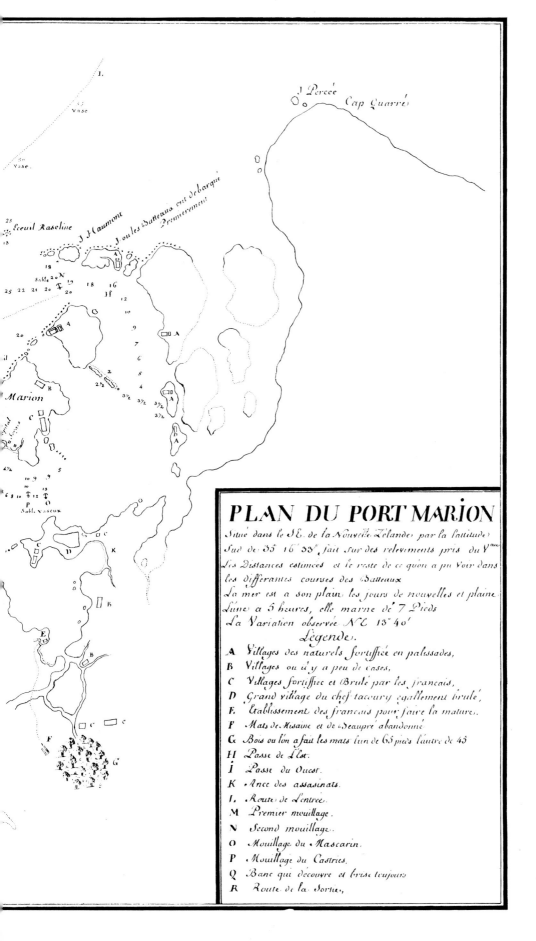

J Percée
Cap Quarré

L.

Vase

Vase.

25 Ecueil Raseline
13
J Haumont
Jou les Batteaux ont debarqué
Premierement

18
A
Sable 20 N
25 22 21 20 T 19 18 16
H 12
10
4
9
20 8
7
6
2 5
2½ 4
3½ 3½ 3½
3½
A
Marion
B
4½ C
5
10 9 4
10 5
6 8 10 T 12 T
P Sabl. vaseux

A

A

C
D K

K

E

B

C C

F
G

PLAN DU PORT MARION

Situé dans le S.E. de la Nouvelle Zelande par la latitude
Sud de 35° 16' 33" fait sur des relevements pris du V
Les Distances estimées et le reste de ce qu'on a pu voir dans
les differentes courses des Batteaux
La mer est a son plain les jours de nouvelles et plaine
Lune a 5 heures, elle marne de 7 Pieds
La Variation observée N.E. 13° 40'

Légende.

A Villages des naturels fortiffiée en palissades,
B Villages ou il y a peu de cases,
C Villages fortiffiée et Brulé par les francais,
D Grand village du chef tacoury egallement brulé,
E Etablissement des francais pour faire la mature,
F Mats de Misaine et de Beaupré abandonné
G Bois ou l'on a fait les mats l'un de 65 pieds l'autre de 45
H Passe de l'Est.
I Passe du Ouest.
K Ance des assasinats.
L Route de l'entrée.
M Premier mouillage.
N Second mouillage.
O Mouillage du Mascarin.
P Mouillage du Castries.
Q Banc qui decouvre et brise toujours
R Route de la Sortie.

the camp on Moturua very often, taking careful note of everything he saw.

Over the next few days the French began to repair their ships, and on 18 May, Marion initiated expeditions to look for wood suitable for remasting the *Marquis de Castries*. Roux went with him in the *Mascarin*'s boat past Taapeka point, which they named 'Cap de Courants' — Currents Cape. After rounding the point in precipitous seas they explored the coastline around Kororareka and Waitangi, where they saw many enticing coves but no suitable trees. Somewhere in this region they landed in a bay where there were two small villages — probably Onewhero Bay, where two undefended settlements are marked on du Clesmeur's sketch 'Plan du Port Marion'. The people of this place brought them fish and they collected oysters from the rocks, and ate a hearty meal. A chief who visited them there arrived in a superb carved canoe sixty-seven feet long and six feet four inches wide, which carried ninety to 100 men and 'travelled extraordinarily well'. His people were very friendly to the French. This may have been one of those leaders mentioned by Roux who sought the French as allies.

On 20 May, Marion du Fresne and others visited the east side of the bay, where there were some fine trees in a ravine but none nearly big enough for a mast. They made their guides understand that they needed to find taller trees than this. One man promised to take them later to a place where there were trees large enough for canoes, some of which three men could not encircle with their arms.

Two days later, Marion and his companions were escorted inland from Manawaora, where they found some magnificent trees, including 'a sort of fir . . . producing resin with a strong scent' with enough wood in a single trunk to mast a seventy-four-gun vessel. These trees were about three miles from the coast, and there were three hills and a swamp between them and the sea. Despite this, Marion decided to send most of his men to this place to establish a masting-camp, where they could cut and trim the masts and then haul them to the water.

During the next four days the weather was bad, but after this the sailors began (no doubt with Maori assistance) to build four 'straw huts' for the coastal masting-camp at Manawaora; one for a guard-house, another for the workers, a third as a store-house and the fourth for the officers. On 25 May four of Marion's black slaves (a man whom he had brought from Île de France and three women purchased during the voyage at Fort Dauphin) were sent to wash table linen at Moturua, where they decided to run away. One of these women must have been called Miki, for she is named in several of the tribal accounts and in a local song about Marion's visit, where she is described as his 'woman'.[41] The man had found a small canoe and persuaded the women to join him, but when they were halfway across a stretch of sea (probably on their way to the mainland) the canoe began to swamp. The man killed one of the women with a paddle, apparently to lighten the canoe, and another (probably Miki) jumped overboard and was able to swim to Motuarohia ('the island where ballast was being collected'), where an officer found her and returned her to the ship. The French were afraid that the male slave might inflame local feeling against them, since 'he was a very bad subject and capable of stirring up in them the desire to undertake something against us', but Te Kauri soon captured the two fugitives and returned them to Marion.

A day or two after this incident a man who was visiting the *Mascarin* spotted a cutlass through the gunroom porthole from his canoe. He managed to make his way into the gunroom and was caught climbing out of the porthole with the weapon. On Te Kauri's advice Marion had him put in chains to frighten him, which suggests that Te Kauri may have seized the opportunity to have a member of a rival descent-group dishonoured by being tied up and treated like a slave. At this, all of the canoes hastily left the ship's side, but shortly afterwards they returned to intercede for their companion. Marion then released the man, and he went off in one of their canoes.

Between 28 and 30 May du Clesmeur established the masting-camp with most of the *Marquis de Castries*'s men, some from the *Mascarin* and a detachment of eight soldiers. The camp was sited behind a wooded hill, with a broad plain to the south, marshy but full of game birds including quail, snipe and duck. Marion arrived at the camp on 30 May and insisted on going to see the trees for the masts. He and du Clesmeur travelled with a party of sailors along a slippery path for about a mile and then crossed a swamp, often sinking up to their waists in water. When they reached the trees Marion was so exhausted that he fell asleep under a tree by a stream while one of the sailors went back to the camp to get food and three armed men. The night was warm and peaceful, and no one troubled the French.

The work on the masts was heavy, for once the logs were cut they had to be trimmed and dragged towards the coast, and the weather was very wet and the men were pestered with stinging gnats. The officers had an easy time of it, however, for only two were required to supervise the work at any time, which left four without any duties. They often travelled about the countryside in groups, exploring the interior and hunting birds. Marion frequently joined them, looking for cultivable lands, minerals, and 'other products the value of which might induce the state to set up a branch of commerce there'. Relationships with the local people during this period were excellent. According to du Clesmeur, 'we led the gentlest, happiest life that one could hope for among savage peoples. They traded their fish and their game with us with the greatest good faith.'[42] Crozet added:

> the savages were always amongst us at our settlements and on board our vessels, and in exchange for nails they furnished us with fish, quail, wood pigeons and wild duck; they ate with our sailors and helped them in their labours; and every time they set to work, the result was very noticeable, for they were extremely strong, and their help relieved our crews very much.
>
> Our young men, attracted by the winning ways of the savages, and by the friendliness of their daughters, overran the villages every day, even making journeys inland to hunt the ducks, and taking with them the savages, who carried them across marshes and rivers as easily as a man would carry a child.[43]

The Maori accounts tell a similar story:

Mariao and his men bartered goods for Maori food — kuumara, fish, and birds — and they stayed at anchor there a long time. The Maori were friendly towards them; they habitually ate together, and the foreigners slept in the Maori houses and the Maori slept on board the ships.[44]

According to Le Dez:

The more we lived among the Zealanders the more we found them gentle and sociable. We went alone and unarmed among them, and we often went rambling even quite a distance; wherever they met us, there were always new signs of friendship . . . When we went hunting, they followed us and showed us the places where there was game . . . When we went into the villages, they opened all the huts to us and showed us their fortifications and their weapons. The young people especially showered us with caresses to the extent that sometimes we were not quite sure how far they would go. They adapted very well to our way of living and found everything that we ate good except the wine and the brandy. Several were more particularly attached to us than the others and gave us to understand that they wanted to come with us when we left. I think however that there were some among them who feared us.[45]

The ambivalence mentioned by Le Dez became increasingly evident in the early days of June. On one occasion the local people arrived at the masting-camp in great numbers, possibly considering a trial of strength with the sailors; and on another day they openly counted their numbers. (Warriors were mustered and counted regularly in the days of tribal fighting, and their numbers reported to other groups.) Soon after this du Clesmeur went on an expedition inland with a guide and a party of two officers and three soldiers. After two hours' brisk walking they arrived at an inlet (probably Pomare Bay) where they found a very large palisaded village on a headland, which du Clesmeur later marked on his chart. The chief of this village greeted them with cries of 'yeremaye' (haeremai) and sat before du Clesmeur to press noses with him. When they were escorted around his village, however, he refused them access to the houses, much to their surprise. The French indicated that they wanted to cross the inlet so the chief summoned three canoes. Halfway across the inlet the paddlers of one canoe attempted to turn back, and were prevented from doing so only when a musket was pointed at their fugleman.

If local people were beginning to consider the possibility of attacking the French, however, this can only have involved some groups, for once on shore again the French officers walked along the coastline until they came to a river, losing their armed guards en route. Despite their vulnerability, their guide returned them five hours later to the masting-camp, where they also found the soldiers safe and sound. In the middle of that night, moreover, a canoe arrived carrying de Vaudricourt, the *Mascarin*'s sub-lieutenant, who had become separated from Marion and his other companions during a hunting expedition that day. Eventually he had found his way back to the coast, where he stumbled upon a small village whose inhabitants had fed him and brought him back to camp. The next morning de Vaudricourt returned to the *Mascarin* and told his story to Marion, 'who, already biased in favour of these people, now placed an utterly blind trust in them'.[46]

Marion du Fresne had probably first learned of Rousseau's ideas of the 'noble savage' during his close contact with Pingré the astronomer, during an earlier voyage to observe the 1761 transit of Venus. It seems likely that he also had had long conversations with Commerson, the botanist on Bougainville's voyage to Tahiti who had afterwards settled on Île de France. Certainly he thought himself in paradise in the bay. According to Crozet:

> It was M. Marion's greatest happiness to live in the very midst of these savages. When he was on board, the council chamber was full of them; he fondled them and with the help of the Taity vocabulary he tried to make himself understood. He overwhelmed them with presents. They on their part recognised perfectly that M. Marion was the chief of the two vessels; they knew that he liked turbot, and every day they brought him some very fine ones. Whenever he showed a desire for anything, he always found them at his orders. Whenever he went ashore, all the savages accompanied him as though it were a day of feasting, and with joyful demonstrations; the women, the girls, and even the children petted him. They all called him by name.[47]

Unlike Cook at Kealakekua Bay in Hawaii, it does not seem that Marion was being feted as a god by the local people but rather as the wealthy, amiable and powerful leader of these strange visitors from the sea. Te Kauri brought his fourteen-year-old son to stay with Marion on the *Mascarin*, and each of the officers had particular friends who accompanied him whenever he went. Crozet, who also evidently knew of Rousseau's (or Commerson's) theories, said of this idyllic period:

> had we departed about this time, we would have brought to Europe the most favourable accounts of these savages; we would have painted them in our relations with them as the most affable, and most humane, and the most hospitable people on the face of the earth. From our accounts philosophers fond of praising primitive man would have triumphed in seeing the speculations of their studies confirmed by the accounts of travellers whom they would have recommended as worthy of belief. But we would all of us have been in the wrong.[48]

On 4 June a chief who had come from inland (perhaps from Hokianga or the area around Lake Omaapere) visited the masting-camp with a large retinue, on his way to see Te Kauri. The men were carrying weapons and the women the supplies. According to Roux, this man was handsome, 'with a very distinguished look about him'. He was accompanied by his wife, whose hair and face were painted red and who wore feathers in her head like her husband. The chief asked the French many questions, which they could not understand, and looked with longing at their tools and other possessions. He was presented with a number of gifts, and then happily went on his way. Although it was pouring with rain, Roux commented that these people did not seem to mind: 'they protect themselves from it easily by means of a cloak made of a sort of reed which the water rolls off and does not penetrate'.[49]

Later that afternoon Roux went hunting by the sea near the shore masting-camp in Manawaora, where he saw a group of about twenty men with their families evicted from their small settlement of about eight or ten houses, by a party of forty warriors who arrived in a canoe. This must have been a *muru* (plundering raid — a way of seeking retribution without war), for their houses were taken and almost all of their property, and they were treated 'very harshly'. The disconsolate refugees were forced to shift to another group of houses about a mile and a half away. Nearby Roux saw a magnificent canoe, seventy feet long and hewn out of a single log, beached under the trees. When he returned to the camp that night he told the other officers what he had seen. They decided to go and take this canoe for the camp, despite Roux's warnings that 'it would be very bad to make themselves masters of it in [such] a way, the more so since it would authorise the natives to steal from us if we took their belongings'.[50] The next day the officers from the guard-post launched the canoe, watched by some local people who offered no resistance. It is certain that its owners, however, must have bitterly resented the theft.

By now the *Mascarin* and the *Marquis de Castries* had been anchored in the bay for more than a month, and the journals recorded a number of incidents that would surely have aggravated various of the descent-groups in the bay. When the sergeant led one group in battle against another, for example; when the French took over houses on Moturua Island; or when the French seized a man who was stealing a cutlass or purloined a large canoe, there would have been groups that were bitterly aggrieved. There must also have been other such events that were neither recorded, nor even recognised by the French. Lesson, a French surgeon who visited the bay in 1824, was told of an incident in which a wood-cutting party from one of Marion's ships was visited by an important chief, who seized a mess-tin of food without being invited to do so and was struck in retaliation by one of the sailors, to his great fury.[51] There is mention, too, of linen being stolen from Miki as she washed clothes for the French at Paeroa, and of quarrels over the distribution of fish.[52]

It also seems probable that by now local women were showing symptoms of venereal disease, and very likely other infectious diseases had been communicated to the local people. Local fishing grounds, shellfish beds and gardens were under pressure from the presence of an extra 200 or so people in the bay, and the felling of trees, shooting of birds, and the constant presence of French visitors in the villages at Manawaora and Moturua no doubt provided other sources of irritation. Perhaps most disruptive of all was the influx of new forms of wealth into the bay — nails, axes, chisels, adzes, garments and probably weapons as well as smaller items — for these must have provoked envy and dissension, particularly amongst those groups whose settlements were more remote and who had less contact with the expedition.

The most virulently offensive of all of the French actions, however, and one that was persistently talked of in the tribal records, was almost certainly committed without the French ever realising what they had done. Marion had developed a habit of going on fishing and hunting expeditions in 'Tacoury's cove' (Manawaora Bay), where fish and oysters were plentiful and there were many large birds to shoot. According to the tribal accounts, however, one of the coves in the bay was intensely tapu at this time, for some members of Te Kauri's

Ngaapuhi descent-group Te Hikutuu had recently drowned and been washed up there on the beach. According to the account from Haakiro recorded by John White, this cove was Opunga,[53] a place where according to later accounts there was also a ritual site to the south where bones were scraped before the tribal dead were finally laid to rest.[54]

On 7 June, Roux accompanied Marion 'to Tacoury's Cove where we enjoyed ourselves fishing and eating some excellent oysters'. It seems likely that on this occasion they inadvertently hauled their nets on Opunga Beach. According to the most detailed Maori account of Marion's visit:

> There came a day when the foreigners rowed ashore in order to net fish on the beach at Manawaora [used here to refer to the entire inlet]. The Maori people scolded them for this, as the beach was tapu to some of Te Kauri's people (the people who lived at Whangamumu) [Te Kauri's people Te Hikutuu also had a large settlement at Orokawa, and a settlement inland from Te Huruhi Bay]. Some people from there had been drowned in the Bay of Islands, and had been cast ashore on this beach. Although the people of Ngaati Pou told them angrily not to do this (for they were afraid that Te Kauri's people would attack them in order to obtain recompense for the violation of their tapu), the foreigners took no notice, and persisted in drawing their net on the beach. Then Ngaati Pou became very sad, and no longer visited the ships and bargained for pieces of hoop-iron the size of a man's hand (these had been given in exchange for food, fish and birds, or for an entire day spent chopping firewood) . . . . The foreigners [had] violated the tapu of Manawaora by netting fish there and eating those fish; it was this that made the desecration of the tapu such a grave offence.[55]

The fish of the bay had been touched by the tapu of death, and had themselves perhaps nibbled on the bodies of the drowned men. To catch these fish was bad enough, but to eat them was tantamount to cannibalism, an attack on the tapu of the corpses and that of their tribe, and on the mana of their tribal gods. It seems that because Ngaati Pou (the people living on the islands at this time) accompanied the French on this fishing expedition in Te Kauri's territory, they were held in part responsible for the offence that the French had committed. It is no wonder that they were horrified by Marion's actions and tried to stop him, and that they avoided him and his people thereafter.

The next morning, 8 June, two chiefs came on board the *Mascarin* looking for Marion. They took him and several officers, escorted by some soldiers, to a high hill near Te Kauri's village. According to Roux, to whom Marion later described this ceremonial:

> On this mountain there were many people and they made him sit down along with the officers who were with him. He received many caresses from them, then they put a sort of crown of feathers on his head, showing him the whole expanse of land and making him understand that they recognized him as their king. They carried out several ceremonies and treated him with much respect; they made him a present of fish and of a stone on which an image of their deity was carved. For his part he also gave them presents and many caresses and they escorted him back on board ship.[56]

Le Dez added that Marion had been seated on cloaks that the people had spread on the ground, and they sang songs to him in which his name was often repeated. As Marion commented to Roux in telling him this story, 'How can you expect me to have a poor opinion of people who are so friendly towards me? Since I do them nothing but good, surely they will not do me any harm?'

Poor Marion du Fresne. Whatever else these ceremonies may have meant, they sealed his death warrant. It is possible that the chiefs that sought him out that day were the leaders of descent-groups who hoped to topple Te Kauri, and who were delighted that so potent a challenge to his tapu had been made. This would explain why they took Marion to a high hill overlooking Te Kauri's village and honoured him with a 'crown of feathers', the mark of a great chief, and presented him with either a greenstone tiki or a mauri (stone resting-place of a god) of some kind. If this interpretation is accurate, then Te Kauri must have been enraged. Not only had the tapu of his dead kinsmen been desecrated, but an open challenge to his mana had been made. The other possibility, which is equally likely, is that Te Kauri knew all about this ceremony, and it was a ritual prelude to the events that were to follow.

The entire district was in an uproar on that day. Ngaati Pou did indeed stop visiting the ship, for according to Crozet, while Marion was ashore that morning

> the young savage for whom I had grown to have a great affection, who came to see me every day and who showed a great attachment towards me, paid me a visit; he was a fine young man, well made, with a sweet expression and always smiling. On this particular day he appeared sorrowful in a way in which I had never seen him before. He brought me as a present some arms, implements, and ornaments of a very beautiful jade which I had expressed a desire to possess. I wished to pay him for these things with iron implements and red handkerchiefs, which I knew would please him, but he refused them. I wished to make him take back his jade, but he would not. I offered him something to eat, he refused again and went away very sorrowfully. I never saw him afterwards.
>
> Some other savages, friends of our officers and accustomed to come and visit them every day, disappeared at this time, but we did not pay sufficient attention to the fact. We had been thirty-three days in the Bay of Islands and lived on very best terms with the savages, who appeared to us to be the best people one could possibly meet with . . .[57]

While Marion du Fresne was being feted at Orokawa, and Ngaati Pou were farewelling their friends on board the *Mascarin*, other groups were gathering near the masting-camp inland. According to the French accounts, during 8 June a large number of local people gathered at the inland workplace where a tent had been set up as a guard-house for the French to leave their belongings. That evening, the men who were working on the masts heard a musketshot. Soon afterwards, one of the sentries from the guard-house came to tell them that while the guards had been eating supper, some local people had slipped into the tent and taken a bag of ships' biscuits, some tools, a musket, a 300-pound anchor, a watchcoat and some great-coats.

The most detailed tribal account identified these people as members of Ngaati Pou, who were stealing goods from the French 'to give to Te Kauri's people as recompense for the desecration of the tapu at Manawaora'.[58] They were spotted as they were leaving the tent, and one of the sentries fired at them. The sentries chased these people into the woods and soon lost them, returning to the guard-house while a crowd of people in the forest 'made a lot of noise' (probably by performing a haka). The sentries sent one man off to the main masting-camp on the coast to get help, and he came back with an officer and twelve men to help protect the masts and guard-tent.

At daybreak when these men went into the woods to look for the culprits, Haumont de Kerbrillant, second lieutenant of the *Mascarin*, ordered a recently abandoned village in the area to be burnt, and seized a chief and a young man whom they encountered during the search. This chief had 'a very fine cloak and his war-feathers in his hair', but despite his evident status, he was tied to a stake (thereby in effect making him a war captive, a man without mana) and the young man was sent under guard to the masting-camp. Haakiro's account identified the chief as a principal chief called Rawhi, while the more detailed White manuscript added that he was of Ngaati Pou. According to the French, this chief hotly denied having anything to do with the raid on the Europeans' property, instead blaming Te Kauri and 'Piquiore'.

When Marion was told of this affair on the morning of 9 June, he was furious with his officers and ordered that both prisoners should immediately be released. Marion's policy was that if property was taken by the local people, restitution should be sought without violence, for 'he was convinced that if we did them no harm they would not try to harm us', a conviction that had been further strengthened by the ceremonies in his honour the day before. The chief was released after being presented with several gifts and fled into the woods, leaving his cloak behind him. The young man, it seemed, had already managed to cut his ropes and escaped during the night. According to one tribal account, his people attributed this escape to their gods, who had severed the ropes that bound him.[59]

That afternoon Roux went hunting in the woods, and while chasing some quail he got lost and wandered for a time. Finally he climbed a high hill to catch a glimpse of the sea, where he noticed two men fighting in a gully. At first he thought they were duelling for exercise, for as he commented, 'I had often amused myself watching them throw darts, lances, assegais etc. at one another, warding them off with singular skill, and in their games they always looked very animated.'[60]

He kept quiet and watched them curiously, enjoying the vigour of their display:

> They were demonstrating the greatest skill and at the same time an astonishing agility. I had been watching them for about six minutes when I saw them suddenly throw aside their weapons and each drew a war-club from his belt, then immediately they fell upon one another with a fury. Their blows missed. They returned to the attack and at that I ran towards them, but I was too late because at that very moment one of them had his skull split open by a blow from his opponent's war-club and he fell down dead. They were so excited that the victor did not see me until I spoke to him. He was so surprised to see me that he ran away as fast as he

could, leaving me beside his victim. I examined this poor fellow and saw that his head was cut open at the level of the eyes as if by a blow from a cutlass.[61]

Roux would have fought in naval engagements where cutlass fighting and serious wounds from cannonfire were common, and he was impressed rather than horrified by what he had seen. He commented that 'this disaster, which took me completely by surprise, convinced me that these natives fight duels and that with great courage', drawing a comparison between this affray and French duelling over matters of honour. From this time on, however, Roux took Maori military power seriously (at least according to his own retrospective account) and often cautioned Marion not to leave himself vulnerable to local attack. Very likely the fight that he had witnessed was part of the growing turmoil in the bay.

Having examined the victim Roux made his way to the shore, where he encountered a group of twelve or fifteen people whom he had previously met on board the *Mascarin*. He tried to tell them what he had just seen but could not make them understand what he was saying. Six of these people offered to guide him back to the camp, giving him a meal of fish on the way at a small village, and they carried him for the last part of the journey, since he was feeling very tired. Roux tried to persuade these people to come to the camp, where he could give them gifts, but they steadfastly refused, leaving him at a little distance. Evidently they had heard about the tying of the chief, but although Roux was completely at their mercy, they did not harm him.

The next morning an axe and a musket that had been taken from the masting-camp were returned to Marion. On shore a great number of armed men gathered around the masting-party as they went on their way to the workplace in the woods. The sailors prepared for battle, but seeing the warriors standing motionless, Roux offered to approach them on his own, apparently unarmed. He hid a cutlass under his coat and stepped forward. As he approached the warriors, four chiefs (two of whom had guided him the day before) came to meet him, embracing him and saying, 'Paye are mai' ('Pai haere mai'), which Roux understood to mean 'Give us peace'. Roux therefore drew out his cutlass and picked up a branch, offering this to the chiefs as a gesture of reconciliation. They took the branch and embraced him, still speaking of peace.

Roux escorted them into the guard-tent, where he gave them gifts, and they asked for the return of their canoe. The canoe was returned to them with some paddles, and the chiefs promised to supply the camp with gifts of fish the following day. The warriors now approached the tent, but their chiefs held them back, and when the people saw that Roux was unarmed they also put aside their weapons. Roux approached their principal chief, who greeted him with friendship, identifying this man by the beautiful feathers that decorated his head and his cloak, his finely carved weapons and his air of grandeur. He presented this chief with the cloaks that the two men captured on 8 June had left behind.

The old chief asked if these men had been killed, and when Roux said that they had not, the chief put the cloaks in a heap and recited some words over them (a karakia), throwing a branch and some 'animal excrement' on the heap in a tapu-raising ritual. He then ordered two young people to carry the cloaks to 'the village on the other side of the river' (presumably the Whakawhiti Stream). Roux commented on this ceremony: 'May not one infer from that that these islanders have a religion and that they recognize a divinity?'

That afternoon Roux made his way back to the vessel, meeting Marion en route in 'Tacoury's cove', where he found him admiring some lovely shells (perhaps paaua) that had been hauled in by the seine. Roux told his captain about the events of the last few days, which Marion ascribed to the humiliating capture of the chief, saying that 'it could be this reason that had made them take up arms and indeed there could be nothing else which could have embittered them against us'. In this comment one sees both Marion's innocence, and his ignorance of Maori ways of life.

Marion now transferred Roux to the guard-post on Moturua Island, where the officer in charge had been sick for several days. Chastened by his experiences on the mainland, Roux immediately set about strengthening the defences around the guard-post, which was manned only by the lieutenant, another officer, the surgeon and four men. Six blunderbusses had been sent ashore to be mounted on wooden tripods, but these had been left lying on the sand. Roux ordered them cleaned and mounted in front of the officers' tent, and posted a sentry at all times. The local people had begun to prowl around the small encampment at night, and at eleven o'clock that evening the sentry woke Roux to say that he had seen five or six men near the tent. When Roux went out these people were running off up the hills behind the camp. From that time onwards Roux thought that they were being spied on and that something ominous was afoot.

Very early in the morning of 11 June Chevillard de Montaison took the longboat to collect ballast near Te Kauri's village. The people in the village had evidently posted sentries during the night, and as they saw his boat approaching in the darkness they made a great noise (on this occasion, probably by blowing war trumpets and calling out a sentry chant, or whakaaraara paa). Soon afterwards beacon fires blazed up in each of the villages along the coastline. It was still only 4 a.m., so de Montaison anchored and waited until daybreak to go ashore. As soon as they landed, he and his contingent of seven unarmed men were surrounded by more than 100 warriors armed with spears, 'bludgeons' (taiaha and tewhatewha) and patu. These men tried to stop them from collecting stones (which they evidently feared were to be used as missiles) and asked repeatedly for 'Mariao' or Marion. The French group loaded the boat with ballast and then returned to the *Mascarin*, where de Montaison told his captain what had happened. Marion said that he had seen the warriors assembling, but that he thought this was only because they had been alarmed by the boat coming ashore so early in the morning.

Shortly after this Marion visited the encampment at Moturua, where Roux told him that prowlers had visited them during the night. Marion commented that people had also begun to prowl around the masting-camp at night, and that he had just sent soldiers there to reinforce the guard post. Roux told him 'that he should not be so trusting with these people, and that I was convinced that the natives were plotting harm. He would believe nothing of it and kept repeating that we had only to treat them kindly and they would never do us any harm.'[62]

During that afternoon de Montaison went on another ballast-collecting expedition near Te Kauri's village, armed only with his hunting-knife. He and his companions were again assailed by the same people who had surrounded them that morning. This time some of the warriors seemed about to attack him, but their principal chiefs (who presumably included Te Kauri) restrained them, and continued to ask for 'Mariao'. He returned to the *Mascarin* and again told his captain that the people were asking for him and that he feared that their intentions were not friendly, but Marion 'did not seem unduly worried about it'.[63]

Also during that afternoon, the chief of Paeroa paa on Moturua (who was probably of Ngaati Pou) came with his people to the island camp with gifts of fish. They were surprised to see the blunderbusses set up in front of the officers' tent, and asked what they were for. Roux took eight or ten balls and loaded a gun with them, whereupon the chief told Roux that he considered these weapons very dangerous. He looked over the camp very carefully and even asked if he could look into the hospital tent, which Roux found disquieting. Later in the afternoon Roux and others went hunting near Paeroa paa, and decided to visit the settlement. The chief welcomed them, then asked several questions about their muskets. He said he had seen them kill birds with these weapons, but that he did not believe that they could kill a man. He gestured towards a dog that was walking past, and asked Roux to shoot it. Roux fired at the dog and killed it, which baffled the chief completely. He looked at the bullet wound with great care, and then examined the musket. Roux handed the chief the unloaded gun and he took aim at another dog, blowing on the musket lock. As Roux remarked, 'I did not seek to instruct him any further, being on the contrary highly satisfied that he did not know how we used our weapons.'[64] The boatswain and the navigator of the *Marquis de Castries* also visited Paeroa paa that evening but were refused entry, something that had never happened before. Fears of imminent hostilities were evidently escalating on both sides. During the night a dozen warriors approached the tents on Moturua Island, but when Roux was woken and went out, they were already running away.

Early on the morning of 12 June the chief of Paeroa paa visited Roux at the island encampment. Roux asked him why his men were prowling around at night and warned him that if they came again they would be shot. According to Roux, 'he understood me well and said Mona which means "Good"; he stayed with me until midday and evidenced the same curiosity as the day before, but I made less effort to satisfy it'.[65] Later that morning du Clesmeur went on board the *Mascarin* to report in detail to Marion about the 'thefts' at the masting-camp and their aftermath. The captain told him that

> we ought to be indulgent with people who know neither 'thine' nor 'mine' [an echo of Rousseau] for what is theft to us is not so to them, and that besides he thought them incapable of hatching any evil plot against us and he recounted, as convincing proof, that a few days earlier he had gone for a walk to a village and the chief has welcomed him at the head of all his people and made him sit down on some mats, after giving back to him the musket stolen at the guard-house of the masting-camp.[66]

That afternoon Te Kauri and some other people came on board to take Marion fishing once more at 'Tacoury's cove'. Marion decided to leave behind his usual escort of several armed soldiers, saying that they made it awkward in the boat. As the captain was about to board the boat he ordered some firearms that had been placed in it taken out again, for he wished to take only his hunting gun. One of the local people who was visiting the *Mascarin*, seeing this, burst into tears and threw himself at Marion's feet. Trying to hide himself from his compatriots he stammered out, 'Marion Tacoury mate terra,' which the French understood to mean 'Marion, if you go ashore Tacoury will kill you.' His officers begged Marion to take notice of this warning, but he would not listen, repeating once again his conviction that people whom he had not harmed would never hurt him.

He boarded the boat with Lehoux, de Vaudricourt, the master of arms, the boatswain, the second pilot, three black slaves and the boat crew, seventeen men in all, who were then joined by Te Kauri, another chief and five or six of their men. Du Clesmeur had gone to take the *Marquis de Castries*'s rudder to Moturua for repairs, and de Montaison, who normally went everywhere with his captain, had taken a set of accounts to the *Marquis de Castries*, so neither of them accompanied him on this expedition. That evening, when the boat did not return to the *Mascarin*, the officers became worried, but consoled themselves by thinking that perhaps Marion had decided to visit the masting-camp and to spend the night ashore.

At 1 a.m. on 13 June Roux was woken at the camp on Moturua by the sentry, who told him that warriors were coming down the hills behind the bay in great numbers. When Roux went outside he saw an estimated 400 fighting men approaching the encampment, and immediately ordered the blunderbusses to be set up in a square. He and the six other able-bodied men in the camp got into the square, and as soon as the warriors saw this they lay down in the ferns. It was bright moonlight and Roux was tempted to open fire, but remembering Marion's strict instructions, he decided to wait until they opened their attack. For about half an hour the Frenchmen and the warriors watched each other intently, and then the local people crept off through the ferns, keeping out of sight as much as possible until they were safely back in the hills. They had evidently been deterred from attacking by the sight of the blunderbusses manned so resolutely. If their attack had succeeded, the French expedition would have been crippled, because the rudders of both ships were on the island, as well as masts, yards, ropes and sixty scurvy-ridden men in the hospital tent who could barely walk.

By daybreak the hills around Waipao Bay were crowded with armed warriors, who had the camp surrounded. A chief who Roux knew came from the mainland approached the tents, apparently unarmed, weeping and calling out, 'Tacoury mate Marion' (Te Kauri has killed Marion). Roux put a brace of pistols in his pocket and went towards him, but could not clearly understand what he was saying, since he believed that Marion was safely on board the *Mascarin*. Suddenly the warriors shouted out, evidently warning the chief that a French boat was approaching, and he retreated. The *Mascarin*'s longboat had been sent ashore with thirty armed men to relieve the island camp, for their lookout had reported that it was surrounded by almost 500 warriors. When these men arrived at the camp their officer told Roux that Marion had gone fishing with several chiefs at the cove near Te Kauri's village at about two o'clock the previous day, and that they had heard nothing from him since. At once Roux understood what the chief had been trying to tell him, and miserably he told the officer that he feared that their captain had been killed. The *Mascarin*'s longboat then went back to the ship, and at seven thirty the next morning this officer returned again to the island camp to tell Roux a terrible story.

Before daybreak that morning the *Marquis de Castries*'s longboat had been sent on shore to fetch firewood, with a volunteer, the boatswain, the quarter-master and nine sailors on board. About an hour later the crew of the *Mascarin* saw a man in the water, swimming for his life. He yelled out for help and they sent their longboat to pick him up, recognising him as one of the crew of the *Marquis de Castries*'s boat. As they hauled him out of the water they saw two spear wounds in his side, and he was evidently in a state of profound shock, for 'he told us such extraordinary and disjointed tales that they suggested the derangement of his mind'.[67]

The wounded man had told them that as their boat had approached the cove near Te Kauri's village that morning, a small number of armed men appeared (evidently at Ongeti in Orokawa Bay[68]) and invited them to land. The boatswain, Raux, seeing good timber at that place for firewood, had decided to go ashore, despite the arguments of the coxswain, who did not like the look of the armed men (whom the tribal accounts identify as men from Ngaati Pou).[69] The warriors came out to the boat and carried the Frenchmen ashore on their shoulders, and then the unsuspecting sailors scattered and went off into the bush to cut wood.

According to this man's account, he had hardly begun his work when he heard a terrible shout, and he and his companion, Lequay, were set upon by about twelve warriors, one of whom immediately wounded him with a spear thrust to the side. He pulled out the spear and killed two of his assailants with his axe, and then tried to go to the assistance of his companion. Seeing that he was hopelessly outnumbered, however, he changed his mind and hid in the under-growth, where he watched his friend Lequay being killed and cut to pieces. Horrified by the sight, he made a run for the longboat, but as he came out of the bush he saw a number of other sailors who had been trying to escape in the long-boat being hacked and speared to death by a group of maddened warriors. In a blind panic he blundered through a little wood and ran past Te Kauri's village, noticing Marion's boat beached at the back of Te Hue Bay. A crowd of children surrounded him, shouting, and, almost unhinged with fear, he leapt into the sea and swam desperately towards the ships.

As the officer told his story to Roux they agreed that Marion's boat must also have been attacked and their captain killed. Roux later recorded his grief at this realisation:

I was filled with successive waves of pity, horror and revenge, but could undertake nothing for the moment. I could only dwell on the thought of this horrible catastrophe which had just robbed us of a man whom we had so many reasons to regret, and of the brave men who had shared his misfortune. We soon felt the enormity of the loss we had just sustained and to what extent it was irreparable. He was a man the like of whom is rarely found for a mission such as the one we were engaged on. He added to all the qualities of a first-class mariner, the greatest gentleness and the highest integrity; no-one was more able than he to make peace and unity prevail and to establish good order on board his ship. Every mistake made by those who replaced him gave us fresh cause to honour his memory. After his death, mistakes became as common as they had been rare while he was alive.[70]

Marion du Fresne was a rare man, indeed. His whole-hearted affection for the local people was both admirable and foolhardy, however, for whether he knew it or not, he and his men had mortally offended some of them and had breached one of their most potent tapu. A breach of the death tapu provoked not only human anger but the wrath of the tribal gods, and if Te Kauri had not been prepared to avenge the desecration of the place where his kinsmen's corpses had rested, their spirits would have hounded him and his gods abandoned him and his people. Further, Marion's innocent lavishing of gifts and friendship cannot have been evenly distributed amongst the descent-groups in the bay. Even before the French expedition had arrived, the place had been in turmoil; and the longer they stayed, the more explosive the situation became.

If, as the tribal manuscript accounts claim, Te Kauri was of Te Hikutuu, then he and his people were part of an ongoing Ngaapuhi infiltration of the bay. If the people on the islands were indeed of Ngaati Pou, a tribe who had previously controlled much of the region[71], then Marion's close friendship with so many of their number must have seemed an unpredictable and ominous threat. When Marion's men, accompanied by Ngaati Pou, had insisted despite the anguished protests of their friends on hauling their nets on a beach that was intensely tapu to Te Kauri's people, the die had been cast for a tragic sequence of events. Not only were Marion and many of his men killed as a result of that decision, but also many local Maori, especially of Ngaati Pou.

With the killing of Marion and his companions from the *Mascarin*, and of the wooding-party from the *Marquis de Castries*, however, the drama was far from over. While the officer was still telling Roux this story they received word from du Clesmeur on board the *Marquis de Castries* that he had despatched a boat armed with fourteen blunderbusses, four stone mortars and twenty armed men to look for Marion, and to reinforce the masting-camp. Roux quickly set about reinforcing his own position, getting the men to fortify an entrenchment large enough to hold the sick men and fifty combatants, and setting up the battery of six blunderbusses on the side most vulnerable to attack. At midday a fleet of ten or twelve canoes arrived from the mainland, landing near Paeroa paa. About 300 to 400 men from these canoes joined the warriors on the hills around Waipao Bay, until the camp was surrounded by 1,000 to 1,200 men. They began to yell insults at the French, telling them that they had killed Marion and showing with their clubs just how it had been done. The latest arrivals came quite close to the camp, led by Te Kauri, who called to Roux by name, and beckoned to him. Roux beckoned back, and when Te Kauri came within musket-range with ten of his men, Roux moved forward with six good marksmen. As Te Kauri abruptly changed his mind and began to retreat, Roux's men fired, and at least one of their bullets found its mark. Te Kauri staggered and fell. His men picked him up and ran off with him, shouting loudly. Roux's men chased after them, firing, while the massed warriors rapidly retreated to a safe distance. According to Roux, 'at the head of those natives were all the chiefs who used to come among us every day and who had been the friendliest towards us, [yet] these wretches had made us believe that they were all at war with one another . . .'[72] These must have been the Ngaati Pou chiefs, who were now fully committed to killing the French in the hope of saving the lives of their own people.

At six o'clock that evening the *Marquis de Castries*'s boat came across to the island, bringing more reinforcements and further news of what had happened on the mainland. They had left the ship that morning to search for Marion, and below Te Kauri's village the officer in charge had noticed their ship's longboat beached in a little cove, with Marion's boat further along the coast (in Te Hue Bay) drawn up under a tree. The boats were surrounded by 1,500 to 2,000 warriors armed with axes, swords and muskets that they had taken from the men they had killed. Some of their chiefs were wearing Marion's and other dead officers' clothes. The French fired a volley at these warriors, and they threw back spears. The longboat was then rowed rapidly to the masting-camp, for by now its crew were desperate to warn their comrades and to avert any further disaster. They found the shore camp almost deserted, surrounded by 500 men armed with spears and clubs. As soon as the boat landed, the warriors ran off into the hills, shouting, 'Marion mate' (Marion is dead). The *Marquis de Castries*'s men relieved Haumont and Barré at the shore camp and marched inland with bayonets fixed, reaching the place where the masts were being hauled towards the coast at 2 p.m. Crozet saw them approaching and came to meet them on his own, and de Montaison told him of the events in Te Hue Bay. Crozet in turn reported that the workplace had been surrounded by 500 to 600 armed warriors that morning, each of whom came carrying a small bundle of fish to show that their intentions were friendly. They had said they were going to make war on Te Kauri and asked the French to join them. When the French refused, however, they began to edge imperceptibly towards them, squatting on their heels and dragging long spears behind them that were hidden in the grass, until finally Crozet had ordered his men to take up arms and drive them off.

Ordering the new arrivals to keep silent about what had happened to Marion, Crozet marched with them to the masting-station. There he stopped all work, had the implements and arms collected, charged the muskets and distributed them amongst his men. The equipment that they could not carry away he ordered buried inside a hut, which was then pulled down and burnt. Crozet then formed his men into two divisions, one party of laden sailors carrying tools surrounded by armed men, and an armed rearguard, about sixty men in all. As they marched out of the station the warriors came down from the hills and took the tools and equipment from the ashes of the burnt hut, then marched in groups beside them taunting them with shouts of 'Tacouri mate Marion' — 'Te Kauri has killed Marion'. The marksmen in the contingent, now realising that their captain was dead, begged to be allowed to fire on their tormentors. Crozet ordered them to hold their fire for fear that they might provoke a mass attack and be over-whelmed by sheer weight of numbers.

As the masting-camp contingent arrived at the longboat the warriors began to crowd around them. Crozet ordered the sailors who were carrying the equipment to load it into the longboat and the masting-camp's boat. After doing this he took a peg and fixed in in the ground, telling the leading chief that if he or any of his men passed the line of this peg he would instantly be shot. Crozet then ordered the warriors in menacing tones to sit down. The chief, seeing Crozet's carbine aimed directly at him, repeated this command, and 1,000 warriors sat down quietly on the beach. The French sailors loaded the boats and climbed on board, some hauling them out into the water. The moment that Crozet embarked, the warriors rose en masse, roaring out a haka, setting fire to the buildings of the shore camp and hurling wooden spears and stones at the laden boat without doing any serious harm. Crozet later claimed that he had hoped to retreat without firing on these people, but when the warriors entered the water to attack he changed his mind:

> Much to my regret I found it advisable and necessary for our safety that I should make these unhappy people understand the superiority of our arms. I had the rowing stopped, and ordered four fusiliers to fire at the chiefs, who appeared more excited and animated than all the others. Every shot told, and this fusilade continued some minutes. The savages saw their chiefs and comrades fall in the most senseless manner, they could not understand how they could be killed by arms which did not touch them like their tomahawks and clubs. At every shot they redoubled their cries and threats; they were most horribly excited, and as they remained on the shore like a flock of sheep, we might indeed have killed every man of them had I desired to continue the firing; but after having killed many more than I wished to, we rowed on to the vessel, while the savages did not leave off shouting.[73]

Cook had decided early on in his voyage around New Zealand that Maori warriors were so formidable and determined that it was necessary to give them a demonstration of firepower early on in each encounter — usually a volley of small-shot, a musketshot or if necessary a cannonball overhead. Marion du Fresne's policy of friendship and goodwill had worked well for several weeks, but finally it led to a catastrophe more destructive than any previously experienced in a Maori-European encounter. The impact of a withering fusilade from experienced marksmen on a mass of warriors who knew nothing of firearms can barely be imagined. Maori accounts of later battles, in which groups who were similarly naive were slaughtered by musketfire, give some idea:

> Now in those days the people . . . were ignorant of the sound of a gun — they did not know what the effect of its noise would be. So these people, who were ignorant in regard to the thunder of guns, went to see what the noise was caused by, and

what the lightening of the strange god was that had been brought there, but these guns were used on these stupids, and many of them fell dead. These stupids saw that many of those who were gazing at the lightening and hearing the thunder were being killed with what they did not know. . . .[74] They could not see what had killed them, but could only hear the voices which the gods uttered. All that could be seen on the corpses. was the blood from a wound . . .[75]

Leaving a tangle of dead and wounded warriors on the beach, Crozet's party returned to their ships. As they passed Te Hue Bay they again saw warriors wearing the clothes of their dead comrades. One chief was wearing the spotted velvet jacket Marion had worn on the day he had been killed, and carried his silver-mounted musket, while others wore other officers' garments, and one man had de Vaudricourt's cutlass slung across his shoulder. Some of the officers on the longboat urged Crozet to fire the blunderbusses and stone-mortars into the bay. Perhaps sensibly, since the boat was loaded almost to the point of swamping, he would not agree. As soon as they returned to the *Mascarin*, Crozet, who was now in command of the vessel, ordered a carronade fired into Te Kauri's village, and sent the longboat with a detachment of soldiers to the camp at Moturua, where great crowds of warriors had gathered. The sailors landed under the cover of a carronade fired by the French vessels at the hills above Waipao Bay. By now it was pouring with rain, so Roux issued the sentries he had posted around the island encampment with pieces of sheepskin to keep their musket-locks dry. All that night they loaded tents, water barrels, the forge and the sick men into boats, and transported them back to the ship. At 11 p.m. the warriors made a feint attack on the forge, where they were forced back by musketfire, and then attacked the entrenchment Roux had constructed, retreating after several volleys were fired, having themselves thrown only a few spears and darts. Picking up their dead and wounded, they vanished into the woods near the forge and made no more attacks that night.

The next morning, 14 June, there were even more warriors on the island than before. They threatened the French, displaying Marion's clothes and musket to try and frighten them into submission. Roux wanted to mount an attack, and at midday he received orders from Crozet to unite his forces, march to the village on the island and drive the warriors off it to protect their access to the local water supply. Crozet also ordered some men, women or children to be captured if at all possible, promising the sailors fifty piastres for every person brought back to the ships alive. Roux selected twenty-six men, twenty soldiers and six volunteers, arming each with a musket, a pair of belt pistols, a cutlass, and forty rounds of ammunition. At one o'clock they set off for Paeroa paa, marching with bayonets fixed and leaving the encampment guarded by an officer and thirty men. When the people of the paa saw them approaching, they loaded their women and children into a fleet of canoes drawn up nearby, and ran into the paa. According to Crozet their chief 'Malou' (Maru?)[76] was with them, with five or six other principal fighting men. Roux described this paa as being built on the end of a peninsula with steep cliffs on three sides, surrounded by three rows of palisades. The neck of the peninsula was fortified by a twenty-five- to thirty-foot fosse and three more rows of palisades, surmounted by a fighting-stage reached by a ladder. To the left side of the paa a narrow track led to the gate, which was only two feet square. As the French approached, the people tossed water on to this track to make it slippery, so that the attackers had to hold on to the palisades as they advanced to stop themselves from falling into the sea. Two chiefs came out and hurled darts at them, using whip-slings. The foremost Frenchmen fired in return, hitting one man in the body and also smashing his thigh. The other man retreated, and as Roux's contingent attacked, they shot the warriors on the fighting-platform so that their bodies blocked it for their comrades who were climbing up to attack the French with darts, stones and spears. They reached the gate without suffering any casualties, only to find it closed and guarded by two chiefs.

The attackers poked the barrels of their muskets through the palisades and shot the two defenders. Others then stepped forward behind 'a kind of lean-to' to take their place and were also shot until five men had been killed. The fifth man who stepped forward lunged at Chevalier de Lorimer with his long spear, wounding him on the nose before he, too, was shot down. The attackers battered down the gate with rocks and the butts of their muskets, and when it finally fell they ran inside to find a rear-guard of warriors covering the evacuation of the paa. These warriors threw themselves behind a rampart and hurled spears at the French, wounding Roux in the thigh and one of the volunteers in the ribs. One old woman stayed back with these men, handing weapons to them with great coolness, but she was very soon shot dead. After about fifty minutes of resolute fighting, all of the chiefs who had led this rear-guard action had been killed, and the survivors were forced to retreat. As the French reached the end of the paa they found two large canoes carrying about 200 men out at sea, and other canoes at the foot of the cliffs still loading people on board. The marksmen took aim and of about 250 people on these last canoes, almost all were shot or drowned. Roux commented that none of the people of this paa seemed to be familiar with firearms, for when they saw the attackers taking aim they lifted up their cloaks in a futile effort to protect themselves from the 'missiles' that were fired.

After taking possession of the paa Roux ordered his men to search the place, but they found no trace of any of their dead comrades, either in the houses or the store-houses. Ngaati Pou, the people of this paa, had joined in the attack on Marion and the wooding-party, but it seemed that all the spoils had gone to Te Kauri's people as utu (compensation) for the desecration of the tapu at Opunga. The Frenchmen tried to follow Crozet's orders by capturing some people alive, but even the wounded men fought and bit so furiously, breaking the cords that bound them as if they were thread, that none of them were taken. When Roux inspected the bodies of the dead (who numbered seven chiefs and forty men) he found that all of the defenders had been grown men, and that the chiefs who had fought with such bravery had taken three or four fatal musket wounds before they collapsed and died. As he commented later, 'Certainly these men put up a resistance such as we had in no way expected.'

The chiefs in particular had controlled the retreat with great coolness, fighting until they dropped, when their followers appeared to lose all hope and retreated in a panic. Evidently the constant display of Marion's garments to the French and the taunt that 'Marion is dead' was likewise intended to dishearten the Frenchmen so that they would panic and run away.

Once the village had been thoroughly searched, a fire was lit on the windward side, so that within an hour and half of all the buildings had been burnt to the ground. The palisades and fighting stage were knocked over and taken for firewood, and the place was completely destroyed. The French feared for a time that the local people may have poisoned their weapons, but after some initial pain and swelling they were reassured to find that their wounds very quickly healed without any complications.

By 15 June the evacuation of the camp on Moturua was completed. Crozet ordered all of the fern at Waipao to be cut down, as it was six feet high and very dense, and would have provided excellent cover for an ambush. He ordered the defenders of the paa to be buried, each with a hand sticking out of the ground 'to let the savages see that we did not eat our enemies'. The local people must have come back to the island shortly after this, because the next time the French paid a visit to Moturua these bodies had been properly buried. During the next week or so the carpenters on board the *Mascarin* worked to rig up jury-masts for the *Marquis de Castries*, which had only a mainmast left, and the new masts had to be abandoned on the mainland. The jury-masts were cobbled together out of spare pieces of timber while the soldiers and sailors collected wood and water from Moturua and loaded it on board.

On one of these expeditions a party of about sixty warriors tried to ambush the French from a remaining stand of fern, but a sentry spotted them before they could attack and they were chased off the island. About twenty-five of these warriors were cut off from their canoes and forced to swim to a rock near Paeroa paa. As they tried to swim from this rock to another island, six of them were shot on the rock and the rest were shot in the sea or drowned. Their canoes were also captured, while the escaping canoes retreated to a village on a nearby island.

On another occasion a larger group of warriors made their way to the far side of the island, where they sent out a warrior dressed in sailor's clothes to approach the French. A sentry challenged this man, but he did not understand what was being said, so he was shot and a large group of warriors, many wearing European clothes, were chased off the island and into their canoes. On 23 June an officer in charge of a working-party on Moturua thought he saw one of the ship's boats on the mainland to the west. He directed the longboat to this place and landed near a small village, finding an excellent piece of shaped timber on the beach which he loaded into the boat. When a few unarmed local people approached him with some fish, he captured one man who managed to escape, fired several musketshots at others and burnt the nearby houses. Le Dez was mystified by the behaviour of these people: 'What is the nature of these people? After hostilities on both sides, how could they have the confidence to come up to us like that?' Since they were close to Te Hue the longboat briefly visited the cove, but they saw only a group of people from Te Kauri's village, who flaunted themselves in European clothes, displaying Marion's musket and de Vaudricourt's cutlass.

On 24 June the officers opened Marion du Fresne's papers but found no instructions relating to the continuation of the voyage. Their men continued to repair the ships as best they could, overhauling the rigging and completing the masts, while the local people stayed in their paa. They posted sentinels who watched the French and called out to the sentries in other paa, reporting every French movement in 'a most surprisingly powerful voice' and signalling to each other at night with fires. The French responded to this hostile scrutiny with fire-power, aiming cannonballs at any group that came within range, one day managing to hit a canoe and cutting it in two.

On 6 July the French captured a canoe that was heading towards the mainland with a load of fish and fernroot, and cut it up for firewood. The next day a formal expedition was sent to Te Kauri's village to try to discover direct evidence of what had happened to Marion. A longboat was sent, well armed with swivel guns and blunderbusses to Te Hue Bay, where they found that the ships' boats had been burnt in order to get the iron used in their construction. The armed contingent then marched to Te Kauri's village, but the chief had retreated. He was spotted on a hill in the distance, wearing Marion's cloak of scarlet and blue English cloth. The village was deserted except for two or three old men, who sat quietly in front of their houses, since they were not fit enough to leave. One of them unhurriedly jabbed at a soldier with his javelin, and was immediately killed.

The contingent searched the village thoroughly, finding Marion's shirt, its neck all bloody and with three or four blood-stained holes at the side. They also discovered some of de Vaudricourt's clothes and his pistols; muskets; ironwork and a rudder and oars from the boats, still stained with blood. In Te Kauri's house they found a head that had been cooked and the flesh partly stripped off; and in a house nearby, a thighbone on a skewer and a shredded heap of rags. As was customary in traditional warfare, the enemies' bodies had been ritually eaten to destroy their mana and to expiate their crimes. According to the most authoritative of the early tribal accounts, 'they took the bodies and cooked them, and Te Kauri and Tohitapu of Te Koroa sub-tribe ate Marion, and Te Kauri took Marion's clothes. The bones of the foreigners who had been killed were made into forks for picking up food, and the thighbones were made into flutes.'[77] The other anonymous account said, 'Marion was cooked and eaten by . . . the chiefs Te Kauri and Tohitapu, as they were priests, and it was for them to eat these foreigners, so that evil might not come on their tribes for the evil of those people for ignoring the tapu of the beach where corpses had lain.'[78] Tohitapu was a celebrated priest and warrior, and evidently the ritual eating of Marion was witnessed by men from various sub-tribes of Ngaapuhi, for according to the detailed tribal account, 'The men who witnessed these acts were Tohitapu of Te Roroa sub-tribe of Ngaa Puhi (who died in 1833), Tarewarewa of Te Patu sub-tribe of Ngaa Puhi, and Takurua of Te Maahurehure (these two men died in 1839).'[79]

The Frenchmen collected all of this melancholy evidence and also the arms and possessions abandoned by the local people, and then burned the village. After this they marched to 'Piquiore's' village at Tangituu Point, which had been hastily evacuated since their landing, and searched it, finding further clothing and remains, and burned this settlement as well. They captured two war canoes and towed them to the vessels for firewood. Although the journals don't say so, it seems that they also burned a village at Paroa Bay, since it is designated 'burned village' on one of du Clesmeur's charts.

On 10 July there were further reports that one of their long-boats had been sighted entering Manawaora Bay, so the *Mascarin*'s longboat was sent to investigate. They found only a few small canoes and about 300 warriors, who threatened them furiously. One man came right to the beach to taunt them, and each time they fired he flung himself on the ground, then leapt up and opened his cloak to show that he had not been hurt.

Roux fumed at the impotence of these gestures, and that attempts at retaliation had come so late. He evidently felt that had a punitive expedition been mounted immediately after the initial attacks, Marion or at least some of the *Marquis de Castries*'s wooding party might have been rescued. Regrets, however, were futile. By 11 July the *Marquis de Castries* had been remasted and the French were ready to leave. The officers held a meeting and resolved that because of the loss of their best men, the shortage of anchors and longboats, their reliance on jury masts, a severe shortage of rations and the fact that some of the men still had scurvy, they should go back to Île de France by the most direct route possible, stopping only at Manila on the way to refresh their crews.

Having once decided on this plan, the officers 'took possession in the King's name of the island of New Zealand', unconsciously echoing Cook; they buried a bottle containing documents formally claiming the country on Moturua Island, 'four feet under ground, fifty-seven paces from the edge of the sea, counting from the high-water mark, and ten paces from the stream'; they named the place 'Treachery Bay' and the country 'France Australe' or Southern France; and at eight o'clock on the morning of 13 July the two ships sailed gladly out of the bay.

In thirty-three days the bay had been transformed for the French from paradise to purgatory. They left, never understanding why they had been attacked, nor why their friends had betrayed them. If the fate of Marion du Fresne and their other comrades seemed terrible to them, however, their fishing expedition at Opunga and their feasting on death-tapu-laden fish had equally horrified the local people. During their time in the bay they had caused great damage, not only by this offence but by many others — only some of which were recorded by either side — which must also have unbearably aggravated existing inter-tribal conflicts. In the end they brought about an alliance between Te Kauri's Ngaapuhi people Te Hikutuu, and Ngaati Pou to drive them from the bay. Even so, Ngaati Pou were never forgiven for their part in Marion's fatal blunder, and after further bitter fighting which lasted for some years they, too, were hounded out of the region.

ETHNOGRAPHIC ACCOUNTS

The French ships had spent thirty-three peaceful days in the bay, and in all they stayed there a little over two months. The officers and sailors had co-existed with Maori groups on terms of friendly intimacy, and enjoyed unprecedented opportunities to become familiar with village life. Although no scientists or artists accompanied the expedition, there were well-educated and thoughtful observers on board, including Marion du Fresne himself, Le Dez and Crozet. Moreover, du Clesmeur's and Marion's charts of the bay, which located a large number of settlements, and the unattributed 'Plan of a New Zealand Fortress' were far more detailed and specific than comparable graphic records from any of the other early voyages to New Zealand. The seriousness of their efforts to understand local life is evident from Le Dez's description of Marion's own activities in the bay:

> In his plan to acquire all the knowledge he could about this country and the character of its inhabitants, he devoted all the time he had left after giving his orders, to this study: a relaxation for him and a pleasure for those of his officers who, off-duty, took a delight in accompanying him on his walks. He knew that to get to know men well it is not always enough to live among them; that if possible he should see them without being seen, that it is only with their peers when they think they owe each other nothing that they are really free, that they observe each other the least and reveal themselves as they really are. Thus, often not seeming to be occupied with anything other than watching them working with their nets, he would observe their least actions. He enjoyed talking to them and, in short, he studied them as much as he thought he could without compromising himself.[80]

The Governor of Île de France had provided Marion with detailed notes on how best to observe new people and places, which directed his attention 'towards objects which might prove most useful to our colonies, and generally towards the advancement of human knowledge'.

The chief shortcoming of this expedition's records, apart from the loss of all of Marion's manuscripts, is the lack of day-by-day journals. Apart from du Clesmeur's navigational journal (which mainly records time spent at sea), all of the surviving accounts are retrospective, written from more detailed daily journals that no longer exist, or from memory, and there is nothing that can be compared with, say, the meticulous daily detail of William Monkhouse's *Endeavour* journal, or even with Joseph Banks's account of the *Endeavour* expedition.

Nevertheless, the accounts of Crozet, Le Dez, du Clesmeur, de Montaison and Roux jointly provide a reasonably detailed version of events during the first part of their stay in the bay (although their dates for particular incidents do not always coincide), and each also included a section of 'Notes on this Country and its Inhabitants' which can be combined to give a graphic description of many aspects of life in the bay. The summary of these notes that follows broadly follows the topics discussed in Le Dez's orderly and systematic description of life in the Bay of Islands in 1772.

Geography

The French accounts located the Bay of Islands, which they named 'Port Marion', at 35°15′ (or 16′) South, and 162°34′ East of the Paris meridian according to their dead reckoning, or 170°39′ East according to their observations.

Climate

The climate was described as mild, temperate and healthy, for even in mid-winter (May to July) the nights were no more than cool, sometimes with a little frost in the morning, which soon vanished after the sun rose. According to Le Dez, until the end of June the prevailing winds were from the east and north-east, when they veered gradually to the south and the west, and during July they turned to the south-west to south-south-east. At each new and full moon a gale blew from the west or the north-east, followed by a brief calm from the south, and then rains from the west.

Terrain

Crozet described the land-mass of the North Island as being mountainous, with a rocky, barely inhabited west coast, which lacked sheltered harbours. His observation that 'from the sea we could not sight any estuaries' was contradicted, however, by the day-by-day entries of other writers, who described a number of inlets and coves along this coastline. He described the eastern coast as 'more cut up with a multitude of islands, bays and harbours, and it seems that all the rivers coming from the mountains have their course and run into the sea on this side. One sees plains which look delicious and appear to be well wooded.'[81]

From the frequent evidence of volcanism in Northland — scoria, blocks of obsidian, basalt and pumice stones — Crozet (or perhaps his editor Rochon) speculated that in the distant past New Zealand had been split off from Australia, the islands of the South Seas or 'some other continent' by a volcanic catastrophe that had sunk all but the mountains of the intervening land mass. This, he thought, might account for the close linguistic similarities observed between Tahitian and Maori, for he dismissed the possibility of inter-island navigation. Crozet concluded these geological speculations by saying:

> I shall not be astonished if those navigators, now occupied with the discovery of an Austral Continent, should find at the Antarctic Pole nothing but islands, being the summits of the mountains which have escaped from volcanic shocks and have been separated from the plains which may formerly have surrounded them. There they will surely find people absolutely similar to those of New Zealand.[82]

In the Bay of Islands itself the French journal writers described the landscape as 'a charming mixture of plains and slopes, valleys and mountains', with mountains of average height, sloping down to plains crisscrossed by small streams. In low-lying areas there were swamps, and the soils in general seemed fertile, being heavy in some places and sandy in others. Du Clesmeur observed black soils and red earth suitable for making pottery, while Crozet recorded deposits of red ochre and white potter's clay, which the master gunner used to demonstrate the potter's art to the local people:

> Our master gunner, a very ingenious man, rigged up a potter's reel, on which in the presence of the savages he made several vessels, porringers and plates, and even baked them under the very eyes of the savages. Some of his essays succeeded perfectly, and he gave the articles to the savages who had seen them turned and baked, but I doubt if they will profit by such an industry as this, which would afford them a thousand conveniences.[83]

Local rocks included 'white marble, red jasper, ideous marble, crystallized quartz, firestone, flint, chalcedonic agates'. In Spirits Bay Crozet noted a spring of very soft water that seemed capable of petrifying objects that had fallen into it. He also commented that a beautiful semi-transparent jade (pounamu), 'one of the hardest stones', was very common, and that the local people had made 'tomahawks', chisels, engraved images and ear ornaments from it, but he was unable to locate its source. This shows that trading networks linking the northern end of the North Island with the South Island greenstone sources were flourishing in 1772.

Plants

According to Le Dez, only the slopes and summits of hills in the bay were cultivated for sweet potato, indicating a strong preference for hill gardening, while the rest of the countryside was covered either with ferns or forest. Ferns, which formed the basis of the local diet, were moderate in height when growing by the sea or on the hills, while those in the valleys and on the foothills grew very tall and produced roots about the thickness of a man's thumb.

The forest trees included 'a very beautiful strong-smelling myrtle 30–40 feet high' (maanuka or kaanuka, whose leaves the French found to be an excellent anti-scorbutic); several 'redwood trees' (probably totara, rimu and matai) and the prevalent 'olive-leaved cedar' or kauri, with trunks up to 100 feet tall and nine to ten feet in circumference, of a light resinous wood, which seemed very suitable for making ships' masts. Although it was mid-winter, none of the trees had shed their leaves, so that the forests were as fresh and green as those in France in mid-summer.

The swamps were full of rushes and reeds, and on stony slopes grew great quantities of 'hoheria' (lacebark or houhere), from which, according to Crozet, 'these savages extract a very beautiful silken thread'. Le Dez noted that cabbage trees (tii kouka) also grew in the bay. It seems likely that Crozet collected some plant specimens during his time in the bay which were later identified by his editor L'Abbé Rochon, for his text included botanical names for a number of plants, including varieties of *Epacris*, *Solanum* and 'Aviculare' as well as 'a very pretty golden immortelle' — evidently a variety of daisy — and a large-leafed watercress. He commented that the local people expressed great astonishment at seeing the French gathering quantities of wild celery and watercress to feed to the sick as anti-scorbutics.

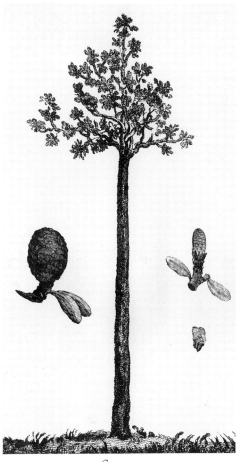

Cedre.

A kauri tree. An engraving from L'Abbé Rochon's edition of Crozet's journal.

According to his own account, Crozet acted as a sort of 'Johnny Appleseed' during his stay in the Bay of Islands:

> I formed a garden on Moutouaro Island [Moturua], in which I sowed the seed of all sorts of vegetables, stones, and the pips of our fruits, wheat, millet, maize, and in fact every variety of grain which I had brought from the Cape of Good Hope, everything succeeded admirably, several of the grains sprouted and appeared above ground, and the wheat especially grew with surprising vigour . . . The garden on [Moturua] Island alone was not sufficient to satisfy my desires; I planted stones and pips wherever I went — in the plains, in the glens, on the slopes, and even on the mountains; I also sowed everywhere a few of the different varieties of grain, and most of the officers did the same. We tried in vain to get the savages to grow some, and explained to them the use of wheat, of the other elementary grains and of the quality of the fruits of which we showed them the stones. But they had no more mind for this than brutes.[84]

Roux, on the other hand, reported that the local people were very satisfied with these plantings and promised to take great care of them.

Game

Under this heading the French described a number of birds, including wild ducks, teal, loons, 'quail like ours only bigger' (which they said were very common), snipe, blue fowl, 'very beautiful wood pigeons about the size of a pullet [with] magnificent sparkling blue and gold plumage' (kuukupa), 'another sort of pigeon the size of a black-bird, dark blue with a crest and barbs of curly little white feathers which look very pretty' (tui), large parrots with black and variegated blue and red plumage, lories, larks, pipits, native robins, and birds 'like wagtails and wheatears'. According to Crozet:

> from the day of our first landing I noticed that all the birds of this country were tame and allowed themselves to be approached so closely that they could be killed with stones and sticks; but when our young men had fired at them for a few days, the game became wild, although the savages could still approach closely, while they fled our sportsmen from afar off.[85]

Among the coastal birds Crozet also listed curlews, snipe, cormorants, black and white egrets like those in France, and grey and white gulls, all of which except the egrets and the gulls were excellent eating.

Quadrupeds

Du Clesmeur remarked, 'we did not come across any wild beasts and indeed we saw no quadrupeds at all other than dogs and rats. I believe that New Zealand has the precious advantage of having not a single noxious animal.'[86] Pieces of dogskin with long white hair were used to decorate weapons, ear ornaments and cloaks, but few people had this form of ornament, and Le Dez was thus led to speculate that it must come from a very rare animal. The kurii, or Polynesian dog, was described as a 'sort of domesticated fox', quite black or white, with a long body, thick tail, short legs, large short paws turned out like those of a basset hound, a head quite like that of a fox, full pointed jaws, straight ears like that of a French wolf-hound and very small eyes. These dogs never barked but had the same cry as a fox. Their hair was about the length of a spaniel's but finer, and many were quite wild. The domesticated dogs were fed on fish and became quite tame, although some that were taken on board the French ships frequently bit the sailors. These dogs were evidently raised to be eaten; but although the French described the kiore, or Polynesian rat, they apparently did not realise that these were hunted and also eaten. On the subject of reptiles Le Dez added 'we have not seen any reptiles other than little lizards'.[87]

According to Crozet, the local people were astounded when they saw livestock — pigs, sheep and goats — on board the French ships, and the chickens and ducks that were kept in pens and coops on deck.

Fish

The French journal keepers agreed that fish were abundant off the coast and in the bay. They mentioned splendid 'barbots' (or labridae), mullet, conger-eels, incredible quantities of mackerel that were much bigger than those caught off the French coast, many 'balistes' (triggerfish), cod and two varieties of red fish like gurnet. Crozet recognised that some species of fish were migratory, and speculated on the basis of his later knowledge of Cook's journals and charts that the fisheries in the strait between the two big islands must be more prodigal still. Lobsters, crabs and shellfish of every variety were readily available, and although no penguins were seen, many whales and white porpoises were sighted out at sea, 'all of which could be hunted'.

People

Accord to Le Dez's very detailed description of the people of the bay, they were tall, robust and healthy:

> The Zealanders are commonly five feet seven to eight inches tall. We saw several who were six feet tall. They are well built and well proportioned. They have a gentle look about them and pleasant faces, although they are disfigured by several strange designs that they like to decorate themselves with, beautiful wide-open eyes, an ordinary-sized mouth and strong white teeth. Some have a nose I could not better describe than chiselled with a great deal of art, patience and as much pain, because they are marked with a lot of little black scars 1/24th of an inch deep, which, linked up, form various patterns according to their taste or perhaps to certain distinctions among them; others have serrations right down the nose and round the outline of the nostrils; others have their faces painted black in different ways — some have half done; others have only a simple design which goes from the inside corner of the eye, widening as it rises to form a double eye-brow; finally, some have no marks at all. I have also seen some who had the edge of the tongue serrated right round.
>
> Their colour is between brown and yellow. Their hair is straight, black and quite soft. They do not wear it long. Some have thinning hair, but most tie it up on the top of their heads. Several rub it with red ochre ground up and mixed with fish oil; there are some who rub this mixture over the whole of their faces. Their legs are well shaped and their feet the same. They almost all have a black voluted pattern on one buttock. I have seen no cripples or any one with a natural defect. Very few of them are thin; they all seemed to me to enjoy good health and to have a robust constitution. Some of them, however, had a sort of dartre and a few pimples. Among the old men, who were numerous, several were extremely aged to judge by their wrinkles. Their hair was very grey, as were their beards, which they often came and asked us to cut for them.[88]

This account included interesting descriptions of partial tattoo patterns on both face and buttocks; a serrated pattern (either cut or tattooed) around the edge of the tongue; thinning hair and some minor skin infections; and an overall prevalence of strong, healthy people without evident disease or defects. The French journal keepers were agreed that these people often lived to a great age, usually keeping all of their hair (which did not whiten much) and their teeth, which according to Crozet were 'more used up than spoiled'. Their descriptions of grey-headed, wrinkled men suggest that the age structure of the population may have included more elderly individuals (probably aged between fifty and seventy) than was usual in Europe at that time, and that the people were generally taller, more robust and healthier than those in other populations with which the French were familiar, either in Europe or French India.

Crozet's comment about teeth being 'more used up than spoiled' probably referred to the harsh patterns of dental wear that resulted from chewing shellfish and fernroot fibres. He added, 'we did not find any traces showing them to be subject to smallpox or venereal diseases . . . neither pock-mark nor cicatrice is to be seen on their skins. There were, however, amongst our crews several sailors who suffered from the usual diseases, which they communicated to the people of the country.'[89] Roux, on the other hand, claimed that venereal diseases were already established on shore (which was not unlikely in view of the *Endeavour*'s recent visit), and that some of the women showed signs of the ravages of these diseases. One may, however, doubt his assertion that none of their crews brought such diseases with them, despite the confidence of the ships' surgeons that 'they had all been cured in the five months we had been at sea.'[90]

According to de Montaison, the women were shorter and less well built than the men, although he added that some were very beautiful, with shapely breasts and quite white skin. Crozet also commented that a number of the people were as white as the sailors, and that several of them had red hair.

Clothing

According to Crozet, both men and married women in the bay wore their hair tied up with plaited fibre into a tuft on the top of their heads, which was then 'cut off in the form of a round brush an inch or two above the cord; for want of scissors for this operation they make use of a shell the edges of which they sharpen'.[91] This style, using a head-tuft rather than a topknot, was also depicted in the 1642 drawing of Taitapu men from Tasman's voyage. This tuft was sometimes dressed with fish oil and powdered with red ochre, and in the case of chiefs it was also decorated with four white feathers. The girls wore their hair loose and cut at about shoulder length. According to Crozet:

> the ears of the men are pierced like those of the women, and they all equally adorn them with mother-of-pearl and lustrous shells, or with feathers, or with small dog-bones. Some wear around their necks pieces of jade of a very fine green of various forms joined together, engraved or carved. Some of this jade glitters very much. They sometimes wear mother-of-pearl, pieces of wood, or bundles of feathers. The women wear necklaces made like rosaries, composed of broken pieces of equal lengths of white teeth alternately with black irregular tubes; others wear necklaces made of small very hard black stones of a fruit I do not know.[92]

Both men and women had 'mantles' or cloaks that they wore over their shoulders, fastened by a plait around the neck, leaving the chest and stomach exposed; or around the waist, held up by a belt plaited either from flax or from 'rushes' (perhaps kuta). Fine cloaks might be 'woven in each corner with threads of various colours in the manner of our stitchwork' (evidently a description of taaniko weaving), or in the case of chiefs, decorated with fringes or well-matched strips of dogskin, or feathers. In cold weather the chiefs often wore their dogskin cloaks reversed, with the fur turned in to keep them warm. The shaggy rain-cloak was described as a long garment bristling with long strings of very coarse flax, which shed the rain like a roof. Quite often the men wore nothing at all, although in that case they tried to hide their genitals from the French. They were, however, very proud of their tattoos, which they willingly displayed. These included S-shaped patterns on the backs of their hands, leg and face tattoos for both men and women, and 'ermine-shaped marks' on their foreheads. According to Crozet, these patterns were pricked into the skin and then rubbed with powdered charcoal to make them indelible.

Food

The basic food in the bay, at least from May to July, was fernroot. The ferns were taller and had larger roots than the bracken fern in France, and their roots were collected in a process that involved first burning off the stalks and then digging up the ground with a digging stick (koo). The firing of fernroot might explain why in so many districts the coastal hills and slopes were relatively bare of vegetation. Repeated firings, both to clear the slopes for gardens and for fernroot gathering, would have discouraged secondary growth. Crozet described the fernroot-digging stick as a pointed spade with a footpiece lashed on to the shaft. Once it had been driven into the ground, two men worked it around to raise a large clod of earth. The roots were then shaken out of the earth, collected up and put on a stand to dry for several days in the sun. After that they were ready to be lightly roasted over a fire, pounded between two stones or with a wooden mallet, and chewed to extract the bitter, pasty juice. When the people were short of food they ate the fibres, but at other times they spat them out. According to Le Dez:

> to judge by the outward appearance of these people, this food must be wholesome and nourishing; they need quite a long time to eat a lot of it and so they spend a long time over their meals, which they usually take in common . . . It is most amusing to see fifteen or so of them gathered together, men, women and children, vying with one another in putting pieces of this root on the fire, beating it over and over again and chewing it with gusto.[93]

Crozet reported that the people ate twice a day, once in the morning and again at sunset, and that they ate great quantities of food when they came on board the ships, especially ships' biscuits. It is possible that because the usual source of carbohydrates, fernroot, had to be eaten in lengthy sessions to get an adequate diet, similar European foods (bread and ships' biscuits) were also eaten in large quantities. According to Crozet, the people were very fond of fat and would eat tallow as a tasty treat, which they took from the sounding-lead or elsewhere on board ship. They also liked sugar and sweet drinks, including sweetened tea and sugar, but disliked wine, any sort of liquor, and salt. They drank vast quantities of water, which Crozet attributed to the dryness of fernroot, their staple food, and chewed a kind of green gum, which the French described as 'very heating', for its flavour.

After fernroot, fish and shellfish were the other staple items in the diet. Fish were either wrapped in leaves and cooked on the coals of a fire, on a skewer over the fire or in an earth oven, along with sweet potatoes, yams, gourds, a 'couch-like root' or the meat of birds (including quails, ducks and other aquatic birds) dogs, rats or enemies. Kitchen shelters in the villages had an oven hole in the ground about eighteen inches to two feet in diameter and about a foot deep. Stones were laid in this hole with a fire on top, and then flat stones were placed on the fire. The food was wrapped in several layers of leaves, and when the stones were hot enough the fire was scraped out and bundles of food laid on the bottom stones. The other stones were placed on top, covered with earth then sprinkled periodically with water. The food cooked quite quickly in these earth ovens and kept all of its flavour.

Fishing

The local fish-hooks were made of wood, mother-of-pearl (paaua or turban shell) or other shells, and some were very large, seven or eight inches across the opening, perhaps for catching sharks. The people preferred the French hooks, however, and eagerly sought these in trading exchanges. Their fishing-lines were 'knotted with the same adroitness as those of the cleverest fisherman of our sea-ports', while the seine nets were often 500 feet long, made of 'reeds' or a well-twisted thread that was coloured red with fish oil. This suggests that nets may have been steeped in a mixture of red ochre and oil, perhaps to preserve the fibres or as a sign of their tapu. Like the nets at Kapowairua, these seines had light wood floats along the top and stone sinkers either in a woven sheath along their base, or individually tied on.

The canoes were generally fifteen, thirty-five or forty feet long and well-made with 'lines well calculated for speed'. A fishing canoe about twenty-five feet long and two and a half to three feet wide carried seven or eight men, while a war

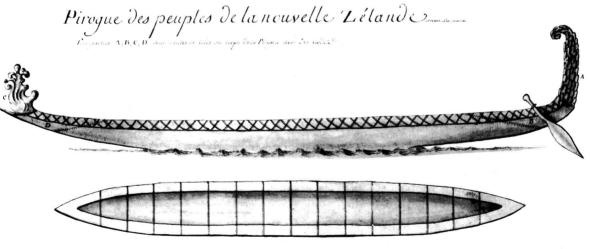

'Canoe of the people of New Zealand' is a crude sketch that inaccurately represents the stern and prow carvings.

canoe eighty to 100 feet long and seven to eight feet wide might carry over 100 warriors. Such war canoes wre held in common by a village, and had decking, benches for the paddlers, gunwhale planks, high carved stern posts and prows, and were painted with a mixture of oil and red ochre. According to Le Dez, the stern-post on such a canoe might be two feet wide at the base and eight to ten feet high, completely covered with openwork carving 'like pieces of Gothic decoration which we see in our old churches'.[94] This was adorned with a plume of black feathers or a 'sort of apron made of feathers'. The paddles were so shaped as to add by the elasticity of the blade to the force of the stroke, and a chief's paddles were finely carved on the back. They did not see sails on these canoes.

Two sketches of canoes that have been attributed to Marion's voyage give crude, rather unconvincing representations of local craft, probably sketched from memory or on the basis of the journal descriptions.

Shellfishing

The women and girls collected shellfish daily from the rocks, putting a rush apron around their waists and carrying a rush basket in which to carry the shellfish they found.

Hunting

Crozet reported that the only local methods for capturing game were the net and the running noose, and that these techniques were used to capture quail, wild ducks, wood pigeon (kuukupa) and other species of birds. Bows and arrows were unknown. Du Clesmeur, however, added that birds were also killed with 'a spear of fern-branch at the end of which is attached the bone from a ray's tail. So armed, they glide as softly as possible into the woods and surprise the birds as they sit on the branch.'[95]

Gardening

It seems that the French did not travel inland as far as the garden lands around Omaapere and elsewhere, for Crozet said that they saw only 'some small fields planted with potatoes [kuumara], gourds, aloes-pite [possibly a variety of tii (cabbage tree)], and very small flax'.[96] Otherwise the countryside seemed to be lying fallow. His comments suggest that tii trees may have been planted in gardens, and he and other French journal writers were definite that flax was also cultivated:

> They cultivate flax and know how to ret it. After retting they beat it in order to detach the hard or woody portion, they then comb their thread with combs made of large sea-shells, and lastly they have a sort of crude and simple wheel and distaff for spinning their thread. They make also a thread of five or six strands of hair that is very strong. Finally they have a method of working which seems to be the commencement of that followed by our weavers, and by which they make cloth of very close tissue and of good wear.[97]

Crozet's statement about the use of a wheel and distaff was evidently a guess, for no such device is known from traditional times. It is possible, however, that he had seen a pump drill lying about and mistaken its use.[98] In his list of foods, in addition to fernroot, sweet potatoes and yams, Le Dez mentioned 'another root like couch grass, only fatter', which he explained was 'as thick as a quill, white, floury and full of threads[99] (possibly poohue or convulvulus).[100] Crozet also commented that gourds were eaten when very young, but otherwise were emptied out and dried when ripe, to make containers that could carry up to ten to twelve pints of water.

Tools

Woodworking tools included adzes hafted to a piece of curved wood, axes, and small greenstone chisels hafted to a handle. According to Roux:

> In all the various places I have been to in this country I have seen only an industrious people. They make their tools of a stone resembling marble, very black and very hard [possibly gabbro]. They make axes and adzes of it. They use the first for cutting down trees but they manage this only after a great deal of difficulty. To lessen the work it gives them, they dig away the earth right around the tree that they want to fell and set fire to it. They take precautions to ensure that the flame burns only the foot. When they have thus felled it, they rough it down with their axes and finish it with their adzes; these stone tools cut quite well. Their chisels are made of a green stone like the one they carve their god from. This stone is extremely hard. They make one end very sharp and fit the chisel to a handle made of a small piece of wood. They attach it in such a way that it does not move when it is struck; they use it for carving and for doing delicate work. All these tools are very well made; they use shells for carving and piercing these stones which are at least as hard as agate; it must take them a pretty long time to carve the figure I have been referring to.[101]

On the basis of this account it appears that stone adzes were hafted both as axes and as adzes for woodworking; and that shells were used in some way to carve and pierce both gabbro and greenstone.

Carving

Le Dez commented that the people of the bay were both patient and skilful in woodwork. 'The posts of their huts, their weapons, their paddles even their tools for working the land — everthing is decorated with a few carvings and I saw boxes, little figures and other trinkets which seem to bear witness to their overriding taste and their principal occupation.'

It seems that like Kapowairua, the Bay of Islands had an active carving tradition in 1772. Chiefs' houses were ornamented with carvings including carved posts in the interior, and in the centre of the village 'parade ground', or marae, stood a carved wooden figure with eyes, a great mouth and a protruding tongue. Weapons including 'lances', 'javelins' and 'pikes'; war trumpets; agricultural tools; 'boxes' (probably papa hou or feather boxes) and paddles were also evidently carved.

413

Weapons and warfare

The various types of spears ('lances', 'pikes', 'sagaies', 'javelins') included some about twenty feet long (huata) which were used to defend the approaches to the palisades of a paa; others about ten feet long with a serrated point which were thrown by hand (tarerarera); and still smaller spears about two feet long (pere), which were thrown inaccurately but quite long distances by 'a sort of whip [kotaha] which works like a sling except for the rotating movement'. According to Le Dez, all of these spears had a very sharp point notched about half an inch from the tip so that it would break off in the body.

Staffs or 'bludgeons' were made of a very hard wood or whalebone. Le Dez described three varieties of this type of weapon:

> Some look quite like an axe and to strike someone they use the back of it, which has been made as sharp as possible without weakening the wood too much [tewha-tewha]. Others are shaped like a pick [possibly pou tangata]; others still like an oar five to six feet long [pouwhenua]. They are all decorated with carvings and pointed at one end.[102]

'Clubs' or 'tomahawks' (mere, patu) were made of greywacke or greenstone about sixteen to eighteen inches long and shaped into an oval with sharp edges, with a handle pierced by a hole for a wrist-cord. These weapons were tucked into the waist-belt and were used to dispatch an enemy who had already been wounded.

War trumpets (puukaea) were made of wood and 'gave out a very disagreeable sound similar to that of shepherds' horns'.

As Crozet (or his editor Rochon) rancorously remarked in his retrospective account:

> All these murderous instruments are carved and worked with care, and the savages possess large quantities of them. Nevertheless all their arms are ridiculous and contemptible when opposed to men armed in European fashion: fifty fusiliers with sufficient ammunition, and who might have to revenge themselves on these people, could without danger destroy them like wild beasts and entirely exterminate them.[103]

Le Dez added that the people were evidently often at war with each other. Most of their villages were fortified (a report borne out by the archaeological evidence from the bay, which shows many fortified headland villages), and at the time of their visit they found several villages that had been abandoned or destroyed. He said:

> I imagine their warfare must be cruel, because we saw neither slaves nor any sign of slavery. What then happened to the inhabitants of the villages we destroyed? I think that they behave amongst themselves as they did towards us. They try to surprise each other and then they massacre each other mercilessly. Then those who manage to escape go wherever they can and leave the sea shore to the victor, that being the part they usually fight over because of the fish and sea-food.
>
> I think that they rarely find themselves in open country. If they do they occupy the heights and when they are within sagaie-range they hurl them at one another

until one of the parties, weakened or intimidated, takes flight or until, well worked up against each other, it becomes a general fray, which I think is quite rare, and it is then bravery and physical force which decides the victory. They use their lances or bludgeons, or they seize each other round the body and fall to the ground and the man who has the upper hand draws his club, which is always in his belt, and splits open his enemy's skull. They explained that to us while we were friends.[104]

Roux concluded that these people were both courageous and enterprising in battle, making war on each other for quite minor reasons and keeping no prisoners. He reported that a chief with whom he had discussed the matter 'gave me to understand that after killing them they put them in the fire, and when they are cooked they eat them. Seeing that that revolted and horrified me, he began to laugh and went on reaffirming what he had just said.'[105] As during Cook's visits to Uawa and the Bay of Islands, local people responded dismissively to European (and Tahitian) criticisms of their custom of eating enemies.

In summary, the French accounts suggest that open combat was relatively rare, with most fighting taking the form of ambush or an attack on fortified positions. Le Dez's comment that sea resources were often fought over is well supported by the evidence of tribal history. It is interesting that he and Roux seem to be agreed that in the Bay of Islands in 1772, captives were killed and not kept as slaves.

Fortified villages

Crozet's 'Description of the Villages of the Northern Portion of New Zealand' is by far the best eye-witness description of the lay-out of fortified villages in the early contact period:

> All the villages are situated on steep cliffs jutting out into the sea, and we noticed that where the inclination of the ground was not great, it had been made steep by hand. We had much difficulty in climbing up, and the savages had often to help us by holding our hands. On arrival at the top, we found first of all a palisade formed of piles, driven straight and deeply into the ground, seven or eight feet high, and the ground well beaten down and grassed at the foot of the palisades. Then followed a ditch about six feet broad, and about five to six feet deep, but this ditch was only placed on the land side, where an enemy might approach. There was then a second palisade, which, like the first, served to enclose the whole village into an oblong shape. The entrance gates are not placed opposite each other. After entering the first circuit one has to go further along a narrow path to look for the entrance through the second palisade. The gates are very small.
>
> From that side from which they fear attacks they have a sort of outworks, equally well palisaded and surrounded by ditches, and which will hold four hundred to five hundred men. This work is only a palisaded oblong and is placed outside the village to act as a defence to the entrance. Inside the village at the side of the gate, there is a sort of timber platform, about 25 feet high, the posts being about 18 to 20 inches in diameter and sunk solidly in the ground. The people climb on to this sort of advance fort by means of a post with footsteps cut into it. A considerable collection of stones and short javelins is always kept up there, and when

they fear an attack, they picket the sentinels there. The platforms are roomy enough to hold fifteen or twenty fighting men. These two outworks are generally placed at the outermost gate, and help to defend it as well as to prevent the ditch being crossed.

The interior of the village is composed of two rows of houses ranged side by side along the two sides of the palisades which form the enclosure, and every house is furnished with a penthouse, which serves as a kitchen. The savages eat their food under these sheds and never take a meal inside the house. The space which divides the two rows of houses, and which is more or less roomy, according to the lay of the ground, serves as a sort of parade ground, and extends the whole length of the village. This parade ground is raised about a foot higher than the surrounding ground on which the houses stand. It is raised by means of soil brought there and beaten down; no grass is to be seen on it and the whole place is kept extremely clean. This whole space between the two rows of houses is only occupied by three public buildings, of which the first and nearest to the village gate is the general magazine of arms. A little distance off is the food storehouse, and still further the storehouse for nets, all the implements used in fishing, as well as all the necessary material for making the nets, etc. At about the extremity of the village there are some large posts set up in the form of gallows, where the provisions are dried before being placed in the stores.

In the centre of this parade ground there is a piece of wooden sculpture representing a hideous figure very badly carved, on which one can only recognize a rude head, eyes, a great mouth, very much like the jaws of a toad and out of which protrudes an immoderately long tongue. All the other portions of the body are still more shapeless, with the exception of the genital parts, occasionally of one sex, occasionally of the other, which are represented in greater detail. This piece of carving is part of a huge pile sunk deeply into the ground.

We entered with the chiefs into the first magazine where the arms are stored; we found a surprisingly large quantity of small wooden spears, some simply with sharpened points, others carved in the form of serpents' tongues, and these carvings continued for the length of a foot from the tip of the javelin, others furnished with very sharp points made from the bones of the whale. We also found bludgeons or clubs made of some very hard wood and of ribs of the whale which are still harder; spears which seemed made on the model of our ancient halberds for spearing at one end and clubbing at the other, these lances being all of a very hard wood and fairly well carved; tomahawks of stone or of bones of whale, the tomahawks being highly polished, well sharpened and neatly carved; sticks furnished at one extremity with knotted cord for throwing darts in the same way as we throw stones with slings; and some varieties of battle-axes in hard wood and fairly well designed for killing people.

In this same magazine we found a collection of their common implements, such as axes, adzes, chisels made of various very hard stones such as jade, granite, and basalt. The magazines are generally about 20 to 25 feet long by 10 to 12 broad. In the interior there is a row of posts which support the ridgeboard of the roof. The savages arranged their arms round these posts like a stand of arms according to variety.

In the second magazine, where the savages keep their food in common, we found sacks of potatoes, bundles of suspended fern-root, various testaceous fishes, cooked, drawn from the shell and threaded on blades of rushes and hung up; a large quantity of fragments of big fish of every variety, cooked, wrapped up in packets in fern leaf and hung up, and an abundance of very large calabashes always kept full of water for village use. This storehouse is almost as big and of the same shape as the magazine house.

The third storehouse contains the rope, fishing lines, the flax for making rope, thread and rushes for making string, an immense quantity of fishhooks of every size from the smallest to the largest, stones cut to serve as lead weights, and pieces of wood cut to serve as floats. In this warehouse they keep all the paddles of their war canoes; it is there that they make their nets, and when they have finished one they carry it to the extremity of the village, or every net in the form of a seine to a separate cabin.

These public storehouses as well as the private houses are made of timber, well squared and fastened by mortise and tenon and pinned together; they are generally oblong in form; instead of planks for the walls of their houses, they make use of well-made straw matting, which they ply doubled or trebled one on top of the other, and which shelter them from wind and rain. The straw mattings also serve as roofs to the houses, but in this case they are made of a sort of very hard grass which grows in the marshes, and which the natives manipulate with great skill. Every house has only one door about three feet high and two feet broad, which they close from the inside by means of a latch very much like the iron one which we use in France for closing our gates. Above the door there is a small window about two feet square furnished with a rush trellis; inside the house there is no flooring, but they take the precaution to raise the soil about a foot and beat it down well so as to avoid damp. In every house there is a square of boards well joined together about six feet long and two feet broad; on these planks are laid seven or eight inches of grass or fern leaves well dried, and upon which they sleep. They have no other beds. In the middle of the house there is always a small fire to drive out the dampness. These houses are very small, being for the most part not more than seven or eight feet long by five or six feet broad. The houses of the chiefs are larger; they are ornamented with pieces of carved wood, and the posts in the interior are also carved. The only furniture we found in these houses were fishhooks of mother-of-pearl and of wood and bone, nets, fishing lines, some calabashes full of water, stone implements such as we had seen in the common storehouses, mantles and other clothing hanging on the partition.

The whole of the villages which we saw during our two months' stay in the Bay of Islands appeared to be constructed on the same plan without any well-defined differences. The construction and form of the private houses as well as those of the chiefs were the same in all the villages; they were all palisaded and placed on high cliffs. At the extremity of every village and on the point which jutted furthest into the sea there was a public place of accommodation for all the inhabitants.[106]

Much of the detail in this account is corroborated by the other French writers, and by a unique pair of plans of Paeroa paa on Moturua Island. These show a palisaded hollow 'outworks' in front of the outer ditch (according to Le Dez these ditches were between twelve to fifteen feet wide and ten feet deep); a rampart backed by a fighting stage with its ladder; and a double row of palisades along the sides of the headland with staggered pairs of gates which allowed entry from narrow tracks along the cliffs. The central 'parade ground' (marae) was raised up with beaten earth and kept meticulously clean. It held various structures including a weapon rack, a chief's house which doubled as an armoury (which held adzes, axes and chisels as well as spears, hand clubs, 'tomahawks' and 'battleaxes', arrayed around the posts by type); a large store-house for food

Plan d'une forteresse zellandoise

de l'isle Marion

1 ouvrage avancé et palissadé
2 fossé sec
3 Rempart
4 Cavalier
5 treilli pour mettre les armes
6 les champs de palissades
7 Case du chef
8 Grand magazin
9 treilli pour pêcher le fougere
10 Postes
11 magazins a vivres
12 Poteau ou fourche de bois
13 ouvriers pour enduire... dans le village, il est vis à vis... long des palissades qu'il n'y a que la largeur du pied

Espace de place d'arme

Profil par la ligne A B

Echelle de 10 Toises

La disposition de leur fortification montre que... qui... s'approche... longuelle font en guerre... ils ont toujours un... facilitaire sur le Cavalier et sur les montagnes voisines... en avant ou l'echange I ils font que leurs palissades puis pour obliger l'ennemi a s'exposer par petites bandes...

toute cette côte escarpée n'est point praticable qu'à celle qui... longuelle... escarpée... est... l'echange I...

(including 'potatoes' in sacks, bundles of fernroot, dried fish and shellfish hung up, and large calabashes of water); a 'public penthouse or shed', which must have been the store-house for nets, lines, sinkers and paddles; and a carved head in the shape of a box, raised on a post, which was probably a place for offerings. At the end of the headland was a fernroot-drying rack and various small store-houses for nets, which had the same shape as other store-houses for kuumara, yams and fernroot. Along either side of the marae were houses and kitchen sheds.

According to marginal notes on these plans, sentries were posted on the fighting stages and on nearby hills in times of war, and stakes were sometimes driven or ditches dug into the ground in front of the palisaded outworks to force an attacking party to divide into several groups. The latrines were sited right at the end of the village, where the cliffs jutted out over the sea. From the amount of

Opposite: *One of two plans of Paeroa paa on Moturua in the Bay of Islands has the following key and captions:*

1   *Outer palisaded work*
2   *Dry ditch*
3   *Rampart*
4   *Raised platform*
5   *Trellis for holding arms*
6   *Rows of palisades*
7   *Chief's hut*
8   *Large storehouse*
9   *Trellis for drying fern*
10   *Gates*
11   *Storehouses for nets*
12   *Stake in the form of a box*
13   *Paths for entering the village; in places along the palisades it is only as wide as a foot.*

Overleaf: *A second plan of Paeroa paa, exhibiting some subtle variations from the first, with the accompanying key:*

E   *Outer palisaded work*
F   *Dry ditch*
P   *Rampart*
R   *Cavalier or raised platform*
1   *Ladder to the said platform*
2   *Second row of palisades*
3   *Rack on which to put the weapons*
4   *Chief's house also used as a magazine for weapons*
5   *Gates*
6   *Large storehouse with food supplies, nets etc.*
7   *Stake with a really hideous head on it in the shape of a box.*
8   *Public penthouse or shed*
9   *Trellis supported by a stake for putting fernroot out to dry*
10   *Small storehouses for nets*
     They have some in the same shape for keeping potatoes, yams and fernroot in. Like their huts, they are waterproof
X   *A little track for entering the village which has parts along the palisades which are no more than a foot-wide so that if one fell*

E Ouvrage avancé et pallisadé
F Fossé Sec
P Rempart
R Cavallier
1 Echelle dudit Cavallier
2 Second rang de Pallisade
3 Trelly pour mettre les armes
4 Maison du Chef Servant aussi de
   Magasin pour les Armes
5 Portes
6 Grand Magasin aux vivres et Seines &
7 Poteau ayant une teste fort hideuse
   et en Forme de Boîte

Plan d'un
de l'Js

Village Zelandois Marion.

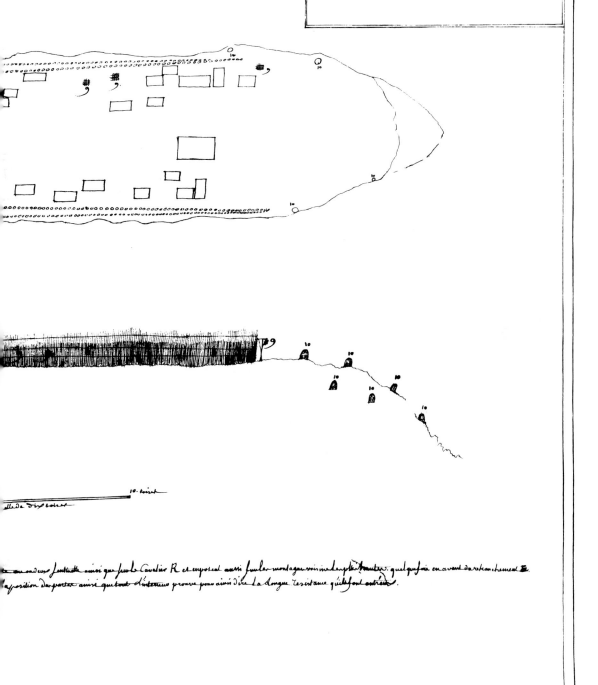

10. toise

... sur deux sentinelle ainsi que par le Cavalier R et exposés aussi sur les montagnes voisine le plus haute ... quelquefois en avant du retranchement E. ... l'exposition des portes ainsi que tout l'intérieur prouve pour ainsi dire la longue résistance qu'ils font entre ...

food and property kept in communal stores in these villages it seems likely that they were permanently occupied, although it is possible that the people had simply shifted into their paa during the French visit for reasons of security. Du Clesmeur added that in their houses each of the chiefs kept 'an intricately carved square box, with a sliding lid, for storing the tufts of white feathers with which they alone have the right to adorn themselves', a good description of papa hou, or feather boxes. According to Le Dez, about a dozen people slept in each of these houses at night, with their heads resting on each other.

Government (Social Relations)

The French accounts described each substantial village as having its own 'chief or king who exercises full and complete authority over his subjects. These chiefs seem [to be] independent of each other.'[107] According to Le Dez, people often presented the gifts they were given by the French to their chiefs, who evidently put them into the communal store-houses. When Te Kauri's village was ransacked the French found many of these items in one of the large stores on the central marae. The French were puzzled in retrospect that they had seen none of the gifts Cook had left in the bay just three years earlier, but probably by then those items had been redistributed to groups outside of the district.

According to de Montaison, the people 'appear to live harmoniously in their villages. The young people greatly respect the old people.'[108] These comments indicate both the esteem in which kaumaatua (elders, both male and female) were held and the relative tranquillity of domestic life. European accounts from the early contact period suggested that compared with Europe, Maori domestic life was relatively free of casual violence, for children were rarely hit and any harm to them was likely to provoke muru (plundering) raids from their kinsfolk. Crozet commented:

> [the women] seemed to be good mothers and showed affection for their offspring. I have often seen them play with the children, caress them, chew the fern root, pick at the stringy parts, and then take it out of their mouth to put it into that of their nurslings. The men were also very fond of and kind to their children. The chief Tacoury sometimes brought his son on board; he was about fourteen years old with a pretty face, and the father seemed to love him very much.[109]

Children were suckled until they had teeth and could walk, and their parents carried them around with them or placed them on mats or dogskins on the floor of their houses. Fathers, like mothers, looked after the physical needs of their children and treated them indulgently. Children appeared to be relatively few, however, and Crozet commented that 'at the sight of these big, hardy and well made men, one suspects that they do not preserve those children who are born sickly or deformed'.[110]

The French writers thought that the men seemed quite indifferent to their women, allowing them to have sexual liaisons without jealousy (a comment contradicted, however, by the explicit prohibition on affairs with married women mentioned earlier), and that the women were very submissive. This impression appears to have been particularly based on the observation that men and women ate separately, the women serving the men their food. Roux commented, 'Indeed, I saw some of these women be so servile as to put the piece of food into their husband's mouth [while] the men stayed sitting quite calmly allowing themselves to be served while they talked to other men, paying no attention to those who were serving them'[111] — a misinterpretation of the custom of feeding a tapu person by hand so that their tapu was not transferred from their own hands to the food (which was noa, or common).

The French were also critical of the local division of labour, saying the men made women do all the heavy work. According to their accounts, women collected and carried bundles of fernroot dug up by the men, carried water up the hills to the fortified villages, collected shellfish, sometimes fished with seine nets, cooked and served food to the men and wove clothing for themselves and their husbands, and cultivated and planted the gardens; while men made nets, did most of the fishing and hunted birds, built houses and canoes, dug fernroot and practised weapon-handling.

Marriage did not appear to be formally celebrated, and men often had several wives, a practice the French attributed to the quantities of fish they ate, which they held to be 'a very warming [aphrodisiac] food'. Polygyny was in fact an aristocratic privilege, with high-born wives who brought mana and diplomatic alliances, and commoner wives who worked to support the kin-group's reputation for wealth and hospitality.

When people died, their kinsfolk mourned them for several days, lacerating their faces and bodies as a sigh of grief, 'assembling in the house of the defunct to weep and utter cries of despair, in recounting his deeds and howling at the end of every account'.[112] Ordinary men, women and children were reportedly buried at sea, while warriors were buried in the earth and spears and javelins were stuck into the burial mound as trophies. On one occasion Le Dez gave a chief some bread and he broke off a piece and put it by a stake nearby, which evidently marked a grave. This may have been a sharing of food with the dead.

Religion

Crozet commented on this topic:

> We did not remain long enough in New Zealand, and I was always too much occupied with the wants of our vessels, to be able to acquire satisfactory notions regarding the worship and belief of the savages. I have, however, sufficient grounds for believing that they have some religion, and these are as follows:
> 1. They have in their language a word which expresses the Divinity; they call it Ea-Toue [atua], a name which describes one who makes the earth tremble.
> 2. When they were asked questions on this subject, they raised their eyes and hands towards heaven with demonstrations of respect and fear, which indicated their belief in a Supreme Being.
> 3. I have already said that in the middle of every village there is a carved figure which appears to represent the tutelary god of the village. In their private

houses are to be found similar figures like little idols placed in positions of honour. Several savages carried similar figures carved in jade or wood around their necks . . .

4. I noticed that the savages who came to sleep on board our vessels were in the habit of communing with themselves in the middle of the night, to sit up and mumble. a few words which resembled a prayer in which they answered one another and appeared to chant. This sort of prayer generally lasted eight or ten minutes.[113]

Crozet's remarks are superficial, but the references to carved figures in the centre of the village as well as inside houses, and carved 'tiki' in greenstone and wood are interesting. Le Dez thought that in war dances the warriors tried to imitate these figures, widening their mouths and sticking out their tongues. The brief exchange of chanted karakia in the middle of the night is reminiscent of the fisherboys on board the *Endeavour* in Tuuranga-nui in 1769, of songs or genealogies recited in the dark by modern elders, or of contemporary Ringatuu services where karakia are still performed at night.

Music

Crozet reported that the people had two or three varieties of flute

from which they extract fairly sweet but at the same time discordant sounds by breathing into them with their nostrils. I have heard them play on those instruments, especially in the evening when they were locked up in their villages, and it appeared to me they sometimes dance to the sound of the flutes.[114]

According to du Clesmeur:

Their music is as monotonous as that of the other Indians, if it is not even more so. We saw only 3 instruments; one being a sort of trumpet [puukaea] which can be heard from a great distance and which I think is used to declare war or summon help. I formed this opinion because we heard the sound of it the day we burned the first village. They also have a type of flute made of two pieces firmly tied together which is blown into at the thick end [puutorino]; the small end and three other holes are stopped up with the fingers and are used to vary the tones a little. The third is more or less the same but much smaller and is played with the nose.[115]

This last instrument was probably the nguru, which, according to ethnomusicologists, can be played only with the mouth.

The local people were evidently fond of singing, which they did in a deep voice, and they often tried to imitate French songs. Le Dez recorded one of their songs (possibly a children's nonsense ditty) as follows:

Qui caye poro, qui quo qui caye pororé, pororé, tigarati, tigarato, tigarata, y a ta, y a ta, concouré pororé, pororé, camoteca yoco.[116]

They also loved to dance, 'singing alternatively warlike and lascivious songs' and dancing so heavily (presumably haka, or war-dances) on the decks of the French ships that on occasion the sailors feared the decking might collapse.

Language

Both Le Dez[117] and du Clesmeur[118] collected vocabularies of Maori, and according to Le Dez, 'there is as little difference between those two languages [Maori and Tahitian] as between those of different provinces in England'. The words can be listed along with more accurate transcriptions of the Maori words where these can be established:

Le Dez		*[Modern transcription]*
Man	Tanée	[taane]
hair	hépoquo	[he upoko (head)]
forehead	eräé	[he rae]
head	hopoquo	[he upoko]
eyebrows	toucamata	[tukemata]
eyes	canonée	[kanohi]
cheeks	Paparigua	[paapaaringa]
nose	aeïou	[he ihu]
mouth	houtou	[ngutu]
lips	hénoutou	[he ngutu]
teeth	hanicho	[he niho]
tongue	ariéro	[arero]
palate	corocoro	[korokoro (throat)]
chin	hécaoné	[he kauwae]
throat	hécaqui	[he kakii]
beard	paréaou	[——]
shoulder	pocoouioui	[pokohiwi]
arm	tapoutapou	[taputapu (intensely tapu)]
hand	hé parou	[paru (dirty)]
fingers	mahicoucou	[maikuku (finger or toenail)]
thumb	coromatou	[koromatua (thumb, great toe)]
index finger	mahio	[maihao]
middle finger	logohiti	[——]
ring finger	coumara	[——]
little finger	coumata	[——]
stomach	héouma	[he uma (chest)]
nipples	théou	[te uu]
navel	hépito	[he pito]
belly	copou	[koopuu]
penis	hérao	[he raho (testicle)]
private parts	héourou	[he ure]
thighs	theoua	[te kuuhaa]
knees	touripona	[turipona (knee joint)]
legs	nëaouye	[ngaa wae]
heels	hétouqué	[he tuke]
foot	ahéparépa	[raparapa]
back	touhara	[tuara]
the behind	erééré	[eneene]
woman	aéné	[wahine]
womb	epouta	[perhaps e puta (emerge)]
to kiss	tétoré	[——]

to piss	mimi	[mimi]
to shit	toutaë	[tutae]
to blow (the nose)	aïoupé	[hupe (nose)]
to drink	éouaye	[inu wai (to drink water)]
to eat	caye	[kai]
to sleep	hémohé	[he moe]
to give	hetou	[hoatu]
fish	ica	[ika]
musket	tapou	[te puu]
their cloaks	coéao	[kahu]
screw pine	mouca	[muka (prepared flax fibre)]
canoe	ouaca	[waka]
paddle	öé	[hoe]
to scratch	théoutou	[perhaps kutu (lice)]
lice	nia	[riha]
enough	tati	[kaati]
to kill	maté	[mate]
bread	taro	[taro (sp.)]
water	taonaye	[perhaps te one (beach)]
sweet potatoes	ceye	[perhaps kai (food)]
clams	pipi	[pipi (cockles)]
conger eels	ahiquoquiro	[he kooiro]
fish-hooks	matao	[matau]
yes	aei — lifting the head a little	[ae]
lobsters	conië	[——]
dogs	couri	[kurii]
axes and chisels	toqui	[toki]
nails	ouaou	[whao]
calabashes	houé	[hue]
sun	erra	[he raa]
moon	hémarama	[maarama]
ashore, over there	terra	[teeraa]
to go below	enticouri	[——]
I want to go away	qui o ouaye	[——]
tomorrow	apopo or abobo	[apoopoo]
come!	Eremaye	[haere mai]
ears	haitaringa	[he taringa]
there is not	cayoré	[kahore]
birds	vourou	[perhaps huruhuru (feathers)][117]

Du Clesmeur

killed	matté	[mate]
fish	ycä	[ika]
water	tavay	[te wai]
potatoes	cay	[kai (food)]
shellfish	pipi	[pipi (cockles)]
clothes	cammée	[——]
fish-hook	matao	[matau]
tomorrow	apopo	[apoopoo]

to urinate	mimy	[mimi]
good	carreca	[ka reka (sweet)]
bird	mannou	[manu]
dog	courry	[kurii]
there is not	cayore	[kahore]
their stone chisel	toquy	[toki]
come to me	yeremay	[haere mai]
canoe	avac	[waka]
over there	terra	[teeraa]
woman	aenée	[wahine]
man	toumanou	[———]
enemies	quinos	[kino (bad)]
friends	pays	[pai (good)]
to eat	taro	[taro (sp.)]
musket	tapon	[te puu][118]

Most of these words refer to body parts or to commonplace and highly visible entities or actions, and collectively they indicate that communications between the French and local people were rudimentary. The absence of phrases suggests that most likely the French had a very limited grasp of the syntax of the language. Le Dez described local speech:

> When they speak they are very appealing, making movements with their heads and eyes which are fixed on the person they are speaking to, drawling on the final sounds a little. Their language seems to me soft and easy; the vowels are often repeated and the consonants rarely used. I even noticed that the words never end with a consonant.[119]

Character

Accounts of the character of the local people by the various French writers reveal at least as much about their own personalities and their reactions to the disastrous expulsion from the Bay of Islands as about Maori characteristics. Crozet's comments, for instance, provide both an angry repudiation of philosophical ideas of the 'noble savage' and a justification of the conduct of the French expedition in the bay:

> I cannot believe that there can be on the face of the earth greater traitors than these savages. I can affirm that not even on the slightest occasion had these savages any reason to complain of us. The friendship which they showed us was carried to the extremest familiarity; the chiefs on boarding our vessels entered our rooms without ceremony, and slept on our beds, examining all our furniture piece by piece; they asked about the meaning of our pictures, and of our mirrors, of which they of course understood nothing. Indeed, they spent whole days with us with the greatest demonstrations of friendship and of confidence. Two days before murdering him they had of their free will proclaimed M. Marion Grand Chief, and on the day on which they had decided to murder him and his companions, in order to feast on them afterwards, they brought him some very fine turbots as a present.
>
> Here then we have a picture of these primitive men, so extolled by those who do not know them, and who attribute gratuitously to them more virtues and less

vices than possessed by men whom they are pleased to call artificial, because for-sooth education has perfected their reason. For my part I maintain that there is amongst all the animals of creation none more ferocious and dangerous for human beings than the primitive and savage man, and I had much rather meet a lion or a tiger, because I should then know what to do, than one of these men. I speak according to my experience. Having been occupied with the art of navigation ever since my childhood, I have never been able to enjoy that happy ease which permits of those studies and contemplations by means of which philosophers improve their minds; but I have traversed the greater part of the globe, and I have seen every-where that when reason is not assisted and perfected by good laws, or by a good education, it becomes the prey of force or of treachery, equally as much so among primitive men as amongst animals, and I conclude that reason without culture is but a brutal instinct.[120]

Le Dez, on the other hand, was less defensive about the French contribution to the cataclysm that befell them in the bay. Like du Clesmeur, he found Maori behaviour puzzling and contradictory, and yet he ended his commentary with a perceptively accurate comment:

> What is the real nature of these people? What judgements can we make about them, having seen them in complete conflict with themselves, their barbarousness following on the greatest gentleness? We have seen nothing but contradictions in them: although brave and bold, they fled before us; although treacherous and secretive, they are without mistrust; although vindictive, they forget or think that others forget the evil they have done. If they had really been what they seemed to us to be at the outset, would they have been able to change as suddenly, would they have meditated our destruction with such tranquillity, would they have been able to hide their dark design so long under the appearance of friendship without letting anything escape which would have given them away? They adopted the subtlest of policies, like men whom habit and success have made familiar with the greatest crimes and bold enough to commit them. However, I do not believe they conspired against us from the time of our arrival: the undertaking was too big. I am even con-vinced that the friendly welcome we received, although motivated by self-interest, was sincere. They came only gradually to the point of trying to bring about our downfall and they were led to it by this same self-interest which had made them welcome us. The great familiarity in which we lived with them probably began to lessen the distance they had placed between themselves and us and from that moment we could only go down in their esteem. First they started to steal a few trinkets and then, emboldened by that, they perhaps planned to seize everything: a few subjects for discontent were then perhaps added to the interest they already had and in no time the plot would have been hatched. We were no longer anything more than dangerous guests that had to be got rid of.[121]

A Maori assessment of the character of their French visitors in 1772 would have been similarly perplexed. These people who seemed so open and friendly, who shared their living quarters and their wealth in chiefly displays of 'manaaki' (hospitality), yet who indulged in inexplicable and unpredictable brutalities, steal-ing houses, a canoe, tying up a chief for no clear reason and finally, in the com-pany of their friends, desecrating a sacred beach belonging to one of the most powerful groups in the bay, must also have seemed full of contradictions. From a local point of view, from the moment that Te Kauri's tapu was attacked the responses of his people were inevitable, and the French were given many warnings of the danger that they were in — from sentry cries and signal fires at night to direct verbal cautions. For some extraordinary reason, however, they chose to take no notice of these signals and walked calmly to their deaths. In light of the violence of their final revenge, the local Maori people might well have judged the French in a precise echo of Le Dez's own words:

> What is the real nature of these people? What judgments can one make about them, having seen them in complete conflict with themselves, their barbarousness following on the greatest gentleness? We have seen nothing but contradictions in them: although brave and bold, they fled before us; although treacherous and secretive, they are without mistrust; although vindictive, they forget or think that others forget the evil they have done. If they had really been what they seemed to us to be at the outset, would they have been able to change as suddenly, would they have meditated our destruction with such tranquillity, would they have been able to hide their dark design so long under the appearance of friendship without letting anything escape that would have given them away?

ANTHROPOLOGY AND HISTORY

The first meetings between Maori and Europeans give a graphic example of the need to bring anthropology and history together in the study of cross-cultural pasts. The puzzlement and perplexity experienced by both sides proved frustrating and sometimes fatal — a reminder, maybe, that one-eyed views of culturally complex situations are not just morally unwise. Categories, cosmologies and customs shaped these early encounters as much as more material imperatives. To attempt to grasp their meaning requires an anthropological imagination as much as the historian's disciplined control of written words. Nor is it just documents that serve as signs of past events — landscapes, sites, ancient objects and remembered stories also speak.

For all the haze of cultural reflections in these records, something of the real world survives. The artists' 'coastal views' can be precisely matched to modern shore-lines; settlements that Spöring sketched can be excavated by archaeologists; and 'artificial curiosities' (tribal taonga — treasures) still held in European museums are readily recognised from their eighteenth-century portraits. Moreover, in the records of these early encounters between Maori and Europeans, the regional variability of tribal life is vividly described. From groups of wealthy agriculturalists practising large-scale fishing in the North, to the gardeners and carvers of the East Coast, the beleaguered inhabitants of Whitianga and bands of hunters and gatherers in Queen Charlotte Sound, settlement patterns, population densities and observable wealth all clearly varied markedly in different parts of New Zealand.

In these first meetings, shiploads of sailors and scientists from different parts of Europe (or its colonial outposts) came together with the inheritors of another sea-borne tradition, which in its way was as restless and turbulent. Once Europeans and the people of various Maori communities met, a process of negotiation and exchange began that continues to this day. There is not much place in this perception of the past for a static Golden Age, a standardised 'traditional society' pieced together from bits and pieces of the colonial past.

'Traditional Maori society' was, in any case, a colonial creation. The ancient patterns of kin-group koorero (talk) about ancestors followed changing genealogical pathways, and told tales of battles, challenges, alliances and migrations. The first Europeans were peripheral to the plot of tribal stories, so recollections of their arrival were usually collected by later Europeans, who prodded the memories of now-elderly eyewitnesses. As Europeans became an established presence, koorero began to include tales of battles with British troops, and Europeans who married Maori men or women were named in whakapapa (genealogies). Tribal historians began to write, chiefs sent letters to each other and speeches at tribal gatherings were recorded in newspapers written in Maori.

It was not until the end of the nineteenth century, in the aftermath of bitter fighting over land and the establishment of the Land Courts that images of 'traditional Maori society' began to be systematically produced. Often the European writers (including S. Percy Smith and Elsdon Best) had been active participants in the wars and the courts. Perhaps that recent history had been too harsh, and in any case 'the Maori race' with its customs and beliefs was thought to be dying out. The pre-European past (in fact the pre-Land War past) was idealised, and 'the Maori as He was' was recorded for posterity in an a-historical mode.

In New Zealand, as elsewhere in the world, however, cultural diversity has proved to be irrepressible. Maori ancestry, traditions and language have not been submerged by global culture; on the contrary, a sense of continuity with an ancestral Polynesian past is vigorous and resurgent. It has also begun to dawn on New Zealanders of European ancestry that their country is in fact a Pacific archipelago, set in a sea of predominantly non-European societies. If cultural diversity is to be a part of New Zealand's future, as it has been of its past, it must be coped with intellectually. In such a case the combination of an a-historical social anthropology and an a-cultural history may not prove ideal.

Two Worlds has been an experimental essay in construing an adequate scholarship of the beginnings of New Zealand's shared history. Tribal as well as European sources and perspectives, and the resources of both history and anthropology have been combined, however imperfectly, in this account. It ends therefore with a chant of binding, used by tribal elders to unite divergent forces and render them creative:

Whakarongo! Whakarongo! Whakarongo!	Listen! Listen! Listen!
Ki te tangi a te manu e karanga nei	To the cry of the bird calling
'Tui, tui, tuituiaa!'	'Unite, unite, be one!'
Tuia i runga, tuia i raro,	Bind above, bind below
Tuia i roto, tuia i waho	Bind within, bind without
Tuia i te here tangata	Tie the knot of humankind
Ka rongo te poo, ka rongo te poo	The night hears, the night hears
Tuia i te kaawai tangata i heke mai	Bind the descent lines
I Hawaiki nui, i Hawaiki roa,	From great Hawaiki, from long Hawaiki
I Hawaiki paamamao	from Hawaiki far away
I hono ki te wairua, ki te whai ao	To the spirit, to the daylight
Ki te Ao Maarama!	To the World of Light!

ERUERA STIRLING, 1980

SOURCES AND TEXTUAL CONVENTIONS

TASMAN'S VISIT

The surviving documentary sources for Tasman's visit to New Zealand in 1642 are relatively few in number.

Two copies of Tasman's 'day register' survive. One, which is lodged in the Netherlands State Archives, includes illustrations and maps and is signed by Tasman, but was evidently produced by a copyist in Batavia at the end of the voyage. The 'Huydecoper' copy in the Mitchell Library, Sydney, includes no illustrations other than maps and coastal profiles (for Tasmania), but otherwise differs only in minor details from the signed version. Details included in the day register indicate that it is based on a collective knowledge of what happened during the voyage, and that it is not simply Tasman's private version of events. This is by far the most informative account of the voyage, and I have quoted here from the signed version as edited by Müller.

Pilot-Major Visscher evidently wrote a day register, which was handed in to the Company at the end of the voyage, but like Tasman's original register this no longer survives. The Netherlands State Archives also holds the copy of a journal by an ordinary seaman on Tasman's expedition, usually known as 'The Sailor's Journal'. This says very little about events in Taitapu (Golden Bay), but gives a useful account of the two visits to Oo-hau (Great Island) in the Three Kings Group. I have quoted here from the translation published in McNab (1914).

In 1671 Arnoldus Montanus made available the first published account of Tasman's voyage in his geographical work *De Nieuwe en Onbekende Weereld*. This appears to have been based on an independent description of the voyage by Henrick Haelbos, a 'wound-healer' and barber on the expedition. This is a lively account that includes additional detail on the encounters both in Golden Bay and in the Three Kings Islands. I am indebted to Barbara Andaya for her excellent translation of the New Zealand sections of this text.

Finally, a number of separate maps survive for this voyage, including the 'Eugene' map, based on a Mercator chart by Visscher, which gives a track of the voyage including the Tasmanian and New Zealand coastlines surveyed en route; and the three 'Vingboons' watercolour charts of those parts of Tasmania, New Zealand and Tonga-Fiji seen on the voyage, also attributed to Visscher. All of these maps are held in the National Library, Vienna.

COOK'S VISIT

The documentation that survives from the *Endeavour* voyage to New Zealand is much more extensive than that from Tasman's visit. Extant journals include those by James Cook (in four manuscript versions), Joseph Banks (in two manuscript versions), a posthumously published journal by Sydney Parkinson, an anonymous published journal that was probably written by James Magra (or Matra), manuscript journals by William Brougham Monkhouse, John Bootie, Peter Briscoe, Charles Clerke, John Gore, Zachary Hicks, Robert Molyneux, Richard Pickersgill, James Roberts, Francis Wilkinson and several anonymous manuscript journals (including one attributed by J. C. Beaglehole to Charles Green which, on internal evidence in the text, appears to have been written by another, unknown writer). The New Zealand sections of the journals by Bootie, Gore, Hicks, Pickersgill and Wilkinson were transcribed and typed out by Jeremy Spencer early in the 'Early Eyewitness Accounts' project. Extant logs include the ship's log, and those written by John Bootie, James Cook, Stephen Forwood, Zachary Hicks, Robert Molyneux, Jonathon Monkhouse, Richard Pickersgill and two anonymous writers.

The New Zealand sections of all of these documents were obtained in copy from the relevant archives, except for those (of Cook, Banks and W. B. Monkhouse) published by J. C. Beaglehole in his meticulous edited versions. There are also several manuscript Maori vocabularies, one evidently written by Sydney Parkinson and the other by Joseph Banks, held in the School of Oriental and African Studies Library in London.

Graphic records from the voyage include numerous sketches and drawings by Sydney Parkinson, Herman Diedrich Spöring and an anonymous artist (probably Joseph Banks); sketches made after the voyage by John Frederick Miller; coastal views by Spöring and Parkinson; and charts by James Cook, Robert Molyneux, and Richard Pickersgill. These have been given close scholarly attention by Rüdiger Joppien, Bernard Smith and Andrew David in two major texts on the graphic records of the *Endeavour* voyage, although these texts include a number of errors in the New Zealand sections which arise primarily from a lack of local knowledge.

Those who wish to know more about the written and graphic records from the *Endeavour* voyage should consult J. C. Beaglehole, 'Textual Introduction' (cxciii–cclxxi) in *The Journals of Captain James Cook*, Volume I, 1968; Andrew David (ed.), *The Charts and Coastal Views of Captain Cook's Voyages: The Voyage of the Endeavour 1768–1771*, 1988; and Rüdiger Joppien and Bernard Smith (eds), *The Art of Captain Cook's Voyages*, Volume I, 1985.

Adrienne Kaeppler's *'Artificial Curiosities': being an exposition of native manufactures collected on the Three Pacific Voyages of Captain James Cook R.N.* also provides a valuable introduction to Maori objects collected on the voyage, although it is often not known on which voyage or in which place particular objects were collected.

The texts from this voyage presented a major challenge, for so many versions of events are not easily correlated. After some experimentation I adopted two techniques. First, Xerox-reduced copies of the texts for each day (as calculated in civil time) were pasted onto A3 sheets, organised into vertical columns for each journal-writer, and horizontal rows for each day. Ten or fifteen of the most informative versions of what happened on each day could then be scanned by placing four or five sheets side by side, and reading the horizontal rows for a particular day across the ten or fifteen vertical columns which gave each journal-writer's account. Second, I purchased the largest engagement diary I could find, one which recorded calendar days by the quarter of an hour, divided the pages into vertical columns for each journal-keeper, and recorded a précis of their accounts to the nearest quarter of an hour (where that was possible). This very precise summary was then checked against the charts in reconstructing both time and place for particular events. Times, places and versions of events given in the above text are thus based on the best generalisations that could be arrived at across sources using these methods, supplemented by local and archaeological knowledge of the relevant landscapes, and any pertinent tribal information or accounts.

VISITS BY SURVILLE AND MARION DU FRESNE

All extant documents from these voyages (texts, charts and sketches) were collected by Isabel Ollivier as part of the 'Early Eyewitness Accounts' project referred to in the Introduction, and the New Zealand sections of the texts have been published in typescript facsimile with parallel translations, and appendices on the graphic records in *Extracts from Journals relating to the visit to New Zealand of the French ship* St Jean Baptiste *in December 1769 under the command of J. F. M. de Surville*, transcription and translation by Isabel Ollivier and Cheryl Hingley, with an appendix of charts and drawings compiled by Jeremy Spencer, 1987; and *Extracts from Journals relating to the Visit to New Zealand in May–July 1772 of the French ships* Mascarin *and* Marquis de Castries *under the command of M. J. Marion du Fresne*, transcription and translation by Isabel Ollivier, with an appendix of charts compiled by Jeremy Spencer, 1985.

The Surville records include the original day-by-day record and accompanying log table kept by Surville himself; copies of day-by-day records and log tables by Labé and Pottier l'Horme; and two retrospective summaries of the voyage by Monneron. The Marion du Fresne records are all retrospective versions, shaped by hindsight and approximate in their recording of time. They include du Clesmeur's historical and navigational journals, Roux's journal, summaries by de Montesson and one attributed by Ollivier to Le Dez, and Crozet's published journal edited by Abbé Rochon. These texts were correlated using the same techniques described for Cook, except that for Marion du Fresne's visit there was no point in attempting a quarter-hourly time reconstruction, since the surviving documents of the voyage did not allow such precision to be attempted.

ACCOUNTS FROM MAORI SOURCES

Tribal sources were used in the research in two different ways.

First, tribal accounts recorded in Native Land Court minute books (particularly those relating to the earlier hearings in each district) and tribal histories written by tribal and other scholars were drawn upon to reconstruct the likely political situation in each district visited by a European expedition. Wherever possible, names cited by the Europeans were located on whakapapa (genealogies), and the stories associated with those individuals and their contemporaries were studied in close detail. This technique could not be applied in the absence of recorded names however, and names recorded by Europeans could not always be located on tribal whakapapa. Much more work could still be done in this area, since the records are voluminous and the prospects of localised reconstructions are excellent.

Second, accounts from Maori sources describing these first European visits were sought, both from manuscript collections and contemporary tribal experts. As I have commented in the Conclusion, the European visits were of marginal interest to tribal historians, since the European protagonists were external to the local genealogical networks that provide the key principle for ordering tribal historical accounts. By far the most useful accounts were those collected from elderly tribal eyewitnesses by early European settlers (such as John White, Joel Polack, and William Colenso), although these versions have the problems associated with all retrospective accounts of remote events — confusions in place, and muddles in the sequence and precise nature of events, etc. I have cited all such accounts, while trying to indicate my opinion of their (varying) reliability in footnotes or in the text itself. Contemporary oral traditions of these first European visits still survive, but these tend to be generalised, and based on key events (especially shootings and kidnappings) and broad impressions of the key protagonists (for instance, both Cook and Marion du Fresne are often — but not always — remembered with anger and resentment). Descent-group names (Ngaapuhi, Ngaati Tumatakokiri, etc.) used in this text are drawn from the earliest manuscripts and Land Court records (usually from 1850 to the 1880s) to describe those groups involved in the first encounters with Europeans. Maori descent-groups, however, periodically change their definitions and names, so these may not have been how those groups would have described themselves in 1642 or 1769–72.

TEXTUAL CONVENTIONS

In the text, double vowels have been used for typographic convenience. Original manuscripts are quoted exactly, with all of their errors of spelling and grammar. Scientific descriptions have not been given for plants and animals except where necessary to sort out a precise identification; instead, their most common name in New Zealand (whether this is in Maori or English) has been used, with the other language equivalent often given in brackets. Place-names are given in Maori in the first instance wherever possible, with names given by the explorers in brackets. Any confusions on this score can be readily resolved by consulting the maps provided. Key terms in Maori have been given with a translation in brackets in the first instance; any confusions can be resolved by recourse to the index, and by looking up the first use of the term.

Notes and References

The Research

1 See Salmond 1980, 1984, 1989.
2 Rolland *et al.*, 1953: 195

Introduction

1 Muller 1965: 17.
2 According to Grahame Anderson, somewhere off Punakaiki on the west coast of the South Island (pers. comm. 1990).
3 Unger 1978: 36–38. A mass-produced Dutch cargo ship, light, full-sectioned, almost flat-bottomed, with bluff bows and a fluted stern, low-masted and long in relation to its breadth.
4 Perahu (prow) was the term for Indonesian sailing craft.
5 Muller 1965: 18–19.
6 The puu taatara, or conch-shell trumpet, played as a signal during hostilities or on other ceremonial occasions.

Chapter One

1 The Dutch navigator Le Maire had sighted land east of Tierra del Fuego in 1616 and supposed it to be part of the great South-land, which he named 'Staten Landt'. Tasman thought the coastline he had discovered might also be part of the South-land, and so he named it likewise. When in 1643 another Dutch navigator established that the land Le Maire had sighted was just a small island, the South-land hypothesis began to fall apart, and Tasman's coastline was renamed (probably by Blaeu, the Amsterdam map-makers) after one of the main provinces in Netherlands.
2 Rarotonga is 1,650 miles north-east from New Zealand; Australia is 1,250 miles to the north-west, and South America 7,450 miles to the east.
3 Davidson in Jennings 1979: 228. Sutton (1987) has argued vigorously for an earlier settlement date, but at present the archaeological consensus rests with the date quoted, or a little later.

4 Green in Siers 1977: 225. This statement, like all those which follow in the paragraph, is a best-guess scenario based on the current results of archaeological and linguistic research in the Pacific.
5 Austronesian is a family of some 500 languages, centred in the Pacific with a western extension in Madagascar, which includes the Malayan and Cham languages on the south-east Asian mainland, the indigenous languages of Taiwan, Borneo, Philippines, Celebes and Indonesia in Island South-East Asia, languages in Melanesia and Micronesia, and all of the Polynesian languages.
6 White in Jennings 1979: 358; Allen *et al.* 1987; Wickler and Spriggs 1988.
7 Kirch 1988: 159. The author argues that since East Polynesia lies beyond the tectonic edge of the Pacific plate, early eastern Lapita sites may have been submerged as the islands to the east underwent relatively rapid subsidence, and have thus eluded discovery.
8 Early texts suggest that in pre-contact times Aotearoa referred to the North Island only, although in more recent times it has become a generalised term to describe the entire New Zealand archipelago. It is uncertain whether there was such a term for the entire country before Europeans arrived. Many placenames that are now used to refer to entire bays or districts were probably originally more specific in their reference (for example, Tuuranga, Tokerau, Taitapu, etc.).
9 Gladwin 1970: 181–89.
10 Lewis in Finney 1976: 20–21.
11 Irwin 1989.
12 Finney 1979: 122.
13 Lewis 1972: 266–68.
14 Levison and Ward 1973: 42, 54–56.
15 Irwin 1989.
16 Lewis 1972: 305–6. Note that obsidian from New Zealand has been found in the Kermadec Islands (Leach, Anderson, Sutton *et al.* 1986).
17 A recent study of regional dialects of Maori (Harlow 1988), along with the diversity of

regional voyaging traditions, and a range of archaeological and physical anthropological evidence all combine to suggest a series of migrations from different island groups in East Polynesia to New Zealand. If, as seems likely, East Polynesia was linked by frequent inter-island voyaging at this early period, sailing directions to New Zealand may well have been passed on to the star navigators of a number of island groups.

18 Walsh 1903: 12.
19 Finney 1987: 190.
20 In Simmons 1976: 22–23; trans. George Graham.
21 Kupe figures in the traditions of Ngaati Kahungunu, Tainui, the tribes of Whanganui, Taranaki, Cook Strait and Northland.
22 Kawau 1880: 8. This direction is puzzling if one assumes a journey from Rarotonga or Tahiti, when the proper bearing would be south-west.
23 For historical approaches to the voyaging traditions see S. Percy Smith 1904 and Simmons 1976; for an analysis of the traditions as myth see Orbell 1985.
24 Kuschel (ed.) 1975: 238–39.
25 Leach and Leach (eds) 1979: 163–70.
26 Prickett (ed.) 1982: 53.
27 Ibid.: 18–19.
28 Leach and Leach (eds) 1979.
29 Duff 1956.
30 Skinner 1912.
31 Houghton 1980: 94–96.
32 Anderson 1983: 12–13.
33 Ibid.: 9–10.
34 Ibid.: 11.
35 Davidson 1984: 123.
36 Ibid.: 106.
37 Leach and Leach (eds) 1979: 34–39.
38 Anderson 1983: 24.
39 Ibid.: 25.
40 Davidson 1984: 136.
41 Anderson 1983: 24.
42 Taylor 1855: 14–16; 1854: 179.
43 Best 1976: 62.
44 White 1887: I 17; and Gudgeon 1907: 109.
45 Smith 1913: 13.
46 Ibid.: 117–18; the translation is amended slightly.
47 Taylor 1855: 16–17.
48 Smith 1913: 117–56.
49 Shirres 1979: 135.

Chapter Two

1 Champion et al., 1984: 27.
2 In Braudel 1981: I 283.
3 In Kamen 1971: 146.
4 Pounds 1979: 28.

5 In Fairbrother 1970: 22.
6 Pounds 1979: 173–74.
7 In Goubert 1969: 46–47.
8 Kamen 1971: 13.
9 Ramazzini in Cippolla 1981: 139–40.
10 Kamen 1971: 13.
11 Pennington 1970: 24.
12 Braudel 1981: 46.
13 In Harrison 1984: 136–37.
14 La Barré in Kamen 1971: 209.
15 Ibid.: 388–89.
16 In Kamen 1971: 294.
17 Pounds 1979:162.
18 Kamen 1971: 42.
19 Ibid.: 379–80.
20 Reed 1986: 205–6. This notion of a geocentric universe had, however, been questioned by Copernicus in 1543. He argued that the cosmos centred upon the sun, and throughout the seventeenth century the theory of a geocentric universe organised in perfect spheres was steadily eroded.
21 The Holy Bible 1611.
22 In Harrison 1984: 157.
23 Harrison 1984: 169–70.
24 In Harrison 1984: 176.
25 Ibid.: 172.
26 Ibid.: 180.
27 Ibid.: 272.
28 Ibid.: 279.
29 Pennington 1970: 127–28. These included Descartes, Kepler, Bacon, Harvey.
30 Kamen 1971: 294.
31 Ibid.: 110.
32 Ibid.: 6.

Chapter Three

1 Andaya 1988: 9.
2 For more detailed argument see Wallis 1988; Hervé 1983; Langdon 1975; and McIntyre 1977. For tribal accounts, see, for instance, ATL MS.189 File 63 (He Waka Pakepakeha by Mohi Turei), which gives a detailed account of a visit by a boatload of white-skinned tuurehu (supernatural people) — evidently to the East Coast — which was said to be well before Captain Cook's arrival.
3 In Boxer 1963: 82.
4 Temple 1673, ed. Clark: 61–63.
5 See Zumthor 1962: 55–78.
6 Vereenigde Oostindische Compagnie.
7 In Boxer 1963: 81.
8 Boxer 1965: 69.
9 Zumthor 1962: 295.
10 Boxer 1965: 99.
11 De Graaf in Taylor 1983: 7.
12 Barlow in Lubbock (ed.) 1934: 242.
13 In Boxer 1963: 98.

14 Muller 1965: 13.
15 Boxer 1963: 87.
16 Wilcocke 1768 in Boxer 1963: 89.
17 Tasman in Muller (ed.) 1965: 131–32.
18 Muller 1965: 135.
19 Ibid.: 151.
20 Ibid.: 139–40.
21 Ibid.: 135.
22 Ibid.: 111.
23 Hocken 1895: 125.
24 Muller 1965: 7.
25 Ibid.: 15.
26 Ibid.: 17. Grahame Anderson identifies the high land first seen as Mounts Rosamond, Rolleston and Murchison, viewed from the north-west (pers. comm. 1990).
27 Mackay 1873: 67–68. White (1887: 315) also notes: 'It was some of the tribe Ngati Tumatakokiri who attacked the boat's crew of Tasman on his visit to Te Taitapu (sacred tide) which locality was by Tasman called Massacre or Murderer's Bay, from the disaster. Te Taitapu is a sandy cove about half a mile from Tata Island, and is pointed out by the Maori as the locality where the attack was made on Tasman's boats.' Taitapu was used as the name for the entire district in several deeds (see Mackay: 67, 68, 311); or to describe the area between Whanganui Inlet and Kahurangi Point in others (see Mackay: 15, 64, 66, 321).
28 Challis 1978: 5.
29 Taylor 1959: 210, 212.
30 Challis 1978: 28–34.
31 Orchiston 1974: 191, 198.
32 Challis 1978: 8.
33 Orchiston 1974: 3.199.
34 Taylor 1959: 207.
35 Newport 1971: 36.
36 Washbourn 1970: 56.
37 Golden Bay Jaycees n.d.: 22.
38 Washbourn 1970:209.
39 Challis 1978: 26.
40 Ibid.: 25.
41 Washbourn 1970: 56.
42 Taylor 1959: 205.
43 Moncrieff n.d.: 45–48.
44 Challis 1978: 5, 8.
45 Beautiful Golden Bay: 33.
46 Newport 1979: 5.
47 Orchiston 1974: 3.177–194; Historic Places Trust 1985; and Brailsford 1981: 79–94.
48 Mackay 1873: I 39; Smith 1901: 104; and Peart 1937: 13.
49 Mackay 1873: I 39, 45; and Peart 1937: 11–16.
50 Ibid. 1873: I 45. See also Nelson Minute Books 2: 170–290; 3: 1–7.
51 D'Urville sketches 1827 set in neighbouring Tasman Bay (see Brailsford 1981: 85–86).
52 Grahame Anderson suggests this anchorage was immediately north of the Wainui Inlet (pers. comm. 1990).
53 Newman 1905: 137.
54 Montanus 1671; trans. Andaya 1988: 4.
55 Muller 1965: 19. Tasman had with him a vocabulary including words recorded by Le Maire's 1616 expedition at Tonga and the Horne Islands, which Le Maire wrongly identified with Mendana's Solomon Islands.
56 Ibid.: 19.
57 My thanks to Janet Davidson and Atholl Anderson for these suggestions.
58 Montanus 1671; trans. Andaya 1988: 4.
59 Muller 1965: 19.
60 Montanus 1671; trans. Andaya 1988: 4.
61 Such small white 'flags' of tapa cloth featured in Tasman's accounts of friendly meetings on land and sea in Tonga, and in other early European accounts of peaceful meetings with Polynesian peoples (see Pearson 1970: 128). I know of no later examples of such a custom in New Zealand, however.
62 Muller 1965: 20.
63 Van Nierop 1674; trans. Andaya 1988: 1.
64 See Smith 1901: 104. However, Heaphy in 1846 talked to a Ngaati Tumatakokiri man who reported that two white men from a ship wrecked near the Mokihinui River on the West Coast many years before had made their way to Totaranui, near Separation Point, where his ancestors killed them. The details do not quite fit, but this and the Mackay account might possibly refer to the same event (see Taylor 1959: 222).
65 McNab 1914: 34.
66 Muller 1965: 24.
67 Montanus 1671; trans. Andaya 1988: 5.

Chapter Four

1 White 1888: V 121–24.
2 Graham 1946: 26–39; and Stack 1879: 159–64.
3 Voltaire, Letters Concerning the English Nation, 1733.
4 Porter 1982: 81.
5 Defoe in Briggs (ed.) 1969: 113.
6 Grub Street Journal, 21 October 1731, in Scott (ed.) 1970: 283.
7 Porter 1982: 151.
8 Owen 1974: 127.
9 Woloch 1982: 135–39; and Owen 1974: 130–31.
10 Porter 1982: 380.
11 For example, Briggs (ed.) 1969: 126–28, 155.
12 Tucker, Instructions for Travellers, in ibid.: 151.
13 George 1965: 266–67.
14 In Porter 1982: 31.

15 George 1965: 39.
16 Smollett 1771 in Scott 1970: 25.
17 In Briggs (ed.) 1969: 54.
18 George 1965: 95–96.
19 Doyle 1978: 130.
20 Porter 1982: 147.
21 George 1965: 146.
22 Ibid.: 302.
23 Porter 1982: 205.
24 Rodger 1986: 369.
25 Porter 1982: 51.
26 In McCormick 1959: 23.
27 Ollivier 1989, pers. comm. Ollivier has compiled a list of fifty European maps published between 1645 and 1763 which represent 'Zeelandia Nova'.
28 See McCormick 1959 for an authoritative listing and commentary.
29 Ibid.: 22.
30 Beaglehole (ed.) 1968: Lxxxviii.
31 Ferguson 1767 in Williams and Marshall 1982: 214.
32 Kames in ibid.: 214.
33 Woolf 1959: 162.
34 Bacon in Robertson (ed.) 1905: 710–32; and Debus 1978: 117.
35 Lyons 1944.
36 McClellan 1985: 214.
37 Ibid.: 210–13, 215–20.
38 A suggestion that was also hinted at by Hornsby in his 1765 *Memoir to the Royal Society on the Transit of Venus in 1769* (Woolf 1959: 162).
39 Beaglehole (ed.) 1968: cclxxix.
40 Ibid.: cclxxxii.
41 Ibid.: cclxxxiii.
42 Woolf 1959: Plate 10.
43 Beaglehole (ed.) 1968: 4.
44 Ibid.: 617; and Howse 1979: 119–35.
45 Beaglehole (ed.) 1968: cxliii.
46 Ibid.: cxxxvi.
47 Carr 1983a: 200.
48 Carr 1983a.
49 Beaglehole (ed.) 1968: 614.
50 Ibid.: 613, 615.
51 Beaglehole (ed.) 1962: 393.
52 Beaglehole (ed.) 1968: cxxiv; and McGowan 1979: 109–16.
53 Villiers 1967: 80.
54 Carr 1983a: 195.
55 O'Brien 1987: 69.
56 Beaglehole (ed.) 1968: 623.
57 Ibid.: 593.
58 Ibid.: 589–600.
59 Ibid.: cxciii.
60 Rodger 1986: 218–29.
61 Beaglehole (ed.) 1962: I 267.
62 Rodger 1986: 64–65.
63 Beaglehole (ed.) 1968: 96.
64 Watt in Fisher and Johnston 1979: 136–43.
65 Ibid.: 346.
66 O'Brien 1987: 74.
67 Beaglehole (ed.) 1968: 8.
68 Beaglehole (ed.) 1962: I 239–40.
69 Beaglehole (ed.) 1968: I 514–15
70 Ibid.: 516–17, 519.
71 In Williams and Marshall 1982: 266.
72 Banks in Beaglehole (ed.) 1962: I 263.
73 Woolf 1959: 148.
74 Hodgen 1964: 425–26.
75 Ibid.: 111–12, 122–24.
76 Beaglehole (ed.) 1962: I 312–13.
77 Ibid.: 371.
78 Ibid.: 396.
79 Ibid.: 397–99. Nicholas Young had probably sighted the inland hills around Te Rimu-a-maru, 108 kilometres from the ship (Anon. 1969). My thanks to Jeremy Spencer for supplying this source.

Chapter Five

1 Gisborne Minute Books 1–4; see also 'Sketch Map of Poverty Bay Distict' [1860s?].
2 Jones 1988; Gisborne Minute Book 1: 243.
3 Jones 1988: 23; Gisborne Minute Book 1: 243.
4 Harris in Mackay 1927: 162–63; Fowler 1974: 1.
5 Jones 1988: 34.
6 Harris in Mackay 1927: 165. The Awapuni lagoon was drained after European settlement.
7 Gisborne Minute Book 2: 178.
8 Fowler 1974: 25.
9 Darcy Ria, pers. comm. 1989.
10 Gisborne Minute Book 2: 172.
11 Ibid.: 178
12 Fowler 1974: 14.
13 Gisborne Minute Book 2: 172.
14 Williams 1936: 75.
15 Jones 1988: 46.
16 Hair (ed.) 1985: 10; Fowler 1974: 24; and Okawhare and Pohuhu 1880.
17 Hair (ed.) 1985: 11.
18 Ibid.: 10.
19 Ibid.: 11. Hinehaakirirangi is said by Te Kani Te Ua to have been the chief priestess of the *Takitimu* canoe (Fowler 1974: 21). See also Ngata n.d.: 24.
20 Hair (ed.) 1985: 11.
21 Fowler 1974: 24.
22 Mitchell 1944: 22.
23 Te Ua in Tai Raawhiti Association 1932: 41.
24 Fowler 1974: 2, 24. According to Ngata, *A Brief Account of Ngaati Kahungunu Origins*, Rua's full name was Ruamatua.
25 Ngata n.d. Lecture 5: 15.
26 Mackay 1966: 36.
27 Fowler 1974: 22–23.
28 Ngata n.d. Lecture 5: 3–7.

29 Lambert 1925: 250.

30 Dates are arrived at here as follows: some journals including Banks's were written in 'civil time' (midnight to midnight); most, including Cook's, were written in 'ship's time' (noon to noon), twelve hours ahead of civil time, with the date referring to the day of the second noon; the dates cited in this text are based on civil time, as given in the journals. To avoid confusion with the primary sources, no extra day is added here for 'westing'.

31 Parkinson 1972: 86.

32 Banks in Beaglehole (ed.) 1962: I 399.

33 Pickersgill Journal 1769: 50. Jeremy Spencer has calculated the exact position of this *Endeavour* anchorage to be just clear of 'The Foul Grounds' in eight fathoms water 38° 41′ 4.2″ South, 178° 00′ 5.3″ East. Offshore from the Cook Monument 2,060 metres 224° (T) SW from monument. (Pers. comm. 1990.)

34 This was Tuamotu Island, which was named 'Morai Island' in some of the later illustrations; 'Tettua Motu' in Parkinson's Journal (Parkinson 1972: 90).

35 Most likely the larger house later described in the coastal fishing village at Te Wai-o-Hii-Harore.

36 Williams 1888: 392.

37 Polack 1838 : I 15.

38 For example, Fowler 1974: 20. The story is that of Pourangahua, who fetched replacement kuumara tubers from Pari-nui-te-raa in Hawaiki, and was brought home on the back of the great bird of Ruakapanga, a chieftain of that place.

39 Monkhouse in Beaglehole (ed.) 1968: 565.

40 This hamlet was marked on Cook's East Coast chart: see David (ed.) 1988: 181.

41 Gisborne Minute Book 2: evidence of Rutene Te Eke, Wi Haronga, Paora Matuakore, Tamihana Ruatapu, Riparata Kahutia: 172–85.

42 Ibid., evidence of Paora Matuakore: 178.

43 Te Kani Te Ua, in Fowler 1974: 25.

44 Parkinson 1972: 87.

45 Wilkinson Journal 1769: 269.

46 Williams 1888: 391; Harris n.d.: 11. Te Maro had been shot with a .75 calibre ball from a Brown Bess Tower musket (Jeremy Spencer; pers. comm. 1990) — a large ball that would have left a terrible wound. These muskets were standard issue in this period.

47 Banks in Beaglehole (ed.) 1962: I 400.

48 Ibid.: 401.

49 Parkinson 1972: 130.

50 Monkhouse in Beaglehole (ed.) 1968: 566.

51 Gore 1769: 130.

52 Ibid.: 566–67.

53 Williams 1888: 393. Cook stated in his rough notes that this rock 'lay nearly in the middle of the river' (Beaglehole (ed.) 1968: I 535), which at this time was an estimated 40 yards wide. Te Toka-a-Taiau no longer exists; in 1877 despite warnings from local elders it was blasted by the Marine Department, although in 1888 it still remained, greatly reduced in size.

54 Banks in Beaglehole (ed.) 1962: I 401.

55 Monkhouse in Beaglehole (ed.) 1968: 568.

56 Ibid.: 568.

57 Ibid.: 568.

58 Polack 1838: I 14.

59 Gisborne Minute Book 3: 113; see also Mackay 1966: 464–67.

60 Harris MS n.d.: 11; Williams 1888: 392.

61 Williams n.d.: 87.

62 Williams 1888: 392.

63 McLean MS32 1851. My thanks to Sir Robert Hall for supplying this quotation.

64 Pickersgill Journal 1769: 51a.

65 David (ed.) 1988: 179, profile No. 4: 'Lagoon' marked by figure 7s. As Banks commented in his key to these views, 'the Indians talkd much of a river of fresh water somewhere hereabouts'. Ibid.: 180.

66 Gore 1769: 131.

67 David (ed.) 1988: 181.

68 Parkinson 1972: 86v.

69 Cook in Beaglehole (ed.) 1968: 515.

70 Or Te Haurangi, Ikirangi and Marukauiti, according to Williams (Williams 1888: 393); Te Hourangi, Ikirangi and Marukauiti, according to Harris (Harris MS n.d.: 11); or Hauraki and Hikurangi, according to Rongo Halbert (Sir Robert Hall, pers. comm. 1989); Ikirangi and Marukawiti in *Te Pipiwharauroa* 104, 1906: 6.

71 Banks in Beaglehole (ed.) 1962: I 403.

72 Pickersgill Journal 1769: 51a.

73 Parkinson 1972: 89. 'Eape' here is evidently an error; Bruce Biggs has pointed out that Parkinson was probably talking to Tupaia, who may have misheard ''ape' (*Colocasia macrorrhisa*) for 'koopii' (karaka berries).

74 Monkhouse in Beaglehole (ed.) 1968: 569.

75 Ibid.: 88.

76 'Taking pieces at one time into their mouths six times larger than we did' (Parkinson 1972: 89).

77 Monkhouse in Beaglehole (ed.) 1968: 569.

78 Fowler 1974: 25; Gisborne Minute Book 3: 113, evidence of his descendant Pimia Aata. See also Mackay 1966: 465–66, and *Te Pipiwharauroa* 104 1906: 6, for claims of another Te Ratu.

79 Fowler 1974: especially plate 14, pp. 11, 24– 25, 28–29, plates 55, 58.

80 Gisborne Minute Book 2: 172–86; 207–14: Minute Book 3: 73–112.

81 Gisborne Minute Book 2: 183–86, evidence

of Riparata Kahutia.

82 Fowler 1974: plate 61.

83 Hall 1984: 1.3, 17.2. Darcy Ria (pers. comm. 1989) has explained to me that this also applied to the relationship between men and women in the bay.

84 Banks in Beaglehole (ed.) 1962: I 403.

85 Beaglehole (ed.) 1968: 514.

86 Cook in ibid.: 171. See also Wilkinson Journal: 269: 'Our Capt and Gentleman have had a very sufficient Proff of their being a Sett of very Obstinate and Stubborn kind of People and Brave withall by Endeavouring to gett master of our Boats, and Fought as long as ever they had any things to throw at us, even a Parcel of Fish which they had in the Canoe they flung, and for all there was 2 men laying in the Canoe by them They Did Not Seem the Least Daunted or Frighted.'

87 Banks in Beaglehole (ed.) 1962: I 404.

88 Ibid.: 404.

89 Monkhouse in Beaglehole (ed.) 1968: 570.

90 Anon. Adm 51/4547/153: 362. The European estimates of number ranged between 52 and 200.

91 Harris MS, n.d.: 11.

92 Williams, quoted in Mackay 1966: 36.

93 Harris MS, n.d.: 11.

94 Monkhouse in Beaglehole (ed.) 1968: 570.

95 Ibid.: 570.

96 Gisborne Minute Book 1, evidence of Riparata Kahutia, Rutene Te Eke and others: 123–26; 232–43.

97 Monkhouse in Beaglehole (ed.) 1968: 571.

98 Colenso 1888: 45.

99 Monkhouse in Beaglehole (ed.) 1968: 571.

100 Gisborne Minute Book 1, evidence of Ihaka Ngarangione: 235–36, also 146.

101 Ibid.: 235.

102 Williams 1932: 8, 87.

103 Parkinson 1972: 89.

104 Polack 1838: I 15–16.

Chapter Six

1 Mitchell 1944: genealogies ix, x, xii, xvii; see also Simmons 1976: 238, 241–51.

2 Simmons 1976: 250–51.

3 Wilson 1939: 190.

4 Fox in Prickett (ed.) 1982: 68.

5 Ibid.: 78; Wilson 1939: 12.

6 Prentice in Wilson 1939: 28.

7 Lambert 1925: 114–15.

8 Ibid.: 275–79; Mitchell 1944: 106–15; Prentice in Wilson 1939: 35–47, 59–63.

9 Simmons 1976: 117–18.

10 Lambert 1925: 114–15; Mitchell 1944: 60–61.

11 Lambert 1925: 262.

12 Buchanan 1973: 5–6.

13 Parkinson 1972: 90.

14 Joppien and Smith (eds) 1985: 211.

15 Kaeppler 1978: 202–3; British Museum NZ150.

16 Mackay 1966: 27

17 Monkhouse in Beaglehole (ed.) 1968: 573.

18 Ibid.: 573.

19 Joppien and Smith 1985: 165–67; British Museum Add. MS 9345 f.12, Add. MS 23920, ff. 55, 56, 67(a–b).

20 Banks in Beaglehole (ed.) 1962: I 407.

21 See Kaeppler 1978: 171–73.

22 Ibid.: 175.

23 Banks in Beaglehole (ed.) 1962: I 408.

24 Parkinson 1972: 90.

25 Monkhouse in Beaglehole (ed.) 1968: 574.

26 Ibid.: 574.

27 Ibid.

28 Banks in Beaglehole (ed.) 1962: I 408.

29 Cook in Beaglehole (ed.) 1968: 174.

30 Monkhouse in ibid.: 575.

31 Ibid.: 575.

32 Probably Ngaati Raakaipaaka of Maahia.

33 Monkhouse in Beaglehole (ed.) 1968: 575.

34 Ibid.: 576.

35 Lambert 1925: 69.

36 The peninsula was said to resemble a man lying prone on the sea, with his right and left arms being represented by Nukutaurua and Long Point (Lambert 1925: 69).

37 Mitchell 1944: 43.

38 Monkhouse in Beaglehole (ed.) 1968: 576.

39 See Joppien and Smith 1985: 200–07.

40 Banks in Beaglehole (ed.) 1962: I 410.

41 Ibid.: 410.

42 Cook in Beaglehole (ed.) 1968: 176.

43 Parkinson 1972: 92.

44 Fox in Prickett (ed.) 1982: 62, 68.

45 Banks in Beaglehole (ed.) 1962: I 411.

46 Prentice in Wilson 1939: 40.

47 Parkinson 1972: 93.

48 Monkhouse in Beaglehole (ed.) 1968: 578.

49 Parkinson 1972: 93. Patrick Parsons has suggested that the chief in the red cloak may have been Hawea Te Marama of Te Awanga.

50 See Joppien and Smith 1985: 200–01.

51 Monkhouse in Beaglehole (ed.) 1968: 578.

52 Banks in Beaglehole (ed.) 1962: I 411.

53 My thanks to Patrick Parsons for this information. The Molyneux map is Add. MS 21593.E.

54 Monkhouse in Beaglehole (ed.) 1968: 579.

55 Ibid.: 579–80.

56 Parkinson 1972: 94

57 Colenso 1851. My thanks to Patrick Parsons for supplying this quotation.

58 Banks in Beaglehole (ed.) 1962: I 414.

59 Forwood 1769: 300.

60 Monkhouse in Beaglehole (ed.) 1968: 581.

61 Ibid.
62 Mackay 1966: 27.
63 Cook in Beaglehole (ed.) 1968: 180.
64 See, for example, Fox in Prickett (ed.) 1982: 68, 70.
65 Hamlyn 1915: 72.

Chapter Seven

 1 Downes 1914: 32, 111; see also Ngata n.d. Lecture 6: 11, 13.
 2 Monkhouse in Beaglehole (ed.) 1968: 582.
 3 Ibid.: 582.
 4 Pickersgill Journal 1769: 53a.
 5 Spöring BM Add MS 23920 f67d, see Joppien and Smith 1985: 167.
 6 Jones 1984: 315–20.
 7 Banks in Beaglehole (ed.) 1962: I 415.
 8 Henare Potae in Waiapu MB 2: 94; Henare Ruru in ibid.: 107.
 9 Lawson 1987: 22.
10 Ngata n.d. Lecture 4: 2–3.
11 Ibid. Lecture 1: 2.
12 Simmons 1976: 137, 126–27.
13 Colenso 1888: 17–26.
14 Ngata n.d. Lecture 4: 10–12.
15 Ruatapu in Iles 1981: 32.
16 Mokai, Hori, 1889 Waiapu MB 8A: 342–46.
17 Taurewa, Heremia, Waiapu MB 8A: 167.
18 Cook in Beaglehole (ed.) 1968: 182.
19 Monkhouse in Beaglehole (ed.) 1968: 583–84.
20 Banks in Beaglehole (ed.) 1962: I 415–16.
21 Cook in Beaglehole (ed.) 1968: 182.
22 Ibid.
23 Wahawaha in Te Waka Maori 1874, in Mackay.
24 Monkhouse in Beaglehole (ed.) 1968: 583–84.
25 Banks in Beaglehole (ed.) 1962: I 417.
26 Monkhouse in Beaglehole (ed.) 1968: 583.
27 Jones 1989b: 54–58.
28 Walsh 1903: 19–20.
29 Cook in Beaglehole (ed.) 1968: 183.
30 Monkhouse in Beaglehole (ed.) 1968: 585.
31 Banks in Beaglehole (ed.) 1962: I 416.
32 Monkhouse in Beaglehole (ed.) 1968: 584–85. Bodies were sometimes mummified (Tregear 1916: 167–72).
33 Banks in Beaglehole (ed.) 1962: I 417.
34 Watt in Fisher and Johnston (eds) 1979: 150–51; Smith 1975: 45.
35 Parkinson Add MS 23920 f60: *a–f*: see Joppien and Smith 1985: 168–69. (But *a* shows a Queen Charlotte style mourning hat, and *b* and *f* show a rei puta and a tattoo pattern respectively, which are probably northern in style. I doubt therefore that these sketches were made in Anaura, despite Joppien and Smith's identification.)
36 Pickersgill Journal 1769: 53a.
37 Pickersgill HD 552/10 in David 1988: 201.
38 Parkinson Vocabulary: 3.
39 Wilkinson 1769: 273.
40 Ibid.: 273.
41 Colenso 1844: 14–16.
42 Te Kani, Himiona, Waiapu MB 8A: 113–25, see also 140–54.
43 Williams 1888: 396–97.
44 Elder 1933: 175.
45 Te Kani, Himiona Waiapu MB 8A: 116; Williams 1888: 397.
46 Jones and Law 1987: 107.
47 Williams 1840 in Porter (ed.) 1974: 75. This figure was for the Uawa Missionary District.
48 See Waiapu MB2, Mangatuna Case: 112–92; Mangaheia No. 2 Case: 325.
49 Colenso MS 1838: 26.
50 Colenso 1844: 19; Moore 1959: 10–11.
51 Ngata n.d. Lecture 6: 15.
52 Mohi Ruatapu in Iles 1981: 35.
53 Arapeta Rangiuia in Waiapu MB 8A: 159.
54 Hone Paerata in ibid: 154.
55 Colenso 1844: 7.
56 Banks in Beaglehole (ed.) 1962: I 418.
57 Parekura Grey and other Hauiti elders, pers. comm. 1989; also *Te Pipiwharauroa* 1906 no. 104: 6.
58 Parkinson 1972: 97.
59 Wilkinson 1769: 274.
60 Parkinson 1972: 97.
61 Ibid.
62 Magra 1967: 77
63 Banks in Beaglehole (ed.) 1962: I 421.
64 Ngata n.d. Lecture 6: 5–6. My thanks to John Laurie for this sensible explanation.
65 Cook in Beaglehole (ed.) 1968: 186.
66 Parkinson 1972: 99
67 Cook in Beaglehole (ed.) 1968: 538.
68 Jones 1986: 23.
69 Banks in Beaglehole (ed.) 1962: I 419.
70 Parkinson 1972: 97–99.
71 Banks in Beaglehole (ed.) 1962: I 421.
72 BM Add MS 23920 f75; see Joppien and Smith 1985: 216.
73 BM Add MS 23920 f52 *a–b*, f77 *b*; see Joppien and Smith 1985: 175–78.
74 Parkinson 1972: 98.
75 Mokena Romio in Iles 1981: 30–31.
76 Parkinson 1972: 98.
77 Cook in Beaglehole (ed.) 1968: 280.
78 Magra 1967: 78.
79 Ibid.: 78–79.
80 Banks in Beaglehole (ed.) 1962: I 420.
81 Ngata n.d. Lecture 4: 11–12.
82 Banks in Beaglehole (ed.) 1962: I 420.
83 Oliver 1974: II 714–15.
84 For example, Cook in Beaglehole (ed.) 1968: 539.
85 Williams 1888: 396.

86 Banks in Beaglehole (ed.) 1962: I 419.
87 Ibid.: 420; Jones 1983: 531–36.
88 Banks in Beaglehole (ed.) 1962: I 419.
89 Ibid.: II 32.
90 Nicholas 1817: II 218–20.
91 Wilkinson 1769: 274.
92 Cook in Beaglehole (ed.) 1968: 538–39.
93 Magra 1967: 79.
94 Brailsford 1984: 26.
95 Wahawaha 1874 in Mackay 1966: 58.
96 Polack 1838: II 127–36; Bain 1986: 167–75.
   A bead said to have been one of these is
   discussed in *JPS* 38: 388–89. (Thanks to
   Jeremy Spencer for the reference.)
97 Williams 1888: 396.
98 Parkinson 1972: 98.
99 In Simmons 1976: 350–51
100 Jones 1983: 531.
101 Jones 1986: 23.

Chapter Eight

1 White 1887: II 189–91.
2 Parkinson 1972: 100.
3 Cook in Beaglehole (ed.) 1968: 539.
4 Pickersgill Journal 1769: 54a.
5 Ibid.: 54.
6 Journal 1771: 82.
7 Banks in Beaglehole (ed.) 1962: I 424.
8 Pickersgill Journal 1769: 54.
9 Banks in Beaglehole (ed.) 1962: I 424.
10 Ibid.: 424–25.
11 Lee 1938: 3–4.
12 Ibid.: 4.
13 Ibid.: 3.
14 Tahatau and Te Uremutu in Simmons 1976: 158–64.
15 Stafford 1967: 17–18; see also 9–38, 81.
16 Te Rangikaheke in Curnow 1983: 266.
17 Lee 1938: 3.
18 White 1889: IV 35.
19 Natanahira Te Hurupa of Ngaati Huarere in Simmons 1976: 175.
20 Coromandel MB 1: 257.
21 A. L. Lee in Kelly 1953: 389.
22 Law 1982: 53.
23 Osborne 1965: 9.
24 Furey 1981: 38; Johnston pers. comm. 1990.
25 Lee 1938: 4.
26 Osborne 1965: 8–9.
27 Paaki Harrison pers. comm. 1989.
28 Wright 1975: 3–14.
29 Parkinson 1972: 103. My thanks to Joan Metge for the interpretation of maakutu.
30 Banks in Beaglehole (ed.) 1962: I 426.
31 Gore 1769: 137.
32 Banks in Beaglehole (ed.) 1962: I 427.
33 Ibid.: 427.
34 Ibid.: 427.

35 Ibid.: 428.
36 Banks in Beaglehole (ed.) 1962: II 19.
37 Banks vocabulary.
38 White 1888: V 126; Te Uri-o-Pou traced their descent from Mapara, a brother of Tama-te-kapua of the *Arawa* canoe, through an ancestor called Pou-tuu-teka. Like Ngaati Hei and Ngaati Huarere, they were of mixed original settler and Arawa lines of descent (Kelly 1949: 112–13, 174; Stafford 1967: 472). See also White 1889: IV 55.
39 Banks in Beaglehole (ed.) 1962: I 429.
40 Cook in Beaglehole (ed.) 1968: 196.
41 White 1888: V 130. The Wynyard account was cited in Grey 1854: 180–81.
42 Ibid.: 127–28.
43 Banks in Beaglehole (ed.) 1962: I 429–30.
44 Cook in Beaglehole (ed.) 1968: 197.
45 Te Taniwha in White 1888: 122–23.
46 Lee 1938: 9.
47 Cook in Beaglehole (ed.) 1968: 197–98.
48 Ema Te Aouru in Coromandel MB 3: 301.
49 Haszard 1903: 30.
50 Banks in Beaglehole (ed.) 1962: I 432.
51 White 1888: 125–28.
52 Cook in Beaglehole (ed.) 1968: 198.
53 Banks in Beaglehole (ed.) 1962: I 432.
54 Cook in Beaglehole (ed.) 1968: 199.
55 Lee 1938: 5.
56 Banks Grey MS 51.
57 Cook in Beaglehole (ed.) 1968: 204.
58 Beaglehole (ed.) 1968: cclxxxiii.
59 Gore 1769: 138.
60 White 1888: V 123–25.
61 Banks in Beaglehole (ed.) 1962: I 434.
62 White 1888: V 131.
63 Wynyard in Lucas 1980: 27–29.
64 Banks in Beaglehole (ed.) 1962: I 434.
65 Ibid.: 435.
66 Parkinson 1972: 106.
67 Banks in Beaglehole (ed.) 1962: I 436.
68 Best 1980: 81–87. Oruarangi is sited seven kilometres from the modern mouth of the Waihou. In reckoning the location of the settlement they saw as 'about 1 mile' upstream, however, there is no knowing where Banks calculated the bay to end and the river to begin.
69 White 1889: IV 48–53, 200–3; Kelly 1949: 175–78.
70 Best 1980: 70.
71 Cook in Beaglehole (ed.) 1968: 207.
72 Banks in Beaglehole (ed.) 1962: I 437.
73 Pickersgill Journal 1769:
74 Wilson in White 1888: V 199.
75 Ibid.: 189.
76 Parkinson 1972: 103.

Chapter Nine

1 Solander sketched one of these fish and described it as *Sciaena abdominalis* (Beaglehole 1962: I 438).
2 Cook in Beaglehole (ed.) 1968: 211.
3 Parkinson 1972: 108.
4 Banks in Beaglehole (ed.) 1962: I 439.
5 Ibid.
6 Banks in Beaglehole 1962: II 14.
7 Gore 1769: 140.
8 Cook in Beaglehole (ed.) 1968: 212–13.
9 Parkinson 1972: 108.
10 Banks in Beaglehole (ed.) 1962: I 439.
11 Ibid.: 440.
12 The modern name Pewhairangi is said to be a transliteration of Bay of Islands (Jack Lee; Bruce Biggs, pers. comm. 1990), although the term is used for the bay in an 1883 manuscript by Hone Ngapua, a nephew of Hone Heke (Freda Kawharu, pers. comm. 1990).
13 This reconstruction of the 1769 environment in the Bay of Islands is based on Shawcross 1966: 204–47; Kennedy 1969: 15–31; *Story of Bay of Islands Maritime and Historic Park* 1965: 79.
14 Lee 1987: 14.
15 Barlow, pers. comm. 1989.
16 Aperahama Taonui in Simmons 1976: 39; Lee 1987: 19.
17 Lee 1987: 32.
18 Hare Matenga in Sissons *et al.* 1987: 111.
19 Lee 1983: 31.
20 Sissons *et al.* 1987: 81. For a valuable discussion of the complexities of descent-group affiliations, in the Bay of Islands as elsewhere, see Schwimmer 1982: 216–17
21 Banks in Beaglehole (ed.) 1962: I 440.
22 Best 1974: 127.
23 Parkinson 1972: 109.
24 White in Orbell (trans., with minor amendments) 1965: 15. Patuone died in 1872, which means he must have lived until he was about 110 years old. The manuscript goes on to say that these 'goblins' were brought ashore at Te Puna, where they lived for 'a month' — apparently telescoping some later arrival together with Cook.
25 Davis 1974: 5.
26 Spencer 1979: 5. This bay is marked on Solander's profile No. 1 of the island, 'there we landed'.
27 Cook in Beaglehole (ed.) 1968: 215.
28 Ibid.
29 Magra 1967: 88–89.
30 Banks in Beaglehole (ed.) 1962: I 441.
31 Cook in Beaglehole (ed.) 1968: I 215–16.
32 Banks in Beaglehole (ed.) 1962: I 442.
33 Ibid.
34 Ibid.
35 Magra 1967: 89–90.
36 Spencer 1979: 8.
37 Banks in Beaglehole (ed.) 1962: I 443.
38 Parkinson 1972: 110.
39 Spencer 1979: 10. Note also Cook Greenwich MS: 'Sent two boats over to the Main to Attend upon Mr. Banks & at the same time to sound the harbour.' (Beaglehole 1968: n. 217).
40 Ibid.: 12.
41 Banks in Beaglehole (ed.) 1962: I 444.
42 Ibid.: 445.
43 Wilkinson 1769: 280.
44 Spencer in Carr 1983: 270–74.
45 Cook in Beaglehole (ed.) 1968: 218–19.

Chapter Ten

1 Cook in Beaglehole (ed.) 1968: 220.
2 Banks in Beaglehole (ed.) 1962: I 446–47.
3 Hollyman 1986: 80.
4 Cook in Beaglehole (ed.) 1968: 222.
5 Banks in Beaglehole (ed.) 1962: I 447.
6 Ibid.: 449.
7 Elvy 1957: 4.
8 Orchiston 1974: T221.
9 Ibid.: T222.
10 O'Regan in Barratt 1987: 139–40; Elvy 1957: 1.
11 Beattie 1915: 103–06; 1918: 138–47.
12 Ibid.: 147–51.
13 Beattie 1915: 130–31; 1917: 75, 78; Elvy 1957: 8.
14 O'Regan in Barratt 1987: 143.
15 Ibid.: 144–45; Elvy 1957: 12–15.
16 Ibid.: 44; O'Regan in Barratt 1987: 153.
17 Ibid.: 149; Elvy 1957: 33–35.
18 O'Regan in Barratt 1987: 154–56; Elvy 157: 44.
19 Banks in Beaglehole (ed.) 1962: I 452–53.
20 Magra 1967: 92.
21 Ibid.: 93.
22 Banks in Beaglehole (ed.) 1962: I 460; Banks vocabulary.
23 Magra 1967: 92.
24 Beaglehole (ed.) 1962: I fn. 453; Habib 1989: 357–60.
25 Cook in Beaglehole (ed.) 1968: 235. The vegetation around Ship Cove still shows the area that was cut by Cook's men during this and later visits.
26 Banks in Beaglehole (ed.) 1962: I 454.
27 Magra 1967: 93–94.
28 Banks in Beaglehole (ed.) 1962: I 454.
29 Joppien and Smith 1985: 188–89, 192.
30 According to Magra, ten were killed, two of whom were women; according to Parkinson, four were killed and two drowned (Magra 1967: 95; Parkinson 1972: 115).
31 Banks in Beaglehole (ed.) 1962: I 455.
32 Pickersgill 1769: 60a.

33 Magra 1967: 95–96.
34 Banks in Beaglehole (ed.) 1962: I 455–56.
35 Cook in Beaglehole (ed.) 1968: 236–37.
36 Banks in Beaglehole (ed.) 1962: I 456.
37 Mackay 1873: 314.
38 Banks in Beaglehole (ed.) 1962: I 457.
39 Parkinson 1972: 116.
40 Ibid.
41 Banks in Beaglehole (ed.) 1962: I 457.
42 Ibid.: 459.
43 Mackay 1873: 314.
44 Beaglehole (ed.) 1968: fn. 238.
45 Banks in Beaglehole (ed.) 1962: I 457–58.
46 Brailsford 1981: 35.
47 Magra 1967: 97.
48 Brailsford 1981: 35.
49 Magra 1967: 97–100.
50 Banks in Beaglehole (ed.) 1962: I 458.
51 Ibid.: 459.
52 Cook in Beaglehole (ed.) 1968: 240.
53 Brailsford 1981: 27.
54 Banks in Beaglehole (ed.) 1962: I 460.
55 Wilkinson 1769: 287.
56 Cook in Beaglehole (ed.) 1968: 242.
57 Ibid.: 243.
58 Pickersgill Journal 1769: 61a.
59 My thanks to Bruce Biggs and Patu Hohepa for these suggestions.
60 Banks in Beaglehole (ed.) 1962: I 461.
61 Wilkinson 1769: 287.
62 Banks in Beaglehole (ed.) 1962: I 462.
63 Ibid.: 462–63.
64 Ibid.: I 463–64.
65 Ibid.: 464.
66 Parkinson 1972: 115.
67 Cook in Beaglehole (ed.) 1968: 247.
68 Parkinson 1972: 116.
69 Ibid.
70 Banks in Beaglehole (ed.) 1962: I 469
71 Orchiston 1974 3: 161–66.
72 Cook in Beaglehole (ed.) 1968: 247.
73 Joppien and Smith 1985: 188–95.
74 Parkinson 1972: 116.
75 Ibid.: 119.
76 Joppien and Smith 1985: 190–91; 199, 200.
77 Cook in Beaglehole (ed.) 1968: 250.
78 Banks in Beaglehole (ed.) 1962: I 465–66.
79 Ibid.: 467.
80 Parkinson 1972: 120.
81 Banks in Beaglehole (ed.) 1962: I 471.
82 Ibid.: 470.
83 Magra 1967: 105.

Chapter Eleven

1 Banks in Beaglehole (ed.) 1962: II 1.
2 Cook in Beaglehole (ed.) 1968: 274.
3 Ibid.
4 Magra 1967: 103.
5 Cook in Beaglehole (ed.) 1968: 276.
6 Banks in Beaglehole (ed.) 1962: II 3.
7 Cook in Beaglehole (ed.) 1968: 278.
8 Ibid.: 277–78.
9 Ibid.: 277.
10 Banks in Beaglehole (ed.) 1962: II 4.
11 Ibid.: 5.
12 Ibid.: 6.
13 Ibid.
14 Cook in Beaglehole (ed.) 1968: 276.
15 For this and other botanical and zoological identifications see footnotes in Beaglehole (ed.) 1962: II 4–10.
16 Ibid.: 9.
17 Banks in Beaglehole (ed.) 1962: II 11.
18 Ibid.
19 Cook in Beaglehole (ed.) 1968: 278.
20 Banks in Beaglehole (ed.) 1962: II 12.
21 Ibid.: 12.
22 Ibid.: 13.
23 Ibid.
24 Ibid.
25 Ibid.: 14.
26 Ibid.
27 Cook in Beaglehole (ed.) 1968: 279.
28 Banks in Beaglehole (ed.) 1962: II 15.
29 Cook in Beaglehole (ed.) 1968: 279.
30 Banks in Beaglehole (ed.) 1962: II 15.
31 Ibid.: 16.
32 Ibid.
33 Ibid.: 17.
34 Parkinson 1972: 127.
35 Banks in Beaglehole (ed.) 1962: II 17–18.
36 Ibid.: 18.
37 Ibid.: 19–20
38 Ibid.: 20.
39 Houghton 1980: 97.
40 Beaglehole 1962: II 22.
41 Ibid.: 23.
42 Ibid.: 24.
43 For example, Kaeppler 1978: 200–1. My thanks to Janet Davidson for this information.
44 Cook in Beaglehole (ed.) 1968: 284–85.
45 Banks in Beaglehole (ed.) 1962: II 25.
46 Ibid.
47 Ibid.: 26.
48 Ibid.
49 Cook in Beaglehole (ed.) 1968: 281–82.
50 Banks in Beaglehole (ed.) 1962: II 29.
51 Ibid.: 32.
52 Ibid.: 32–33.
53 Cook in Beaglehole (ed.) 1968: 281.
54 Banks in Beaglehole (ed.) 1962: II 33.
55 Ibid.: 34.
56 Ibid.: 34–35.
57 Magra 1967: 105–06.
58 Banks in Beaglehole (ed.) 1962: II 35.
59 Magra 1967: 107–09.
60 Banks in Beaglehole (ed.) 1962: II 37.

Chapter Twelve

1 In Ollivier and Hingley 1987: 211.
2 Gossman 1972: 54.
3 Woloch 1982: 51.
4 Ibid.: 145.
5 Ibid.: 46.
6 Goubert 1969: 20.
7 Ibid.: 11–12.
8 Gossman 1972: 11.
9 Goubert 1969: 177–78.
10 Woloch 1982: 108.
11 Ibid.: 71.
12 In Goubert 1969: 118.
13 Woloch 1982: 166.
14 Ibid.: 92.
15 Darnton 1985: 136.
16 Goubert 1969: 262.
17 Darnton 1985: 9–65.
18 Goubert 1969: 260.
19 Montaigne in Frame (ed.) n.d.: 152.
20 Ibid.: 155.
21 Ibid.: 158–59.
22 Rousseau in Cranston (ed.) 1986: 115–16.
23 Voltaire in Rolland *et al.* (ed.) 1953: 220–24.
24 Sen 1958: 46.
25 Voltaire in ibid.: 31.
26 Buffet in Dunmore 1965: 124.
27 Chevalier to the Minister, in Dunmore 1981: 21– 22.
28 Dunmore 1981: 21–27.
29 Rochon in ibid.: 23.
30 Ollivier and Hingley 1987: 147.
31 La Gravière in Dunmore 1965: 39.
32 My thanks to Isabel Ollivier for this insight.
33 Dunmore 1981: 32; 1965: 123.
34 See Ollivier and Hingley 1987: 209–11; Dunmore 1981: 32–33.
35 I am indebted to Isabel Ollivier for pointing out the echoes of Buffon in Pottier's descriptions of the people at 'Lauriston Bay'.
36 Dunmore 1981: 273–87.
37 Picard *et al.* in Dunmore 1981: 14.
38 Pottier in Dunmore 1965: 148.
39 Labé in Dunmore 1981: 235.
40 Ibid.: 236.
41 Prévost in Ollivier and Hingley 1987: 209.
42 Pottier in ibid.: 96.
43 'Mangoonui', or 'Oruru', were also sometimes given as the name of the entire harbour. This seems to reflect a naming strategy that used the names of prominent features (a beach, a river, a bay or a hill) as a handy label for some larger geographic unit, such as an extensive harbour.
44 Johnson 1986.
45 Waitangi Tribunal 1988: 260.
46 Phillips 1987.
47 Waitangi Tribunal 1988: 68–74.
48 Grey 1961: 221–24.
49 Waitangi Tribunal 1988: 260–61.
50 Ollivier and Hingley 1987: 181.
51 Ibid.: 154.
52 Ibid.: 102.
53 Ibid.: 156.
54 Ibid.: 67. The paa locations given in the next sentence were identified by Jeremy Spencer, using the bearings given by the French and correlating these with archaeological site surveys. (Spencer 1991: pers. comm.)
55 Ibid.: 17. Identification of the 'second row of mountains' by Jeremy Spencer (pers. comm. 1991).
56 Ibid.: 67.
57 My thanks to Patu Hohepa for this suggestion.
58 Ollivier and Hingley 1987: 106–7.
59 Ibid.: 18.
60 Ibid.: 15.
61 Ibid.: 69.
62 Lloyd and Coulter 1961: 293–95.
63 Ollivier and Hingley 1987: 20.
64 Ibid.: 22.
65 In Dunmore 1965: 41–42.
66 Ollivier and Hingley 1987: 71.
67 Ibid.: 71.
68 Ibid.
69 Ibid.: 107–8.
70 Ibid.: 71.
71 Ibid.: 23. My thanks to Dame Joan Metge for her suggestions about maakutu in this context.
72 Ollivier and Hingley 1987: 73.
73 Ibid.: 23.
74 Ibid.: 109.
75 Ibid.: 110.
76 Ibid.: 25.
77 Ibid.
78 Ibid.
79 Ibid.: 77.
80 Ibid.: 75–77.
81 Ibid.: 77.
82 Ibid.
83 Ibid.
84 Ibid.: 79.
85 Ibid.
86 Ibid.: 81.
87 Ibid.
88 Ibid.: 27.
89 Ibid.: 81.
90 Ibid.
91 Ibid.: 111–13.
92 Ibid.: 81.
93 Ibid.: 31–32.
94 Ibid.: 33.
95 Ibid.
96 Ibid.: 118–19.
97 Ibid.: 85.
98 Colenso 1868: 24–25.
99 Ollivier and Hingley 1987: 173.
100 White MS n.d. Folder B19: 87.
101 Ollivier and Hingley 1987: 36.

102 Ibid.: 87.
103 Ibid.: 164.
104 Ibid.: 119.
105 Houghton 1980: 33.
106 Banks in Beaglehole (ed.) 1962: II 16.
107 Ibid.: 13.
108 Ollivier and Hingley 1987: 120.
109 Ibid.: 41.
110 Ibid.: 120–22.
111 Ibid.: 39.
112 Ibid.: 132.
113 Ibid.: 122–24.
114 Ibid.: 124.
115 Ibid.
116 Ibid.: 125.
117 Ibid.: 167.
118 Ibid.: 169.
119 Ibid.: 125–27.
120 Ibid.: 127.
121 Ibid.: 166.
122 Ibid.: 128.
123 Ibid.: 129–30.
124 Ibid.: 130.
125 Ibid.
126 Buffon 1797: IV 312.
127 Ollivier and Hingley 1987: 130–31.
128 Cook in Beaglehole (ed.) 1968: 281.
129 Olliver and Hingley 1987: 132.
130 Ibid.: 134.
131 Ibid.: 167–68.
132 Ibid.: 135.
133 Ibid.
134 Ibid.
135 Ibid.: 168.
136 Ibid.: 136.
137 Banks in Beaglehole (ed.) 1962: II 21.
138 Lloyd and Coulter 1961: 72.
139 Ollivier and Hingley 1987: 38.
140 Ibid.: 138.
141 Ibid.: 139.
142 Ibid.
143 Ibid.: 43.
144 Ibid.: 141.

Chapter Thirteen

1 Ollivier 1985: 255.
2 Dunmore 1965: 169.
3 Kelly 1951: 23.
4 Ross 1978: 118–20.
5 Ling Roth 1891: 69.
6 Dunmore 1965: 166–67.
7 Kelly 1951: 23.
8 D'Après de Mannevillette in Ollivier 1985: 364.
9 Ling Roth 1891: 29.
10 My thanks to Isabel Ollivier for this identification.
11 Le Dez in Ollivier 1985: 259–60.
12 Ollivier 1985: 261–62.
13 Ibid.: 276.
14 Roux in Ollivier 1985: 125.
15 Ling Roth 1891: 23.
16 Hayward 1987: 160.
17 De Montaison in Ollivier 1985: 227.
18 Roux in ibid.: 129–31.
19 Roux in ibid.: 134–35.
20 De Montaison in ibid.: 231.
21 Ibid.
22 Roux in ibid.: 139.
23 Du Clesmeur Journal in ibid.: 23.
24 Roux in ibid.: 139.
25 Ibid.: 139–41.
26 Crozet in Ling Roth (ed.) 1891: 25.
27 White MS papers 75 B19: 83, 88.
28 Roux in Ollivier 1985: 141.
29 Du Clesmeur Journal in ibid.: 23.
30 Crozet in Ling Roth (ed.) 1891: 26.
31 Ibid.: 27–28.
32 Roux in Ollivier 1985: 143.
33 Crozet in Ling Roth (ed.) 1891: 28.
34 White (MS papers 75, B19: 8) in Orbell (trans.) 1965: 16.
35 White APL NZ MSS 30.
36 Kelly 1951: 34
37 Jack Lee pers. comm. 1990.
38 Roux in Ollivier 1985: 145.
39 Du Clesmeur Navigational Journal in ibid.: 109. Spencer (pers. comm. 1991), for instance, characterises Cook's charts of the bay as 'far superior in execution and exactness'.
40 Roux in ibid.: 147.
41 Kelly 1951: 89–90.
42 Du Clesmeur Journal in Ollivier 1985: 25.
43 Crozet in Ling Roth (ed.) 1891: 47.
44 White in Orbell (trans.) 1965: 16.
45 Le Dez in Ollivier 1985: 291.
46 Du Clesmeur Journal in ibid.: 27.
47 Crozet in Ling Roth (ed.) 1891: 48.
48 Ibid.: 49.
49 Roux in ibid.: 157.
50 Ibid.: 157.
51 Kelly 1951: 87–88.
52 Ibid.: 88.
53 White 1857 NZMSS 30: 11.
54 Abraham 1954: 244–46.
55 White in Orbell (trans.) 1965: 16.
56 Roux in Ollivier 1985: 175.
57 Crozet in Ling Roth (ed.) 1891: 49–50.
58 White in Orbell (trans.) 1965: 17. This account claims, however, that the clothes were stolen on the coast and the chiefs were tied up on board one of the ships; these are probably locational slips due to the oral transmission of the story over a period of at least seventy years. Note too, a translation slip in Orbell, which collapses the phrases 'ngaa kahu i taahaetia ra e Ngaati Pou, hei hapainga maa raatou ki Te

Hikutu, ki te iwi o Te Kauri' (the clothes stolen by Ngaati Pou, for them to give to Te Hikutuu, the people of Te Kauri) into a very misleading translation: 'The clothes had been stolen by Te Hikutuu to give to Te Kauri's people').

59   White in Orbell (trans.) 1965: 17.
60   Roux in Ollivier 1985: 161.
61   Ibid.: 163.
62   Roux in ibid.: 175.
63   De Montaison in ibid.: 237.
64   Roux in ibid.: 177.
65   Ibid.: 265.
66   Du Clesmeur in ibid.: 28.
67   De Montaison in Ollivier 1985: 239.
68   Kennedy 1969: 37.
69   White in Orbell (trans.) 1965: 17; White MS papers 75, B19: 88.
70   Roux in Ollivier 1985: 183.
71   Ngaati Pou, Ngaati Wai and Ngare Raumati were all essentially remnant hapuu of Ngaati Awa; and at this time the distinction between Ngaati Wai and Ngaati Pou was ill defined (Jack Lee, pers. comm. 1990).
72   Roux in Oliver 1985: 185–87.
73   Crozet in Ling Roth (ed.) 1891: 55.
74   White 1888: 158.
75   Ibid.: 172.
76   Kelly 1951: 54, 110. This man was identified by Dumont d'Urville as 'Tupahia or Malu', and by Kelly as Maru, the son of the famed fighting chief Whakaaria, an identification disputed, however, by local Maori at the time.
77   White in Orbell (trans.) 1965: 17.
78   White MS papers 75 B19: 88.
79   White in Orbell (trans.) 1965: 17.
80   Le Dez in Ollivier 1985: 292.
81   Crozet in Ling Roth (ed.) 1871: 70.
82   Ibid.: 71.
83   Ibid.: 76.
84   Ibid.: 75.
85   Ibid.: 77.
86   Du Clesmeur in Ollivier 1985: 35.

87   Le Dez in ibid.: 317.
88   Ibid.: 317–19.
89   Crozet in Ling Roth (ed.) 1891: 66.
90   Roux in Ollivier 1985: 169. Men suffering from syphillis would certainly still have been infectious after five months at sea, and some of those with gonorrhea were likely to be still infectious also (Dr Rick Franklin, STD Clinic, Auckland Hospital, pers. comm. 1911).
91   Crozet in Ling Roth (ed.) 1891: 37.
92   Ibid.: 38.
93   Le Dez in Ollivier 1985: 323.
94   Ibid.: 325.
95   Du Clesmeur in ibid.: 34.
96   Crozet in Ling Roth (ed.) 1891: 40.
97   Ibid.: 43–44.
98   My thanks to Janet Davidson for this suggestion.
99   Le Dez in Ollivier 1985: 323.
100   My thanks to Janet Davidson for this suggestion.
101   Roux in Ollivier 1985: 165.
102   Le Dez in ibid.: 327.
103   Crozet in Ling Roth (ed.) 1891: 44.
104   Le Dez in Ollivier 1985: 329.
105   Roux in ibid.: 169.
106   Crozet in Ling Roth (ed.) 1891: 29–35.
107   Roux in Ollivier 1985: 163.
108   De Montaison in ibid.: 247.
109   Crozet in Ling Roth (ed.) 1891: 66.
110   Ibid.
111   Roux in Ollivier 1985: 167–69.
112   Crozet in Ling Roth (ed.) 1891: 66.
113   Ibid.: 45.
114   Ibid.
115   Du Clesmeur in Ollivier 1985: 35.
116   Le Dez in ibid.: 335.
117   Ibid.: 338–41.
118   Du Clesmeur in ibid.: 35.
119   Le Dez in ibid: 335.
120   Crozet in Ling Roth (ed.) 1891: 40.
121   Le Dez in Ollivier 1985: 337.

Bibliography

Abel Tasman National Park Board, 1962, *Abel Tasman National Park: A Handbook for Visitors*. Nelson.

———— 1985. *A Park for all Seasons: The Story of Abel Tasman National Park*. Welllington, Lands and Survey Department.

Abraham, A. C. T., 1954. Some Bay of Islands Maori Place Names. *Journal of the Polynesian Society*, 63: 243–46.

Adams, Brian, 1986. *The Flowering of the Pacific: Being an Account of Joseph Banks' Travels in the South Seas and the Story of his Florilegium*. Sydney, Collins.

Adams, J. W., 1981. Consensus, Community and Exoticism. *Journal of Interdisciplinary History*, XII (2): 253– 66.

Akerblom, Kjell, 1968. *Astronomy and Navigation in Polynesia and Micronesia*. Stockholm, The Ethnographical Museum.

Allan, Ruth, 1965. *Nelson: A History of Early Settlement*. Wellington, Reed.

Andaya, Leonard and Barbara, 1988. *Glimpses of Indonesian history*. Auckland, New Zealand Asian Society.

Anderson, Atholl, 1983. *When All the Moa Ovens Grew Cold*. Dunedin, Otago Heritage Books.

———— 1986. Mahinga Ika o te Moana: Selection in the pre-European fish-catch of Southern New Zealand in ed. A. Anderson, *Traditional Fishing in the Pacific*. Bishop Museum, Honolulu.

Anonymous, 1969. Was Young Nicks Head the First Piece of Land Seen by Captain Cook and His Crew? *New Zealand Surveyor*, 236: 208–10.

Babayan, Chad, *et al.*, 1987. Voyage to Aotearoa. *Journal of the Polynesian Society*, 96: 161–200.

Bacon, Francis (ed. J. M. Robertson), 1905. *The Philosophical Works of Francis Bacon*. London, Routledge.

Badger, G., 1988. *The Explorers of the Pacific*. Kenthurst, Kangaroo Press.

Bain, Pamela, 1986. A Reappraisal of the Maori Rock Drawings at Cook's Cove, Tolaga Bay. *New Zealand Archaeological Association Newsletter*, 29: 167–75.

Barratt, Glynn (ed.), 1987. *Queen Charlotte Sound, New Zealand: The Traditional and European Records, 1820*. Ottawa, Carleton University Press.

Barton, G., 1978. A History of the Landscape of Kennedy Bay, Coromandel Peninsula — an archaeological and historical geographical investigation. Typescript, University of Auckland Anthropology Reading Room.

Baudet, Henri, 1965. *Paradise on Earth: Some Thoughts on European Images of Non-European Man*. Connecticut, Greenwood Press.

Beaglehole, J. C. (ed.), 1942. *Abel Janszoon Tasman and the Discovery of New Zealand*. Wellington, Department of Internal Affairs.

———— 1961. *The Discovery of New Zealand*. London, Oxford University Press.

———— (ed.), 1962. *The Endeavour Journal of Joseph Banks 1768–1771, Vols I and II*. Sydney, Angus and Robertson.

———— (ed.), 1968. *The Journals of Captain James Cook on His Voyages of Discovery: Vol. I. The Voyage of the Endeavour 1768–1771*. Cambridge, at the University Press, for The Hakluyt Society.

———— 1974. *The Life of Captain James Cook*. London, Hakluyt Society.

Beattie, H., 1915–1922. Traditions and Legends Collected from Natives of Murihiku (Southland, New Zealand), in *Journal of the Polynesian Society*, XXIV 1915: 98–112, 130–39; XXV 1916: 9–17, 53–65; XXVI 1917: 75–85; XXVII 1918: 137–61; XXVIII 1919: 152–59, 212–25; XXIX 1920: 128–38, 189–98; XXXI 1922: 134–44, 193–97.

Begg, A. C. and Begg, N. C., 1970. *James Cook and New Zealand*. Wellington, Government Printer.

Bellwood, Peter, 1978. *The Polynesians: Prehistory of an Island People*. London, Thames and Hudson.

Berg, Maxine, 1985. *The Age of Manufactures, 1700–1820*. London, Fontana.

Best, Elsdon, 1974. *The Stone Implements of the Maori*. Wellington, Government Printer.

———— 1976. *Maori Religion and Mythology: Part 1*. Wellington, Government Printer.

450

——— 1982. *Maori Religion and Mythology: Part 2*. Wellington, Government Printer.

Best, Simon, 1980. Oruarangi Pa: Past and Present Investigations. *New Zealand Journal of Archaeology*, 2: 65–91.

Binney, Judith, 1987. Maori Oral Narratives, Pakeha Written Texts: Two Forms of Telling History. *New Zealand Journal of History*, 21 (1): 16–28.

Bithell, Jenny, n.d. *Guide to the History of Whitianga*. Thames, Thames Historical Printers.

Black, V., 1985. *The Spirit of Coromandel*. Auckland, Reed Methuen.

Borofsky, Robert, 1987. *Making History — Pukapukan and Anthropological Constructions of Knowledge*. Cambridge, Cambridge University Press.

Boxer, C., 1963. The Dutch East-Indiamen: Their Sailors, Their Navigators, and Life on Board, 1602–1795. *Mariner's Mirror*, 49 (2): 80–104.

——— 1965, *The Dutch Seaborne Empire 1600–1800*. London, Hutchinson.

Brailsford, Barry, 1981. *The Tattooed Land: The Southern Frontiers of the Pa Maori*. Wellington, Reed.

——— 1984. *Greenstone Trails: The Maori Search for Pounamu*. Wellington, Reed.

Braudel, Fernand, 1981. *The Structures of Everyday Life*. London, Collins.

Brewer, J., 1980. Laws and Disorder in Stuart and Hanoverian England. *History Today*, 30: 18–27.

Briggs, Asa (ed.), 1969. *How They Lived, Vol. III 1700–1815*. London, Blackwell.

Broad, Lowther, 1892. *The Jubilee History of Nelson, from 1842 to 1892*. Nelson, Bond, Finney.

Buchanan, C., n.d. Ahuahu (Great Mercury Island): Memoirs of Cameron Buchanan, Resident of Mercury Island 1859–1873. Typescript, Auckland Public Library.

Buchanan, J. D. H., (ed. D. R. Simmons), 1973. *The Maori History and Place Names of Hawke's Bay*. Wellington, Reed.

Buffon, (trans. Barr), 1797. *Buffon's Natural History, containing a Theory of the Earth, A General History of Man, of the Brute Creation, and of Vegetables, Minerals Ec. Ec., Vol. IV*. London, Symonds.

Butts, David, 1978. Rotokura: An Archaeological Site in Tasman Bay. *Journal of the Nelson Historical Society*, 3 (4): 5–17.

——— 1979. Archaeology in Tasman Bay. *Journal of the Nelson Historical Society*, 3 (5): 40–44.

Campbell, I. C., 1980. Savages Noble and Ignoble: Preconceptions of Early European Voyagers in Polynesia. *Pacific Studies*, 4 (1): 45–59.

Carr, D. J., 1983a. The Books That Sailed with the Endeavour. *Endeavour*, 7 (4): 194–201.

——— 1983b. *Sydney Parkinson: Artist of Cook's Endeavour Voyage*. Sydney, Nova Pacifica.

Carter, Harold B., 1988. *Sir Joseph Banks 1743–1820*. London, British Museum (Natural History).

Caselberg, J. (ed.), 1975. *Maori is My Name: Historical Maori Writings in Translation*. Dunedin, McIndoe.

Challis, Aidan, 1978. *Motueka: An Archaeological Survey*. Auckland, Longman Paul.

Champion, T., *et al.*, 1984. *Prehistoric Europe*. London, Academic Press.

Charlton, D. G., 1984. *New Images of the Natural in France*. Cambridge, Cambridge University Press.

Cipolla, Carlo M., 1976. *Public Health and the Medical Profession in the Renaissance*. Cambridge, Cambridge University Press.

——— 1981. *Before the Industrial Revolution: European Society and Economy 1000–1700*. London, Methuen.

Cohn, Bernard S., 1981. Anthropology and History in the 1980s: Toward a Rapprochement. *Journal of Interdisciplinary History*, XII (2): 227–52.

——— An Anthropologist among the Historians: A Field Study, in *An Anthropologist among the Historians and Other Essays*. Delhi, Oxford University Press.

Colenso, William, 1844. *Excursion in the Northern Island of New Zealand in the Summer of 1841–42*. Launceston, Launceston Examiner.

——— 1868. On the Maori Races of New Zealand. *Transactions and Proceedings of the New Zealand Institute*, 1: 339–424.

——— 1881. Historical Incidents and Traditions of the Olden Times, pertaining to the Maoris of the North Island (East Coast), New Zealand. *Transactions and Proceedings of the New Zealand Institute*, 13: 3–38; 14 3–33.

——— 1888. *Fifty Years Ago in New Zealand: A Commemoration: A Jubilee Paper: A Retrospect, Read before the Hawke's Bay Philosophical Institute October 17 1887*. Napier, R. C. Harding.

Comaroff, J. and Comaroff, J., 1988. Through the Looking-Glass: Colonial Encounters of the First Kind. *Journal of Historical Sociology*, 1: 6–32.

Cruise, R. A., 1824. *Journal of a Ten Months' Residence in New Zealand*. London, Longman, Hurst, Rees, Orme, Brown and Green.

Curnow, Jennifer, 1983. Wiremu Maihi Te Rangikaheke. MA Thesis, University of Auckland.

Dalrymple, Alexander, 1770. *An Historical Collection of the Several Voyages and Discoveries in the South Pacific*

Ocean. London, Nourse.

Darnton, Robert, 1985. *The Great Cat Massacre, and other Episodes in French Cultural History*. New York, Random House.

David, Andrew (ed.), 1988. *The Charts and Coastal Views of Captain Cook's Voyages: The Voyage of the Endeavour 1768–1771*. London, Hakluyt Society.

Davidson, Janet, 1984. *The Prehistory of New Zealand*. Auckland, Longman Paul.

Davis, C. O. B., 1855, *Maori Mementoes. A Series of Addresses by the Native People to Sir George Grey . . . A Small Collection of Laments*. Auckland, Williamson and Wilson.

———— 1974. *The Life and Times of Patuone, The Celebrated Nga Puhi Chief*. Auckland, Field.

Davis, N. Z., 1981. The Possibilities of the Past. *Journal of Interdisciplinary History*, XII (2): 267–75.

Debus, Allen G., 1978. *Man and Nature in the Renaissance*. Cambridge, Cambridge University Press.

Dening, Greg, 1966. Ethnohistory in Polynesia. *Journal of Pacific History*, 1: 23–42.

———— 1988. *History's Anthropology: The Death of William Gooch*. Lanham, Maryland, University Press of America.

Doak, Wade, 1984. *Fishes of the New Zealand Region*. Auckland, Hodder and Stoughton.

Downes, T. W., 1914. History of Ngati-Kahungunu. *Journal of the Polynesian Society*, 23: 28–33, 111–24, 219–25; 24: 57–61, 77–85, 121–29; 25 1–8, 33–43, 77–88.

Doyle, William, 1978. *The Old European Order 1660–1800*. Oxford, Oxford University Press.

Duchet, Michèle, 1971. *Anthropologie et Histoire Au Siècle des Lumières*. Paris, Flammarion.

Duff, Roger, 1956. *The Moa-Hunter Period of Maori Culture*. Wellington, Government Printer.

Dunmore, J., 1965. *French Explorers in the Pacific, Vol I*. Oxford, Clarendon Press.

———— 1981. *The Expedition of the St Jean-Baptiste to the Pacific 1769–1770*. London, Hakluyt Society.

During, Simon, 1989. What was The West? Some Relations between Modernity, Colonisation and Writing. *Meanjin*, 48 (4): 759–76.

Edson, S., and Brown, D., 1977. Salvage Excavation of an Archaic Burial Context, N44/97, Hahei. *Records of the Auckland Institute and Museum*, 14: 25–36.

Elder, John (ed.), 1933. *The Letters and Journals of Samuel Marsden 1765–1838*. Dunedin, Coulls Somerville Wilkie, and Reed, for the Otago University Council.

Elvy, W. J., 1957. *Kei Puta Te Wairau: A History of Marlborough in Maori Times*. Christchurch, Whitcombe and Tombs.

Fairbrother, Nan, 1970. *New Lives, New Landscapes*. Harmondsworth, Penguin Books.

Fanning, Pauline, 1970. *James Cook: His Early Life and the Endeavour Voyage*. Canberra, National Library of Australia.

Farris, N. M., 1987. Remembering the Future, Anticipating the Past: History, Time and Cosmology among the Maya of Yucatan. *Comparative Studies in Society and History*, 29: 566–93.

Field, A. N., 1942. *Nelson Province 1642–1842: From Discovery to Colonisation*. Nelson, Betts.

Finney, Ben R. (ed.), 1976. *Pacific Navigation and Voyaging*. Wellington, Polynesian Society.

———— 1979. *Hokule'a: The Way to Tahiti*. New York, Dodd, Mead.

Fowler, Leo, 1974. *Te Mana o Turanga*. Auckland, Historic Places Trust.

Fox, Aileen, 1902. Hawke's Bay, in Prickett (ed.), *The First Thousand Years*.

Friedman, Jonathan, 1985. Captain Cook, Culture and the World System. *Journal of Pacific History*, XX (4): 191–201.

Furey, M. L., 1981. Field Recording and the Coromandel Region: A Discussion of Site Survey Methodology and Data Analysis. MA Thesis, University of Auckland.

———— 1982. Review of Coromandel Peninsula Excavation Literature. *New Zealand Archaeological Association Newsletter*, 25 (1): 30–46.

Fry, Howard T., *et al.*, 1970. *The Significance of Cook's Endeavour Voyage: Three Bicentennial Lectures*. Townsville, James Cook University of North Queensland.

George, M. Dorothy (ed.), 1928. *England in Johnson's Day*. London, Methuen.

———— 1965. *London Life in the Eighteenth Century*. Harmondsworth, Penguin Books.

Geyl, Pieter, 1961. *The Netherlands in the Seventeenth Century, Pts 1 and 2*. London, Benn.

Gladwin, Thomas, 1970. *East is a Big Bird: Navigation and Logic on Puluwat Atoll*. Cambridge, Mass., Harvard University Press.

Glass, D. V., and Eversley, D. E. C. (eds), 1965. *Population in History: Essays in Historical Demography*. London, Edward Arnold.

Gossman, Lionel, 1972. *French Society and Culture: Background for Eighteenth Century Literature*. New Jersey, Prentice-Hall.

Goubert, P., (trans. S. Cox), 1969. *The Ancien Régime: French Society 1600–1750*. London, Weidenfeld and Nicolson.

Grace, John Te H., 1959. *Tuwharetoa: A History of the Maori People of the Taupo District.* Wellington, Reed.

Graham, George, 1920. The Wars of Ngati Huarere and Ngai-Maru-Tuahu, of Hauraki Gulf. *Journal of the Polynesian Society,* 29: 37–41.

———— 1946. Some Taniwha and Tupua. *Journal of the Polynesian Society,* 55: 26–39.

Grayland, E. and Grayland, V., 1968. *Coromandel Coast.* Wellington, Reed.

Green, Roger, and Pawley, A., 1974. Dating the Dispersal of the Oceanic Languages. University of Auckland, Department of Anthropology.

Grey, Sir George, 1854. Copy of a Despatch from Governor Sir George Grey. *Further Papers Relative to the Affairs of New Zealand.* London, Eyre and Spottiswoode.

———— 1961. *Polynesian Mythology: An Ancient Traditional History of the Maori as Told by their Priests and Chiefs.* Christchurch, Whitcombe and Tombs.

Gudgeon, W. E., 1894–97. The Maori Tribes of the East Coast of New Zealand: Parts I–V. *Journal of the Polynesian Society,* 3: 208–19; 4: 17–32, 177–82; 5: 1–12; 6: 177–86.

———— 1907. A Maori Cosmogony. *Journal of the Polynesian Society,* 16: 109–19.

Habib, G., 1989. *Report on Ngai Tahu Fisheries Evidence.* Auckland, Waitangi Tribunal.

Haddon, A. C., and Hornell, James, 1936. *Canoes of Oceania: Vol. I.* Honolulu, Bernice P. Bishop Museum.

Hair, A., 1985. *Muriwai and Beyond.* Gisborne, Gisborne Herald for Muriwai School Centenary Book Committee.

Hamlyn, Rev. J., 1915. Estimate of the Maori Population in the North Island Circa 1840. *Journal of the Polynesian Society,* 24: 72–74.

Hammond, L. D. (ed.), 1970. *News from New Cythera: A Report of Bougainville's Voyage 1766–1769.* Minneapolis, University of Minnesota Press.

Harlow, Ray, n.d. Maori Dialects and Multiple Origins. Conference paper, typescript.

Harris, Marvin, 1987. Population Regulation in the Age of Colonialism, in *Death, Sex and Fertility.* New York, Columbia University Press.

Harrison, J. F. C., 1984. *The Common People: A History from the Norman Conquest to the Present.* London, Fontana.

Haszard, H. D. M., 1903. Foot-tracks of Captain Cook. *Transactions and Proceedings of the New Zealand Institute,* XXXV, 24–45.

Hayward, B. W., 1987. Prehistoric Archaeological Sites on the Three Kings Islands, Northern New Zealand. *Records of the Auckland Institute and Museum,* 24: 147–61.

Heninger, S. K., 1977. *The Cosmographical Glass: Renaissance Diagrams of the Universe.* San Marino, Calif., Huntingdon Library.

Herdendorf, C. E., 1986. Captain James Cook and the Transits of Mercury and Venus. *Journal of Pacific History,* XXI (1): 39–55.

Hervé, Roger, (trans. John Dunmore), 1983. *Chance Discovery of Australia and New Zealand by Portuguese and Spanish Navigators between 1521 and 1528.* Palmerston North, Dunmore Press.

Hoare, Michael, 1977. *In the Steps of Beaglehole: Cook Researches Past and Prospect.* Dunedin, Hocken Library.

Hocken, T. M., 1895. Abel Tasman and His Journal. *Transactions and Proceedings of the New Zealand Institute,* XXVIII: 117–40.

Hodgen, Margaret T., 1964. *Early Anthropology in the Sixteenth and Seventeenth Centuries.* Philadelphia, University of Pennsylvania Press.

Hollyman, K. L., 1986. Les Emprints Polyngiens Dans les Langues de la Nouvelle-Calédonie et Des Îles Loyauté. *Cahiers de Lacito,* 1: 67–88.

Holy Bible, 1611. *The Holy Bible, Conteyning the Old Testament and the New.* Robert Barker.

Hongi, H., 1918. On the Greenstone Tiki: What the Emblem Signifies. *Journal of the Polynesian Society,* 27: 162–63, 199–201.

Horrocks, L. C., 1976. A Study in Intercultural Conflict: The du Fresne Massacre at the Bay of Islands, New Zealand 1772. *The Artefact,* I (1): 7–29.

Houghton, Phillip, 1975. The People of Wairau Bar. *Records of the Canterbury Museum,* 9 (3): 231–46.

———— 1977. Prehistoric Burials from Recent Excavations on Motutapu Island. *Records of the Auckland Institute and Museum,* 14: 37–43.

———— 1977. Human Skeletal Material from Excavations in Eastern Coromandel. *Records of the Auckland Institute and Museum,* 14: 45–56.

———— 1980. *The First New Zealanders.* Auckland, Hodder and Stoughton.

Howse, Derek, 1979. The Principal Scientific Instruments Taken on Captain Cook's Voyages of Exploration 1768–80. *Mariner's Mirror,* 65 (2): 119–35.

Hughes, Robert, 1987. *The Fatal Shore: A History of the Transportation of Convicts to Australia 1787–1868.*

London, Collins Harvill.

Huizinga, J. H., 1968. *Dutch Civilization in the Seventeenth Century, and other essays.* London, Collins.

Iles, Mark, 1981. A Maori History of Tokomaru Bay. MA Thesis, University of Auckland.

Irwin, G., 1989. Against, Across and Down the Wind: A Case for the Systematic Exploration of the Remote Pacific Islands. *Journal of the Polynesian Society*, 98 (2): 167–206.

Jennings, Jesse (ed.), 1979. *The Prehistory of Polynesia.* Cambridge, Mass., Harvard University Press.

Johnson, Leigh, 1986. Aspects of the Prehistory of the Far Northern Valley Systems. MA Thesis, University of Auckland.

Jones, C., n.d. *New Zealand's Bay of Islands: The Land and Sea Guide.* Auckland, Deddings Press.

Jones, Kevin, 1983. Joseph Banks' 'Fence of Poles' at Cook's Cove, East Coast, North Island, New Zealand. *Journal of the Polynesian Society*, 92: 531–36.

———— 1984, A 1761 George III Medalet from the East Coast, North Island, New Zealand: relic of Cook's first voyage? *Journal of the Polynesian Society*, 93: 315–20.

———— 1986. Polynesian Settlement and Horticulture in Two River Catchments of the Eastern North Island, New Zealand. *New Zealand Journal of Archaeology*, 8: 5–32.

———— 1988. Horticulture and Settlement Chronology of the Waipaoa River Catchment, East Coast, North Island, New Zealand. *New Zealand Journal of Archaeology*, 10: 19–51.

———— 1989a. Traditional Maori Horticulture in the Eastern North Island. *New Zealand Journal of Agricultural Science*, 23: 36–41.

———— 1989b. 'In Much Greater Affluence': Productivity and Welfare in Maori Gardening at Anaura Bay, October 1769. *Journal of the Polynesian Society*, 98: 49–75.

Jones, K., and Law, G., 1987. Prehistoric Population Estimates for the Tolaga Bay Vicinity, East Coast, North Island, New Zealand. *New Zealand Journal of Archaeology*, 9: 81–114.

Jones, Stephanie, 1986. The Builders of Captain Cook's Ships. *Mariner's Mirror*, 70 (3): 299–302.

Joppien, R., and Smith, B., 1985. *The Art of Captain Cook's Voyages, Vol. I.* Melbourne, Oxford University Press.

Journal of a Voyage around the World in H.M.S. Endeavour . . . 1768–1771, 1771. (Attributed to James Magra or Matra.) 1967 reprint, Amsterdam, N. Israel.

Kaamira, Himiona, 1957. Kupe. *Journal of the Polynesian Society*, 66: 216–48.

Kaeppler, Adrienne, 1978. *'Artificial Curiosities': being an exposition of native manufactures collected on the three Pacific voyages of Captain James Cook, R.N.* Bernice P. Bishop Museum Special Publication 65, Honolulu, Bishop Museum Press.

Kamen, Henry, 1971. *The Iron Century: Social Change in Europe 1550–1660.* London, Weidenfeld and Nicolson.

Kawau, Piri, 1880. Aotea Migration. *Appendix to the Journals of the House of Representatives* 1880, v. 2, G-8. Translation of extract of Aotea Migration from Nga Tupuna Maori by Sir George Grey.

Kelly, Florence, 1963. *O Te Raki: Maori Legends of the North.* Auckland, Paul's Book Arcade.

Kelly, L. G., 1933. In the Path of Marion du Fresne. *Journal of the Polynesian Society*, 42: 83–98.

———— 1938. Fragments of Ngapuhi History: The Conquest of the Ngare Raumati. *Journal of the Polynesian Society*, 47: 163–72.

———— 1949. *Tainui: The Story of Hoturoa and his Descendants.* Wellington, Polynesian Society.

———— 1951. *Marion du Fresne at the Bay of Islands.* Wellington, Reed.

———— 1953. Wharetaewa Pa, Mercury Bay, 1952. *Journal of the Polynesian Society*, 62 (3): 384–91.

Kennedy, Jean, 1969. *Settlement in the Bay of Islands 1772: A Study in Text-Aided Field Archaeology.* Anthropology Department, University of Otago.

Kereama, Matire, 1968. *The Tail of the Fish: Maori Memories of the Far North.* Auckland, Maxwell Printing.

Kirch, Patrick V., and Green, R. C., 1987. History, Phylogeny and Evolution in Polynesia. *Current Anthropology*, 28 (4): 431–56.

———— 1988. The Talepakemalai Lapita Site and Oceanic Prehistory. *National Geographic Research*, 4 (3): 328–42.

Kirch, P. V., and Hunt, T. L. (eds), 1988. *Archaeology of the Lapita Cultural Complex: A Critical Review.* Seattle, Burke Museum.

Küschel, G., 1975. *Biogeography and Ecology in New Zealand.* The Hague, Junk.

Ladurie, E. Le Roy, (trans. B. Bray), 1984. *Montaillou: Cathars and Catholics in a French Village 1294–1324.* Harmondsworth, Penguin Books.

Lambert, T., 1925. *The Story of Old Wairoa and the East Coast.* Dunedin, Coulls Somerville Wilkie.

Langdon, Robert, 1975. *The Lost Caravel.* Sydney, Pacific Publications.

Laurie, John, 1987. *Tolaga Bay: A History of the Uawa District.* Gisborne, Gisborne Herald.

Law, Gary, 1982. Coromandel Peninsula and Great Barrier Island, in Prickett (ed.) *The First Thousand Years.*

Lawson, Lloyd, 1987. *Wharekahika: A History of Hicks Bay.* Hicks Bay, the author.

Leach, B. Foss, and Leach, Helen M. (eds), 1979. *Prehistoric Man in Palliser Bay.* Wellington, National Museum of New Zealand.

Leach, Helen M., 1984. *1000 Years of Gardening in New Zealand.* Wellington, Reed.

Leach, B. Foss., *et al.*, 1986. The Origin of Obsidian Artefacts from the Chathams and Kermadec Islands. *New Zealand Journal of Archaeology*, 8: 143–70.

———— 1989. Traditional Maori Horticulture — Success and Failure in Aotearoa. *New Zealand Agricultural Science*, 23:34–41.

Lee, A. L., 1938. *Whitianga, Auckland Province, New Zealand.* Auckland, Abel, Dykes Printers.

Lee, J. R., 1970. Historical Map of the Bay of Islands. Wellington, New Zealand Historic Places Trust.

———— 1983. *I Have Named it the Bay of Islands.* Auckland, Hodder and Stoughton.

———— 1987. *Hokianga.* Auckland, Hodder and Stoughton.

Levack, Brian P., 1987. *The Witch-hunt in Early Modern Europe.* New York, Longmans.

Levison, M.; Ward, R. G.; and Webb, J. W., 1973. *The Settlement of Polynesia: A Computer Simulation.* Canberra, Australian National University.

Lewis, David, 1967. *Daughters of the Wind.* London, Gollancz.

———— 1972. *We, the Navigators.* Canberra, Australian National University Press.

———— 1978. *The Voyaging Stars: Secrets of the Pacific Island Navigators.* London, Collins.

Ling Roth, H., 1891. *Crozet's Voyage to Tasmania, New Zealand, and the Ladrone Islands, and the Philippines in the Years 1771–1772.* London, Truslove and Shirley.

Lloyd, C., and Coulter, J. L. S., 1961. *Medicine and the Navy 1200–1900; Vol. III 1714–1815.* Edinburgh, Livingstone.

Lucas, J. H., 1980. *Coromandel: Vol. I, Early Settlement — Maori and Pakeha.* Coromandel, Coroprint.

Lyons, Sir Henry, 1944. *The Royal Society 1660–1940: A History of its Administration under its Charters.* Cambridge, Cambridge University Press.

Lysaght, A. M. (ed.), 1980. *The Journal of Joseph Banks in the Endeavour.* Adelaide, Rigby.

Lubbock, B. (trans.), 1934. *Barlow's Journal of his Life at Sea in King's Ships, East and West Indiamen and other Merchantmen from 1659 to 1703, Vols I and II.* London, Hurst and Blackett.

McCallum, G. K., 1971. A Date With Cook. *Journal of the Royal Australian Historical Society*, 57 (1): 1–9.

McCaskill, K. W., 1981. *Scenic Reserves of Marlborough.* Wellington, Department of Lands and Survey.

McClellan, James E., 1985. *Science Re-organized: Scientific Societies in the Eighteenth Century.* New York, Columbia University Press.

McCormick, E. H., 1959. *Tasman and New Zealand: A Bibliographical Study.* Wellington, Government Printer.

———— 1977. *Omai: Pacific Envoy.* Auckland, Auckland University Press/Oxford University Press.

McGowan, A. P., 1979. Captain Cook's Ships. *Mariner's Mirror*, 65 (2): 109–18.

McIntyre, K. G., 1977. *The Secret Discovery of Australia: Portuguese Ventures 200 years before Captain Cook.* Medindie, South Australia, Souvenir Press.

Mack, P., and Jacob, M. C., 1987. *Politics and Culture in Early Modern Europe: Essays in Honour of H. G. Koenigsberger.* Cambridge, Cambridge University Press.

Mackay, Alexander, 1873. *A Compendium of Official Documents Relative to Native Affairs in the South Island, Vols I and II.* Wellington, Government Printer.

Mackay, Joseph A. (ed.), 1927. *Life in Early Poverty Bay: joint golden jubilees.* Gisborne, Gisborne Publishing.

———— 1966. *Historic Poverty Bay and the East Coast, N.I., New Zealand.* Gisborne, Poverty Bay-East Coast Centennial Council.

McKenzie, D. W. (ed.), 1987. *Heinemann New Zealand Atlas.* Auckland, Heinemann.

McNab, Robert, 1914. *Historical Records of New Zealand, Vols I and II.* Wellington, Government Printer.

Maddock, S., 1969. *As Far As a Man May Go: Captain Cook's New Zealand.* Auckland, Collins.

Mahuika, Apirana T., 1973. Nga Wahine Kai-Hautu o Ngati Porou: The Female Leaders of Ngati Porou. MA Thesis, University of Sydney.

Mander-Jones, P., 1972. *Manuscripts in the British Isles Relating to Australia, New Zealand and the Pacific.* Canberra, Australian National University Press.

Medick, Hans, 1987. 'Missionaries in the Row-Boat'? Ethnological Ways of Knowing as a Challenge to Social History. *Comparative Studies in Society and History*, 29: 76–98.

Meek, Ronald, 1976. *Social Science and the Ignoble Savage.* Cambridge, Cambridge University Press.

Meilink-Roelofsz, M. A. P., 1962. *Asian Trade and European Influence in the Indonesian Archipelago Between 1500 and about 1620.* The Hague, Nijhoff.

Millar, D. G. L., 1967. Recent Archaeological Excavations in the Northern Part of the South Island. *Journal of the Nelson Historical Society*, II (2): 5–12.

455

Milligan, R. R. D., 1958. Ranginui, Captive Chief of Doubtless Bay, 1769. *Journal of the Polynesian Society*, 67: 181–203.

Milton-Thompson, G. J., 1974. The Changing Character of the Sailor's Diet and Its Influence on Disease, in *Problems of Medicine at Sea*. London, Trustees of the National Maritime Museum.

Mitchell, J. H., 1944. *Takitimu: A History of the Ngaati Kahungunu People*. Wellington, Reed.

Moncrieff, Perrine, n.d. *People Came Later*. Nelson, Stiles.

Montaigne, M. de, (trans. D. M. Frame), 1960. *The Complete Works of Montaigne*. London, Hamish Hamilton.

Montanus, Arnoldus, 1671. *De Nieuwe en Onbekende Weereld: of beschrijving van America en 't Zuid-land*. Amsterdam, Jacob Meurs. Translated by Barbara Andaya, 1988.

Moon, G., and Lockley, R., 1982. *New Zealand's Birds, A Photographic Guide*. Auckland, Heinemann.

Moore, Tiniku, 1959. How our Great Grandparents Lived. *Te Ao Hou*, 26: 10–11.

Morris, E. E., 1900. On the Tracks of Captain Cook. *Transactions and Proceedings of the New Zealand Institute*, XXXIII: 499–514.

Morris, Roger, 1987. *Pacific Sail: Four Centuries of Western Ships in the Pacific*. Auckland, Bateman.

Morton, Harry, 1975. *The Wind Commands: Sailors and Sailing Ships in the Pacific*. Dunedin, McIndoe, and Vancouver, University of British Columbia Press.

Motuti Community Trust, 1986. *Karanga Hokianga*. Hokianga, Motuti Community Trust.

Muller and Co. (eds), 1965. *Abel Tasman's Journal*. Los Angeles, Kovach.

Munn, Dan, 1981. Ngati Manu: An Ethnohistorical Account. MA Thesis, University of Auckland.

Newman, A. K., 1905. On the Musical Notes and Other Features of the Long Maori Trumpet. *Transactions and Proceedings of the New Zealand Institute*, XXXVIII: 134–39.

Newport, J. N. W., 1971. *Collingwood: A History of the Area from the Earliest Days to 1912*. Christchurch, Caxton Press.

———— 1975. *Golden Bay: One Hundred Years of Local Government*. Blenheim, Golden Bay County Council.

———— 1979. Some Industries of Golden Bay. *Journal of the Nelson Historical Society*, 3.5: 5–31.

New Zealand Historic Places Trust, 1985. *Historic Places Inventory: Golden Bay County*. Wellington, New Zealand Historic Places Trust.

New Zealand's Heritage, 1971. Paul Hamlyn.

Ngata, A. T., 1949. The Io Cult — Early Migration — Puzzle of the Canoes. *Journal of the Polynesian Society*, 58: 335–48.

———— n.d. *Rauru-Nui-a-Toi Lectures and Ngati Kahungunu Origins*. Reprinted 1972 by Victoria University of Wellington, Department of Anthropology.

Nicholas, J. L., 1817. *A Narrative of a Voyage to New Zealand, 1814–1815, Vols I and II*. London, Black.

Nierop, Dirk Van, 1674. *Eenige Oefeningen in God-lijcke . . . Pt 2*: 56–64: 'Een kort Verhael uyt het Journael van den Komm. Abel Jansen Tasman'. Translated by Barbara Andaya, 1989.

Norman, Waerete, 1987. Muriwhenua. MA Thesis, University of Auckland.

O'Brien, Patrick, 1987. *Joseph Banks: A Life*. London, Collins Harvill.

Okawhare, Paratene, 1880. History of the Horouta Migration. *Appendix to the Journals of the House of Representatives*, Vol. II, G–L.

Oliver, Douglas, 1974. *Ancient Tahitian Society, Vols I, II, III*. Honolulu, University Press of Hawaii.

Oliver, W. H., 1971. *Challenge and Response: Study of the Development of the East Coast Region*. Gisborne, Gisborne Herald.

Ollivier, I., 1983. French Explorers in New Zealand 1769–1840: A List of Manuscript Material. *Turnbull Library Record*, 16 (1): 5–19, (2): 95–110.

Ollivier, I., and Spencer, J., 1985. *Extracts from Journals relating to the Visit to New Zealand in May–July 1772 of the French ships* Mascarin *and* Marquis de Castries *under the command of M. J. Marion du Fresne*. Wellington, Alexander Turnbull Library Endowment Trust with Indosuez N.Z. Ltd.

Ollivier, I.; Hingley, C.; and Spencer, J., 1987. *Extracts from Journals relating to the Visit to New Zealand of the French ship* St Jean Baptiste *under the command of J. F. M. de Surville*. Wellington, Alexander Turnbull Library Endowment Trust with Indosuez N.Z. Ltd.

Ong, W., 1982. *Orality and Literacy: The Technology of The Word*. London, Methuen.

Orbell, Margaret, 1965. The First Pakehas to Visit the Bay of Islands. *Te Ao Hou*, 51: 14–18.

———— 1985. *Hawaiki: A New Approach to Maori Tradition*. Christchurch, University of Canterbury.

Orchiston, Wayne, 1972. Maori Neck and Ear Ornaments of the 1770s: A Study in Proto-historic Ethno-archaeology. *Journal of the Royal Society of New Zealand*, 2 (1): 91–107.

———— 1974. Studies in South Island New Zealand Prehistory and Protohistory. PhD Thesis, University of Sydney.

Owen, John B., 1974. *The Eighteenth Century 1714–1815*. London, Nelson.

Parkinson, Sydney, 1972. *A Journal of a Voyage to the South Seas in His Majesty's Ship, The Endeavour.* Facsimile ed., Adelaide, Libraries Board of South Australia.

Parry, J. H., 1971. *Trade and Dominion: The European Oversea Empires in the Eighteenth Century.* London, Weidenfeld and Nicolson.

Pearson, W. H., 1969. European Intimidation and the Myth of Tahiti. *Journal of Pacific History,* 4: 199–217.

———— 1970. The Reception of European Voyagers on Polynesian Islands, 1568–1797. *Journal de la Société des Oceanistes,* 26: 121–54.

———— 1984. *Rifled Sanctuaries: Some Views of the Pacific Islands in Western Literature,* Auckland, University of Auckland.

Peart, J. D., 1937. *Old Tasman Bay.* Nelson, Lucas.

Pennington, D. H., 1970. *Seventeenth Century Europe.* New York, Longman.

Phillips, C. A., 1987. Locational Analysis on the Karikari Peninsula. MA Thesis, University of Auckland.

Phillipps, M. A. L., 1980. An Estimation of Fertility in Prehistoric New Zealanders. *New Zealand Journal of Archaeology,* 2: 149–67.

Piripi, Morore, 1961. Ko Te Timatatanga Mai o Ngatiwai. *Te Ao Hou,* 37: 18–21; 38: 43–46; 39: 46–49.

Pohuhu, Nepia, 1880. History of Ngatiira, of the Takitimu Migration. *Appendix to the Journals of the House of Representatives,* Vol. II, G–L.

Polack, J., 1838. *New Zealand: Being a Narrative of Travels and Adventures, Vols I and II.* London, Bentley.

Ponder, W. Frank, 1986. *A Labyrinth of Waterways: The Forgotten Story of New Zealand's Marlborough Sounds.* Blenheim, Wenlock House.

Pool, D. Ian, 1977. *The Maori Population of New Zealand 1769–1971.* Auckland, Auckland University Press/Oxford University Press.

Porter, Frances, 1978. *A Sense of History: A Commemorative Publication for John Cawte Beaglehole.* Wellington, Government Printer.

Porter, Roy, 1982. *English Society in the Eighteenth Century.* Harmondsworth, Penguin Books.

Pounds, N. J. G., 1979. *A Historical Geography of Europe 1500–1840.* Cambridge, Cambridge University Press.

Price, Richard, 1983. *First-Time: The Historical Vision of an Afro-American People.* Baltimore, Johns Hopkins University Press.

Prickett, Nigel (ed.), 1982. *The First Thousand Years: Regional Perspectives in New Zealand Archaeology.* Palmerston North, Dunmore Press.

Priestly, H. I., 1939. *France Overseas Through the Old Regime.* New York, Appleton Century.

Pullar, Allan, 1959. Archaeology in the Gisborne District. *New Zealand Archaeological Association Newsletter,* 2 (2): 26–28.

Quaife, G. R., 1987. *Godly Zeal and Furious Rage: The Witch in Early Modern Europe.* Beckenham, Kent, Croom Helm.

Reed, Michael, 1986. *The Age of Exuberance 1550–1700.* London, Routledge and Kegan Paul.

Regnier, Corry, 1987. *Coromandel Ecological Region (Mainland Ecological Districts): Protected Natural Areas Programme: Compilation and Assessment of Ecological Information.* Wellington, Department of Conservation.

Rich, E. E., and Wilsom, C. H. (eds), 1967. *The Cambridge Economic History of Europe: Vol. IV: The Economy of Expanding Europe in the Sixteenth and Seventeenth Centuries.* Cambridge, Cambridge University Press.

Rodger, N. A. M., 1986. *The Wooden World: An Anatomy of the Georgian Navy.* London, Collins.

Rolland, R., Maurois, A., and Herriott, E., 1953. *French Thought in the Eighteenth Century.* London, Cassell.

Root, Deborah, 1988. The Imperial Signifier: Todorov and the Conquest of Mexico. *Cultural Critique,* 6–7: 197–219.

Ross, John O., 1982. *Captain F. G. Moore, Mariner and Pioneer.* Wanganui, Wanganui Newspapers.

Ross, Michael, 1978. *Bougainville.* London, Gordon and Cremonesi.

Rousseau, Jean-Jacques, (trans. M. Cranston), 1984. *A Discourse on Inequality.* Harmondsworth, Penguin Books.

Rowe, John H., 1964. Ethnography and Ethnology in the Sixteenth Century. *Kroeber Anthropological Society Papers,* 30, Berkeley, Department of Anthropology, University of California.

Ryan, Michael T., 1981. Assimilating New Worlds in the Sixteenth and Seventeenth Centuries. *Comparative Studies in Society and History,* 23: 519–38.

Sahlins, Marshall, 1985. *Islands of History,* Chicago, University of Chicago Press.

Salmond, Anne, 1975. *Hui: A Study of Maori Ceremonial Gatherings.* Wellington, Reed. (4th edition 1985.)

———— 1976. *Amiria: The Life Story of a Maori Woman.* Wellington, Reed.

———— 1980. *Eruera: The Teachings of a Maori Elder.* Auckland, Oxford University Press.

———— 1984. Maori Epistemologies, in *Reason and Morality,* ed. Joanna Overing: 240–63. London, Tavistock.

457

———— 1989. Tribal Words, Tribal Worlds: The Translatability of Tapu and Mana, in *Culture, Kin and Cognition In Oceania: Essays in Honour of Ward Goodenough*, eds M. Marshall and J. L. Caughey, Washington, D.C., American Anthropological Association.

Schama, Simon, 1987. *The Embarrassment of Riches*. London, Fontana Press.

Scott, A. F. (ed.), 1970. *Every One a Witness: The Georgian Age*. London, Martins.

Sen, S. P., 1958. *The French in India 1763–1816*. Calcutta, Mukhopadhyay.

Sharp, Andrew, 1968. *The Voyages of Abel Janszoon Tasman*. Oxford, Clarendon Press.

Shawcross, K., 1966. Maoris of the Bay of Islands 1769–1840: A Study in Changing Maori Attitudes Towards Europeans. MA Thesis, University of Auckland.

Shirres, Michael P. W., 1977. Tapu: Being with Potentiality for Power. MA Thesis, University of Auckland.

Sider, Gerald, 1987. When Parrots Learn to Talk and Why They Can't: Domination, Deception and Self-Deception in Indian-White Relations. *Comparative Studies in Society and History*, 29: 3–23.

Siers, James, 1977. *Taratai: A Pacific Adventure*. Wellington, Millwood Press.

———— 1978. *Taratai II: A Continuing Pacific Adventure*. Wellington, Millwood Press.

Simmons, D. R., 1976. *The Great New Zealand Myth: A Study of the Discovery and Origin Traditions of the Maori*. Wellington, Reed.

Simpson, R. A., 1955. *This is Kuaotunu*. Thames, Thames Star.

Sissons, Jeff, 1984. Te Mana o Te Waimana. PhD Thesis, University of Auckland.

Sissons, J.; Wihongi, W.; and Hohepa, P., 1987. *The Puuriri Trees are Laughing: A Political History of Ngaa Puhi in the Inland Bay of Islands*. Auckland, Polynesian Society.

Skelton, R. A. (ed.), 1969. *The Journals of Captain James Cook on His Voyages of Discovery*. Cambridge, published for the Hakluyt Society at the University Press.

Skinner, H. D., 1912. Ancient Maori Canals, Marlborough, N.Z. *Journal of the Polynesian Society*, 21: 104–08.

———— 1916. Review: On the Significance of the Geographical Distribution of the Practice of Mummification. *Journal of the Polynesian Society*, 25: 122–24.

Smith, Bernard, 1984. *European Vision and the South Pacific*, 2nd ed. Sydney, Harper and Row.

———— 1985. The Functions of Art on Cook's Voyages, Lectures 1–3. *Pacific Islands Monthly*, 56 (10): 42–43; 56 (11): 42–44; 56 (12): 42–44.

Smith, C. T., 1978. *A Historical Geography of Western Europe before 1800*. London, Longman.

Smith, H. M., 1975. The Introduction of Venereal Disease into Tahiti: a re-examination. *Journal of Pacific History*, 10 (1): 38–45.

Smith, S. P., 1901. Traditions of Tasman's Visit. *Journal of the Polynesian Society*, X: 104.

———— 1896. *The Peopling of the North*. Supplement to the *Journal of the Polynesian Society*.

———— 1904. *Hawaiki: The Original Home of the Maori; with a sketch of Polynesian history*. Christchurch, Whitcombe and Tombs.

———— (ed.), 1913. *The Lore of the Whare-Wananga, Part I — Te Kauwae-runga, or Things Celestial*. New Plymouth, Avery.

Spencer, J. H., 1979. A most Spatious and well sheltered harbour: The *Endeavour*'s visit to the Bay of Islands, 29 November–5 December 1769. Typescript, University of Auckland.

———— Coastal profiles and landscapes, in Carr, D. J., 1983b: 260–74.

———— 1984. A New Zealand draught chart by James Cook R.N. *Cartography*, 13 (4): 316–22.

———— 1985. The Visit of the *St Jean-Baptiste* expedition to Doubtless Bay, New Zealand, 17–31 December 1769. *Cartography*, 14 (2): 124–43.

———— 1990. Review of A. David (ed.), The Charts and Coastal Views of Captain Cook's Voyages, Vol. I. The Voyage of the *Endeavour* 1768–1771. *The Globe* (in press), Australian Map Circle, Victoria.

Stack, James W., 1877. Sketch of the Traditional History of the South Island Maoris. *Transactions and Proceedings of the New Zealand Institute*, 10: 57–92.

———— 1879. Remarks Concerning Mr Mackenzie Cameron's Theory Concerning the Kahui Tipua. *Transactions and Proceedings of the New Zealand Institute*, XII: 159–164.

———— 1898. *South Island Maoris: A Sketch of their History and Legendary Lore*. Christchurch, Whitcombe and Tombs.

Stafford, J. M., 1967. *Te Arawa: A History of the Arawa People*. Wellington, Reed.

The Story of the Bay of Islands Maritime and Historic Park, 1965. Auckland, Lands and Survey Department.

Sutton, Douglas, 1987. A Paradigmatic Shift in Polynesian Prehistory: Implications for New Zealand. *New Zealand Journal of Archaeology*, 9: 135–55.

Tairawhiti Maori Association, 1932. *Echoes of the Pa*. Gisborne, Gisborne Publishing.

Tapu-kereta School, 1979. *Tapu-kereta School and District Reunion. 18??–1979*. Auckland Public Library.

Tawhai, Mohi, (trans. G. Graham), 1939. Nukutawhiti. *Journal of the Polynesian Society*, 48: 221–33.

Taylor, A. C., *et al.*, 1971. *The Opening of the Pacific: Image and Reality.* London, National Maritime Museum.

Taylor, E. G. R., 1968. Navigation in the Days of Captain Cook. *Journal of the Institute of Navigation*, 21: 256–76.

Taylor, Jean Gelman, 1983. *The Social World of Batavia: European and Eurasian in Dutch Asia.* Madison, Wis., University of Wisconsin Press.

Taylor, Nancy M., 1959. *Early Travellers in New Zealand.* Oxford, Clarendon Press.

Taylor, Richard, 1855. *Te Ika a Maui, or New Zealand and its Inhabitants.* London, Wertheim and Macintosh.

Temple, William, 1932. *Observations Upon the United Provinces of the Netherlands (1673).* Cambridge, University Press.

Te Pipiwharauroa, 1906. Kapene Kuki, No. 103: 6–8; Nga Korero o Kapene Kuki, No. 104: 6–7.

Todorov, Tzvetan, (trans. R. Howard), 1984. *The Conquest of America: The Question of the Other.* New York, Harper and Row.

Tregear, E., 1916. Maori Mummies. *Journal of the Polynesian Society*, 25: 170–72.

Trustees of the British Museum, 1979. *Captain Cook and the South Pacific.* London, British Museum Publications.

Tuhua, Tanguru, 1906. Incidents in the History of Horehore Pa, Te Takapau, Hawkes Bay District. *Journal of the Polynesian Society*, XV: 69–93.

Turei, Mohi, 1912. The History of Horouta Canoe and the Introduction of the Kumara into New Zealand. *Journal of the Polynesian Society*, 21: 152–63.

Unger, Richard W., 1978. *Dutch Ship-building before 1800.* Amsterdam, Van Gorcum.

Van Klaveren, J. J., 1953. *The Dutch Colonial System in the East Indies.* Rotterdam, Drukkerrij Benedictus.

Veit, Walter (ed.), 1972. *Captain James Cook: Image and Impact, South Seas Discoveries and the World of Letters, Vols I and II.* Melbourne, Hawthorne Press.

Villiers, Alan, 1967. *Captain Cook, The Seamen's Seaman: A Study of the Great Discoverer.* London, Hodder and Stoughton.

Waitangi Tribunal, 1988. *Muriwhenua Fishing Report.* Wellington, Waitangi Tribunal.

Wallis, H., 1988. Did the Portuguese Discover Australia? *History Today*, March 1988: 30–35.

Walls, J. Y., 1974. Argillite Quarries of the Nelson Mineral Belt. *New Zealand Archaeological Association Newsletter*, 17 (1): 37–43.

Walsh, Archdeacon, 1903. The Cultivation and Treatment of the Kumara by the Primitive Maoris. *Transactions and Proceedings of the New Zealand Institute*, XXV: 12–24.

Washbourn, Enga, 1970. *Courage and Camp Ovens.* Wellington, Reed.

Washburn, W. E., 1962. The Meaning of Discovery in the Fifteenth and Sixteenth Centuries. *American Historical Review*, LXVIII (1): 1–21.

Watt, J., 1979. Medical Aspects and Consequences of Cook's Voyages, in *Captain James Cook and His Times*, eds R. Fisher and H. Johnston. Seattle, University of Washington Press.

Watts, Sheldon J., 1984. *A Social History of Western Europe 1450–1720.* London, Hutchinson.

White, John, 1887. *The Ancient History of the Maori: Horouta or Takitimu Migration, Vol I.* Wellington, Government Printer.

——— 1887. *The Ancient History of the Maori: Horouta or Takitimu Migration, Vol II.* Wellington, Government Printer.

——— 1889. *The Ancient History of the Maori: Tainui, Vol IV.* Wellington, Government Printer.

——— 1888. *The Ancient History of the Maori: Tainui, Vol. V.* Wellington, Government Printer.

——— 1890. *The Ancient History of the Maori: Tainui, Vol. VI.* Wellington, Government Printer.

Wilkes, Owen, 1961. Site Survey of West Nelson. *New Zealand Archaeological Association Newsletter*, 4: 21–31.

Williams, Glyndwr, 1966. *The Expansion of Europe in the Eighteenth Century.* London, Blandford Press.

Williams, Glyndwr, and Marshall, P. J., 1982. *The Great Map of Mankind: British Perceptions of the World in the Age of Enlightenment.* London, Dent.

Williams, H. W. and Williams, M., 1936. Letters and Journals written by the Rev. Henry and Mrs Marianne Williams and the Rev. Williams and Mrs Jane Williams 1822–64. Typed copy from the originals in the possession of Mr Hal Williams, London, University of Auckland Library.

Williams, W. and Williams, J. (ed. Frances Porter), 1974. *The Turanga Journals 1840–1850: Letters and Journals of William and Jane Williams, Missionaries to Poverty Bay.* Wellington, Price Milburn for Victoria University Press.

Williams, W. L., 1888. On the Visit of Captain Cook to Poverty Bay and Tolaga Bay. *Transactions and Proceedings of the New Zealand Institute*, XXI: 389–97.

——— 1932. East Coast Historical Records. Reprinted from the *Poverty Bay Herald*, Gisborne.

459

463

Index